Rome, the Greek World,

and the East

Studies in the History of Greece and Rome

P. J. Rhodes and Richard J. A. Talbert, editors

Rome, the Greek World, and the East

VOLUME I

The Roman Republic and the Augustan Revolution

Fergus Millar

Edited by Hannah M. Cotton and Guy M. Rogers

The University of North Carolina Press
Chapel Hill and London

Set in a Bembo revival
by Tseng Information Systems, Inc.
Manufactured in the United States of America

⊚ The paper in this book meets the guidelines
for permanence and durability of the Committee on
Production Guidelines for Book Longevity
of the Council on Library Resources.

Library of Congress Cataloging-in-Publication Data

Millar, Fergus.
Rome, the Greek world, and the East / Fergus Millar;
edited by Hannah M. Cotton and Guy M. Rogers.
p.   cm. — (Studies in the history of Greece and Rome)
Includes bibliographical references and index.
Contents: v. 1. The Roman Republic
and the Augustan revolution
ISBN 0-8078-2664-2 (cloth: alk. paper)
ISBN 0-8078-4990-1 (pbk.: alk. paper)
1. Greece—Civilization. 2. Rome—Civilization.
I. Title. II. Series.
DE3 .M52   2002
938—dc21   2001027500

Cloth 06 05 04 03 02   5 4 3 2 1

Paper 06 05 04 03 02   5 4 3 2 1

Contents

Preface   vii

Introduction: Polybius Was Right, by Guy M. Rogers   xi

Abbreviations   xvii

Author's Prologue
1

Part I. Conceptions and Sources

1. Taking the Measure of the Ancient World
25

2. Epigraphy
39

Part II. The Roman Republic

3. Political Power in Mid-Republican Rome:
Curia or Comitium?
85

4. The Political Character of the
Classical Roman Republic, 200–151 B.C.
109

5. Politics, Persuasion, and the People,
before the Social War (150–90 B.C.)
143

6. Popular Politics at Rome in the Late Republic
162

7. Cornelius Nepos, "Atticus,"
and the Roman Revolution
183

8. The Last Century of the Republic:
Whose History?
200

9. The Mediterranean and the Roman Revolution:
Politics, War, and the Economy
215

Part III. The Augustan Revolution

10. Triumvirate and Principate
241

11. The Emperor, the Senate, and the Provinces
271

12. State and Subject:
The Impact of Monarchy
292

13. "Senatorial" Provinces:
An Institutionalized Ghost
314

14. Ovid and the Domus Augusta:
Rome Seen from Tomoi
321

15. Imperial Ideology in the Tabula Siarensis
350

16. The Roman City-State
under the Emperors, 29 B.C.–A.D. 69
360

Index
377

Preface

Fergus Millar, Camden Professor of Ancient History in the University of Oxford, is one of the most influential ancient historians of the twentieth century. Since the publication of *A Study of Cassius Dio* by Oxford University Press in 1964, Millar has published eight books, including two monumental studies, *The Emperor in the Roman World* (Duckworth, 1977) and *The Roman Near East, 31 B.C.–A.D. 337* (Harvard, 1993). These books have transformed the study of ancient history.

In his study of the role of the emperor in the Roman world Millar argued that the reign of Augustus inaugurated almost three centuries of relatively passive and inert government, in which the central power pursued few policies and was largely content to respond to pressures and demands from below. After more than twenty years of scholarly reaction, *The Emperor in the Roman World* is now the dominant scholarly model of how the Roman Empire worked in practice.

Reviewers immediately hailed Millar's magisterial study of the Roman Near East as a "grand book on a grand topic" (*TLS*, 15 April 1994). In this grand book, displaying an unrivaled mastery of ancient literary, epigraphical, papyrological, and archaeological sources in Greek, Latin, Hebrew, Aramaic, and other Semitic languages, Millar made the indigenous peoples of the Roman Near East, especially the Jews, central to our understanding of how and why the three great religions of the book, Rabbinic Judaism, Christianity, and Islam, evolved in a cultural context that was neither "eastern" nor "western." There can be no doubt that *The Roman Near East 31 B.C.–A.D. 337* will be the standard work on the subject for a long time to come.

More recently, Millar has challenged widely held notions about the supposed oligarchic political character of the Roman Republic in *The Crowd in Rome in the Late Republic* (Michigan, 1998). In the future, Millar intends to return to the Roman Near East for another large-scale study, to be entitled *Society and Religion in the Roman Near East from Constantine to Mahomet*. In this study Millar will bring the story of Greco-Roman culture in the Near East from the early fourth century up to the Islamic invasions of the seventh century A.D.

During the same period in which he has produced these ground-breaking books, Millar also has published over seventy essays on aspects of Greco-Roman history, from the Hellenistic period until the middle of the fifth century A.D. These essays have laid the foundations for or supplemented the ideas and arguments presented in Millar's very well known books. Some of these essays, such as "The Emperor, the Senate and the Provinces" (*Journal of Roman Studies* 56 [1966]: 156–166), or "Emperors, Frontiers and Foreign Relations, 31 B.C.–A.D. 378" (*Britannia* 13 [1982]: 1–23), have appeared in hitherto accessible journals and are widely regarded as classics of scholarship. But other outstanding essays, published in specialty journals or edited volumes, such as Millar's study, "Polybius between Greece and Rome" (published in *Greek Connections: Essays on Culture and Diplomacy* [1987]: 1–18), have been more difficult to locate, even for professional historians doing research in the field.

Therefore, the primary goal of our collection, *Rome, the Greek World, and the East*, is to bring together into three volumes the most significant of Millar's essays published since 1961 for the widest audience possible. The collection includes many articles which clearly will be of great intellectual interest and pedogogical use to scholars doing research and teaching in the different fields of the volume headings: Volume 1, *The Roman Republic and the Augustan Revolution*; Volume 2, *Government, Society, and Culture in the Roman Empire*; and Volume 3, *The Greek World, the Jews, and the East*. At the same time, we have conceived and organized the three volumes of *Rome, the Greek World, and the East* especially in order to make Millar's most significant articles readily available to a new generation of students.

The principle of arrangement of the essays in each of the three volumes is broadly chronological by subject matter treated within the ancient world, after an initial section on "Conceptions and Sources" in volume 1. We believe that this chronological arrangement of essays (rather than by publication date of the essays) gives intellectual coherence to each volume on its own and to the collection as a whole. Overall, as Millar himself has defined it in the prologue, the subject of this collection is "the communal culture and civil government of the Greco-Roman world, essentially from the Hellenistic period to the fifth century A.D."

Publication of a three-volume collection of essays, drawn from a wide variety of journals and edited volumes, over nearly four decades of scholarly production, presents editors with some major stylistic challenges. Our collection contains more than fifty essays. Most of these essays originally were published in learned journals or books, each of which had its own house style. Some learned journals also have changed their house styles over the time that Millar has published in them. For these reasons we have not attempted to bring all of the citations in the texts or notes of the articles in the collection into perfect stylistic conformity. Conformity for the sake of conformity makes no sense; moreover, to achieve such conformity would delay publication of the collection for years.

Rather, the stylistic goal of our collection has been to inform readers clearly and consistently where they can find the sources cited by Millar in his essays. To help achieve that goal we have included a list of frequently cited works (with abbreviations for those works) at the beginning of each volume. Thus, in the text or notes of the essays, readers will find abbreviations for frequently cited journals or books, which are fully cited in our lists at the beginning of each volume. For example, references in the notes to the abbreviation *JRS* refer to the *Journal of Roman Studies*. For the abbreviations themselves we have relied on the standard list provided in *L'Année Philologique*. In certain cases, where there have been individual citations in the original texts or notes to more obscure collections of inscriptions or papyri, we have expanded the citations themselves in situ, rather than endlessly expanding our list of frequently cited works.

In accordance with Professor Millar's wishes, for the sake of readers who do not know Latin or Greek, we have provided English translations of most of the extended Greek and Latin passages and some of the technical terms cited by Millar in the text and notes of the original essays. In doing so, we have followed the practice Professor Millar himself adopted in *The Emperor in the Roman World* in 1977. We believe that providing these translations will help to make Millar's essays more widely accessible, which is the essential goal of the collection. Readers who wish to consult the original Greek and Latin passages or technical terms which we have translated in the collection can look up those passages or technical terms in the original, published versions of the essays.

The editors would like to thank the many friends and colleagues who have helped us in the process of collecting these essays and preparing them for publication. We are indebted first of all to Lewis Bateman, formerly senior editor at the University of North Carolina Press, who suggested the basic arrangement of the essays into three volumes. We are also grateful to David Perry, editor-in-chief, and Pamela Upton, assistant managing editor at the University of North Carolina Press, for their flexibility, advice, and support of the project.

Gabriela Cerra, Asaph Ben Tov, Tamar Herzig, Masha Chormy, Ori Shapir, and Andrea Rotstein in Israel and Desirée Garcia, Molly Maddox, and Dr. Nancy Thompson of the Metropolitan Museum of Art in New York in the United States provided editorial assistance. Our thanks also to Mark Rogers for his help with the maps. We owe a great debt to Priscilla Lange for her helpfulness and kindness to us in Oxford. We also would like to express our gratitude to the Fellows of Brasenose College Oxford and All Souls College Oxford for their hospitality while we were working on this project.

Above all, however, the editors would like to thank Fergus Millar, for his scholarship, his generosity, and his friendship over more than two decades.

Hannah M. Cotton	Guy M. Rogers
The Hebrew University	Wellesley College
Jerusalem	Wellesley

Polybius Was Right

At the beginning of the three-volume collection of essays entitled *Rome, the Greek World, and the East*, Fergus Millar, in a prologue written for volume I, looks back at the essays collected here and contends that "Ancient History" is meaningful and intelligible to us precisely because it is comparatively so recent and we are still so close to it in so many important ways.

Following the author's prologue, the essays of Millar in this volume defend the continued significance of the study of classics, argue for expanding the definition of what constitutes classics, and challenge the dominant twentieth-century scholarly interpretation of Roman politics. According to Millar, the Roman people, not the Senate, was the sovereign power in Republican Rome.

After a brief survey of the contents of volume I, *The Roman Republic and the Augustan Revolution*, following the logic of Millar's argument, in this introduction I set out some of the relatively unexplored interpretive implications of accepting that Polybius was right about the role of the people in the structure of the Roman Republic.

In the first essay of this volume, "Taking the Measure of the Ancient World," Millar reminds classicists and others of the enormous substantive and temporal boundaries of the field. Classics is, or should be, the study of the culture, in the widest sense, of any population using Greek and Latin from the late Bronze Age to the Islamic invasions of the seventh century A.D. at the earliest. The importance of classics as a major part of human experience stems from its sheer extensiveness in space and time.

Having defined the vast scope of the field of classics, Millar then argues persuasively for studying Greek and Roman history together. We should do so because the histories and cultures of Greece and Rome were closely connected from the eighth century B.C. and became even more inextricably intertwined as time went on. Within the same essay a compelling case is made for including Jewish and Christian texts in our conception of classics. Indeed, scholars familiar with Millar's books, especially his revision of E. Schürer's classic three-volume study, *A History of the Jewish People in the Age of Jesus Christ, 175* B.C.–A.D. *135* (along with G. Vermes, M. Black, and M. Goodman), will recognize that Fergus Millar has done as much as any classical scholar in the twentieth century to make the historical experience of the Jewish people during the Hellenistic and Roman imperial eras central to the study of classical history.

In the second essay of the volume, "Epigraphy," Millar then provides a uniquely succinct survey of inscriptions from the Greco-Roman world and their uses to historians. In his survey Millar cites a number of illustrative epigraphical texts to show what inscriptions can and cannot tell us about the ancient world. He points out, for instance, that the existence of a single inscription, documenting a particular practice from the geographical or temporal limits of the classical world, allows us to deploy a kind of "double-negative" reasoning. The existence of such a text proves that it is *not* the case that there are *no* examples of a phenomenon from a particular place and time. Thus, the existence of one inscription can destroy a possible negative generalization about Greek or Roman history. Here, and elsewhere in this volume, readers will find that Millar's "rules of evidence" characteristically derive from very wide reading and analysis of the ancient evidence itself, including manuscripts, papyri, and inscriptions. Indeed, the originality of Millar's scholarship has been sustained over decades by his deep and continued engagement with the ancient evidence itself.

Deep engagement for Millar with respect to inscriptions has involved reading epigraphical texts in bulk and analyzing them as examples of literature in their own right. As an example of the value of such an approach, Millar's essay "Imperial Ideology in the Tabula Siarensis" (chapter 15) shows how close reading of a number of related inscriptions can be used to control distortions in Tacitus' account of events in Rome in relation to the posthumous honors for Drusus, the son of Tiberius, in A.D. 23. In this essay and, indeed, throughout this collection, readers will discover just how remarkable the scholarly results can be when inscriptions are treated as literature in their own right *and* are historically contextualized.

In part II Millar calls into question the assumption found in much scholarship since the publication of M. Gelzer's *Die Nobilität der römischen Republik* (The nobility of the Roman Republic) in 1912 that Republican Rome was dominated by a homogeneous "patrician-plebeian" élite (the Senate), which rendered popular participation in politics passive and nominal through a network of patronage relationships. Rather, Millar argues, in a series of essays presented here and in part III, such patronage relations cannot serve as the key to understanding the political process in Rome. The citizen body of Rome was too large for such a system to have operated effectively, and our evidence also reveals that those who aspired to office in Rome competed for popular favor. Most important, however, we need to remember that the Roman citizen body voted directly on legislation, elected all the annual holders of political and military office, and judged cases in popular courts constituted by the centuriate assembly (*comitia centuriata*) and the tribal assembly (*comitia tributa*).

If we believe that sovereignty resides within those institutions which have the power to legislate or judge capital cases, then the sovereign power in Rome during the Republic—whose *imperium* (military and legal jurisdiction) was extended throughout Italy and to the provinces in the course of the Republic—was ultimately, at least in theory, the Roman citizen body. Moreover, according to Millar, at the center of the practice of Roman politics was not the Roman patron (*patronus*), imposing his will upon a client, but rather the orator, addressing the crowd in the Roman Forum. As Millar has put it (in chapter 4, "The Political Character of the Classical Roman Republic, 200–151 B.C."), some people made speeches and other people voted.

In sum, Polybius, the Greek politician from Megalopolis, who wrote forty books of *Histories* explaining Rome's rise to power to a Greek-reading audience after 168 B.C., was right about the role of the Roman people in the formal structure of the *res publica* and his modern critics are wrong, when he wrote:

> After this we are naturally inclined to ask what part in the constitution is left for the people [δήμῳ], considering that the Senate controls all the particular matters I have mentioned, and, what is most important, manages all matters of revenues and expenditure, and considering too that the consuls have uncontrolled authority as regards preparations for war and operations in the field. But nevertheless there is a part, and a very important part left for the people. For it is the people which alone has the right to confer honors and inflict punishment, the only bonds by which kingdoms and states and in a word human society are held together. For where the distinction between these is overlooked or is observed but ill applied, no affairs can be properly administered. How indeed is it possible when good and evil men are held in equal estimation? It is by the people then, in many cases, that offenses punishable by fine are tried, especially when the accused have held the highest office; and they are the only court which may try capital charges. As regards the latter they have a practice which is praiseworthy and should be mentioned. Their usage allows those on trial for their lives when

found guilty liberty to depart openly, thus inflicting voluntary exile on themselves, if even only one of the tribes pronouncing the verdict has not yet voted. Such exiles enjoy safety in the territories of Naples, Praeneste, Tibur, and other allied states. Again it is the people who bestow office on the deserving, the noblest reward of virtue in a state; the people have the power of approving or rejecting laws, and what is most important of all, they deliberate on the question of war and peace. Further, in the case of alliances, terms of peace and treaties, it is the people who ratify all these or the reverse. Thus here again one might plausibly say that the people's share in the government is the greatest, and that the constitution is a democratic one (Polybius, *Histories* 6, 14)

Although Polybius goes on to recount how each of the three parts of the state (consuls, Senate, people) was able to counteract or cooperate with the other parts if it wished, it should be obvious from Polybius' account that he believed that no one could understand either the theory or practice of Roman republican politics if his view did not somehow encompass the power of the Roman people as represented directly, if imperfectly, in their assemblies.

But, as Millar notes, the interpretive implications of accepting the fact that Polybius was right, and most modern historians have been wrong, about the theory and practice of Roman Republican politics, extend far beyond the narrative history of the second century B.C. Republic. Major events in late republican history, such as the Social War of 90 B.C. between Rome and its Italian allies, the Sullan counter-revolution of 82 B.C., the outbreak of the civil wars in 49 B.C., and the emergence of the triumvirs, all need to be viewed in the context of popular politics, or crowd politics.

Most important of all, however, Millar's restoration of the citizen body to its rightful place within the constitutional structure of the *res publica* and its politics provides the analytical framework for a very different understanding of what happened in 27 B.C. than we might gather from reading the *Annales* of Tacitus. Octavian's alleged restoration of the *res publica*—or the foundation of the monarchy—was not the seizure of sovereign power from the Senate by Octavian, because the Senate was not the sovereign power in the first place. It was to the discretion of the Senate *and* the Roman people that Augustus later claimed to have transferred the *res publica* from his power ("rem publicam ex mea potestate in senatus populique Romani arbitrium transtuli," *Res Gestae*, 34). Moreover, it was to the *populus Romanus* that the *imperium*, and at least some of the provinces of the empire, belonged in constitutional theory. That, at any rate, seems to have been the point of view of Augustus himself, who claimed to have added Egypt "to the imperium of the Roman people" (*Res Gestae* 27).

Even if this claim is taken to be mendacious or merely symbolic, as some scholars have argued, the question for historians is why it was important for Augustus to have made such a claim publicly in A.D. 14, long after the establishment of the monarchy. In other words, if popular politics were only a symbolic charade during the Republic, why was it necessary for the most powerful man in the Mediterranean world to keep up the charade during the empire?

Whatever we make of Augustus' public claim to have added Egypt to the jurisdiction of the Roman people, it should be obvious that we cannot understand either the politics of the Roman Republic or the historical transition from the *res publica* to the monarchy—what Ronald Syme deemed the "Roman Revolution"—if we leave the Roman citizen body (*Quirites*) or the Roman people (*populus Romanus*) out of our account. Indeed, although Millar himself never says so explicitly in any of the essays collected here, it is possible to argue on the basis of the evidence he cites in these essays that the second Roman monarchy itself was one of the (unintended) consequences of the struggle between some of the *nobiles* and the *populus Romanus* over the question of who was the sovereign power in the *res publica*. If we look at the breakdown of the Roman Republic from this perspective, we might see the emergence of a monarch from among the *nobiles* in 27 B.C. as an ironic victory for that democratic element in the Roman constitution, the Roman people.

Indeed, articles included in part III, "The Augustan Revolution," which, at the time of publication, rightly achieved classic status for the way they used a variety of literary and documentary sources from around the Mediterranean world to re-define the nature of the change from republic to monarchy, as reflected upon by contemporaries, now can be seen to have foreshadowed Millar's later and implicit challenge to our interpretation of the nature of the "Roman Revolution" itself. For instance, we now should see the case Millar made for the persistence of votes by the Senate *and* the people through the Triumviral period in his 1973 article, "Triumvirate and Principate" (chapter 10) to have laid the foundations for arguments made in later articles, such as "Imperial Ideology in the Tabula Siarensis" (chapter 15), published in 1988, about the continuing significance of the people in the passage of legislation, even during the early imperial period.

Similarly, Millar's full exposure in 1989 of how modern scholars unjustifiably have imposed on the ancient evidence an item of terminology, "the senatorial provinces" in " 'Senatorial' Provinces: An Institutionalized Ghost" (chapter 13), which wrongly implies a division of responsibility between the emperor and the Senate for the provinces, can be traced directly back to arguments made in the earliest article included in volume 1: "In no sense whatsoever did the Senate 'control' the senatorial provinces, and the proconsuls were not 'responsible to' it. Both the emperor and the Senate, predominantly of course the former, made regulations (sometimes jointly) affecting all the provinces" (chapter 11, "The Emperor, the Senate and the Provinces," *JRS* 56 (1966): 165). In the articles of part III, which were published later, the style of argumentation is often tighter and more explicit, but the concerns and themes of the articles, from 1966 to the present, remain substantially the same. Substance abides.

When a historian has challenged long-held scholarly orthodoxies about who the sovereign power in republican Rome was and how Roman politics were practiced, we should expect specialists in the field of Roman republican history either to lend support to his arguments (e.g., A. Yakobson, "*Petitio et Largitio*: Popular Participation in the Centuriate Assembly of the Late Republic," *JRS* 82 [1992]: 32ff.), or to critique his work. (For a valuable contribution to the debate about Roman "democracy," see M. Jehne, ed., *Demokratie in Rom? Die Rolle des Volkes in der Politik der römischen Republik* [Stuttgart, 1995].) Such diverse scholarly responses are a clear sign of the importance of the debate and, perhaps more important, of the vitality of the field of Roman history itself at the beginning of the new millennium.

But whatever scholarly consensus eventually emerges about who the sovereign power in republican Rome was and what the nature of Roman politics was, there can be no doubt but that in the essays of this volume Millar has revivified Roman republican history by having the courage to ask what is surely a deeper, and even more important question than the question of who was the sovereign power in republican Rome: that is, who, or what community, or communities, ought to be the subject of the history of Rome?

For Millar, the answer to this question is that the history of Rome is, or should be, under the Republic as under the Empire, the history of the whole community, not just the Senate. If Millar is right about the answer to this fundamental question—and I believe he is—large parts of the history of the Roman Republic *and* the early Roman Empire need to be rewritten. Therein lies the scholarly challenge for the next generation of Roman historians.

Guy MacLean Rogers
West Lodge
5 September 2001

Abbreviations

Abbott and Johnson
   F. F. Abbott and A. C. Johnson, *Municipal Administration in the Roman Empire* (1926)
AC
   L'Antiquité Classique
Acta Ant. Acad. Sc. Hung.
   Acta Antiqua Academiae Scientiarum Hungaricae
AE
   L'Année Épigraphique
AJA
   American Journal of Archaeology
AJAH
   American Journal of Ancient History
AJPh
   American Journal of Philology
Amer. Hist. Rev.
   American Historical Review
Ann. Arch. Arab. Syr.
   Annales Archéologiques Arabes Syriennes
Ann. Sc. N. Sup. Pisa
   Annali della Scuola Normale Superiore di Pisa
ANRW
   Aufstieg und Niedergang der römischen Welt. Geschichte und Kultur Roms im Spiegel der neueren Forschung
Ant. Class.
   L'Antiquité Classique
Arch. esp. de arqu.
   Archivo Español de Arqueología

Arctos

    Arctos. Acta philologica Fennica

Ath. Mitt.

    Mitteilungen des Deutschen Archäologischen Instituts, Athenische Abteilung

Athenaeum

    Athenaeum. Studi periodici di Letteratura e Storia dell'Antichità

BAR Supp.

    British Archaeological Reports, Supplements

BCH

    Bulletin de Correspondance Hellénique

BE

    Bulletin Épigraphique, published in *Revue des Études Grecques*

BGU

    Aegyptische Urkunden aus den Königlichen (Staatlichen) Museen zu Berlin, Griechische Urkunden

BICS

    Bulletin of the Institute of Classical Studies of the University of London

Brit. Journ. Sociol.

    British Journal of Sociology

Bull. Epig.

    Bulletin Épigraphique, published in *Revue des Études Grecques*

Bull. Inst. Cl. Stud.

    Bulletin of the Institute of Classical Studies of the University of London

CAH, CAH[2]

    Cambridge Ancient History

Cavenaille, *Corp. Pap. Lat.*

    R. Cavenaille, *Corpus Papyrorum Latinarum* (1958)

Charlesworth, *Documents*

    M. P. Charlesworth, *Documents Illustrating the Reigns of Claudius and Nero* (1951)

CIL

    Corpus Inscriptionum Latinarum

Coll. Int. du CNRS

    Colloques internationaux du Centre National de Recherche Scientifique

Coll.

    Mosaicarum et Romanarum Legum Collatio (*FIRA*[2] I, 541–89)

CQ

    Classical Quarterly

CR
  Classical Review
CRAI
  Comptes-rendus de l'Académie des Inscriptions
Degrassi, *Ins. It.*
  A. Degrassi, *Inscriptiones Italiae*
Dial. d'hist. anc.
  Dialogues d'Histoire Ancienne
Dial. di Arch.
  Dialoghi di Archeologia
Diz. Epig.
  Dizionario Epigrafico
Econ. Hist. Rev.
  Economic History Review
Ehrenberg and Jones
  V. Ehrenberg and A. H. M. Jones, *Documents Illustrating the Reigns of Augustus and Tiberius*² (1955; repr. with addenda 1976, 1979)
FGrH
  F. Jacoby, *Die Fragmente der griechischen Historiker*
FHG
  C. Müller, Th. Müller, et al., *Fragmenta Historicorum Graecorum* I–V (1853–70)
FIRA²
  S. Riccobono, J. Baviera, C. Ferrini, J. Furlani, and V. Arangio-Ruiz, *Fontes Iuris Romani Anteiustiniani*² I–III (1940–43)
G&R
  Greece and Rome
*Gesch. d. röm. Lit.*⁴
  Geschichte der römischen Literatur
GRBS
  Greek, Roman and Byzantine Studies
HSCPh
  Harvard Studies in Classical Philology
I. K. Eph. = I. K. Ephesos
  Inschriften griechischer Städte aus Kleinasien: Ephesos
I. K. Kyme
  Inschriften griechischer Städte aus Kleinasien: Kyme
IG
  Inscriptiones Graecae

IGBulg.

   G. Mikailov, *Inscriptiones Graecae in Bulgaria repertae*

IGLS

   Inscriptions greques et latins de la Syrie

IGR

   R. Cagnat et al., *Inscriptiones Graecae ad Res Romanas Pertinentes*

*ILLRP*²

   Inscriptiones Latinae Liberae Reipublicae

ILS

   H. Dessau, *Inscriptiones Latinae Selectae* I–III

Ins. Didyma

   A. Rehm and R. Harder, eds., *Didyma* II: *Die Inschriften*

Int. Hist. Rev.

   International History Review

Ist. Mitt.

   Mitteilungen des Deutschen Archäologischen Instituts, Istanbuler Abteilung

Iura

   Iura. Revista internazionale di Diritto romano e antico.

Jahreshefte Öst. Arch. Inst.

   Jahreshefte des Österreichischen Archäologischen Instituts

JEA

   Journal of Egyptian Archaeology

JJS

   Journal of Jewish Studies

JRS

   Journal of Roman Studies

LTUR

   E. M. Steïnby, *Lexicon Topographicum Urbis Romae* I–VI (1993–2000)

McCrum and Woodhead, *Select Documents*

   M. McCrum and A. G. Woodhead, *Select Documents of the Principates of the Flavian Emperors* (1961)

MEFR(A) and *MEFR*

   Mélanges d'Archéologie et d'Histoire

MRR

   T. R. S. Broughton, *The Magistrates of the Roman Republic*

NC

   Numismatic Chronicle

Num. Chron.

   Numismatic Chronicle

OGIS
> W. Dittenberger, *Orientis Graeci Inscriptiones Selectae* I–II (1903–5)

*ORF*³
> H. Malcovati, *Oratorum Romanorum Fragmenta*³

P.Köln
> *Kölner Papyri*

Platner-Ashby
> S. B. Platner and T. Ashby, *A Topographical Dictionary of Ancient Rome* (1929)

Pap. Brit. Sch. Rome
> *Papers of the British School at Rome*

P. Oxy
> B. P. Grenfell, A. S. Hunt, et al., eds., *The Oxyrhynchus Papyri* (1898–)

P.Ryl.
> *Catalogue of the Greek papyri in the John Rylands Library at Manchester*

PBSR
> *Papers of the British School at Rome*

PCPhS
> *Proceedings of the Cambridge Philological Society*

Peter, *HRR*
> H. Peter, *Historicorum Romanorum Reliquiae*

*PIR*¹, *PIR*²
> *Prosopographia Imperii Romani* (1897–98 and 1933–)

Proc. Roy. Irish Acad.
> *Proceedings of the Royal Irish Academy*

P-W
> Pauly-Wissowa, *Realencyclopädie der klassischen Altertumswissenchaft*

REA
> *Revue des Etudes Anciennes*

R.I.C.
> H. Mattingly and E. A. Sydenham, eds., *Roman Imperial Coinage* I– (1923–)

RFIC
> *Rivista di Filologia e di Istruzione Classica*

RG
> *Res Gestae*

RIDA
> *Revue Internationale des Droits de l'Antiquité*

Röm. Mitt.
> *Mitteilungen des Deutschen Archäologischen Instituts, Römische Abteilung*

Rostovtzeff, *SEHRE*[2]
  M. Rostovtzeff, *Social and Economic History of the Roman Empire*[2], ed.
  P. M. Fraser (1957)
RRC I (1974)
  M. Crawford, *Roman Republican Coinage* I (1974)
Sardis, VII.1
  W. H. Buckler and D. M. Robinson, *Sardis* VII.1: *Greek and Latin
  Inscriptions* (1932)
SB
  Sammelbuch griechischer Urkunden aus Aegypten 1915–
SEG
  Supplementum Epigraphicum Graecum (1923–)
Sel.Pap.
  A. S. Hunt and C. C. Edgar, *Select Papyri*, I–III. Loeb Classical Library.
  (1932–42)
Stud. Class. e Or.
  Studi Classici e Orientali
Syll.[3]
  Sylloge Inscriptionum Graecarum[3] I–IV (1915–24)
TAPhA
  Transactions of the American Philological Association
TLS
  Times Literary Supplement
YCS
  Yale Classical Studies
ZPE
  Zeitschrift für Papyrologie und Epigraphik

Rome, the Greek World,
and the East

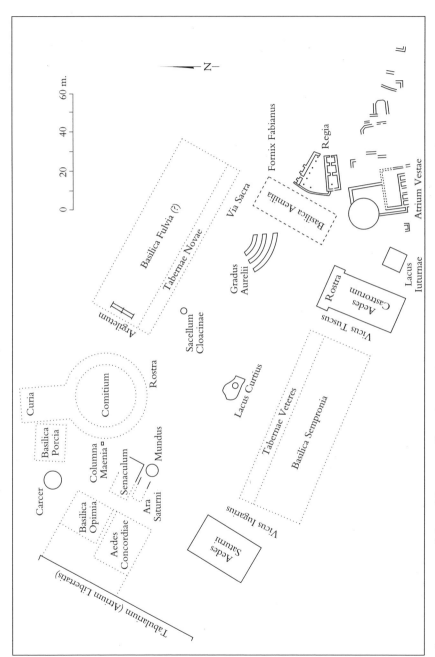

The Forum, c. 53 B.C. (adapted from F. Millar, *The Crowd in Rome in the Late Republic* [Michigan, 1998], p. 40)

Augustan Rome

To Praeneste

Aqua Iulia

Aqua Claudia

To South Italy

Horti Maecenatiani

ESQUILINE

Republican Wall

QUIRINAL

VIMINAL

Forum Augustum

Temple of Mars Ultor

Roman Forum

Temple of Deified Iulius

Sacra Via

Domus Aurea

Temple of Apollo Palatinus

Domus Augusta

CAELIAN

PALATINE

Domus Tiberiana

Circus Maximus

Republican Wall

Horti Luculliani

Campus Agrippae

Aqua Virgo

CAPITOL

Theatre of Balbus

Mausoleum of Augustus

Ara Pacis

Horologium

Pantheon

Campus Martius

Saepta Iulia

Theatre of Pompey

Porticus of Octavia

Theatre of Marcellus

AVENTINE

To Ostia

Tiber

Emporium

Bridge of Agrippa

Tiber

Nemus Caesarum

Italy during the late Republic

ATLANTIC
OCEAN

BELGICA

LONG-HAIRED GAUL

TRANSPADANA Verona
Po R.

**TRANSALPINE
GAUL**
Massilia · Pisa
Narbo

SALONA

ILLYRICU

Corsica
Aleria · Heba
Tarraco · Rome

**HISPANIA
ULTERIOR**

**HISPANIA
CITERIOR**

Sardinia

Corduba
· Italica
Siarum

Carthago Nova

Tingi

Epizephy
Locris

Sicily
Syracuse

Cirta · Carthage

NUMIDIA

Malta

AFRICA

MEDITERRANEA

Lepcis Magna

0   300 mi.

The Roman Empire and the eastern Mediterranean, c. 27 B.C.

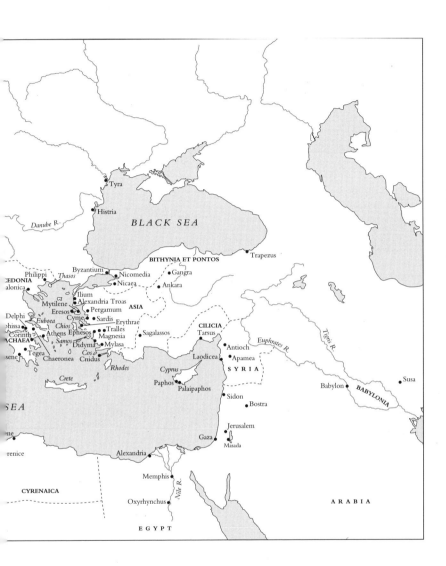

Tyra

Histria

Danube R.

BLACK SEA

Trapezus

BITHYNIA ET PONTOS

Byzantium   Nicomedia   •Gangra
Philippi   *Thasos*   •Nicaea   •Ankara
CEDONIA
alonica   Ilium
Mytilene   Alexandria Troas   ASIA
Delphi   Eresos   •Pergamum
Euboea   Cyme• •Sardis   Erythrae
ohissa   *Chios*   •Tralles   Sagalassos   CILICIA
Corinth   Athens Ephesos   Magnesia   Tarsus
ACHAEA   *Samos*   Didyma •Mylasa   Antioch
sene•   Tegea   *Cos* Cnidus   Laodicea   •Apamea   Euphrates R.   Tigris R.   Susa
Chaeronea   *Rhodes*   SYRIA
Crete   *Cyprus*   Babylon •   BABYLONIA
SEA   Paphos   Sidon
ene•   Palaipaphos   •Bostra
renice   Jerusalem
Gaza•   Masada
CYRENAICA   Alexandria
Memphis•   *Nile R.*   ARABIA
Oxyrhynchus•
EGYPT

Author's Prologue

For someone who claims to be a historian of the ancient world, to look both back on what he himself has written and forward to what might be written by others is salutary and stimulating, but also disturbing. For a start, what we conventionally call "the ancient world," namely the Mediterranean and the areas which were in contact with it, from the second millennium B.C. to (perhaps) the reign of Justinian or the early Islamic conquests, was not "the world" at all, but only a modest part of it. Central Asia, Afghanistan, the Indian sub-continent, and Sri Lanka do indeed come into the story. But the northern part of the Eurasian landmass only does so very obscurely and indirectly, while China, Japan, south-east Asia, and the early history of human habitation in Australia and sub-Saharan Africa, as in the Americas, are entirely outside what is meant by "the ancient world" in this sense.

More clearly still, Graeco-Roman history, far from being "ancient," is, comparatively speaking, the study of a very recent phase of human history. Humans evolved several million years ago (perhaps some 7 million years) and had spread from Africa into south-east Asia by around a million years ago and into Europe half a million years ago. On present calculations, almost all parts of the world where humans now live, except some Pacific islands, had been populated by humans before the emergence of the first writing in the Greek language (though not yet in the Greek alphabet) in the second millennium B.C. If we think in the categories of time and space, by far the larger part of the "ancient history" of humans is pre-history, illuminated by no written texts, and discernible now only through its physical remains.

To realise how recent and how close, in every sense, to ourselves, the Graeco-Roman "ancient world" is, is both disconcerting and encouraging. Disconcerting, because the study of that "ancient world" is revealed as a parochial pursuit, in which the danger is that everything from the structure of the languages involved, to the two main alphabets, to literary forms, architecture, political formations or philosophical ideas, will seem too readily accessible and intelligible. It is so, as is obvious, not only because of the dependence of "Western" civilisation on that of the Graeco-Roman world, but because it is all so close to us in time. To put it in graphic terms, if we look back from the end of our second, Christian, millennium, the lifetimes of a mere twenty-five people aged eighty, imagined as following in sequence on each other, would take us back to the reign of Augustus and the birth of Jesus. Even the legendary date of the Trojan War is, in these terms, only some forty lifetimes away, while the Islamic conquest of Syria and the Near East in the seventh century is a mere seventeen.

The Graeco-Roman "ancient historian" therefore needs a dose of modesty and an awareness of just how much more is involved in the genuinely "ancient" history of humans, and of how much had already happened before his or her subject matter comes into view, even in that limited part of the world in which Graeco-Roman history took place, or with which the classical world had connections.

Many readers will have begun to suspect, rightly, that these very general thoughts owe everything to the seminal work by Jared Diamond, *Guns, Germs and Steel*.[1] This reading indeed has given me a sense of how parochial our activities as "ancient historians" are, and in that sense it is certainly disconcerting. In other senses, however, it is not. For, firstly, one of the central messages of the book is the overwhelming importance of the possession, or absence, of inherited capacities, and inherited physical and technical resources, for the contacts and conflicts between different societies. But, for the moment, I want to leave that theme aside, to look at two other themes which emerge from Diamond's study of early human evolution, both of them fundamental to seeing Graeco-Roman "ancient history" in perspective. One is the very restricted and limited nature of the domestication of plants and animals, and the other is the immense importance of lateral communications from east to west across the Eurasian landmass. In a way which is quite striking, and indeed encouraging, to the conventional "ancient historian," the study of the earliest domestication of food plants (wheat, peas, olives) and of animals (sheep and goats) gives a crucial predominance to the Fertile Crescent, where these developments may have occurred around 8500 B.C., or some 10,000 years or more ago. The adoption of these domesticated crops and animals in the Mediterranean zone and Europe seems to have been a function of their dissemination from the Fertile Crescent, and to have taken place between 6000 and 3500 B.C. In an extraordinary way, therefore, we

1. J. Diamond, *Guns, Germs and Steel: A Short History of Everybody for the Last 13,000 Years* (1997).

can now discern the real roots and origins of Western civilisation, which are mirrored in the mythical story of Abraham, and his migration from Mesopotamia to the Holy Land, there to serve as the founder figure of a sacred story which, diffused in Greek and Latin as Christianity, would embrace all of the Mediterranean zone and Europe; and, transmitted into Arabic, would travel back across the Eurasian landmass to Iran, Central Asia, India, and south-east Asia.

More particularly, the story, or rather the set of different stories, told by Jared Diamond, focusing, as regards the early period, on the basic features of human exploitation of the plant and animal world, ought to serve to invite historians of the Graeco-Roman world also to go back literally to basics. The first question to ask might then be: off what stock of plants did communities which spoke Greek or Latin in fact live, and how were these plants grown and harvested, and their products stored and cooked? The second concerns animals. One of the most striking messages of Diamond's book is also how narrow and limited, at all times, has been the range of animals which have genuinely been domesticated and bred, to be used for food, clothing, leather, carrying burdens, pulling wheeled carts or sledges or ploughs, and war.

The question of diet and food supply has at least now been brought firmly to the attention of classical ancient historians, above all in the work of Peter Garnsey,[2] while the late Joan Frayn opened up quite new perspectives in making us think about wild and cultivated plants, or about sheep-rearing and the wool trade.[3] There is no need to multiply examples: all that is underscored here is the need for awareness, on the part of those whose access to the classical world is essentially mediated through words, of the desirability of understanding the terms of human interaction with, and exploitation of, the natural world. Of course, in that area too, we neither can nor should attempt to work without the aid of the words in which classical writers reflected this relationship, whether it is Galen's treatise *On the Properties of Foodstuffs*,[4] or the *Naturalis Historia* of Pliny the Elder. Mary Beagon's study has shown that the *Natural History* has an intellectual structure, and is more than just a random

2. See Peter Garnsey, *Famine and Food Supply in the Graeco-Roman Cities* (1988); *Cities, Peasants and Food in Classical Antiquity: Essays in Social and Economic History* (1998); *Food and Society in Classical Antiquity* (1999).

3. J. M. Frayn, "Wild and Cultivated Plants: A Note on the Peasant Economy of Ancient Italy," *JRS* 65 (1975): 32; *Subsistence Farming in Roman Italy* (1979); *Sheep-Rearing and the Wool Trade in Italy during the Roman Period* (1984).

4. Galen, *On the Properties of Foodstuffs* I–III (*De alimentorum facultatibus*), *Opera*, ed. Kühn, VI, 453–748 (1823). See V. Nutton, "Galen and the Traveller's Fare," in J. Wilkins, D. Harvey, and M. Dobson, eds., *Food in Antiquity* (1995), 359.

assembly of items of evidence.[5] But in fact we should not be wary of using the *Natural History* also as just that, as an endless series of sidelights on human interaction with and exploitation of, the varied components of the natural world, whether organic (plants, animals, and fish) or inorganic, which means above all metals and stone, as it took place in the classical world.

The latter theme is one area with which, at least as regards the era before there were "guns," Jared Diamond's infinitely stimulating and suggestive book does not really deal. That is to say, the evolution of tools, and with them the expansion of human capacity to dig, to quarry, to cut both wood and stone, and to construct wheeled vehicles, ships, houses, temples, and public buildings, as well as the ability to make weapons for killing animals and other humans, both at close quarters and at a distance.

Yet, even if it were the case that we possessed no literary record (transmitted through medieval manuscripts) of the classical world, and had no idea of its history as constructed by those who wrote within it, the arrival, evolution, and spread—over most of the area from Hadrian's Wall to Afghanistan—of a very distinctive material culture would be clearly visible in the archaeological record. For what that record would show first of all is a vast production of manufactured objects, particularly pottery vessels and containers of innumerable kinds, accompanied by a high level of construction in stone, of both private and monumental communal buildings, and by representational art, coins bearing both words and images (of which there must literally be millions now preserved), and documents inscribed on stone or bronze, or on perishable materials. In the case of written texts in many of the languages involved—for instance (obviously), Latin, Greek, Hebrew, and Syriac—no complex process of decipherment, such as there is with Akkadian, would even be necessary. For in these languages the letter forms, the grammar, and much of the vocabulary are essentially still current today.

Of course this picture of a hypothetical re-discovery *de novo* of a hitherto unknown "classical" world, known only from archaeology, is a fantasy, because the close connections between it and ourselves are a function of the fact both that the classical world itself evolved an elaborate literature, and that subsequent generations have not only never lost contact with that literature, but have been profoundly shaped by contact with it. If nothing else, there has never been a break in the cultural history of the Near East, the Mediterranean and Europe, of a sort which would have led to a break in the continuous reading of the Bible, in Hebrew, in Greek, and in Latin. It

5. M. Beagon, *Roman Nature: The Thought of Pliny the Elder* (1992); note also R. French, *Ancient Natural History: Histories of Nature* (1994).

should be stressed that all three of these versions of the Bible, as canonical assemblages of texts, are products of the classical world: the latest book of the Hebrew Bible (Daniel), was composed in the second century B.C., and the Hellenistic period saw the translation of it, and of all the other books, into Greek; and both the "Old Latin" and the Vulgate, as Latin versions of the Bible, are products of the Roman Empire.

The fact that continuous use of texts, pagan and Christian, in Greek and Latin, links us directly to the classical world, and that there is no way in which we either can escape their influence or should seek to, does not mean that we should not try to look beyond them, to discern the material development of human life and settlement in the whole vast range of different areas which at one time or another came within the orbit of Graeco-Roman civilisation. Vast regions of the Graeco-Roman world are in any case hardly illuminated by any literary texts, or, if they are so at all, it is only by passing allusions to peripheral societies made by writers from the main stream of the classical tradition. A total history of human society in all the areas concerned, from southern Scotland to northern India—something which is currently (and for all foreseeable futures) completely unattainable—would have to encompass the fundamental issues of nutrition and of interactions with the physical world with which I began, and would involve an understanding of an immense series of complex questions: health, patterns of disease, expectation of life, demography, family structure, housing, and sanitation. Beyond these would lie the question of dependence on household production for subsistence, or alternatively of access to markets for food, and dependence or otherwise on the market for access to manufactured goods, furniture, or clothing. As indicated already, virtually the entire geographical area which saw the flourishing of Graeco-Roman civilisation, a period which in terms of human history is very recent indeed, has left a vast stock of physical evidence, from potsherds to buildings to organic remains, which is potentially relevant to all these questions. But one need only sketch the ideal of answering fundamental questions of human life in the way suggested to make it obvious that all that can be hoped for at the moment is partial studies, often of what are in fact very small archaeological sites, and which at best can give only very limited and localised answers.

None the less, the purpose of spelling out these unattainable ideals is that the wider background of our almost all-embracing ignorance should be kept in mind when we think of the more limited, but still enormously extensive, evidence which we do have—evidence which is accessible, which in itself can be understood, and which will yield at least partial and suggestive answers to major questions.

For instance, the physical remains of construction, from the foundations of small huts to the Pantheon in Rome, with its dome still complete as Hadrian built it, can be found almost anywhere in the area covered by Graeco-Roman civilisation. In Diamond's picture of the relative capacities of different societies, the topic of quarrying, stonecutting, the carving of decoration in stone, and the haulage of stone to the intended sites for building might have played a larger part. We can think of this area of enquiry as an aspect of the history of technology, or of education and training (how was it possible, in so many modest local contexts, to train generations of stonecutters, who could cut marble for use in building, or produce elaborate marble sarcophagi by the thousand?), or of artistic styles. But quarrying too is a fundamental aspect of the interaction of humans with the natural world, brilliantly explored, for instance, in a recently published "geological companion" to Greece.[6]

But sanctuaries, cemeteries, villages, and cities are of course not only the product of physical efforts and technological skills, but are expressions of the values and priorities of the societies which produced them, and can be "read" and interpreted in a way quite similar to the interpretation of written texts—which is, of course, to say also that, by the nature of interpretation, they can be "read" and interpreted wrongly, or at any rate in ways which have no defensible logical foundation. But here again, it would be futile and counter-productive to pretend that we either can, or should attempt to, "read" buildings and urban landscapes without doing so in the light of what is recorded of them in literary or documentary texts. Interpretation of physical remains in terms set by the ancient literary tradition has its dangers, of course, above all that of failing to distinguish what we are told in words from what is actually to be seen and encountered on the relevant site now.[7] But the fact remains that some of the most successful advances in understanding during the past few decades have involved the interpretation of architectural complexes and of urban landscapes through the combination of literary, archaeological, and documentary evidence. One may think for instance of what is (very surprisingly) the first overall attempt to interpret the history, function, and meaning of the Athenian Acropolis and the

6. M. D. Higgins and R. A. Higgins, *A Geological Companion to Greece and the Aegean* (1996).

7. The fact that the book maintains this distinction with such firmness and clarity is one of the many merits of Amanda Claridge's excellent *Rome: An Oxford Archaeological Guide* (1998).

buildings on it.[8] But the prime case, extremely relevant to at least some of the essays in this volume, must be the study of ancient Rome itself. In terms of style of approach and of interpretation, the tone has been set by Filippo Coarelli, whose work is not essentially *archaeological*, in the sense of the excavation and analysis of objects, but interpretative, in combining very detailed topographical knowledge, and a profound sense of place, with the use of written evidence. This, above all, has brought the Roman Forum to life as never before.[9] In parallel with this has come the new direction given to the study of Roman history by the combination of history, architectural history, art history, iconography, and topography in Paul Zanker's classic work on the power of images in the reign of Augustus.[10] This approach has now found its most systematic expression in the triumphant production, all within the last decade of the century, of the six volumes of Margareta Steinby's *Lexicon Topographicum* of the city of Rome.[11]

If the reader were to look at the articles collected in this volume in the order of the dates of their original publication, and not, as they are in fact arranged, in the chronological order of the subjects which they cover, he or she would see at least a pale reflection of the revolution of perception which has affected Roman history. That is to say, the earlier papers are wholly dependent on written evidence, literary or documentary, and show absolutely no sense of the physical or symbolic environment against which the narrative of Roman history is set. I hope at least that the reader would detect a change in the mid-1980s, as a direct consequence of a month spent in 1983 at the British School in Rome, walking around the city with Filippo Coarelli's *Guida Archeologica di Roma* in hand. The effect is (I hope) clearly visible in chapter 4, "The Political Character of the Classical Roman Republic, 200–151 B.C.," and chapter 12, "State and Subject: The Impact of Monarchy," both published in 1984.

The latter essay makes some allusions to numismatic evidence and uses the excellent British Museum pamphlet on Augustus, published in 1981.[12] But here the scene has been completely transformed in the 1990s by the publication of a work whose significance has perhaps still not been fully felt.

8. J. M. Hurwit, *The Athenian Acropolis: A History, Mythology and Archaeology from the Neolithic Era to the Present* (1998).

9. F. Coarelli, *Il Foro Romano I–II* (1983–85).

10. P. Zanker, *Augustus und die Macht der Bilder* (1987), translated as *The Power of Images in the Age of Augustus* (1988).

11. E. M. Steinby, ed., *Lexicon Topographicum Urbis Romae I–VI* (1993–99).

12. Susan Walker, *Augustus: Handlist of the Exhibition and Supplementary Studies* (1981).

I refer to the first volume of *Roman Provincial Coinage*, covering the period 44 B.C.–A.D. 69.[13] Now for the first time, it is possible to "read" the images and the written legends presented by the entire range of local coinages in the Graeco-Roman world over the crucial period of the establishment of monarchic rule in Rome. The coinages of the different local communities reveal at once the transformation of the symbolic landscapes—even, one might say, the "imagined communities"—to which they now belonged: each community representing itself as something with an independent political identity; but nearly all explicitly reflecting the existence at the centre of a single ruler, whose image is reproduced almost everywhere.

To collect and display the coins in this way is, of course, deliberately to give priority to their explicit messages, expressed in words and in images. But, to revert to a theme touched on earlier, coins, like other physical products of ancient societies, belong in several different fields of enquiry. Once again, there is the human interaction with the physical world: the mining, smelting, and transport of base metals, silver or gold; and then the design of type faces, and the production of the coins (one should not say production by a *mint*, or still less "by the mint of city x," for no one can define what, if anything, a "mint" in antiquity was). But there is also the question of volume of production, of circulation, and, beyond that, the problem of whether we should see economic relations at all levels in the Graeco-Roman world as having been monetised.[14] "Monetised" will mean two things, not entirely identical: the expression of value in terms of coin ("two denarii," "one million sesterces"); and the question of whether everyone had access to coins in circulation, with which they would make payments. These issues arise in a profound way and are very far from being solved, as regards the extraction of value by the Roman state in the form of taxation, and its subsequent redeployment, mainly in payments to soldiers. How far were these obligatory exchanges of value conducted by the use of coin?[15] Moreover, given that there was no paper money, and no system of credit transfer on paper, and

13. A. Burnett, M. Amandry, and P. P. Ripollès, *Roman Provincial Coinage* I.1–2: *From the death of Caesar to the death of Vitellius (44 B.C.–A.D. 69)* (1992). See now also the second volume, A. Burnett, M. Amandry, and I. Carradice, *Roman Provincial Coinage* II.1–2: *From Vespasian to Domitian (A.D. 69–96)* (1999).

14. For a few key studies, see, e.g., K. Hopkins, "Taxes and Trade in the Roman Empire (200 B.C.–A.D. 400)," *JRS* 70 (1980): 101; C. J. Howgego, "Why Did Ancient States Strike Coins?," *Num. Chron.* 150 (1990): 1; "The Supply and Use of Money in the Ancient World," *JRS* 82 (1992): 1; *Ancient History from Coins* (1995).

15. See R. Duncan-Jones, *Structure and Scale in the Roman Economy* (1990), chap. 12: "Taxation in Money and Taxation in Kind."

that therefore the physical transport of coin around the empire was necessary, how was this achieved? This issue brings us back once again to the evolution of physical resources and capacities: the construction of wheeled waggons, and the employment of animals for traction; and the role of shipping for official transport, as well as for wider economic exchanges.

Some brief remarks on the minting and redistribution of coins are made in another essay, "Cash Distributions in Rome and Imperial Minting," which appears for the first time in English as chapter 7 of volume 2. But in general it would have to be acknowledged that the work collected in these three volumes does not deal with the physical bases of human life in Graeco-Roman antiquity, or with economic history, or with state finance, in the sense of the exchange of value between subject and state. The only, partial, exception is that one essay, chapter 9, in this volume, "The Mediterranean and the Roman Revolution: Politics, War, and the Economy," does sketch some aspects of how this exchange worked in the erratic, violent, and fluctuating circumstances of the end of the Roman Republic.

War was in fact endemic in the Graeco-Roman world until we reach the Roman Empire. This was true of the Greek city-states, as it was of what in effect was an under-recognised category of city-states, those of Italy in the first millennium B.C. War was certainly endemic in all the "barbarian" societies which bordered on the Graeco-Roman area, as it was equally in the Persian Empire and the Phoenician-Punic world of the central and western Mediterranean in the period up to the achievement of Roman domination in the second century B.C. As a masterly article by Michel Austin has shown, military ambition was integral also to the nature of the Hellenistic kingdoms.[16] Discussion of Roman imperialism in the Republic, fundamental though some recent studies have been,[17] has perhaps not been conducted with sufficiently explicit attention to the fact that the Romans were not the only imperialists who were currently active: Pyrrhus, Hannibal, Philip V, Antiochus III, Mithridates, Tigranes of Armenia, and Cleopatra were all in the business of the active expansion of the areas under their control. It is certainly the case also that, if we look at "the Greek city" as a political and communal structure, far more attention has gone to the citizen as voter, official, or juror than to the citizen as soldier.[18]

16. M. M. Austin, "Hellenistic Kings, War, and the Economy," *CQ* 36 (1986): 450.

17. Note esp. W. V. Harris, *War and Imperialism in Republican Rome, 327–70 B.C.* (1979; repr. 1985); W. V. Harris, ed., *The Imperialism of Mid-Republican Rome* (1984); J. Rich and G. Shipley, eds., *War and Society in the Roman World* (1993).

18. Note however L. A. Burkhardt, *Bürger und Soldaten: Aspekte der politischen und militärischen Rolle athenische Bürger im Kriegswesen des 4. Jahrhunderts v. Chr.* (1996).

But all ancient political communities were in fact by their nature military organisations, and it is one of the most significant aspects of the originality of Polybius that, in thinking about the Roman *politeia* in book 6, he gives a large amount of space to the organisation of the Roman army. I have been as guilty as most others of not wanting to make wars and armies the focus of my attention; and, insofar as military history and military structures play any part in these volumes, it is more as a general context than as serious topics in their own right. But, it should be emphasised here that, right down to the battle of Actium, not just the major powers but, as it seems, every small community within their shadow had to be prepared to exert itself in its own defence.

In default of any other serious attention to military history, I would like to suggest that we ought at least to ask ourselves whether it is not the battle of Actium (rather than, say, the conquests of Alexander and the emergence of the Hellenistic monarchies) which marks the most significant turning point in the history of the Greek city-state. For up to Actium (it seems) Greek cities might still be under the necessity to produce military or naval forces, for their own protection or in the service of others; but after Actium (or so it seems) this essential communal function simply vanishes, at least until the drastically changed circumstances of the third century. A similar change, of immense importance, was one of the most profound consequences of the Social War of 90–87 B.C., and of the extension of Roman citizenship to all the communities of Italy. For this was the moment at which the allied communities of Italy, and the *coloniae Latinae*, ceased to provide and pay for their own contingents for the Roman army. Instead, their men were drafted into the Roman legions. I will return to this theme very briefly later, in looking more closely at the topic of the chapters in this volume, Roman history of the Republican and Augustan periods. But it will be worth noting here that the military and naval roles of Greek *poleis* in the late Republic on the one hand, and of Italian *civitates* up to the Social War, but not after, are specifically compared by Cicero in the fifth Verrine oration, written in the summer of 70 B.C.[19] So far as I know, no provincial governor under the Empire had the specific opportunities for malpractice which his deployment of ships provided by the Greek cities of Sicily offered to Verres. One key element in the relations between provincial communities and the ruling power had changed, and at the same time (as it seems) the military role of the self-governing community had disappeared.

19. Cicero, *Verr.* II 5, 60. The passage is translated in chapter 8 in this volume, "The Last Century of the Republic: Whose History?"

That role has never been fully explored, nor have the consequences of its end been examined. I stress it here only to emphasise that I believe it to be important, and also (once again) to indicate that it is not among the topics covered in the chapters of this volume, or, in any significant way, in the two following ones.

The subject of all three volumes could be summed up as the communal culture and civil government of the Graeco-Roman world, essentially from the Hellenistic period to the fifth century A.D. In one sense at least, as the author of the articles and review articles assembled as chapters in these three volumes, I have to admit that both the questions asked in them and the material deployed to answer these questions are traditional and even old-fashioned. They show expertise neither in the biological and demographic history of mankind over the seven or eight centuries concerned, nor in the material evidence, nor, except in a very modest and peripheral way, in urbanism, architecture, or visual imagery. The evidence used is fundamentally that provided by words, whether literary texts reaching us through medieval manuscripts, or original documents, inscriptions above all, but also papyri and coin legends. If any originality can be claimed, it is not as such in the type of material used, namely the written word, but in the extension of the cultural and linguistic range of the written words concerned, to cover Jewish literary sources and documents in Greek, Hebrew, and Aramaic, as well as material in other Semitic languages—for instance, Palmyrene and Nabataean inscriptions, and Syriac documents (inscriptions and parchments) and literary texts. But the theme of the co-existence and interpenetration of cultures and traditions in the Near East, of the interpretation of classical and Jewish traditions, and of the early stages of Arab self-identification in terms of descent from Abraham, belongs in volume 3. For the moment, it will be enough to call attention to an article by Hannah Cotton, Walter Cockle, and myself, which it was not appropriate to include in these volumes, and which surveys the papyrology of the Near East in the imperial period.[20] It may be worth noting that the texts listed there include examples in Latin, Greek, Hebrew, Jewish Aramaic, Nabataean, Palmyrene, and Syriac. To me, it must be said, the Near East represents the most significant part of my work, and, if fate allows, I hope after all to return to its history in the period between Constantine and Mohamed.

Within the strictly Graeco-Roman sphere, and accepting that the articles collected here derive fundamentally from written material, literary and

20. H. M. Cotton, W. E. H. Cockle, and F. G. B. Millar, "The Papyrology of the Roman Near East: A Survey," *JRS* 85 (1995): 214.

documentary, it would also have to be admitted that many major themes of contemporary historiography have found no place, or very little: pagan religion, magic, women's history or gender studies, or the history of medicine, either as an applied art, or as encompassing a significant proportion of the literary texts surviving from antiquity, or as containing immensely important material, both for social history and for ancient conceptions of the body and the human self.[21] On reflection, there are not many excuses for this. For, unexpected as it may seem, when I began graduate work in 1958 under the late Sir Ronald Syme, with the idea of writing a thesis on Cassius Dio,[22] the first work I was told to read was the classic article of 1905 by J. Ilberg, "Aus Galens Praxis."[23]

Ronald Syme was an inspiring supervisor, to whom I owe an enormous debt. But I cannot pretend ever to have been consumed by his passion for prosopography and the history of families, in either of its two main manifestations. One was the study of careers in the imperial period, above all as recorded in thousands of honorific inscriptions. The other main manifestation was, of course, in the political history of the Republic and the Augustan period, and the focus which has been of central importance in the writing of classical Roman history throughout the twentieth century on the Senate and on the "nobility," or "aristocracy," which was believed to have dominated it, and which in the end compromised with remarkable ease with the monarchic regime of Augustus.[24]

Here, to come finally to the specific subject matter of this volume, it is obvious that my work on Roman history has, broadly speaking, taken not merely a different direction from that of Ronald Syme, but in many respects one which runs directly counter to his. In case it needs saying, this has never been seen by me, and was never seen by him during his life, as representing any sort of personal challenge or conflict. So far as he was concerned, as he always made clear, if someone had something to say, that was fine, and all the more so if what was written showed some sense of style or of the capacity for structure and composition. So far as I was, and am, concerned, I could never hope to achieve a masterpiece of literary composition like *The Roman Revolution* (finished, it may be noted, when its author was thirty-five), am not a classicist in anything like the same sense, and suffer from the further

21. Note esp. H. King, *Hippocrates' Woman: Reading the Female Body in Ancient Greece* (1998).

22. *A Study of Cassius Dio* (1964; repr. 2000).

23. J. Ilberg, "Aus Galens Praxis," *Neue Jahrbücher für das Klassische Altertum* 15 (1905): 276.

24. See, of course, the remarkable, and somewhat undervalued, work of Syme's old age, *The Augustan Aristocracy* (1986).

crippling disadvantage that I find it impossible to remember details of family relationships and genealogy. I only trust that my turning away from interpretations resting on such relationships has been motivated by something more profound than simply not being able to remember who was whose cousin, or nephew, or brother-in-law.

There are however two very important aspects of *The Roman Revolution* in respect of which I would like to think that there is some continuity, rather than a sharp break. One is the intention to see Augustus and his reign very specifically through the literature of the period, and through the precise vocabulary in which views of it, by followers or by more detached observers, were expressed. The other was—in spite of Ronald Syme's reputation as a passionate observer of the "aristocracy"—to widen enormously the cast of characters who could be perceived as having been participants in the Roman "revolution," by bringing in the minor figures, down to centurions or local town councillors, mentioned in passing in literary sources or recorded on inscriptions, who played a part in the march of events, and perhaps gained, for themselves or their descendants, a place in the upper levels of Roman society. How many other books on the political history of the late Republic have found a place (*Roman Revolution*, 354) for "T. Flavius Petro, from Reate, a Pompeian veteran"? This was, of course, the grandfather of the emperor Vespasian.[25]

This sense of a wider social range, and of the innumerable different petty localities from which men might come to play a part in the wider Roman system, is a major development in Roman history in the twentieth century, expressed for instance in Claude Nicolet's first great work, on the equestrian order under the Republic,[26] and later in Ségolène Demougin's remarkable study of the same status group under the Julio-Claudians.[27] Who would have imagined that our evidence would reveal the names of no less than 770 *equites* of that period?

The stage on which what we think of as "Roman history" can be seen being played out has thus become incomparably more populated than could possibly have been the case before the composition of the great works of prosopography which began in the late nineteenth century. This is not the place to list these, except perhaps to note the inception and completion of the *Prosopography of the Later Roman Empire*, covering the period from A.D. 260

25. Suetonius, *Div. Vesp.* I.

26. C. Nicolet, *L'ordre équestre à l'époque républicaine, 312–43 av. J.-C.* I–II (1966–74).

27. S. Demougin, *L'ordre équestre sous les julio-claudiens* (1988); *Prosopographie des chevaliers romains julio-claudiens* (1992).

to 641, begun soon after the Second World War, and reaching its last entry, "Zudius", in volume IIIB, published in 1992.[28]

Reference works in the field of prosopography, whether structured alphabetically, person by person, or as lists of office-holders, are an indispensable tool, which we now almost take for granted. But they can of course lead to an overestimate of the importance of the occupation of office, and can at the worst embody unquestioned assumptions which tend to equate the pursuit of office with the entire political process in the community concerned. The danger is even greater when the study of which individuals—or of which families over successive generations—held office is projected back into a period from which there is no contemporary literary or documentary evidence. In spite of the superlative scholarship displayed in Friedrich Münzer's great work of 1920 on Roman noble "parties" and families, now translated for the first time into English,[29] and while doing honour to the tragic personal history of Münzer himself in the Nazi period,[30] it ought in my view to be acknowledged that the book served to stimulate a curiously distorted manner of "seeing" Roman republican history, and of interpreting the narratives of it which we have, which was to dominate the study of republican history for at least the next half century.

Of course the emphasis on competition for the consulship in Münzer's work was not gratuitous, for it followed the lead given by our narrative sources themselves and, very notably, by the two great Augustan inscriptions, the *Fasti Consulares* and the *Fasti Triumphales*, which literally set in stone a certain view of the Roman past, in listing all those who had held triumphs, back to Romulus himself, and all the pairs of consuls since the foundation of the Republic. But to say that is to say that *as texts* these inscriptions are every bit as much ideological representations of the Roman past as Livy's *History*, or Ovid's *Fasti*, or the last part of Ovid's *Metamorphoses*. As a *text*, the all-too-perfect listing of the supposed holders of the consulate in the fifth century B.C., each equipped with the *praenomen* of both his father and his grandfather, deserves to be studied as a literary construct, not as a documentary record; and *as inscriptions*, as Margareta Steinby's study of the east side of the Forum

28. A. H. M. Jones, J. R. Martindale, and J. Morris (eds.), *The Prosopography of the Later Roman Empire* I: *A.D. 260–393* (1971); J. R. Martindale, ed., II: *A.D. 395–527* (1980); III A–B: *A.D. 527–641* (1992).

29. F. Münzer, *Römische Adelsparteien und Adelsfamilien* (1920); translated by Thérèse Ridley, *Roman Aristocratic Parties and Families* (1999).

30. See the very moving account by A. Kneppe and J. Wiesehöfer, *Friedrich Münzer. Ein Althistoriker zwischen Kaiserreich und Nationalsozialismus* (1983).

showed, everything is uncertain about the original location, the conception, the date, and the function of both sets of *Fasti*.[31]

There is thus an organic connection between the *Fasti*, as a product of Augustan—or rather, in origin, pre-Augustan—culture, politics, and antiquarianism, and a great modern work like T. R. S. Broughton's *The Magistrates of the Roman Republic*. The one leads to the other, and both represent choices in the construction of the past. As for the early Republic, the alleged sequences of named holders of major offices are an unreliable basis for historical reconstruction. For the later Republic we can accept that the data are essentially reliable. But they represent only one aspect of the political history of the wider community of Romans.

There is also another important aspect of prosopography which has played a large part in twentieth-century writing on Rome, and which is also directly rooted in the Romans' perceptions of their own history. I mean by this the study of the very distinctive and important theme in Roman history and historiography, by which the category of "Romans" was not closed, but was repeatedly expanded to include ever wider groups, not forgetting all slaves legally freed by Roman citizens. This theme is expressed most prominently in the famous inscription from Lyon recording the speech in which the emperor Claudius urged the Senate to take a positive attitude to the admission of leading men from Gaul (who were themselves, by definition, already Roman citizens) into the Senate. Such a policy had been an aspect of the history of Rome from the very beginning, Claudius explained; and, more recently, Augustus and Tiberius had wished to see "the whole flower of the *coloniae* and *municipia* everywhere, provided that they were respectable men and rich, in this *curia*."[32] This theme came very quickly to appeal to the young "provincial" from New Zealand, Ronald Syme, decades before it bore fruit in his two-volume work on Tacitus, published in 1958. The proof of this was provided in 1999 in the form of the publication of the original text of the study entitled *The Provincial at Rome*, which Syme had referred to, as begun but never completed, in the Preface to *Tacitus*. It bears the date 1934.[33]

31. E. M. Steinby, "Il lato orientale del Foro Romano. Proposte di lettura," *Arctos* 21 (1987): 139; see pp. 156–57 on the Fornix Fabianus. This article is not discussed in the otherwise excellent article of C. J. Simpson, "The Original Site of the *Fasti Capitolini*," *Historia* 42 (1993): 61. Between them, the two essays show very clearly how the study of both inscriptions needs to be undertaken *de novo*.

32. *ILS*, no. 212.

33. Ronald Syme, *The Provincial at Rome and Rome and the Balkans, 80 B.C. to A.D. 14*, ed. Anthony Birley (1999).

Such a prosopographical approach evidently formed an essential starting point for anyone who, like myself, began as a doctoral student under Ronald Syme, and (as it happens) in the same year as *Tacitus* was published. If we look at such an approach in the light of the much wider perspectives evoked earlier, the long-term demographic, institutional, medical, and geographical history of mankind, it will of course appear limited and conventional, closely tied to texts—literary or documentary—which are accessible only through an education in Greek or Latin. And, indeed, it not only *seems* relatively restricted, but is. Furthermore, a much wider approach—though nowhere coming close to the wider biological history of humans—had already been demonstrated before *The Roman Revolution* was published. By that I mean, of course, Rostovtzeff's *Social and Economic History of the Roman Empire*, first published in 1926. Once again, this is not the place to attempt to characterise Rostovtzeff's work in detail, or to evoke the very active and creative studies of him, both in Russia and in the West, in the 1990s.[34] But it is relevant to stress that Rostovtzeff brought into a narrative of imperial history, firstly, a vast range of physical evidence, visited in situ or inspected in local museums; and secondly, an equally vast range of local documentary evidence, above all inscriptions and papyri. In that way he exploited innumerable local "voices" or testimonies as evidence for the wider history of the Empire. But Rostovtzeff was not just assembling data, he was telling a story. But that story, we should frankly admit, was in itself a quite conventional one, of growing prosperity and stability in the Empire up to the Antonine age, followed by a military monarchy and the beginnings of anarchy in the third century; in short, it is precisely the story told in the last part of the *Roman History* of Cassius Dio.

Rostovtzeff's *History* was both the symbol and the first large-scale product of the revolution produced in the nature and scale of our access to the ancient world that had been made possible by the apparently dry labour of producing *corpora* of inscriptions and papyri, catalogues of coins, volumes of excavation reports, descriptions of buildings and categorisations of small finds which had gone on since the nineteenth century. Rostovtzeff's own interests also embraced, if in very varying degrees of intensity, the whole geographical area of the Roman Empire and (as regards Asia) far beyond it.

The range and variety of possible historical approaches to the ancient world is thus now incomparably greater than was possible even a century

---

34. Note esp. the excellent introduction by Jean Andreau to the French translation, *Histoire économique et sociale de l'empire romain* (1988); and also the papers and documents edited by G. Bongard-Levin, *Skifskii Roman* (1997).

ago. An infinity of different emphases, or starting points, is possible, from studying the rhetoric of Cicero or the biblical exegesis of Saint Jerome, or examining the literary character of Tacitus' portrait of Tiberius, to assessing the organic remains from excavations as evidence for diet, surveying whole landscapes, excavating settlements, analysing the chemical composition of pottery, assembling the coins of a small Greek city, reading multilingual documents from the shores of the Dead Sea—or asking how, if at all, we can understand what we mean by "Roman" religion.

If I reflect on my own path within this trackless forest of possibilities, it is easy to see that the work done belongs very clearly, and fairly consistently, at a definable logical level. That is to say, it has been almost wholly dependent on verbal evidence, documentary and literary. But it nowhere approaches literary criticism in the proper sense, nor on the other hand has it been concerned with the initial publication of newly discovered documentary texts. The area of operation can thus be seen as stretching from strictly political history on the one hand, to political institutions and forms of behaviour, social values, and conceptions—and not least conceptions and expectations directed to rulers by those below them and in contact with them—to social life proper, in the sense in which it is accessible through literary and documentary texts. The arrangement of the studies in this volume, in the broad chronological sequence of the topics of periods covered, serves to obscure their chronological sequence in the other sense, the time of writing, which is not far from being the complete converse. That is to say, the earlier studies represented here focus on Augustus and his regime, and do so primarily through the medium of the way in which the new emperor, and his personal role, his form of government, and his actions, are conceptualised in contemporary literary and documentary texts. There is no need to rehearse any of this here. But I would wish to underscore one principle of method and one conclusion. The principle of method is in a sense a democratising one, or at any rate is concerned with seeing the imperial rule through the eyes, or at least the words, of as wide a geographical and social range of his subjects as the evidence allows. Put another way, it affirms that "the emperor," conceived of as the addressee of a letter and decree of a Greek city, to be borne to him by ambassadors, is at least as validly the "real" emperor as the one represented in a later Latin narrative.

The one conclusion which may be worth re-stating here is that nothing anywhere in the evidence justifies the idea that it was ever claimed officially that Augustus had "restored the republic" in the sense of re-creating a republican system. It was, of course, claimed that the *res publica* had been *restituta*; but that is not the same thing. If anyone had wished to claim that Augustus had given up personal power, they might have said that the *res publica* had been *reddita* by him. But they did not, and could not have; and one of the most well-placed and well-informed of Augustus' contemporaries, the geographer Strabo, said unambiguously the exact opposite: that "his native land entrusted to him the care of the government, and he was established for life as master of war and peace."[35]

The studies of the Republic in this volume have a rather different origin. One aspect of it has been touched on already: the experience of absorbing a sense of the topography of Rome in 1983. Otherwise, this sequence of studies of republican politics, culminating in my book on the crowd in Rome,[36] have a very different character from most of the rest of my work. For what is precisely lacking so far in our evidence for the Republic is, on the one hand, a mass of local documents expressing the identity and concerns of subordinate participants in a wider structure; and, on the other, a range of contemporary literary works written by observers who were not themselves at the heart of events. It is frustrating in many ways that the most explicit, detailed, and immediately revealing contemporary documents for republican history tend to come from the Greek East;[37] and among these an important place must go to the late Republican and Triumviral texts from Aphrodisias.[38] Also, major new documents remain to be fully studied: for instance, the extensive inscription on *portoria* from Ephesos; and, above all, the last legacy of the great Louis Robert, namely the two long inscriptions of leading citizens from Colophon who acted as intermediaries between their city and the Roman authorities in the early decades of the province of Asia.[39]

These texts, of immense potential value, have (surprisingly) not been studied in great detail in the decade since their original publication. But what they serve to emphasise is also, by contrast, the dearth of literary and documentary "voices" from inside republican Italy—and, paradoxically perhaps,

35. Strabo, *Geography* XVII, 3, 25 (840). See now K. Clarke, *Between Geography and History: Hellenistic Constructions of the Roman World* (1999).

36. *The Crowd in Rome in the Late Republic* (1998).

37. Note R. K. Sherk, *Roman Documents from the Greek East: Senatus Consulta and Epistulae to the Age of Augustus* (1969).

38. J. M. Reynolds, *Aphrodisias and Rome* (1982).

39. For the *monumentum Ephesinum*, see still H. Engelmann and D. Knibbe, *Das Zollgesetz der Provinz Asia. Eine neue Inschrift aus Ephesos* (*Epigraphica Anatolica* 14, 1989); *SEG* XXXIX, no. 1180; *AE* 1989, no. 681; and for the inscriptions of Polemaios and Menippos, see Louis Robert and Jeanne Robert, *Claros* I: *décrets hellénistiques*, fasc. 1 (1989), with J.-L. Ferrary, "Le statut des cités libres dans l'Empire romain à la lumière des inscriptions de Claros," *CRAI* (1991): 217. A full commentary is still needed.

an even greater dearth from inside Rome itself. This is the great weakness of republican history, in spite of its endless fascination, the powerful narratives which record it, and the profound nature of its impact on the outside world, from Britain to Mesopotamia. It is also the reason why the influence of anthropology has not been felt in Roman history as it has in Greek. For, in order to be able to borrow (as we should) approaches developed in social anthropology, we require a society to apply them to, or at least one which we can convince ourselves that we can in some sense observe and understand. But when we speak of "Roman" society, what do we mean? The inhabitants of the city, about whose life we know almost nothing? Or of the *vici* which surrounded it? Or the citizen farmers occupying the territory stretching north across Italy to the Adriatic, or south-east to Campania? Or the people of small, ancient urban centres and political communities like Arpinum, enjoying a full dual citizenship, Roman and local, after 188 B.C.? The truth is that there is not even one of these several very contrasting component elements of the Roman citizen body of before 90 B.C. of which we can gain any serious conception at all.

This problem shows up perhaps most clearly of all when we discuss "Roman religion"—or "the religions of Rome," as a remarkable and important recent work puts it.[40] For even this book concentrates on the evolution of cults and religious practices in the city of Rome itself. But what of the cults of Tusculum, or of the Sabine county, or Picenum? What temples were there in Arpinum, how were priests chosen, what was the form of their religious calendar? Even more profoundly, our view of Roman religion, in spite of the fact that most Roman citizens must have lived by agriculture, fails to give a central place to the offerings and prayers which a farmer was advised to carry out if he wanted his crops to flourish. Indeed, we hardly have any impression of the religious practice of agriculture at all except from Cato's *De agri cultura*. One example will suffice:[41]

> The following is the Roman formula to be observed in thinning a grove: A pig is to be sacrificed, and the following prayer uttered: "Whether thou be god or goddess to whom this grove is dedicated, as it is thy right to receive a sacrifice of a pig for the thinning of this grove, and to this intent, whether I or one at my bidding do it, may it be rightly done. To this end, in offering this pig to thee I humbly beg that thou wilt be gracious and merciful to me, to my house and household, and

40. M. Beard, J. North, and S. Price, *The Religions of Rome* I–II (1998).
41. Cato, *De agri cultura*, 139–40 (Loeb trans.).

to my children. Wilt thou deign to receive this pig which I offer thee
to this end?"

If you wish to till the ground, offer a second sacrifice in the same
way, with the addition of the words: "for the sake of doing this work."
So long as the work continues, the ritual must be performed in some
part of the land every day; and if you miss a day, or if public or domestic
feast days intervene, a new offering must be made.

The effect of the limited nature of the evidence for the republican period,
therefore, is that, instead of having the evidence to write a social history, in
the light of which we could interpret the political narratives which we have,
we have to use those narratives themselves (together, in Cicero's time, with
speeches, and the narratives contained within them) to construct a picture of
the constitutional structure of the *res publica*, of the political relations which
lay behind voting and elections, and of the structure of Roman society itself.
Cato is exceptional in speaking of the religious life of the countryside at all.
But it is typical that we owe even this testimony to the pen of an ex-consul
writing for contemporary upper-class landowners.

If such limitations affect our knowledge of "Roman" society, in or near
the city and out in the countryside and in small towns, it is even more true of
the "Latin" communities of old Latium and of the *coloniae Latinae*, or of the
very diverse groups who came under the heading of *socii* or *foederati*. What
we can at least perceive through our narrative sources is in fact something
very remarkable, namely the fact that the Italian peninsula in the republican
period was a world without kings or hereditary aristocracies or castles. If we
only had the evidence, republican Italy would claim a place, just as much as
classical Greece, in the history of the self-governing city-state. It could not,
of course, be proved that every Italian community had a functioning "constitution" and annual magistrates. But the progress of Italic epigraphy and the
work of M. Cébeillac-Gervasoni and others has allowed us at least glimpses
of these magistrates in office over large parts of the peninsula.[42] None the
less, we are still a long way from being able to "see" any Italian communities
(Roman, Latin, or federate) from inside, or to understand what changes the
extension of the Roman citizenship after the Social War will have brought
about. One of these is mentioned earlier: the end of the military role of Latin
and federate *civitates*, and the enrolment of their young men into the Roman

42. See, e.g., P. Poccetti, *Nuovi documenti italici* (1979); A. Morandi, *Epigrafia Italica* (1982).
See M. Cébeillac-Gervasoni, ed., *Les "bourgeoisies" municipales italiennes aux IIe et Ier siècles av.
J.-C.* (1983); *Les élites municipales de l'Italie péninsulaire des Gracques à Néron* (1996); *Les magistrats
des cités italiennes de la Seconde Guerre Punique à Auguste: le Latium et la Campanie* (1998).

legions. It is frustrating that it remains the case that the new situation of Italy, as something which approximated to a nation-state—what Augustus, looking back to 32 B.C., was to call "tota Italia"—is still best grasped through local copies of *leges* passed by the people in Rome, or, in the case of the Tabula Heracleensis, of a local compilation, then inscribed, of sections from different laws passed in Rome. None the less, the work done on these documents in recent years is of primary importance.[43]

With the reigns of Augustus and Tiberius, we suddenly enter a world where, in a certain sense, our evidence is transformed in scale and in the richness of the meanings which it conveys. This is true, clearly enough, of literature, both Latin and Greek; of the explosion of "the epigraphic habit," also in both Latin and Greek; and, as mentioned earlier, of the huge range of local coins mirroring the predominance of the distant and largely unseen emperor. Even if "Augustan" literature hardly reveals to us the life of the broad masses of the population, its complexity as a cultural, ideological, and political product is sufficient to ensure that interpretation and reinterpretation will never run dry.[44] Moreover, this is one field of study which is truly "inter-disciplinary," in the sense that physical and iconographic evidence, along with a flood of epigraphic material, can be brought into conjunction with the literary sources. It is also no surprise that we have ever more epigraphic "sidelights" on the imperial regime from the Greek world, from the relations of Miletos to Augustus, to a Bosporan king thanking one of the Greek cities of his kingdom for maintaining tranquillity while he was off to Rome to see the emperor.[45] But now older elements in the Latin epigraphic record—for instance, the two inscriptions from Pisa which give us the first detailed picture of the politics of a *colonia*—are now joined by long texts, composed in Rome, but dutifully inscribed in Italy or Baetica, which completely renew our sense of the institutions of Rome under the emperors, of contemporary conceptions of the Empire (themes touched on in chapters 15 and 16 in this volume), of the tone and language of deferential politics in a monarchic setting, and of the machinery of communication to Rome's subjects. I refer of course to the two new, infinitely rich and complex, Latin epigraphic texts, the *Tabula Siarensis* and *Tabula Hebana* (overlapping epigraphic

43. All the relevant texts are re-edited, translated, and commented on in M. Crawford, ed., *Roman Statutes* I–II (1996).

44. Note, for instance, K. Galinsky, *Augustan Culture: An Interpretative Introduction* (1996).

45. See P. Herrmann, "Milet unter Augustus. C. Iulius Epikrates und die Anfänge des Kaiserkults," *Ist. Mitt.* 44 (1994): 203; H. Heinen, "Zwei Briefe des bosporanischen Königs Aspurgos (*AE* 1994, 1538)," *ZPE* 124 (1999): 133.

copies of a single original text), and the *Senatus Consultum de Cn. Pisone patre*.[46] I am not sure whether to be encouraged or discouraged by the reflection that nearly all of what I have written on the early imperial regime will have to be read in future as pre-dating the new era created by these texts.

In "inscriptions" such as these, the barrier between "literature" and "documents" essentially dissolves, and we are forcibly reminded that all documents, even the most apparently simple (which these are decidedly not), are constructs with a logic and rhetoric of their own. But that reflection brings us back to the central point of the observations in this prologue. That is to say that what we are pleased to call "ancient history" is meaningful and intelligible to us precisely because it is so recent, and because we are in every sense so close to it. Above all, a huge and ever-growing stock of words written in classical antiquity, in scripts and languages which have remained fully accessible ever since, is available for us to read. Much the same is true of the art and iconography, the coins with legends and images, and the architectural styles and the urban plans which characterised Graeco-Roman civilisation. That may seem rewarding, and in many senses it is, above all if we take within our view also Jewish tradition, culture, and belief, and follow the emergence of Christian monotheism from within the context of Graeco-Roman paganism. But all this profusion of evidence necessarily tends to obscure from us the fact that what we can encounter by these means is the history of a culture, rather than the whole history of a human society, or rather of a set of linked societies, over many centuries. In the present state—and all imaginable future states—of our knowledge of human history in the long period and the varied regions which we label the "ancient" or "classical" or "Graeco-Roman" world, we just have to accept that a very large part of it is beyond our grasp. But what we can grasp is enormously rich and varied, and increasing every day.

Fergus Millar

46. For the *Tabula Siarensis* and the *Tabula Hebana*, we can now refer to the edition in M. Crawford (n. 43), no. 37/8. It remains the case that the joint text still needs detailed study from many points of view—linguistic, institutional, cultural, and political. For the *Senatus consultum* all that is already provided, in the exemplary publication by W. Eck, A. Caballos, and F. Fernández, *Das Senatus Consultum de Cn. Pisone Patre* (1996), with the review article by M. Griffin, "The Senate's Story," *JRS* 87 (1997): 249, and the special issue of the *American Journal of Philology*, edited by C. Damon and S. Takács, *The Senatus Consultum de Cn. Pisone Patre*, *AJPh* 120, no. 1 (1999).

PART I

Conceptions and Sources

CHAPTER ONE

Taking the Measure
*of the Ancient World**

Almost exactly forty years ago, I was in my last term at a Scottish public school on the shores of the Firth of Forth, where the climate would have made that of Durham, by comparison, seem positively tropical, and the boys were prevented from freezing only by being permanently occupied in playing rugby football. But, fundamental as rugby football ("rugger" in common language) was to the ideology of the school, even I was surprised when the then head boy approached me, and said in despairing tones: "Millar, I get depressed sometimes. There are *some* people in this school who think that rugger is just something like Latin, which you never *think* about except when you're doing it."

I do not tell this story in order to mock my own origins. For one thing, in a world where we can be told by our prime minister that there is "no such thing as society," the values of "team spirit" and mutual responsibility which Loretto really did instil now seem less self-evident, and more important, than they might have done. Secondly, when, with the onset of the second infantilism common to middle-aged gentlemen, I came back years later to watching international rugger matches, I realised that the head boy had been right, on one side at least: we *had* just played and played, without actually thinking about how the game might be played better.

So, thirdly, might he have been right also in implying that Latin was also something which one tended just to "do," and that we do not always ask ourselves what our subject is, what it really amounts to, or how are we or our pupils might best approach it? This is the opportunity which I would like to

---

* Presidential address at the Classical Association, Durham, April 1993, *Proceedings of the Classical Association* 90 (1993): 11–33.

take now: not, at least in the first instance, by way of self-questioning and self-criticism, but rather the opposite. By defining what our subject amounts to, we might also remind ourselves, and others, just how vast its scope is.

Let me begin by offering a possible definition: classics is the study of the culture, in the widest sense, of any population using Greek and Latin, from the beginning to (say) the Islamic invasions of the seventh century A.D.

Since Michael Ventris' decipherment of Linear B, "the beginnings" ought of course to cover the later second millennium B.C.; and certainly we can on no account leave the late Bronze Age out of our conception of Greek history. None the less, we could still choose to treat that as a sort of Greek "pre-history," and to take the decisive beginning as falling in the eighth century B.C. To do that would be to use two interrelated markers: the appearance of the earliest scraps of writing which are not only in Greek but in the Greek alphabet; and the works of Homer and Hesiod.

Whether we ought, or ought not, to talk of a real, historical world of Homer (following M. I. Finley's brilliant *The World of Odysseus*), it remains very important that a remarkable range of the basic features of Greek culture and Greek social and political life is already represented for us in the poems of Homer: a multiplicity of gods and goddesses; sacrifices offered to them; temples; cities, and newly founded "colonial" cities; war; competition; honour; oratory; popular assemblies; competitive sport. Thus the history of European sports journalism begins, very appropriately, with *Iliad* 23, and a famous row as to whether victory in a chariot race had been legitimately won. (Perhaps, in view of the farce of the Grand National in 1993, the Classical Association could offer a prize for fifty lines of Homeric hexameters describing a race which never got started because some deity maliciously dulled the wits of the officials?).

But if we are to begin with Homer, it is absolutely essential not to let that mislead us into thinking of "Greek history" as something which happened first, followed sometime after by "Roman history." For the two histories and the two cultures were closely connected from the eighth century onwards, and became even more inextricably intertwined as time went on. Thus, we must recall that imported Greek vases were already reaching Rome around the notional, or legendary, date of its "foundation," 753 B.C. And from around that time too we have the East Greek Geometric skyphos discovered on the island of Pithekoussai (Ischia), the earliest Greek settlement in the West, and not much over one hundred miles from Rome. The famous graffito written on it, "I [am] the cup of Nestor, good to drink from," both reflects a knowledge of epic, and, being written from right to left, illustrates the (probably very recent) borrowing of the Greek alphabet from Phoenicia. Almost all that we can hope to know of the eighth-century Mediterranean is embodied in a single fragmentary pot.

We come, however, a great deal closer to early Rome with the krater of the following century found at Caere, a mere twenty miles from Rome, painted with a scene showing Odysseus and his companions blinding Polyphemus; or, a century later again, with Herodotus' story (I, 167) of how a Greek *agōn* was instituted at Caere (Agylla) on the instructions of Delphi, in expiation for the murder of some Phocaean captives, and was still maintained in the next century. It is not merely that the early evolution of Rome took place within the orbit of Greek culture, as that the preconditions for the Romans' self-perception of themselves as descended from Aeneas existed almost from the very beginning.

From the archaic period onwards, we have to see Greek and Roman culture as evolving in parallel. Rome did lag behind, of course. Greek cities dotted the eastern and western Mediterranean, and the Black Sea, several centuries before Roman expansion began. Moreover, and crucially for our knowledge, Roman literature begins some five centuries later than Greek. The fact is more surprising than one might think. Rome of the late sixth century was already a major city, with at least one massive temple on the Capitol. And if the inscription, in an early form of Latin, on the Lapis Niger from the Forum is really of the mid-sixth century, then it is earlier than any known public inscription from Athens. Why a Latin literature did *not* develop before the third century B.C. is a real puzzle.

The moment when the two linked but separate histories do really start to become one is the late fourth century B.C. For Philip and Alexander's conquests, carrying Macedonian armies into Greece, and Greek-speaking armies all over the Near East, Egypt, Babylonia, Persia, and central Asia, are exactly paralleled by smaller-scale, but even more significant, developments in Italy. I mean the break-up of the Latin league in 338 B.C., and then half a century of wars against Samnites, Etruscans, Celts, and Greeks. Even before the Romans crossed the Straits of Sicily in 264 B.C., a long list of Greek cities had already come under Roman domination, and Rome was already a known power on the edges of the Greek world.

We do have to accept that both the interweaving of Greek and Roman culture and history, to produce a single "Graeco-Roman" world, and the vast extension of that world were produced by imperialism and colonisation. However complex the accompanying factors, and the mutual reactions between different cultural groups, it was, quite simply, imperialism and the desire for conquest which carried Greek culture to Afghanistan and northern India, and Graeco-Roman culture to Hadrian's Wall. As I am trying to stress, we have everything to boast of in the sheer extensiveness, in space and in time, of Graeco-Roman culture. But in emphasising the importance of our field as a major part of human experience, we must not, just because both "imperialism" and "colonialism" are unpopular concepts in modern culture, falsify history by obscuring the fact that it was, in the first instance, war, conquest, and overseas settlement, both Greek and Roman, which created the vast and long-standing Graeco-Roman world.

As for that process itself, we do not need to follow all the details here. It will be enough to recall that the two major phases were indeed Alexander's conquests in Asia in the later fourth century, and Roman conquest, in both the Greek East and what was to become the Latin West, which reached a decisive phase in the first century B.C.

From within the context of the imposition of Greek culture in Asia, it will be worth just picking out three areas where the consequences were particularly striking. The first is Egypt, which is given a particular significance by the survival of papyri. So, firstly, we can actually meet the settlers from the Greek world who established themselves there from the late fourth century onwards. Perhaps most notable of all, because so early, is the Greek papyrus of 311 B.C. from Elephantine, nearly six hundred miles south from the mouth of the Nile. The papyrus records a marriage contract between two Greek settlers:

> In the 7th year of the reign of Alexander son of Alexander, the 14th year of the satrapship of Ptolemy, in the month of Dius. Marriage contract of Heraclides and Demetria. Heraclides takes as his lawful wife Demetria, Coan, both being freeborn, from her father Leptines, Coan, and her mother Philotis, bringing clothing and ornaments to the value to 1,000 drachmae, and Heraclides shall supply to Demetria all that is proper for a freeborn wife, and we shall live together wherever it seems best to Leptines and Heraclides consulting in common. . . . Witnesses: Cleon, Gelan; Anticrates, Temnian; Lysis, Temnian; Dionysius, Temnian; Aristomachus, Cyrenaean; Aristodicus, Coan.

More important, perhaps, because from now on until the Arab conquests Egypt was to be a bilingual land, in which both Egyptian and Greek were used, the tens of thousands of surviving papyri preserve for us a large, if erratic, cross-section of Greek literature, in which Homer predominates above all else. We can now read Greek (and a little Latin) literature, not as transmitted by medieval scribes, but as read in the ancient world.

The second area of immense significance was of course Judaea, for one of the long-term consequences of Alexander's conquests was to be that post-biblical Judaism, and of course early Christianity, would be formed within a Greek environment. Looking back from the end of the first century A.D., the great Jewish historian Josephus, writing in Greek the whole history of his people from the Creation to A.D. 66, was to incorporate a wonderful folktale, or (one might say) historical *novella*, about Alexander's visit to Jerusalem:

> Then he went up to the temple, where he sacrificed to God under the direction of the high priest, and showed due honour to the priests and to the high priest himself. And, when the book of Daniel was shown to him, in which he had declared that one of the Greeks would destroy the empire of the Persians, he believed himself to be the one indicated; and in his joy he dismissed the multitude for the time being, but on the following day he summoned them again and told them to ask for any gifts which they might desire. When the high priest asked that they might observe their country's laws and in the seventh year be exempt from tribute, he granted all this.

We need not hesitate to say that the story as told is legend, for the Book of Daniel, in which this pseudo-prophecy does indeed appear (8:21), had not yet been written. It was to be composed, in the form in which we have it, in the heart of the Hellenistic period, to be precise in the 160s B.C., during the persecution of Judaism by the Seleucid king Antiochus IV Epiphanes.

Alone of all the other cultures which were to be submerged by Greek culture, Judaism continued to produce works written in its two native languages, Hebrew and Aramaic (Daniel uses both), and to have its own canonical works translated into Greek. The legend of how the Bible, or at least the Pentateuch, came to be translated into Greek, involves both Egypt, under Ptolemy II Philadelphus (283–246 B.C.), and Judaea. For the king is said to have sent a mission to Jerusalem to bring translators to carry out the work in Alexandria. The story does indeed seem to be legend, though the seventy (or seventy-two) translators have given its name to the Greek version of the Bible, the Septuagint. But it is a fact that the work of translation had at least been begun in the third century; and with it a quite new vision of the world, and how it came into existence, came to be expressed in Greek. How many classes for the translation of Greek prose, I wonder, have ever found before them the opening words of the first chapter of Genesis?

Ἐν ἀρχῇ ἐποίησεν ὁ θεὸς τὸν οὐρανὸν καὶ τὴν γῆν. Ἡ δὲ γῆ ἦν ἀόρατος, καὶ ἀκατασκεύαστος, καὶ σκότος ἐπάνω τῆς ἀβύσσου καὶ πνεῦμα θεοῦ ἐπεφέρετο τοῦ ὕδατος. καὶ εἶπεν ὁ θεός Γενηθέτω φῶς. καὶ ἐγένετο φῶς.

Yet this view of the nature of the world and of the divinity was, as time went on, to be at least as important, for millions of people whose language of culture was Greek—and later, as we will see, Latin—as anything contained in the pagan classics. It is therefore essential for us to see it too as part of ancient culture. The third century was thus also the moment when the two strands of our inherited culture came together.

Before we go on to look at the later Graeco-Roman world, it is worth taking a glance sideways at another conjunction of cultures and religious systems which might have led to an equally long-lasting new civilisation, but in the end did not. In the time of Ptolemy Philadelphus large parts of India and Afghanistan, profoundly affected by the arrival of Alexander, but given up by Seleucus Nicator, were ruled by a great emperor of the Mauryan dynasty, Asoka, one of whose epithets was "piodasses," which apparently means "of benevolent countenance." Having an important message to communicate to his people, Asoka had a series of proclamations inscribed at different points across his empire. One of these places was Kandahar, where he put up an edict in Aramaic and Greek. Since this quite remarkable document, first published in 1958, has never become generally well known to classicists, it deserves quotation in full here:

> When ten years had been fulfilled, Piodasses demonstrated piety before men, and from that time on has made men more pious, and all has prospered throughout the land. For the king abstains from (eating) living things, and other men—even such as are the king's hunters or fishermen—have abandoned the chase. And if any are lacking in self-control, they have left off their excesses so far as they can. Moreover they are obedient each to their father and mother, and to the elders, to an extent greater than previously. For the future, acting according to all these principles, they will live more agreeably and better.

Why was the king impressing these ideals on his people? Because he had recently converted to the teachings of Buddha. The document is one of only two (the other being another edict of Asoka, published in 1964) in which Buddhist beliefs are expressed in classical Greek.

That remarkable conjunction turned out, so far as we know, to be abortive. In the end, the world of Greek cities would stretch no further than the Tigris, or at the most Seleucia on the Eulaeus, the ancient Susa. But in the wider Mediterranean region, Roman expansion, beginning, as we have seen, exactly at the moment of Alexander's conquests, absorbed nearly all of the region where those conquests had left long-lasting effects, and at the same time carried Latin culture all over Mediterranean North Africa, western

Europe, including eventually Britain, and central Europe down the Danube to the Black Sea, with a striking extension into Dacia, present-day Romania. The effect, therefore, was to produce, by the first few centuries A.D., a dual Graeco-Roman culture, expressed in Greek, Latin, or both, from the Tigris to the Atlantic, or from Elephantine on the Upper Nile to Hadrian's Wall.

It is worth emphasising the sheer scale of this process. Modern estimates (or rather guesses) would put the population of the Roman Empire at something like 50 million people. It is important to stress that what was produced was a dual culture, Greek and Latin, in which the constituents of Latin culture owed far more to Greek culture and tradition than the other way round. The Roman army did of course carry the Latin language, and even Latin literature, to every corner of the Empire. Within the past few years new discoveries have demonstrated how the army took the text of the *Aeneid* with it to its furthest outposts: a line of the *Aeneid* (9, 473) from Vindolanda is echoed by another (4, 9) from Masada, the great rock by the Dead Sea which the Roman army occupied after its defenders, in the last stage of the Jewish Revolt, had committed suicide in A.D. 73 or 74.

But the first of the two fundamental facts which one needs to grasp about the Roman Empire, is that "Latinisation," never in any case seriously attempted, made very little progress in the Greek-speaking East. There is for instance no certain proof that anyone translated any of Virgil into Greek until in the early fourth century the emperor Constantine produced some of the *Fourth Eclogue* in Greek for the benefit of an assembly of bishops.

More important, in the eastern half of the Empire, the language of ordinary life, and even (largely) of public business, remained Greek. It would be a reasonable estimate that, at all stages in the history of the Roman Empire, it contained more native speakers of Greek than of Latin. Thus it was that there survived a continuous tradition of Greek culture through the Hellenistic period, through the Roman Empire of the first three centuries A.D., past the foundation by Constantine of Constantinople, situated at the strategic point on the route between Danube and Euphrates, past the fall of the Roman Empire in the West in the fifth century, and on into the Byzantine world.

But the other essential fact about the Roman Empire is equally important. That is the diffusion of Latin so as to become not just the language of Empire, but that of ordinary speech, in the non-Greek regions. When, forty years ago, my head boy just assumed that one did not really "think about" Latin, I fear that he was right. In the case of Italy itself, Gaul, and Spain, we can be certain that in the end a popular language which had evolved out of Latin did become the main language of ordinary speech. But when, by what stages, and by what social or educational processes? Had the same been true of North Africa before the Islamic invasions? Was it true of Britain by the time of the Roman withdrawal in the early fifth century? We can meet the ordinary Latin of the street and the market-place in (for instance) the curse tablets from the temple of Sulis Minerva at Bath, splendidly edited by R. S. O. Tomlin. But was Celtic none the less spoken all through the nearly four centuries of the Roman occupation of Britain, while leaving hardly a written trace? Similar problems present themselves also for all of central Europe, not to speak of Romania with its Latin-derived language. We do need to "think about" Latin; and the social history of the spread of Latin and its adoption as the language of ordinary speech has hardly begun to be written.

In any case, in thinking of the expansion of Latin, we are not concerned just with a language, but with an entire culture and historical consciousness. It is an extraordinary tribute to the attraction of Latin culture that virtually no trace survives of any pre-Roman literature, oral or written, or of any conception of their own previous history, on the part of any of the peoples of the western Mediterranean and of north-western and central Europe. The only literature they inherited was Latin, and the only history Roman—except insofar as they acquired also a consciousness of Greek culture and, with Christianity, of Old Testament tradition.

Very few people, either then or now, have allowed themselves to be sufficiently surprised by this. One person who did so allow himself, however, was Aurelius Augustinus, born in A.D. 354 and brought up in the little one-horse town of Thagaste in Roman North Africa. Looking back in his *Confessions*, written in the 390s, Augustine did find it possible to ask himself why his education had been as it was:

> Even now I have not yet discovered the reasons why I hated Greek literature when I was being taught it as a small boy. Latin I deeply loved, not at the stage of my primary teachers but at the secondary level taught by the teachers of literature called "grammarians." The initial elements, where one learns the three Rs of reading, writing and arithmetic, I felt to be no less a burden and an infliction than the entire series of Greek classes.

But why, in any case, had his education been about the passions of Dido and not about his own soul?

> What is more pitiable than a wretch without pity for himself who weeps over the death of Dido dying for love of Aeneas, but not weeping over himself dying for his lack of love for you, my God, light of my

heart, bread of the inner mouth of my soul, the power which begets
life in my mind and in the innermost recesses of my thinking.

The question expressed the irresolvable tensions between the two traditions, Judaeo-Christian and classical, which now made up the culture of the
Graeco-Roman Empire — which, at the very time when Augustine was writing, was reaching, in A.D. 395, the first step in the eventual division of Latin
West and Greek East.

Where we should see the story of Graeco-Roman culture as ending is of
course an insoluble problem. In one sense the answer, of course, is never. In
another, 1453 and the fall of Constantinople. Or perhaps the Islamic invasions
of the seventh century. Or perhaps, if we wish to choose a terminal date,
with the reign of Justinian in Constantinople, in 527–565. For not only did
his reign see the last attempt to re-unify East and West by military means,
but it also produced one of the greatest monuments of Latin prose and of
Roman culture, the *Digest*. It seems odd, again, that, in an educational context, no one (to my knowledge) ever uses extracts from it. For, first, whatever
Justinian may have intended, what the compilers of the *Digest* actually produced was something very familiar to us all: a source book. What they did
was to select extracts from the main writers of classical Roman law, primarily
those of the early third century A.D., Ulpian, Papinian, and Paulus, and ar-
range them under headings. Through the *Digest* we thus gain access to a vast
corpus of Roman prose writing from the height of the Empire, the best part
of 1 million words in all. Not only that, the main manuscript of the *Digest*,
now in Florence, was written, in Latin of course, somewhere in the Greek
world in the late sixth or the seventh century A.D. It is thus extremely close
in time to the original compilation.

Suppose that we imagined that the writing of this vast Latin manuscript
had taken place in A.D. 622, the year of Mahomet's *Hegira* from Mecca to
Medina. We might then choose to use these two events as marking a symbolic terminus for the ancient world. That date belongs almost exactly 1,400
years since the first Greek settlers had arrived in Pithekoussai, and since their
immediate successors brought with them an awareness of "Nestor's cup" and
Homeric epic. The interval concerned happens to be slightly longer than the
timespan from A.D. 622 to now. In defending our subject, and in emphasising its significance in human history, and its sheer scale in space and time,
we should not be too modest.

At the same time, we ought to be prepared to ask ourselves some questions. For a start, why have we allowed our "canon" of what is worth reading
in Greek and Latin to be narrowed to whatever counts as "literature"? Might

not extracts of Roman legal texts, with their repeated use of ordinary-life situations, seem more accessible to pupils than (for instance) Ovid with his complex web of mythological allusions? Equally, might not pupils respond to Roman architectural or military handbooks? Or to Greek medicine, in the form of the Hippocratic corpus? Or to papyrus letters, for instance, from errant sons to irate fathers? But above all, why do we exclude from the standard conception of what a classical education is about Jewish and Christian texts in Greek, and Christian texts in Latin? (To the best of my knowledge there is no Jewish literature in Latin from antiquity.) To end this exclusion would be, as I suggested earlier, to bring the Septuagint within the canon of Greek literature, not to speak of those two immensely powerful narratives (in Greek) of the Jewish resistance to Hellenism in the second century B.C., namely I and II Maccabees. These texts, conveniently available either in the Catholic Bible or Protestant editions of the Apocrypha (translated for instance in the New Jerusalem Bible or the New English Bible), are not only immensely powerful pieces of writing, but bear directly on the nature and impact of Greek culture in the Hellenistic period. Take for instance the account in II Maccabees 4 of how the high priest of the 170s B.C. "was pleased to found immediately below the acropolis a gymnasium, and conducted there the noblest of the ephebes wearing the *petasos* [a Greek sun-hat]. That was the moment of the height of *Hellenismos* and advance of foreign customs [*allophylismos*] through the pollution of the impious Jason, no true high priest, so much so that the priests were no longer eager to conduct the services of the altar, but, despising the Temple and neglecting the sacrifices, they rushed to take part in the exercises of the *palaistra*, when summoned by the sound of the *diskos*."

If we allowed ourselves this angle of vision on the classical world, we could also accept the centrality of the works of Josephus, written in Greek in Rome in the later first century A.D., but representing to the pagan world a tradition and a local history going back to the Creation. We might even read in Greek classes those vivid views of provincial society in the Roman Empire provided by the Gospels and Acts.

There are furthermore two other important reasons for allowing ourselves to include Jewish and Christian texts in our conception of "classics." One is that, in the case of Christianity, we can follow the transmission of the new faith from a Greek into a Latin context, and with that arrive once again at the Graeco-Roman world of late antiquity, where pagan culture and tradition lived in uneasy co-existence with Judaeo-Christian beliefs, traditions, and literature. We ought to remind ourselves also that it was probably in the late Roman world of (say) the fourth and fifth centuries A.D. that the largest number of people had either Greek or Latin as their primary language. In one way, as Augustine's picture of his education in his little home town shows, this was the most "classical" of all periods.

But the second reason is more relevant to how we introduce people to the classical world today. For the two important processes mentioned just now, the transfer of Christianity and its sacred scriptures into a Latin-speaking environment, and the clash between Christianity and paganism, are illustrated for us by texts of outstanding dramatic force, combined with great linguistic simplicity, the *Acts of the Christian Martyrs*. These *Acts* are not, though they may seem to be, authentic verbal records of the trials of martyrs. But they are ancient literary evocations of those trials, which both, in reality and as presented in martyr acts, served to focus on just what was at stake in the clash of two views of the world.

One aspect of these complex processes is perfectly caught in the earliest of the known martyr acts in Latin, which represents the trial before the proconsul of Africa in A.D. 180 of some Christians from a small place called Scilli. One of the proconsul's questions evokes a response of far greater significance than the very simple language might suggest:

Saturninus the proconsul asked: What things are there in your box?
Speratus answered: The books and letters of Paulus, a righteous man.

With that we have the very earliest evidence for the translation of the New Testament into Latin, a process which was to culminate in Jerome's great work of revision, and the production of the Vulgate, which has remained ever since the Bible of the Catholic Church:

In principio creavit Deus caelum et terram. terra autem erat inanis et vacua et tenebrae super faciem abyssi. et spiritus Dei ferebatur super aquas. dixitque Deus "fiat lux"; et facta est lux.

From one point of view, the diffusion of this view of what the world was is surely of some importance for our understanding of the ancient world. But from another, might not these simple, pregnant sentences provide for beginners a good way into the Latin of later antiquity (as Jewish texts do into the Greek of the Hellenistic period)? But if we did wish to use Christian Latin as a way in for beginners, there could be no better choice than the martyr act which represents the trial of Fructuosus, bishop of Tarragona, before the governor (*praeses*) in A.D. 259. Note the very loaded and meaningful use of tenses, the deployment of subordinate clauses, the contrast of singular and plural (*deum* and *deos*) in speaking of the divine order, and the stark clarity in which the clash of religious understandings is presented:

Aemilianus praeses Fructuoso dixit: Audisti quid imperatores
 praeceperunt?
Fructuosus dixit: Nescio quid praeceperunt. ego Christianus sum.
Aemilianus praeses dixit: Praeceperunt deos coli.
Fructuosus dixit: Ego unum Deum colo, qui fecit caelum et terram et
 mare et omnia quae in eis sunt.
Aemilianus dixit: Scis esse deos?
Fructuosus dixit: Nescio.
Aemilianus dixit: Scies postea.

. . . .

Aemilianus praeses Fructuoso dixit: Episcopus es?
Fructuosus dixit: Sum.
Aemilianus dixit: Fuisti.

Aemilianus, the governor, asked Fructuosus: Have you heard what the
 emperors have ordered?
Fructuosus answered: I do not know what they have ordered. I am a
 Christian.
Aemilianus, the governor said: They have ordered that the gods are to
 be worshipped.
Fructuosus answered: I worship the one God, who made heaven and
 earth and sea and all that is in them.
Aemilianus asked: Do you know that there are gods?
Fructuosus answered: I do not know.
Aemilianus said: You will know later on.

. . . .

Aemilianus, the governor, asked Fructuosus: Are you a bishop?
Fructuosus answered: I am.
Aemilianus said: You were.

Enough has been said to illustrate the three main themes which I want to put
forward: the sheer scale in time and space of what we call the "ancient world";
the significance within it of those Jewish and Christian texts in Greek or
Latin which we would do well to include in our view; and the use to which
some of these texts could be put, as being grammatically simple but pregnant
with meaning, in introducing beginners to classical culture and beliefs.

 If space allowed, I would say something about the hundreds of thousands
of inscriptions and tens of thousands of papyri which give us direct access
to the words written in the thousands of small towns and villages of the ancient world (many of these texts would also serve for beginners starting to

read Greek or Latin). But instead I will indulge myself by quoting from my favourite work from late antiquity, Jerome's brilliantly journalistic account of the life of Hilarion, an inhabitant of the ancient city of Gaza, who was born in the 290s and converted in the early years of the fourth century to the life of a Christian ascetic.

The ancient Philistine city of Gaza was now in fact a perfect example of a "Graeco-Roman" place. Long since Hellenised, it had been given in the third century the status of a Roman colony. Hence (in principle at least) it used Latin in its public affairs, and its two chief annual magistrates had the Latin title *duumviri*. As a Roman *urbs*, Jerome reports, the city held an annual festival in honour of the god Consus, to commemorate the rape of the Sabine women. As part of the festival, a Christian, Italicus, was due to enter a *quadriga* (four-horse chariot) against one owned by a pagan *duumvir* and feared the effect of spells. So Hilarion was asked to provide holy water to scatter over the Christian-owned horses and *quadriga*, and their charioteer.

Thus, Jerome records, "when the signal was given, they [the Christian horses] flew off, and the others were held up." Jerome picks up here the tradition of sports journalese inaugurated in *Iliad* 23, and turns to using the historic present: "Under the Christian chariot the wheels grow red hot; they [the pagan horses] can scarcely see their rival's backs as they fly past" (Sub horum curru rotae fervent; illi praetervolantium terga vix cernunt). "Marnas has been conquered by Christ!" (Marnas victus est a Christo), shouted the crowd. So indeed it was to be in the end, but only after several hundred years when worshippers of Christ and of the pagan deities co-existed, and more people were educated in Greek and Latin language, culture, and tradition than ever before. We should not be afraid, in the modern world, to boast of just how much of human history all this represents. But, equally, we should allow ourselves to "think about Latin," and about how the modern beginner can best be helped to approach the Graeco-Roman world.

A Note on the Sources

For anyone who wants to follow up any of the texts mentioned in this lecture, a note of some places where they are printed follows:

1. The papyrus of 311 B.C. is most easily found in A. S. Hunt and G. C. Edgar, *Select Papyri* 1 (1932), no. 1, Loeb edition.
2. Josephus' account of Alexander in Jerusalem comes from his *Jewish Antiquities* 11, 8, 5 (329–39); the passage quoted is 336–38 (Loeb).
3. The Buddhist inscription of Asoka was first published by D. Schlum-

berger, L. Robert, A. Dupont-Sommer, and E. Benveniste in *Journal Asiatique* 246 (1958): 1. Text and French translation also in J. Pouilloux, *Choix d'inscriptions grecques* (1960): no. 53. The second Greek text was published by E. Benveniste in *Journal Asiatique* 252 (1964): 137, and by D. Schumberger in *Comptes-rendu de l'Académie des inscriptions* (1964): 1, and is reproduced in P. Steinmetz, ed., *Beiträge zur hellenistischen Literatur und ihren Rezeption in Rom* (1990), on pp. 47–49.

4. Constantine's translation of the *Fourth Eclogue* into Greek is contained in his *Address to the Assembly of the Saints*, usually printed along with Eusebius' "biography," *On the Life of the Blessed Constantine*. The passage referred to is *Address*, chaps. 19–20. The only English translation known to me is that of P. Schaff and H. Wace in *Select Library of Nicene and Post-Nicene Fathers* I (1890; repr. 1952). But see now A. Cameron and S. Hall, *Eusebius' Life of Constantine*, translated with introduction and commentary (1999).

5. R. S. O. Tomlin's edition of the curse tablets from Bath can be found in B. Cunliffe, ed., *The Temple of Sulis Minerva at Bath* II (1988).

6. The translation of the *Confessions* (1, 13) is taken from that by H. Chadwick, *Saint Augustine, Confessions* (World's Classics, 1992).

7. The Greek text of I and II Maccabees can be found in editions of the Septuagint, for instance, that by A. Rahlfs, originally published in 1935; and also, with French translations and commentary, in F.-M. Abel, *Les livres des Maccabées* (1949).

8. The Christian martyr acts can be found with a (very poor) English translation, in H. Musurillo, *The Acts of the Christian Martyrs* (1972). The text of the acts of the Scillitan martyrs is no. 1, and that of the acts of Fructuosus no. 12.

9. Jerome's *Vita Hilarionis* is printed in C. Mohrmann, ed., *Vita dei Santi* IV (1975), 69ff., and translated in R. J. Deferrari, ed., *Early Christian Biographies* (1952), 245ff.

CHAPTER TWO

*Epigraphy**

Introduction

There can have been few major civilisations in which the incision of words on stone or metal for permanent display or record has played no part at all. But if the making and display of inscriptions is attested in many cultures, it was so distinctive a feature of Graeco-Roman civilisation that it deserves consideration as a major cultural phenomenon in its own right. As a consequence of this, the sheer volume of inscriptions from the ancient world, primarily but not only in Greek and Latin, gives epigraphy a central importance in the study of its history and culture, in a way which is not characteristic of historical approaches to most other periods or areas. Thus, it was to an epigrapher of the classical world that the editors of a post-war French encyclopaedia turned when they wanted to include a section on epigraphy as a historical discipline in general.[1]

The sheer profusion of epigraphic evidence—from tiny graffiti on walls or fragments of pottery, to stamps on jars, to the sepulchral inscriptions of innumerable individuals, to vast monumental inscriptions which may run to several hundred lines—creates its own problems. It would be a Herculean (and pointless) labour to work out even approximately how many Greek and Latin inscriptions have now been published; a guess of something over half a million might not be far out. Though many major projects for *corpora* of inscriptions have been undertaken—the great classics being the *Corpus Inscriptionum Latinarum* and, to a lesser extent, *Inscriptiones Graecae*—none ever

* First published in M. Crawford, ed., *Sources for Ancient History* (Cambridge, 1983), 80–136.

1. L. Robert, "Épigraphie," in *L'histoire et ses méthodes* (*Encyclopédie de la Pléiade*, Paris, 1961), 453–97; German translation by H. Engelmann, *Die Epigraphik der klassischen Welt* (Bonn, 1970), with added notes by Robert.

has been, or ever could be, completed without being already out of date. Even to offer an extended guide to the basic bibliography of classical epigraphy in general,[2] of Greek inscriptions[3] or of Latin ones,[4] is now a considerable enterprise which itself will be out of date immediately on publication. The most successful of epigraphic publications remain those great collections of the late nineteenth and early twentieth centuries which aimed to provide a very large representative *sample* of Greek or Latin inscriptions. W. Dittenberger's *Orientis Graeci Inscriptiones Selectae* I–II (1903–5) and *Sylloge Inscriptionum Graecarum*[3] I–IV (1915–24), R. Cagnat's *Inscriptiones Graecae ad Res Romanas Pertinentes* I–IV (1906–27), and H. Dessau's *Inscriptiones Latinae Selectae* I–III (1892–1916) remain the best places to begin the practice—which is of fundamental importance for understanding the ancient world and arriving at an original view of it—of reading inscriptions *in bulk*. Though we must always be conscious of how much inscriptions will *not* tell us—and a large part of this chapter is concerned with precisely those limitations—it is still the case that inscriptions, read in bulk, provide the most direct access which we can have to the life, social structure, thought, and values of the ancient world. Papyri and parchments, which may preserve public documents but also offer us thousands of examples of private, informal texts—letters, complaints, records of dreams, private financial accounts—are potentially even more revealing.[5] But the very special circumstances required for their preservation, which are consistently present only in the desert areas of Middle and Upper Egypt and in parts of the Near East, inevitably create a marked geographical bias in the evidence which they present.

2. Note the valuable work of A. Calderini, *Epigrafia* (Turin, 1974), which would provide an excellent orientation in this field for anyone undertaking research in any area of Graeco-Roman history.

3. The essay by Robert mentioned in n. 1 is almost entirely devoted to Greek epigraphy. More systematic surveys are given by G. Klaffenbach, *Griechische Epigraphik*[2] (Göttingen, 1966), and G. Pfohl, ed., *Das Studium der griechischen Epigraphik* (Darmstadt, 1977). Note also A. G. Woodhead, *The Study of Greek Inscriptions*[2] (Cambridge, 1981). The fullest survey of the types of material is M. Guarducci, *Epigrafia greca* I–IV (Rome, 1967–78), who reproduces and discusses a large number of texts, with illustrations.

4. See I. Calabi Limentani, *Epigrafia Latina con un appendice bibliografica di Attilio Degrassi* (Milan, 1968), and E. Meyer, *Einführung in die lateinische Epigraphik* (Darmstadt, 1973). The classic work of R. Cagnat, *Cours d'épigraphie latine*[4] (Paris, 1914), has still not been replaced as an introduction to the subject. See now G. L. Susini, *Epigrafia romana* (Rome, 1982).

5. The standard, and very good, introduction to papyrology is E. G. Turner, *Greek Papyri* (rev. ed., Oxford, 1980) with his *Greek Manuscripts of the Ancient World* (Oxford, 1971). Note also O. Montevecchi, *La papirologia* (Turin, 1973; suppl., 1988).

For these reasons it is the reading of inscriptions, even more than of papyri, which will provide the essential direct acquaintance, the "feel" for ancient society, without which the formulation of precise historical questions or hypotheses is an empty exercise, indeed cannot properly proceed at all. But as soon as a student does formulate any specific question, even in the vaguest outline, he or she will want to be able to trace all the relevant evidence. It is here that the difficulties begin, and some of them are fundamental. Firstly, it is abundantly clear that only a very limited range of human activity and experience formed the subject matter of inscribed material. Literature, archaeology, numismatics, or papyrology may in certain cases provide an intelligible context which the inscriptions, in spite of the explicit character of the evidence they provide, do not. But epigraphy can never escape from the conundrum posed by all the vast, varied, but irremediably partial evidence surviving from the ancient world: how are we to construct an intelligible and not grossly misleading framework within which to interpret that fragmentary evidence which does happen to be left to us from antiquity?

That brings us to the second problem. What was originally inscribed was inevitably partial in what it chose to present to the contemporary reader; but what happens to have survived happens to have been seen or excavated in the modern world, and happens subsequently to have been published—a consequence which may follow very belatedly or not at all—is infinitely more partial. In seeking to gather "all the evidence" on a particular point we are at best summing up a minute sub-category of various infinitely receding larger categories. But can we do even that? Given the multiplicity of forms of "publication," which include local antiquarian journals which never reach a wider market, it is in fact never possible to be certain that all the published evidence has been collected. But some approximation to this can be achieved by reading—and using the indexes of—the three major annual (or more or less annual) surveys of Greek and Latin epigraphy: the *Supplementum Epigraphicum Graecum* (*SEG*), published, with interruptions, since 1923, and designed to reproduce texts of new Greek inscriptions and note improvements in ones already known; *L'Année Épigraphique* (*AE*), published since 1888 and devoted to the reproduction of the texts of new Latin inscriptions and of Greek ones relevant to Roman history; and, above all, the *Bulletin Épigraphique* (*BE* or *Bull. Épig.*), a survey and analysis of Greek inscriptions, published in the *Revue des Études Grecques*. From 1938 onwards this last was the work of Jeanne and Louis Robert, and it has been—and will remain—essential reading for anyone who wishes to understand Greek civilisation as it was in antiquity, above all in the post-classical period and in Asia Minor (present-day Turkey), the focus of the Roberts' own interests. To read the *Bulletin Épigraphique* is prob-

ably the best way to gain a sense both of one's own overwhelming ignorance
and of the excitement of exploring the vast, and ever-expanding mass of
Greek which survives in inscriptions.[6]

Any reader of these publications would also gain a vivid impression of
the immense geographical area over which Greek and Latin inscriptions are
found, from Ai Khanum, which lies on the Oxus on the border of Afghanistan and the USSR, to Iran and the Persian Gulf, Mesopotamia, the Caucasus,
the north coast of the Black Sea,[7] Romania, the whole of Europe within the
Danube and Rhine, and North Africa from the Atlantic to Egypt. Egypt is
also a conspicuous case of a phenomenon which by their very nature collections and surveys of Greek and Latin inscriptions tend to obscure—the interpenetration of Graeco-Roman culture with a considerable range of other
cultures. Many of the Greek inscriptions of Egypt come from temples and
monuments of a specifically Egyptian character;[8] in Jewish funerary practice
in Palestine, Hebrew, Aramaic, and Greek texts are closely intermingled.[9]
Similarly it is a fundamental (and to some extent neglected) fact about the
"Romanisation" of the Latin-speaking areas of North Africa and the West
that neo-Punic texts, sometimes written in Latin characters, continued to be
inscribed in North Africa at least until the end of the second century A.D.,[10]
and extended texts in neo-Punic appear in Sardinia until about the same

6. An index to the *Bulletin Épigraphique* has now been published in various parts: *Index
du Bulletin Épigraphique de J. et L. Robert, 1938–65*, I: *les mots grecs* (Paris, 1972); II: *les publications*
(Paris, 1974); III: *les mots français* (Paris, 1975); *Index du Bulletin Épigraphique de J. et L. Robert,
1966–73*, IV (Paris, 1979).

7. For Ai Khanum, see L. Robert, "De Delphes à l'Oxus: Inscriptions grecques nouvelles
de la Bactriane," *CRAI* (1968): 416; for the Black Sea region, note, e.g., V. V. Struve, *Corpus
Inscriptionum Regni Bosporani* (Leningrad, 1965).

8. See the fully illustrated collections by A. Bernand: (1) (with E. Bernand), *Les inscriptions grecques et latines du Colosse de Memnon* (Paris, 1960); (2) *Les inscriptions grecques et latines
de Philae* I–II (Paris, 1969); *De Koptos à Kosseir* (Leiden, 1972); (3) *Le Paneion d'El-Kanais:
les inscriptions grecques* (Leiden, 1972); *Pan du désert* (Leiden, 1977); E. Bernand, *Recueil des
inscriptions grecques du Fayoum* I (Leiden, 1975), II–III (Leiden, 1981).

9. The documentary evidence for linguistic usage in Palestine (which also includes the
well-known papyri and parchments from the Judaean desert and Qumran) is summed up
in E. Schürer, *History of the Jewish People in the Age of Jesus Christ* II, ed. G. Vermes, F. Millar, and M. Black (Edinburgh, 1979), 20–28. See now H. M. Cotton, W. E. H. Cockle, and
F. G. B. Millar, "The Papyrology of the Roman Near East: A Survey," *JRS* 85 (1995): 214.

10. See F. Millar, "Local Cultures in the Roman Empire: Libyan, Punic and Latin in
Roman Africa," *JRS* 58 (1968): 126.

time.[11] Palmyra, where the local branch of Aramaic was clearly the main language of ordinary speech, produces public inscriptions in either Greek or Palmyrene (heavily impregnated with Greek, and a few Latin, loan-words) or in parallel texts, throughout the three hundred years of its history.[12] The Semitic-language epigraphy of the classical period, taken in all its branches from the western Mediterranean to Afghanistan, is a sufficiently important parallel phenomenon to Greek and Latin epigraphy to deserve a special emphasis here.[13] In this area too there is an excellent running survey, the "Bulletin d'épigraphie semitique" published by J. Teixidor in the journal *Syria*.

The Geography of Languages

There is no need to catalogue here the substantial range of evidence — largely from inscriptions — for the multiplicity of languages used in the Graeco-Roman world; those attested in the Roman Empire are surveyed in a useful recent volume.[14] But it is worth emphasising how complex and interesting a world is revealed for instance by the late-Phrygian inscriptions of the imperial period, all written in the Greek alphabet,[15] or the neo-Punic inscriptions from Africa written not only in the local variety of the Semitic alphabet but sometimes (as we have seen) in Latin characters or in Greek ones.[16] By contrast the epigraphic remains of Celtic from France are all written in Latin or Greek characters, and no trace of a non-classical script survives.[17] In this instance the very fact of composing a text for inscription must surely be regarded as a borrowing from Graeco-Roman culture.

11. E.g., M. G. Guzzo Amadasi, *Le inscrizioni fenicie e puniche delle colonie in Occidente* (Rome, 1967), 133, no. 8.

12. For examples, see J. B. Chabot, *Choix d'inscriptions de Palmyre* (Paris, 1922), and note M. G. Bertinelli Angeli, *Nomenclatura pubblica e sacra di Roma nelle epigrafi semitiche* (Genoa, 1970).

13. The standard collection is *Corpus Inscriptionum Semiticarum* (*CIS*) (Paris, 1881–). Note also G. A. Cooke, *A Textbook of North-Semitic Inscriptions* (Oxford, 1903), and H. Donner and W. Röllig, *Kanaanäische und aramäische Inschriften*[3] I–III (Wiesbaden, 1973).

14. G. Neumann and J. Untermann, eds., *Die Sprachen im römischen Reich der Kaiserzeit*, Beihefte der *Bonner Jahrbücher* 40 (1980).

15. O. Haas, *Die phrygischen Sprachdenkmäler* (Sofia, 1966).

16. For this phenomenon, see, e.g., H. G. Horn and C. B. Rüger, eds., *Die Numider* (Bonn, 1979), 107.

17. For a relatively recent example, see the discussion by K. H. Schmidt, "The Gaulish Inscription of Chamalières," *Bulletin of the Board of Celtic Studies* 29 (1981): 256.

Grossly inadequate as our often isolated fragments of inscriptional evidence are, they are often the best (or the only) evidence we have for the use of a language, or the contrasting uses of different languages, in a particular time and place. In western and central Europe, for instance, there is still nothing to suggest that any "native" language was ever used in public documents in parallel with Latin, or indeed came into regular use in public inscribed documents separately from Latin. It does not of course follow that none was spoken, or even used in writing on perishable materials. However, in Tripolitania in North Africa, for instance, neo-Punic texts accompanied Latin ones on public inscriptions at least until the end of the first century A.D. But the excellent volume of the *Inscriptions of Roman Tripolitania*, by J. M. Reynolds and J. B. Ward Perkins (1952), merely alludes to but does not print or discuss these parallel texts.

That this should be so is a product both of the inevitable limitations of human knowledge, energy, and skill and of the costs of printing; the effort and expense of producing a volume of Latin and/or Greek inscriptions is great enough without the extra problems presented by other ancient languages and scripts. Yet it does deserve emphasis that this restriction, serious enough for our understanding of the local culture of Tripolitania, is a much more fundamental handicap when we come to the even richer mixture of cultures in the Near East, where we find a number of major documents inscribed from the beginning in parallel texts in two or more languages — and where the texts in different languages have tended to be published and discussed separately. This is the case even with the Rosetta stone from Egypt, a decree of the Egyptian priesthood passed in 196 B.C., and reproduced in a Greek text and two Egyptian ones, written in hieroglyphic and demotic. The Greek text is available as Dittenberger, *Orientis Graeci Inscriptiones Selectae*, 90. But although, as is well known, it was the parallel texts which enabled Champollion to decipher the hieroglyphic script in the 1820s, the three versions have since then very rarely been discussed within the same covers.

Egypt is perhaps the most marked case where the skills necessary to study Greek inscriptions, papyri, and ostraca (fragments of pottery with writing inked or scratched on them), on the one hand, and Egyptian ones, on the other, have for understandable reasons been deployed as if in separate compartments. But it may be worth noting three relatively recent discoveries of major multilingual texts, which serve to show up both the present limitations of and the infinite possibilities of epigraphy in the Near East and central Asia.

1. The trilingual inscription, in Aramaic, Lycian, and Greek, from Xanthos in Lycia, almost certainly to be dated to 337/6 B.C., that is, in the last

years of the Persian Empire. The three texts, which concern the setting up of an altar and associated priesthood in the sanctuary of Leto at Xanthos, have had to be published by separate authors, if within the same volume, both in the initial publication and in the final report.[18]

2. The two Greek inscriptions of the Indian king Asoka, of the mid third century B.C. These are so far the only two Buddhist documents surviving in Greek. Both come from Kandahar. The first, published in 1958, has a parallel Aramaic text and is an invitation to the king's subjects to follow him in abstaining from meat.[19] The second was published in 1964.[20] In this case there is no parallel text in the epigraphic sense, but the inscription is a Greek version of the end of Edict XII and the beginning of Edict XIII of Asoka, already known from inscriptions of his put up elsewhere. The first contains moral precepts, and the second gives an account of the king's remorse and conversion after the casualties and destruction brought about in a war which he fought in Kalinga. It does not seem that these truly remarkable documents have yet had their full impact on our conception either of the use of the Greek language in central Asia or of the nature of "Hellenisation."[21]

3. The "Res Gestae" of Shapor I. The record of the achievements of the early Sassanian king Shapor I (241–72) is carved on a stone wall at Naqsh-i-Rustam near Persepolis, and written in three languages, middle Persian (the original text), Parthian, and Greek. The complete Greek text, accompanied by the two Iranian versions in transcription, was published for the first time

18. For the initial publication, see *CRAI* (1974): 82 (the Greek text); 115 (Lycian); 132 (Aramaic). The final report is *Fouilles de Xanthos* VI: *la stèle trilingue du Letoon* (Paris, 1979), 33ff. (the Greek inscription); 49ff. (Lycian); 129ff. (Aramaic). The correct date is that established by E. Badian, "A Document of Artaxerxes IV," in K. H. Kinzl, ed., *Greece and the Eastern Mediterranean in Ancient History and Prehistory: Studies Presented to F. Schachermeyr* (Berlin, 1977), 40.

19. The Greek text is republished in *SEG* XX, 326, and, with a French translation, by J. Pouilloux, *Choix d'inscriptions grecques* (Paris, 1964), no. 53, and both texts are reproduced and discussed by G. Pugliese Carratelli and G. Garbini in *A Bilingual Graeco-Aramaic Edict by Asóka* (Rome, 1964). Note also R. Thapar, *Asóka and the Decline of the Mauryas* (London, 1961; 2nd ed., Oxford, 1997).

20. Published and discussed contemporaneously by D. Schlumberger, "Une nouvelle inscription grecque d'Açoka," *CRAI* (1964): 1, and by E. Benveniste, "Édits d'Asóka en traduction grecque," *Journal Asiatique* 252 (1964): 137.

21. Note however J. Harmatta, "Zu den griechischen Inschriften des Asoka," *Acta Ant. Acad. Sc. Hung.* 14 (1966): 77, and R. Schmitt, "EX OCCIDENTE LUX. Griechen und griechische Sprache in hellenistischen Fernen Osten," in P. Steinmetz, ed., *Beiträge zur hellenistischen Literatur und ihren Rezeption in Rom* (1990), 41.

only in 1958.[22] It represents not only, in its second part, an immensely detailed account of the religious position and activities of an early Sassanian king but, in its first part, the only detailed account of a Roman war which we have from a non-Graeco-Roman source. More important, like the other major documents just mentioned—the Rosetta stone, the tri-lingual inscription from Xanthos, and the edicts of Asoka—it gives some hint of the complexity of the mixture of cultures in these areas of Asia which were touched (at least) by Hellenisation. For any scholars who—individually or in collaboration—can deploy the varied linguistic skills required, there are whole areas whose social and cultural history in the Graeco-Roman period has hardly yet begun to be written. We have only to think of Egypt at almost any period, Hellenistic Phoenicia, Hellenistic Babylonia, with its combination of Greek and cuneiform documents,[23] Mesopotamia in the period of the Roman occupation, or Nabataea as a kingdom and as the Roman province of Arabia.

It may be noted in passing, since this area is wholly beyond the competence of the author, that inscriptions are inevitably of the greatest importance for the study of the history of language—not only Greek and Latin but all the others used within the orbit of Graeco-Roman civilisation—as they are also for grammar, spelling, orthography, and pronunciation. These subjects themselves have great historical significance. The sixteen hundred or so fifth-century B.C. ostraca from the Agora and Kerameikos of Athens so far published—and potentially the several thousand found in the Kerameikos in the 1960s and not yet published—give uniquely important evidence for the letter forms, spelling, and grammar used (in very varied ways) by ordinary Athenians of the classical period. If and when these ostraca are published and properly studied they would in principle allow an attempt to reconstitute the text of (say) Aeschylus' *Persae* of 472, with the lettering and grammatical forms which would actually then have been in use. If that seems too farfetched a possibility, it is still worth pointing out that the Athenian decree relating to Chalcis of (probably) the 440s remains the earliest documentarily attested piece of continuous Attic prose.[24] It would be agreeable to think that it is often introduced as such to students of classics.

22. A. Maricq, "Res Gestae Divi Shaporis," *Syria* 35 (1958): 295; the Greek text is reproduced in *SEG* XX, 324. Note M. G. Bertinelli Angeli, "In margine alle Res Gestae Divi Saporis," *Parola del Passato* 27 (1972): 40.

23. Note, e.g., M. Rostovtzeff, "Seleucid Babylonia: Bullae and Seals of Clay with Greek Inscriptions," *YCS* 3 (1932): 1; A. K. Grayson, *Assyrian and Babylonian Chronicles* (Locust Valley, N.Y., 1975); G. J. P. McEwan, *Priest and Temple in Hellenistic Babylonia* (Wiesbaden, 1981). There is considerable further evidence in both languages.

24. *Syll.*³ 64; *IG* I², 39; R. Meiggs and D. M. Lewis, *Greek Historical Inscriptions* (Oxford,

In the same way the vast body of Hellenistic inscriptions is the essential source for the evolution of the *koine* or common Greek language of the post-Alexander period (which did not exclude the preservation of dialect forms in some cities, for instance, Doric in Rhodes or Cyrene), while the local inscriptions of Italy are the only basis for our knowledge of the various Italic tongues, and the gradual spread of Latin—itself a key element in the Romanisation of Italy.[25] Similarly, surviving Latin inscriptions provide our only evidence of how Latin was written and spoken in eastern Europe in the Roman imperial period.[26] Whereas monumental inscriptions necessarily present a formalised language which may yield little trace of that used in ordinary life, graffiti on walls (best known, of course, at Pompeii), and pottery provide a means of access, comparable to that of the ostraca for the Greek of classical Athens, to the grammatical forms and pronunciations actually used by ordinary people.[27] For the evolution of vulgar Latin, the third-century A.D. ostraca written by soldiers stationed at the frontier post of Bu Ngem in Tripolitania will be of exceptional importance.[28] Beyond that, in favourable circumstances, the graffiti of a town such as Pompeii may be extensive enough to allow an attempt to define the elements of a popular culture.[29] All of this is simply to point out the obvious, that the inscriptions of the classical world are first and foremost a body of texts, an ever-increasing mass of language, which inevitably outstrips all attempts at lexical or grammatical analysis. In one particular area of language, the history of nomenclature, the importance of inscriptions—above all because of their primarily local character—has long been obvious. A major conference was devoted to Latin onomastics,[30] and the *Lexicon of Greek Proper Names*, currently being prepared under the direction of P. M. Fraser, has required the efforts of a whole team of researchers and the use of a computer. From this it is quite

---

1969), no. 52; now re-edited by D. M. Lewis in *IG* I³ (1981), no. 40. Photograph in B. D. Merritt, H. T. Wade-Gery, and M. F. McGregor, *The Athenian Tribute Lists* II (Cambridge, Mass., 1949), pl. 10.

25. See, e.g., E. Pulgram, *The Tongues of Italy: Prehistory and History* (Cambridge, Mass., 1958), and *Italic, Latin, Italian, 600 B.C.–A.D. 1260: Texts and Commentaries* (Heidelberg, 1978); E. Vetter, *Handbuch der italischen Dialekte* I (Heidelberg, 1953); P. Poccetti, *Nuovi documenti italici* (Pisa, 1979).

26. See H. Mihaescu, *La langue latine dans le sud-est de l'Europe* (Bucharest, 1978).

27. See, e.g., V. Väänänen, *Le latin vulgaire des inscriptions pompéiennes*³ (Berlin, 1966), and *Introduction an latin vulgaire*² (Paris, 1967).

28. See R. Marichal, *Les ostraca de Bu Njem* (Tripoli, 1992).

29. See M. Gigante, *Civiltà delle forme letterarie nell' antica Pompeii* (Naples, 1979).

30. *L'onomastique latine*, Coll. Int. du CNRS, no. 564 (1977).

clear that only work with a computer—and perhaps not even that—could enable lexicographical work on Latin, and especially Greek, to do any justice to the ever-growing volume of epigraphic material. The immense bulk of the computer index to *CIL* VI, containing the Latin inscriptions of Rome, gives some idea of the problems involved.

For any serious attempt at social or cultural history we normally require (as will be stressed again later) a substantial concentration of documents which can mutually illuminate each other. But it is precisely on the margins—at the geographical or temporal limits of a culture or civilisation—that the single document, however slight, may have a disproportionate importance. At the very least it may allow that form of reasoning which deploys a double negative—it will show that it is not the case that there are no examples of *x* from a particular time or place. That being so, the form of other arguments on larger issues will also be affected.

Let me take a final example from an area mentioned several times already, Afghanistan. Asoka had at least two proclamations inscribed in Greek at Kandahar. Could it be argued that he was just following contemporary royal fashion and had no real Greek-speaking public in the locality to address and convince? No, because P. M. Fraser has published a fragmentary Greek dedicatory epigram from a statue base in Kandahar which dates to the first half of the third century and indicates that there was a sanctuary (*temenos*) there, and almost certainly shows that the place was a Greek city or settlement (and possibly even one of Alexander's foundations).[31] All that, with considerable consequences for our understanding of the area, can be revealed by four very fragmentary lines of Greek text.

If we move further west, a number of similar examples of marginal cases, where individual documents are of great importance, can be taken from the early history of Italy, which, because of new archaeological and epigraphical discoveries, has become one of the most interesting areas in the history of the ancient world. It is perhaps worth pointing out that the documents mentioned here, dating from between the late eighth century and around 500, are in four different languages: Greek, Latin, Etruscan, and Punic.

1. A very well known example, "Nestor's cup" from the eighth-century Greek settlement on the island of Pithekoussai (Ischia) near Naples. The cup has this nickname because on its body are scratched three lines of verse in Greek, written from right to left and beginning "Of Nestor I am, a cup pleasant to drink from."[32] The cup and the graffito seem to belong towards the

31. P. M. Fraser, "The Son of Aristonax at Kandahar," *Afghan Studies* 2 (1979): 9.

32. See, e.g., L. H. Jeffery, *Local Scripts of Archaic Greece* (Oxford, 1961), 235–36 and pl. 47; Meiggs and Lewis (n. 24), no. 1.

end of the eighth century. The consequences which can be drawn from these few lines are momentous. Firstly, this is among the earliest attested uses of the Greek alphabet. Secondly, while it has never been denied, even in the classical period itself, that the Greek alphabet is a borrowing, with varied adaptations, from the twenty-two-letter Phoenician-Hebrew alphabet, the consistent right-to-left writing here seems to indicate a particular closeness to the Phoenician source. That itself might not be correct (though evidence has been presented for a Phoenician presence on Ischia), for it has been argued that the earliest examples of Greek writing which we have (from the eighth century) reflect the Phoenician script not of that period but of some three centuries earlier.[33] The theory, based on letter forms and other strictly palaeographical considerations, naturally has to contend with the fact (which could, of course, be altered by new discoveries at any moment) that there are no examples of Greek alphabetic writing before the eighth century. But in any case, if we look to the immediate context in Ischia, the double-negative form of argument is still relevant. It cannot be argued that all the Greek colonists on Ischia were illiterate, because at least one of them was literate. What is more, the graffito is in verse and appears to contain a literary allusion, if not to the *Iliad* at any rate to the content of a story incorporated in the *Iliad*. Moreover, since it is an undoubted fact that a version or adaptation of the Phoenician alphabet passed also to the Etruscans (who continued to write right-to-left), the graffito at least illustrates a possible channel through which these fundamentally important cultural transmissions may have passed.

2. The "Black Stone" (*lapis niger*) from the Forum in Rome. This famous stone contains an inscription, written vertically, in lines running alternately up and down, which is almost entirely unintelligible, but certainly in Latin. The latest archaeological discussion of the *comitium* (the archaic meeting place of the people) area of the Forum where the stone was found (and remains in situ) suggests that the construction dates to the sixth century B.C. What is more, the presence of a fragment of Athenian black-figure pottery datable to *c.* 570–560 and containing a representation of Hephaestus strongly suggests that the monument should be identified with the Volcanal or shrine of Vulcan (= Hephaestus) which is known to have been situated in this area.[34] Since the identification cannot be certain, the argument is one of coherence, and cannot be conclusive. If it *is* correct, it naturally implies that the identification of the Greek Hephaestus and Vulcan was consciously made not later

33. J. Naveh, "The Greek Alphabet: New Evidence," *Biblical Archaeologist* 43 (1980): 22.

34. See F. Coarelli, "Il Comizio dalle origini alla fine della Repubblica," *Parola del Passato* 32 (1977): 166; note the survey by T. J. Cornell, "Rome and Latium Vetus, 1974–79," *Archaeological Reports for 1979–80* (1980), 71ff., on pp. 83–84.

than the sixth century. But whether that is valid or not, the clear indications are that the inscription presents quite a complex Latin text of the regal period; it is thus one of a number of items of evidence for some degree of literacy *in Latin* (as opposed to Etruscan) in the archaic period. The Rome of that period emerges as a relatively advanced community, a conclusion which is of some importance, even if it makes it all the more puzzling to understand why the close contacts with the Greek world which existed from the beginning took so long—until the third century B.C.—to engender a literary culture.

3. The inscription of Sostratus from Gravisca. Another strikingly important item of evidence for Greek influence in Italy in the archaic period is represented by the inscription discovered in 1970 at Gravisca, the port of Tarquinia in Etruria.[35] The inscription is on a stone anchor, dates to about 500 B.C., and runs "I am of Aeginetan Apollo. Sostratus (son of) . . . had me made." It is difficult to exaggerate the importance of the discovery. Firstly, together with the other evidence from the sanctuary of Hera, it shows Greeks solidly established on the Etruscan coast in the late sixth century. Secondly, it would be carrying academic caution too far if we declined altogether to associate this Sostratus with the Sostratus mentioned in a passing aside in Herodotus (4, 152) as the man who made the largest trading profit ever known (among Greeks, as is surely implied). This Sostratus, or at the very least a relative, now acquires a firm location and approximate date (roughly contemporary with the foundation of the Roman Republic). Furthermore, a large number of Attic vases of this period from Etruria bear the stamp $\Sigma O\Sigma$, which it is surely not too rash to associate with Sostratus. In that case we have an important indication of the character of Greek long-distance trade in the late archaic period. The vases were manufactured in Athens but carried to Etruria in substantial quantities by an Aeginetan trader, whose personality and profits were sufficiently well known to be alluded to by Herodotus more than half a century later. The *combination* of different types of evidence—a literary reference, a dedication in situ, and marks on a large number of vases—is therefore certainly sufficient to re-open the question of long-distance trade in archaic Greece as a significant activity, deliberately aimed at producing profits. Whether it would also suggest the existence of a *class* of traders is a different and much more complex question.

4. The gold leaves from Pyrgi. Pyrgi was one of the ports of the southern

35. M. Torelli, "Il santuario di Hera a Gravisca," *Parola del Passato* 26 (1971): 44; F. D. Harvey, "Sostratos of Aegina," *Parola del Passato* 31 (1976): 206; J. Boardman, *The Greeks Overseas*[3] (London, 1980), 206.

Etruscan city of Caere, and the three gold leaves, discovered in the excavation of a sanctuary there, apparently record a dedication made, probably early in the fifth century, by Thefarie Velianas, king of Caere. Their most immediate significance lies firstly in the fact that the dedication is to the Phoenician goddess Astarte and secondly that while two are in Etruscan the third is in Punic. Leaving aside the whole question of Phoenician-Punic influence and activity in the western Mediterranean in the archaic period,[36] the leaves have a very precise relevance, as a marginal case, to the issue of the first Roman-Carthaginian treaty. Polybius (3, 22) quotes this from an ancient and almost unintelligible document and dates it to the first pair of consuls in the Republic, who held office, according to him, twenty-eight years before Xerxes' invasion of Greece. The existence of these gold leaves, inscribed in Punic and Etruscan, probably a few decades later, will not, of course, serve to *prove* that there ever was such a treaty, or (still less), that Polybius' text, if genuine at all, is rightly dated to that period. But what it will do is to alter the terms of the argument, once again by the insertion of a double negative: it can *not* now be taken as a starting point that the notion of written documents exchanged between Carthage and an Italian community in this area is an unacceptable anachronism.

Place and Date

The form of argument which relies on the fact that there is (at least) one epigraphic example of something from a particular time or place, thus destroying a possible negative generalisation, will often, of course, have a place in much better-attested periods also. For instance, the fact that even a few inscriptions in Etruscan should be discovered in the Republican province of Africa,[37] used on boundary markers, opens up new perspectives relating to emigration from Italy and also to the use of the Etruscan language in secular, ordinary-life contexts. Or, alternatively, in a very crude and simple sense the discovery of a Latin military inscription (*CIL* III, 13430) recording a legion wintering at Leugaricio (Trencin in Czechoslavakia, some eighty miles north of the Danube) and of another from the neighbourhood of Baku on the coast of the Caspian Sea indicating the presence of a legionary detachment (*AE* 1951, 263 — the easternmost Latin inscription so far discovered), serves to demonstrate the extension of a Roman military presence at least

36. See J. Heurgon, "The Inscriptions of Pyrgi," *JRS* 56 (1966): 1.

37. J. Heurgon, "Inscriptions étrusques de Tunisie," *CRAI* (1969): 526; O. Carruba, "Nuova lettura dell' inscrizione etrusca dei cippi di Tunisia," *Athenaeum* 54 (1976): 163.

as far as these places. It is precisely the fact that the vast majority of inscriptions come from contexts which can be located at least within reasonable limits that gives them their very special significance both in contrast to and in combination with literary texts handed down in a manuscript tradition.

Many inscriptions can also be dated, either precisely—if they contain a date using a known system (e.g., the Seleucid era, Roman consuls, or the titles of a Roman emperor)—or approximately, from considerations of archaeological context, style of monument, letter forms of the inscription, use of formulae, nomenclature, or language. But even formal, public inscriptions may sometimes be very difficult to place in a chronological context; and even greater problems may be presented, for instance, by private tomb inscriptions from the Roman provinces.

Epigraphy as Literature

The very close links and resemblances between classical literature and Greek and Latin inscriptions, which can be considered and analysed as a sub-species of literary texts, have not, of course, escaped notice.[38] But it is relevant to suggest that for the classically trained student approaching Greek and Latin epigraphy one relevant stratagem might be to begin with one or more of those extended texts which can without any difficulty be seen as minor literary compositions; some of them are indeed prime specimens of narrative or rhetorical prose. A strictly literary analysis of methods of composition, introduction of themes, repetition, and forms of explanation and justification addressed to the potential reader would be of exceptional value, for instance in relation to extended legislative inscriptions, particularly for example the long and complex inscriptions containing Roman laws which appear in the later second century B.C.[39] Given the difficulty of following the structure of these texts, it is not surprising that historical works devoted to this period show a distinct tendency to allude in passing to isolated aspects of them rather than treating them as what they are, by far the most important surviving products of the political processes of the period.

It may be worthwhile therefore to give a few examples of extended epigraphical texts which could be analysed as minor literary products, and which

38. Note for instance the compilation by R. Chevallier, *Épigraphie et littérature à Rome* (Faenza, 1972).

39. For relevant analyses, see D. Daube, *Forms of Roman Legislation* (Oxford, 1956); A. Watson, *Law Making in the Later Roman Republic* (Oxford, 1974). But see now A. N. Sherwin-White, "The Lex Repetundarum," *JRS* 72 (1982): 18.

independently embody and reveal important aspects of the ideology or structure of the societies which produced them. I begin with two closely related
examples from early Hellenistic Greece, in that notable period when a real
struggle, both ideological and military, was fought to preserve the traditional
freedom of the Greek city against the claims of the rival monarchies.

   1. Kallias of Sphettus. The inscription of 109 almost completely preserved
lines honouring an Athenian named Kallias was voted in 270/69 B.C. and set
up in the Agora.[40] The first part of the decree contains a highly allusive account, none the less giving many new specific details, of the revolt of Athens
against Demetrius Poliorcetes in 287 or 286 B.C. and the role played in these
events by Kallias, who (as the inscription reveals) was acting as the commander of a Ptolemaic garrison on Andros. The political and military background of the 280s is highly complex, and the chronological framework of
the story is open to various different interpretations.[41] What matters in this
context is the revelation of a new and quite extensive piece of early Hellenistic narrative prose; the ideology of liberation and attachment to democracy
which informs the document throughout; by contrast with that, the dependence on Ptolemaic military assistance and the highly evolved diplomatic
and ritual relations of Athens with Alexandria; and the very full specification
of the communal and ceremonial institutions of Athens which come into
play in the allotment of appropriate honours to Kallias—who at the time of
the document's composition was a Ptolemaic official on duty at Halicarnas-
sus. No document could reveal more clearly the tensions and contradictions
between the ideal of the freedom of the city-state and the power of the conflicting monarchies.

   2. Decree of the *Koinon* of the Greeks at Plataea in honour of Glaucon.[42]
This beautiful and almost complete text of the mid third century B.C. was inscribed at Plataea by the common council (*Koinon*) of the Greeks in honour
of Glaucon, the brother of the Athenian Chremonides, who had proposed in
Athens in the 260s the alliance with Sparta and other states which led to the

40. T. L. Shear, *Kallias of Sphettos and the Revolt of Athens in 286 B.C.* (*Hesperia* Supp. XVII,
1978).

41. See Chr. Habicht, *Untersuchungen zur politischen Geschichte Athens im 3. Jahrhundert v.
Chr.* (Munich, 1979); M. J. Osborne, "Kallias, Phaidros and the Revolt of Athens in 287 B.C.,"
ZPE 35 (1979): 181.

42. R. Étienne and M. Piérart, "Un décret du Koinon des Hellénes à Platées en l'hon-
neur de Glaucon, fils d'Étéoclès, d'Athènes," *BCH* 99 (1975): 51; J. Pouilloux, "Glaucon, fils
d'Étéoclès d'Athènes," *Le monde grec: hommages à Claire Préaux* (Brussels, 1975), 376. This inscription is also translated in the excellent collection by M. M. Austin, *The Hellenistic World
from Alexander to the Roman Conquest* (Cambridge, 1981), no. 51.

ultimately unsuccessful "Chremonidean War" against Antigonus Gonatas.
The inscription perfectly illustrates the use of Plataea as a symbolic rallying
point and the attachment to the ideal of freedom, and on the other hand the
limitations imposed by the power structure of the time, which meant that
(as in the case of the previous inscription) aspirations to freedom from the
rule of one major power inevitably meant being drawn into the diplomatic
or military orbit of another. Rather than summarise or isolate particular features—which tends in any case to allow the all-important ceremonial, ritual,
and religious context to be obscured—I give a translation of the complete
document:

> At the time when Nicocleides son of Chacreas was priest and Archelaus
> son of Athenaeus was agonothete, decree of the Hellenes. Euboulus son
> of Panormostus the Boeotian spoke:
>
> Since Glaucon son of Eteocles, the Athenian, when formerly he was
> dwelling in his native city, never ceased to show his goodwill either
> publicly to all the Hellenes or privately to those who visited the city,
> and afterwards when he held office at the court of King Ptolemy
> showed the same attitude, wishing to make clear the extent of his good-
> will toward the Hellenes, and adorned the sanctuary with offerings and
> revenues which it is appropriate to reserve for Zeus the Liberator and
> the Harmony [*Homonoia*] of the Hellenes, and also enriched the sac-
> rifices offered to Zeus the Liberator and to Harmony, as well as the
> contest which the Hellenes celebrate over the tombs of the heroes who
> fought against the barbarians for the liberty of the Hellenes—in order
> that all may be aware that the common council of the Hellenes returns
> to those, both living and dead, who honour the sanctuary of Zeus the
> Liberator, thanks appropriate to the benefits they have bestowed, it has
> been decided by the Hellenes to praise Glaucon and to offer precedence
> to him and his decendants in respect of any occasion when the ath-
> letic contests are being celebrated at Plataea, on the same basis as other
> benefactors, and that the agonothete should have this decree inscribed
> on a stone *stele* and dedicated beside the altar of Zeus the Liberator and
> Harmony, and that the treasurer in charge of the sacred funds should
> make the expenditure for this purpose.

It hardly needs to be emphasised how complex are the administrative, religious and ceremonial institutions which provide the machinery and framework of the honours voted here. The significance of the ceremonials at the
site of the battle of Plataea in 479, which were still carried out in Plutarch's

time (*Life of Aristides* 21), is if anything increased by the fact that the decree was passed after the defeat of the Greeks in the Chremonidean War and the garrisoning of Athens by the forces of Antigonus Gonatas. The purpose of quoting the inscription here, however, is not to offer any detailed commentary, but simply to illustrate how individual inscriptions of sufficiently rich content, even ones which—like this—are quite short, can provide a focus of study through which the nature of a whole society or period could be analysed. Epigraphic texts of this sort can be taken (in a sense) individually and placed in a wider context in the same way as literary texts may be.

3. The *senatus consultum* of 39 B.C. from Aphrodisias. This document of 95 long lines represents almost the fullest text of any *senatus consultum* so far published. It is perhaps the most important of the large dossier of inscriptions illustrating the relations of the Carian city of Aphrodisias with Rome published by Joyce Reynolds.[43] Without repeating the very detailed commentary given by Miss Reynolds, it is enough to say that the document both provides detailed evidence about, and raises many problems in relation to, a host of issues: the meeting places of the Senate, its procedures and their documentation, Julius Caesar and his attachment to the cult of Venus/Aphrodite, the role of the Triumvirs in relation to republican institutions, the nature of *asylia* (rights of asylum) and the privileges of "free" cities. But the most complex and difficult question of all relates to the composition of the document as we have it. What exactly is it that the inscription is a record of? The proceedings of the Senate? The consul's (consuls'?) speech? A motion passed on his (their) proposal? Why is the document, whose text is badly damaged in many places, marked by so many repetitions of the same subject matter, which none the less do not exhibit exact verbal repetitions? And, in any case is the Greek text a complete translation of the Latin original or a set of extracts, or something more like a summary? What appears at first sight to be a documentary record soon turns out to show considerable ambiguities, not lessened by the fact that the actual inscription as we have it was inscribed more than two centuries later. Somewhere behind the actual physical object, the inscription carved in Greek in the early third century A.D., lies a set of proposals passed in Latin by the Senate in Rome in 39 B.C. How close we can come to the latter must depend in part on a detailed "textual" and structural analysis, comparable to that applied to literary texts.

4. The "Laudatio Turiae." This famous inscription, containing an address by an unknown Roman to his unnamed deceased wife, recording her devo-

---

43. Joyce Reynolds, *Aphrodisias and Rome* (London, 1982), doc. 8.

tion to him and her services in the troubled period of the Triumvirate of Octavian, Antonius, Lepidus, has recently received renewed attention.[44] If nothing else, it would deserve this attention as one of the few pieces of narrative or rhetorical prose to survive from the reign of Augustus, the most important era of Latin poetry. Like the already famous Latin papyrus containing a few lines of the poetry of Cornelius Gallus,[45] it is thus of prime importance as evidence for the style, grammar, orthography, and spelling in use in this period. It is also one of the few extended biographical, or at any rate personal, records of an individual, probably of equestrian rank, available to use from this period. The text offers not only reflections of historical events (the purchase of the house of Milo, the proscriptions of 43, the husband's flight, the wife's prostration before the feet of Lepidus to petition for his restoration), but evidence on inheritance and the handling of family property, the conduct expected of wives and the importance of child-bearing to marriage. In other words, it is a central document for the values of Roman society. In this connection it may be significant that the surviving text, which is packed with expressions relating to moral duties and obligations, contains only a single passing reference to religious observance.

5. The Tabula of Banasa. The bronze tablet from Banasa in Morocco, finally published in 1971, is perhaps our finest documentary item of evidence for the archival procedures of the Roman emperors and for the limits and consequences of the granting of citizenship, as well as affording some glimpses of social structure in a marginal area of the empire.[46] In view of the almost complete state of the text and its exceptional character as a formal document, it seems worthwhile to reproduce it in full (omitting a few technical details):

[c. A.D. 168] Copy of a letter of our emperors Antoninus and Verus, Augusti, to Coiiedius Maximus: we have read the *libellus* [petition] of Julianus the Zegrensian attached to your letter, and although the

44. _ILS_ 8393; M. Durry, _Éloge funèbre d'une matrone romaine_ (Paris, 1950); new edition with photographs by E. Wistrand, _The So-Called Laudatio Turiae_ (Göteborg, 1976). See N. M. Horsfall, "Some Problems in the 'Laudatio Turiae,'" _BICS_ 30 (1983): 85.

45. R. D. Anderson, P. J. Parsons, and R. G. M. Nisbet, "Elegiacs by Gallus from Quasr Ibrîm," _JRS_ 69 (1979): 125, with pls. 4–6.

46. W. Seston and M. Euzennat, "Un dossier de la chancellerie romaine, la Tabula Banasitana, étude de diplomatique," _CRAI_ (1971): 468; A. N. Sherwin-White, "The _Tabula_ of Banasa and the _Constitutio Antoniniana_," _JRS_ 63 (1973): 86; W. Williams, "Formal and Historical Aspects of Two New Documents of Marcus Aurelius," _ZPE_ 17 (1975): 37 on pp. 56–57; F. Millar, _The Emperor in the Roman World_ (London, 1977), 130, 216, 223, 261–62, 473; U. Schillinger-Häfele, "Der Urheber der Tafel von Banasa," _Chiron_ 7 (1977): 323.

Roman citizenship is not normally granted by imperial *indulgentia* to those tribesmen unless earned by the highest deserts, yet since you affirm that he is among the most prominent among those peoples of his and most loyal in his prompt obedience in our interests (and we do not think that many households from among the Zegrenses will be able to claim the same of their services), and since [?] we wish as many as possible to be aroused by the honour conferred by us on that house to emulate Julianus, we do not hesitate to give the Roman citizenship, without prejudice to the law of the tribe, to him, his wife Ziddina, and their children Julianus, Maximus, Maximinus, Diogenianus.

[A.D. 177] Copy of a letter of the emperors Antoninus and Commodus, Augusti, to Vallius Maximianus: we have read the *libellus* of the chief of the tribes of the Zegrenses and have noted the favour with which he is regarded by your predecessor Epidius Quadratus, and also moved by the latter's testimonies, and the services and evidence of his conduct which he himself puts forward, have given to his wife and children the Roman citizenship, without prejudice to the law of the tribe. In order that this may be recorded in our *commentarii* [records] find out what the age of each is and write to us.

Copied down and checked from the record [*commentarius*] of those given the Roman citizenship by the Divine Augustus (names of preceding emperors) . . . which the freedman Asclepiodotus produced, as it is written below:

In the consulship of Imperator Caesar L. Aurelius Commodus Aug. and M. Plautius Quintilius, on the day before the nones of July, at Rome [July 6, 177].
Faggura, wife of Julianus, *princeps* of the tribe of the Zegrensians, age 22, Juliana, age 8, Maxima, age 4, Julianus, age 3, Diogenia, age 2, children of Julianus mentioned above:
At the request *per libellum* of Aurelius Julianus, princeps of the Zegrensians supported by Vallius Maximianus by letter [*suffragante . . . per epistulam*], to these we have given the Roman citizenship, without prejudice to the law of the tribe, and without diminution of the *tributa* [taxes] and *vectigalia* [revenues] of the people and the *fiscus* [the emperor's treasury].

Carried out on the same day in the same place under the same consuls. Asclepiodotus, freedman: I have checked it:

Witnesses:

M. Gavius Squilla Gallicanus	[consul, 150]
M'. Acilius Glabrio	[consul, 152]
T. Sextius Lateranus	[consul, 154]
C. Septimius Severus	[consul, 160]
P. Julius Scapula Tertullus	[consul, 160/6]
T. Varius Clemens	[ex–*ab epistulis*]
M. Bassaeus Rufus	[ex–praetorian prefect]
P. Taruttienus Paternus	[praetorian prefect by 179]
Sex. (Tigidius Peren)nis	[probably praetorian prefect]
Q. Cervidius Scaevola	[lawyer, prefect of *Vigiles*, 175]
Q. Larcius Euripianus	
T. Flavius Piso	[prefect of the corn supply, 179]

Firstly, the procedures recorded fall clearly within the wider category, fundamental to the nature of imperial government, of petition-and-response. Secondly, the document clearly illustrates one sub-category of this procedure, the way in which provincial governors might send on petitions from private individuals to the emperor, with a covering letter of recommendation. In this case the terminology used (*suffragante Vallio Maximiano per epistulam*) perfectly exemplifies G. E. M. de Ste Croix's justly famous demonstration—given long before this inscription was known—of how the meaning of words with the root "suffrag-" shifted from votes by equals to petitions for favours addressed by intermediaries to superiors. In other words it is a clear example of how language was distorted by the impact of monarchy.[47] Thirdly, the right to grant the Roman citizenship was from the beginning one of the perquisites of the monarchic rule exercised by the Roman emperors. We had known already from Pliny's correspondence with Trajan (10, 95; 105) that there were imperial *commentarii*, or archives, in which the names of the recipients of *beneficia* (grants) were entered; but not that there was a "*commentarius* of persons granted Roman citizenship" by all the emperors (other than subsequently unrecognised pretenders) back to Augustus himself. Nor, before the publication of this inscription, did we possess a single documentary text from these archives. The bulk of such an archive—in which, as the extract given implies, the individual entries were written up in remarkable detail—must have been very considerable. The document also confronts us with major unanswered questions as to the nature of archives on perishable materials, their organisation, location, form of storage, and (?) transport-

47. G. E. M. de Ste Croix, "'*Suffragium*': From Vote to Patronage," *British Journal of Sociology* 5 (1954): 33.

ability. For did they remain permanently in Rome or accompany the emperors on their increasingly frequent travels and campaigns? If not, in what sense could they be used by an emperor who might be a thousand miles away? The list of imperial *amici*, first consulars in order of seniority and then the leading *equites*, also seems to give a perfect representation of the emperors' advisers as they were in 177. These distinguished gentlemen are listed as witnesses to a document which, seen from Rome, must have been of very minor local importance. If they really did attend in person to affix their seals, that is quite a striking fact. But did they also discuss the *content* of Imperial written decisions and letters? If not, since so much of the emperor's work concerned the issue of written decisions in various forms, the significance of the role of advisers or *amici* must have been much less than often supposed.

The document also raises important questions about the citizenship itself, as it does about the nature of the taxes and revenues of the people and the *fiscus* (the emperor's treasury). But perhaps more significant is the fact that the bronze tablet, with all the information and problems which it presents to us, is only available, firstly, by the accident of survival (and bronze is for obvious reasons highly vulnerable) and of discovery and, secondly, because it was originally in the interest of someone—presumably Julianus, the *princeps* of the Zegrenses—to have it inscribed and put up. It is the fundamental limitation and problem of epigraphy that in reading an inscription we are always reading what someone wished to tell not us but his contemporaries. The very notion of putting up an inscription in Latin will have been a cultural import which came to Banasa with the extension of Graeco-Roman culture. But the occasion would only arise, firstly, when some success, such as a favourable reply to a petition, had been secured and, secondly, when there was some need to record this in a local context. None the less, in spite of all the problems of context and background, this is a beautifully explicit document which has almost infinite lessons to give us about the nature of the Roman Empire.

6. The Tetrarchic Edict on Maximum Prices. The two imperial letters in the Tabula of Banasa are highly typical of the workings of imperial government in the first three centuries in being *replies* to requests from interested parties. In the period of the Tetrarchy an important change seems to appear in the aspirations of government, the level of innovation which it sought, and the degree of social and economic intervention at which it aimed.[48] This

---

48. For a brief indication of the novelty and importance of the Tetrarchic edicts, see Millar (n. 46), 257–58. See now S. Corcoran, *The Empire of the Tetrarchs: Imperial Pronouncements and Government* (Oxford, 1996).

very distinctive phase, accompanied by major attempts at systematisation of the law,[49] was also marked by much more explicit and deliberate attempts to explain and justify imperial decisions to the public. By far the most significant product of this development was the well-known edict on maximum prices, now known from a large number of fragments in the Greek East.[50] For our knowledge of its text we are (once again) bound to be dependent on whether in each province the choice was made to inscribe it on stone. So far, the fragments come from a quite restricted range of provinces, in the Greek-speaking part of the empire.[51] This is not the place to enter into any discussion of the products and services for which the edict lays down maximum prices, or of the perplexing problems of relative monetary and bullion values in this period, also the subject of another contemporary edict of which one fragment has been published.[52] What may be emphasised here is the vast preamble in which the emperors explain and justify their measures. As with the earlier documents mentioned, this could be considered first of all as a specimen of the official Latin prose of the early fourth century. Secondly, *whose* prose is it? The problem of the actual authorship of the texts of all forms of imperial pronouncement, from speeches to *subscriptiones* (replies written under petitions given in by individuals or groups), is acute (and insoluble) in all periods, and is made all the more complex by the Tetrarchic system. What we have is at any rate a piece of extended propaganda and self-justification issued in the name of all four of the Augusti and Caesares. We can study it

49. See T. Honoré, " 'Imperial' Rescripts AD 193–305: Authorship and Authenticity," *JRS* 69 (1979): 51 on pp. 60–63, and *Emperors and Lawyers* (London, 1981; 2nd ed., Oxford, 1994), chap. 4.

50. For a full text as known to that date, with extensive commentary, see S. Lauffer, *Diokletians Preisedikt* (Berlin, 1971); note also M. Giacchero, *Edictum Diocletiani et Collegarum de Pretiis Rerum Venalium* (Genoa, 1974). Extensive epigraphic work on the texts, especially that from Aphrodisias, is, however, still in progress. See K. T. Erim and Joyce Reynolds, *JRS* 63 (1973): 99; J. Reynolds, *ZPE* 33 (1979): 46 (Aphrodisias); M. H. Crawford and J. M. Reynolds, *ZPE* 26 (1977): 125; 34 (1979): 163 (Aezani); *AE* (1977): 776–7 (Achaea).

51. On the question of publication on stone and the importance of the role of the provincial governor, note M. H. Crawford and J. Reynolds, "The Publication of the Prices Edict: A New Inscription from Aezani," *JRS* 65 (1975): 160. The geographical pattern there suggested is slightly extended by the publication of a new fragment from Odessus on the west coast of the Black Sea; see G. Mihailov, *Stele (Memorial to N. Kontoleon)* (Athens, 1980), 147.

52. K. T. Erim, J. Reynolds, and M. Crawford, "Diocletian's Currency Reform: A New Inscription," *JRS* 6 (1971): 171; see M. Crawford, "Finance, Coinage and Money from the Severans to Constantine," *ANRW* II.2 (1975), 560, on pp. 578–81.

as a major expression of the new imperial ideology, while recalling that the only contemporary observer from whom we have a surviving mention of it, Lactantius (*De mortibus persecutorum* 7, 6–7), saw the edict as the work of Diocletian alone, and regarded it as a total failure.

With that we may leave this minute selection, inevitably quite unrepresentative, of that vast number of inscriptions (certainly far more numerous in Greek than in Latin) which can be read like—or even as—literary texts, and which have a sufficiently full and complex content for them to form a focus of study in themselves. That study itself, however, would have to consist of extended explorations of the wider context from which these documents come and to which they refer. In consequence, no clear line could or should be drawn between this approach and what must, obviously enough, be the normal one, the study of inscriptions in groups. The vital questions are, firstly, what types of groups and, secondly, what are the limits and nature of the questions which can be asked of them?

Handling Inscriptions in Bulk

Two preliminary points must be made. If the activity of increasing our knowledge and understanding of the past is valid at all, then every scrap of information, from a couple of letters scratched on a sherd onwards, potentially has a place in some wider framework of understanding. Hence comes the value of the apparently thankless task of producing reports and publications of endless archaeological and epigraphic finds, which at the moment do not seem to have any intelligible context or to make the slightest contribution to understanding. That may require several different levels or stages of work, not necessarily by the same person: a study of script and grammar in the Latin of a western province; an analysis of the linguistic patterns prevailing there; broader conclusions on the nature of "Romanisation." Or, just occasionally, someone with the energy and vision of a Rostovtzeff may be able to gather up a whole mass of disparate fragments of information and combine them to form an intelligible pattern.

But for the ordinary student of the ancient world who is not going to become an epigraphist himself, but who sees that the published inscriptions provide both an extraordinarily privileged and immediate means of access to the life of antiquity and a (literally) inexhaustible mass of data, the choice of an area or theme, and the construction of questions which the inscriptions will actually answer, are all-important. There are, it is true, very few aspects of life which are referred to nowhere in the hundreds of thousands of surviving inscriptions. If it were a reasonable or adequate objective to cata-

logue isolated references to (say) agricultural production, the marketing of
vegetables, the customs of non-urban communities, diet, childbirth, or religious observances within the family, then that could always be done. But it
does have to be accepted that whole areas of life will only appear tangen-
tially, if at all, in the inscriptions, and that there are many areas, however
desirable in themselves, where the inscriptions will not allow of any serious
social history. One of these areas, for instance, is slavery. There are indeed
important concentrations of documents, such as the manumission inscriptions of Delphi or Thessaly, which are highly *relevant* to slavery and brilliantly
illuminate its social framework from a very specific angle.[53] But an actual *history* of slavery in any particular region cannot be written. Again, for almost
all areas of economic life and activity inscriptions will provide the names of
trades and occupations, regulations affecting markets or prices, or the limits
of the privileges enjoyed by the members of particular groups. But they will
bring us very little nearer to an economic *history*. Similarly, the most detailed
inscriptions which we have relating to agriculture, those concerned with
imperial estates in Africa,[54] resemble the inscriptions of imperial mines in
the Iberian peninsula[55] in being *regulations* which allude to many important
aspects of economic and social life, but cannot by their nature take us further
than that. These documents too would be best studied in the first instance
as texts, in order to establish a clear view of their internal structure and purpose. But the limitation which faces us in collecting either isolated items of
economic evidence (say on the names of trades or occupations, whether generally or in a particular place) or extended formal documents relating to economic life, is that we still cannot place this evidence within any worthwhile
framework. We have no idea of how or where the produce of the emperor's
estates in Africa was marketed or consumed, nor what happened to the silver
from his mines in Spain.

   This is not to say that ancient economic history should not be pursued—
only that no one has so far escaped from the alternatives of having interesting ideas which do not relate to the evidence in a wholly satisfactory way, or

53. For an interesting historical study of the manumission inscriptions from Delphi, see
K. Hopkins, *Conquerors and Slaves* (Cambridge, 1978), 133–34; for some Thessalian manumission documents, see B. Helly, "Actes d'affranchissements thessaliens," *BCH* 99 (1975): 199,
and "Lois sur les affranchisements dans les inscriptions thessaliennes," *Phoenix* 30 (1976): 143.
   54. These texts are reproduced, e.g., in *FIRA*² I, nos. 100–103; Tenney Frank, ed., *Economic Survey of Ancient Rome* IV (Baltimore, 1938), 83–102.
   55. *FIRA*² I, nos. 104–5; translation and notes in Tenney Frank, ed., *Economic Survey of
Ancient Rome* III (Baltimore, 1937), 167–74.

collecting evidence which cannot in any real sense be interpreted. All serious work on ancient economic history using inscriptions would have to be conducted with the consciousness that all that can be achieved is preliminary collection and analysis of groups of relevant data.[56]

The Case of the Greek City

Significant historical work with inscriptions, leading to results which are more than merely preliminary or indicative, must (I would suggest) satisfy two conditions: that there is a sufficient concentration of evidence either by locality, type, or theme; and that it can be placed within some intelligible framework. Given the formality of nearly all types of inscription, and therefore the all too clearly defined and limited nature of what they are designed to say, the prospects of serious historical analysis are greatly improved if the inscriptions can be related to other evidence—literature above all, but also (in certain areas) papyri, and also coins, archaeological evidence, and studies of topography. Granted these conditions—that is, granted that in many areas the concentration of evidence will be too thin to allow any coherent results—the study of the history, topography, and institutions of particular areas or cities will always be an avenue worth exploring. The work of Louis Robert, heavily emphasised at the beginning of this chapter, provides innumerable examples of studies of cities and areas in Asia Minor, using the evidence of inscriptions.[57] But we may note also, as examples, studies of the history and cults of Thasos,[58] of Cos,[59] and of Gonnoi in Thessaly.[60] It is not an accident that all these are places in the Greek East, whose inscriptions tend both to be fuller and more revealing individually (i.e., to be, as suggested already, a minor form of literature in themselves), and to come in denser concentrations. Perhaps the only two towns in the Latin West of which real "histories" can be written are Pompeii and Ostia, both being cases where a

---

56. For instance, the invaluable work of R. Duncan-Jones, *The Economy of the Roman Empire: Quantitative Studies*[2] (Cambridge, 1982), is more accurately characterised by the second than the first half of its title.

57. E.g., L. Robert, *Études anatoliennes* (Paris, 1937); *La Carie* II (Paris, 1954) (by L. Robert and J. Robert); *Villes d'Asie Mineure*[2] (Paris, 1962); *À travers l'Asie Mineure* (Paris, 1980).

58. J. Pouilloux and C. Dunant, *Recherches sur l'histoire et les cultes de Thasos* I–II (Paris, 1954–58).

59. S. M. Sherwin-White, *Ancient Cos: An Historical Study from the Dorian Settlement to the Imperial Period* (Göttingen, 1978).

60. B. Helly, *Gonnoi* I–II (Amsterdam, 1973).

relatively rich stock of inscriptions can be placed in an archaeological setting of wholly exceptional character.[61] In the Greek East even a single sanctuary can produce a major series of inscriptions, allowing historical studies at various levels: so, for instance, the Asclepieion at Pergamum,[62] the great temple of Apollo at Didyma near Miletus,[63] or the sanctuary of Zeus at Labraunda in Caria.[64] An incomparably more extensive mass of inscriptions comes from the sanctuary of Apollo at Delphi.[65] The several hundred inscriptions of Delphi, stretching from the classical to the imperial period (for which there is an extensive series of Imperial letters concerned with the sanctuary) serve to create a not uncommon situation: that while we normally complain of a dearth of evidence for the history of the ancient world, here we find ourselves with *too* heavy a concentration of documents of very specialised types (accounts, dedications, letters) which, together with the vast archaeological remains, make a "history" of Delphi in the ancient world an almost unimaginable task. We have such a history for part of the Hellenistic period;[66] but, for instance, no one has yet published a historical analysis of the role of Delphi in the Graeco-Roman world of the Empire. Much the same could be said of Delos,[67] where the pattern of the inscriptions is complicated by the island's special relationship to Athens and by its brief but very important role as a major international trading centre between 166 B.C. and the Mithridatic wars. It is, once again, as yet impossible to imagine serious historical work, using the epigraphic and archaeological evidence, which is not strictly

61. For Ostia there is the classic study of R. Meiggs, *Roman Ostia*² (Oxford, 1973); for Pompeii, see now P. Zanker, *Pompeii: Stadtbild und Wohngeschmack* (Mainz, 1995), translated as *Pompeii: Public and Private Life* (Cambridge, Mass., 1998). For work based on inscriptions and graffiti, note the work of Gigante (n. 29) and Väänänen (n. 27). See also H. Castrén, *Ordo Populusque Pompeianus: Polity and Society in Roman Pompeii* (Rome, 1975). The graffiti from Pompeii are collected in *CIL* IV and Supplements.

62. Chr. Habicht, *Altertümer von Pergamon* VIII.3: *die Inschriften des Asklepieions* (Berlin, 1969), with an exemplary historical introduction.

63. A. Rehm, *Didyma* II: *die Inschriften* (Berlin, 1958).

64. J. Crampa, *Labraunda: Swedish Excavations and Researches* III.1–2, and *The Greek Inscriptions* (Lund, 1969–72).

65. Volumes of inscriptions appear among the reports of the French excavations, *Fouilles de Delphes* III, in a series of separate fascicules divided by the architectural setting of the inscriptions and published at intervals since 1909.

66. R. Flacelière, *Les Aitoliens à Delphes* (Paris, 1937); G. Daux, *Delphes au IIme et du Ier siècles* (Paris, 1936).

67. The inscriptions are again published in the reports of the French excavations, *Inscriptions de Délos*, and so far run to 2,879 items. Note therefore G. Durrbach, *Choix d'inscriptions de Délos* I.1–2 (Paris, 1921–22).

divided, as such work has been so far, by periods or themes.[68] Here at least there has been a beginning of analytical historical writing. But if we turn, to take only the most obvious example, to Ephesus, from where some five thousand inscriptions, stretching from the sixth century B.C. to the sixth century A.D., have been collected,[69] the evidence seems to call out for a historical study embracing topography and urban development, architecture, institutions, ceremonials, and cults. It is curious, however, that the late antique and Byzantine period of Anatolian Greek cities (notably Ephesus itself) has been better studied recently than the classical period.[70]

However, all these considerations pale into insignificance beside the fact that there is no serious analytical study of the one place where all the necessary conditions for a fully historical use of inscriptions are fulfilled, namely the most obvious of all, classical Athens. Hellenistic Athens was the subject of a beautifully balanced, but now antiquated, history by W. S. Ferguson;[71] a new history, using the vast mass of new inscriptional material has now been published by Chr. Habicht.[72] But classical Athens, of the fifth and fourth centuries, more than anywhere else in the ancient world, presents a concentration of literary, archaeological, and very extensive epigraphical evidence which should allow a fully integrated historical treatment of a society and its evolution through time; and here, alone among all ancient cities, the evidence of public inscriptions can be set against the background of a detailed contemporary analysis of the working of the constitution, the Aristotelian *Athenaion Politeia*.[73] As yet, to take only a few examples of those aspects to which the inscriptions are most relevant, we have detailed studies of the treasurers,[74] an excellent account of the working of the council,[75] studies of the

---

68. See, e.g., P. Roussel, *Délos, colonie athénienne* (Paris, 1916); or the important recent work of Ph. Bruneau, *Recherches sur les cultes de Délos à l'époque hellénistique et à l'époque impériale* (Paris, 1970).

69. In the series *Inschriften griechischer Städte Kleinasiens* and under the title *Die Inschriften von Ephesos* Ia (Bonn, 1979); II (Bonn, 1979); III–VI (Bonn, 1980); VII, 1–2 (Bonn, 1981).

70. See C. Foss, *Byzantine and Turkish Sardis* (Cambridge, Mass., 1976); *Ephesos after Antiquity: A Late Antique, Byzantine and Turkish City* (Cambridge, Mass., 1979).

71. W. S. Ferguson, *Hellenistic Athens: An Historical Essay* (London, 1911).

72. Chr. Habicht, *Athen: Geschichte der Stadt in hellenistischen Zeit* (Munich, 1995), translated as *Athens from Alexander to Antony* (Cambridge, Mass., 1997).

73. Note the massive recent commentary on this work by P. J. Rhodes, *A Commentary on the Aristotelian Athenaion Politeia* (Oxford, 1981).

74. W. S. Ferguson, *The Treasurers of Athena* (Cambridge, Mass., 1932).

75. P. J. Rhodes, *The Athenian Boule* (Oxford, 1972). Cf. B. D. Merritt and J. S. Traill, *The Athenian Agora* XV: *Inscriptions: The Athenian Councillors* (Princeton, 1974).

political geography of Attica,[76] and a very full prosopography of the richer Athenians and their families.[77] The combination of literary and epigraphic evidence also makes possible a very full understanding of Athenian festivals.[78] Without multiplying further examples, it is enough to pose the question, in concluding this section, as to why classical Athens has attracted no major historical study.

A strictly geographical concentration of inscriptions, such as lies relatively unexploited not only in the individual areas and cities mentioned but also in a host of others, is not the only type of concentration which would allow serious study. Few would now dare to attempt a synthetic view of the functioning of "the Greek city" over many centuries in the manner of that great historian, A. H. M. Jones, even if his work remains essential reading for all students of the Greek world.[79] But there remain major themes where substantial series of documents are available, stretching over wide areas in time and space. One example is the major subject of the formal, diplomatic, military, and financial relations between Greek cities and Hellenistic kings, involving, for instance, the evolution of royal cults,[80] the form and content of royal letters to cities,[81] the prosopography of royal emissaries and office-holders,[82] or the forms of control and exploitation in the overseas possessions of the Ptolemies.[83] Subjects such as these can be effectively studied for two reasons. Firstly, because, in spite of diversities over time and space, it is reasonable to start from the hypothesis that the Hellenistic monarchies were functioning systems, in which each item of evidence will make some contribution to the understanding of the whole.[84] Secondly, we are dealing with

76. J. S. Traill, *The Political Organization of Attica: A Study of the Demes, Trittyes and Phylae and Their Representation in the Athenian Council* (*Hesperia* Suppl. XIV, 1975).

77. J. K. Davies, *Athenian Propertied Families, 600–300 B.C.* (Oxford, 1971).

78. See L. Deubner, *Attische Feste* (Berlin, 1932); A. W. Pickard-Cambridge, *The Dramatic Festivals of Athens*[2], rev. J. Gould and D. M. Lewis (Oxford 1968); H. W. Parke, *Festivals of the Athenians* (London, 1977). See now R. Parker, *Athenian Religion: A History* (Oxford, 1995).

79. *The Greek City from Alexander to Justinian* (Oxford, 1940).

80. Chr. Habicht, *Gottmenschentum und griechische Städte*[2] (Munich, 1970).

81. The collection by C. B. Welles, *Royal Correspondence in the Hellenistic Era* (New Haven, 1934), could now be greatly extended, for instance by the third-century letters from Labraunda (see n. 64).

82. E. Olshausen, *Prosopographie der hellenistischen Königsgesandten* I: *von Triparadeisos bis Pydna* (Louvain, 1974).

83. R. S. Bagnall, *The Administration of the Ptolemaic Possessions outside Egypt* (Leiden, 1976).

84. Note the classic, if perhaps too schematic, study of E. Bikerman, *Institutions des Séleucides* (Paris, 1938), and D. Musti, "Lo stato dei Seleucidi," *Studi Classici e Orientali* 15 (1966): 61–200.

explicit documents which not only name and locate offices and functions, but also reveal at least some elements of the values pertaining to the system. The honorific or cult inscriptions for kings, the texts of decrees honouring men who protected a city's rights against royal encroachment, or the letters of the kings themselves will all reveal at least the formal public values accepted in Hellenistic society. But behind the diplomatic history of the relations of city and monarch, which has many elements of continuity stretching from the fourth century B.C. to the late Roman Empire, and whose primary documents could (once again) be seen as constituting a minor branch of literature with its own themes and variations, lies the major historical theme of the vitality of the Greek cities and the vigour with which they competed with each other and demanded acceptance of their claims from the successive monarchs under whose rule they fell.

This activity in itself is only a product of the communal, political, and ceremonial life of the Greek cities, which can be studied not only locality by locality, but also thematically. Here again there are strict limits on what the formal, public inscriptions available to us will reveal. We cannot hope to gain more than passing hints of the overall social composition of a Greek city, of its economic life, or of the relations of town and country. Indeed the inscribed documents will hardly mention the peasant villages of the countryside except when a king makes a grant of some of them to a favourite. The inscriptions will rarely even make clear the sources of the surplus wealth which evidently did pass into the hands of the upper classes of the cities. What they will do is to illustrate public expectations as to the semi-voluntary deployment of that wealth on building, the provision of shows or food, offerings and sacrifices, or embassies to a king—in short, the system of *euergetisme* whose importance in the early Hellenistic city was adumbrated by Paul Veyne.[85] These values and expectations—and the specific roles performed—can legitimately be compared across a whole range of cities. Simply by way of example, I offer a translation of one of these honorific decrees, which comes from Erythrae and probably dates to the 330s, just before the opening of the Hellenistic period proper:[86]

> It was voted by the Council and People on the proposal of the Prytaneis, Generals, and Auditors. Since Phanes, son of Mnesitheus, is a good man

85. P. Veyne, *Le pain et le cirque: sociologie historique d'un pluralisme politique* (Paris, 1976), translated as *Bread and Circuses: Historical Sociology and Political Pluralism* (London, 1990), ch. 2.

86. H. Engelmann and R. Merkelbach, *Die Inschriften von Erythrai und Klazomenai* I (Bonn, 1972), no. 21.

and both shows every willingness in being constantly well disposed towards the People of Erythrae and has contributed money without interest both towards the sending away of the soldiers and the razing of the acropolis, it has seemed right to the Council to crown Phanes son of Mnesitheus with a gold crown worth fifty Philippic staters, and to proclaim this at the Dionysia. Zenodotus the *agonothete* is to see to the proclamation. He [Phanes] should be granted maintenance in the *prytaneion*. This decree is to be inscribed on two *stelai*, of which one is to be placed in the sanctuary of Athena and one in the sanctuary of Heracles, so that all may know that the People knows how to return appropriate thanks for the benefits [*euergetemata*] conferred on it.

It was precisely this perfectly conscious and explicit convention of the re-payment of concrete benefits (in this case, it seems, simply bribing a Persian, or perhaps early Hellenistic, garrison to go away) with honours and ceremo-nial rights and the immortalisation of these on stone in appropriate places, which was the source of so many of the tens of thousands of public inscrip-tions surviving from the Greek cities. Taken individually, they may often do no more than allude to elements of social, economic, and religious life; the use of a particular currency, the observance of festivals, the role of city officials, public maintenance for them and a variety of honorands in the *pry-taneion*, or the existence of certain important sanctuaries. Taken collectively, they may allow the exploration of a vast, but not infinite, range of ques-tions about ancient Greek society and its institutions; and all the more so if considered along with literary, numismatic, and archaeological evidence.[87] Given the volume and complexity of the epigraphic evidence and the vari-ous strategies available for approaching it—whether on a local basis, or by studying vocabulary, concepts, and ideologies, or by isolating particular insti-tutions—there is almost infinite scope for exploring what the inscriptions do tell us, whether explicitly in what they report or implicitly in the funda-mental structures of the values and assumptions which they embody. In the vast mass of the inscriptions of the Greek cities and sanctuaries, above all in Asia Minor, which stretch from the fourth century B.C. to the third century A.D., we can for once perhaps afford not to worry too much about the many areas of social and economic life to which they will only allude (or which they will pass over altogether) until we have explored more fully how much they do convey.

In one particular area the (relatively) unexplored possibilities are obvious,

87. For a relevant example, see S. G. Miller, *The Prytaneion: Its Function and Architectural Form* (Berkeley, 1978).

namely the religious life of the cities. Naturally there has been a vast range of studies of particular aspects, including collections of the sacred regulations from Greek cities.[88] But the standard modern work on Greek religion is not alone in its tendency, when it reaches the Hellenistic and Roman period, to concentrate on the general and the abstract, on "ruler cult," philosophy, oriental cults, monotheistic tendencies, or astrology.[89] In other words the tendency is to select out those aspects which seem to represent religious systems logically comparable to Christianity. To do so is to fail to do any real justice to the complex cult and ceremonial institutions of the communal life of the Greek cities.[90] For any enquiry into this area the inscriptions are central, not only for the vast range of customs and institutions on which they contain information, but also for the religious concepts, values, and distinctions which they explicitly and implicitly express.[91]

For reasons which it would be very interesting—if exceedingly difficult—to explore, the voting and putting up of monumental inscriptions, though still known, ceased to be so distinctive a feature of Greek city life after the third century A.D.[92] The spread of Christianity and the increasing dominance, and (apparently) increasing demands, of the Roman state and its representatives were clearly all of some relevance here. We may however note, in leaving this area, a perfect example, from an inscription, of the transference into the role of bishop of the values of secular city life. The inscription comes from Laodicea Combusta in Phrygia and dates to the crucial turning point, the reign of Constantine.[93]

> I, M. Julius Eugenius, son of Cyrillus Celer of Kouessos, town councillor, having served on the governor's staff in Pisidia and having married Flavia Iulia Flaviane, daughter of Gaius Nestorianus, a senator, and having served honourably in the meantime, when an order went

88. F. Sokolowski, *Lois sacrées le l'Asie Mineure* (Paris, 1955); *Lois sacrées des cités grecques: supplément* (Paris, 1962); *Lois sacrées des cités grecques* (Paris, 1969).

89. M. P. Nilsson, *Geschichte der griechischen Religion* II: *die hellenistische und römische Zeit*[2] (Munich, 1961).

90. For a serious, if still too brief, attempt to represent the communal religious institutions of the ancient world in their local contexts, see R. MacMullen, *Paganism in the Roman Empire* (New Haven, 1981).

91. For a valuable analysis of the vocabulary of sacrifice as directed towards the Roman emperors, see S. R. F. Price, "Between Man and God: Sacrifice in the Roman Imperial Cult," *JRS* 70 (1980): 28.

92. For an example of a major series of inscriptions from a late antique city, see C. Roueché, *Aphrodisias in Late Antiquity* (London, 1989).

93. *Monumenta Asiae Minoris Antiqua* I, 170.

out under Maximinus that the Christians should sacrifice and not be allowed to resign the service, endured very many torments and succeeded in leaving the service under the governor Diogenes while keeping the Christian faith. After staying in Laodicea for a short time I was by the will of the all-powerful God installed as bishop. For twenty-five years I administered my bishopric with much honour, built the whole church from the foundations, and also all the surrounding ornamentation, consisting of porticoes and tetraporticoes and paintings and mosaics and a fountain and gateway, and fitted it all with dressed stone, and in a word with everything. Being about to depart from human life, I have made for myself a plinth and tomb, on which I have had the foregoing inscribed to the glory of the church and my family.

The Latin World

Turning away from the central areas of Greek culture, it is worth noting that the region of which the most complete and thoroughly edited collection of Greek inscriptions has been made is present-day Bulgaria.[94] But when we come to the Latin-speaking world it must be stressed that although in many areas inscriptions are of prime importance—sometimes as limiting cases in the way discussed earlier—they rarely rise to either the complexity of content or the density of concentration found in the inscriptions of the Greek cities. In the history of Rome for example, though, as we saw, public inscriptions had begun even in the regal period, neither the inscribing of laws or regulations nor the presentation on inscriptions of individual careers became a major feature until quite late in the Republic. The career inscription, giving a man's public offices in great detail, is a distinctive phenomenon of the imperial period. None the less the Republican inscriptions of Rome and Italy are prime documents for the history of the Latin language, as they are also for its orthography and spelling, and must therefore be studied on the stones or at any rate with the aid of photographs.[95] The relatively few ex-

94. G. Mihailov, *Inscriptiones Graecae in Bulgaria Repertae* (Sofia, 1956; rev. 1970); II (Sofia, 1958); III.1 (Sofia, 1961); III.2 (Sofia, 1964); IV (Sofia 1966).

95. The main Latin inscriptions of the Republic, except for the laws and *senatus consulta*, are collected by A. Degrassi, *Inscriptiones Latinae Liberae Reipublicae* (Florence, 1957; rev. 1965); II (Florence, 1963); *Inscriptiones Latinae Liberae Reipublicae; Imagines* (Berlin, 1965), with excellent photographs. It is unfortunate that not all the earliest inscriptions, i.e., those of the regal period (e.g., the Lapis Niger; see text to n. 34 above), are included. For texts and linguistic discussions (but no photographs), see the excellent Loeb volume of B. H. Warm-

tensive texts embodying laws or decrees of the Senate begin in the second century B.C. and have been collected and discussed many times.[96] There is still room, however, for treatments of these texts which do not aim so much at either restoration of lost sections (often involving prolonged and fruitless arguments about line lengths) or reconstructions of their political context and purpose, as at using them as evidence for the history of language and (as mentioned earlier in "Epigraphy and Literature") at understanding their composition as texts. Even more profound ambiguities attend the question of what can be considered a companion group of texts, the so-called municipal laws of the late Republic. We owe to the late M. W. Frederiksen a fundamental discussion of the nature of these documents. Are they in fact "laws," generated in some way from the centre of power in Rome? How and from what sources was each text as we have it put together? When, by whom, and for what reason was it inscribed?[97] Not all of the questions which were thus so effectually opened up have yet been answered. It will not seem paradoxical, in view of what has been said here, that a significant proportion of the most detailed, clear, and explicit republican documents is in fact drawn from the repertoire of the epigraphy of the Greek cities and is thus available to us only in Greek translation.[98] The inter-play between Greek and Latin as the vehicles of official prose, in both the republican and the imperial periods, thus becomes a major historical subject in its own right.[99] The volume of these texts (and the difficulty of the problems associated with them) has been considerably increased by the publication in 1974 of several extensive

---

ington, *Remains of Old Latin* IV: *Archaic Inscriptions* (Cambridge, Mass., 1940). The time has arrived, with many new discoveries, for a new edition of this work.

96. E.g., I. Bruns, *Fontes Iuris Romani Antiqui*[7] (1907); S. Riccobono, *Fontes Iuris Romani Anteiustinianae*[2] (1941). See K. Johannsen, *Die lex agraria des Jahres 111 v. Chr.: Text und Kommentar* (Diss. Munich, 1971). Note now also A. W. Lintott, *Judicial Reform and Land Reform in the Roman Republic* (Cambridge, 1996), and esp. M. Crawford, ed., *Roman Statutes* I–II (London, 1996), no. 2.

97. M. W. Frederiksen, "The Republican Municipal Laws: Errors and Drafts," *JRS* 55 (1965): 183.

98. See R. K. Sherk, *Roman Documents from the Greek East: Senatus consulta and epistulae to the Age of Augustus* (Baltimore, 1969).

99. Note two fundamental older works, P. Viereck, *Sermo Graecus* (Diss. Göttingen, 1888); L. Hahn, *Rom und Romanismus im griechisch-römischen Osten* (Leipzig, 1906). See now H. J. Mason, *Greek Terms for Roman Institutions: A Lexicon and Analysis* (Toronto, 1974); M. Kaimio, *The Romans and the Greek Language* (Helsinki, 1979); E. García Domingo, *Latinismos en la Koine* (Burgos, 1979).

new sections, found at Cnidus, of the Roman "pirate law" of circa 100 B.C.[100] As noted earlier (text to n. 43) the important new series of republican docu-ments in Greek from Aphrodisias also brings extensive further evidence, and further problems. But, the major individual documents apart, there are only limited categories of inscriptions which are important for the history of the Republic. One such category, which is best considered as being even closer to literature than most others, is the historical (or pseudo-historical) inscrip-tions put up in Rome and representing one aspect of the Augustan revival: the lists (*fasti*) of the pairs of consuls since the beginning of the Republic and of the *triumphatores* (the generals who celebrated a triumph in Rome); and also the *elogia* (eulogies) recording the achievements of the great military commanders of the Republic, which were designed to accompany the statues of these men put up in the Forum of Augustus.[101] As contemporary products, direct documentary parallels to the literary works of Virgil and Livy, these are of great interest. As "documentary" attestations of alleged historical facts their status cannot be any higher than that of the literary sources of the same period.

The epigraphic record of the Roman Republic in the provinces is still sparse, except — as always — in the Greek East,[102] and it is perhaps only in the rapidly developing epigraphic material of Italy, which can be followed in the annual survey "Rivista di epigrafia italica," published since 1973 in *Studi Etruschi*, that it is beginning to be possible to trace major themes (cf. also text to n. 25).

It is one of the most marked features of the culture of the imperial period that this situation alters progressively. In the East, as mentioned earlier, the mass of city inscriptions continues as before, closely associated, above all in the second century A.D., with very extensive public building. From the first century A.D. onwards the same is true of Latin-speaking North Africa, con-trasting sharply with the almost total absence of epigraphic record from the first one and a half centuries of Roman rule there. It is obvious that in a gen-

100. M. Hassall, M. Crawford, and J. Reynolds, "Rome and the Eastern Provinces at the End of the Second Century B.C.," *JRS* 64 (1974): 195. For subsequent discussions, see the survey by J. Reynolds, M. Beard, R. Duncan-Jones, and C. Roueché, "Roman Inscriptions, 1975–80," *JRS* 71 (1981): 123.

101. Collected and edited in A. Degrassi, *Inscriptiones Italiae* XIII.1: *Fasti consulares et tri-umphales* (Rome, 1947); XIII.3: *Elogia* (Rome, 1937).

102. Note, e.g., K. Tuchelt, *Frühe Denkmäler Roms in Kleinasien: Beiträge zur archäologi-schen Überlieferung aus der Zeit der Republik und des Augustus* I: *Roma und Promagistrate* (Tubin-gen, 1979); R. Mellor, *ΘΕΑ 'ΡΩΜΗ: The Worship of the Goddess Roma in the Greek World* (Göttingen, 1975).

eral way the putting up of inscriptions was a quite important facet of the city life which was characteristic of the Graeco-Roman world, and therefore spread steadily along with urbanisation. Thus we have a substantial harvest of inscriptions also from the Mediterranean coast of Spain and from the south (Baetica/Andalusia), and progressively less until we reach the northwest, which seems hardly to have been touched by Graeco-Roman patterns of life at all. Gaul too, while some Latin inscriptions are found in all regions, produces relatively few, and only a very short list of extended documents of individual importance: the best known are the famous bronze tablet from Lyon with the text of the emperor Claudius' speech on the admission of Gallic nobles to the Senate,[103] and a complex document of the 230s honouring one Sennius Sollemnis.[104] But from Britain, whose civil and military inscriptions have been collected and edited with exceptionally lavish care,[105] to Dalmatia and the middle Danube, the scattered Latin inscriptions, often slight and insignificant in themselves, are the primary evidence for the spread of Roman civilisation, the Latin language, and the institutions of the self-governing town. They also provide evidence (for example) for nomenclature, occupations, and the observation of the cults of local or imported deities. But it is important to stress once again that the historical value of relatively scattered inscriptions can only be indicative or illustrative. Valid negative conclusions can almost never be drawn from such evidence; in France in particular the fact of continuous occupation of urban sites in the intervening centuries means that no negative conclusions or even statistical inferences can ever be drawn from what happens to survive. The double-negative form of argument can, however, be validly used. If (for instance) even a few persons used Latin to scratch imprecations on lead tablets deposited in Gloucestershire,[106] it follows that it cannot be argued that Latin was in use in Britain only in official or military contexts.

Even more than in the Greek East there is much that we can never hope to learn from the epigraphy of the Latin West. None the less, it is a historical fact of the greatest importance that the Roman period saw the spread of forms of city or communal self-government, invariably using Latin; in con-

---

103. *CIL* XIII, 1668; *ILS* 212.

104. *CIL* XIII, 3162; H. G. Pflaum, *Le Marbre de Thorigny* (Paris, 1948).

105. See R. G. Collingwood and R. P. Wright, *Roman Inscriptions of Britain* I: *Inscriptions on Stone* (Oxford, 1965).

106. M. W. C. Hassall and R. S. O. Tomlin, *Britannia* 10 (1979), 341–44. Note the publication by the same authors of four of a find of over forty lead tablets from Bath, *Britannia* 12 (1981): 370–76. For full publication, see now R. Tomlin, *Tabellae Sulis: Roman Inscribed Tablets of Tin and Lead from the Sacred Spring at Bath* (Oxford, 1988).

sequence it is possible to collect and analyse the surviving texts of municipal decrees.[107] The most vivid evidence for local self-government comes from the well-known *leges* (charters?) of Domitian's reign from Baetica in Spain. These documents, which preserve extensive, and partly overlapping, extracts from the constitutional codes of several *municipia* (cities with Roman-style constitutions), suffer from a lack of comparative material, and leave unanswered fundamental questions about the authorship or legal source of the codes (delivered by the emperor or the governor of Baetica or generated locally?), the degree of innovation intended (since both places had magistrates in office already), and the relation of the production of these codes to the two towns' status as *municipia*—a term whose definition is controversial—and to their possession of "Latin rights."[108] The two texts, which have not been re-studied in detail for some time, would deserve an epigraphical and historical re-examination. At the moment, granted that we know that there were many Punic towns in the western Mediterranean (of which Malaca had been one, according to the geographer Strabo), which must also in their Punic phase have had "constitutions," and that we can find also communities, like the Vanacini in Corsica,[109] with the institutions of local self-government but without either of the specifically Roman statuses of *municipium* or *colonia*, the whole question of the "Romanisation" of communal institutions in the West remains in a state of conceptual confusion.

However, it is precisely in the Roman Empire that the detailed study of the formal types of information which inscriptions are designed to reveal has been most successfully pursued. The genre of the honorific inscription, immortalising the record of a man's offices, statuses, and (sometimes) benefactions, continued to be very common in the East, and also spread to the West. On the one hand the carefully graded *cursus* or "career" laid down for Roman senators in the Republic and expanded by a large number of new functions under the Empire, comes to be illustrated by literally hundreds, perhaps thousands, of inscriptions giving the offices held by individuals. On the other hand the honorific inscriptions from towns in Italy and the provinces, both Greek- and Latin-speaking, reveal the major historical development that people from many (though not all) of these places served as

---

107. R. K. Sherk, *Municipal Decrees of the Roman West* (Buffalo, 1970). The number of texts found by Sherk (65) is strikingly small.

108. For the essential documentation, including the long new text from Irni in Baetica, see J. González, "The Lex Irnitana: A New Copy of the Flavian Municipality Law," *JRS* 76 (1986): 147.

109. *CIL* X, 8038; F. F. Abbott and A. C. Johnson, *Municipal Administration in the Roman Empire* (Princeton, 1926), no. 59.

"equestrian" officers in the Roman army, or rose higher into the so-called equestrian civil service which developed in the first century and a half of the Empire. This relative openness of access to Roman offices is a very significant aspect of the political character of the Empire. A nexus thus developed between office-holding and *euergetisme* (see text to n. 85) in small towns, service as an officer in the Roman army, posts as an equestrian civil official, the rank of senator, and even the position of emperor. The link between local institutions, the imperial service, and the patronage of the emperor is nowhere better illustrated than in the Latin inscription of Q. Domitius Marsianus, put up in his home town, Bulla Regia in the province of Africa, in the 170s A.D.:[110]

> To Q. Domitius Marsianus, son of Lucius, tribe Quirina, procurator of Augustus of the *patrimonium* [imperial property] of the province of Narbonensis, procurator of Augustus for the iron mines, procurator in Gaul for receiving the census declarations of the province of Belgica throughout the districts of the Tungri and Frisavones and of Germania Inferior and of the Batavi, *praefectus militum* [commander of an auxiliary unit], adlected into the *decuriae* [jury panels in Rome] by the Emperors M. Aurelius Antoninus and L. Aurelius Verus, Caesares. When the Town Council had voted to put up an equestrian statue of him at public expense, his brother L. Domitius Fabianus erected it at his own expense, thus sparing expenditure on the part of the city.

> Copy of the *codicilli* (letter of appointment):
> Caesar Antoninus Augustus to his own Domitius Marsianus greetings. Having long since been eager to promote you to the splendour of a ducenariate procuratorship, I am now making use of the opportunity which presents itself. Succeed therefore to Marius Pudens with an expectation of my unfailing favour so long as you retain the conscious possession of probity, diligence, and experience. Farewell my Marsianus, dearest to me.

The inscription comes in fact from the base of the equestrian statue (which has not survived) which stood in Bulla Regia to record for his fellow citizens the favour which Marsianus had earned in the imperial service. His brother Fabianus, if not actually a member of the city council (as he probably was), was at least a well-off resident of the town. The inscription thus offers a very clear example of the roots in local communal life which are a primary char-

---

110. *AE* (1962), 183; cf. H. G. Pflaum in *Bonner Jahrbücher* 171 (1971): 349.

acteristic of those who entered the imperial service. But there is a catch here which typifies the limits of what epigraphical evidence can tell us. For in a very large number of cases we owe our knowledge of the careers, and indeed of the existence, of these men precisely to the fact that a local community had some motive to commemorate them on an inscription. If there were men who rose in the imperial service but retained no local roots, and neither kept a family connection nor served as town councillors or annual officials nor held priesthoods nor acted as a *patronus* of the town, the chances of their being recorded on inscriptions will have been greatly reduced.

A rather similar limitation affects imperial letters, of which one sub-category, the imperial letter of appointment addressed to a member of the senatorial or equestrian order, is best represented by Aurelius' letter in this inscription. No one ever recorded in an inscription an imperial letter informing him that he could *not* have a particular post; and similarly cities never put up inscriptions displaying imperial letters rejecting requests or informing them that they had lost a dispute with a neighbouring city. We have a small number of documentary texts of such letters only because cities involved in disputes sometimes inscribed unfavourable letters or replies addressed to their neighbours, which were therefore implicitly or explicitly favourable to themselves.[111] None the less, the genre of the imperial letter, together with the more informal type of imperial reply known as a *subscriptio*, is represented by several hundred documentary texts in both Latin and Greek, preserved on inscriptions and papyri and in legal and literary sources, and is therefore both a sub-literary type, which deserves study in its own right, and a prime source for the nature of the Roman Empire as a system.

The Marsianus inscription is unusually rich in both giving the text of the imperial letter and retailing the circumstances of the erection of the statue (which will not have been wholly unlike the famous one of Marcus Aurelius from the Capitol). More commonly, such inscriptions concentrate on the successive steps of the man's career—often in reverse chronological order to bring the most important posts to the beginning. In spite of the many severe limitations on what these inscriptions *can* by their nature tell us—limitations frequently not recognised in modern work, as we shall see—there is no question of the scale and importance of the information which, by retailing equestrian and senatorial careers, they have revealed about the workings of the Empire. The two editions of the *Prosopographia Imperii Romani* (1897–98

111. For this category of letter, see Millar (n. 46), 431–32; 436–37; 438–39; J. Reynolds, "Hadrian, Antoninus and the Cyrenaican Cities," *JRS* 68 (1978): 111; *Aphrodisias and Rome* (London, 1982), docs. 10, 13, 14.

and 1933 onwards, so far up to P) bear witness to the vast store of information from this and other sources which has now been reduced to intelligible
order.[112] Given the steady flow of new inscriptions, the technical work of
compiling lists of the holders of particular offices, recording the earliest or
latest appearance of a particular office, following the rise of successive generations of a family, and so forth, can continue indefinitely. There are also
a number of broad and indisputable historical conclusions which arise from
this material. Firstly, an equestrian "career" following a succession of posts
in (at least) roughly graded orders of seniority and prestige did evolve in the
course of the first century and a half.[113] Secondly, entry to equestrian posts
and the Senate was gained by men from many (but, so far as the inscriptions
can tell us, not all) provincial areas. Thirdly, the career of Marsianus, which
took him solely to the region of Gaul, seems to have been exceptional, in that
both equestrian and senatorial careers generally show a marked absence of
geographical specialisation. If we take the usual characteristics of the succession of posts followed as our evidence, then in this respect the Empire seems
to have been an integrated system, which showed no tendency to regional
compartmentalisation.

Our difficulties arise as soon as we step outside the confines of the formal
evidence actually presented to us by those inscriptions which happened to be
created in the ancient world and happen to have been preserved and to have
been published in the modern era. Is our picture of the geographical areas
from which *equites* and senators came simply dictated by the accident of what
happened to be inscribed? Or could we reasonably relate the communal in-
vestment in monumental inscriptions to the social conditions which would
allow at least some families in a local community to rise into the equestrian
service and the Senate—and thus regard them as parallel products of socio-
economic conditions which were present in some places and not in others?
Or again, even if such varying regional patterns really existed and are significant to us, were they of any conscious significance at the time? Marcus
does not imply that it was of any importance to him that Marsianus came
from Bulla Regia, or from the province of Africa. It is we who impose the
categories of "the African contribution to the imperial service" or suppose
(for instance) that Hadrian might have favoured Italians as opposed to pro-

112. Note also the supplementary collection by B. Thomasson, *Senatores Procuratoresque
Romani* (Göteborg, 1975), collecting and analysing careers documented, or more fully documented, since the appearance of the relevant volumes of *PIR*[2].

113. Note the classic analysis of these careers by the late H. G. Pflaum, *Les carrières procura-
toriennes équestres* I–III (Paris, 1960–61), with the review by F. Millar, *JRS* 53 (1963): 194–200.

vincials in appointments to the senatorial office of *praefectus aerarii Saturni* (prefect of the *aerarium* of Saturn—the state treasury in Rome). But even if we can be sure of the identification of men's local origins (as we can with Marsianus, but often cannot), we have no clear indications that such categories had any relevance at all to the appointments made by emperors. These and similar ambiguities, both statistical and conceptual, haunt—and have so far almost entirely vitiated—all attempts to go beyond the formal records which the inscriptions present, to conclusions involving choices, values, and intentions.[114]

The same ambiguities attend all attempts to interpret the succession of posts previously held by a man as the basis of his specific claims (in terms of relevant experience or qualifications) to a more senior post. But the fact that a list of posts is the only evidence which we happen to have does not mean that we should be confident that it provides a sufficient explanation, or any explanation at all. We can never know the relevance of personal qualities (including quiescence and lack of dangerous ambitions), family background, the influence of intermediaries, or simply the fact of having been available and of the right seniority at the right time. It may be indicative that Aurelius' letter—one of the rare items of evidence which even alludes to the motives of imperial choice—implies that the promotion was a personal favour, dependent on the personal moral and social qualities of the recipient. Personal patronage may or may not have been an important factor; but what is clear is that the formal evidence of the inscriptions fully demonstrates a pattern of variety rather than concentration of "relevant experience" in the case (say) of prefects of Egypt[115] and in general fails to show consistent patterns of promotion in equestrian careers.[116] The same difficulties of interpretation attend senatorial careers. Were men picked for their abilities? If they rose rapidly— that is, gained the consulate early or had few intermediate posts—is that a sign of the recognition of their abilities? But, if so, their background "experience" when they reached the major military posts will have been less, not greater.[117] Or (again) did men rise by virtue of their social background, connections, or personal charms? But in any case the whole area may be one

---

114. For demonstration of the dangers inherent in such attempts, see the review of a number of prosopographical works by G. P. Burton in *JRS* 70 (1980): 203–9.

115. See the demonstration by P. A. Brunt, "The Administrators of Roman Egypt," *JRS* 65 (1975): 124.

116. See R. P. Saller, "Promotion and Patronage in Equestrian Careers," *JRS* 70 (1980): 44, and *Personal Patronage in the Early Empire* (Cambridge, 1982).

117. See B. Campbell, "Who were the 'Viri Militares'?," *JRS* 65 (1975): 11.

of conceptual confusion, for we may be imposing irrelevant and anachronistic categories on the business of holding public office, which may have been a prize to be won and exploited, a recognition of wealth and social status, or a burden to be avoided. All that is clear is that the genre of the monumental inscription, formally listing a man's successive offices, is a very distinctive feature of the society and culture of the High Empire. It would well deserve study as such, in particular because it is not, to anything like the same degree, characteristic of either the preceding or the following period.

It is worth the emphasis given here partly because it is a specific instance of the wider phenomenon of the place of inscriptions in the culture of the ancient world, and partly because it offers a particularly clear example both of the extensive information which inscriptions can make available when treated collectively and of the dangers which lurk everywhere as soon as we go beyond the formal analysis and arrangement of that information and attempt wider historical and social judgements. To take only one example, there is no harm in pursuing the much-practised genre of assembling the names, dates, and careers of those who held office in a particular province.[118] Such a study will always be useful as a work of reference. But as soon as we ask — and attempt to answer from the career inscriptions — (say) what sort of men the emperor sent to Britain and on what principles his selection was based, we enter issues which touch on the values of the entire society, and which we can solve, if at all, only by the consideration of all the other evidence.

Very similar problems would emerge if we were to look in detail at the vast epigraphic (and papyrological) documentation now available for the structure and working of the Roman army in the High Empire. A significant proportion of the evidence owes its existence to the same very important element in imperial culture, the honorific inscription. This genre of inscription, for instance, provides our only substantial body of evidence for what was evidently a highly important class of office-holders whose rank came just below — and overlapped with — that of *equites*, namely the centurions and "first centurions" who might rise from the ranks or might be directly commissioned, and might proceed further in a form of career known only from inscriptions, to important equestrian civil positions. The framework of a significant element in the Roman state is thus revealed — but, equally, basic questions about functions, social background, and criteria for promotion must remain unanswered.[119]

118. See, e.g., A. R. Birley, *The Fasti of Roman Britain* (Oxford, 1981).
119. See B. Dobson, "The Significance of the Centurion and 'Primipilaris' in the Roman

This survey of the inscriptions from the Graeco-Roman world and their uses to the historian cannot do justice to the sheer volume of the surviving examples or to their infinite variety of type and scale; probably the most common single type of inscription from the Latin West, for instance, is the brief tomb inscription of a private individual who held no public office. It is, of course, this genre which has lasted most successfully into the modern world and continues to have a place in contemporary culture. The ancient tomb inscription, for instance, like the modern, very commonly mentioned the person's age at death. So, granted the enormous number of such inscriptions, do we for once dispose of a valid body of statistical data, illuminating the fundamentally important question of the expectation of life in the ancient world? The answer appears to be no, for the graphs thus produced are both impossible in their overall patterns and tend to show a marked concentration on ages of death which are multiples of five. In other words, what the epitaphs reveal is not an objective sample of ages at death but a pattern produced by choices as to who was commemorated; they also cast light on wider social issues such as the level of literacy.[120]

But it is the formal monumental inscription—containing a law, communal decision, letter from a superior, regulation of cult practices, accounts of a temple, or vote of honours—which is the most distinctive and historically important product of the role in ancient culture of the inscribing of words on stone or bronze. The motives for the inscription of particular documents are quite often made explicit in the documents themselves without our thereby being enabled to understand the very marked prevalence of the public inscription in ancient society as a whole, or what deductions we should draw from this evidence about the extent of popular literacy. All that is clear is that each and every public inscription is the result of a deliberate choice, whether motivated by the need to proclaim rules or privileges in permanent form or to give equally permanent expression to the highly competitive value systems of most ancient communities. This explicit and formal character is both the great strength and the limitation of the inscriptions as historical evidence. But whatever caution must be observed in drawing conclusions from them, the ever-growing mass of inscriptions in Greek and Latin, and also in other languages, from the ancient world still represents a major cultural phe-

---

Army and Administration," *ANRW* II.1 (1975), 392; *Die Primipilares. Entwicklung und Bedeutung, Laufbahnen und Persönlichkeiten eines römischen Offiziersranges* (Cologne, 1978).

120. See, e.g., R. P. Duncan-Jones, "Age-Rounding, Illiteracy and Social Differentiation in the Roman Empire," *Chiron* 7 (1977): 333.

nomenon in itself.[121] Some branches of it also can and should be considered as minor (but, in bulk, very extensive) literary genres, which provide a whole range of deliberately composed prose and verse to set against the remains of ancient literature surviving in the manuscript tradition. But the extent of the latter, however inexhaustible its interest, can only increase marginally, largely through the publication of papyrus fragments. Epigraphy provides our most direct access to ancient society and culture, and shows every sign of being able to add indefinitely to the stock of available texts. It thus represents the best guarantee we have that our understanding of the ancient world need never be static.

121. Compare the fundamental essay by R. MacMullen, "The Epigraphic Habit in the Roman Empire," *AJPh* 103 (1982): 233.

PART II

The Roman Republic

CHAPTER THREE

Political Power in Mid-Republican Rome: Curia or Comitium?*

The earlier history of Rome presents us with a very familiar, inescapable, and apparently insoluble paradox. On the one hand, the historiography of Rome begins only in the late third century, with Fabius Pictor's *History* in Greek and (not to be neglected) Naevius' *Bellum Punicum* in Latin. As for the First Punic War itself, Naevius had been born early enough to serve in it. But the narration of it could, on the other hand, be set in the framework of the Foundation and of the earliest history of the city, rooted in the legendary emigration from Troy (fr. 25 [3] Strzelecki):

> After Anchises caught sight of the bird in Apollo's temple,
> the sacred objects were put in order on the table where the
> Penates are laid;
> he prepared to sacrifice the beautiful golden victim.

To Fabius, as the remarkable inscription of the second century B.C. from Taormina makes clear (*SEG* XXVI, no. 1123, fr. ii, col. A), the mythical history of Rome went even further back, to Herakles: "Quintus Fabius, called Pictorinus, a Roman, son of Gaius: who related the arrival of Herakles in Italy and the return of Lanoios, an ally of Aeneas and Ascanius; much later there were Romulus and Remus and the foundation of Rome by Romulus, who was the first to be king." That is the paradox: that when people finally came to write the history of Rome, a "history" stretching back centuries was appar-

---

*First published as a review article on Kurt A. Raaflaub, ed., *Social Struggles in Archaic Rome: New Perspectives on the Conflict of the Orders* (1986), and K.-J. Hölkeskamp, *Die Entstehung Der Nobilität: Studien zur Sozialen und Politischen Geschichte der Römischen Republik im 4. Jhdt. V. Chr.* (1987), in *JRS* 79 (1989): 138–50.

ently already there to be written. But "stretching back" is perhaps not quite
the right expression. Instead, like other "histories," it stretched *forward*, from
the earliest mythical origins, then tapered off rather sharply, and expanded
again with the period within, or more or less within, human memory. Naevius in fact provides the perfect model: three books on the mythical past,
and then in the fourth straight to the narrative of the war (fr. 32 [39]):

> the Roman army crossed over to the island of Malta,
> set fire to the whole island,
> pillaged, laid waste, disposed of the enemies' property.

But, on the other hand, the history of the earlier Republic, which was not
(could not be?) described in full-scale narratives in the late third century,
was to be written later, in the greatest detail and colour. This process was
analysed in T. P. Wiseman, *Clio's Cosmetics* (1979), pt. I; and the whole issue
is re-surveyed by Raaflaub in the first chapter of his book, where he does,
however, suggest that comparison, above all with Greece, may help us to res-
cue some elements otherwise lost. That still leaves us with the problem of
whether we can make anything of the vast narratives of Livy and (in even
greater detail) Dionysius, written just at the moment of the monumentalization of the Roman past by Augustus in the form of the *Fasti Triumphales* (the
list of generals who celebrated a triumph in Rome) and the *Fasti Consulares*
(the list of consuls) and the *elogia* (eulogies) of his new Forum. Put like that,
the facts seem to demand from us a clear decision: so far as "real" history goes,
we should forget the earlier Republic, and begin where contemporary evidence begins, in the time of Hannibal. The fourth century and the "conflict
of the orders" belong in the realm of myth.

Yet so apparently purist a decision will not really do either. Firstly, we
could reasonably stretch the definition of "contemporary," in relation to the
late third century, to include the previous two to three generations, over
which, as most would agree, collective memory will provide some more or
less veridical representation of the past. Romans of the late third or early second centuries certainly represented to each other versions of family or collective history over such a time scale. So for instance Cato, born in 235, said
(in what context?) that his father (born in the 260s?) had been a brave man
and a good soldier, while his great-grandfather (born in the 320s?) had often
won *aristeia* (prizes), and had had five horses killed under him, receiving the
price of them from public funds as a reward for his courage. He himself might
have been new in terms of rank and fame, so he said, but in terms of the deeds
and virtues of his forefathers he was very long established (Plutarch, *Cato* 1).
Either the father or the great-grandfather, from this family of local gentry of

Tusculan origin, with lands in the Sabine country, cavalry-men rather than (as yet) "equestrians," might have stood for office, and then perhaps have been enrolled in the Senate. The notion of that body as an "aristocracy" in the modern sense has confused the study of the Republic for decades.

But there were of course families which were indeed relatively "aristocratic." One was that of the Cornelii Scipiones, and here too we can see how a family history was represented in the early second century. In the family tomb on the Appian Way an earlier inscription on the sarcophagus of L. Cornelius Scipio Barbatus, consul in 298, censor in (?)280, was erased, and a new one created, addressed to passers-by. See J. van Sickle, "The Elogia of the Cornelii Scipiones and the Origin of Epigram at Rome," *AJPh* 108 (1987): 41; J. van Sickle, "The First Hellenistic Epigrams at Rome," in N. Horsfall, ed., *Vir Bonus Discendi Peritus: Studies in Celebration of Otto Skutsch's Eightieth Birthday*, BICS suppl. 51 (1988), 143; F. Coarelli, *Il sepulchro degli Scipioni a Roma* (1988). The new inscription read:

> Cornelius Lucius Scipio Barbatus
> son of Gnaeus /, a brave and wise man,
> whose looks matched his virtue /
> he was consul, censor, aedile amongst you,
> he captured Taurasia Cisauna? / in Samnium,
> reduced the whole of Lucania and took hostages.

Incidents from the Roman conquest of southern Italy of about a century before were thus rehearsed, as was the holding of civil offices, as censor and aedile, in the community — "apud vos." This form of address is of some significance, as will be seen later.

It would thus be needlessly hypercritical not to accept that, at least in broad outline, the major stages of Roman history back to around 300 B.C. were within recall when Roman historiography began. But we can certainly go beyond that. For whether later annalists could, or we now can, reconstruct valid year-by-year narrative sequences, or not, which frankly matters little, it remains beyond question that a range of important developments can be seen to have occurred in the fourth and early third centuries, which formed the background of the great campaigns at the end of that period, above all Pyrrhus' invasion and the outbreak of the First Punic War. That is to say the emergence of Rome from within the framework of the Latin League, the foundation of further "Latin" colonies, the extension of Roman full or half citizenship, and the subjugation or bringing into alliance of all the communities or peoples in the southern two-thirds of the Italian peninsula. However hypercritical we are, this process cannot be argued to have

occurred *later* than the early part of the third century; it is also of course presupposed by Polybius' account of the Gallic invasion of the 220s (2, 14–35),
and by the entire narrative of the Hannibalic War. But it also cannot belong
earlier than the first half of the fourth century, when Rome was the subject
of a Gallic raid, of which Aristotle and Heraclides Ponticus knew (Plutarch,
Cam. 22). Polybius was later to be absolutely confident that he could locate
this event precisely by reference to Greek history (1, 6, 1, Loeb trans.):

> In the nineteenth year after the naval battle at Aigospotamoi, and
> the sixteenth year before the battle of Leuktra, in the year in which
> the Lakedaimonians ratified the so-called Peace of Antalkidas with the
> King of the Persians, and the Elder Dionysios, having defeated the
> Greeks of Italy in the battle on the River Elleporos, was besieging Rhe-
> gion, the Gauls took Rome by force and held all of it except the Capitol.

Polybius then summarizes the successive stages by which Rome arose from
that low point, overcoming the other Latins and then the Etruscans, Gauls,
and Samnites, and victoriously confronting Pyrrhus (1, 6, 3–8). If there are
arguments for regarding the hundred-year sequence of events presented by
Polybius as being fundamentally erroneous, I do not know what they are. A
broad external framework can be established.

As regards narrative history it seems to me impossible to go much further
back, no further probably than the capture of Veii. But perhaps, again, we
do not need to. For the traces of the archaic Roman community, even that of
a still earlier stage, are quite clear enough in the record of its institutions in
the historical period, just as they are in large measure in the archaeological
record. The structure of the Roman community in the middle Republic still
clearly reflected the fact that Rome had once had kings (*reges*), who left behind them a cult building called the Regia, and an Atrium Regium, as well
as officials in the form of a *rex sacrorum* and, when needed, an *interrex*. It also
preserved the traces, and even the workings, of archaic social divisions, between patricians (*patricii*) and plebeians (*plebeii*), whose origins were (and
are) a matter of pure speculation. A fine example of such speculation is to
be found in J.-C. Richard's paper, "Patricians and Plebeians: The Origin of
a Social Dichotomy" (Raaflaub et al., 105 ff.).

In the historical period some Romans (very few) were identified as patricians, a rank which was gained solely by birth (descent through the father),
and which gave exclusive access to some major priesthoods, a guaranteed
share of other collegial priesthoods, and, until 172, a reserved place as one of
the two annual consuls. The later tradition both asserted a very clear association of patricians with Romulus' original enrolment of a Senate of *patres*, and

with the holding of individual positions concerned with the community's relation to the divine order, and narrated a prolonged evolution whereby plebeians, defined negatively as *non*-patricians, also gained access to some, though not all, of these positions. The strictly religious aspect of the patrician-plebeian distinction—the question of who can be permitted to take the auspices on behalf of the community—is rightly stressed by R. E. Mitchell, "The Definition of *patres* and *plebs*: An End to the Struggle of the Orders" (Raaflaub et al., 130ff.), even if the idea that we should think of *patres* as "priests" should be taken merely as a salutary device to provoke re-thinking. It is certainly important that this distinction of birth was in no way reflected in the structure of the popular assemblies, the centuriate assembly (*comitia centuriata*) and the tribal assembly (*comitia tributa*), as they were in the historical period. Nothing was, or is, certain about the earliest history of these assemblies except that they went back to before the historical period; that the tribes (*tribus*) had reached their ultimate limit of thirty-five in 241, and that the structure of the centuriate assembly reflected a stage in the early history of the Roman army.

What I mean to suggest by these extensive preliminaries is, firstly, that the history of the early-middle Republic (say 390–218 B.C.) is indeed inescapable, for it was then that the institutions of Rome were either created or took on their established form and functions: for example, the dual consulate, the praetorship (and later praetorships), the censorship, and the enrolment by them of the Senate, and so forth. It was also then that there took place that very sudden—and even more important—expansion of Roman domination over Italy, of which the most crucial phase was exactly contemporary with Philip's victory at Chaeronea and then with Alexander's conquests and the wars of the Diadochoi. This period cannot, therefore, help being a central problem in Roman history. But it is a paradoxical and insoluble problem only if we insist, like the Roman annalists, on knowing too much. It is all the more unfortunate that those who deal with it, in spite of ritual expressions of caution, do insist on knowing too much.

What is more, like many of the authors whose work appears in the two exceptionally interesting, learned and stimulating volumes under review, we tend to insist not only on knowing too much, but on knowing precisely those things which the ancient sources themselves, in their better moments, warn us that we cannot know. That is to say the attribution to datable individuals of particular actions and achievements, and the grouping of individuals into supposedly reliable family trees. Cicero, as is well known, said it all (*Brutus* 62, Loeb trans.):

Yet by these laudatory speeches our history has become quite distorted; for much is set down in them which never occurred, false triumphs, too large a number of consulships, false relationships and transitions of patricians to plebeian status, in that men of humbler birth professed that their blood blended with a noble family of the same name, though in fact quite alien to them; as if I, for example, should say that I was descended from Manius Tullius the patrician, who was consul with Servius Sulpicius ten years after the expulsion of the kings.

The same warning, though without the crucial mention of bogus family trees, is repeated later by Livy (8, 40, 4–5, Loeb trans.):

The records have been vitiated, I think, by funeral eulogies and by lying inscriptions under portraits, every family endeavouring mendaciously to appropriate victories and magistracies to itself—a practice which has certainly wrought confusion in the achievements of individuals and in the public memorials of events.

Livy is speaking here of the year which we call 322 B.C., and of only a marginal variation in his sources. Much more fundamental problems would attend any modern attempt at narrative history of the fifth century, of which in my view no serious account can be written.

But even in the relatively historical, or semi-historical period, from the earlier fourth century to the mid-third, with which we are concerned here, any attempt to write a narrative history focusing on internal political issues seems to me open to serious question for the following reasons. Firstly, as mentioned already, far greater importance attaches to the overall, and historically indubitable, transformation in the structure of Italy in the same period. Secondly, there are insuperable uncertainties as to the precise date or meaning of many internal changes which, viewed broadly, undoubtedly took place. Thirdly, in talking of the "conflict of the orders" (Raaflaub et al.) or the "evolution of the *nobilitas*" (Hölkeskamp), terms are being used which are at best not clearly defined and at worst profoundly misleading; H. in particular is looking at the period retrospectively, interpreting it in terms of the coming into being of something which is itself open to radical re-thinking. Finally, both he and the authors of the articles collected by Raaflaub et al. make too little use of the archaeological and antiquarian evidence for early Rome analysed and made available above all by Filippo Coarelli and Mario Torelli, which allows us to see the evolution of the political structure of the archaic Roman state in a wholly different light. One lesson which might be drawn from this evidence is that we have tended to look in the wrong direc-

tion, at what might be supposed to have gone on in what it would be salutary to see as a relatively marginal and anomalous institution, the Curia; but
where we should be looking is to the centre of power in Rome, the Rostra,
the Comitium, and the Forum as a whole. The year 338, one might well say,
was the crucial moment in the history of the Republic, and not only because
of the break-up of the Latin League. Victory was symbolized, as everyone
knows, by the bringing to Rome of the prows (*rostra*) of captured ships from
Antium. But they were used to decorate not the Curia, where we imagine
power to have lain, but the speakers' platform on the opposite side of the
Comitium. It was from the Rostra that speakers would address the sovereign
people, who gathered to vote originally in the Comitium, and then, after
145 B.C., in the wider Forum.

We will return later to the importance of the symbolic, political, and functional landscape which evolved around the Comitium, and in the Forum
area as a whole. Its significance lies above all in the fact that the citizens who
gathered there did so in order to exercise their sovereign powers of voting:
on legislation, in non-capital jurisdiction, and in (some) elections. That is
one aspect of what "the conflict of the orders," as represented in later narratives, meant: that is the assertion of sovereign collective voting rights. Then
there is something different, and much more difficult to assess historically,
because wholly dependent on whether the available narratives of events have
any claim to accuracy: that is, the actual content of legislation, or proposed
legislation, on broad social and economic issues, such as debt, *nexum*, or the
use of public land (*ager publicus*). Thirdly, there is the aspect which is the central topic of Hölkeskamp's book, and the concern of several of the essays in
Raaflaub et al., namely the right of plebeians (not definable in social or economic terms, but solely negatively, as *non*-patricians) to hold elected office
(as consul, praetor, or censor) or have a share in (at least many) priesthoods.

These three issues cannot of course have been wholly unrelated. But they
are none the less not the same. To call a book *Social Struggles in Archaic Rome:
New Perspectives on the Conflict of the Orders* is to suggest in advance that the
question of access to office was itself in some way a "social struggle" affecting broad social classes definable in terms of wealth or occupation. Similarly, Hölkeskamp can call his very learned, and very valuable, analysis of
the political-military history of Rome from 366 to 287 B.C., *Die Entstehung
der Nobilität* only because, as the title itself implies, he sees the period as that
of the birth of a particular political order which is known and is beyond
serious question: that is to say the domination of Rome by a homogeneous
"patrician–plebeian" *nobilitas*, or aristocracy.

From time to time in what follows the discussion will inevitably return to certain presuppositions which run through Hölkeskamp's book, and will do so from a totally divergent point of view. It is therefore only right to stress here that the work is a considerable achievement and is indeed the most detailed and serious treatment we have of the political history of Rome in the fourth and earlier third centuries. Its intention is not, however, to present a mere narrative, but to get away from the obsession with alleged "Adelsparteien," a conception, as Hölkeskamp rightly says (p. 13), simply assumed by Münzer and not "problematisiert" by him. In its place there will be a step-by-step analysis of the actual political, constitutional, military, and social issues which formed the subject matter of politics. In this sense the book represents a real advance, in seeing Roman politics in the context of Rome's wars, and of the progressive domination of Italy. But its central focus remains the steps which gave access to public roles to a new plebeian "élite" which however was rapidly absorbed by the existing patrician élite to form the homogeneous "patrician-plebeian élite" mentioned earlier.

As a study and discussion of all that we know, or hope that we know, of the political history of Rome in this period, the book will henceforward be indispensable. My divergence from it springs, however, from the view that, while its "problematization" of Münzer's views is entirely justified, it has not rid itself of the quite unsupported assertions about Roman political and social structure set out in Gelzer's *Die römische Nobilität* of 1912, and which have been so dominant ever since (note the English translation, *The Roman Nobility*, by Robin Seager, 1969). But the history of the Republic is already seeing a radical revision of these preconceptions also, a point to be discussed further. The alternative view argued here is that we could with profit abandon Gelzer's view of a homogeneous élite (or "aristocracy" or "nobility"?) controlling the mass of the people through a network of patronage relationships, and start all over again by looking at the Roman community and political system from the bottom up, that is starting from the broad mass of the people, settled in Rome and round about it, and progressively also further away. For to focus on the political process in Rome itself, as it was in this period, is to give relatively marginal attention to far more important developments: the progressive domination of Italy, the spread of Latin colonies and Roman settlement, and the expansion of the Roman tribes between 390 and 241.

This expansion, in two senses, both in numbers (from twenty-one to thirty-five) and in geographical location, is extremely important. Firstly, because we know that it happened; for the end effects of this process are visible in the political map of Italy in the historical period (L. R. Taylor, *Voting Districts of the Roman Republic* [1960]). Moreover, T. J. Cornell is surely right in his claim ("The Value of the Literary Tradition concerning Archaic Rome," Raaflaub et al., 52ff.) that this is one "structural element" which has survived through the legendary accretions of later tradition. It is also worth stressing that this is one area where there are no fundamental contradictions, and no rival story. We have no serious alternatives to the story that in 495 Roman tribal territory was occupied by four urban tribes and by seventeen rural ones, territorial groupings, spread in a radius round the city. The territory covered suggests a population of perhaps some 35,000 (Cornell, 69, following Ampolo). Then no source even claims any expansion for roughly a century; but, after that, expansion began again in 387 with the incorporation of the territory of Veii and the creation of the *tribus* Stellatina, Tromentina, Sabatina, and Arnensis (Livy 6, 5, 8; Taylor, *Voting Districts*, 48). After that the broad lines of the successive creation of new tribes, in pairs, down to 241, are not the subject of any major conflicts in our sources. Along with the parallel process of the "export" of Roman citizens into Latin colonies, they represent *the* major known element in the social and constitutional history of Rome in this period. If we want to concentrate on what can actually be known of Roman history in the fourth and earlier third centuries, and also on what was to be important in subsequent history, we would be better employed studying the first volume of Toynbee's *Hannibal's Legacy* than the topics which form the main focus of these two books.

There is, however, also another reason for beginning at the bottom, with the mass of the citizenry, and that is the importance of popular sovereignty, and of the complex structures within which the citizen could vote. C. Nicolet's fundamental work *Le métier de citoyen* (1976), translated as *The World of the Citizen in Republican Rome* (1980), seems to have had surprisingly little influence on the way that the authors represented here approach republican politics. The long-established notion of a system wholly manipulable from above, and marked by the domination of the richest groups, is of course coloured in large part by the representations in later sources of the "Servian" centuriate assembly, with its eighteen centuries of *equites* voting first, followed by the eighty centuries of the (*prima*) *classis* ("first census class," Livy 1, 43; Dionysius 4, 16–21). But, while the principle of voting priority according to wealth always remained, it is easy to minimize the significance of the *relative* transformation of this system which had taken place by the outbreak of the Second Punic War. By then, as is well known, voting began with the now seventy centuries (two from each of the thirty-five tribes) which constituted the first class (Livy 24, 7, 12, on 215 B.C.; cf. 26, 22, 2–13, 27, 6, 3). Two quite new principles were involved: the removal of the voting priority of the *equites*, and the division of the centuries of the first class among the tribes, a century of *iuniores* and one of *seniores* from each. Strictly speaking, such a new principle might have been instituted at any time. But it is probably right that, as Livy implies (1, 43, 12), it belongs after 241 — "after the full number of 35 tribes had been reached." It was surely this that Dionysius meant in saying that there had been a subsequent remodelling by which the centuriate assembly was made more democratic — μεταβέβληκεν εἰς τὸ δημοτικώτερον (4, 21, 3). See, for example, L. J. Grieve, "The Reform of the Centuriate Assembly," *Historia* 34 (1985): 278, rightly seeing this as a significant change. I would only ask why it should be assumed (Grieve, "Reform of the Centuriate," 309) that the relevant law will have been put through by a consul or censor. Why not a tribunician law? At all events its full importance will only appear when it is put in the context of a much wider range of constitutional legislation in this period; within that context, it is of course significant that this partial measure of democratization came very late.

That the centuriate assembly was still biased in favour of the upper classes is, and was, patent, and it was indeed precisely for that reason that Cato and Cicero approved of it (Cicero, *De rep.* 2, 22/39–40). But the tribal assembly was not so structured, and no source claims that it ever had been. That this fact is not more clearly stressed in analyses of the Roman political system is due in part to the excessive emphasis on elections, above all elections to the consulship, and a consequential failure to give sufficient importance to legislation.

The question of the conditions under which acts of collective voting constituted legislation in the early Republic of course represents a minefield of confusion. But it would be carrying scepticism too far to reject the unanimous view of our sources that the Lex Hortensia of 287 B.C., passed by a *dictator* after the last secession of the *plebs*, represented a major landmark, and did so because it laid down that votes of the plebs were binding on the whole people — "ut plebiscita universum populum tenerent" (Gaius, *Inst.* 1, 3); or "ut eo iure quod plebs statuisset omnes Quirites tenerentur" (Aulus Gellius 15, 27, 4; full sources in Marina R. Torelli, *Rerum Romanarum Fontes* [1978], 69–71). The key point, if we may believe Gellius, is that an assembly called by a tribune was only a *concilium*, not a meeting of the *universus populus* (the whole people), because it had excluded patricians. How we reconcile that with repeated reports of tribunes of the previous period passing what looks remarkably like "legislation" in common-language terms (for instance, the Lex Ogulnia of 300 B.C. adding plebeians to the previously patrician colleges of priests) is notoriously unclear. But suppose that what was at stake in 287 was the right of the *concilium plebis* (plebeian assembly) to give instructions to any citizen, including a patrician magistrate exercising military or political functions? If so, that might indeed explain why, very soon after, it was to the tribune of the plebs, Aelius, that the people of Thurii publicly erected a statue in Rome; Pliny the Elder (*NH* 34, 32), in reporting this, seems to imply, but does not explicitly state, that this was the first statue in Rome to be voted by a foreign community. They did so because Aelius had had a law passed against the Lucanian Sthenius Stallius, who had twice attacked Thurii. This public honour, accompanied by a gold crown, will surely not have related to some mere expression of hostility. The vote passed by Aelius clearly commanded action against the Lucanians, which duly followed, perhaps already in 285 or 284 (Livy *Per.* 11 *ad fin.*: "it contains the exploits against the Vulsinienses and the Lucanians, against whom it had seemed right to give help to the people of Thurii"), but definitively in 282 under C. Fabricius, to whom the Thurini also voted a statue (Pliny, *NH* 34, 32).

Unless we find some reason to reject the story altogether, we have to accept that the people of Thurii knew who could have a binding law passed in Rome, in spheres including those of foreign relations. Pliny's report is thus precious testimony to the sovereign powers of the people, shown again, in a different way, in 264, when the consuls, against the will of the Senate, successfully persuaded the people, with momentous consequences, to send aid to the Mamertini in Messene (so Polybius 1, 11, 1–3).

These facts represent one reason why the entire picture of the evolution of the Roman state as presupposed by Hölkeskamp, following a long tradition, can be called in question. It should not, for instance, simply be asserted that the Senate was the central "governing body" of the *res publica* (10). More problematic still is the definition of the "aristocracy" in terms of its alleged monopoly of office, quoted, with approval, from Christian Meier: "Whoever played a part in politics belonged to the aristocracy, and whoever belonged to the aristocracy played a part in politics" (Hölkeskamp, 248). But this definition is circular; if we wished to say that an aristocracy controlled office and the exercise of active political functions, we would have to be able to define that aristocracy in terms which were *independent* of their occupation of office. Furthermore, the whole picture depends in part on the identification of the occupation of the consulship with "Politik." Of course, the same families reappear frequently in the consulship, though Hölkeskamp's own analysis shows new families arriving and then dropping out again. Was Q. Publilius Philo (*consul* 339, 327, 320, 315, *dictator* 339, *censor* 332, and so forth) an "aristocrat"? We could say that only if we had independent evidence of the family's established role and standing in the earlier period. But we have not: at the very best a dubious tradition records a Q. Publilius as tribune of the plebs in 384. Moreover, Publilius created no line of successors from his own family, no "plebeian aristocrats" playing any role in the third century: one T. Publilius, perhaps a son, is recorded as becoming *augur* in 300.

But the fact that some families played a predominant role in the consulship is of course beyond dispute. In part at least that was a function of the fact that one consulship, between 342 and 172, always went to a patrician, and patrician *familiae* were relatively few. It seems odd to me that neither of these books provides a list of patrician *familiae*, of which only twenty-one to twenty-three still existed in 366; so P. Ch. Ranouil, *Recherches sur le Patriciat 509–366 avant J.-C.* (1975), 236. Nor does either offer any definition of what a *familia* or a *gens* was. But never mind; if one hundred consulates per century were already "reserved" for whatever members of these few patrician *familiae* were in evidence and of the right standing, that alone will have given a somewhat "aristocratic" look to the *Fasti*. What we would then need is a picture of the "heritability" of the consulship among plebeians, quite a different issue.

But we are begging the question anyway. For the consulship was primarily a military office, though certainly consuls could and did consult the Senate (and introduce embassies to it), and put legislation to the people before going on campaign (a time sequence which Polybius sets out with perfect clarity, 6, 12, 1–4). There were other elective offices, a praetor (after 366), then subsequently two, and from 227, four; a pair of censors every five years; quaestors, military tribunes (of whom more were progressively subject to popular election) and so forth. But every year there were also ten elected tribunes of the plebs, who stayed in Rome all year, sat daily on their *subsellia* (benches) beside the Curia fronting on the Comitium, were available to give *auxilium* (aid), and could also mount the Rostra to address the people and to put forward legislation, in some sense already before 287, and certainly after that. Were they all, or even characteristically, "aristocrats," or from a definable social élite? Hölkeskamp, 244, speaks of "the plebeian élite which controlled the tribunate." How do we know that? Between 366 and (say) 219 a simple calculation will show that well over one thousand men will have held the tribunate. Inspection of Broughton, *MRR*, suggests that our sources report (accurately or otherwise) the names of about thirty. What does it mean to say that they were an "élite" except (circularly) that they held the tribunate? Does it mean that they also (some of them) are known to have held other offices? But, to be precise, of the mere thirty or so whose names are known, eight are attested as having held other offices. Is this a sign of the absorption of the tribunate into a wider office-holding élite, leading to the political neutralization of the office? Quite the contrary, for *either* we cannot in any case rely on the traditions about them, *or* (if we can, to any degree) these men are almost all represented as conspicuously plebeian leaders. In 358, for example, there was C. Poetilius, one of the most prominent early plebeian consuls (360, 346, 326), and as *tribunus* the author of a law restricting canvassing to the Forum (Livy 7, 15, 12); in 311, C. Marcius (Rutilius Censorinus), the author of a law on the popular election of military tribunes, consul in 310; in 310, P. Sempronius (Sophus?), consul 304; in 300, Q. Ogulnius, joint author of the major law on plebeian priesthoods, consul in 269; in 298, M'. Curius Dentatus, associated with a step to secure prior authorization by the senate (*patrum auctoritas*) before elections, consul 290, 275; in 270, M. Fulvius (Flaccus), who is recorded as having protested against the execution of Campanian mutineers captured in Rhegium on the grounds that they were Roman citizens (Valerius Maximus 2, 7, 15), consul in 264. It is surely worth stressing that M. Fulvius (Flaccus) is in fact the earliest consul in the history of Rome who is recorded as such in contemporary documentary evidence. It consists of two fragmentary but evidently identical inscriptions from the bases of statues erected by him in the *area sacra* of S. Omobono in the Forum Boarium after his capture of Volsinii: they originally read "M. Folvio, son of Quint(o?), consul, dedicated (it) after Volsinii had been captured" (M. FOLVIO Q.F. COSOL. D. VOLSINIO CAPTO); see M. Torelli in *Roma Medio Repubblicana* (1973), 103–4, and now F. Coarelli, *Il Foro Boario* (1988), 213–16.

Archaeological evidence is bound to be to a certain extent a matter of luck. But the erection of this early victory monument, inscribed with his own name, in the Forum Boarium by a consul whose only known previous office was as tribune of the plebs cannot be without significance. It perhaps deserved a mention at the beginning of the interesting book by C. Pietilä-Castrén, *Magnificentia Publica: The Victory Monuments of the Roman Generals in the Era of the Punic Wars* (1987). We should recall that it was the two consuls of this year who, according to Polybius, persuaded the People, against the will of the Senate, to intervene in Sicily. Only one (Appius Claudius) gained that province, and it seems certain that he won no triumph for his pains. But the connection of populism with imperialism is clear enough. There is also another coincidence, of time and place: for it was in this consulship, in the Forum Boarium, that the first-ever gladiatorial show on the occasion of a funeral was put on for the entertainment of the People (Livy, *Epit.* 16; Valerius Maximus 2, 4, 7; G. Ville, *La gladiature en Occident* [1981], 42).

Finally there is C. Flaminius, tribune of the plebs in 232, praetor in 227—the first to have Sicily as his province—consul in 223 and 217, censor in 220. In this case it is superfluous to argue the case for his role as a champion of the *plebs*, since the tradition is unanimous and emphatic. The Circus Flaminius

and the Via Flaminia were to serve as his memorials on the map of Rome and
of Italy. But here too it should be stressed that Polybius (2, 21, 7–8) emphasizes both the demagogic character of his law for the distribution of Gallic
land, and its military consequences.

The tendency of our evidence is thus perfectly clear. In terms of wealth or
social class we have no means whatever of characterizing the tribunes of this
period. The vast majority cannot even be named. Of those about whom we
know a little more, and who held other offices (in most cases the consulship),
almost all are clearly identified in the tradition as champions of the *plebs* or
of popular rights.

The evidential basis for any assertions about "who" tribunes typically were
in this period, and from what families or social strata they came is thus almost
non-existent. But no one will deny that there was a certain integration on
a social level, that holding a tribunate came to be something perfectly com-
patible with holding other offices (which themselves, of course, steadily expanded in number); tribunes also gained the right to summon the Senate
themselves, and the expectation that they would be enrolled in it by the censors. We can, of course, insist on seeing this as a take-over of the tribunate by
the "patrician-plebeian élite," or by the Senate: we may then see a "a change
of function of the tribunate from a plebeian, 'party' instrument of struggle to
magistracy under the control of the senate and in its service" (Hölkeskamp,
196–97).

But suppose that we were to try the stratagem of looking not from the
Curia to the Comitium but from the Comitium to the Curia? A whole range
of evidence would then suggest a quite different interpretation, and, firstly,
give considerable support to the notion argued by J. von Ungern-Sternberg,
"The End of the Conflict of the Orders" (Raaflaub et al., 353ff.), that a real
political tension survived at least to the Second Punic War, or even after.
Polybius notoriously saw Flaminius' proposal in 232 about the Ager Gallicus
as the *beginning* of demagogy (2, 21, 7–8). Why should we not see the first
half of the second century, not as the period of untroubled control of the
"People" by the "élite," but as that in which popular rights had become quite
well established, and popular demands, for victories, booty, and land, were
quite easily met? Such is the thesis argued in "The Political Character of the
Classical Roman Republic, 200–151 B.C." *JRS* 74 (1984): 1 (chapter 4 in this
volume). In this period, for instance, it was obligatory on every magistrate,
within five days of entering office, to take an oath to obey the laws. If he did
not, he could continue in office no longer (Livy 31, 50, 6–7). No evidence
relating to an earlier period attests this rule. But we must surely see such an
oath, unquestionably taken in public, in the Forum, as a means by which

the People attempted to impose appropriate behaviour on those whom they elected.

If we were to take Flaminius' law as an aspect of the "conflict of the orders," we would be focusing on the second of the possible senses of the phrase mentioned earlier: the actual content of legislation, in this case a law for the distribution of conquered land to citizens. But a second effect of seeing the whole political structure from the Comitium would be to focus on an aspect of the first sense, the assertion of sovereignty by the people: that is, the use of legislation (*plebiscita*, i.e., laws passed by the plebeian assembly—the *concilium plebis*—or *leges*, laws passed by the other assemblies), whether to ensure the protection of the rights of citizens or to restrict within limits the actions which could be taken by office-holders, or the terms under which office could be held. There remain problems about how (or even if) such items of legislation were effective at all before 287; and, of course, intrinsic problems about dating, and the apparent reduplication of laws, for example, on *provocatio* (appeal). But even the most selective of tabulations will show how our sources *represent* a long series of items of legislation as having been passed, mainly by tribunes, in the fourth and third centuries. Table 1 illustrates certain general tendencies, and omits some particularly controversial cases. The conception which all of these acts of legislation, even the last-mentioned, embody, is that the constitutional structure of the state, the conditions of office-holding, and the duties of office are for determination by the People via the medium of *leges*. This latter aspect is also particularly clear in the case of the tribunician Lex Papiria, of uncertain date between 242 and 124 (Festus 468L, based on J. D. Cloud's trans.):

> Concerning this matter it was ordained by a law of the tribune of the plebs, Lucius Papirius, in these words: "whoever hereafter shall have been made the praetor, who shall have jurisdiction between citizens, let him propose to the people [the election of] three men in charge of capital cases [*tresviri capitales*]), and those three men in charge of capital cases, whoever <hereafter> shall have been <made> let them enforce the taking of an oath, adjudicate cases" etc.

The law lays a duty both on future praetors and on the *tresviri capitales* whose election they are to conduct. So equally does the Lex Silia, a tribunician law of (probably) the second half of the third century, making it an offence for any magistrate to alter the established weights and measures (Festus 288L): "If any magistrate contrary to these rules with wrongful deceit shall have made the official weights, dry measures and vessels too small or too large, or shall have ordered (these things) to be done" (trans. J. D. Cloud).

Table 1. Political Power in Mid-Republican Rome

362	Law for the election of 6 military tribunes, rather than selection. Livy 7, 5, 9.
357	Tribunician law "ne quis populum postea sevocaret," i.e., forbidding the summoning of an assembly beyond the first milestone. Livy 7, 16, 8.
?318/12	Tribunician Lex Ovinia entrusting the enrolment of senators to the censors rather than to the consuls. Festus 290L.
311	Tribunician Lex Atilia Marcia on election, rather than selection, of 16 military tribunes. Livy 9, 30, 3.
300	Tribunician Lex Ogulnia adding plebeian *pontifices* and augurs. Livy 10, 6, 1–9, 2.
287	Lex Hortensia.
242 or later	Tribunician Lex Plaetoria on jurisdiction of the urban praetor.
?292/219	Lex Maenia on *auctoritas patrum*.
218?	Tribunician Lex Claudia, limiting shipping activity by senators and their sons. Livy 21, 63, 3.
217	*Plebiscitum* releasing ex-consuls from an existing ban on repetition of office. Livy 27, 6, 7.

Such a provision can be understood only in relation to a formally constituted public space, under magisterial supervision, for the sale of products by citizens. Equally, a clear conception of place (and time) is essential for us if we are to envisage what is meant by the tribunician Lex Plaetoria, of not earlier than 242 (Censorinus, *De die natali* 24, 3, trans. J. A. Crook):

> M. Plaetorius the tribune passed a *plebiscitum*, in which it was written "Whoever is now urban praetor and whoever <shall be appointed> hereafter is to have two lictors with him and he is to have jurisdiction between citizens <through> the last hour right down to sunset."

We would begin to gain a sense of the middle republican Roman community if we were to relate to this Varro's comment (*LL* 6, 5, Loeb trans.): "The
Lex Plaetoria declares that this time also should be 'last' at which the praetor
[better 'the herald,' *praeco*?] in the Comitium has announced to the people
the 'end of the session.'" The scene is therefore the Comitium, and the obligation laid down in the law is for the praetor to be available to give justice
to the People all day until dusk falls.

How was that moment to be determined? It might well be an offence to
the popular sense of justice if a praetor could leave of his own volition, before an aggrieved litigant were heard. The evidence preserved by antiquarian
sources, whose resurrection and deployment is one of the great services of
the modern school of Italian archaeology, gives a wonderful sense of location and of the role of public action, in the open, in front of the crowd,
in the archaic community. I rely here, as will be evident, on F. Coarelli, *Il
Foro romano* II (1985), in my view the essential work for understanding the
political structure of the Republic as a social system—a system of interaction
between people, in the most concrete sense.

How the end of the day was determined in the earliest Republic is as obscure as everything else about that period. But in 338 and the following years
the monumentalization of the Comitium and Forum began, not merely with
the Rostra, but with the Maeniana, or spectators' galleries, above the *tabernae*
(shops), and the erection of the *Columna Maenia* to the west of the Comitium. All three were recorded as having been the work of the consul of 338,
C. Maenius, either after his capture of Antium in that year, or as censor in
318. There was now an agreed and simple means of determining both the
midday and nightfall: an *accensus* (a herald, *praeco*, presumably) of the consuls proclaiming (*pronuntiante*) midday when, looking out from the Curia,
he saw the Sun between the Rostra and the Graecostasis; sunset was when
he saw the Sun between the *Columna Maenia* and the Carcer (the alignments
are marked in the plan in Coarelli, *Il Foro romano* II, 23). In the rapidly developing Rome of the first half of the third century that procedure must have
begun to seem somewhat primitive and arbitrary. So, according to Varro, in
the consulship of M. Valerius (Maximus) Messala, 263 B.C., a *horologium* taken
in the capture of Catane was installed on a column near the Rostra. In fact
it was inaccurate, but was used for nearly a century until the censors of 164
erected a better one. But neither solved the problem of cloudy days, finally
overcome when the next censors (of 159) put up a water clock. The whole
story is told by Pliny the Elder (*NH* 7, 212–15), and is a perfect mirror of the
evolution of Rome in this period.

It is not necessary to rehearse here more of the literary and archaeological evidence deployed by Coarelli to bring to life the architectural, artistic
and functional evolution of the Comitium. But his demonstration (*Il Foro
romano* II, 22–23) that the *tribunal praetoris* (the praetor's tribunal) was duly
situated on the eastern perimeter of the Comitium, near the *Puteal*, until
moved west into the wider spaces of the Forum proper, is essential. For the
proper satisfaction of individual claims it had to be known exactly both
when and where justice could be seen to be done. It was of course also in the
Comitium that the thirty-five tribes could be found voting in order (both
functions are reflected in the speech of 161 B.C. quoted by Macrobius 3, 16,
14–18), until they too (probably in 145 B.C.) moved out (for legislation and
trials) into the "seven *iugera*" of the wider Forum, and for elections down to
the Campus Martius like the centuriate assembly.

Nearer to the Curia Hostilia, on the left as you entered, the tribunes of
the plebs had their *subsellia* (benches). From there they could offer *auxilium*
to the *plebs* in the event of oppressive magisterial action, and also watch the
door of the Curia and what went on inside; from there, as Zonaras (7, 15)
says, following Cassius Dio, they were in the course of time drawn in to the
Curia itself (Loeb trans.):

> Now at first they did not enter the Senate-house, but sat at the entrance
> and watched proceedings, and in case anything failed to please them,
> they would there and then oppose it. Next they were invited inside.
> Later, however, the ex-tribunes became members of the Senate, and
> finally some of the senators sought to be tribunes.

We could accept, as Hölkeskamp does, the common view of this as their absorption and neutralization by the governing élite. But, as argued earlier, a
quite different view of the entry of the tribunes into the Curia remains possible; on this view what mattered was the constitutional power of the people,
accompanied in the period from the later fourth century to the middle of
the third by a vast process of settlement on the land, resumed in the 190s and
apparently coming to a halt in the middle of the second century. There was,
of course, for a relatively brief period in the first half of the second century, a
degree of neutralization of the role of the tribunes of the plebs as the champions of popular rights. But for that the explanation given by Dio/Zonaras
is at least as good as any other: the disunity and mutual jealousy of a board
of ten with equal powers.

The Comitium, even after it ceased to be the only place where one could
agere cum populo (transact business with the people) retained those major
historical monuments which marked it as the focus of communal life: the

Rostra, adorned with various ancient statues, the Volcanal, with the Lapis Niger, the ficus Ruminalis, and beside it the statue of the She-wolf and the Twins erected by the Ogulnii in 296. In the same period, that of the Samnite wars, there were erected on the instructions of Pythian Apollo the statues of Pythagoras and Alcibiades, respectively the wisest and bravest (?) of the Greeks; the statues lasted until Sulla's enlargement of the Curia (Pliny, *NH* 34, 26). It was almost certainly also in the same period that there was erected the statue of Marsyas. The arguments for its origin at this point are no more than circumstantial, as are those for the belief that it already symbolized liberty: the representation of the statue on *denarii* of L. (Marcius) Censor(inus) of 82 B.C.; a statue of Marsyas from the Forum of the Latin colony of Paestum, 273, held to be an imitation of the one already erected in Rome; a possible association, as with later provincial statues of Marsyas, or Liber Pater, with *libertas*; and a possible candidate as the dedicator in an ancestor of Censorinus, namely C. Marcius Rutilus, tribune of the plebs 311, consul 310, one of the first plebeian augurs under the Lex Ogulnia, and censor in 294 and 265. See M. Torelli, *Typology and Structure of Roman Historical Reliefs* (1982), 98–99; Coarelli, *Foro* II, 91–92; T. P. Wiseman, "Satyrs in Rome," *JRS* 78 (1988): 1, on p. 4. It should, however, be noted that M. H. Crawford, *RRC* I (1974), 377–78, rejects any connection with *popularis* ideology.

Contrast with all (much more than sketched here) that we know of the Comitium and the surrounding area how little any source has to say of the Curia itself. We know, of course, that it was there, on the north side of the Comitium, and it is not unlikely that a comparable relationship of Comitium and Curia was created when Latin colonies were founded; see C. Krause, "Zum baulichen Gestalt des republikanischen Comitiums," *Röm. Mitt.* 83 (1976): 31, esp. 53–54; F. Coarelli, *Il Foro romano* I (1983), 141–42. But it seems to me to be only at Cosa (273) that this parallel is at all clear. It is, moreover, notorious how little any of our sources have to say about the size, shape, internal disposition, internal or external adornment, or symbolic character of the Curia Hostilia. We ought also to pose a question which is more puzzling than it appears at first sight. Why did the Senate meet in a *building*, and under a roof, at all? For every other public function of the Roman community took place in the open air (there is no Republican evidence for the use of the basilicas for jury courts).

The fact that the site of a legitimate meeting of the Senate had to be an inaugurated *templum* did not of itself imply that it had to be a "temple" with walls and a roof, though of course the majority of the regular alternative meeting places of the Senate were (the temples of Capitoline Juppiter, Castor and Pollux, Concordia, Bellona, and so forth; see M. Bonnefond, "Espace, temps et idéologie: le Sénat dans la cité romaine républicaine," *Dial. di Arch.*, 3rd ser., I [1983]: 37). For the Rostra was also an inaugurated *templum*. But, given that the Curia was exclusively a meeting place for the Senate, the lack of any clear image or symbolic associations remains baffling. Almost all that we hear of it concerns its external features: the two statues of Alcibiades and Pythagoras outside it, removed when Sulla enlarged the building; the statue of Attus Navius which stood somewhere before it, and was burned in 52 (Pliny, *NH* 34, 20; Coarelli, *Il Foro romano* II, 29–30); and the *tabula Valeria*, a picture representing his victory over the Carthaginians and Hiero in 263, which was placed on the side wall by M'. Valerius Maximus Messala (Pliny, *NH* 35, 22); it was put on the left side as you faced the Curia, just above the *subsellia* (benches) of the tribunes of the plebs (Coarelli, 53–54). Once again, as with Fulvius Flaccus' dedications of the previous year, in the Forum Boarium, victories now needed to be exhibited in permanent form before the eyes of the people.

The indistinctiveness of the Curia as a building may not be entirely accidental, for it oddly mirrors the indistinctiveness of the Senate itself in the early period. Our sources for the mythical history of early Rome, of course, narrate the summoning of a Senate of *patres* by Romulus, relate this term to patricians, and speak of *maiores* and *minores gentes*. But as to the composition, role, and function of the Senate in the early Republic, they provide no very clear picture. Insofar as we are told by our sources the story of a "conflict of the orders" relating to personal status, it concerns either elective annual offices or the membership of the priestly colleges. It is in no way about the right to be a senator. All that we can (at best) claim to know is that before the tribunician Lex Ovinia, of indeterminate date before 312, the Senate seems to have been enrolled by the consuls; but that enrolment now became a duty laid on the censors and conducted by a public reading of the list. As such, this step forms a clear partial parallel to the progressive removal of the power of appointment of some military tribunes by the consuls, in favour of popular election.

As is self-evident, no history can be written except with the benefit of hindsight. This is doubly so in the case of the middle Republic, where almost all our evidence is itself retrospective. What this discussion—more a reflection on the period than any attempt at a review of these two interesting, suggestive, and important books—is intended to suggest is that our retrospection has been governed by a false presupposition: that what the political history of the middle Republic led to was the formation of a "patrician-plebeian governing class" which exercised a real control both social and political, a control which ended and neutralized the "conflict of the orders." But, all else apart, many of the pillars on which such a view rests have been demolished in the recent work of P. A. Brunt, first in "*Nobilitas* and *Novitas*," *JRS* 72 (1982): 1, and now in *The Fall of the Roman Republic* (1988), above all in the chapters on *clientela* and on *factiones*. Whoever wants to argue for the genealogical continuity of the governing élite, the importance of lateral groupings within the Senate, or the socio-political function of those vertical links allegedly constituted by *clientela* will at any rate now have to start all over again. As for genealogical continuity, any discussion will also have to deal with K. Hopkins, *Death and Renewal* (1983), chap. 2: "Political Succession in the Late Roman Republic (249–50 B.C.)." Moreover, as soon as we attempt to follow *gentes* and *familiae* back into the archaic period, we have to face the fact that at least some "family-histories" were antiquarian constructions; see T. P. Wiseman, "Legendary Genealogies in Late-Republican Rome," *Greece and Rome* 21 (1974): 153 = *Roman Studies* (1987), 207. Our notions of which *familiae* were which also depend essentially on the combination of *nomen* and *cognomen* as attributed in later narratives, and in the inscribed Augustan *Fasti*, to individuals reported to have held offices, passed laws, or fought wars. But how many of the *cognomina* appearing in these later sources were really in use at the dates implied? There is no simple answer, and I do not wish to imply that a wholly negative conclusion can be justified. See, for a start, I. Kajanto, "On the Chronology of the Cognomen in the Republican Period," *L'Onomastique Latine* (1977): 63. For what can be done by "reading" the meanings of *cognomina* in their historical context, see also E. L. Wheeler "*Sapiens* and Strategems: The Neglected Meaning of a Cognomen," *Historia* 37 (1988): 166. More generally, without a history of names, based on contemporary documents, "histories" of *familiae* and *gentes* are premature.

It may of course be that the "patrician-plebeian nobility" can be restored to the unchallenged domination which it has enjoyed posthumously for most of this century. But I for one doubt it. For we *could* read the history of the middle Republic as recording the imposition on office-holders of public rules and obligations, coupled with an ever-accelerating need for individuals to advertise themselves to the People and to compete for their favour. The first of these themes is brought out best of all by A. N. Sherwin-White in "The Lex Repetundarum and the Political Ideas of Gaius Gracchus," *JRS* 72 (1982): 18, a seminal contribution to our understanding of republican politics. The second is plainly visible in the record of shows put on in Rome, in the literary record of statues and monuments in Rome, and in the archaeological record. See above all the classic article by T. Hölscher, "Die Anfänge römischer Representationskunst," *Röm. Mitt.* 85 (1978): 315. As Hölscher showed, and Hölkeskamp duly recognizes, the record of representational art, portraying contemporary individuals and their deeds, beginning (if we reject some legendary items from the fifth century or earlier) in the second half of the fourth century, is as good evidence as we have for the emergence of politics as a sphere of individual activity which would be demonstrated in permanent form before the people, sometimes with the sanction of specific votes by them. Ennius was to express this with perfect succinctness: "so many statues will the Roman people vote, so many columns, which will speak of your deeds" (Vahlen, *Varia* II; Skutsch, *Annales*, p. 130, fr. iv).

Seen in this light, the institution of the funeral oration, which in the second century at least was delivered to the people in the Forum from the Rostra, falls into the same pattern: the celebration of distinctive political and military roles before the community. The best evidence is of course the much-quoted funeral oration of 221 B.C., delivered by Q. Caecilius Metellus on the death of his father, L. Caecilius Metellus, consul in 251 and 247. The competitive presuppositions of the speech as summarized by Pliny the Elder (*NH* 7, 139–40), have been stressed recently by T. P. Wiseman in *Roman Political Life, 90 B.C.–A.D. 69* (1985), 3–4: "outstanding . . . the best . . . the bravest . . . the greatest deeds . . . the greatest distinction . . . the greatest wisdom, the foremost senator . . . the most celebrated in the state." It goes along with that final emphasis on popular fame that he should have been recorded as the first to lead elephants in a triumph, to have had a statue recording his services erected on the Capitol (Dionysius 2, 66, 4), and have been voted, by the Roman people, the right to use a *currus* (chariot) to ride in on his way to the Curia (Pliny, *NH* 7, 141). As Pliny explicitly states, the people had never conferred such a right on anyone else. A secure domination by a socially and politically unified "patrician-plebeian nobility"? It is perhaps worth stressing that on the later definition of *nobilis* (whatever that was)—which we have absolutely no reason to suppose was in use in the period concerned—L. Caecilius Metellus may not even have been one; it is no more than a possible reconstruction that the consul(?) of 284 may have been his father. At all events no securely attested Caecilius Metellus is known to have held office in Rome before the *triumphator* who was to be renowned for his display of elephants.

As confessed already, what has been said here is not so much a review of these two books as a reaction to them. The proposal made here is threefold. Firstly, that it is hopeless to work "forward" from the legendary beginnings of Rome—what were patricians? How did the *plebs* "originate"? Or even to ask detailed questions about the holders of office in the fifth and earlier fourth centuries. For that, if it were worth attempting at all, we would have to start, as suggested already, from the history of names, not as reconstructed in the Augustan *Fasti*, but as actually used at the time, not just in Rome but in Latium and neighbouring areas. As Cicero already warns us, there were Tullii both in Rome and Arpinum, once a Volscian town. For all we know, the now famous POPLIOS VALESIOS recorded on an archaic inscription from Satricum could just as well have been a Satrican as a Roman, or even a Sabine (see H. Versnel in C. M. Stibbe et al., *Lapis Satricanus* [1980], 128–29); and into what *familia* or *gens* should we fit the "Tiberius Claudius son of Gaius from Antium, made curator of the city" attested at Entella in Sicily in the first half of the third century? (See now M. Corsaro, "La presenza romana a Entella: una nota su Tiberio Claudio di Anzio," *Ann. Sc. N. Sup. Pisa* 12 [1982]: 993). Moreover, persons with the name "Claudius," in its Etruscan form ("Klavtie" or "Clavtie"), turn up in the fifth century B.C. at Aléria in Corsica and at the end of the fourth at Caere; see J. Jehasse and L. Jehasse, *La nécropole préromaine d'Aléria* (1973), 551, a reference which I owe to T. J. Cornell, to whom I am grateful for generous (and sceptical) comments on this chapter. As for these "Claudii," J. Heurgon, ap. Jehasse, 551, speaks engagingly of "la vitalité expansionniste de ces Claudes," descending from their Sabine homeland. But surely, in seeing all the attested Claudii, in Rome and elsewhere, as members of an original *gens Claudia*, we are indulging in a classic example of mythic history, and really ought to start again.

What we should do is to work *back* from the historical period, first (in my view) revising our conceptions of it itself, and then examining what types of social and political structure are already presupposed by what we find at each stage. In looking at these structures, the sheer size of mid-republican Rome, as both a city and a community, becomes more and more significant. It is much to be regretted that Chester G. Starr's small but very suggestive book, *The Beginnings of Imperial Rome: Rome in the Mid-Republic* (1980), has never been published on this side of the Atlantic, and has never really attracted the attention which it deserves. In working back into the later archaic community, the antiquarian evidence, as deployed by Coarelli and Torelli, is a crucial, but also, inevitably, a controversial, tool. (Perhaps the time has come for a collection and critical study of the scattered reports on early Rome in Pliny's *Natural History*.) But we are not confined to later reports of buildings, works of art, triumphs, shows and other manifestations of communal life. The archaeological evidence collected, not perhaps in the clearest way, in *Roma Medio Repubblicana* (1973) remains to be used to the full, as do the results of Coarelli's work on the Forum and now the Forum Boarium. As was noted briefly, an image of mid-republican Rome can perhaps now be gained also from excavations at the Latin colonies of Alba Fucens (304), Paestum (273) and Cosa (273). The Italian dimension, and not least the connections with Neapolis and Capua, must be essential in comprehending the Rome of the later fourth and earlier third centuries, as it so clearly is in M. Crawford, *Coinage and Money in the Roman Republic* (1985). Here perhaps the perspective imposed by Polybius may need some correction, as we work back from the historical period to the first phase of Rome's existence as a major local power. For to us the outbreak of the First Punic War must indeed, in retrospect, seem the crucial event of 264 B.C., as it did to Polybius. But to Romans at the time perhaps equal significance attached to the capture of Volsinii, and to the victory monument erected in the Forum Boarium, and inscribed with his own name, by the plebeian consul of that year, M. FOLVIO (which is the name which he actually used, whatever later tradition was to claim). Unless of course the people were even more interested in the gladiatorial show, the first ever, which was put on in the same year, and also in the Forum Boarium. Before many years had passed such shows were to move to the Forum proper, long since established as the central arena of communal life, where the Rostra had since 338 served simultaneously as a monument of victory and the platform for addressing the people.

CHAPTER FOUR

The Political Character of the Classical Roman Republic, 200–151 B.C.*

Polybio nostro

Introduction

In any attempt to understand Roman history the first half of the second century B.C. must have a special place. Victory in the Hannibalic war had laid the foundations of a general dominance of the Mediterranean world, but had hardly yet produced an empire. Outside Italy, only Sicily, Sardinia, and two commands in Spain were normally allotted as provinces for annual magistrates; and this list was not increased by the famous victories in the Greek East, Cynoscephalae, Thermopylae, Magnesia, and Pydna. Roman *imperialism* is too crude a term for what we can observe between 200 and 151 B.C. Roman *dominance* was felt everywhere, from Spain to Carthage, Alexandria, Jerusalem, Antioch, and Ankara; Roman *militarism* was demonstrated consistently in northern Italy and Spain, at various periods in Greece and Mace-

---

* First published in *JRS* 74 (1984): 1–19. A version of this chapter was given as a lecture on 9 December 1983, in London, as part of the obligations of the holder of the Balsdon Senior Fellowship at the British School in Rome. I hope that it may serve as an expression of thanks for that opportunity, which I enjoyed in Spring 1983, and may also bear witness to what I then learned, or tried to learn, of the public spaces of republican Rome. Successive subsequent versions were given as lectures at Berkeley, Stanford, Santa Barbara, and Princeton, and in particular as the Gerald F. Else Lecture in the Humanities, which I had the honour to give at Ann Arbor, Michigan, on 28 March 1984. I am indebted for points and criticisms to Professors P. A. Brunt, Erich Gruen, and Alan Astin, as also to Mary Beard. More fundamentally, whatever I have come to understand about the Roman Republic was learned from John North and Tim Cornell during the eight years at University College London; this remains so, even though both (like the persons named above) might disagree with much that is said here. Finally, this article is a tribute to Frank Walbank, to whom we all owe everything when it comes to Polybius.

donia (200–194, 191–187, 171–168), and for one period of three years in Asia Minor (190–188). Roman *colonialism* was still confined, with one very marginal exception, to the Italian peninsula.

Any discussion of what we mean by Roman "imperialism" in this period would have to maintain some such distinctions—and its main focus ought to be Spain, and, more important still, northern Italy.[1] It was in Liguria, in the Celtic lands of the Po Valley, and in Venetia and Histria that the Romans of this period exhibited a consistent and unremitting combination of imperialism, militarism, expansionism, and colonialism. T. Quinctius Flamininus gained his chance to win the great victory of Cynoscephalae only because in March 197, when the new consuls had entered office, the Senate decided to keep both of them in Italy to confront the Celts (Pol. 18, 11–12).

That illustrates the point that if we talk about Roman imperialism we must, at least at one level, try to make clear whose imperialism we are discussing. Who, in the Roman political system, actually decided the declaration of war or the making of peace, the scale of the military call-out for each year and its allotment to different areas, the answers to be given to Italian and foreign embassies, the despatch of colonies: the consul or proconsul in the field, the Senate, or the Roman people in their assemblies?

Thus to understand Roman imperialism, but not that alone, we must understand the Roman political system itself. That is of course hardly a novel observation, since precisely that was the purpose of Polybius' analysis of the Roman constitution in book 6. By the purest of accidents, Polybius' seventeen years as a hostage in Rome (167–150) began at exactly that point in time where our text of Livy now breaks off. I do not, however, wish to imply that Polybius' evidence complements that of Livy in illuminating this half century. On the contrary, Livy's narrative is at least equalled in significance by Polybius' account, combined with contemporary documents, the vivid images of the Roman political community in Plautus, Ennius, and Caecilius, and the fragmentary remains of the political speeches of the time.

This half century can also be seen by us, as it was later in antiquity, as presenting the classic phase of the working of the Roman constitution. The "struggle of the orders" had ended in 287. The number of tribes had reached its permanent limit of thirty-five in 241; soon after, as it seems, came the obscure reform which related the centuries in the centuriate assembly (*comitia centuriata*) to the tribal system. The temporary strains which had produced

---

1. For this point (and much else), see A. N. Sherwin-White, *Roman Foreign Policy in the East, 168 B.C.-A.D. 1* (1984), esp. 8 and 11–12.

recurrent dictatorships and repeated consulships in the Hannibalic war were
also over. The phase of major constitutional reforms, tensions, and crises,
which began in 149 and continued with the ballot laws of the early 130s (see
text to nn. 70–72), had not yet been reached. By any reasonable standards
the constitution worked smoothly. There was no interruption in the annual
election of office-holders, and not a single Roman is known to have been
killed, or even injured, in political violence during the period.

That is not to say that there was no change and no internal debate. There
were repeated public issues about war and peace, the internal regulation of
the constitution, the moral regulation of society, the inclusion of marginal
groups within the citizen body, the despatch of colonies, and the occupation
and exploitation of the public land within Italy. Nor is it to say — as often
has been said — that the period was marked by the secure domination of the
Senate as a body, or the *nobiles* as a group. The main purpose of this paper is to
argue that Polybius was right and his modern critics are wrong. We do have
to see the power of the people as one significant element in Roman politics.
Polybius, it is claimed, failed to see the social structures which ensured the
domination of the *nobiles*;[2] that must mean the relationships of patronage and
dependence which supposedly dominated Roman political decision making
and rendered popular participation passive and nominal. But the existence
of these structures is itself a modern hypothesis, which has very little support
in our evidence. It is time to turn to a different hypothesis, that Polybius did
not see them because they were not there.

Or rather, vertical links of obligation can of course be found in Roman
society. But for at least three reasons they cannot serve as the key to the political process; so Polybius was right to ignore them. First is the sheer size of
the citizen body. Second, all our evidence shows that those who aspired to
office engaged in vigorous mutual *competition* for popular favour. Why else
should Antiochus Epiphanes have carried back with him from his years as a
hostage in Rome that vivid image of Roman political behaviour which he
then exhibited to the baffled inhabitants of Antioch? Dressed in the white
toga of a candidate he would go around the agora grasping men by the hand
and embracing some, and asking for their votes for him as tribune or aedile
(Pol. 26, 1, 5).

Electoral support had to be sought at the time and also prepared in advance
by building up the right reputation. Scipio Aemilianus, so Polybius records
(31, 29, 8), was unlike the other young men of his class. He went hunting;

2. F. W. Walbank, *Polybius* (1972), 155.

they devoted themselves to speaking in court and greeting people, spending their time in the Forum, "and by these means attempted to recommend themselves to the many."

The people enjoyed the three basic constitutional rights of direct voting on legislation, including declarations of war and the making of peace treaties; of electing all the annual holders of political and military office; and of judging in popular courts constituted by the centuriate assembly and tribal assembly (*comitia tributa*). This last element is not given its full significance in modern work. Gelzer, for instance, could list as a "struggle between cliques" what were in fact prosecutions before the popular courts (*iudicia populi*).[3]

In the end I will want to say no more than what Polybius said: that we cannot understand Roman politics if our view does not encompass, along with the power of individuals holding office and the collective power of the Senate as a body, the power of the people as represented, however imperfectly, in their assemblies. This is not to say that it is worth trying to argue that Rome was a democracy. It *is* to say that in many respects it was more like, say, the classical Athenian democracy than we have allowed ourselves to think. Certainly the people were subject to influence from above. But it was in a large number of cases a matter of competing, conflicting, or contradictory influences: invariably when they acted as jurors or decided election to office, and very frequently when they voted on laws, the people were exercising the power to decide between claims or proposals made to them from above. This brings us to the third reason why the traditional picture is misleading. The vehicle through which such claims or proposals reached them was oratory. It is the greatest weakness of the presuppositions about social and political structure which have dominated much modern writing—at least in English and German—on the Roman Republic for more than half a century, that they have made us deaf both to the voice of the orator and to the reactions of the crowd gathered in the Comitium (the archaic meeting place), and Forum, on the Capitol or in the Campus Martius.

Polybius witnessed the exercise of Roman political and military power first from a distance, as an increasingly important member of an allied state, the Achaean League, and then, from close up, as a deportee in Rome. It will be convenient to do likewise and come gradually to the real centres of power, the Senate house, the Comitium, and the Forum.

---

3. M. Gelzer, *Die Nobilität der römischen Republik* (1912), 106 = *The Roman Nobility*, trans. R. Seager (1969), 127.

Political Authority and External Relations

To the peoples of the Mediterranean world Roman commanders—consuls or praetors in their year of office, or prorogued for a second year (and very occasionally more)—could seem like kings, disposing of large armies, sending and receiving embassies, corresponding with kings or negotiating with them in person, destroying or sparing cities, selling whole populations into slavery. In the Greek world they could take on quite precise roles fulfilled by kings: Flamininus presided at the Nemean games (Plut., *Flam.* 12), which Philip V had attended a few years before (Pol. 10, 26, 1); Aemilius Paullus placed his own statue on a base intended for one of Perseus at Delphi (Plut., *Aem.* 28, 2), and used the royal library and hunting grounds (*Aem.* 28, 6; Pol. 31, 29, 3–6). If only one Roman *imperator*, Scipio Africanus, had actually been hailed as a king, by the Spaniards (Pol. 10, 38; 40), the comparison was quite conscious, and was formally expressed in the decorations which the Senate sent as honours to allied kings.[4]

But of course this "monarchic" power was confined in time and space and restricted by the processes of the Roman constitution. Ennius might represent Scipio as claiming the sole right to immortality (*Epig.* 23–24 Vahlen/3–4 Warmington); but individual power and ambition were still effectively restrained. No office could be gained without popular election. The provinces to be allotted each year, and the prorogations of last year's office-holders, were decided, almost invariably, by the Senate, as soon as the consuls entered office on 15 March. Almost invariably, because even after the prorogations and provinces had been decided and the lot drawn, the arrangements could be changed by a decree of the Senate (*senatus consultum*) followed by a *plebiscitum* (a law passed by the plebeian assembly—the *concilium plebis*) (Livy 35, 20, 9); or the tribunes, by a law proposed directly to the people, could attempt to upset a prorogation which had been decided in advance (41, 6, 2). In normal times the lot decided which consul or which praetor took which province,[5] and the lot thus gave or removed what might be a man's only chance for a famous victory. If the chance were not taken in the year of office, it was either lost forever to a man's successor (see, e.g., Pol. 38, 8, 3, on 147 B.C.), or could only be kept alive by prorogation. Hence, as Polybius records (18, 9–12), the terms offered by Flamininus to Philip V depended on whether he

---

4. E. Rawson, "Caesar's Heritage: Hellenistic Kings and Their Roman Equals," *JRS* 65 (1975): 148.

5. For a contemporary reflection of this, see Ennius, *Ann.* 329 Vahlen/325 Warmington: "Greece was assigned to Sulpicius by the lot, and Gallia to Cotta" (200 B.C.).

would be prorogued or not. Relatively mild terms could have been proposed, and the war ended in spring 197. But prorogation was decided, and the consuls were both allotted Gaul; therefore Flamininus' emissaries to the Senate recommended offering harsh terms to Philip, and peace was not made. Only then was the way open for Cynoscephalae.

The spheres of activity of office-holders, the forces available to them, and the finances allotted all depended, therefore, on a debate and vote conducted in the Senate at the beginning of each year. Thereafter, for the rest of the year, time and distance might remove immediate strategic and diplomatic decision making from the collective political process in Rome, and leave it to the discretion of the commander in the field. But yet a consul on campaign, at least in Italy, might think of consulting the Senate (Livy 41, 1, 1), or actually do so (40, 16, 5–6). Communities in the area concerned might report to the Senate that a consul had left his province, and emissaries be sent by the Senate to tell him to return (43, 1, 7–12). When one consul suffered defeat in Histria in 178, the Senate instructed the other to leave Liguria and cross over to Gallia, raising troops from the communities there (41, 5, 5). The Senate might even circulate allied cities and leagues in the Greek East with a decree of the Senate to the effect that they should not obey requests for forces from Roman commanders in the area, unless these were in accordance with the terms set by the Senate (Pol. 28, 13, 11; 16, 1; Livy 43, 17, 2).

Moreover, all the dealings and agreements of Roman commanders with foreign peoples were conditional and were subject to subsequent ratification in Rome by the Senate and (surprisingly often) by the people. It is not merely that Polybius repeatedly records that treaties made in the field were subject to ratification by the people;[6] but documentary evidence shows how office-holders abroad spoke as the representatives of Senate and People. Or rather the other way round. For in the only surviving contemporary Latin document which illustrates decision making in the provinces, Aemilius Paullus, as proconsul in Further Spain in 189, lays down that a group of people should be free and retain their land, "so long as the Roman People and Senate wish it."[7] The sequence is instructive.

Had this group been dissatisfied, however, their only recourse would have been to send an embassy to the Senate, and to the Senate alone. For there is no evidence that foreign embassies were ever brought to speak before the people. In this crucial respect Rome did offer a marked contrast to the Athenian democracy. Hence there arose the image abroad, perfectly reflected in

6. E.g., Pol. 21, 17, 9; 24, 2–3; 30, 16; 32, 1; cf. Livy 32, 23, 2.
7. *ILS* 15; Degrassi, *ILLRP*² 514.

the first book of Maccabees (8), of the 320 counsellors sitting every day and deciding major affairs of state. It is not necessary to give examples of the endless sequence of foreign embassies which came to speak in the Senate. One documentary example of a response by the Senate will do, namely the letter in which Spurius Postumius, praetor in 189, wrote to tell the Amphictyonic League what the Senate had decided in response to its embassy on rights of asylum.[8] The Senate was also the only body in Rome which sent ambassadors. Thus we find the young Aemilius Lepidus, as ambassador to Philip V in 200, reminding the king of what the Senate had decided (Pol. 16, 34, 3); or Popilius Laenas beginning his famous confrontation with Antiochus IV outside Alexandria in 168 by handing the king the text of a decree of the Senate (Pol. 29, 27, 2).

The Senate thus exercised a real governmental, even, one might say, parliamentary, function in debating the replies to foreign embassies. It was of course in the Senate in 167, and in response to an embassy, that Cato delivered his speech on behalf of the Rhodians.[9] People in the Greek cities knew very well that their diplomatic efforts might need to extend beyond Roman commanders in the field to reach the Senate itself in Rome (*Syll.*[3] 591); and also that, once there, they must also go the rounds of the houses of individual senators, to pay their respects and gain support.[10]

Thus, as Polybius explicitly states (6, 13, 6–9), those who came on diplomatic business to Rome in the absence of the consuls could not but think of Roman government as essentially aristocratic. Yet, as Polybius himself makes clear, that was not the whole story, even as regards war and foreign affairs. The declaration of war and the making of peace treaties both depended on the votes of the people. Often, of course, the people simply ratified proposals put to them by a magistrate, following a decree of the Senate. So it was with the declaration of war on Antiochus III in 191 (Livy 36, 1, 4–6), with Scipio's settlement of Asia in 189 (Pol. 21, 24, 2–3), with peace with Aetolia in the same year (21, 32, 1), and with the declaration of war on Perseus in 171 (Livy 42, 30, 10–11). But the great issues of foreign relations did not always pass without public debate. In 201 the consul, Cn. Lentulus, had vetoed a decree of the Senate on peace with Carthage, whereupon two tribunes had carried

8. R. K. Sherk, *Roman Documents from the Greek East* (1969), no. 1.

9. Aulus Gellius, *NA* 6, 3 = *ORF*[3], Cato XLII; cf. Livy 45, 25, 2. See G. Calboli, *Marci Porci Catonis Oratio pro Rhodiensibus* (1978).

10. See, e.g., Livy 45, 20, 10 (cf. n. 60), and, far more important, *Syll.*[3] 656, on ambassadors from Teos acting on behalf of Abdera, on which see L. Robert, *BCH* 59 (1935): 507–13, and *REA* 62 (1960): 327, n. 2, and P. Herrmann, *ZPE* 7 (1971): 72.

a *plebiscitum*, which was followed by a vote of the Senate (Livy 30, 43, 1–4). In 200 the Senate voted for war against Philip V, and the consul, Sulpicius Galba, put a bill *(rogatio)* proposing war to the centuriate assembly. But a tribune of the plebs had made public speeches against war and accused the Senate. The proposal was rejected; when it was subsequently passed, it was after a speech to the people by the consul (Livy 31, 5, 1–8, 1). In 196 emissaries from Flamininus arrived in the Senate with proposed terms for peace with Philip. The Senate approved, but the newly elected consul, M. Claudius Marcellus, wanting the chance to fight in Greece himself, so Polybius says, spoke against peace before the people. They none the less accepted the terms, and the Senate sent ten emissaries to carry them out (Pol. 18, 42, 1–5; cf. Livy 33, 25, 4–7). In 167 a praetor, M'. Iuventius Thalna, made a speech proposing to the people the declaration of war on Rhodes, only to be dragged from the Rostra by the tribune Antonius (Pol. 30, 4, 4–6). It is in relation to this episode that Livy states that the bill had been introduced without a vote of the Senate, but that the tribunes had been reluctant to veto it; for it was the custom not to veto a proposed law until private individuals had had the opportunity of speaking for and against it (45, 21).

I will come back later to the question of the reality or otherwise of public debate in Rome. But I would emphasize here the importance of public announcement and report by office-holders to the people on matters of war and foreign affairs. When the Senate had decreed the enrolment of troops, the consul would make his announcement of the call-up before a public meeting (e.g., Livy 37, 4, 1). On one occasion, in 171, when an appeal against call-up was made to the tribunes of the plebs by twenty-three former centurions, the issue was debated before a public meeting of the people. If we follow Livy's account (42, 32, 6–35, 2), speeches were made by an ex-consul, by the consul of the year, and by a former centurion, and the appeal was then dropped.

A consul might also address the people on the subject of a war before leaving for his command, as Aemilius Paullus did in 168 (Livy 44, 22, 1–16; see Pol. 39, 1), or might return to report on the situation in a public meeting, as did Claudius Pulcher in 177 (Livy 41, 10, 13). When a victory had been won, the commander's letter might be read first in the Senate and then in a public meeting, as with Flamininus' letter in 197 (Livy 33, 24, 4). More commonly the emissaries sent by the victorious general are described as appearing in the Senate and then as being brought before a public meeting—that is, as coming out from the Senate house to the Rostra a few yards away, to make a speech reporting the victory to the people.[11]

11. E.g., Livy 36, 21, 7–8; 37, 52, 2; 45, 2, 2–6.

When the victorious *imperator* himself returned, it was again the custom that he should address the people; or so Livy reports in recording the public speech (*contio*) given to Aemilius Paullus by the tribunes of 167 (45, 40, 9). It was in this speech that Aemilius recalled his prayer that any misfortunes which threatened the Roman people might fall on his own house—as had just happened, with the deaths of his two sons.[12]

Aemilius' triumph, in which one of the sons had appeared, only to die a few days later, had been the subject of violent public debate. Normally, as Polybius records (6, 15, 7–8), it was the Senate on whom the *imperator* was dependent for his triumph, a process which was a crucial means of collective control in an age of great individual victories.[13] But on this occasion (at least) a bill was also required, to allow Paullus, Anicius Gallus, and Cn. Octavius to retain their *imperium* on the day of the triumph. A tribune of the plebs put the bill to the people meeting on the Capitol. Here too, Livy says, the opportunity was given for private individuals to speak, and a military tribune, Servius Sulpicius Galba, an enemy of Paullus, spoke against. M. Servilius, consul of 202, intervened after the first tribes had voted against Paullus; and Cato, ignored by Livy, also spoke. Here Livy's narrative breaks off; but the triumph was of course held.[14]

The issue in this case had been the lack of generosity which Paullus had shown to his soldiers, who themselves were present in force at the voting. More often the *imperator* after his return faced accusations of corruption over the vast sums which now became available as booty. Once again, these repeated accusations, which certainly served the function of preventing a brief eminence in the field from being translated into a continued dominance at home, are quite inadequately interpreted in modern accounts as representing simply personal or factional struggles among senators. They were public accusations, enacted on public stages—which is what the Forum and Campus Martius were—and voted on by the assemblies. In considering them we should recall the frequent prosecutions of generals (*strategoi*) in the Athenian democracy. Like them, if less often, the Roman *imperator* faced the prospect of accusation in a popular court after his return home. Hence for instance Cato's speech recording and defending his conduct in Spain as consul of 195;[15] or the prosecution brought against Acilius Glabrio before the people by two

12. Val. Max. 5, 10, 2 = *ORF*³, 1 (p. 101).

13. See J. S. Richardson, "The Triumph, the Praetors and the Senate in the Early Second Century B.C.," *JRS* 65 (1975): 50.

14. Livy 45, 35, 4–39, 20. Cato's speech: Aulus Gellius, *NA* 1, 23 = *ORF*³, Cato XLIII.

15. *ORF*³, Cato IV, F. 21–55*.

tribunes in 189 (Livy 37, 57, 12–58, 1); or the accusation of Scipio Africanus. To save notorious confusions I will quote simply Polybius' account (23, 14, 1–4): there was an accusation before the people *according to the custom of the Romans*; Scipio spoke in his own defence and the people dispersed, unwilling to hear the case further. By contrast, complaints by a Chalcidian embassy in the Senate in 170 led to C. Lucretius Gallus, praetor of 171, being brought before a public meeting, a day being set (*dies dicta*) for his trial, and his condemnation to a fine by all thirty-five tribes (Livy 43, 7, 5–8, 10). When the issue arose of the improper enslavement of the Statiellates in Liguria in 173, the Senate ordered restitution; then in 172 there was a decree of the Senate and a bill setting up an enquiry, to be conducted by a praetor. But this was not a popular court, and the praetor allowed the case to lapse, overcome by influence and supplications (Livy 42, 7–9; 21–22). In this case, therefore, popular sovereignty was exercised indirectly, with ineffective results. Absolution might also be achieved by a direct appeal to the people; so, when in 149 a tribune moved a bill over the conduct of Servius Sulpicius Galba as praetor in Lusitania, and Cato supported the proposal, Galba brought his own sons and the orphaned son of C. Gallus before the people; by these means he just escaped, "having stirred the pity of the People."[16]

Cicero describes this bill as being like a *privilegium*, that is, a law passed in respect of an individual. But comparable issues could also be presented in impersonal terms, as in 187, when a bill was moved for the setting-up of an enquiry into the money acquired from Antiochus III. Public speeches were made on either side, including Cato's *de pecunia regis Antiochi*, and the bill was passed by all thirty-five tribes (Livy 38, 54–55).

Thus the great victories gained by Roman commanders were fought by annual magistrates who gained their chance by a combination of election, the lot, and, sometimes, prorogation. Their actions were liable to investigation and prosecution, and the terms on which they concluded their wars were subject to senatorial approval and the votes of the people. These processes were of course frequently ineffective in practice. For instance L. Licinius Lucullus, as consul of 151, made war on the Vaccaei in Spain, contrary to a treaty, without, as Appian says, ever being put on trial for it (*Iber.* 51–55/215–33). None the less, Polybius perhaps hardly stressed sufficiently the limits which, as yet, confined the "monarchic" element in the Roman state.

---

16. Cicero, *Brut.* 90 = Peter, *HRR*, *Origines*, F. 106 = *ORF*³, Cato LI; cf. Appian, *Iber.* 60/255, stating that he used his wealth to escape condemnation.

Italy and Rome

The situation was not wholly different as regards the relations of Italy with Rome. What is sometimes called "the Italian confederation" was not a confederation at all; this term would have surprised Polybius, who knew what a real confederation was, namely something like his own Achaean League. Rome's formal relations with Italian communities, other than citizen or Latin colonies, consisted of individual treaties, which bound the other to provide troops or naval forces; but, on a less formal and less regular basis, Roman demands for military support also affected many of its allies overseas, for instance the Aetolians, or the Achaeans themselves. Polybius had been personally involved in the contentious issue in 169 as to whether the Achaean League should assent to Appius Cento's demand that they should send a force of 5,000 men to Epirus (28, 13). Some time later, as a deportee in Rome in the mid-150s, he assisted the Epizephyrian Locrians to gain exemption from their treaty obligation to send ships for the Spanish and Dalmatian wars. It is typical of the presuppositions which we now impose on Roman politics that it can be assumed that this will have been achieved through private influence with Scipio Aemilianus (who had so far held no public office).[17] We should rather presume that the Locrians sent an embassy to the Senate, and that Polybius was asked to speak for them.

The so-called Italian confederation had in fact no collective decision-making structure. Decisions relating to Italy, or to communities within it, depended on Rome, which retained the institutions of a nuclear city-state. In other words Rome applied its normal procedure in foreign relations, the reception of embassies by the Senate. This was true even of the Latin colonies, such as Placentia and Cremona in 190 (Livy 37, 46, 9–47, 2), or Aquileia in 171 (43, 1, 5–6), just as it was of allied states. Indeed, even an embassy from a citizen colony might appear in the Senate to dispute territorial claims by a neighbouring community, as the colonists (*coloni*) of Luna did in 168 (45, 13, 10–11). It was colonisation, the spread of the citizenship, and the confiscation of land for settlement which distinguished Italy, not the supposed confederation. Otherwise, Italian allied communities differed from overseas ones only in the degree of regularity of their military obligations, and various regions of the peninsula repeatedly served as the provinces for the operations of Roman magistrates. Complaints about these operations, again, came to the Senate through embassies (e.g., Livy 39, 3, 1–2), just as with communities overseas.

17. Pol. 12, 5, 1–3. For the assumption mentioned, see Walbank's commentary.

This assumption about the standard means of communication is clearly
reflected in the decree of the Senate about the Bacchanalia in 186. It lays
down as regards the allies (*foederati*): "Let none of them have a Bacchanal. If
there are any who decide that they require to have a Bacchanal, they should
come to the urban praetor in Rome, and when their words have been heard,
the Senate should decide on the matter."[18] The Senate did indeed begin in
this period, as is well known, to issue instructions to communities in Italy.[19]
But documentary evidence shows it doing so equally abroad, as in the decrees of the Senate about Thisbae in 170, about the Serapeum of Delos circa
164 or about the territorial dispute between Priene and Magnesia some time
in the mid-century.[20]

But when the Senate replied to a self-exculpatory embassy from Tibur in
154, it is noticeable that the senators made quite explicit their role as representatives of the Roman people: "Since as regards these matters you have
been freed of blame by the Senate, you ought, we believe, to assume that you
will similarly be freed of blame by the Roman People."[21] The slight hesitation is interesting, and is to be seen against the repeated involvement of the
people in measures affecting Italy, especially those concerning land, colonies,
and the boundaries of the citizen body; the passing of such laws indeed marks
an important distinction between Italy and the other regions under Roman
domination. Only if no legislation was required could matters be handled
solely by the Senate; so, when Latin allies (*socii Latini nominis*) complained
in 187 that their citizens were migrating to Rome, the Senate could give a
praetor the task of seeking them out and sending them home (Livy 39, 3,
4–6). Equally, the Senate could rule that men from Latin colonies who had
put down their names for Roman citizen colonies could not count as Roman
citizens until the colonies were actually established.[22] But when in 177 embassies complained in the Senate about Latin immigration to Rome and also
of Samnite and Paelignian immigration to Fregellae, a Latin colony, a law
had to be passed to change the rules (Livy 41, 8, 6–12; 9, 9–12), just as it had
in 193 to extend the laws relating to loans made to Roman citizens to cover
Latins and allies (35, 7, 1–5).

When embassies came to the Senate from Latin colonies asking for supplementary *coloni*, the Senate (it seems) could decide on a favourable reply. But,

18. *ILS* 18; *FIRA*² I, 30.

19. See, e.g., A. H. McDonald, "Rome and the Italian Confederation (200–186 B.C.)," *JRS* 34 (1944): 11.

20. Sherk (n. 8), nos. 2, 5, and 7.

21. *ILS* 19; *FIRA*² I, 33.

22. Livy 34, 42, 5–6; for this interpretation see Briscoe's commentary.

to carry out the decision, *triumviri* still had to be elected by the people.[23] New colonies certainly involved the full procedure of a decree of the Senate followed by a *plebiscitum* for the election of three men (*triumviri*), conducted by one of the praetors (Livy 34, 53, 1–2; cf. 35, 40, 5–6). But when in 197 the tribune of the plebs C. Atinius passed a law to establish five new citizen colonies on the coast (32, 29, 3–4), Livy does not expressly state that the Senate had already approved, though it may have done so. The basic principle that Roman public land in Italy was available for the profit of the Roman people had been reflected already in the tribunician law passed in 232 by Flaminius, without prior senatorial assent, for the viritane distribution of land in the Ager Gallicus. It is surely significant that Polybius, writing his second book long before the tribunate of Tiberius Gracchus, saw this as the beginning of the corruption of the people.[24] As yet there was little open conflict over colonies or the use of public land, though cattle breeders could be tried before the people (33, 42, 10), and a tribune of 172 could pass a law to compel the censors to lease out the Ager Campanus (42, 19, 1). Seven years later the Senate gave the urban praetor, P. Cornelius Lentulus, the task of buying out the private landholders who occupied large parts of the Ager Campanus, and thus restoring it to effective public use. It is noteworthy that he had a bronze map of the land in question put up for public inspection in the Atrium Libertatis (Gran. Licin., 9–10 Flem.). But, at least down to the late 170s, newly conquered land was still available for distribution in northern Italy (Livy 13, 4, 3–4). It was to be when major conflict arose over the existing stock of public land in Italy that the Roman revolution began.[25]

Equally, it was for the people to extend the Roman citizenship if they so wished. Our only illustration of the large-scale process by which (as it seems) all the communities with the citizenship without the vote gained the full citizenship is the law of 188 passed by a tribune to give the citizenship to Formiae, Fundi, and Arpinum. Four other tribunes interceded because there had been no prior decree of the Senate but desisted "when instructed that it was the right of the people, not the Senate, to give the vote to whom it wished" (38, 36, 7–9). This evidence forms a useful complement to Polybius' observation, which he relates to the use of the veto, that the tribunes' role is to carry out the wishes of the people (6, 16, 5).

23. Livy 37, 46, 9–47, 2; 39, 55, 4–9; 43, 17, 1.

24. Pol. 2, 21, 7–8; see *MRR* 1, 225. For a discussion of the view that this remark was inserted after 133 B.C., see Walbank's commentary.

25. For the best exposition of various related themes, see P. A. Brunt, "The Army and the Land in the Roman Revolution," *JRS* 52 (1962): 69.

The Internal Regulation of Society and Government

If controversy is rarely attested as regards the exploitation and management of Italy, the same is hardly true of the internal regulation of the Roman community itself. Here too, we should give the proper emphasis to the rules which expressed the power of the people over its elected magistrates.[26] Already from the previous century we may note not merely the Lex Claudia, but the tribunician law of 242: "Let the urban praetor now in office, and any future holder, have two lictors in attendance and give justice between the citizens up to the last hour of the day."[27] In similar vein the tribunician Lex Silia of the second half of the third century had established fixed weights and measures, and imposed a fine on any magistrate who contravened them.[28] Then, at some point between 242 and 124, a tribunician Lex Papiria obliged the urban praetor to see to the election of "three men in charge of capital cases" (*tresviri capitales*), and laid on them in their turn the duty of judging in accordance with the laws.[29] A tribune could also carry a *plebiscitum* to compel the magistrates in office in a particular year to follow a certain course, as Terentius Culleo did in 189, in obliging the censors to enrol all of free birth (Plut., *Flam.* 18, 1).[30] Perhaps even more significant is the standing obligation on all magistrates to take an oath to obey the laws within five days of assuming office (Livy 31, 50, 6–7).

It hardly needs to be said that this period saw a steady evolution of the rules and conventions regulating the conditions of access to office; L. Villius' tribunician law of 180 on the ages at which magistracies might be held is merely the most prominent of them.[31] Changes in the rules, or the creation of new offices, required a vote of the people, as in the creation of "three men in charge of the public feasts" (*tresviri epulones*) in 196 (Livy 33, 42, 1), or the law to allow military tribunes to be appointed by the *imperatores* in 171 (42,

26. For the notion of a *lex* as the expression of the collective power of the people, see, e.g., F. Serrao, *Classi, partiti e legge nella repubblica romana* (1974), 63ff.

27. Censorinus, *De die natali* 24, 3; *FIRA*[2] I, 3; P. F. Girard, F. Senn, and V. Giuffrè, *Les Lois des romains*[7] (1977), no. 3 (p. 83). See now M. Crawford, ed., *Roman Statutes* I–II (London, 1996), no. 44.

28. Festus 288L; *FIRA*[2] I, 1; Girard et al. (n. 27), no. 1. See now Crawford (n. 27), no. 46.

29. Festus 468L; *FIRA*[2] I, 2; Girard et al. (n. 27), no. 2. See now Crawford (n. 27), no. 45.

30. It has long been disputed what groups are really referred to here. For a recent discussion, see M. Humbert, *Municipium et civitas sine suffragio* (1978), 351–52, suggesting *cives sine suffragio* (citizens without the vote) rather than sons of freedmen. In that case this issue would be closely related to that of 188.

31. Livy 40, 44, 1. See A. E. Astin, *The Lex Annalis before Sulla* (1958); G. Rögler, "Die Lex Villia Annalis," *Klio* 40 (1962): 76; R. Develin, *Patterns in Office-Holding, 366–49 B.C.* (1979).

31, 5). Much more significant is the fact that problems over office-holding, and disputes between office-holders, were resolved either by legislation by an assembly, or by a trial before a popular court. Thus the tribunes of 200 passed a *plebiscitum* to allow the flamen Dialis to have a substitute take his oath as curule aedile for him (31, 50, 7–9); by contrast, in 189 when the pontifex maximus forbade a later flamen Dialis to go to his province as praetor, and imposed a fine, appeal was made to the tribunes, and the case was heard before the people (37, 51, 1–5). In 180 the pontifex maximus ordered a *duumvir navalis* (an official in charge of the fleet) to abdicate before being appointed to a priesthood as *rex sacrorum*. When he refused, the pontifex again imposed a fine, the *duumvir* appealed and the case was heard by the thirty-five tribes (40, 42, 8–10). In 169 a complex conflict between the censors and a tribune of the plebs involved a series of moves, all in public—the imposition of a fine before a public meeting, the promulgation of a bill, speeches on either side, and finally the trial of the censors for treason before the centuriate assembly. A public demonstration by the first men of the state was just enough to ensure acquittal, with a mere eight centuries lacking for condemnation (43, 16).

We do not always know whether laws for the regulation of society occasioned public controversy or not. What we do know is firstly that they were seen as being imposed by the people—"many laws did the people pass on your account," as Curculio says to the money-lenders in Plautus' play (*Curc.* 509). Secondly, the office-holder concerned will have made a speech proposing a law to the people; but others might also speak, for or against, as we know (for example) of the Lex Cincia of 204 (Cic., *Cato* 10) or the Lex Voconia of 169.[32] Equally, Cato as consul of 195 spoke in public against the abrogation of the Lex Oppia, as proposed by two tribunes; but it was abrogated all the same (Livy 34, 1, 1–8, 3). He seems to have spoken similarly against abrogation of the tribunician Lex Orchia of 182, regulating expenditure on dinners; whether it was in fact abrogated remains unclear (*ORF*[3], Cato XLV).[33]

Even when a formal vote by the people may not have been in question, we can see a tendency (as with reports of military operations) both to direct persuasion and information at the people in the form of speeches, and to conduct ritual actions in public before them (see text to nn. 78–80). Thus, as Polybius records (31, 25, 5), it was in a speech to the people that Cato made his complaint that slave boys sold for more than fields, and jars of pickled

32. *ORF*[3], Cato XL, F. 156–60. Cato's advocacy of the law "loudly and vehemently" was clearly in public, addressed to the people.

33. *ORF*[3], Cato XXXV; cf. H. H. Scullard, *Roman Politics, 220–150 B.C.*[2] (1973), 263–66.

fish for more than slaves employed as ploughmen. The sumptuary laws of this period may indeed be understood "in the context of the urgent need of the second-century aristocracy to preserve the cohesion of the group."[34] But popular attitudes are relevant also. As Cicero was to say, commenting on an incident in 129, the Roman people appreciated public magnificence and hated private luxury (*Mur.* 75–6). Plutarch, however, alleges that Cato also spoke to the people against the distribution of corn or money (*Cato* 8, 1). The occasion for some or all of these speeches may have been his censorship, when we know that he justified in a speech to the people his omission of L. Quinctius Flamininus from the Senate.[35] Similarly, in the Bacchanal affair the actual steps were taken by the Senate (see text to nn. 18–20); but the consuls still ascended the Rostra, addressed the people on the issue and announced rewards for informers (Livy 39, 15, 1–17, 3). For these rewards the Senate had been able to vote money from the state treasury (*aerarium*); but on the question of allowing P. Aebutius exemption from military service, and from being assigned a public horse (*equus publicus*), and of granting special rights in private law to Faecenia Hispala, a tribune of the plebs had to put a *plebiscitum* to the people (39, 19, 3–7). For these were exceptions as against the normal rules of the community.

Election to Public Office

I do indeed wish to suggest that we have somehow left out of our conceptions of the working of the Roman state both open conflict on issues and the importance of all forms of oratory addressed to the people. The second of these at least, so it has often been held, does not apply to elections. The elections, on this view, were determined from above by the operations of *clientela* and other forms of dependence. Not programmes or political attitudes, but persons — or even membership of a particular *familia* or *gens* — decided the results; it is a sign of this that the candidates did not make election speeches to the people. The entire process, therefore, although formally democratic in varying degrees, depending on whether it involved the tribal assembly or *centuriata*, was in reality a charade, determined by a self-perpetuating oligarchy, the *nobiles*.[36]

34. M. Crawford, *The Roman Republic* (1978), 79.

35. Plut., *Flam.* 18–19; Livy 39, 42, 5–12, does not make it explicit that the speech was to the people.

36. For the conventional view, see, e.g., J. Suolahti, *The Junior Officers of the Roman Army in the Republican Period* (1955), 15: "For in the elections no real freedom of choice existed

This view would have surprised Plautus, who reflects the conception that public office was an *honor* bestowed by the vote (*suffragium*) of the people (*Bacch.* 438). It is entirely in consonance with this that it was the custom for a consul designate to ascend the Rostra and make a speech of thanks to the people (Plut., *Aem. Paul.* 11, 1). The standard view rests on a series of presumptions, in the light of which the evidence can be read; some of these presumptions have already been disproved in recent work. As for *clientela* and dependence, there will be more to say later (text to nn. 66–69). However, as regards *familiae* and *gentes* no one, of course, will dispute the importance of descent in Roman public life. It is Polybius himself (6, 53–4) who records both the display of ancestral death masks (*imagines*) at the funerals of prominent Romans, and the custom by which a son or other relative mounted the Rostra and discoursed to the people on the virtues of the deceased, and then of his ancestors, beginning with the most ancient. But, here again, we have information and persuasion addressed to the people, publicly, from the Rostra. To Cato it was a custom which belonged in the past that after dinner, in private, the diners had sung "the praises and virtues of famous men."[37] In his own day it was in public, in the Forum, and by the medium of oratory that the services of office-holding families were rehearsed repeatedly before the people at large.

Since 264 the occasion of a prominent funeral had been further underlined by recommendations of a more concrete kind, in the form of funeral games, first with gladiatorial displays, then with theatrical performances as well. The scale of the shows grew rapidly, from three pairs of gladiators performing in the Forum Boarium in 264, to twenty-two in 216, twenty-five in 200, and sixty in 183, accompanied by a distribution of sacrificial meat (*visceratio*) and a dinner in the Forum. In 174 a mere thirty-seven pairs fought in the funeral games for Flamininus, but accompanied by a distribution of sacrificial meat, a banquet, and theatrical shows for four days.[38] We know from Polybius, speaking of the gladiatorial show which accompanied the funeral of Aemilius Paullus, that a good performance cost some thirty talents, or 720,000 HS (31, 28, 5–6). Once again, these were displays directed to the public at large.

---

among the electorate, since their decisions were guided by numerous bondages and ties, from family relations and friendships to factors such as *clientela* and bribery." Earlier critiques of this view are P. A. Brunt, *Social Conflicts in the Roman Republic* (1971); Crawford (n. 34), 35–37; K. Hopkins, *Death and Renewal* (1983), 36–37.

37. Cic., *Tusc. Disp.* 4, 2, 3; Peter, *HRR, Origines,* F. 118.

38. See G. Ville, *La gladiature en Occident des origines à la mort de Domitien* (1981), 42–43.

But if the importance of direct descent from former holders of office was ever more emphatically stressed to the public, the more general presumptions of modern scholarship can now be seen to be exaggerated. Firstly, there is no clear proof, as regards the historical period, that a Roman *gens* was a significant element in society, with a known membership and boundaries, defined functions or common interests. Recent demolitions of the long-supposed fundamental importance of the *genos* in Greek society should make us very cautious here.[39]

Secondly, it has recently been demonstrated by Brunt, and in even more detail by Hopkins and Burton, that there was more fluidity in the occupation of office over generations than previous theories presupposed.[40] These analyses of course confirm what is undeniable, that the higher the offices reached by a man's immediate ancestors the better his chances of high office himself. Yet succession to office-holding in the same family depended on the birth of sons and on their survival to the right age, on the financial resources of the family, and on willingness to enter public life. As a result, for instance, while two-fifths of consuls were the sons of consuls, as many as one-third had no consular ancestor in the previous three generations; only one-third of consuls had a son who was also consul. This very figure, however, demonstrates a substantial degree of social bias in the occupation of the consulate. The prestige of families and the importance of descent certainly made high office harder to obtain the lower the rank achieved by immediate ancestors. But there was constant fluidity; and in exceptional cases, like that of Cato, a man with no office-holding ancestors could rise, by election, to be consul and censor.

Thirdly, the much-used term "the patrician-plebeian nobility" is variously misleading. *Nobilis*, or *nobilitas*, was never a technical term, like peerage, referring to a closed and legally defined group; these words are *descriptions*, appearing in late republican literature. Even the late-republican semi-technical usage—whether confined, as Gelzer thought, to descendants of consuls or their equivalents, or applied, as Brunt has shown, to those of a wider group of office-holders—happens not to be specifically attested in the (admittedly slight) surviving literature of our period.[41] We are not entitled to *assume* that

39. See F. Bourriot, *Recherches sur la nature du Genos* (1976); D. Roussel, *Tribu et cité* (1976). See S. C. Humphreys, "Fustel de Coulanges and the Greek 'Genos,'" *Sociologia del Diritto* 3 (1982): 35.

40. P. A. Brunt, "*Nobilitas* and *Novitas*," *JRS* 72 (1982): 1; Hopkins (n. 36), chap. 2: "Political Succession in the Late Republic, 249–50 B.C." (with G. P. Burton).

41. Brunt (n. 40). The word *nobilitas* is attested, Plautus, *Captivi* 299, but in a related, non-specific sense.

this semi-technical usage was already current. Moreover, the application of these terms, both in the late Republic and in modern works, to any descendants, however remote, of the relevant office-holders conceals considerable fluctuations in the occupation of office over generations.

Finally, as regards our conception of office-holding in this period, we have perfectly clear evidence as to what succession to office would have been like if there had in fact been no open competition, and if the apparently democratic elections had in reality masked an effective process of co-optation managed from above. For the colleges of priests were still filled by co-optation, and the occupation of priesthoods shows the common acquisition of the role at an early age, retention for life, and a high rate of succession within families, including direct succession from father to son.[42] It is hardly surprising that transfer of the right of appointment to be in the gift of the people was to be put forward as a bill in 145 (Cic., *Lael.* 96), and achieved in 103.

If we go back, once again, to Polybius, he tells us, firstly, that cavalrymen were liable for ten years' military service and, secondly, that no one could hold office who had not completed ten years' service (6, 19, 2–4). It is thus reasonable, if not absolutely certain, to accept the view of Gelzer, argued more fully by Nicolet, that the census rating of an equestrian, whatever it was in this period, was a prerequisite for public office.[43] Public life was thus not only strongly influenced by descent, but was, in a strict sense, timocratic. That is all that Polybius says about qualification for office, other than his remark that it is one of the prerogatives of the people to bestow honour ($\tau\iota\mu\acute{\eta}$)—or, in different words, "to give magistracies to those who are worthy, which is the fairest reward of excellence [$\kappa\alpha\lambda o\kappa\alpha\gamma\alpha\theta\acute{\iota}\alpha$] in the state" (6, 14, 4 and 9). This is a significant aspect of what he means by the "aristocratic" element in the Roman system.

The only other point which Polybius makes about elections is that, whereas at Carthage people gain office by openly offering gifts, in Rome the penalty for that is death (6, 56, 4). Laws on bribery (*ambitus*) are known to have been passed in 181 and 159, though nothing is known of their content. But the fact that the need was felt to take measures against electoral malpractice is a clear hint that adequate support could not be secured on the basis of personal relations of dependence. So too is the rising level of display and munificence directed to the public at large. Triumphs, which were the subject of repeated debate in the Senate, and on one occasion by the people

42. See D. E. Hahn, "The Roman Nobility and the Three Major Priesthoods, 218–167 B.C.," *TAPhA* 94 (1963): 73; G. B. Szemler, *The Priests of the Roman Republic* (1972).

43. Gelzer (n. 3), 7; C. Nicolet, "Le cens sénatorial sous la République et sous Auguste," *JRS* 66 (1976): 20.

(see text to n. 14), could also be accompanied by shows lasting many days, as in that of Scipio Africanus in 201 (Pol. 16, 23, 7). Polybius also records the temporary theatre erected in the Circus by L. Anicius in association with his triumph in 162 (30, 22). More common was the device of votive games. If the Senate approved, a sum could be set aside from the money carried in a triumph to fulfil the vow made to a god in the event of victory. So L. Fulvius Nobilior's triumph over Aetolia in 186 was distinguished by performers from Greece, the first athletic competition ever held in Rome, and a hunt of lions and panthers (Livy 39, 5, 7–10; 22, 1). But by 182 the Senate felt the need to restrict the means of gathering resources for games, and in 179 laid down that expenditure should not exceed the total spent on Nobilior's triumph in 186 (Livy 40, 44, 8–12).

Such displays by consuls or proconsuls could be of direct relevance to the future electoral prospects of the man himself (as opposed to his sons) only in the rare case of a possible second consulship, or for the most vigorously contested election of all, for the censorship — an office which, as we sometimes forget, gave far more, and more continuous, political power *in Rome* than any other. So M'. Acilius Glabrio, who had triumphed in 190 (Livy 37, 46, 2–6), was a formidable candidate for the censorship in 189, above all "because he had given largesses, by which he had attracted a large part of the population to himself" (37, 57, 10–11). But at a lower level, the curule aedileship, the giving of elaborate shows was becoming regularly associated with office — for instance, the first theatrical shows to be put on at the Megalesia, in 194 (34, 54, 3), or the sixty-three panthers and forty bears and elephants shown at the circus games in 169 (44, 18, 8). It is impossible not to see these as competitive gestures designed to win popular favour and enhance future electoral prospects. Like funeral orations and games, and like triumphs (whose public image is reflected in Plautus, *Bacchides* 1069–75), these displays were directed to the public at large — not to defined groups of supporters but to whatever section of the populace happened to turn up.

As regards the elections themselves, we had better start by admitting how little we know. Granted that ten years' military service was a prerequisite, as was (almost certainly) the census of an equestrian, how many men typically sought any public office in each generation, and how many tried, and failed, to reach the higher offices? In other words how far did unwillingness to stand, lack of funds, or an anticipation of failure serve to limit competition from the beginning? We know for instance that Cato's great-grandfather, presumably born around 330, had served as a cavalryman, and was thus probably qualified for office (Plut., *Cato* 1, 1). Did neither he, nor the grandfather, nor the father choose to stand, or did they try and suffer defeat?

It was clearly common, though in no way formally required, that a man's first public office should be as one of the twenty-four military tribunes elected each year by the tribal assembly; this is at any rate known of all three of the figures from this period of whom we have biographies: Cato, Flamininus, and Aemilius Paullus. Was there competition already at this level? All we know is that in 151 a crisis was created by the *absence* of candidates (Pol. 35, 4, 4), which clearly implies that in normal years there were at least enough. If we think only of the normal twenty-four successful candidates (subtracting the older men, even ex-consuls, who might still hold this post), mortality alone will clearly not have reduced competition to the two who would hold the consulship twenty to twenty-five years later. But our literary evidence hardly ever dwells on the competition for offices lower than the consulship or censorship, and not always even there. A single chance item records that Aemilius Paullus had twelve competitors for the aedileship of 193 (Plut., *Aem. Paul.* 3, 1), all of whom were said to have subsequently reached the consulship; the implication is evidently that it would have been normal that not all of them would achieve the consulship. However, Antiochus Epiphanes' performances in the agora of Antioch strongly suggest that competition was normal in elections for the aedileship and tribunate. We should also remember the normal preliminaries to a political career which Polybius notes— greeting men in the Forum and engaging in advocacy in order to recommend oneself to the people. That point is exactly matched by Plautus' representation in *Menaechmi* (571–601) of men seeking as many *clientes* as possible, in cases before the people or *in iure* (before the praetor) or *ad iudicem* (before a judge)—all taking place in the Forum. Alternatively Plutarch implies (*Cato* 1, 4) that Cato built up his earliest support by advocacy in towns and villages outside Rome; what courts Plutarch means to refer to is not clear.[44]

Advocacy must have created some obligations on the part of the persons represented (it is significant that the tribunician Lex Cincia of 204 had made illegal more concrete expressions of gratitude); it will also, perhaps more important, have established a reputation as an orator among the citizens who voted in judicial assemblies, or just those who were anyway to be found in the Forum area, and might provide an audience. But when we come to the electoral process itself, as has often been noted, we do not seem to find formal election speeches either by the candidates themselves or by their supporters. In one case, however, the censorial election of 184, Livy (39, 41, 3–4) does

44. Possibly the reference is to cases before the *Praefecti iure dicundo* (as Professor Brunt suggests to me). See P. A. Brunt, *Italian Manpower* (1971), 528–35, and Humbert (n. 30), 356–57.

seem to imply that Cato made public statements in support of his own candi-
dature and that of Valerius Flaccus, and Plutarch explicitly states that he made
speeches from the Rostra (*Cato* 16, 5–8). The normal pattern, however, was
different: the candidate in his white toga appeared in the Forum (cf. Polybius 10, 4, 9–5, 1) and solicited votes, and his supporters did likewise on his
behalf. It was only because he was actually consul, and about to conduct the
election himself, that it was thought improper that Claudius Pulcher canvassed for his brother in the elections in spring 184. His canvassing consisted
of rushing about the Forum, accompanied by his brother, to the shouts of
his opponents and the majority of the Senate (Livy 39, 32, 5–13). A similar
scene is presented by Livy's description of the consular elections of spring
192 (35, 10). The patrician place was contested by Cn. Manlius Vulso, eventually consul in 189; P. Cornelius Scipio, successful in the following year, 191,
supported by his cousin, Scipio Africanus; and L. Quinctius Flamininus, supported by his brother, who exploited his more recent military glory, and his
brother's role in it, to win the place.

All six competitors for the consulship of 192 were in fact successful within
a few years. One or two unsuccessful campaigns could indeed be expected;
but Livy is probably right to imply elsewhere that to be rejected three times
could be a source of reproach (39, 32, 6–8; 40, 37, 6). If so, it is more than
likely that there was a degree of self-selection and that men would be wary
of the public shame of rejection. Even at the level of the consulship we can
hardly pursue this point further, for Livy does not record for every year even
who the unsuccessful candidates were.[45] It is possible to list 174 holders of the
praetorship between 218 and 166 who never held the consulship;[46] but we
cannot tell how many of them ever stood for it. Especially for men of relatively undistinguished ancestry, a lower office may often well have seemed
to confer glory enough.

Finally, as regards the censorship, all the known candidates in this period
were ex-consuls. Contested elections were common, again on the basis of
one patrician and one plebeian place, but are not attested for every occasion.[47]
It is more than likely that not all ex-consuls sought this office.

It is better in any case to leave aside the special conditions of the quinquennial election of two censors, and to look at the entire process of the

45. For contested consular elections, see, e.g., Livy 35, 24, 4–5 (for 191); 37, 47, 6–7 (189);
39, 32, 5–13 (184); 41, 28, 4 (173, no names given).

46. Hopkins (n. 36), 46.

47. Contested elections for the censorship: 32, 7, 2 (199, no names given); 37, 57, 9–58,
2 (189); 39, 40, 1–41, 4 (184); 43, 14, 1(169).

annual elections. This produced in each year twenty-four military tribunes, ten tribunes of the plebs, two curule and two plebeian aediles, probably ten quaestors,[48] six praetors from 197 onwards (six and four alternately from perhaps 181; Livy 40, 44, 2), and two consuls, not to speak of minor offices such as the *tresviri capitales* (three men in charge of capital cases); the total, therefore, comes to more than fifty annually elected offices. We have of course some hints as to factors which were relevant in producing success or failure. As emphasized earlier, descent from office-holding ancestors was repeatedly stressed before the Roman people. It is clear too that a man's relatives in his own generation, a brother or a cousin, would lend active public support in an electoral campaign. In a different context, that of a trial, Livy records that P. Cornelius Nasica, speaking in defence of Scipio Africanus, recalled in a speech the glories of the Cornelian *gens* in general and of his own branch (*familia*) of it in particular (38, 58, 3–59, 10). Beyond that, Livy implies that it was surprising that P. Cornelius Scipio should have been rejected for the consulship for 192, although not only was his cousin Africanus canvassing for him, but the *Cornelia gens* was supporting him, and a Cornelius (L. Cornelius Merula) was conducting the election (35, 10, 9). In this last point there has long seemed to lie one of the keys to the electoral process; but Rilinger's study has shown that the role of the person conducting the elections was severely restricted by convention, public opinion, and the essential fact that the entire process was conducted in public.[49]

What factors were most important over the entire range of annual elections we do not know.[50] We can, however, reasonably accept that an important part was played by descent, by the support of relatives if a man came from a famous family, gratitude on the part of former *clientes* in court, by reputation as an orator, and by glory won on the field of battle. But all these factors had to be re-emphasized in a public process of competition immediately before the election. No source explicitly attests that a *cliens* was under an obligation to vote for his *patronus*, still less for a political ally of his *patronus*.

That descent played a more important part the higher the office concerned is not surprising, and should not of itself lead us to characterize the entire process as non-democratic. Aristotle had regarded the direct popular election of archons in Solon's constitution as an aristocratic aspect of it (*Pol.* 2,

48. W. V. Harris, "The Development of the Quaestorship 267–81 B.C.," *CQ* 26 (1976): 92.

49. W. Rilinger, *Der Einfluss des Wahlleiters bei den römischen Konsulwahlen von 336 bis 50 v. Chr.* (1976).

50. For a useful discussion, see A. E. Astin, *Scipio Aemilianus* (1967), 28–29, and 337, note B.

12, 1273b). The implied contrast is with appointment by lot, which played no role in Rome—except of course in the vital area of the distribution of provinces. But in the fifth-century Athenian democracy, to which appointment by lot was fundamental, the people, so the Old Oligarch observed (1, 3), none the less had the sense to fill the major military offices of the *strategia* and the *hipparchia* by election, and to leave them to their social superiors.

The voting behaviour of the Athenian *demos* (and the self-selection of candidates for the *strategia*?) in the first two-thirds or so of the fifth century clearly did in fact exhibit a marked class bias, as is shown not least by the reaction to the rise of the "new politicians" in the Peloponnesian War.[51] But it would be quite wrong to draw from the evident fact of deferential voting the conclusion that Athens of the earlier fifth century was not a democracy. To raise the same question about Rome in the first half of the second century is not of course to assert an identity, or even close resemblance. It is to ask whether we have not misconstrued the character of republican politics by not taking seriously enough the democratic element which Polybius believed himself to have observed.

The Democratic Element and Its Limits in the Classical Republic

Two of the three elements which Polybius discovered in the republican political system are hardly controversial today. Firstly, no one will dispute the "monarchic" power wielded by consuls and praetors, proconsuls and propraetors, when actually in the field. Even so, I have tried to indicate the extent of their real dependence, in various ways, on Senate and people (see text to nn. 11–16). Nor will anyone dispute the "aristocratic" (not, it should be noted, "oligarchic") element, namely the centrality of the role of the Senate. To talk of it as a "government,"[52] however, is quite misleading; for the term itself is anachronistic when applied to an ancient city-state. But on the other hand Nicolet has emphasized in important recent work that it is also unrealistic to see all the Senate's functions as "advisory."[53] Its votes produced effective decisions on (for instance) the provinces to be filled each year, the size of the forces to be raised, the answers to be given to embassies and the award of triumphs. It is indeed precisely in such areas that our sources show it debating, and providing an arena for personal conflicts, in a manner analo-

51. See W. R. Connor, *The New Politicians of Fifth-Century Athens* (1971).

52. So, perhaps surprisingly, even M. I. Finley, *Politics in the Ancient World* (1983), 88.

53. C. Nicolet, *Rome et la conquête du monde méditerranéen 264–27 avant J.-C.* I: *les structures de l'Italie romaine* (1977), 373ff.

gous to a true parliament. But once again it must be stressed how little we know of the Senate as a whole, as a political body. Under the terms of the tribunician Lex Ovinia of the later fourth century its 300 members were enrolled by the censors, in office for eighteen months out of each five-year period. If about twelve new members were needed per annum to keep up the full complement,[54] each pair of censors will have enrolled about sixty, or a fifth of the total. However, hardly any evidence from this period even illustrates the relevant criteria. For that we have to go back to the emergency enrolment of 216, when 177 were chosen, in the following order of preference: men elected to a curule magistracy since the last censorship; former aediles, tribunes of the plebs, and quaestors; holders of minor magistracies; those who had set up captured spoils at home or won a civil crown (Livy 23, 22, 10–23, 7). Similarly, it was evidently significant when a tribune of the plebs was *not* enrolled by the censors of 169/8 (Livy 45, 15, 9).

Each pair of censors will in fact have enrolled rather more than sixty members, because they also normally ejected some, often a small number; these are several times identified by Livy as men who had not held a curule office.[55] But in a famous incident Valerius Flaccus and Cato in 184/3 ejected an ex-consul, L. Quinctius Flamininus, and (see text to n. 35) justified this step in speeches before the people. In 174 the nine ejections included a praetor and an ex-praetor (n. 55).

It is clear, therefore, that membership of the Senate normally depended, in the loose way described, on election to public office; the class of elected office-holders and the class of senators were thus roughly co-extensive. Beyond that, it would be absurd to pretend that we have anything like enough evidence to characterize the attitudes, voting behaviour or personal or group attachments of its 300 members at any one time. All that we can observe is that, in those areas where the Senate had an effective right of decision, recognizable elements of political behaviour came into play. Greek ambassadors might make the rounds of senators' houses to gather support (see text to nn. 8–10). A consul might attempt by a speech in the Senate to get it to reverse the allotment of provinces for the year (Livy 38, 42, 8–13). In the highly contentious area of the granting of triumphs the friends and relatives of the *imperator* would try to use their influence. Thus a praetor of 200 returned to Rome from campaign, and speeches by himself and his friends persuaded the

54. Hopkins (n. 36), 47.

55. Thus seven of non-curule rank in 204, Livy 29, 37, 1; three in 194, 34, 44, 4; four in 189, 38, 28, 2; three in 179 (no rank given), 40, 51, 1; nine in 174, 41, 27, 2 (see below, otherwise no rank given); seven in 169, no rank given, 43, 15, 6.

Senate, against the wishes of the absent consul, to vote a triumph (Livy 31, 47, 6–49, 3). The relatives and friends of Manlius Vulso performed a similar function in 187 (38, 44, 9–50, 3), and his friends later persuaded the Senate "to curry favour with the people" by paying back the tax collected for the war (39, 7, 4–5). In the same year M. Fulvius Nobilior returned to ask the Senate to vote him a triumph. When a tribune said he would veto this until the return of the consul, M. Aemilius Lepidus, Fulvius spoke of the enmity between himself and the consul, and Sempronius Gracchus is reported to have reminded the tribune that his office had been entrusted to him by the people "for rendering assistance to and protecting the freedom of private citizens, not for bolstering up consular domination" (39, 4, 1–5, 6).

As regards the politics of senatorial decision making, what we know therefore is, firstly, the operation of publicly acknowledged individual friendships and enmities, *amicitiae* and *inimicitiae*, on the part of a few prominent persons only. The most public of all was the enmity between these same two, Aemilius Lepidus and Fulvius Nobilior, who were formally reconciled in a public ceremony after their joint election as censors for 179 (40, 45, 6–46, 15). What we do *not* know, and have no right to presume, is the existence of larger groupings or associations, "Scipionic" or "Fulvian" parties or factions,[56] covering any significant proportion of the 300 members of the Senate, or (still less) extending over successive generations. We cannot ignore the fact baldly and correctly stated by P. A. Brunt: "No such stable groups are explicitly attested at any period."[57] That being so, expressions of reservation or caution, which have often been registered,[58] are not sufficient. On the contrary, it is for those who follow the "factions hypothesis" to state what its logical and evidential foundations are.

Until that is done, we should start from what is explicitly present in the evidence. The Senate met in a variety of locations, all of which were were technically *templa* (places formally rendered sacred by inauguration) and of which the most important was the Curia Hostilia.[59] The Curia lay directly adjacent to the traditional meeting place of the people, the Comitium, so that the Senate could actually be described in contemporary documents as

56. The inapplicability and unhelpfulness of this term was demonstrated very well by R. Seager, "*Factio*: Some Observations," *JRS* 62 (1972): 53.

57. *Gnomon* 37 (1965): 189.

58. See, e.g., Astin (n. 50), 80ff., and esp. Chr. Meier, *Res Publica Amissa*[2] (1980).

59. On the meeting places of the republican Senate, see now M. Bonnefond, "Espace, temps et idéologie: le Sénat dans la cité romaine républicaine," *Dial. di Arch.*, 3 ser., 1 (1983): 37.

meeting "in the Comitium."[60] In consequence emissaries from victorious generals could go directly from the Senate to address the people from the Rostra (see text to nn. 9–11); and Livy may not be relying entirely on imagination in describing some Rhodian ambassadors in 167, when excluded from the Senate, as standing in the Comitium imploring the by-standers not to credit the charges against them (45, 20, 4–10).

For most of each year the consuls were away from Rome, as were (normally) four of the six praetors, the holders of prorogued commands, military tribunes, *legati* (emissaries), and others absent on public business. We have no means of knowing how these absences affected senatorial opinions and voting, or even what the typical level of attendance was (the *s.c. de Bacchanalibus*, however, prescribes a quorum of 100). All that is probable is that the Senate will have been summoned and consulted more often by the urban praetor — that is, the one of the six praetors on whom, after election, the lot for this province had fallen — than by any other magistrate.[61] Once the Senate had met, we know very little, for this period, about how the order of speaking or the method of voting was determined; a report by Polybius relating to 155, however, makes clear that after opinions had been expressed the presiding urban praetor was free to choose which motions to put to the vote (33, 1). Here and elsewhere it is certain that the making of speeches played a central role. We have already seen various examples of speeches in the Senate, of which Cato's speech for the Rhodians in 167 is the best preserved (see text to n. 9). It is unfortunate for our entire conception of the Senate that so few speeches are explicitly attested as having been made *in the Senate* on the subject of proposed legislation. But even with that limitation we can surely accept the implication that the proceedings of the Senate took the form of a succession of speeches. Its decisions *may* indeed have been effectively predetermined by personal or group allegiances among its members; but such allegiances, if thought of as extending throughout the 300 members at any one time, are entirely hypothetical. If there is evidence for them it should be produced. For the moment, there is no reason not to assume that it was debate in the Senate which gave rise (for instance) to the complex considerations upon which, as Polybius records, it decided on operations in Illyricum in 157 (32, 13, 1–9). Here, but not in legislation, the Senate could *decide*, by making Illyricum a province for the year, and allotting forces to it. When it

60. See Sherk (n. 8), nos. 2, 4, 5, 7, and other examples from after the mid-second century.

61. For documentary examples, see, e.g., *FIRA*² I, nos. 32–3; Sherk (n. 8), nos. 2, 4, 5; cf. 9 (*c.* 140 B.C.).

came to legislation, or to war and peace, the Senate could not decide; and its wishes could be translated into action only by an elected magistrate with the power to step outside, proclaim his intention to propose a law, and later summon the people, address them, and call them to vote.

For if oratory was, so far as our evidence tells us, the chief influence brought to bear on voting within the walls of the Senate, the same was true of the open-air meetings of the citizens. In seeking a valid conception of this we might start from the touching image in the *Annales* of Ennius (7, 234–51 Vahlen/210–27 Warmington) of Servilius Geminus (the one who died at Cannae) returning home tired after spending most of his day directing the affairs of state "by his counsel in the broad Forum and the sacred Senate." We might also recall Ennius' description of M. Cornelius Cethegus, "the honey tongued" consul of 204, nicknamed by his fellow countrymen (*populares*) "the choice flower of the People and the marrow of persuasion."[62]

Legislation, war, and peace were decided by the people, who were summoned to the Forum or to the Capitol to be addressed in speeches, and who voted (for legislation) as the tribal assembly in the Forum and (for war and peace) as the centuriate assembly in the Campus Martius.[63] No less important, and no less subject to oratory, were the meetings of these same two assemblies to hear capital cases or vote on fines imposed by magistrates. Great uncertainties, as is known, attend the question of the juridical character of these popular courts, and the range of offences and persons which they actually judged.[64] But we ought to be impressed by the image of the criminal trial before the assembly, as it appears in Plautus.[65] The forty-four accusations which Cato underwent in the course of his career will all have been before these popular courts, and provide an extreme instance of the importance of the political trial before the people (Pliny, *NH* 7, 200). But we know too, from the *Annales* of Calpurnius Piso (*cos.* 133), that ordinary citizens could

62. Cicero, *Brutus* 58; Ennius, *Ann.* 9, 303–8 Vahlen/300–5 Warmington.

63. For the fullest study of the forms of popular participation, see of course C. Nicolet, *Le métier du citoyen* (1976) = *The World of the Citizen in Republican Rome* (1980), esp. chap. 7, which however deals with the entire republican period and does not offer conclusions as to the nature of power within the system.

64. See W. Kunkel, *Untersuchungen zur Entwicklung des römischen Kriminalverfahrens in vorsullanischer Zeit* (1962); H. F. Jolowicz and B. Nicholas, *Historical Introduction to the Study of Roman Law*[3] (1972), 305–17; A. H. M. Jones, *The Criminal Courts of the Roman Republic and Principate* (1972), chap. 1; A. W. Lintott, "Provocatio," *ANRW* I. 2 (1972), 226; A. Giovannini, "Volkstribunat und Volksgericht," *Chiron* 13 (1983): 545.

65. Plautus, *Captivi* 475–6; *Pseudolus* 1232–3; *Aulularia* 700; *Truculentus* 819.

stand trial before the tribe, and address the citizens in their own defence (Pliny, *NH* 18, 41–3; Peter, *HRR*, F. 33).

Was all this a charade managed from above—the election of over fifty office-holders a year, the declaration of war and the voting on treaties, the passing of legislation, the trials of office-holders and private citizens? For over half a century modern books have asserted and reasserted in varying terms the proposition that the citizen body was powerless, largely because it was bound by relations of dependence, sometimes all subsumed under the term *clientela*.[66] It can even be claimed that we are entitled to apply to ancient societies the now established common-language (or sociological) use of terms like "clientage" and "patronage" without regard to the presence, or precise use, of equivalent terms in the society in question.[67] But to say that is to say that curiosity about the exact nuances of ancient social and political relationships is superfluous. Of course it does matter what words were used, and what forms of relationship are actually attested in any particular period. It is of considerable significance that the major re-examination of *clientela* by N. Rouland, published in 1979, concludes that the institution of *clientela* was in decline in the second century B.C.[68] If there is clear evidence for *clientela* as a *dominant* factor in voting behaviour, either in legislation or in elections, it is time for it to be produced. By contrast the importance of measures directed to the acquisition of favour among the population at large, and the significance of the *substance* of major political issues, and their relevance to the interests of the population, are patent in our sources.[69] Once again, as with the supposed factions, or lateral connections, which allegedly dominated voting in the Senate, it would have to be proved that these supposed vertical relations of obligation and attachment constituted a dominant factor in the behaviour of voters *throughout* a by now very large citizen body. No such demonstration has ever been offered; until it is, we should

66. The source of these presumptions is of course Gelzer (n. 3), see esp. pp. 49–56 (trans. Seager, pp. 62–69) and the conclusion, pp. 115–16 (p. 139). It is needless to cite a long series of examples of later adhesion to them. It may suffice to point to the presumptions still present in the work of J. Bleicken, *Staatliche Ordnung und Freiheit in der römischen Republik* (1972), 64–65; *Lex Publica* (1975), 244–45; *Die Verfassung der römischen Republik*² (1978), and, in the most sophisticated and interesting modern treatment of Roman politics, Chr. Meier, *Res Publica Amissa*² (1980), esp. 34ff.

67. So Finley (n. 52), 40–41.

68. N. Rouland, *Pouvoir politique et dépendance personelle* (1979), 258–59.

69. For this point, see Brunt (n. 36), and, with specific reference to this period, Finley (n. 52), 98–99.

attend to what our sources tell us, that some people made speeches and other people voted.

On the other hand, the sheer size of the citizen body, which in this period numbered some 200,000 to 300,000 adult male voters, and its geographical distribution, has its own relevance to the question of democracy. P. A. Brunt once wrote (*Italian Manpower*, 3): "The citizen body was so numerous and so scattered that in the absence of the representative principle the democratic features which they (Roman political institutions) seem to manifest were bound to be illusory in practice, and Rome could consequently not enjoy a genuinely popular government." There was indeed no notion of representation or local ballot stations. The archaic institution of the assembly in the Forum, the Capitol, or the Campus Martius remained the only means by which the citizen could record his vote. But Roman citizens now occupied blocks of territory which stretched north-eastwards to the Adriatic coast and southwards into Campania, a maximum distance of about 100 miles in each direction; furthermore, in northern Italy a few Roman citizen colonies were established at a greater distance — Parma and Mutina in 183, Luna in 177. Distance, social status, and economic resources must have exerted a fundamental influence in determining which persons out of the vast number with theoretical voting rights actually came to vote. The consular and praetorian elections, held towards the end of each year of office (15 March–15 March), were at least predictable, and more voters may have come for them. But the rule which laid down publication of proposed laws for three successive *nundinae* (eight-day periods), which Rutilius Rufus, consul of 104, was to emphasize as a means of public information (Macrobius, *Sat.* 1, 16, 34), was itself a primitive institution, best adapted for peasants coming in to market from a few miles around the city.

It could not be claimed, therefore, that the system created, or even allowed, an equal opportunity to vote for all citizens. For comparison, the citizens of the Athenian democracy lived at a maximum distance of some thirty miles from the Pnyx, where alone they could cast their votes. This too will have meant, for those who lived furthest away, a round trip of up to two days. In Athens too, therefore, distance and social class will have exercised a profound effect on who voted. Rome shows the same pattern in a much more extreme form.

To Polybius the Roman voters were simply "the people" (ὁ δῆμος). It is perhaps the most significant gap in what survives of his account of the Roman constitution that he does not describe the system of voting in groups, or differentiate between centuriate assembly and tribal assembly, or indicate either the stratification by social class or the sequential voting which characterized the *centuriata*. This form of assembly, whose functions covered the election of censors, consuls, and praetors, the making of war and peace and (as a court) capital condemnations, was thus "popular" in only a limited and specific sense. The same considerations did not, however, apply to the tribal assembly, on which all legislation depended. None the less the procedure of group voting by the thirty-five tribes will have served to prevent any possibility that decisions could have been dominated, by simple majority, by those who lived in Rome or nearby.

That the form of meeting, the order of voting, and the custom of giving each man's vote orally, in the hearing of others, were indeed all felt as restrictions on the liberty of the people is clear from the legislation, proposed or carried through, of the following half century. Licinius Crassus, as tribune in 145, took some step, which remains not quite clear, to shift the location of voting from the confined space of the ancient Comitium to the large and still uncluttered area of the Forum [70]—which was easily large enough, after all, to accommodate as large a crowd as could have heard an unaided human voice. Gaius Gracchus is said to have proposed that the centuries of the centuriate assembly should no longer vote in the fixed order of the census classes (*classes*).[71] The four laws which established voting by secret ballot—in 139 for elections, 137 on popular courts, 131 or 130 on legislation, and 104 on trials for *treason*— were reactions to a perceived restriction on the liberty of the people, as was Marius' law of 119 on the width of the "bridges" (*pontes*) along which people came up to vote (Cicero, *De leg.* 3, 33–9). Yet the first three of these laws must themselves have been passed by open voting. They belong, like much of the Gracchan legislation, like the law of 104 subjecting the appointment of the priestly colleges to a form of popular election, and like the "pirate" law from Delphi and Cnidus, to a movement which can be regarded as an assertion of popular sovereignty.[72]

That was a new phase, closely connected with increased popular pressure for the exploitation of the empire and the effective conduct of military operations;[73] there is again a parallel with classical Athens. But if we return to our period, to the first half of the century, we should none the less not dismiss too readily the democratic, or at least "popular," features which were inher-

70. Cicero, *Laelius* 96; Varro, *De re rust.* 1, 2, 9. See L. R. Taylor, *Roman Voting Assemblies* (1966), 22–23.

71. [Sall.], *Ep. ad Caes.* 2, 8, 1. See C. Nicolet, " 'Confusio Suffragiorum'. À propos d'une réforme électorale de Gaius Gracchus," *MEFR* 71 (1959): 145.

72. See, e.g., Serrao (n. 26), 176ff.; and L. Perelli, *Il movimento popolare nell'ultimo secolo della Repubblica* (1982).

73. Cf. E. Badian, *Roman Imperialism in the Late Republic*[2] (1968), chaps. 2–4.

ent in the system. This remains so in spite of a number of obvious limitations: the restriction of actual office-holding to a narrow social class;[74] the highly imperfect fit between the custom of collective voting in Rome and the geographical spread of the citizen body; the class stratification of the centuriate assembly; the primitive system of open oral voting; the limited proportion of the total citizen body which either did vote, or could have voted, in the established voting areas;[75] and the evident absence of class-consciousness and presence of political acquiescence and deference to rank which characterized the period.[76] There is also the fact, which has often been stressed, that the assemblies (like the Senate) had no fixed agenda or dates of meeting, and could be called only by a magistrate; they could also only vote on matters which a magistrate put before them. But to emphasize all these aspects is also to miss, firstly, the sheer range of issues over which a popular vote, however we choose to characterize it, was indispensable. Democracy, as Guarino has emphasised, is first of all a strictly constitutional concept.[77] Secondly, it is to miss, as has been stressed repeatedly, the extent of the rhetorical persuasion and the visible display which were directed, often in a context of mutual competition or accusation or conflict, by the office-holding class to the populace at large. But, thirdly and most important of all, it is to miss the symbolic importance of the public spaces of Rome and of the performance of communal acts there before whatever persons happened to be present.

The central importance of publicity in the Gracchan extortion (*repetundae*) law has recently been brought out, for the first time, by Sherwin-White.[78] Similar conceptions inform the Latin law of Bantia.[79] Within five days office-holders were to take an oath standing "before the temple of Castor in public during daylight, facing the Forum" (ll. 16–18); senators were to do so "before the quaestor at the aerarium in public during daylight" (ll. 23–24). This documentary evidence may give added significance to literary reports from the first half of the century: the censors of 169/8 resolving a dispute by agreeing to select an urban tribe for the freedmen to vote in by lot, publicly, in

---

74. Note on this aspect the pertinent remark by Finley (n. 52), 70, n. 3: "It surely does not require argumentation to reject the view . . . that popular participation is reduced to a charade by the fact that leadership was monopolised by the élite."

75. See R. MacMullen, "How Many Romans Voted?," *Athenaeum* 58 (1980): 454.

76. For some interesting observations on this aspect, see W. G. Runciman, "Capitalism without Classes: The Case of Classical Rome," *Brit. Journ. Sociol.* 34 (1983): 157.

77. See, e.g., A. Guarino, *La democrazia a Roma* (1979).

78. A. N. Sherwin-White, "The Lex Repetundarum and the Political Ideas of Gaius Gracchus," *JRS* 72 (1982), 18, on pp. 21–23.

79. *FIRA*² I, no. 6; Girard et al. (n. 27), no. 6. See now Crawford (n. 27), no. 7.

the Atrium Libertatis (Livy 45, 15, 5); a praetor of 176 being required either to go to his allotted province or to take an oath before a public meeting (*pro contione*) that his sacrificial obligations prevented him (41, 15, 6–9); or Sempronius Gracchus swearing "in public" that he had not regained the friendship and favour of Scipio Africanus (Aulus Gellius 6, 19, 6). It was to the Forum also that the citizen could think of going to seek justice. We should remember the wronged father in Caecilius' play *Plocius* (175–76) saying: "we are going to the plebs"; "our defence is to be made in public" and "I shall go to the *forum* and I shall act in protection of poverty." We should recall too the evocation in Plautus of the various types of men to be found, at law, at business, and at leisure, around the Comitium, the shrine of Cloacina, the basilica, the Forum Piscarium, the lower Forum, before the temple of Castor, along the Vicus Tuscus (*Curculio*, 470–82). The rapid construction in this period of the great basilicas which fronted on the Forum area — the Porcia of 184, the Aemilia of 179, and the Sempronia of 170 — is itself an indication of the concentration of public and private activity here. The Forum was a public stage where an audience was permanently to hand.

We may still not want to characterize this as democracy. Nor did Polybius. On the contrary, when he needs to give a one-word characterization of the Roman political system (23, 14, 1), he calls it "aristocratic":[80] "Publius (Scipio), who sought honour in an aristocratic *politeuma*, won goodwill among the masses and trust among the Senate." This very passage thus clearly illustrates why he found it necessary to emphasize also the democratic and popular element in the working of the state. It was the Roman people which gave public honours,[81] and issued criminal condemnations; they voted on laws, on colonies, on admission to the citizenship, on war and peace. In the light of recent work it is time to abandon the once established presuppositions of a hereditary "nobility," of aristocratic factions, and of an all-embracing network of dependence and clientship. We might then be able to see the public life of the classical Republic in a rather different light: as an arena in which those who sought and held office competed before the crowd by advertisement of their glorious descent if they could; by the exercise of rhetoric in defence of citizens; by reports and demonstrations of military victory. They also fought out

80. For this point and a good analysis of Polybius' conception of the political character of the Roman system, as expressed both in book 6 and elsewhere, see now C. Nicolet, "Polybe et la 'constitution' de Rome: aristocratie et démocratie," in C. Nicolet, ed., *Demokratia et Aristokratia. À propos de Caius Gracchus: mots grecs et réalités romaines* (1983), 15.

81. Note the public demonstration over the consular elections of 149 B.C.: "and they [the people] were exclaiming that by the laws handed down from Tullius and Romulus the people were the judges of the elections" (Appian, *Pun.* 112).

their most bitter rivalries before juries constituted by the citizen assemblies. Their ability to legislate depended on the tribal assembly; and the necessary persuasion was applied, often in open conflict and debate, by the means of speeches, which were made not only, or even primarily, in the "sacred Senate," but in the open space of the Forum, before the ever-available crowd consisting of whoever was already there, or whoever turned up. It was this crowd which, however imperfectly, symbolized and represented the sovereignty of the Roman people.

CHAPTER FIVE

Politics, Persuasion, and the People before the Social War (150–90 B.C.)*

The purpose of this chapter is to present a particular model of how Roman politics worked, and of what Roman politics before the Social War was "about." In essence I want to place in the centre of our conception the picture of an orator addressing a crowd in the Forum; a picture of someone using the arts of rhetoric to persuade an anonymous crowd about something.[1] The

* First published in *JRS* 76 (1986): 1–11. This chapter represents the text of a lecture given at the Roman Society on 19 March 1985. As is obvious, it continues the themes and pre-occupations of my article "The Political Character of the Classical Roman Republic, 200–151 B.C.," *JRS* 74 (1984): 1 (chapter 4 in this volume). As will be equally obvious, it pretends to be no more than an essay, or sketch, recommending one way of seeing the politics of this period; it does not attempt to give a full or balanced account. Hence the text remains essentially in the form in which it was given as a lecture, and no attempt has been made to give full references to modern works, or more than the minimum essential ancient evidence. I am grateful for comments to the Editorial Committee of the *JRS* and also to Jean-Louis Ferrary.

1. I use the word "particular" to emphasize that this chapter, like its predecessor (chapter 4), can be seen as one reflection of a general reconsideration of the nature of Roman politics, as a reaction to interpretations which emphasise prosopography or the influence of *clientela*. In retrospect many of the most important considerations can be seen to be expressed already in P. A. Brunt, *Social Conflicts in the Roman Republic* (1971), closely followed in many respects by M. I. Finley, *Politics in the Ancient World* (1983), who went some distance, though in my view not far enough, in recognizing the reality of political issues in second-century Rome. The fluidity and competitiveness which marked political life and the holding of office are well emphasized by K. Hopkins and G. Burton in *Death and Renewal* (1983), chap. 2, esp. 107ff. The same competitiveness and individualism is also rightly stressed by T. P. Wiseman, *Roman Political Life, 90 B.C.–A.D. 69* (1985), chap. 1. Similarly, note W. M. Beard and M. Crawford, *Rome in the Late Republic* (1985). My approach has de-

most important subject of oratory—and the most important fundamental right exercised by whoever came to vote—was legislation. Yet the greatest of all the extraordinary distortions which have been imposed on our conception of republican politics in the twentieth century is that the process of legislation and the content of the legislation passed by the people have both ceased to be central to it. With that we have ceased to listen sufficiently to the actual content of oratory addressed to the people, to the arguments from rights, from the necessities of the preservation of the *res publica*, from historical precedents, both Roman and non-Roman, and from social attitudes and prejudices. In the second century above all, we can see how the prestige which the office-holding class derived from family descent and personal standing on the one hand was matched on the other by popular demands for appropriate conduct, and by popular suspicions of private luxury, of profiteering from the conduct of public affairs, and of improper collaboration with wrongdoers both at home and abroad.

Those who spoke to the people in the Forum, from one or other of the two main stages used for the purpose—the Rostra and the podium of the temple of Castor and Pollux—could use these popular prejudices and suspicions against each other, just as they could play on the crowd's knowledge of the individuals concerned. For a public meeting (*contio*) was indeed a stage performance; this idea is expressed by Cicero in words which he puts into the mouth of Laelius in *De amicitia* 97: "on stage, that is at a *contio*." The Forum itself was a stage on which there steadily encroached monuments representing individuals, or recalling their achievements, or associated with their names. Before the middle of the second century the Forum area was already lined with statues of individuals, and in 158 the Senate decreed the removal of those which had not been voted by Senate and People (Pliny, *NH* 34, 30, from the *Annales* of L. Piso). In 117 L. Caecilius Metellus restored the temple of Castor and Pollux. Seven decades later, defending Metellus' grandson, Scaurus, in a case in the Forum, Cicero could remind the jurors: "his grandfather appears to have established the most holy gods in that temple, in your sight, so that they can plead for the safety of his grandson" (*Pro Scauro* 24). After Marius' victory over the Cimbri, Cimbrian shields hung as tro-

---

rived much from all these studies, as also from L. Perelli, *Il movimento popolare nell'ultimo secolo della Repubblica* (1982). None, however, has shared the particular stress which I would like to put on the element of oratorical persuasion addressed to the crowd. Note, however, C. Nicolet, "La polémique politique au deuxième siècle avant Jésus-Christ," in C. Nicolet, ed., *Demokratia et Aristokratia* (1983), 37.

phies on the Tabernae Novae in front of the Basilica Aemilia. Iulius Strabo could put them to demonstrative use, saying to Helvius Mancia in an altercation before a crowd "I will show what you are like," and pointing to the grotesque head of a Gaul painted on one of the shields (*De or.* 2, 266). Before that, the first arch ever to appear in the Forum, the Fornix Fabianus, had been erected by Q. Fabius Maximus Allobrogicus, to commemorate his triumph in 121. It gave Licinius Crassus the opportunity to say in a public meeting, about the tribune Memmius, "Memmius thinks himself so big that on his way down to the Forum he bends his head as he goes under the Fornix Fabianus" (*De or.* 2, 267).

As we will see, orators of the office-holding class played on the prejudices and suspicions of the crowd to deploy much more significant and loaded mutual criticisms than that, both when speaking about legislation, before the popular courts constituted by the tribal assembly (*comitia tributa*), and before the new jury courts. These too of course met in the Forum, before a crowd of spectators. The jurors both *represented* the people at large and functioned under its gaze. The mode of oratory, the forms of persuasion, and the bases of argument and justification used here might not always be very different from those before a public meeting or before the assembly functioning as a court.

Yet it is precisely here that we can see the remarkable distortion imposed on our conceptions of republican public life by the most influential of all twentieth-century approaches to it; I mean of course Gelzer's *Die römische Nobilität*, published in 1912 — "the key that unlocked the door from the 19th to the 20th century in historical research on the Roman Republic," as Badian described it.[2] The attempt which Gelzer made, to look behind the constitutional façade to the social reality, was in itself wholly justified. And no one will ever have read this slim volume for the first time — or indeed many more times — without a constant sense of illumination. Yet it is clear that it has actually been too successful. On some points, such as the definition of *nobilitas*, it is misleading, as Brunt has shown.[3] On others, such as the importance of relations of personal obligation and dependence in Roman politics, its conclusions go far beyond the evidence which it itself cites: "The entire Roman people, both the ruling circle and the mass of voters whom they ruled, was, as a society, permeated by multifarious relationships based on *fides* and on

2. E. Badian, *JRS* 57 (1967): 217, quoted by R. Seager, in the introduction to his translation, *The Roman Nobility* (1969), xi.

3. P. A. Brunt, "*Nobilitas* and *Novitas*," *JRS* 72 (1982): 1.

personal connections, the principle forms of which were *patrocinium* in the courts and over communities, together with political friendship and financial obligations. *These relationships determined the distribution of political power.*"[4]

This conclusion, to repeat, goes far beyond what the body of the book contains, namely illuminating observations on various social dimensions of the exercise of power. It is an explicit claim that these social dimensions constitute an adequate global explanation of the political process. More insidious still, however, is the implicit—and never openly acknowledged—direction of attention and selection of material which shapes the work as a whole. For instance, the only context in which Gelzer gives any attention to oratory is that of cases heard in the courts. There is not even the barest allusion to oratory deployed for or against the passing of laws—that "popular kind of oratory," which, as Cicero says, enabled Sp. Thorius to get through a law relating to the public land (*ager publicus*) (*Brutus* 136), or that personal presence (*auctoritas*) and oratorical power which enabled Marcus Octavius to have C. Gracchus' corn law (*Lex Sempronia frumentaria*) abrogated by the votes of a plenary meeting of the people (*Brutus* 222), to be replaced by something more moderate.

This emphasis on forensic oratory and its political function both implicitly ignores one major focus of the political process, legislation, and explicitly attributes a primary significance to trials: "political struggles were for the most part conducted in the courts."[5] Moreover, the major trials, which of course were indeed "political," are interpreted solely, by careful selection and emphasis, in terms of the established conventions of personal obligation and connection among the upper classes. These conventions were naturally of some significance. As Gelzer duly notes (trans. Seager, pp. 76–77), when M. Antonius, in the mid-90s, defended Norbanus on a charge of high treason (*maiestas*), he openly stated his obligation to do this for his former quaestor. But you would not guess, from reading Gelzer, that he had said much else, of a wholly different sort. Yet we have the clearest possible evidence that he did. In *De oratore* 2, 198–99, Antonius is made to recall what his speech contained:

> I gathered together all types of civil discords, with their associated wrongs and dangers, and made the speech a survey of all the successive phases of our *res publica*, and concluded by saying that even though all civil discords had always been an affliction, some none the less had been just and even necessary. . . . Without dissension among the *nobiles*, the kings could not have been driven from this state, nor tribunes of

4. Gelzer, trans. Seager (n. 2), 139 (my emphasis).
5. Gelzer, trans. Seager (n. 2), 85.

the plebs created, nor the consular power [*potestas*] have so often been limited by *plebiscita* [laws passed by the plebeian assembly—the *concilium plebis*], nor the right of appeal [*provocatio*] granted to the Roman people, guardian of the state and the defence of its freedom.

The argument from historical precedent was fundamental to the nature of the public political process. But there was also another aspect to the issue at stake in this case, an argument which was more specific in its terms and of more immediate contemporary relevance than that. The entire case (*tota illa causa*) depended on the definition of "damage to the majesty of the state" (*maiestas minuta*), as laid down—for the first time ever—in the Lex Appuleia passed by Saturninus, probably in his second tribunate in 100.[6] What then were the terms in which *maiestas* was defined in Saturninus' law, the earliest to give formal legal expression to this concept? Cicero supplies the definition in the *De inventione* 2, 53:

> To detract in any way from the dignity (*dignitas*) or the greatness (*amplitudo*) or the power (*potestas*) of the people, or of those to whom the people has given power.

It might be worth considering in what light we would understand these words if we were told that they derived from the political life of a Greek city. Indeed it might help us to escape from the shackles of what we *think* we know about the Roman Republic if we were to read all the information which we are given about Rome between 150 and 90 B.C. as if it related to a Greek city. Nor would this be wholly inappropriate. Polybius, who should have known, did suppose that the categories of political analysis relevant to Greek cities could be applied to Rome. Moreover, there had never been a time, from the eighth century onwards, when Rome had not been within the orbit of the Greek world, and profoundly affected by Greek influences.[7] And, specifically from this period, there is perfectly clear evidence that precedents from Greek history were regularly deployed in political reasoning in Rome.

Even without these innumerable real interconnections and influences, it would be a useful logical device for us to relocate the available evidence in a context to which we would apply different presuppositions. Nothing could

---

6. For the ideological content and revolutionary implications of Saturninus' legislation see above all the very important articles of J.-L. Ferrary, "Recherches sur la législation de Saturninus et de Glaucia," *MEFR(A)* 89 (1977): 619; "Les origines de la loi de majesté à Rome," *CRAI* (1983): 556.

7. Note now esp. A. D. Momigliano, "The Origins of Rome," *Settimo Contributo* (1984): 379.

then be easier than to read the wording of Saturninus' law in terms comparable to those which expressed the sovereignty of the Athenian people, and the status of elected officials or commanders as the delegates of the people. If we then returned to the year 101/0 in Rome and to the extensive law on the eastern provinces, known in texts from Delphi and Cnidus, we would of course find exactly that presupposition, together with an assertion that the revenues of a newly gained part of the empire shall be gathered as the people instructs.[8]

Another parallel suggests itself with the case of classical Athens. A. H. M. Jones demonstrated some decades ago how the ideology of democracy in Athens has to be reconstructed from the attitudes taken up, and criticisms expressed, by writers who were largely, or wholly, unsympathetic to it. The same is largely true of that period of acute crisis in the Roman state which stretches from the middle of the second century to the Social War. We cannot help the plain fact that a high proportion of our evidence derives from the writings of Cicero. But we should read his judgements as reactions to a political system and not as descriptions of it, still less as expressions of the values which actually prevailed in it. Cicero's conception of the Roman state—or rather his aspirations and hopes for a Roman state dominated by the example set by "the respectable and the best" (*boni* and *optimates*), and controlled politically by the Senate—has had far more success with posterity than it ever had in his lifetime, except for a single decade, or before it. Cicero was of course not alone in his view that it was the essential function of the Senate to guide political decision making; the same view is for instance reflected, in the 80s, in *Ad Her.*, 4, 35/47. But it is a mistake to elevate this aspiration into a description of an actual state of affairs. As a result, modern writing on the political history of the Republic is haunted still by the utterly misleading, unconscious presupposition that the Senate was a sort of parliament, which exercised the powers of government. So the question now becomes, How, within the walls of the Senate, within the circle of this governing body, did you gain power? The answer then becomes, By having an extensive set of connections, which of course it is naive to call a "party" and which we now know that we cannot call a faction (*factio*) either. No other name will do instead, however, because, if we want to locate the exercise of power, this is the wrong question; we are looking in the wrong direction. Firstly, within the governing class, the thing which above all distinguished

8. M. Hassall, M. Crawford, and J. Reynolds, "Rome and the Eastern Provinces at the End of the Second Century B.C.," *JRS* 64 (1974): 195; note R. K. Sherk, *Rome and the Greek East to the Death of Augustus* (1984), no. 55 (translation and commentary).

the exercise of power was its individualistic character.[9] This aspect might of course have been confined to the pursuit of office, and military glory. But it was precisely the second half of the second century which saw the break-up of the relative (but by no means complete) consensus which had obtained among the governing class before, and which consequently led to the presentation to the people of political and constitutional propositions of strongly diverging ideological content. It is commonplace to stress the limitations on the people's power: they could only accept or reject laws put to them by an office-holder. This, though true, ignores, firstly, the conflicting opinions expressed in public meetings held before a law was put to the vote; secondly, the fact that to achieve office a man had previously to have been elected; and, thirdly, that effective legislative power still resided with those who, for whatever reason and in whatever numbers, came to the Forum to vote.

Gelzer's assertion—and it was no more than that—that the patterns of personal obligation, which he was able to illustrate so vividly, actually *determined* the political behaviour of the whole mass of voters, did of course have one very convenient corollary. It offered a blanket explanation of voter behaviour; or rather it dispensed us from troubling with the problem of explaining voter behaviour at all, of explaining who came to vote and what sorts of reason they might have had for voting the way they did.[10] Furthermore, by silently omitting legislation altogether from his portrayal of the political process, he inevitably obscured the crucial distinction between electoral voting and legislative voting. The process of election to office may well often have had little or no ideological content. Even so, anyone who had already held public office will have had the opportunity, if he wished, to establish a public identity, and political posture, which would be relevant when it came to his next office: "So, Citizens (*Quirites*), when *I* set out from Rome I took with me belts full of silver which I brought back empty from my province; as for others, the *amphorae* full of wine which they took out with them *they* brought back filled with silver" (*ORF*[3], p. 112). This of course is Gaius Gracchus, speaking about his quaestorship in Sardinia in 126–24; in the context of repeated public debates and altercations over personal conduct by office-

9. Cf. the works referred to in n. 1.

10. No such explanation is offered in this chapter, and it is not clear to me whether any is possible. It is, however, worth noting the discussion, relating to a later period, in Lily Ross Taylor's *Party Politics in the Age of Caesar* (1949), chap. 3. It is interesting to note the presuppositions embodied in the title of this section, "Delivering the Vote." I hope to return to this question elsewhere, in the context of the popular politics of the last decades of the Republic.

holders, it is a highly political statement. He was, after all, soon to propose to the people legislation taking the extortion court out of the hands of senators.

It is, however, primarily a statement about himself, addressed to a crowd of citizens. The unconscious fiction of the collective parliamentary rule of the Senate has obscured the centrality of this much more important relationship, that is, of the one to the many, of the individual orator and/or office-holder and the crowd.[11]

In the longer term it is only if we brush aside the fiction of senatorial government that the Roman revolution becomes intelligible. It was by popular laws, against the will of most senators on most occasions, that power was given successively to individuals like Pompey and Caesar. Once we allow ourselves to think of republican Rome as a system having significant democratic features, as Polybius saw, we might then attach rather more importance to a passage in which Polybius discusses how a democracy breaks down.[12] Trouble arises through the inordinate ambition of politicians:

> Setting out to seek power, and unable to gain their objectives by their own resources and through their own qualities, they dissipate their property, using every means to bribe and corrupt the masses. Then again, when they have rendered the many receptive and greedy for largesse through their insane appetite for prestige, the essential character of democracy is destroyed, and it evolves into a state of violence and government by force. The populace, once it is accustomed to feed off the property of others, and expects to live off the property of their neighbours, and when it finds a champion who is ambitious and daring, but is excluded by poverty from political rewards, brings the rule of force to completion, and gathering together, carries out murders, exiles, and redistributions of land—until, having come to live in the manner of beasts, it finds once again a master and monarch.

To explain all that, we would indeed have to have some access to voter behaviour, which of course we do not. All we can recapture is, firstly, something of the forms of self-representation and of persuasion which were addressed to the voters; and, secondly, something—in certain cases rather a lot—of the actual content and wording of the laws which the people passed.

---

11. There is much to be learned from the analyses of the relation of the individual and the people in Z. Yavetz, *Plebs and Princeps* (1969).

12. Polybius 6, 9, 6–9. I am very grateful to John North for pointing out to me in conversation that this passage can be read as an implicit prediction of the course of events in the last century of the Republic.

As regards self-representation, senators can be found repeatedly contrasting themselves with others, named and unnamed, just as Gaius Gracchus did after his quaestorship. They never, to my knowledge, proclaim their own attachment to any group; if they underline their associations with anyone, it is with members of their own families, both past and future. Association with past members of the family was precisely the function of the public funeral oration, delivered from the Rostra; Q. Lutatius Catulus, consul of 102, was the first to deliver one for a woman, his mother Popilia (*De or.* 2, 44), thus setting a precedent for Caesar. Nothing could more clearly have underlined the public significance of the prominent family. The next generation too could be publicly presented; in his hour of danger, as Sempronius Asellio recorded, Tiberius Gracchus produced his male children in public and commended them to the care of the people (Aulus Gellius, *NA* 2, 13). By comparison, C. Papirius Carbo Arvina, tribune in 90, was to recall in a public meeting the contrast between Livius Drusus, the deceased tribune of the previous year, and his father, Livius Drusus, consul in 122. The young Cicero heard him speak (*Orator* 213):

> O Marcus Drusus—I call on the father—you used to say that the *res publica* was sacred, and that all those who had violated it had paid the penalty. The wisdom of the father's saying was proved by the rash conduct of the son.

Both father and son had, of course, held office at moments when major issues of principle were at stake—about the exercise of power in the state, the use of public property for the individual benefit of the citizens, and the extension of the citizenship itself. That, finally, is one particular reason for concentrating here on the six decades before the Social War. Moreover, as is obvious, the Social War itself was a major turning point, which introduced a new era in Roman politics. But how significant the war was is brought out only if we realise that the Romans lost. And we will only see that in perspective if we look at the legislation, and proposed legislation, of the previous half century. A whole range of fundamental issues was put to the Roman people, and voted on by them. Among these questions there repeatedly came forward ones which affected the constitutional rights of Latins and Italian allies. Those proposed laws which would have extended such rights without exception failed to pass, or were never even put to the vote; those which restricted them did pass. The only, partial, exception to the rule was the law of Saturninus in 100 which granted land in Gaul—probably Cisalpina—to former soldiers of Marius, including Italians, some of whom were to gain citizenship in the new colonies. It was passed only in the face of mob violence in the Forum; and some at least of the colonies envisaged were never sent.

This issue — of the extension, or rather non-extension, of citizen rights — was only one of a whole series of issues on which the Roman people were called upon to vote between 150 and 90 B.C. These issues were not all controversial, and the passing of a law might on occasion be a mere formality. But they did include the setting-up of permanent courts (*quaestiones*), for the prosecution of extortion (*repetundae*) and high treason (*maiestas*) at least, and the qualifications and duties of the jurors; the procedures in voting — that is, above all, the series of laws on the use of the ballot passed in the 130s and 104; the establishment of the basic constitutional principle that only the people could set up a court with capital jurisdiction; the transfer to the people of the election of members of the priestly colleges, proposed in 145, passed in 104; the use of the public land in Italy, and in Africa; the use to be made of the legacy of Attalus of Pergamon; and the conduct of wars — in at least three forms: the direct appointment of commanders to wars, overriding the normal distribution of provinces by lot; the use of tribunician legislation passed by the people to give direct instructions to holders of *imperium*, as in the law of 101/0 on the eastern provinces; and the passing of laws to establish special ad hoc courts to examine misconduct in diplomatic and military affairs.

Many of the known sumptuary measures too were also laws, though decrees of the Senate (*senatus consulta*) could perform a similar function, as in 161 B.C. (Aulus Gellius, *NA* 2, 24, 2). Those which were laws were voted by the people, and involved persuasion and discussion before the people, as earlier in Cato's speech to the people about the growth of private luxury (Polybius 31, 25, 5). One important aspect of all this was precisely the arousal, by oratory, of popular resentment and suspicion about the life-styles of the rich. A notable example was the public altercation between the censors of 92, revolving specifically round the luxurious character of Crassus' house (*ORF*[3], pp. 248ff.). But the restrictions in the laws which the people passed might later come to seem too burdensome on the voters themselves. As the tribune Duronius said to the People from the Rostra in 97, when proposing the abrogation of a sumptuary law, "Reins have been placed on you, Citizens, which are not to be tolerated" (Val. Max. 2, 9, 5).

This list does not exhaust all the categories of legislative activity in this period. It has also to be seen in immediate conjunction with those trials before the people which involved questions of the constitution, or of the safety of the state. Three examples of these will suffice: firstly, the prosecution of Opimius, consul of 121, by the tribune Decius in 120. The trial was brought before the people, and the issue was whether the passing of the novel decree of the Senate enjoining action for the safety of the state constituted a legal justification for the murder of Gaius Gracchus and the imprisonment of citizens (Livy, *Epit.* 61). As is well known, Opimius was acquitted. So too were the two ex-consuls against whom Cn. Domitius Ahenobarbus, as tribune in 104, brought actions for the imposition of a fine (*multa*), before the thirty-five tribes. Both concerned the safety of the state. M. Iunius Silanus, consul of 109, was tried for his defeat by the Cimbri in that year: the charge was that he had acted without being authorized to do so by the people (*iniussu populi*), and that his defeat had been the beginning of the disasters which the people had since suffered (Asconius 80C). Aemilius Scaurus, probably then a *pontifex*, was accused on the grounds that the public rites of the Roman people had been damaged by his fault; to be precise, the rites of the *Dei Penates* at Lavinium had been improperly conducted. He too was acquitted, but more narrowly: only three of the thirty-five tribes voted for condemnation, but in the remaining thirty-two a majority for acquittal was achieved by only a few votes (Asconius 21C).

It was in this same year that Domitius Ahenobarbus carried his law that the priestly colleges should be filled by popular election, a measure already proposed unsuccessfully in 145, when Laelius, speaking against the law, had discoursed to the people, going into the details of religious observance "which Numa left to us" (*Nat. Deor.* 3, 43). Domitius' law, when finally passed, obliged anyone nominating a new augur for election, in the place of (to replace) one who has died, to do so at a public meeting.

The principle of the accountability of office-holders, and the popular suspicion of impropriety and profiteering, themes which run through all the politics of this period, had their place in the regulation of religious observances also. Thus when L. Caecilius Metellus as pontifex maximus, along with the College of Pontifices, tried three Vestal Virgins for breaking their vows, acquitting two, a tribune of 113, Sextus Peducaeus, accused them of corrupt judgement (*male iudicasse*), and the people voted to appoint L. Cassius to enquire into the issue. Here as elsewhere, no one need suppose that Roman politicians were devoid of personal motives. On the contrary, these motives could even be openly paraded before the people. We may recall Gaius Gracchus at a public meeting telling the attendant to go and summon Piso to appear, that is before the people. "Which Piso?" enquired the attendant. "You force me to say, my enemy, Frugi" (Cicero, *Font.* 39). But, "enmities" or not, it is essential not to forget, firstly, that the proposal of laws and opposition to them, the setting-up of ad hoc or permanent courts, and the conduct of trials before the people might all involve basic issues of the nature of the state, or sovereignty within it, or the disposition of its resources and of the management of its affairs. And, secondly, that all these issues were presented before the people at large through the medium of speeches. It was, after all, the people who voted.

It was also the same Calpurnius Piso Frugi himself who made a point of appearing in person to collect the fixed-price corn made available to the people by the Lex Frumentaria of Gaius Gracchus, which he had opposed: "I would prefer, Gracchus, that it were not your pleasure to distribute my property to individuals [*viritim*]; but if you do it, I will seek my share" (Cicero, *Tusc.* 3, 48).[13] That again was a public expression, before the crowd, of a political judgement about the resources of the state. There was also another dimension to this question, the fear of domination (*dominatio*). Just as accusations of aspiring to tyranny or kingship had been brought against Tiberius Gracchus, so it may have been Gaius Fannius, the consul of 122, who argued, against Gaius Gracchus, that by "largess" (*largitio*) Peisistratus, Phalaris, and Dionysius of Syracuse had corrupted the citizens and sought domination. Thus these and other precedents from Greek history have considerable significance.[14] Even after Gracchus' death it was possible for a tribune, by use of oratorical persuasion, to cause a crowded popular assembly to abrogate his law for corn distribution, and replace it with something less radical.

The questions of the public funds, of public property and its possible distribution, of the right form of management of public revenues, all therefore involved issues of principle; but they also exhibited fluctuations and inconsistencies in popular attitudes—or, at any rate, in the way that those people would vote who turned up on any one occasion. The subject matter of politics also kept within certain bounds. Almost every aspect of the state itself was subject to legislative votes in this period, and in particular it lay in the nature of laws (*leges*) that they set down rules for the holders of office. Laws might also, but less characteristically, define criminal offences with which ordinary people might then be charged. Hence, of course, the famous distinction made in the advice of Servilius Glaucia to the people on how to listen when laws were read out. If the laws began "Dictator, consul, praetor, magister equitum . . .," they need not be concerned. But if they heard the words "Whoever the passage of this law . . .," they should take note, in case

13. See now P. Garnsey and D. Rathbone, "The Background to the Grain Law of Gaius Gracchus," *JRS* 75 (1985): 20.

14. *ORF*[3], pp. 44–85. See J.-L. Ferrary, "À propos de deux fragments attribués à C. Fannius, cos. 122," in C. Nicolet, ed., *Demokratia et Aristokratia* (1983), 51, arguing that the quotations are not contemporary, but come from later declamations on the subject of Gaius Gracchus.

they would be subject to a new court (Cicero, *Rab. Post.* 14). What the operations of politics did *not* yet touch was private property. The only hint of a threat to that which we hear of in this period came in a speech, or speeches, of L. Marcius Philippus as tribune in perhaps 104. He said a great deal in demagogic style including the claim that there were not 2,000 men in the community who had any property. The speech at least implied the possibility of equal distribution of property; but his land law, of unknown content, was rejected (Cicero, *De off.* 2, 73).

None the less, the scope of the subject matter of politics was enormously extended in this period; and the issues at stake embodied basic questions about the rights of citizens, the location of sovereignty in the state, the control of foreign relations and military affairs, and the access of individual citizens to a share in the resources which the state had at its disposal. The best proof that what we see happening in this period represents "real" politics, embodying serious challenges to the established order, is precisely the irruptions of violence which ended the lives of Tiberius and Gaius Gracchus and of Saturninus; this last event was, of course, to be celebrated in evocative detail by Cicero in the *Pro Rabirio*.[15]

We can hardly help seeing all this through the eyes of Cicero, whose youth was spent under the guidance of the major conservative figures of just this period.[16] But there do remain two other avenues of access to the ideas which were embodied in popular legislation in this period, or which were expressed in speeches addressed to the people. The first and most important access is provided by the inscribed laws from this time. It cannot be stressed too often that these represent the only direct testimonies to the political mentality, conceptions, and vocabulary of the period. As for the great inscription of the extortion law, which we may take to be that of Gracchus, many aspects of its true significance were brought out, for the first time, by Sherwin-White.[17] He rightly stressed the emphasis which is placed in this law on publicity, that is the necessity of the observance, under the eyes of the people, of the rules on the part of both the praetor and the jurors themselves. That must give a possible clue to the real point of another law of Gracchus, that about the censorial farming out (*censoria locatio*) of the revenues of Asia. It should be seen not just as a political scheme to benefit the *equites* or tax collectors, but as aimed, firstly, at securing the revenues due to the people; and, secondly, at

15. See most recently E. Badian, "The Death of Saturninus," *Chiron* 14 (1984): 101.

16. On this, see esp. T. N. Mitchell, *Cicero: The Ascending Years* (1979), chap. 1.

17. A. N. Sherwin-White, "The Lex Repetundarum and the Political Ideas of Gaius Gracchus," *JRS* 72 (1982): 18.

ensuring the allocation of the contracts by the censors, in Rome, before the people. Cicero himself emphasizes this point in arguing, before the people, against the Rullan agrarian bill of 63 (*De leg. ag.* 2, 55, Loeb trans.): "it is not permitted to farm out the revenues anywhere except in this city, from this place [i.e., the Rostra], before you all in full assembly." The inscribed Latin law of Bantia, whatever its precise date or purpose, embodies a similar concern: not only must office-holders and senators swear within five days to obey the law, but they must do so in public, during daylight, at specified locations bordering on the Forum — either in front of Castor's temple or *ad aerarium*, that is, before the temple of Saturn.[18] Moreover, just enough is left of the inscribed decree of the Senate of a treaty with Astypalaea in 105 to reveal (perhaps) the traces of a highly populist law, or laws, of the Gracchan period. The relevant clause may have read as follows, and may refer to Rome rather than Astypalaea: "that according to the Rubrian and Acilian law [or laws] a copy [of this alliance] should be set up in a public and conspicuous place, exposed where the majority of citizens walk by, and that each year it should be read aloud [? in the assembly]."[19]

But the major new item which must affect our view of the nature of the state in this period is the law of 101/0 on the eastern provinces (see n. 8); firstly, it *is* a popular law; secondly, it too obliges office-holders (other than the tribunes) to take an oath; thirdly, it gives detailed instructions to both consuls and governors. Most significant of all, perhaps, are the provisions laid down as to what steps the governor of Macedonia should take with regard to a newly conquered area in eastern Thrace; he is to proceed there, to see to the collection of the public revenues (i.e., those of the Roman state), and in future to spend there a period of not less than sixty days.

The notion that the funds of the Roman state were a perquisite of the Roman people, and should be at its disposition had been expressed most clearly of all in Gaius Gracchus' speech to the people about a law apparently intended to re-adjust royal territories in Asia Minor, at some point in the 120s. Almost all the themes and forms of persuasion which I have been trying to emphasize are embodied in the quotation by Aulus Gellius of part of this speech (*NA* 11, 10). Gracchus is speaking to the people:

18. Riccobono, *FIRA*² I, no. 6; P. F. Girard, F. Senn, and V. Giuffré, *Lois des romains*⁷ (1977), no. 6. See now M. Crawford, ed., *Roman Statutes* I–II (1996), no. 48.

19. For text and discussion of this document, long since destroyed, see R. K. Sherk, *Roman Documents from the Greek East* (1969), no. 16; Sherk (n. 8), no. 53 (text and discussion). For a comparable publicity clause, note the Fragmentum Tarentinum, Girard et al. (n. 18), no. 9, ll. 13ff. See now Crawford (n. 18), no. 8.

As for you, Citizens, if you wish to display wisdom and virtue, you will, even if you search, find none of us coming forward here without reward. All of us who make speeches are seeking something, and no one comes forward before you for any reason except to gain something. I myself, who am speaking before you in order that you may increase your revenues, and that you may more readily control your assets and the *res publica*, am not coming forward for nothing; but I seek from you not money but your good opinion and honour. Those who come forward to dissuade you from accepting this law do not seek honour from you, but money from Nicomedes; those who persuade you to accept it do not seek good opinion from you, but profit and reward for their pockets from Mithridates. But those from the same station and order [*ordo*] who maintain silence, these are the sharpest of all, for they take profit from all, and deceive all. You who believe that they are innocent of such things, accord them good opinion; but the embassies from the kings, since they believe them to be maintaining silence in their interests, offer them lavish gifts of money.

He concludes with a story from fourth-century Greek history, of how the orator Demades boasted that he had received ten talents from the king (Philip) for holding his peace.

Once again some knowledge of Greek history is assumed and is used to hold a mirror to current events. But the important point is the right of the people to the profits of empire, and the suspicion that senators are lining their private pockets by not pressing the public interests of Rome as against those of allied kings. This speech of Gaius Gracchus is the essential background to much of the tribunician agitation which fills Sallust's account of the Jugurthine War. Not many people in the streets of Rome would have swallowed the view that senatorial inaction after Jugurtha's seizure of power should be put down to "natural unwillingness to think ill of an old friend."[20] The quotation from Gaius Gracchus shows that we do not need to disregard as a historical fiction the speech which Sallust gives to Memmius, tribune of 111 (*Jug.* 31). The counter-reaction to Gaius Gracchus, Memmius says, had labelled as "an attempt at kingship" what was in fact an attempt "to restore its own to the *plebs*." In subsequent years the people (he says) have watched in silent indignation the pillaging of the state treasury (*aerarium*), and kings and free peoples paying revenues to a few *nobiles*. Sallust also represents Memmius as referring to the early secessions of the plebs. There is no reason whatever

---

20. So E. Badian, *Roman Imperialism in the Late Republic*[2] (1968), 25.

to think that the making of such a reference must be an unhistorical elaboration by Sallust himself. We know, for instance, that M. Antonius, in the 90s,
retailed civil discords by which the liberties of the people had been secured
(see text to n. 5); and Cicero notes the existence of a popular (*popularis*) tradition of the history of Rome (e.g., *Acad.* 2, 13). If we were to doubt the public
relevance of earlier history in this period we have only to look at the irrefut-
able contemporary, and documentary, evidence of the coins, on which an
emphatic break is marked by the appearance of historical themes and political symbols from 137 onwards; perhaps most notably "I appeal" (PROVOCO)
on coins of 110–109.[21] Moreover, as Peter Wiseman has argued, it was in this
period that there came to be a great deal more *of* Roman history in written
form than there had ever been before.[22] Whether this was "true history" or
"false history" does not matter in this context. What matters is the way that
beliefs about history could be put to current use. Appian could well be right
in reporting that in 148 the people shouted that by the "laws of Tullius and
Romulus" the people were sovereign in the elections and could validate or
invalidate the laws (*Lib.* 112/531).

The elements of a popular, even a democratic, tradition and ideology in
a Roman context could easily be put together even from the evidence we
have.[23] But, significant though this is, it is not the intention of this chapter
to attempt to restore the Roman people to their proper place in the history
of democratic values. On the contrary, its purpose is to present a neutral, or
purely functional, model of how politics worked: that of the individual orator using persuasion, and addressing his words to the crowd which has the
right of voting and decision. This in the end was to lead to just the conclusion
which Polybius had implicitly predicted.

But we also see another side, in relation to the half century before the
Social War, if we remember that all the measures, taken or proposed, in relation to the Latins and Italians were laws, put to the people, argued for and
against by the medium of oratory, and voted or rejected by the people. We
should not think of these laws simply as actions "of" the person who proposed them: the alien law "of" Pennus in 126; the law "of" Licinius Crassus
and Mucius Scaevola as consuls of 95. As noted already, many laws extending
the rights of Latins and Italian allies were proposed, or at least mooted, in
this period. Not one was passed. Those which were passed were those which

---

21. See M. Crawford, *Roman Republican Coinage* I (1975), 266ff; for 110/9, p. 313.

22. T. P. Wiseman, *Clio's Cosmetics* (1979), chap. 2.

23. The use of historical examples in various public contexts is one mode which, *pace*
Finley (n. 1), 126ff., the Romans of this period did possess for representing political conflict.

restricted those rights. Tiberius Gracchus perhaps intended to offer citizenship to the Italians; in any case such a law was certainly not voted; nor (in my view at least) did Italians share in his allotments of Roman public land.[24] More certainly, Iunius Pennus, as tribune in 126, did get a law passed prohibiting foreigners (*peregrini*) from the city. Gaius Gracchus seems, once again, to have used historical examples to argue against it: "Those nations destroyed their *res publica*, among other things, by avarice and stupidity."[25] In 125 Fulvius Flaccus made a proposal for extension of the citizenship, which seems never to have come to a vote.[26] Gaius Gracchus did propose a law, which, as it seems, gave Latin voting rights to the Italians and full citizenship to the Latins. This too, if ever put to the vote, was not passed.[27] But we know from Cicero (*Brut.* 99) of a speech of Gaius Fannius, consul of 122, *De sociis et nomine Latino contra Gracchum*. It is evidently from this that there comes one highly illuminating fragment, addressed to the people: "If you were to give the citizenship to the Latins, do you suppose that you would have any room in the public meeting, in the same way as you have now assembled, or would be able to attend the games [*ludi*] or days of public business?"[28]

I mentioned earlier the violent conflicts in 100 over land allotments which would have included Italian along with Roman ex-soldiers.[29] If a share in the profits of Empire, for which they had to fight, was one of the things which the Italians wanted, they must surely have noted this episode. Worse was to come. A law passed by the consuls of 95, Licinius Crassus and Mucius Scaevola, set up a procedure to enquire into citizen rights improperly enjoyed, or

24. For an interesting and valuable, but not ultimately persuasive, attempt to argue that under Tiberius' agrarian law Italian allies could receive both allotments of public land and a simultaneous grant of the citizenship, see J. S. Richardson, "The Ownership of Italian Land: Tiberius Gracchus and the Italians," *JRS* 70 (1980): 1.

25. Festus 286M/362L. Cicero, *De off.* 3, 47, suggests, without quite proving, that the law was actually passed. Was it directed specifically against Italian allies, or against all (or overseas?) foreigners? In the latter case it may not be quite certain that Gaius Gracchus was opposing the law. Might he not have been arguing that "these nations" (e.g., the Greek cities) had suffered disaster by their own fault?

26. Val. Max. 9, 5, 5; Appian, *BC* I, 21/86–87; 34/152.

27. Appian, *BC* I, 23/99–101. I would not put any weight on the various proposals and counter-proposals vaguely recorded by Plutarch, *Gaius Gracchus* 5 and 8–9.

28. Iulius Victor 6, 4 (C. Halm, *Rhetores Latini Minores* (1863), p. 402).

29. Appian, *BC* I, 29–30/129–40. For a detailed discussion of this passage, the only item in our evidence to mention popular hostility to benefits for Italian ex-soldiers, see now H. Schneider, "Die politische Rolle der *plebs urbana* während der Tribunate des L. Appuleius Saturninus," *Ancient Society* 12–13 (1982–83): 193.

claimed, by Italians: no one was to be considered who was not in fact a citizen.[30] It is easy and natural to see this step as an action "of" the two consuls; but it was not only theirs. Like any other law it had to be notified in advance, and proposed in public meetings before the people. Innumerable proposed laws met opposition, by counter-persuasion or force, and many were never passed. This one *was* passed, by the votes of the people. Contrast this with the events of 91–90, which might reasonably be taken as the prime example of divisions within the office-holding class, of the presentation of conflicting views before the people, and of the people's effective right to call members of the senatorial class to account, and (until military necessity dictated otherwise) to protect its own constitutional powers. It is instructive to compare the law mooted by Livius Drusus, to give citizenship to the Italians, which (as it seems) never came to a vote, with that of Varius, directed against those who had helped the Italians, which was passed.

There seems to be no direct evidence as to what was said in support of, or against, Drusus' law to enfranchise the Italians; nor is it quite certain that the matter ever reached the stage of being debated in public meetings. The public meeting held by Drusus which the consul, L. Marcius Philippus, tried to interrupt, only to suffer physical violence for his pains, apparently concerned the agrarian law, or laws (Val. Max. 9, 5, 2; *De vir ill.* 76, 9). Cicero does, however, describe the public meeting which Philippus held in September, and in which he raised popular feeling against the Senate, saying that he would need to seek another advice (*consilium*); for with that Senate (as it then was) he could not conduct the affairs of the *res publica*. Drusus then summoned the Senate, to report on the consul's speech, and Licinius Crassus delivered his swan song, a denunciation of the consul's attack on the place of the Senate in the state. The celebrated narrative (*De or.* 3, 1–11) in which Cicero retails all this surely reveals enough to suggest that the real issue at this moment was popular hostility to Drusus' proposal, and suspicion of those within the Senate who were believed to support it. A few days later Crassus died. A few days after that Gaius Cotta was "expelled from the tribunate through rancour"— that is, through rancour he failed to gain the tribunate for which he was a candidate (*De or.* 1, 25). The reason is surely clear from the fact that some months later he was exiled under the law proposed by the tribune Q. Varius, and passed, perhaps in 90 rather than 91, by the people. This law set up a court into the actions of those "by whose assistance or advice the [Italian] allies had taken up arms against the Roman people" (Asconius 22C). All those persons known to have been condemned were Roman senators. They did not of

---

30. See esp. Cicero. *De off*, 3, 47; Asconius 67–68C.

course include Livius Drusus himself, who had been murdered in October of 91; nor apparently, did they include the aged Aemilius Scaurus, whom Varius summoned separately before the people and accused of having incited the Italians to arms; but he rebutted the accusation by a direct demand to the citizens to believe his word (Asconius 22C). Popular opinion could always be swayed by an effective personal plea. But when Drusus' opponent, the consul Marcius Philippus, denounced the Senate to the people; when Cotta lost the tribunate through rancour; and when Varius could persuade the people to vote a law to investigate and punish those who had betrayed them from above by encouraging the Italians in the hope of sharing their rights — all that was surely as clear a demonstration as we could possibly have of the power of popular politics, and the strength of popular feeling for the retention of the people's exclusive rights to the exercise of political power: "he [Crassus] did not [live to] see Italy ablaze with war, the Senate inflamed with passion, the leading citizens arraigned for a nefarious crime" (*De or.* 3, 8, Loeb trans.).

Within a few months the war forced the people to pass the first of the laws by which they were after all to share those rights with the Italians. With that there began a new phase in the nature of the Roman political system, one in which military force and organized violence were to play a part in a way unknown before, and in which any crowd which gathered in the Forum bore an even more erratic relationship to the vastly increased number of qualified voters. It was also to be the greatest age of Roman oratory, much of it directed to the people at public meetings. Persuasion was still vital; and the votes of those few who did vote played a crucial part in the last decades of republican history.

CHAPTER SIX

Popular Politics at Rome
in the Late Republic*

"After this, Curio delivered before the people a lengthy denunciation of Pompey and the consuls, and when he had finished his term of office at once set off to join Caesar." Few people who have studied Roman history will have difficulty in identifying the moment which these words describe. It is of course December of the year 50 B.C., when the incoming consuls-elect had made up their minds to resist Julius Caesar by force, and when Curio, coming to the end of his tribunate, due on December 9, held his last meeting to address the Roman people. Caesar's crossing of the Rubicon was not far away. We are exactly at the major turning point in Roman history. We are also, and this is surely no accident, exactly half way through the great *Roman History* in eighty books, written in the third century A.D. by Cassius Dio, a Greek from Bithynia, a Roman senator, and *consul ordinarius* in A.D. 229. The words which I have quoted are in fact the very last sentence of book 40.[1]

Dio thus displayed considerable artistry and sense of overall design in choosing the last moments of the tribunate of Curio to end the first half of his

* First published in I. Malkin and Z. W. Rubinsohn, eds., *Leaders and Masses in the Roman World: Studies in Honor of Zvi Yavetz* (1995), 91–113. This chapter, which it is a deep pleasure to offer to Zvi Yavetz, owes much to a lecture given at the Classical Association in Glasgow in 1986, and subsequently, in various forms, at a number of universities in the United Kingdom and Ireland, at New York University, and—on a memorable occasion in January 1989—at Tel-Aviv. I have kept the style of a lecture, with only minimal notes, partly as a tribute to one of the great masters of the spoken word, in English and other languages, and partly because it is itself a *Vorarbeit*. The topic is explored more fully in my Jerome Lectures of 1993–94, "The Crowd in Rome in the Late Republic"; now published as *The Crowd in Rome in the Late Republic* (1998).

1. Dio 40, 66, 5.

History. These were not however to be the last words addressed to the people before the civil war broke out. Among the ten tribunes taking up office on 10 December 50 B.C., were Marcus Antonius and Q. Cassius Longinus. By 25 December, Cicero and Pompey, then at Formiae, more than 100 kilometres away, had in their hands the text of a *contio*, a speech before the people, delivered by Antonius on 21 December: "containing," as Cicero reported to Atticus, "a denunciation of Pompey since he came of age [*a toga pura*], a protest on behalf of the persons condemned, and threats of armed force."[2] After the new consuls, C. Claudius Marcellus and L. Cornelius Lentulus, had entered office on 1 January 49, Antonius held another public meeting (*contio*), at which he read out the text of a letter from Caesar; in it Caesar put proposals which, as Plutarch reports, were "persuasive to the people": that he and Pompey should both give up their provinces, dismiss their forces, submit to the judgement of the people, and render an account of their actions.[3] But the Senate on 7 January passed what Caesar calls that "extreme and ultimate decree . . . that the consuls, praetors, tribunes of the plebs, and whichever proconsuls were in the neighbourhood of the city, should see to it that the *res publica* suffered no loss," thereby misleading modern scholars into thinking that there was a legal entity called the *senatus consultum ultimum*.[4] Immediately after this vote, Antonius and Cassius also left to join Caesar, and the civil war began.

How had such a crisis arisen? What was the nature of the political system which gave rise to the civil war and, as a result of it, to a monarchical regime which was to last, in Rome and in Constantinople, for a millennium and a half? What was the place within it of the Senate on the one hand, and the Roman people on the other?

It is still common to say that the Senate represented the "government" of the Roman Republic. A typical formulation is that offered even by P. A. Brunt, whose work has done more than that of anyone else to rid us of stereotypes which are in fact quite recent, but have become hardened into dogma: "The true governing organ of the Roman Republic was the senate which acted through annual magistrates elected by the people but drawn from its own ranks. The senate itself was dominated by a few noble families whose power reposed on their wealth and on the number of their dependents and

2. Cic., *Att.* 7, 8, 5 (Shackleton-Bailey, no. 131).

3. Plut., *Pomp.* 59.

4. Caesar, *Bell. Civ.* 1, 5, 3, on which see the text, translation, and commentary by J. C. Carter, *Julius Caesar, The Civil Wars Book I and II* (1991) (taking, however, a more definite view than I do of the *senatus cunsultum ultimum* as an institution).

on the prestige they derived from their past services to the state." He goes on to talk of the theoretical power of the people, the practical restrictions imposed on their voting, and the manipulation of those conditions by the ruling class: "At Rome there were too many checks and balances in the constitution, which operated in practice only in the interest of the ruling class. Reformers had to use force, or at least to create conditions in which the senate had reason to fear its use."[5]

I think that most people would accept this as a fair description of the structure of politics in the late Republic: an oligarchical system, dominated by noble families; a stable system progressively destabilised, in part at least, by eruptions of mob violence. It is significant indeed that the well-known article from which these quotations are drawn is called "The Roman Mob," and ends with a catalogue of acts of political violence in Rome in the last century of the Republic.

I am not going to suggest that this standard view is wholly wrong. Indeed it lies in the nature of analyses of political systems that they cannot be, in any simple sense, right or wrong. But I do want to suggest that we could see the whole system in rather different terms. For a start we need to establish some different perspectives.

Firstly, the traditional model assumes that popular quiescence or passivity was the norm; popular action running counter to the interests or the wishes of the Senate, or of the upper classes as a whole, represents a breakdown, normally accompanied by violence. No one will dispute that group violence, fuelled by various political motivations, often occurred in the politics of the late Republic. Alternatively, John North's very valuable discussion of the nature and limits of democratic politics at Rome asserts "The popular will of the Roman people found expression in the context, and only in the context, of discussion within the oligarchy."[6] The formulation seems convincing. But by importing the words "the oligarchy" it presupposes that we can define such a group in a way which is not circular, that is, which does not depend on the mere fact of election to office. It also presupposes that mass reactions had, and could have, no influence. And it (again) invites to take as the norm a state of affairs (when?) in which there were no divisions among

5. The quotations are from P. A. Brunt, "The Roman Mob," *Past and Present* 35 (1966): 3, on pp. 4–5 and 8; this article was unfortunately not reprinted with other important papers in *The Fall of the Roman Republic* (1988), 4. But it was *Social Conflicts in the Roman Republic* (1971), which took the first significant step in removing the stereotypes which have obscured the reality of communal politics at Rome.

6. J. A. North, "Democratic Politics in Republican Rome," *Past and Present* 126 (1990): 3, on p. 18.

the "oligarchy." But, more important still, the standard formulation does not take sufficiently into account the central fact that the sovereign body in the Roman *res publica* was not the Senate, but the Roman people. Roman laws expressed this fundamental conception with perfect clarity: the tribunician law of (almost certainly) late 101 B.C. had spoken of the "nations outside [Italy] who are in the friendship of the Roman people";[7] Saturninus' law of 100 on *maiestas* (treason) defined it in terms which Cicero reflects in the 80s: to detract in any way from the dignity (*dignitas*) or the greatness (*amplitudo*) or the power (*potestas*) of the people, or of those to whom the people has given power.[8] And in 58 B.C., when the consuls, Gabinius and Piso, passed a law establishing the immunity from taxation of the sacred island of Delos, the text of the law incorporated the notion that this measure "was in accordance with the dignity and majesty of the Roman people."[9]

Using "democracy" in a strictly neutral sense, it is undeniable that the constitution of the Roman Republic was that of a direct democracy. Firstly, in Rome all office was conferred by election in the assemblies. Our sources reflect repeatedly the conception that office was a favour (*beneficium*) conferred by the Roman people, something which had to be asked for from the people.[10] As Cicero emphasised in his speech in defense of Plancius of 54 B.C., it was essential for a candidate to present the public image of someone petitioning humbly (*submisse supplicare*), and particularly essential for a *nobilis*, someone with at least one ancestor who had already held a major office.[11] Given this public expectation, it was also the norm that a consul, on entering office on January 1, should make a speech of thanks to the populace to give thanks for the favour conferred on him.[12] It is not for us to say that all this was mere pretence: firstly, because office could in fact not be gained without election, preceded by the well-known processes of *ambitus*, that is, literally going around soliciting votes; and, secondly, because the public ideology of a system is itself a fact about it, which we cannot ignore if we wish to understand it. It is noteworthy that it has now been demonstrated by Alexander

7. M. Hassall, M. Crawford, and J. Reynolds, "Rome and the Eastern Provinces at the End of the Second Century BC," *JRS* 64 (1974): 195, Cnidos Copy, col. III, ll.33–34.

8. Cic., *Inv.* 3, 53.

9. C. Nicolet et al., *Insula Sacra: la loi Gabinia Calpurnia de Délos (58 av. J-C)* (1980), restored text on p. 149, l. 18.

10. See, e.g., Lucretius 3, 995–98: "Sisyphus in this life also appears before our eyes, gasping to solicit from the people the *fasces* [rods] and the sacred axes, and always retires sad and defeated."

11. Cic., *Pro Plancio* 12–13; 50.

12. Cic., *De leg. ag.* 1, 1.

Yakobson that because the elections were *competitive*, even elections in the centuriate assembly (*comitia centuriata*) represented a power of choice by the people which could and often did extend beyond the highest classes.[13]

Secondly, and even more important, it was the people, and not the Senate, who could legislate; they did so by voting in person; a *lex* or *plebiscitum* was by definition something put to the *populus* or *plebs*, and formally voted on by them; as is well known, in the late Republic the assembly which voted on *leges* was almost always the tribal assembly (*comitia tributa*) of the thirty-five tribes. In the relatively rare cases where such a law conferred a right or privilege on an individual, this too could be seen as a favour conferred by the Roman people: so Julius Caesar in early 49 complained that the Senate and consuls were denying him the right conferred by the law proposed by the ten tribunes in 52, and passed by the people, namely that he would be allowed to stand for the consulship in absence: "he was grieved that the favour conferred on him by the Roman people should be injuriously denied him by his enemies."[14] It is more important to recall that the right to propose legislation to the people had been removed from the tribunes in Sulla's legislation in the late 80s, was the subject of repeated popular pressure through the 70s, and was restored in 70. Thereafter, the process of legislation became again what it had been before, one of the central elements in the public political process, and the main agent of *change*. This needs to be stressed: the passing of new laws by the people was *the* essential vehicle by which rapid and fundamental change came about in the last twenty years of the Republic.

Should we see this twenty-year period, from 70 to 50 B.C., on which I intend to concentrate, as itself representing the breakdown of a previously successful and stable political order? In a wider perspective, that would indeed be paradoxical. For it was precisely in this period that Roman direct rule, and Roman taxation, suddenly expanded through Asia Minor to Syria, the banks of the Euphrates, and the edge of the desert in one direction, and to the North Sea in the other. As Pompey claimed in a speech addressed to the people some time after his return in 62, "he had received Asia as the furthest of provinces and restored it to his homeland as a central one (in the Empire)."[15] It should be noted that this claim was made in a *contio*, a speech addressed to a meeting of the people. There followed the great triumph celebrated in Rome by Pompey in 61, in which the extent of his conquests, the

13. A. Yakobson, "*Petitio et largitio*: Popular Participation in the Centuriate Assembly of the Late Republic," *JRS* 82 (1992): 32.

14. Caesar, *Bell. Civ.* 1, 9, 2, on which see Carter (n. 4).

15. Pliny, *NH* 7, 99; *ORF*³, Cn. Pompeius Magnus V/19.

scale of the booty, and, what is more, the vast increase in the recurring taxation income of the Empire were all demonstrated in visual form before the people.[16] It is not surprising that the law of 58 B.C. about Delos, referred to earlier, not only looks back to the law of 67 which Gabinius had passed as tribune (against almost universal opposition from the Senate); as a result of it, the law of 58 recalls, the pirates had been "overcome and destroyed"; but the text of the law also describes the present state of affairs as one in which the *imperium* had been expanded (*amplificatum*) and peace achieved throughout the world.[17] In 58 also, of course, Caesar was to begin his campaigns in Gaul, a chance which he too owed to a law proposed by a tribune, and passed by the people, in 59; in 58 itself another law proposed by Clodius as tribune, would send Cato to annex the Ptolemaic kingdom of Cyprus. The constitutional and political issue which was at stake in this case was also presented quite explicitly to the people. Cicero twice records that Caesar wrote from Gaul to congratulate Clodius on putting Cato in this position; his acceptance of this commission would prevent him from complaining in future about grants of extraordinary powers. More important, however, is the fact that this letter was then read out by Clodius to the crowd assembled at a public meeting.[18] If Cato was embarrassed by this mission, he did not show it when he returned in 56 B.C. He sailed back to Rome in one of the royal galleys, and had the royal treasures paraded through the Forum, to the amazement of the people. Once again, the profits of the Empire were literally demonstrated to the public.[19]

Yet another law of Clodius, passed in January 58, established for the first time that the monthly grain distribution made to the people of Rome should be free of all charge. To Cicero this law seemed, as such laws always did, a misuse of the revenues of the state: "with the remission of the charge about a fifth of the revenues would be removed." To others it was clearly, as Asconius says, "extremely popular"; to them it will surely have seemed the fulfilment of the principle put forward earlier, by the Gracchi: "what could be more just than that the impoverished *people* should be supported from their own treasury"?[20]

I would like to suggest that we should, among other perspectives, also try to see the evolution of the Roman Empire, and the pattern of Roman

16. See esp. Plut., *Pomp.* 45.
17. See n. 9; see ll. 16–19 of text.
18. Cic., *Dom.* 22; *Sest.* 60.
19. Plut., *Cato Min.* 39.
20. Cic., *Sest.* 55; Asconius, ed. Clark, 8; Florus, *Epit.* 2, 1.

political life, from the point of view of the people of Rome. In doing so we need not in the least deny the important role of the upper classes: the inherent militarism of Roman upper-class life; the competitiveness and search for personal and family glory; the vast scale of personal profiteering; and the steadily rising standards of personal wealth, luxury, and display. All that is beyond question, and the expansion of the Roman Empire would not have taken place in the same way without it. But we can still try the stratagem of adopting a perspective which is not that of the upper classes, and seeing whether it does not make as good or better sense of the evidence before us. Suppose, that is, that we consider the Roman political system, Roman military activities, and the expansion and exploitation of the Empire, in terms of how far they satisfied the interests of the voters, the Roman people.

The political quiescence of the first half of the second century B.C. would then appear not as domination by the Senate, but as the result of a series of relatively brief, successful, profitable, and glorious wars in the East on the one hand; and, on the other, of the continued availability in Italy of newly conquered land, which could be divided out for settlement, at any rate down to the 170s.[21] The political turmoil of the second half of the second century would then be seen as arising, for instance, from involvement in long and unprofitable major wars in Spain, from 153 B.C. onwards; then from suspicions of improper conduct and profiteering on the part of senatorial commanders—we should recall the famous trial of Sulpicius Galba before the Roman people in 149, and the passage in the same year of the first tribunician law to set up a court to try senatorial governors and office-holders for extortion;[22] but, above all, conflicts now arose over the occupation and use of a now fixed and limited stock of public land in Italy.

I do not need to rehearse again all the themes of popular politics in the later second century: the use of the funds left by Attalus of Pergamon to Rome; the exploitation of the revenues of Asia; suspicions over corruption and bribery on the part of senators; the laws on grain distribution in Rome, so far at a fixed price, not free; the treason law of Saturninus, whose terms were quoted earlier; the first laws for establishing colonies or land allotments overseas; the major law of 101 B.C. laying down what was to be done in Asia Minor and in Macedonia, and imposing on office-holders the obligation to

21. For my view of this period, obviously not the only one which is possible, see "The Political Character of the Classical Roman Republic, 200–151 BC," *JRS* 74 (1984), 1 (chapter 4 in this volume).

22. See J. S. Richardson, "The Purpose of the Lex Calpurnia de repetundis," *JRS* 77 (1987): 1.

swear within five days to obey its provisions. Taken together, these and other measures of the period represent both an assertion of popular sovereignty and repeated attempts to reap the benefits of empire for the people.[23]

The Social War of 90 B.C., the extension of the Roman citizenship to all of Italy, and the consequent doubling of the number of persons in principle qualified to vote in Rome represented one major disturbance of this political pattern; I will come back later to some of its consequences. Another disturbance of course was the establishment by force of Sulla's counter-revolution in 82, and the constitutional changes which were then imposed. It is important to stress how profound a counter-revolution this was. Whatever the exact form of the removal of tribunician legislation, the very fact that this step was taken demonstrates the centrality of the operation of popular sovereignty. So does the force of the reaction in the following decade. For by 70 B.C. all the essential elements of popular politics had reasserted themselves. When C. Aurelius Cotta, as consul in 75 B.C., passed a law to give back to the tribunes the right to stand for further office, it was "against the will of the *nobilitas*, but with great popular enthusiasm."[24] L. Quinctius, as tribune in 74, is described by Cicero as having brought back the "tribunician voice" to the Rostra, abandoned since Sulla, and caused the people to become once again accustomed to public meetings.[25] M. Seius, aedile in the same year, provided oil and grain at a modest price for the Roman people, apparently contributing the cost from his own pocket. As a result he became a popular hero; statues of him were dedicated on the Capitol and the Palatine, and on death he was carried to his cremation by the people.[26] The consuls of the next year, 73, carried a law for the purchase of grain in the provinces, for consumption in Rome. Demands for the restoration of the tribunate continued, coupled with popular suspicion of the operations of the extortion court, as conducted by the senatorial jurors. Indeed, if we may believe Cicero, the latter question aroused even more feeling than the former. For in his first speech against Verres, of 70 B.C., he recalls an occasion in the previous year:[27]

> Finally, when Cn. Pompeius himself, as consul designate, held his first
> public meeting near the city, in which, as seemed to be the thing most

23. For a sketch of the ways in which these issues played a role in oratory addressed to the People, see F. Millar, "Politics, Persuasion and the People before the Social War," *JRS* 76 (1986): 1 (chapter 5 in this volume).

24. Asconius, ed. Clark, 66–67.

25. Cic., *Cluent.* 110–12. See Broughton, *MRR* II, 103.

26. Cic., *De off.* 2, 58; Pliny, *NH* 15, 2; 18, 16.

27. Cic., *Verr.* 1, 45.

expected of him, he made clear that he would restore the powers of the tribunes, there arose in response a noise and a contented murmur on the part of the crowd. But when he himself in the same speech had said that the provinces were being ravaged and harried, and the courts becoming a shame and disgrace—this was something which he intended to provide for and take steps about; then indeed, not with a mere noise, but with a mighty shout the Roman people made known their will.

Time and again in the orations against Verres, Cicero alludes to the force of popular opinion in Rome, as it bore on the conduct of the courts, and emphasises the hostility of the Roman people to Verres. A law transferring control of the courts had indeed not yet been passed; that was precisely the threat which he was holding over the heads of the senatorial jurors. "What can we say against that praetor [L. Aurelius Cotta] who daily occupies the *templum* [i.e., the Rostra in the Forum] and who says [i.e., in speeches to the people] that the *res publica* cannot stand unless the courts are transferred to the equestrian order?"[28]

Thus the various elements of a political system based on popular power and directed to popular gratification had either survived the Sullan regime or, by 70, been restored after it. Cicero can allude casually in the Verrine orations to the fact that "in our *res publica*" people gain office by *largitio*, by largesse to the voters.[29] The series of games and shows offered to the people had even increased in this period. The summer in which Cicero was speaking was taken up not only by the traditional Roman Games, but by the Victory Games established by Sulla himself, and the Votive Games given by Pompey as consul.[30] Cicero himself could look forward to the power and public role which he would enjoy as aedile in 69; if Verres were not condemned, he would be able, as aedile, to accuse him before a popular court.[31] More important, occupation of this office will give him a central role in the life of the city: the conduct of games in honour of the gods, the care of the sacred buildings, the care of the whole city.[32]

Immediately after 70, and the restoration of the right of the tribunes to propose legislation to the people, the course of popular politics duly resumed the pattern which it had shown until the year 100. Within a couple of years laws put to the assembly by tribunes became the means by which provincial

28. E.g., *Verr. II* 3, 7; 223.
29. *Verr. II* 2, 138.
30. *Verr.* 1, 31.
31. *Verr. II* 5, 173.
32. *Verr. II* 5, 36–37.

commands were transferred, and detailed questions relating to the provinces settled. It was surely by means of a law that, in 68, the province of Cilicia was removed from Lucullus' command and given to Q. Marcius Rex;[33] and it is virtually certain that the law on the privileges of Termessos in Pisidia, put to the plebs by a group of tribunes, also belongs to 68; among other things the text of this law declares that the people of Termessos are to be "friends and allies" of the Roman people, and it instructs magistrates and promagistrates not to billet soldiers there, or make any illegal demands on them.[34]

This phase came to a head in 67. One law passed by the tribune Gabinius gave to the consul, M'. Acilius Glabrio, the province of Bithynia and Pontus, and another gave Pompey his historic Mediterranean-wide command against the pirates. In the following year Cicero, speaking to the people, was to recall the scene when this latter law was passed.[35]

> Do you think that there is any shore so deserted, that the fame of that day has not reached it, when the whole Roman People, with the forum packed, and every temple crowded from which this place [the Rostra] can be seen, demanded Cn. Pompeius as sole *imperator* for the common war on behalf of all peoples?

It would be possible to devote an entire paper to the complex patterns of popular politics — or of *public* politics conducted in the open in a central public place, the Forum Romanum — as they showed themselves in this law, and other legislation of the year 67. But a few episodes will suffice by way of illustration. The two prominent ex-consuls (*consulares*), Hortensius and Catulus, both spoke against the law, to the people.[36] Catulus did so in part by question-and-answer to the crowd, as Cicero recalls:[37]

> When he asked of you (the people), if you were to confer all power on Pompey, and if anything happened to him, in whom you would repose your hopes, he gained a striking reward for his own virtue and dignity, when you all with one voice said that it would be in him himself.

Here, as in the following year, a fundamental argument about the nature of the constitution on the one hand, and the needs of imperial security on the other, was being conducted in public through the medium of speeches.

33. Dio 36, 2, 2.
34. See J.-L. Ferrary, "La Lex Antonia de Termessibus," *Athenaeum* 63 (1985): 419.
35. Cic., *Man.* 44.
36. *Man.* 51–53, 56.
37. *Man.* 59.

Cicero's *Pro lege Manilia* itself, a literary version of a public speech delivered by Cicero to the people, is our best evidence of that. One should note especially the elaborate arguments from historical precedent, and, as always, the fear of the effects in Rome of losing the revenues of Asia. Particular significance attaches to the quotation of Hortensius' speech against this law: *if* all power were to be granted to one man, Hortensius had said, Pompey was the most worthy; but it was *not* proper to grant all power to one man.[38]

Of course political decisions were not made solely on the basis of reasoned public argument about past precedent and present necessity. The complex machinery of the Roman constitution could be invoked to crush opposition; in 67, when another tribune, Trebellius, was persuaded to veto the law about Pompey's command, Gabinius had called in the thirty-five tribes one by one to vote on his deposition. Only when seventeen tribes had voted, and the eighteenth was going to, did he give in.[39] In the same year another tribune, Cornelius, raised the issue of profiteering by the medium of loans being made to foreign ambassadors present in Rome; this question too became a constitutional issue, when he proposed that the steps taken by the Senate were inadequate, and that law passed by the people was required.[40] The attempt to pass the law led to a veto by another tribune; this veto had the effect of stopping the scribe from reading out the text of the law to the people; so Cornelius took the text (*codex*) and read it out himself. Note that custom required that the whole text of the law should be read out before the people—and that no one had established whether one tribune could veto another acting in person. When the consul declared publicly that a veto of this type was improper, he was greeted with abuse by the people; when he ordered his lictors to arrest some of them, their *fasces* (rods) were broken, and stones were hurled from the back of the crowd.[41]

This issue was in the end settled by a compromise. But it involved basic questions as to who might profit from the power conferred by Empire, and where sovereignty lay. The atmosphere of the year 67 is, however, perhaps best recaptured in another incident which Cicero retails eleven years later in his speech in defence of Sestius. Gabinius, as tribune in 67, had displayed to the crowd a picture of a villa, with the object of bringing a prominent citizen

38. *Man.* 52.

39. Asconius 37, ed. Clark.

40. I make no attempt in this context to go into the complex series of events associated with this tribunate. See, e.g., M. Griffin, "The Tribune C. Cornelius," *JRS* 63 (1973): 196.

41. Asconius 57–59, ed. Clark.

(Lucullus) into disrepute.[42] The purpose was clearly to arouse popular suspicion of profiteering and luxurious private life-styles. "The Roman people," as Cicero recalled, defending Murena in 63, "hates private luxury, and delights in public magnificence."[43] Visual messages, as well as verbal ones, had their place in popular politics.

With the mid 60s, we have of course returned to the period from which I started: the period of the clearing of the pirates from the Mediterranean, and of the great conquests by Lucullus and Pompey, soon to be followed by those of Caesar, when the Empire was indeed expanded, as the law of 58 proudly stated. I have emphasised above all two things. In the short term, in the 60s and 50s, there was the essential role of laws passed by the people in establishing the major commands which made the conquests possible. The laws already mentioned were followed by those of 58 which gave Piso the province of Macedonia, and Gabinius first Cilicia and then Syria; and then the laws of 55 which gave Pompey Spain and Crassus Syria, each for five years, and another which prolonged Caesar's command in Gaul.

The second essential point is the extent to which all this led to benefits which themselves reflected the fact of the sovereignty of the Roman people. Suppose, as I suggested earlier, that we ask how the whole story would look if we saw it from the perspective of the people of Rome. The most obvious example is the fact that a free corn ration was established by a law passed by Clodius in 58; this right to free corn was to last late into the Empire. Then there were laws to use the resources of the state to acquire land for individuals. The law proposed by Rullus on entering the tribunate in December 64 aimed to raise funds by selling public assets in the provinces, and to use these funds for buying private land on which individual citizens could be settled. The text of Rullus' law was put up in public, where interested parties could copy it; and Rullus explained his proposals to the people in a speech which, Cicero says, was so long and so complicated that no one understood it.[44] We do not know whether the bill was rejected, or was never finally put to the vote; only that it did not become law. Nor do we know why; we only know Cicero's public speech against it, his second oration *De lege agraria*, using, among others, the arguments that the proposal was in reality a device to gather power into a few irresponsible hands. But the same issue returned in 60 with the bill about land distribution proposed by Flavius, when

42. Cic., *Sest.* 93.
43. Cic., *Mur.* 76.
44. Cic., *De leg. ag.* 2, 13–14.

again Cicero made a detailed speech against it, addressed to the people; here he defended the interests of private property "with a favourable reception from the public meeting," or so he reports.[45] The bill of 60 also did not become law; but the two agrarian bills of Caesar in 59 did, to be followed in his dictatorship by the first-ever extensive programme of colonisation overseas, involving some 80,000 people. Conquest, overseas colonisation, and the political change which we call "the Roman Revolution" are three aspects of the same process.

One other argument which Cicero had used in 63, against Rullus' proposal for procuring agricultural land on which to settle citizens, was the fact that they would then be deprived of the delights of the city:[46]

> You indeed, Citizens, if you will listen to me, keep hold of what you have, your political influence [*gratia*], your freedom, your votes, your dignity, your city, forum, games, festivals, and all your other assets.

These were indeed real assets. It would be a mistake to see public shows and ceremonials, and the steadily rising level of the public magnificence which was demanded of office-holders by the people, as trivial features of the way that Roman politics worked.[47] Looked at structurally, they were both a price paid to the people for office, and a means by which the benefits of Empire could be felt by the mass of the people in Rome. There is no need here for a long catalogue of shows and liberalities. It may be sufficient to mention, for example, the dinner and the three-month supply of grain given to the people by Crassus as consul in 70;[48] or Caesar's ruinously expensive displays as aedile in 65; or the famous games given by Scaurus as aedile in 58, which involved the construction of a temporary theatre three storeys high, of which the first was veneered in marble; the theatre allegedly seated 80,000 spectators, and contained 3,000 statues.[49] Scaurus was also to display 150 female leopards, the first hippopotamus ever shown in Rome, and 5 crocodiles for which a special water-channel had to be cut. From Jaffa he brought what was said to be the skeleton of the monster to which Andromeda had been exposed.[50] The point was not solely to exhibit magnificence, or to amaze the public. Scaurus had

---

45. Cic., *Att.* I, 19, 4 (Shackleton-Bailey, no. 19).

46. *De leg. ag.* 2, 70–1.

47. The best treatment of the role of public magnificence in the late Republic is P. Veyne, *Le pain et le cirque* (1976), pt. iii, trans. as *Bread and Circuses* (1990). See also Yakobson (n. 13).

48. Plut., *Crass.* 2, 12.

49. Pliny, *NH* 36, 113–15.

50. Pliny, *NH* 8, 64 (leopards); 96 (hippopotamus and crocodiles); 9, 11 (monster from Jaffa).

been left by Pompey as the first governor of Syria, with the anomalous rank of *proquaestore propraetore*, in 63–62, immediately after it had been conquered. The legendary monster from Jaffa, like the coins of 58 naming both Scaurus as *aid(ilis) cur(ulis)* and King Aretas of Nabataea (which he had in fact invaded, but then retreated), was thus another comforting reminder to the people of the rapid recent extension of the boundaries of Roman power.[51]

This extension was aptly mirrored also, in the 50s, by major building projects instituted and paid for by the great conquerors out of the profits of conquest. These buildings have many levels of significance, but one is precisely the channelling for public benefit of profits which could have been spent privately. Pompey's permanent stone theatre, the first ever constructed in Rome, was said by Pliny to have seated 40,000 spectators; the true figure is perhaps 10,000, which is striking enough. This too was also a symbol of Roman expansion: the design was copied from the theatre at Mitylene; and in and around the theatre stood fourteen statues of personified nations, evidently those conquered by Pompey. Above the *cavea* stood a temple of Venus Victrix, and in theory the seats of the *cavea* were merely the steps leading up to the temple. In his edict addressed to the people Pompey invited them to the dedication of this temple "to which we have subjoined seats for the shows." Like his triumph of six years before, but in permanent form, the theatre offered the Roman people a symbol of his, and its, victory. Before the battle of Pharsalus Pompey was to dream that he was entering the theatre to make offerings to Venus Victrix, and receiving the applause of the people.[52]

A permanent inscription, with Pompey's name, was placed on the theatre only three years later, during his third consulship in 52.[53] By that time he was already in danger of being outdone. For Caesar's building projects, financed by his victories in Gaul, were planned to occupy an even more central place in the political life of the Roman people. The sum of 100 million sesterces from the spoils of war in Gaul was used merely to purchase the ground for his new Forum.[54] By mid 54 Cicero himself, as he records in a letter to Atticus, was in some way involved in plans for extending the Forum as far as the Atrium Libertatis, and 60 million sesterces had already been spent. In the

---

51. Broughton, *MRR* II, 168, 175; M. Crawford, *Roman Republican Coinage* I (1974), no. 422.

52. Pliny, *NH* 35, 115 (40,000 spectators); 41 (*nationes*). Tertullian, *Spect.* 10, 5 (*edictum*); Plut., *Pomp.* 68, 2 (dream). See E. Frézouls, "La construction du *theatrum lapideum* et son contexte politique," in *Théatre et spectacles dans l'Antiquité (Colloque Strasbourg 1981*, 1983), 193. See P. Zanker, *Augustus und die Macht der Bilder* (1987), 30ff.

53. Aulus Gellius, *NA* 10, 1, 7.

54. Suet., *Div. Jul.* 26.

same letter of 54, Cicero alludes to even more spectacular plans for building on that other essential public space, the Campus Martius, where the elections were held (all elections, as it seems, since the mid second century). Here the plan was to build for the electoral assemblies a marble enclosure, the Saepta, roofed and surrounded by a portico 1,000 paces in length. This building was in fact to be completed in 26 B.C., one year after Senate and People had finally recognised the power of Augustus.[55] That may seem to be a paradox. In fact it is not. For it was precisely this two-way relationship between *princeps* and *plebs* which broke up the Republic.

These lavish buildings and elaborate, apparently pointless, displays are not a trivial or superficial aspect of Republican politics. To understand their significance we have to consider them together with the distributions of grain, which was now free, and reached some 300,000 people; Cicero may be exaggerating in saying that these distributions used up a fifth of the public revenues; but the scale of the provision is still striking.[56] Similarly, buildings and shows meant the deployment in Rome of major organisational efforts in relation to the rather slight overall functions which the Roman *res publica* performed. In sheer terms of scale and cost these things cannot be regarded as trivial. As I suggested earlier, we could reasonably look at the whole course of Rome's expansion and exploitation of its empire in terms of its capacity to provide benefits for the Roman people. In that context it is very significant that by 57 the people saw themselves as entitled, not merely to a free ration of corn, but to active measures on the part of the state to provide corn for the market in Rome. In September of 57 the crowd gathered spontaneously in the temporary theatre erected for the Roman Games and then rushed to where the Senate was meeting; according to Cicero, in a letter to Atticus, Clodius inspired the crowd to shout that the shortage was his, Cicero's, fault. They also demanded that Cicero propose that the care of the corn supply be given to Pompey. After he had duly proposed this, and the Senate had passed a decree in these terms, the text of it was immediately read out to the crowd outside. When the crowd applauded "in the silly, new-fangled fashion," by

55. Cic., *Att.* 4, 16, 8, Shackleton-Bailey, no. 86. On the Forum Iulium, whose scanty surviving remains are in any case of the imperial period, see esp. Platner-Ashby s.v., and J. C. Anderson, *The Historical Topography of the Imperial Fora* (1984), chap. 1. For the Saepta, Platner-Ashby s.v. Completion in 26 B.C.: Dio 53, 23, 2, and L. R. Taylor, *Roman Voting Assemblies* (1966), esp. 47ff. See now R. B. Ulrich, *AJA* 97 (1993): 49, and N. Purcell, *PBSR* 61 (1993): 125.

56. For Cicero's claim, see text to n. 20. For the grain distributions, see the succinct treatment in G. E. Rickman, *The Corn Supply of Ancient Rome* (1980), chap. 7.

chanting Cicero's name, he himself made a speech before them.[57] Dio may be over-dramatising in recording that the mob in fact rushed to the Capitol, where the Senate was meeting in the temple of Concordia, and threatened to slaughter the senators and burn down the temples.[58] But the essential points are clear: the presumption of a public right to beneficial measures on the part of the state; the highly exposed position of the Senate when popular feeling was aroused; and (to look forward) the permanent acceptance later, under the Empire, both of a free corn distribution and of the state's obligation to protect the market price of corn. The demands of the Roman people were to find their most important reflection in the *Res Gestae* of Augustus.

In the late Republic, however, the term Roman people was already a highly ambiguous one. Almost all the benefits which it successfully demanded were felt in the city itself—the shows put on by office-holders and others, the triumphs which literally demonstrated the profits of Empire before the people, the distributions of corn, the provisions for the supply of market corn. So too of course all the active functions of a citizen could only be performed in Rome, by voting in person in the traditional locations of the Forum or the Campus Martius. But, as was mentioned earlier, the effect of the Social War of 90 B.C. had been to win the citizenship for everyone in Italy—that is, of course, all free, adult males—living south of the Po, not far short of a million people in all. They were not in practice registered as voters, however, until twenty years later, in the consulship of Pompey and Crassus in 70, which saw the effective doubling of the registered citizen body. As Cicero was delivering his first oration against Verres in the summer of 70 B.C., he could refer to "this crowd [*frequentia*] from all over Italy, which has gathered at a single moment from all directions, for the elections, the games, and registration in the census."[59]

As is well known, the structure of the Roman city-state was not changed in the slightest to reflect its progressive numerical and geographical expansion. All political activity was still carried out in Rome, in person. But what Lily Ross Taylor, in her much underestimated book on Roman politics in the time of Caesar, called "delivering the vote" could now involve canvassing as far

57. Cic., *Att.* 4, 1, 6, Shackleton-Bailey, no. 73, translates "<cum multitudo> more hoc insulso et novo plausum meo nomine recitando dedisset" as "the people applauded after the silly new-fangled fashion *when* my name was read out," surely wrongly. The new fashion will have been that of applauding *by* repeating his name.

58. Dio 39, 9.

59. *Verr.* 1, 54.

away as the Po Valley.[60] In elections, all might thus depend on which groups, from which areas, might feel the enthusiasm, or be persuaded, to make the journey in to Rome to vote. Defending Plancius in 54, Cicero points out that it was precisely *because* he came from a rather obscure place, Atina, that everyone in that neighbourhood had come in to vote for him in his campaign for the aedileship; so had large numbers from the small towns nearby, Arpinum, Sora, Casinum, Venafrum, Allifae. In Tusculum, from where his defeated rival came, the prospect of a local man reaching the aedileship was commonplace, and of no interest.[61] These small places which had supported Plancius lay over 100 kilometres from Rome; but for a particular reason, when a local man was standing, it was possible to "get out the vote" from there.

But this was an election, happening at a more or less predictable time, and support could be prepared in advance. The various factors and influences which were relevant to Roman elections have often been studied. Too often indeed; for we have allowed our overall picture of the Roman political process to be determined by that. The consulate, for instance, was dominated by *nobiles*, the descendants of office-holders.[62] Does that of itself prove that in political terms the *res publica* was, or could be, run by an oligarchy for its own benefit? No: firstly, public office was, as indicated earlier, conceived of as a favour conferred by the people. Secondly, and more important, in the case of the two annual consuls, we should remember what Cicero said: the people, in electing consuls, were choosing *imperatores* (generals). Only secondarily, and in particular circumstances, might people look to rhetorical ability: "[then] a consul is sought who by speaking may sometimes repress the furor of the tribunes, turn aside the excited people, resist largess."[63] Four fundamental points are relevant here; firstly, elections to the consulship tell us a lot, but not everything, about Roman political life. Secondly, other offices, and above all the tribunate, were also reflections of popular support, and vehicles of popular politics; thirdly, the use of words, oratory, before the people, was central to the political process in Rome; and fourthly—the most important thing of all—the central focus of politics was *not* election to office but conflict about laws.

Here too the gross discrepancy between the total number of voters and the relatively small numbers who did, or even could, vote in the traditional

60. L. R. Taylor, *Party Politics in the Age of Caesar* (1949), chap. 3. See, e.g., *Comm. Pet.* 30–31; Cic., *Att.* 1, 1, 2.

61. Cic., *Planc.* 19–22.

62. For a clear demonstration of this, see now E. Badian, "The Consuls, 179–49 B.C.," *Chiron* 20 (1990): 371.

63. Cic., *Mur.* 38; 24.

public assembly, the Forum, played a major part. In this context also, research is only now beginning to examine forms of leadership or political influence which might be brought to bear within the context of a large city, made up of different quarters (*vici*), in order to bring large crowds to the Forum or the Campus Martius.[64] As to what happened when a crowd did assemble, it is crucial to recall that there was no organised force on which elected officials could depend. As Wilfried Nippel has shown, the very limited level of force which could be exercised by the lictors who accompanied the consuls was hardly more than symbolic, and depended for its effectiveness on communal deference.[65] When that disappeared, the way was open to mob violence, or to the organised gangs of Clodius and Milo. Time and place were all; a crowd occupying the Forum might pass a law there, and be succeeded within the same day by a different crowd protesting. So, in 55, one tribune by occupying the Forum in advance got a law passed to give long-term commands to Pompey and Crassus; as the crowd was departing, another tribune appeared, showed the people one of his colleagues who had been injured, and "by saying those things which would have been expected, profoundly stirred their feelings."[66] In the same year, after Vatinius and others had been elected as praetors with the aid of force, to serve for that same year, those who had voted for them left the Campus Martius. Then a tribune called a public meeting there, which was addressed by Cato, who told the people what would come from the domination of Pompey and Crassus. Plutarch claims that he was then escorted home by a larger crowd than had accompanied any of the elected praetors.[67]

These violent and erratic fluctuations are well known, and indeed have an established place in pictures of the breakdown of the republican system. All that I wish to emphasise is that they are themselves a product of what one cannot quite call democratic politics, and certainly not a class struggle; but it was a matter of popular politics, or crowd politics, and it was about the passing of laws and measures to do with the empire. For it is absolutely crucial to emphasise that a Roman crowd occupying one of the established centres of political activity was—or could be—something fundamentally different from the "urban mob" familiar from many periods of history. For such a crowd, as soon as it was organised into its voting units, whether tribes or

64. See now P. J. J. Vanderbroeck, *Popular Leadership and Collective Behaviour in the Late Roman Republic (ca. 80–50 B.C.)* (1987), a valuable work from which there is much to learn.

65. W. Nippel, "Policing Rome," *JRS* 74 (1984): 20, and *Aufruhr und "Polizei" in der römischen Republik* (1988).

66. Dio 39, 35.

67. Plut., *Cato Min.* 42.

centuries, was not *protesting* against the actions either of a legal sovereign or of an effective "governing organ." For it was itself the sovereign body, and in many respects it was also the governing organ. Moreover, and this is my final point, we underestimate how large a part in all this was played by persuasion, mainly in the form of oratory, but also by question-and-answer, or by various forms of visual presentation. In all of this we are looking at various aspects of the *contio*—a word which, depending on the context, means an informal public meeting called by an office-holder, a speech delivered at such a meeting, or the actual crowd attending it.

It is important to stress that the Senate itself functioned within this context of crowd politics. As I mentioned earlier, it met in exposed locations in the centre of the city, normally of course in the *curia* on the edge of the Forum itself. The noise of an angry crowd gathered around the Comitium outside could be heard inside. Moreover, interested persons from within the Senate could also easily step outside and report to the crowd on what had been said inside. So in 52, on the day after the murder of Clodius, T. Munatius Plancus delivered a public speech to explain what decree the Senate had intended to pass, who had asked for a division, who had interposed a veto, and why.[68] Or, again, Clodius could report in a public meeting that the college of *pontifices* had ruled that the destruction of Cicero's house was legal, and that Cicero was trying to regain possession of it by force; the people should follow him in defence of their liberty.[69] Alternatively, prominent persons, office-holders or members of the colleges of priests, could be brought before public meetings to give public testimony in person. So Cicero, speaking as if addressing Clodius, recalls what the latter had done as tribune in 58:[70]

> You produced Bibulus before a public meeting, as you did also the augurs; in response to your interrogation the augurs replied that when someone was watching the heavens for *auspicia*, it was not legal to put measures before the people.

Two years later, C. Cato, as tribune of 56, compelled members of the college of fifteen people called *Quindecimviri sacris faciundis* to read out verses from the Sibylline Books before a public meeting.[71] In the same year the consul, Cn. Cornelius Lentulus Marcellinus, complained in a public meeting

---

68. Asconius, ed. Clark, 44–45.
69. Cic., *Att.* 4, 2 (Shackleton-Bailey, no. 74).
70. Cic., *Dom.* 40.
71. Dio 39, 15, 1–16, 1.

about the excessive power (*potentia*) of Pompey and Crassus and was met with roars of approval from the people.[72] He also brought these two in person before a public meeting, and questioned them as to whether they intended to stand for the consulship—"the many," according to Plutarch, "bidding them answer,"[73] that is, shouting out that they wanted an answer. To Cicero this sort of dialogue with the crowd was a dangerous innovation which was all too like the uncontrolled licence of Greek democracies—as was the scandalous idea of the populace being able to debate things sitting down, a point on which he speaks at length in his speech in defence of Flaccus.[74] Thus he writes of Appius Claudius Pulcher, the brother of Clodius, and praetor in 57:[75]

> That praetor, in the fashion not of his father, grandfather, and great-grandfather, but of mere Greeks, used to interrogate the crowd at a public meeting on the subject of myself, asking "did they wish me to be restored"?—and when he was answered by the half-dead voices of some hired hacks would proclaim that the Roman people said no.

It would be possible to go on with many more examples of speeches before the people, and reactions from them, speeches which might continue up to the last moment before people divided into their tribal voting units to vote on a law.[76] The notion current in modern books that there was no debate at meetings of the Roman people is a pure technicality, which distinguishes the voting process itself from the highly politicised public meetings (*contiones*) which preceded it. We would understand late republican politics much better if we took the content of what Antonius said to the people in December of the year 50 as seriously as Cicero did. Antonius, it may be recalled, had denounced the public role of Pompey throughout his career; had protested about improper condemnations in the courts; and had threatened civil war. Four days later a written text of the speech was being studied by Cicero, over 100 kilometres away in Formiae. If we paid equally close attention to the actual words addressed to the sovereign people in Rome, we would be better placed to understand the nature of Roman politics, the evolution of the republican empire, and that very direct relationship between speaker and crowd which played so fundamental a part in the workings of the republican system. That it continued to do so was one legacy, among many others, of

72. Val. Max. 6, 2, 6.
73. Plut., *Pomp.* 51.
74. Cic., *Flacc.* 15–18.
75. Cic., *Sest.* 126.
76. See Asconius, ed. Clark, 71.

the nuclear city-state, with an urban centre and surrounding territory, which Rome had been until the early fourth century. Hence the workings of politics in Rome were always marked by those direct exchanges between *plebs* and *princeps* whose subtleties were first explored by Zvi Yavetz.[77] It is only a seeming paradox that it was this primitive feature of the Republic, direct addresses to the crowd followed by their voting as the sovereign People, which was to contribute so much to the emergence of monarchy.

77. Z. Yavetz, *Plebs and Princeps* (1969); reissued with a preface by C. Nicolet and an avant-propos by the author, as *La plèbe et le prince: foule et vie politique sous le haut-empire romain* (1984).

CHAPTER SEVEN

Cornelius Nepos, "Atticus," and the Roman Revolution[*]

The biography of Atticus by Cornelius Nepos, covering the last eight decades of the Republic and written at the precise moment of the establishment of monarchy by Octavian, ought always to have been treated both as one of the best introductions to the period, and as an exposition, from a unique angle, of some of the values expressed in Roman society. But now, more than ever, there may be a place for a brief essay which attempts to bring out both some values exhibited in this particular text and the way in which these were taken up, distorted, and deployed in the propaganda of the Augustan regime. For, firstly, the larger background of late-Republican scholarship, antiquarianism, historiography, and biography has been fully explored by Elizabeth Rawson;[1] secondly, Joseph Geiger has argued for the originality of Nepos as a writer of political biography;[2] thirdly, we have a major study of the ethical models which it is the purpose of the biography to hold up for emulation.[3] Finally,

[*] First published in *Greece and Rome* 35 (1988): 40–55. This chapter represents a lightly edited version of a lecture given in 1983 to the London Branch of the Classical Association. It seemed on reflection worthwhile to publish it, as an essay suggesting various lessons which might be drawn from this extremely interesting and informative text. I am very grateful for comments to Nicholas Horsfall, whose *Cornelius Nepos: A Selection, including the Lives of Cato and Atticus* (1989) is now essential, and to the late Elizabeth Rawson, who saved me from many errors.

1. E. Rawson, *Intellectual Life in the Late Roman Republic* (London, 1985), chaps. 15–16, on historiography and antiquarianism. This paper, as will be evident, makes no attempt to explore the wider deployment of antiquarian studies in the Augustan period.

2. J. Geiger, *Cornelius Nepos and Ancient Political Biography*, Historia Einzelschriften 47 (Stuttgart, 1985).

3. M. Labate and E. Narducci, "Mobilità dei modelli etici e relativismo dei valori: il

John North, in an important review article on recent works on Roman religion,[4] has identified three significant characteristics of late republican religiosity: a scholarly or antiquarian perception of religious change, often seen as decline; the identification of religion as the subject of a particular form of discourse; and a shift in focus within the sphere of religion, from the community as a whole to great men within it. All three come together, as we will see below, in the passage of Nepos' biography in which he records how, some time in the 30s B.C., Atticus suggested to Octavian that the now roofless temple of Iuppiter Feretrius on the Capitol should be repaired.

But first the main characteristics of Nepos' representation of Atticus need to be outlined. It should be stressed that the subject of what follows is not the "real" Atticus, even supposing that any valid conception of that entity were attainable, but the "Atticus" whom Nepos delineates for us. Before that it will be useful to recall who Cornelius Nepos was, what he wrote, and why.[5] Like Catullus, whose first poem is addressed to him, and like Virgil, he came from the Po Valley, perhaps from Mediolanum. If this is correct, his home town gained Latin rights in 89 B.C. and the citizenship not until 49; and the area ceased to be a province only in 42.[6] Yet, like others from that region, he not only seems to have spent his time in Rome, but wrote as a Roman, composing short biographies which contrasted distinguished foreigners with distinguished Romans, in various categories: of these biographies, the lives of non-Roman generals survive, as do, of Roman historians, the *Cato* and the *Atticus*. Earlier, he had written the *Chronica*, which set out in chronological order parallel events and persons in the Roman and Greek past. Nepos had already written this work in three books when Catullus addressed poem 1 to him in the 50s.[7] He was also a personal friend of Atticus,

---

'personaggio' di Attico," in A. Giardina and A. Schiavone, *Società romana e produzione schiavistica III: modelli etici, dirrito e trasformazioni sociali* (Rome and Bari, 1981), 127.

4. J. North, "Religion and Politics, from Republic to Principate," *JRS* 76 (1986): 251.

5. The sparse biographical data are collected in M. Schanz and C. Hosius, *Geschichte der römischen Literatur*[4] I (Munich, 1927), 351–52.

6. See U. Ewins, "The Enfranchisement of Cisalpine Gaul," *Pap. Brit. Sch. Rome* 23 (1955): 73; C. Peyre, *La Cisalpine Gauloise du IIIe au Ie siècle avant J-C* (Paris, 1979). Nepos himself might therefore have gained the Roman citizenship by holding a magistracy (*per magistratum*) or, as any well-placed foreigner might, through a viritane grant. He would remain none the less an example of the "outsiders" from this region to whom we owe so much of our conception of Rome.

7. Fragments in P. K. Marshall, *Cornelii Nepotis Vitae cum fragmentis* (Teubner, 1977), 101–2. Catullus 1, 5–7: "When you took courage, long ago, you alone of Italians, to set forth the

and had written most of his biography of Atticus before the latter died at the end of March 32 B.C. He then added chapters 19–22. For reasons which we will see, it is particularly unfortunate that we cannot tell which, if any, of the events of the following years had already happened before he wrote these concluding chapters. At any rate Nepos himself can hardly have been born later than the 80s B.C., and perhaps considerably earlier. His statement (*Att.* 19, 1) that *Fortuna* willed that he should survive Atticus, may suggest that his birth fell before the beginning of the first century.

Nepos is thus someone who in his modest way reflects many of the major tendencies of Roman society and culture in the first century B.C. The fact that he can be seen as representatively "Roman" is however itself a reflection of that well-known process by which the greatest age of Roman literature, and with it our conceptions of "Rome," were the product of people of non-Roman origin.

Atticus himself, however, was different, for he came from a long line of native Romans "descended as he was from the remotest origins of the Roman race" as Nepos says (1, 1). It may be that in stressing this Nepos was indeed speaking from the standpoint of a "new Roman." More important however for the significance of the model which the *Life* set out to present is the fact that Atticus was an *eques*. The significance of that lies firstly in the terminology which Nepos uses to describe Atticus' rank: "retained uninterrupted the equestrian rank [*dignitas*] inherited from his forbears" (1, 1). It is striking that *dignitas* can be used of a personal status not associated with any public office,[8] or still less with any positive achievement. In fact, although Nepos cannot have meant to say that Atticus formally inherited equestrian rank from his ancestors, he certainly does represent this *dignitas* as having been in a real sense derived from them. The bias of our evidence means that we normally see social status in Rome from above. Nepos here affords us a rare glimpse of the status of a long-standing equestrian family, as seen from below, or from outside.

The *Life* is thus a literary presentation of the biography of an equestrian — the only one in the whole of Roman literature. As such, the closest parallel to it is not a work of literature in the normal sense, but something which, though preserved on an inscription, should be seen as a literary work, namely

---

whole history of the world in three volumes, learned volumes, by Jupiter, and laboriously wrought" (Loeb trans.).

8. Compare the discussion by J. Hellegouarc'h, *Le vocabulaire latin des relations et des partis politiques dans la République*[2] (Paris, 1972), esp. 397–411.

the so-called *Laudatio Turiae*, for which Nicholas Horsfall's recent study is now essential.[9] In its vivid reflection of the troubled fortunes of a wealthy Roman family which eventually survived the Triumvirate and the proscriptions, to achieve peace under Augustus, this funerary oration is very close in content, and location on the social hierarchy, though not in all of its presuppositions, to Nepos' *Life*. As an oration, it is also one of the most substantial surviving specimens of Augustan prose, and the only one emanating from a private person which survives (in part) as inscribed at the time.

At least two features however serve to give a much greater importance to Nepos' biography. Firstly the life of his subject can be portrayed over an exceptionally long and eventful period, from Atticus' birth in 110/9 B.C. to his death on 31 March, 32. Born in the early stages of the Jugurthine War, he survived, as Nepos records (19, 4), to see his one-year-old granddaughter, Vipsania, the child of his daughter Pomponia and of Agrippa, betrothed to Tiberius Claudius Nero, the future Emperor Tiberius.

The biography thus presents the most troubled period of Roman history from the angle of a man who was at the heart of Roman society, but was not a political actor in the events of the day; it is the biography of one who endured and survived, not who acted. But this is no mere negative point, or mere reflection of facts. For the model which the biography holds up is that in which the virtues of the hero and the appropriateness of his responses to circumstances must be demonstrated by the options which he might have taken up but did not; in short it is a representation of what its hero did not do, of the temptations presented by public life, and changes of political fortune, to which he did not succumb. By contrast, the positive virtues and activities which are exhibited are those of private life, of scholarship, antiquarianism, and concern for the traditions and antiquities of Rome. It is incontestable, as we will see, that Nepos himself was at the least reserved and neutral, and very likely hostile, in the face of Octavian's rise to power. The irony of it all is that it was precisely the type of irreproachable private scholarship to which Nepos' "Atticus" is shown devoting himself that was to be taken up and deployed in the propaganda of the new regime.

But before that it is worth looking at some examples of what, as portrayed by Nepos, Atticus did not do. For example, in the 80s, when the state was divided between Sulla's party (Sullani) and Cinna's party (Cinnani), he saw no chance of living as befitted his rank (*pro dignitate*), for fear of offending one or other party—so he withdrew to Athens and took no part (2, 1–2). Then, when Sulla came to Athens on his way back from the East in 84–83, he

9. N. Horsfall, "Some Problems in the 'Laudatio Turiae,'" *Bull. Inst. Cl. Stud.* 30 (1983): 85.

wanted Atticus to accompany him on the invasion of Italy. But Atticus again enunciated his standing principle of neutrality: "I would not wish you to lead me against those with whom I would not bear arms against you, leaving Italy to avoid this." Sulla praised his sense of duty (*officium*) and departed (4, 1–2). What we see here is a striking reversal of the principle allegedly laid down by Solon: that the citizen has a duty to take sides in a civil dispute. The overriding duty here is private; civil war is, potentially or actually, a disturbance of a network of mutual private obligations.

Public life and public office were not for Atticus. What Nepos says in this connection is perhaps worth quoting in full (6, 1):

> As regards public life he conducted himself in such a way that he both was [in fact], and had the reputation of being, of the "best party" [*optimae partes*] but he would not commit himself to the billows of civil strife; for he considered that those who did so were no more in control of their own destiny than those who trusted themselves to the billows of the sea.

This passage continues with a whole series of negatives. He *could* have sought public office, having the necessary influence (*gratia*) and dignity—but did not because office could no longer be gained or held without corruption. He did *not* purchase any properties of condemned persons, when sold off by the state. He did *not* engage in accusation, or private litigation. When many consuls and praetors conferred prefectures on him, he accepted these only on condition of *not* going to the province in question—he was content with the *honour* (i.e., the mere title), ignoring the profit to his estate. This is quite an important passage for the way in which the Roman state worked in the late Republic. For it is a reflection of the right which senatorial provincial governors exercised, of conferring the position of prefect by patronage on equestrians—and thereby, as we see with Cicero's experience in Cilicia, giving them on occasion an actual military command, with the possibility of using force.[10] The state thus devolved some of its functions, leaving them to be exercised by private patronage. There is also an unmistakable implication in what Nepos says, that such a position, when occupied, could be expected to lead to an increase in personal wealth at the expense of the provincials. Perhaps more important, these military prefectures, conferred by consuls and praetors as provincial governors, were in fact the origin of the public roles of equestrians as they evolved under Augustus and later emperors.[11]

---

10. See, e.g., C. Nicolet, *L'ordre équestre à l'époque républicaine* I (Paris, 1966), 434–35.

11. For the functions of *equites* under Augustus, and their predominantly military char-

Atticus would also not go with Quintus Cicero as proconsul of Asia (in 61), when offered the rank of a legate: since he could have been a praetor himself, Nepos says, he would not be a hanger-on of a praetor: he thus preserved both his dignity and his peace avoiding suspicions of wrongdoing. His attention was all the more valued, because people saw that it must be attributed to his sense of duty rather than to fear or to hope (6, 4–5).

With the office of legate we again see, of course, the origins of a key element in the Augustan system. A legate, as is clear in this context, *might* still, in the late Republic, be an equestrian, rather than, as was normal (and as was to be a firm rule under the Empire), a senator.[12] More significant for the late Republic is, once again, what Atticus is described as avoiding. He is refusing, that is, to blur the domains of private duty and public rank, and public profit. The normal rule, as is clearly implied, was that everybody did just that. Public functions, private social relations and obligations, and personal profiteering were closely interrelated.

The civil war broke out in 49, when Atticus was about 60. When Pompey left Italy, Atticus stayed in Rome, profiting from the exemption conferred by age; but he caused no offence by doing so, or at any rate not to his personal friend Pompey. By contrast, those who had earlier accepted wealth or offices from Pompey now had the choice of joining him reluctantly in his camp or of mortally offending him by staying at home (7, 1–2). Atticus' inactivity indeed so pleased Caesar that, when he obliged others, by letter, to make contributions of money, he exempted Atticus. Thus, as Nepos says, by keeping to his old rule of conduct he escaped these new dangers (7, 3).

Then, after the Ides of March, some persons conceived the idea of setting up a fund into which the Roman equestrians would make contributions to assist the assassins of Caesar. A friend of Brutus (himself a friend of Atticus) called upon Atticus to take the lead, or to be in charge—"ut eius rei princeps esse" (8, 3). Again, what follows is worth quoting:

> But, he [Atticus], on the grounds that he was someone who thought that services [*officia*] should be offered to friends without taking sides, and who had always kept himself clear of such schemes, replied as follows. If Brutus wished to make any use of his resources, he should do

---

acter, see esp. C. Nicolet, "Augustus, Government and the Propertied Classes," in F. Millar and E. Segal, eds., *Caesar Augustus: Seven Aspects* (Oxford, 1984), 89.

12. This passage is not taken into account in *P-W*, s.v. "Legatus," xii (1925), cols. 1141–3. Note however B. Schleussner, *Die Legaten der römischen Republik* (Munich, 1978), 154, noting the parallel provided by Diodorus, 37.8.1.

so, to the extent that they were available; but he himself would enter into no joint discussions, or plans, on this matter with anyone.

Once again private services had to be observed, but public action avoided. The principle is presented, as it is consistently throughout the biography, as something praiseworthy. But of course the price paid for it was rather high. Brutus and Cassius were the last to fight in the name of liberty.

The following paragraphs (8–12) give a devastating impression of the swings of fortune which confronted Roman society in the later 40s and the 30s B.C. In the first part of 43 B.C. there was the campaign of Mutina; Antonius was declared a public enemy (*hostis*), so everyone attacked his wife, Fulvia, his children, and his friends. Atticus, however, gave Fulvia financial support at crucial moments (9). Then came the reversal of 43 ("fortune suddenly turned" [conversa subito fortuna est], 10, 1), the arrival in Rome of the *imperatores* (Antonius, Lepidus, and Octavian), the Triumvirate, and the proscriptions. Atticus went into hiding. But Antonius remembered Atticus' *officium* (i.e. his conduct to Fulvia) and wrote a letter with his own hand to offer him protection (10, 4). Now in favour, Atticus could have used the occasion of the proscriptions to increase his own property. But instead he used his influence solely to seek relief for friends facing danger or loss — "in deprecandis amicorum aut periculis aut incommodis" (12, 2). But here too, of course, we can see a foreshadowing of the Empire. As in Cicero's *Pro Marcello*, or in the petitions addressed to Lepidus and Octavian by the brave wife praised in the *Laudatio Turiae*, power was now held by non-responsible rulers to whom the appropriate form of address was a *deprecatio*, a "begging-off," as a matter of favour, or clemency, on behalf of those in danger or disfavour.

With that we have already crossed the border between what Atticus abstained from doing and what he did in fact do, in the public, or semi-public arena. Obviously enough, this boundary, for someone of Atticus' wealth and social position, could never be securely maintained. Thus, if we go back over Nepos' biography of him, though he would never join any faction or conspiracy, he did in fact deploy his wealth repeatedly to assist individuals in public life who needed it: he gave money to help the younger Marius, in flight in 88/7 (2, 2), and also gave 250,000 sesterces to Cicero, in exile in 58/7 (4, 4). In 49, though he stayed in Rome himself, he gave money to others setting off to join Pompey (6, 7); and in 44, though he would not join an organization to help Brutus and Cassius, he nonetheless sent Brutus successive gifts of 100,000 and then 300,000 sesterces (8, 2–3) — just as he soon afterwards helped the family and friends of Antonius (8, 3), and then (by contrast) those of the opposite party, in flight from the proscriptions and from Philippi (11).

Nepos presents this even-handed generosity as having a moral basis, that is
the maintenance of private *officium* regardless of circumstances. But it also
had another purpose, of course—that of personal survival through drastic
swings of fortune: why, Nepos says (10, 6), should one not regard as remarkable the prudence of a man who amid so many and so terrible civil storms
wins through to safety?

A prominent equestrian in this period could not in fact help being part
of the political scene, even if he did not accept prefectures or take up public
contracts (6, 3: "for no enterprise did he become a surety or a contractor,"
may refer to this). As Nepos' biography shows, along with a mass of other
evidence, there was no social barrier between equestrian families and senatorial ones; indeed, even to put it like that is misleading, since what we are
concerned with is a single social class, people of sufficient landed wealth to
live off their income. Within that class some families had a continuous, or
relatively continuous, tradition of holding public office, and thus entering
the Senate. Other families might come into, or drop out of, the Senate. Since
Syme's *The Roman Revolution* attention has always tended to concentrate on
upward mobility, that is, the entry of "new men" from the Italian municipali-
ties into the Senate.[13] But often these "new men" were in one sense not new
at all; they had already enjoyed from youth onwards personal connections
and friendships with prominent senators. This is particularly well attested in
the case of Cicero.[14] Such people were new to the electoral process in Rome,
or at least to the apex of it, election as consul. But they were very often not
new to senatorial society, even the most aristocratic elements of it.

If this was true of a man from a *municipium* like Cicero, it was of course
even more true of a rich equestrian from an old Roman family, like Atticus. The wealth which he inherited from his father was already considerable,
2 million sesterces according to Nepos (14, 2); but we also know from Nepos
(5, 1–2) that his uncle, Q. Caecilius, who died in 58, adopted him by will
and left him a further 10 million sesterces—that is, ten times the level that
Augustus was later to establish as the minimum senatorial census. Nepos,
however, tactfully leaves out the information which Valerius Maximus supplies (7, 8, 5), that Caecilius had previously implied that he would leave all
this to Lucullus; public indignation at this breach of trust was such that the
mob dragged Caecilius' body through the streets of Rome.

That connection with Lucullus is just one indication of the absence of
any social barrier between equestrians and senators; and Atticus himself, as

13. See esp. T. P. Wiseman, *New Men in the Roman Senate, 139 B.C.–A.D. 14* (Oxford, 1971).
14. For a good account of this, T. Mitchell, *Cicero: The Ascending Years* (New Haven, 1979).

Nepos records (1, 3), "had a notable reputation among his contemporaries"; his outstanding skill in rhetoric was not easy to bear for his aristocratic fellow students (*generosi condiscipuli*). It is very apposite that Nepos names as Atticus' friends and fellow students in youth the following three persons, who between them illustrate the variety of social levels within the Senate: firstly, L. Torquatus, that is, L. Manlius Torquatus, a patrician and later consul of 65 B.C.; then the younger Marius, a second-generation senator; and finally Cicero, not yet a senator (1, 4).

Another sign which indicates how senators and equestrians should be seen as a single class is marriage connections. Of course, no one has ever suggested that senators formed a legally, or conventionally, closed group, who married only among themselves. But we still tend to use terms like "senatorial aristocracy" or "senatorial oligarchy" which are in many ways misleading. Among senators there were certainly families with outstanding office-holding traditions (indeed we shall see that the lifetime of Atticus was just the period when, more than ever before, people took to emphasising genealogy, genuine or otherwise). But to enter the Senate, of some 300 and then after Sulla, some 600, members, was a *choice*, a choice of role and life-style, made by members of a wider social class.

The marriage connections of Atticus' family may serve to illustrate this. Atticus' cousin, Anicia, for instance, was married to the brother of Sulpicius Rufus, the tribune of 88;[15] this fact was one reason for Atticus' prudent withdrawal to Athens in the mid 80s (2, 1–2). His sister was married to Quintus Cicero (5, 3), who was also of course embarked on a senatorial career. Later, as we saw, Atticus' daughter Pomponia was married to Agrippa. In this case Nepos does emphasize that such a choice on Agrippa's part was something worthy of note: Agrippa, Nepos says, on account of his influence and power of Caesar (i.e., Octavian), could have made any match he pleased; but he preferred an alliance with Atticus, and chose the daughter of a Roman equestrian rather than an aristocratic bride (*generosarum nuptiae*, 12, 1).

Nepos' use of the word *generosus* is of some interest. As noted earlier, it is quite clear that within the Senate some families stood out as having a particularly distinguished history. We do, however, now have to avoid using the word "noble" here, or rather to be extremely careful about how we use it. For P. A. Brunt has conclusively shown that Gelzer in his *Roman Nobility* was wrong. *Nobilis*, as used in the late Republic, was not in any case a constitu-

---

15. Most editors read "(M.) Servio, fratri Sulpicii." But see H. Mattingly, *Athenaeum* 53 (1975): 265, and n. 14 in favour of retaining the reading of the Leiden manuscript: "M. Servilio fratri Sulpicii."

tional term; and as a *social* term it does not refer to a small in-group of the descendants of consuls and their equivalents, but to anyone who could boast of any ancestor who had held public office. And this still applied even after a long gap, during which no members of a family had held office.[16]

Perhaps then we ought to start using instead the word *generosi*, for those Romans whose ancestry really was, in a loose sense, "aristocratic"—or was thought to be. For, if one thing is certain about the self-consciousness of the Roman upper class in the late Republic, it is, firstly, that there was an outburst of interest in family histories, and, secondly, that not all these histories wholly corresponded to historical reality. It is hardly necessary to recall Julius Caesar, as quaestor in 69, addressing the Roman populace from the Rostra on the occasion of his aunt's funeral. Among other things he gave them the following historical information (Suetonius, *Div. Jul.* 6):

> The maternal descent of my aunt Julia sprang from the kings and her paternal descent was linked with the gods. For Ancus Marcius was the ancestor of the Marcii Reges, from which family her mother came. From Venus there descended the Julii, a *gens* of which our *familia* is a branch.

This information would probably have occasioned some surprise if it had been contained in a speech delivered not in 69 but in 269 B.C. (five years before the custom began of marking prominent funerals with a gladiatorial show). For the first Julius Caesar known to have held office in Rome did not appear until 208, and the first Marcius Rex not until the middle of the second century.[17] The claim is in fact typical of the genealogies linking often quite new families to mythical ancestors which were widely evolved in the last two centuries of the Republic.[18] The essential warning about bogus genealogies is provided by Cicero in the *Brutus*. We all quote this paragraph (62), but by and large we then contrive to ignore it. I think it is worth quoting once again:

> The various *familiae* used to preserve them [i.e., laudations of the dead] as their adornments and monuments so to speak, and also for use, if anyone of that stock [*genus*] died; also as a memorial of the honours of the house, and to adorn their *nobilitas*. However, the effect of these

16. P. A. Brunt, "*Nobilitas* and *Novitas*," *JRS* 72 (1982): 1.

17. Broughton, *MRR* I, 290 (Sex. Iulius Caesar, praetor in 208); 418 (P. Marcius Rex, *legatus* in 171); 471 (Q. Marcius Rex, praetor in 144).

18. See esp. T. P. Wiseman, "Legendary Genealogies in Late-Republican Rome," *G&R* 21 (1974): 153, now reprinted in his *Roman Studies, Literary and Historical* (Liverpool, 1987), 207.

laudations has been to falsify our history. Many events are recorded in them which never took place, bogus triumphs, multiple consulates, false genealogies, and transitions to the plebs, so that men of lower birth were insinuated into another *genus* of the same name; as if I [i.e., M. Tullius Cicero] were to claim descent from Manius Tullius, who as a patrician was consul with Servius Sulpicius in the tenth year after the expulsion of the kings.

In fact we can see a perfect example of such an alleged transition of a family (from patrician to plebeian status) embedded in the first paragraph of Suetonius' *Life* of Augustus:

> That family [the Octavii] was adlected into the senate by King Tarquinius Priscus among the "minor families," then transferred by Servius Tullius to the patrician families; later it crossed over to the plebs; and then, after a long interval, returned to the patriciate by the agency of Divus Julius.

The relevance of this growth of interest in family histories is Atticus' own role in the matter, as Nepos describes it. This was again an aspect of his central role in Roman society, this time as an antiquarian and scholar in close contact with senators sharing these interests. Such concerns partly represented a genuinely scholarly activity, at least in intention; but partly they were studies pursued in the interests of particular *familiae*. Nepos describes this function of Atticus as follows (18, 1):

> He was also an extreme devotee of ancestral custom [*mos maiorum*], and lover of antiquity, of which he had so close a knowledge that he set it all out in that volume in which he arranged the magistracies in order. For there was no law nor peace treaty nor war nor famous deed of the Roman people, which was not recorded at its correct point in time; moreover, he added, as was particularly difficult, the origins of the various families, in such a way that from it we might be able to identify the descendants of famous men.

This last motive is very striking, and will need further discussion. For the moment it is worth stressing that this task needed to be performed: without scholarly research, if that is the word, people did not necessarily have a clear idea of from whom, in the Roman past, their contemporaries descended. But there is another aspect to this. Like so many elements of Atticus' life and activity, as Nepos presents them, this one looks forward to the values which were to be institutionalized in the reign of Augustus. In the period of Caesar and Augustus the old Forum, a large open space for public use, began its transformation into a crowded site for dynastic monuments, whose highly confusing remains confront us today. The central element in it was now the temple of the Deified Julius, dedicated in 29 B.C. Between it and the ancient temple of Castor and Pollux stood a new arch of Augustus, constructed to celebrate the victory of Actium. On the other side of the temple, between it and the Basilica Aemilia, there may subsequently have been constructed another triple arch, built to celebrate the recovery of the standards from Parthia, and completed in 18–17 B.C. It was on the sides of the central span of this arch, so Coarelli has argued, that there were placed the great marble slabs whose remains we can now see in the Capitoline Museum, and which contained the inscriptions of the *Fasti Triumphales* and *Fasti Consulares*.[19] The lists of people who had held a triumph in Rome (*triumphatores*) and of consuls were thus perpetuated on stone, and put up on an imperial monument at the very centre of Rome, for the instruction and edification of the public. The history of republican Rome was thus formally re-emphasized just at the moment when it was becoming, in a certain sense, irrelevant.

The list of *triumphatores*, as inscribed, concludes with L. Cornelius Balbus, proconsul of Africa, whose triumph was celebrated in 19 B.C. But after 19 B.C., as it turned out, no one would ever again celebrate a triumph, except members of the imperial family;[20] and the consulate would rapidly become something which was given out, by patronage, by the emperor. At all events the process of establishing fixed lists of *triumphatores* and consuls, and of freezing the official version on stone, was one which derived directly from the antiquarian obsessions of the late Republic, and from the scholarly activities of which Atticus' work was one example.

But Atticus had also had a second purpose, to enable contemporaries to know from which famous men in the past individuals in their own time descended. Not unnaturally, his senatorial friends found this gratifying. As a consequence, therefore, he found himself composing a whole series of separate family histories, beginning with a history of the Junian family, which he wrote at the request of Brutus. In this he listed the members of the family, from its origin to the present day, recording who was whose son, and what

19. On the transformation of the Forum, see P. Zanker, *Forum Romanum: die Neugestaltung durch Augustus* (Tübingen, 1972), and now of course the major re-examination by F. Coarelli, *Il Foro Romano* II: *periodo repubblicano e augusteo* (Rome, 1985), esp. 258–59; his re-construction of the placing of the *Fasti* is followed here.

20. On the progressive monopolization of public honour by the Imperial family, see esp. W. Eck, "Senatorial Self-Representation: Developments in the Augustan Period," in Millar and Segal (n. 11), 129.

public offices (*honores*) they had gained at what dates (18, 2–3). In the same way, Nepos says, Claudius Marcellus asked him for a history of the Marcelli, and Cornelius Scipio and Fabius Maximus for one of the Aemilii and the Fabii (18, 3). Perhaps it is not an accident that this genealogical element in the history of Rome came so definitely into fashion just at the moment when power was passing out of the grasp of a network of prominent families and into the hands of a succession of individual rulers.

There were however other reasons for taking an interest in the deeds of famous men in the past. One was simply the pleasure of recalling them. As Nepos puts it, "nothing can be more pleasurable than these books—i.e., Atticus' books—for those who have any longing for knowledge of famous men" (18, 4). It seems to have been in a separate volume that Atticus further satisfied this longing, firstly, by presenting portraits of men who had excelled other Romans in honour and in the grandeur (*amplitudo*) of their deeds; and, secondly, by accompanying each of these portraits (*imagines*) by four or five lines of verse in which the essentials of their achievements were summed up (18, 5–6). Here too he was following a fashion of the time. For his famous contemporary Varro, among his many other historical and antiquarian works, published one which contained no less than 700 *imagines* of famous men, both Greek and Roman (Pliny, *NH* 35, 11). These too seem each to have been accompanied by both a prose text and an epigram in verse; the evidence of Aulus Gellius seems to show that the work was produced in 39 B.C., under the Triumvirate (*NA* 3, 10).[21]

Once again a literary and antiquarian fashion of the late Republic was taken up by Augustus, immortalized in stone, and (in this case) put to an explicitly propagandist purpose. For the great temple of Mars Ultor, dedicated in 2 B.C., formed the centre-piece of Augustus' new Forum, the Forum Augustum.[22] In front of the temple stood a four-horse chariot (*quadriga*) dedicated to Augustus himself. Along the two sides of the Forum, both opening into wide, semi-circular apses, stood a line of statues of famous figures from the history of Rome: on the one side Aeneas, the kings of Alba Longa, and

---

21. For the details, see *P-W*, Supp. VI (1935), cols. 1227–9; Rawson (n. 1), 198–99; 230–31. If we knew what Varro's "literary picture-gallery" was (Cicero, *Att.* 16, 11, 3), we might have to conclude that some version of the *Hebdomades* or *De imaginibus* was in circulation in 44 B.C.

22. On this P. Zanker, *Forum Augustum: das Bildprogramm* (Tübingen, 1968); J. C. Anderson, *The Historical Topography of the Imperial Fora, Collection Latomus* 182 (Brussels, 1984), chap. 2. For the *elogia*, the standard edition by A. Degrassi, *Inscriptiones Italiae* XII.3: *Elogia* (1937), with S. R. Tufi, "Frammenti delle statue dei summi viri nel Foro di Augusto," *Dial. di Arch.* 3 (1981): 69.

members of the Julian house; on the other Romulus, and a line of legendary or historical heroes of the Republic. Here too each statue was equipped with an inscribed text, giving the offices which each man had held, and a brief account of his achievements. Augustus, as we know from Suetonius, intended something more by all this than just the pleasure of contemplating the great deeds of the past. He explained in an edict, couched in his usual somewhat tedious and moralizing style, that he had intended these statues to serve as an example, in terms of which the appropriate conduct could be demanded, by his fellow citizens, both of himself while he lived and of the *principes* of succeeding periods (Suetonius, *Augustus* 31). With these propagandist overtones added, the programme of the Forum of Augustus thus exactly matched, and followed from, that of the antiquarian works composed by innocent scholars in the last years of the Republic.

Moreover, as Nepos' biography of Atticus shows, there was still another area in which the antiquarian interests of the late Republic were to be put to propagandist and programmatic use by the new regime. In the last decade of Atticus' life, that is in the later forties and the thirties, Atticus became a friend of "Imperator Divi filius" (normally now called "Octavian"), as Nepos says in the concluding section which he wrote after Atticus' death. Caesar used to correspond frequently with him, whether he was in Rome or away: in his letters he would ask Atticus to resolve some point of antique learning, or would put to him some literary puzzle (19, 1–20, 2). At this time, Nepos records, the temple of Iuppiter Feretrius on the Capitol, which had been established by Romulus, was lying in ruins, and was roofless through age and neglect. It was at the prompting of Atticus that Octavian undertook the task of restoring it (20, 3).

This step therefore appears here as an isolated measure of the 30s B.C., which was taken before there was any general programme for the restoration of temples; and it owed its origin to the initiative not of Octavian but of Atticus. But, of course, this picture was soon to change. Livy, writing book 4 in the 20s, refers to Augustus as "the founder or restorer of all the temples," and makes a specific mention of the temple of Iuppiter Feretrius, "which he restored when collapsed through old age." He also refers to Augustus' claim that he had personally discovered there evidence that Cornelius Cossus had been consul, rather than military tribune, when he won the *spolia opima* (spoils removed from an enemy general by the Roman commander who had personally killed him in battle) and deposited them there;[23] hence there was no

23. Livy, 4, 19–20, with the invaluable comments of R. M. Ogilvie, *Commentary on Livy Books 1–5* (Oxford, 1965).

exception to the alleged rule that only those fighting under their own auspices could gain these *spolia*. It is by no means clear that Livy in fact believed
the testimony of Augustus, which he felt obliged to record, in an excursus,
with very marked reservations—and without altering his introduction of
Cossus as a military tribune (4, 19, 1). Augustus was later of course to include
this ancient temple of Iuppiter Feretrius in the list of restored temples which
he duly recorded for posterity in his *Res Gestae* (19). He did not, however,
feel obliged to recall that this restoration had not, in the first instance, been
his own idea, but someone else's. This passage, as noted earlier (text to n. 4),
thus represents a significant conjunction between late-Republican scholarship and concern about religion as a distinct area, on the one hand, and the
growing dependence of politics on great individuals, on the other.

This correspondence between Atticus and Octavian, along with the marriage of Pomponia to Agrippa, and the betrothal of the one-year-old Vipsania to Tiberius, might well make one think that Atticus, towards the end of
his long life, will have been represented by Nepos as a committed supporter
of Octavian. For, even if he had not in fact been, one might have expected
that Nepos would have made the most of any connections which he had had
with Octavian, and any commitment which he had felt to him. It is all the
more surprising, therefore, to see that Nepos in fact does just the opposite,
that he manifests no enthusiasm for the rise of Octavian to sole power, and,
if anything, emphasizes (once again) Atticus' neutrality.

In the section of the biography which had been written and made public ("edita," 19, 1) before Atticus' death in March 32 B.C., Octavian appears
simply as "the young Caesar" (*adulescens Caesar*) to whose friendship and
power Agrippa had owed the fact that he could have married anyone he
chose; however, Nepos specifically notes—"it is not to be concealed"—that
the mediator (*conciliator*) of the marriage had in fact been M. Antonius (12,
1–2).

In the final section, written after Atticus' death, Octavian has become "Imperator Divi filius"; his full official name, from about 38 B.C. onwards, had
of course been "Imperator Caesar Divi filius."[24] It seems clear that Nepos
wrote this concluding section before the name "Augustus" was conferred in
January 27. But was he writing before or after the battle of Actium in 31, or
the death of Antonius in the following year? This seems wholly uncertain.
What is clear is, firstly, that Nepos says that Atticus owed his friendship with
Octavian to the same elegant style of life (*elegantia vitae*) which had attracted

24. R. Syme, "Imperator Caesar: A Study in Nomenclature," *Historia* 7 (1958): 172 =
Roman Papers I (Oxford, 1979), 361.

other first men of the state, of equal dignity but lesser good fortune. The second point is that this—good fortune—is the wholly neutral light in which he places Octavian's rise to power. "For such prosperity accrued to Caesar that Fortune denied him nothing which she had ever granted to anyone else, and won for him what up to that point no Roman citizen had been able to acquire" (19, 2–3).

The marriage relationship served, Nepos says, to strengthen their personal friendship. At this point (20, 1–3) he describes the frequent correspondence between Atticus and Octavian on antiquarian and literary questions, and Atticus' advice about restoring the temple of Iuppiter Feretrius. But then, in a very striking way, Nepos goes on to say that even now Atticus preserved his political neutrality, and kept up a similar relationship with Marcus Antonius. The paragraph which he devotes to this relationship, and to the lessons which were to be drawn from it, is the last in his biography before he comes to Atticus' final illness and death, at the end of March 32 B.C. It cannot, obviously enough, have been written earlier than 32, when according to the *Res Gestae* (25) all of Italy was spontaneously swearing loyalty to Octavian, and asking for him as general (*dux*) in the war which was to be decided at Actium. This is what Nepos writes (20, 5):

> His friendship was no less cultivated from a distance, by letter, by Marcus Antonius, to the extent that he kept Atticus informed in detail, from the ends of the earth, as to what he was doing and what his concerns were. The significance of this can be weighed by anyone who is capable of judging what a sign of wisdom it is, to retain the friendship and goodwill of men between whom there was not only rivalry for supreme power, but that degree of personal hostility which was inevitable as between Caesar and Antonius, given that each sought to be the first man [*princeps*] not only of the city of Rome, but of the entire world.

We have no reason to disbelieve the statement made by Nepos, that Atticus continued through the 30s to correspond with Antonius. What attitude Atticus himself had had to the rivalry of Octavian and Antonius we cannot know. But there is nothing to show that it was very different from that of Nepos; and Nepos at any rate saw it as a naked competition for power, in the face of which one showed one's wisdom by maintaining good relations with both sides.

This attitude of neutrality and non-partisanship cannot of itself explain why things turned out as they did. For, of course, there were others who did not act on this principle. Not only Roman senators, but—what is more puzzling—whole armies had earlier fought in the name of liberty. Equally, not only members of the Roman upper class, but large armies of ordinary men, both Romans and non-Romans, fought under Antonius and Octavian. Why and how they came to do so still seems remarkably difficult to explain. But part of the total picture is surely that many others remained throughout passive, uncommitted, and neutral, preferring private duties and the glories of the past to the urgent issues of the present. As Nepos himself wrote elsewhere, the *res publica* was now governed not by "right" (*ius*) but by "force" (*potentia*) (*Cato* 2, 2); and elsewhere again he complains that the state was endangered by the fact that army veterans claimed the right to give orders themselves, rather than receive them (*Eum.* 8, 2). But no one offered a serious alternative to force, or presented a programme to solve the problems of the veterans. And the philosophic quietism and neutrality, which Atticus observed and Nepos praised, only served to smooth the path to monarchy. Under that new monarchy political neutrality was to be the enforced fate of everybody; and an antiquarian interest in the Roman past could be put to use in the propaganda of the newly established dynasty, and immortalized in stone in the monuments which it put up in the centre of Rome.

CHAPTER EIGHT

The Last Century of the Republic: Whose History?*

Intellectual Approaches

Any reader of this massive volume would be justified in feeling a mixture of emotions: for a start, amazement, admiration, and perplexity. Firstly amazement at the sheer scale of the publishing, editing, and writing involved. Then admiration: the whole enterprise is an extraordinary tribute to the devotion to learning and education on the part of the academic profession; neither on the part of the editors nor of the contributors could the expenditure of so much effort (and thereby its diversion from other activities) be explained by the (very modest) prospect of monetary gain.

But perplexity too is appropriate. For whether this self-sacrifice is as much a sign of wisdom as of virtue is a more complex question. From the beginning, the very notion of the massive, multi-author, "authoritative" *Cambridge History* has been open to obvious fundamental objections: that any "representation" of the past constitutes a personal point of view, bounded, if not precisely determined, by time and circumstance; that this essential starting point is not altered, but its relevance is simply confused, when reality is divided up by a committee and allotted to different authors; and that the contributor is, inevitably, stretched uneasily between his or her own vision of what matters, and of how the field in question should be interpreted, on the one hand, and the prescriptions of the editors, on the other.

In fact, neither this volume nor the new edition of the *CAH* as a whole can be seen as professedly and explicitly the mouthpiece of a group with an ideological message about how we should approach the complex business of

---

*First published as a review of J. A. Crook, A. Lintott, and E. Rawson, eds., *The Cambridge Ancient History*² IX: *The Last Age of the Roman Republic, 146–43 B.C.* (Cambridge, 1994), in *JRS* 85 (1995): 236–43.

understanding the ancient world. Implicitly, however, it is rather curious to observe, it seems rather to represent traditional "ancient history," structured round ancient narrative sources, of a type which seems to have no relationship at all to the "Cambridge" style of self-conscious critical analysis of what we are about which was fostered by the late M. I. Finley. What has actually been produced, I observe quite without satisfaction, is closer to being an "Oxford" Ancient History than a "Cambridge" one.

Even if a *CAH* volume has no explicit methodological or philosophical programme of its own, should its contents none the less be structured so as to enter into explicit dialogue with modern interpretations, naming the authors concerned, and overtly discussing the propositions they have put forward? This is done here to a limited degree, but the overall *tendency* is merely to present each individual author's version, often essentially a narrative, and to relegate reference to other modern writers to a footnote, which itself embodies a reference to the bibliography at the end (efficiently organised into sections). This procedure is consistent, and carried out in an economical way. But it hardly brings the reader, especially the student reader, into any real relationship with modern views and debates.

More serious, to my mind, is the very slight use made overall of explicit quotation and discussion of ancient texts, whether literary or documentary. Ancient texts appear predominantly as footnote references, not as items embodying the representation of present circumstances or past events, which themselves require discussion and interpretation. Naturally, practicalities prevent this being done on every occasion. But the effect is both to suggest that narrated "facts" are unproblematic, and to limit the student's direct acquaintance with the diverse materials out of which we construct "our" ancient world.

Even leaving aside these fundamental problems of theory, approach, and method, the editors of every volume in such a series confront difficult questions of principle. Is the series to be conceived of as a whole, so that the reader will need to read across, or forward and back, from one volume to another? It is an equally insoluble question, when the material is divided up into short chronological sections, to know which geographical areas should be considered on a regional basis, and how that treatment should be distributed. Thus, for instance, early Hellenistic Sicily benefits from a chapter on Agathocles in volume VII.1, 384ff., but then vanishes altogether from VII.2, except for a narrative chapter on Pyrrhus (456ff.); it appears only in passing in VIII, and gets two and a half pages (25–27) to itself in the volume under review, surfacing later in connection with Verres and provincial government.

The student reader of the *Verrines* could thus not find anywhere in *CAH*² a coherent presentation of the geographical, historical, and social context in which Verres had been functioning.

To presume on a discussion to which I will return later, this volume could only have been given coherence by a focus on Rome, and not every related region could have been given separate treatment. But it does seem a major lack that the heart of the late Hellenistic world, namely Greece, the Aegean, and western Asia Minor, appears only as the battleground for Roman or Mithridatic armies (there is a splendid chapter by J. G. F. Hind on the latter, as also an excellent one by the late A. N. Sherwin-White on "Lucullus, Pompey and the East").

Given the priority allotted, as a quite reasonable choice, to Graeco-Roman culture within "ancient history" as *CAH* conceives it, the Aegean and its periphery were essential both in economic and social terms, and as the immediate source of Hellenism in Italy and Rome. Its omission as a topic thus obscures even Athens itself (see now Chr. Habicht, *Athen in hellenistischer Zeit, Gesammelte Aufsätze* [1994]), not to speak of Delos (see F. Coarelli et al., *Delo e l'Italia* [1983]) or Rhodes, not merely a cultural centre, but still a major independent naval power, as it appears in the Roman law on the eastern provinces of 101/0 B.C.; its history is discussed by R. M. Berthold, *Rhodes in the Hellenistic Age* (1984).

One effect of this omission is that nowhere in *CAH*² IX is there a view of the world of the main late Hellenistic cities as such, nor of the illuminating viewpoints which, through a large number of inscriptions, they provide on the evolving Roman Empire. We are left with the wonderful, and so far unchallenged, account by Rostovtzeff in the last part of his *Social and Economic History of the Hellenistic World*. For the inland part of Asia Minor, dominated by the Galatae, we now have also the major work of Stephen Mitchell, *Anatolia* I (1993), which is essential for understanding the Roman impact, and the process of province formation.

Important formal questions also remain obscure, such as the conditions, meaning, and extent of freedom (*libertas*) as enjoyed by Greek cities. See, for example, R. Bernhardt, *Polis und römische Herrschaft* (1988), or J.-L. Ferrary, "Le statut des cités libres dans l'Empire romain à la lumière des inscriptions de Claros," *CRAI* (1991): 557. The reference is to the two extraordinarily rich honorific inscriptions published by L. and J. Robert, *Claros* I: *décrets hellénistiques* (1989), which illustrate the complex way in which local notables managed the relations between their cities and Rome. It is one inevitable penalty of the huge task of bringing such a massive volume into existence that neither these texts nor the vast Greek inscription from Ephesos, *Epigra-*

phica Anatolica 14 (1989), with provisions for tolls (*portoria*), dating from the 60s B.C. onwards, have found a place in it (except the latter, in a footnote on p. 35).

Similar, but worse, problems affect the history of the Jews in the Hellenistic period, which is not treated at all in *CAH*² VII.1. The fundamental topic of the impact of Hellenism on Judaism before the Maccabees, the subject of major modern works, such as Victor Tscherikover, *Hellenistic Civilisation and the Jews* (1959), Martin Hengel, *Judentum und Hellenismus* (1969; trans. as *Judaism and Hellenism*, 1974), and the late Elias Bickerman's posthumous *The Jews in the Greek Age* (1988), is thus tackled nowhere in *CAH*². Tessa Rajak's excellent chapter in this volume (274ff.) on "The Jews under Hasmonean rule," intended for a period beginning in 146 B.C., can only pick up the Maccabean revolution, one of the few unquestionable "turning points" in human history, after it is already under way.

Rome and "The Romans"

The question of what the intended subject of a *CAH* volume on republican Rome should be is emphasized still more by the existence of another *Cambridge History*, the *Cambridge History of Classical Literature* II: *Latin Literature* (1982). Rather typically of an older attitude, "literature" is conceived of there as something which happens within the texts of individual works by well-known authors. There is nothing whatsoever in it which renders superfluous the splendid chapter in *CAH*² IX, 689ff., by Miriam Griffin on "The Intellectual Developments of the Ciceronian Age."

Unfortunately, the two projects between them still leave unfilled two enormous gaps, which come close to rendering the Latin-speaking culture, society, and politics of the period empty and unintelligible. Firstly, nobody can dispute that the dominant form of public "literary" expression in the period was oratory. Without some systematic discussion of the shape and content of speeches, as well as of their public contexts and audiences—the Senate, public meetings, popular and permanent courts (*contiones, iudicia populi*, and *quaestiones*), not to speak of the repetition of comparable contexts in towns outside Rome—we can hardly conceive of what being a "Roman" meant in the late Republic. Some aspects of this are covered in the massive volume by J.-M. David, *Le patronat judiciaire au dernier siècle de la République romaine* (1992).

More problematic still is the absence from either volume of any attempt even to pose the problem of the "Latinization" of Italian culture. "Romanization" is important enough on the political (and military) plane, of which more later, and the absence from *CAH*² IX of post–Social War Italy is more than unfortunate. But the *Latinization* of the culture of Italy, and with it the focusing of creative literary effort on Roman society and Roman tradition, is a more important, and difficult, question. Somehow, any meaningful account of "Rome" must pose the problems of why it was not only Latin, but expressly "Roman" literature which was to be written by Catullus from Verona, Virgil from Mantua, Livy from Patavium, and Horace from Venusia, all born in the period covered by this volume, as well as by Ovid from Sulmo, born in the year of its terminal point, 43 B.C. The "Republican Rome" which we can know is very largely the Rome which they constructed for us. Their testimony rivals that of Cicero from Arpinum, who came from within the somewhat longer established zone of Roman citizens (Arpinum had gained the full Roman citizenship eighty-two years before Cicero's birth, in 188 B.C.), and is followed later by that of Greek-speaking Roman citizens of the imperial period, Plutarch, Appian, and Cassius Dio.

This missing problem simply serves to emphasise the wider problem which makes republican history so deceptively difficult: who, or what community, or communities, ought to be the subject of the history of late republican "Rome"? It is time to turn, all too belatedly, to the years 146–43 B.C.

It follows from all that is said that I accept the practical and logical impossibility of finding a perfect structure within which to incorporate the material. Whatever choice is made, some meaningful and significant viewpoints will be lost. It was, therefore, wholly defensible to take "Roman" history as the focus of this volume, and to treat coherently only some of the areas on which the Empire progressively impinged (note also a fair shot at the very difficult and not very well documented topic of late Ptolemaic Egypt, chapter 8c, covering however a mere eighteen pages). As it happens, however, all the non-Roman zones or topics treated are eastern (Mithridates, Egypt, the Jews). Africa, Spain, and Europe thus play a role only in the survey in chapter 2 on "The Roman Empire and Its Problems in the Late Second Century," or as and when the narrative reaches them. For a global view of the interaction between Rome and a variety of societies and cultures, *CAH*² IX cannot compare with C. Nicolet, ed., *Rome et la conquête du monde méditerranéen II. Genèse d'un empire* (1978). If one western region (other than Sicily) deserved to be picked out, it was surely Gallia Transalpina, the subject of much debate and detailed work in recent years; see now E. Hermon, *Rome et la Gaule Transalpine avant César, 125–59 B.C.* (1993).

The shape which the volume actually takes is first a chapter on the crisis of the Republic and on sources; then the previously mentioned chapter on the second-century Empire and its problems; then a long section of over 400 pages which is essentially political-military narrative, with the three eastern sections interspersed. The final section, of nearly 300 pages, takes a number of separate themes: the constitution and public criminal law (largely on the permanent courts); Roman private law; the administration of the Empire; economy and society (an extremely stimulating section by Claude Nicolet, explicitly designed to raise wider questions); the city of Rome and the urban plebs, by Nicholas Purcell, of which more later; intellectual developments (the first-class chapter by Miriam Griffin); religion, by Mary Beard; and finally an epilogue, by the three editors.

It will quickly be seen that no one could reasonably complain of the richness or quality of the material offered. There is an infinite range of themes which could be discussed, so I will select just three: "the Senate"; the mass of Roman citizens, in Rome itself, in Italy, and (increasingly) in the provinces; and the role of the provincial populations in the military structure of the Empire.

Being a Senator in the Late Republic

Richard Saller, reviewing volume VIII in *JRS* 81 (1991), rightly commended the serious attempt by the late Alan Astin to discuss the basic features of Roman political life (VIII, 163–96). Andrew Lintott, in a helpful and clear, if fairly brief, initial section of this volume (40–53), does likewise. Yet, it seems to me, we need to start further back, and to look much more carefully at the social context of the functions of a senator. Surprising as it may seem, given the centrality of the topic, there is actually much about "the Senate" of the Republic which still calls out for examination and clarification. Polybius, as we all know, defined the Senate as the "aristocratic element" of the Roman mixed constitution. But does that mean essentially a role defined by achievement, personal prominence, and office-holding, or by descent? (To say, as some have, that all office-holders were by definition "aristocrats" is circular.) Many problems arise. What *was* a *gens*, or a *familia*? How many patrician *familiae* (*gentes*?) were there in 146–43 B.C., and what was the significance of belonging to one? What proportion of the 300 and then (after Sulla) 600 members of the Senate really did descend from previous holders of curule office, with or without a break of one or more generations? The question partly, but only partly, depends on the late republican informal usage of the terms *nobiles* and *novi* (literally "new men"), re-opened by P. A. Brunt in *JRS* 72 (1982): 1. Equally important, and not yet absorbed by republican historians, is the nuanced treatment by K. Hopkins and G. P. Burton in chapter 2 of *Death and Renewal* (1983), looking (for once) at *all* grades of senatorial office (or senate-related, like the twenty-four annually elected military tribunes). We must at all costs distinguish occupation of the *consulship*, which E. Badian in "The Consuls, 179–49 BC," *Chiron* 20 (1990): 371, has confirmed as having been very heavily influenced by "noble" descent, from that of the wider range of less prestigious public offices. Should we really see all of the 100 tribunes of the plebs, or the 200 quaestors, of the 60s as part of an aristocracy of birth?

The question of how much we really know of the long-term history of "senatorial" families (*gentes? familiae?*) is radically confused in this period by the invention of family histories (and retrojection of cognomina) by the Romans themselves. It will be enough to refer to the fundamental article by Peter Wiseman, "Legendary Genealogies in Late-Republican Rome," *Greece and Rome* 21 (1974): 153 = *Roman Studies, Literary and Historical* (1987), 207, with further material in O. Wikander, "Senators and Equites v. Ancestral Pride and Genealogical Studies in Late Republican Rome," *Opuscula Romana* 19 (1993): 77. This very emphasis on ancestors, expressed through household portraits (*imagines*), on coins minted from the 130s onwards, and in literary reconstructions, as by Atticus (Nepos, *Atticus*, 18, 2–6), of course itself confirms that descent was regarded as important. But how significant was the availability of "noble" ancestors for that large majority of holders of public elected office, and consequently senators, who never held the consulship? The modern emphasis on the consulship, as the key to "politics," is in any case rendered problematic by the fact that it was only after Sulla, in the first period which we know well from contemporary evidence, that consuls tended to stay in Rome for most of their year of office before going to their provinces. As we know from J. P. V. D. Balsdon, "Consular Provinces under the Late Republic," *JRS* 29 (1939): 57, and A. Giovannini, *Consulare Imperium* (1983), the consuls' provinces were already allotted during their year of office, and they could (it seems) go off to them when they wished. But they did in fact tend to stay in Rome, and thus to function as politicians, thus marking a vast change as against the earlier and middle Republic, when consuls (like the *strategoi* of fifth-century democratic Athens) were in essence elected generals (*imperatores*) who left Rome soon after taking up office.

Oddly enough, neither in *CAH*² VIII nor in IX is there any real discussion of the evolving "senatorial" cursus, and the pattern of a senator's public military/civilian office-holding over an adult life-time. Nor is there (for instance) any discussion that I can find of the role of the lot (*sortitio*) in allocating provinces. Yet it was the lot which had given Macedonia to Flamininus as consul of 198, and also the lot (Appian, *BC* I.55/241) which had given Sulla the command against Mithridates, before tribunician intervention temporarily overrode it. Volume IX also misses the significant formal change which also seems to go back to Sulla, namely that praetors now underwent a double sortition, one for an urban function during their year in office, and a second one for a provincial command. The sequence is clearly attested for Verres: see *Verr.* II 1, 104: "he obtained the urban province by lot" (i.e., became urban praetor); and II 2, 17: "the province of Sicily fell to him by lot." There are also wider issues of social structure which ought to be examined, precisely as a way of *not* taking the notion of "the Senate" for granted. Was the wealth which was a prerequisite for being an elected magistrate, and hence (by censorial enrolment until Sulla) a senator, always predominantly derived from agricultural properties? If so, how should we envisage the typical pattern of the geographical distribution of a senator's landed properties? What about urban properties (in Rome or elsewhere)? Or semi-industrial production (pottery, bricks) from landed properties? Or income from commercial activities?

Where in Rome did senators live, and what were their houses like? How large a household did each maintain? These questions are not antiquarian, or part only of "social history." For one of the fundamentals of "government" in republican Rome was precisely that there were, apart from the Senate house (*Curia*) itself, almost no "government buildings." A senator's house functioned as his political base, both in the sense that large numbers of people were received there, and in that he proceeded ceremonially from there, escorted by followers, to go down to the Forum and Curia. Many, but clearly not all, would literally "go down" the Via Sacra, because they lived, like Cicero, on the northern slopes of the Palatine, in the area of substantial houses, aligned along a major drainage system of the archaic period, partly excavated recently by Andrea Carandini. The symbolic importance of the aristocratic house (*domus*), its positioning and architectural character, simply cannot be left out of any account of what "being a senator" amounted to. See now E. M. Steinby, ed., *Lexicon Topographicum Urbis Romae* II (1995), with hundreds of entries under "domus."

The spatial distribution of the *domus* of senators is a significant question, as is the configuration and forms of occupation of the *domus* themselves. Exactly parallel issues arise with the meeting places of the Senate, not only the Curia Hostilia in its exposed location on the edge of the Forum, but a variety of other *templa* (places formally rendered sacred by inauguration), for example, those of Concordia, Iuppiter Stator, and Bellona. The relations of these buildings to their urban contexts, and their size and internal configuration (how many persons could actually get into the temple of Concordia on its narrow ledge below the Capitol?), are also important questions if we are to envisage realistically how "public life" really worked (see M. Bonnefond-Coudry, *Le sénat de la république romaine* [1989]).

In terms of wider social relations, whether lateral, as between (approximate) social equals, or vertical, towards *clientes* or other protégés or followers, everything has been thrown into an entirely beneficial state of confusion by the two fundamental chapters in P. A. Brunt's *The Fall of the Roman Republic* (1988), namely chapter 9, "Factions," and chapter 8 "*Clientela*." Students of the late Republic have hardly begun to absorb the effects of these demonstrations that our evidence does not allow us to say that *either* lateral connections *or* vertical forms of dependence can legitimately be deployed to explain political behaviour and political developments. Once more, we need to start all over again. Brunt's major work is, of course, alluded to in *CAH²* IX (whose bibliography contains items up to 1990), but the fundamental nature of the problem of how to understand Roman politics is hardly brought out.

One way to approach the issue is to look at forms of personal and social influence as they appear in contemporary evidence, above all in the letters of Cicero. That task has been carried out now by Élizabeth Deniaux, *Clientèles et pouvoir à l'époque de Cicéron* (1993), an exemplary study of Cicero's letters of recommendation (and, like the book by Bonnefond-Coudry, a *thèse* supervised by Claude Nicolet). It shows that written interventions in favour of either communities or individuals played an immensely important role in the functioning of the *res publica*—but does nothing (and could have done nothing) to support the quite misleading notion that mass voting by *clientes* ever affected the making of decisions, that is to say, the passing of laws by the assemblies.

Instead, far more space needs to be given to the operation of magnificence and largess (*magnificentia* and *munificentia*) directed to the people at large, in the form of votive games, gladiatorial shows, buildings, dinners, or distributions of benefits in cash or kind. But that topic would take us to the wider, and extremely difficult, problem of what the Roman people was.

The Urban Plebs and the Roman People

If we start, as *CAH²* IX does, from political history, the first and most important thing that the Roman people "was" was whoever turned up at public meetings, or to meetings of the tribal assembly, in the Forum Romanum. The configuration of this primary public space is thus the first thing that needs to be understood. Which is another way of saying that F. Coarelli's *Il foro romano* I–II (1983–85) is not an antiquarian or archaeological *adjunct* to the history of the Republic, but the context from which everything has to start. For, if we are to explain anything, we have to begin from the proposition that, with the exception of meetings of the Senate, everything happened out of doors, "under the eyes of the Roman people" (*sub conspectu populi Romani*), and nearly everything happened in this particular space—public meetings, assemblies, (except for elections, now held in the Campus Martius), triumphal processions, the procession (going in the opposite direction) to the Roman Games in the Circus Maximus, permanent courts, theatrical performances (sometimes in elaborate temporary theatres), gladiatorial shows, funeral orations from the Rostra. In *CAH*² IX Peter Wiseman's remarkable narrative of the politics of the 60s and 50s is indeed, as one would expect, imbued through and through with a consciousness of the urban context (displayed on a modest sketch-map on p. 370). Furthermore, the wider social context of the city is evoked, in vivid and highly original style, by Nicholas Purcell in chapter 17, "Rome and the Plebs Urbana." There is too much here to comment on, or even (as yet) to absorb. But somehow a sense of the city, and its vast population, as of the Forum as an open-air political stage (evoked perhaps more vividly in the *Verrines* or the *Brutus* than anywhere else) belongs earlier, perhaps indeed (or also) in volume VIII. To give only one example, it is hardly meaningful to record the "imprisoning" of the consuls by the tribunes of the plebs, if the reader does not already know that it was about forty metres from the Curia and Comitium to the Carcer, and that this was a symbolic gesture played out before the crowd in the Forum.

Belatedly or otherwise, however, the city and its population come alive in Nicholas Purcell's chapter as never before. But the urban plebs was not the whole Roman people, even before the Social War. It is, however, very important that, of the nearly 1 million Roman citizens who finally get themselves registered in 70 B.C., up to 320,000 (the maximum figure recorded) lived *either* in Rome *or* near enough to collect Clodius' ration of free corn in the years after 58 B.C. Thus, in spite of vast expansion, before and especially after the Social War, a huge population, and a very substantial proportion of citizens, always lived within a shortish distance from the political centre.

Beyond that, however, if what we are trying to write is first of all a history of "the Romans," we surely ought to give a prominent place to the formal structure of the integration of the Roman citizen in the *res publica*, as voter and soldier, an integration achieved primarily by the census. Perhaps equally important to explain, especially for the student reader, is (once again) the spatial configuration of Roman citizens in Italy, firstly before the Social War, when, apart from Rome and its surrounding area, they occupied primarily two broad zones, of which one stretched south-east into Campania, and the other more or less due north, diagonally across Italy, to the Adriatic. This area included many long-established, internally self-governing communities (*civitates*), such as Arpinum; but its primary importance was that its people (the adult males) belonged to Roman tribes, were enrolled by the censors, had the right (in principle) to vote in Rome, and (above all) were recruited directly into the Roman legions. This vast politico-social structure, already an uneasy combination of a nuclear city-state and an extended nation-state, does need to be *explained* before anything at all is intelligible in the history of the later Republic. So also do the other two major elements of "Roman" Italy. Firstly there were places of Latin status, a combination of ancient communities like Tibur and Praeneste, colonies created by the Latin League before its dissolution in 338 B.C., and post-338 colonies established by Rome, from Aquileia to Brundisium or Vibo Valentia. The failure to find a place for Italy as such in *CAH*² IX, the only fundamental fault of the volume, shows up painfully here. For, to take only one example, Praeneste can show the single most spectacular monument of late second-century Italy, the temple of Fortuna Primigenia. Equally, four of the Latin colonies have been extensively excavated: Cosa, Alba Fucens, Paestum (the former Greek city of Poseidonia), and Fregellae. See, for general discussions, F. E. Brown, *Cosa: The Making of a Roman Town* (1980); J. R. Mertens, *Alba Fucens* (1981); J. R. Mertens, "Alba Fucens: à l'aube d'une colonie romaine," *Journal of Ancient Topography* I (1981): 93; J. G. Pedley, *Paestum: Greeks and Romans in Southern Italy* (1990); F. Coarelli, ed., *Fregellae II: il santuario di Esculapio* (1986).

These Latin colonies shared with the other element, that is, the noncitizen allies, the essential characteristics of self-government on the one hand, and of the obligation to provide, officer, and pay contingents for the Roman army; but they did not pay any tribute in money. "Rome and Italy in the Second Century B.C." had been very well discussed by E. Gabba in *CAH*² VIII, chapter 7, and the theme is taken up again by him, in IX, chapter 4, "Rome and Italy: The Social War." But surely the political *geography* of late second-century Italy needed to be re-surveyed, and a map indicating the different communal statuses provided? Equally, in 776 pages of text on ninety years, published in the 1990s, space should have been found for a survey of the different ethnic groups, cultures, languages, and settlement patterns of Italy before the Social War, from Liguria to Etruria, Umbria, the Samnite or Oscan zone, and the Greek cities, surveyed now by Katherine Lomas, *Rome and the Western Greeks* (1993). There is a growing mass of local inscriptional and archaeological evidence which it would be futile to try to survey here. But, without such an attempt, we miss even Pompeii, whose urban evolution from an Oscan town into its imperial form was analysed recently by Paul Zanker, *Pompeji. Stadtbilder als Spiegel von Gesellschaft und Herrschaftsform* (1988).

The relevance of all this to the Roman state is, of course, that the Social

War brought all of Italy (up to the Po?) into the citizenship. Gabba, in his first-class account of the Social War, by far the best available, stresses the progressive military success of the Romans. I would emphasise more their comprehensive political *surrender*, by which they granted almost immediately, in the Lex Iulia of 90, the fundamental principle over which the war had broken out.

The consequences were momentous but remain extremely difficult to discuss in detail. It is therefore here, in the absence of any chapter on post–Social War Italy, or on first-century Cisalpina, that the only major weakness of *CAH*² IX lies. If we think of progressive integration into the Roman *res publica*, Cisalpina is a particular problem. Was this process of integration fundamentally different north and south of the Po? What happened to the pre-existing Latin colonies (e.g., Cremona, Placentia, Aquileia) after 89 B.C.? In spite of important modern studies, the reviewer must confess to remaining wholly confused. See, however, R. Peyre, *La Cisalpine gauloise du IIIe au Ier siècle avant J.-C.* (1979); R. Chevalier, *La romanisation de la Celtique du Pô* (1983); F. M. Ausbüttel, "Die Eingliederung Oberitaliens in das römische Reich," *Prometheus* 15 (1989): 165; D. Foraboschi, *Lineamenti di storia della Cisalpina Romana. Antropologia di una conquista* (1992).

As for the rest of Italy, immense problems persist and cannot be treated here. It does seem clear at least that, as the Tabula Heracleensis shows (ll. 142–56), the census of Roman citizens in Italy was now conducted in their local community (*municipium, colonia,* or *praefectura*), and the details then delivered by delegates (*legati*) to the censors in Rome. Secondly, as a consequence of the citizenship, all now served in the legions (legionary service—for instance, as a qualification for local office—is also one of the recurrent presuppositions of the Tabula Heracleensis). What we can, and cannot, know of these and other fundamental changes in the life of Italian communities, and of their relation to the political centre, should have formed a major chapter of *CAH*² IX. As it is, at least we can be certain that the ending of the obligation to organise, officer, and pay their own contingents must have represented a fundamental change in the life of both the Latin colonies and the allied communities of Italy. The integration into the Roman legions of those of their young men who were recruited must also have been a major social change, with considerable long-term consequences. Post–Social War Italy still awaits a comprehensive historical treatment. Curiously enough, this is not provided either in the other major, multi-volume, multi-author series which is being published in parallel with the Roman volume of *CAH*², the *Storia di Roma*. Volume II of this series, *L'impero mediterraneo* I: *La repubblica imperiale* (1990), which covers the period from the fourth century to Actium in 965 pages of text, gives only a few pages (706–10) to "L'Italia dopo la guerra sociale," with a few more pages later (831–43) on "Sistemazioni urbane in Italia tra II e I secolo."

Provincial Allies and Roman Military Power

The regular calling-up of contingents of Italian allies, on the basis of the *formula togatorum* (the list of males of military age), had been one of the bases of Roman military power before the Social War, just as direct recruitment of Italians into the legions was after it. But was the basis of Rome's overseas empire fundamentally different, structured instead on direct and indirect taxation in cash or kind? Clearly the imposition of taxation, and the consequent inflow of revenues to Rome (but not to the allied communities of Italy) was crucial. But what Cicero writes in the *Verrines* about one of the many areas of Verres' malpractice suggests explicitly that we should not make too radical a distinction between Italy and provinces (*Verr. II* 5, 60):

> Each *civitas* [in Sicily] had always been accustomed to entrust to a naval commander of its own all the funds for its fleet, for supplies, pay, and everything else. . . . That was, as I say, always the established practice, not only in Sicily but in all provinces, also as regards the pay and expenditure of the [Italian] allies and the Latins, in the period when we used to make use of their forces.

Verres, however, had demanded that all these sums should first be handed over to himself, and then dispensed by him to whomsoever he chose. What is important for us is, firstly, the close comparison made between pre–Social War Italy and the provinces and, secondly, the general nature of Cicero's account, which explicitly relates to all provinces, and does not seem to take into account differences of status between communities which were free or had a treaty, or were merely tribute-paying. In *CAH*[2] IX Rome's late republican Empire is in general very well treated, first in Andrew Lintott's excellent overview in chapter 2, "The Roman Empire and Its Problems in the Late Second Century"; for a further treatment we can turn now to his *Imperium Romanum: Politics and Administration* (1993). Then, in the second, thematic, half of the volume, there is chapter 15 by J. S. Richardson, "The Administration of the Empire." But in general, given that we are talking of a major period of conflict and conquest, not to speak of great civil wars in the 80s and 40s, even the strictly "Roman" army plays a relatively small part—no systematic part at all indeed, after four pages (36–39) devoted to "Military Strength and the Empire" in the later second century. Equally, the question of the large proportion of the "Roman" army made up of contingents from the Italian allies is not prominent. It is thus not surprising, though it is regrettable, that the quite difficult and obscure question of the basis on which Cicero made his generalisation is not really broached at all. Cicero had, at least on the face of it, been talking about naval contingents, as he does elsewhere in the *Verrines* in recording Verres' outrageous behaviour when, as a legate in Asia Minor in 80/79, he sold off a ship (a *myoparos*) supplied by Miletus, while its soldiers and oarsmen were told to make their own way home. This vessel counted as part of the navy of the Roman people, and was one of ten ships built by the people of Miletus from its own resources for the Roman people (*Verr. II* 1, 86–90). Similar obligations applied, it seems clear, to land forces. Hence we have the very explicit indication in the decree from Lete in Macedonia of 119 B.C. in honour of the quaestor, M. Annius, that it was a benefaction on his part not to have called out more soldiers from the Makedones to confront a Celtic invasion, in order to spare the cities (*Syll.*³, no. 700, ll. 23–25). The same right to call out troops clearly applied also in the western provinces. Hence Cicero says of Fonteius as propraetor of Gallia in 74–72 that "as for those (Gauls) who had often been conquered in great wars, so that they were personally obedient to the Roman people, he required of them great forces of cavalry for all those wars which were then being waged throughout the world by the Roman people, great sums of money for their pay, and a very large quantity of grain for the support of the war in Spain" (*Font.* 13).

There is no need to pursue the question here. To understand what being under Roman power meant, however, it would be important to know what distinctions, if any, we should draw in this respect, between ordinary, tribute-paying provincial communities on the one hand, or free cities, or ones with a treaty, whether lying within or outside the geographical bounds of a province on the other. Royal forces, very prominent in the civil wars, are also relevant. Is the despatch of a contingent by Aphrodisias to help Oppius in Laodicea in 88 B.C. (Reynolds, *Aphrodisias and Rome*, nos. 2–3) to be seen as the voluntary gesture of an ally, or the obligation of a subject? Such forms of recruitment became particularly important in the large-scale civil wars which Romans fought, largely on provincial territory, in the 40s and 30s. Moreover, as is clear, the regular Roman auxiliary forces of the Principate go back to these provincial auxiliaries of the later Republic; see D. B. Saddington, *The Development of the Roman Auxiliary Forces from Caesar to Vespasian (49 B.C.– A.D. 79)* (1982). Since these later auxiliary forces come into view precisely by virtue of the discharge certificates (*diplomata*) which gave them the citizenship on discharge, the republican provincial auxiliaries do belong also, in the longer term, to the history of Roman citizens.

Conclusions

*CAH*² IX, for all its very high intellectual level, and the coherence and sense of purpose with which it had been designed and edited, still makes a somewhat old-fashioned impression. For that, there seem to me to be three reasons. One is that the last few decades have perhaps not been as creative in the history of this period as they have for other periods and areas of the ancient world. Another is that, as indicated already, too large a proportion of the volume has been devoted to year-by-year political-military narrative. "Events," of course, cannot be avoided, and the notion that there ever was a (more or less) timeless world of peasants to which politics and wars were irrelevant, might have seemed extremely odd to the hundreds of thousands of peasants who found themselves, in the later Republic, with their villages assaulted by Roman or other armies, subjected to new governmental systems, recruited into armies, taken away by pirates, or sold into slavery. But to say that rapid change is fundamental to the period does not really mean that even the most subtle and perceptive of narratives really has to take up so much of the volume.

Secondly, it surely would be possible now to broaden the basis of what we take to be the subject: to the social and spatial context of the "aristocratic" *familia* and its *domus* (and this, surely, would have been the place for considerations of marriage and property, slavery and manumission); to the voters meeting in the Forum or the Campus Martius; to the urban plebs of the metropolis (a broadening which is achieved here); to the Roman, Latin, and allied communities of pre–Social War Italy, and to the now (in principle) Roman-citizen communities of post–Social War Italy; to the Roman armies; to the provincial populations; and to all those groups, not yet ruled by Rome, on whom Roman power, sometimes divided against itself, made so great an impact. We do after all have many different view-points on this rapidly changing world. Not least of these is Diodorus, who not only gives the fullest, almost contemporary, account of the slave wars and the Social War, but happened to be in Egypt in 60–59 B.C. when Ptolemy Auletes was seeking recognition from Rome, and every effort was being made to seek Roman favour. But a visiting Roman accidentally killed a cat, and nothing that royal agents could do could prevent his being lynched by the mob (Diodorus 1, 83, 8–9). This minor incident might serve to symbolize the instability of social and political relations in the Mediterranean area under the growing pressure of Roman power, and the complexity of the history which we might one day be in a position to write.

CHAPTER NINE

The Mediterranean and the Roman Revolution: Politics, War, and the Economy*

If we want to understand the violent history of the late Roman Republic, which in a few decades saw both a vast extension of Roman conquest and the establishment of monarchy by Augustus, we might begin with an anecdote told by Plutarch about Julius Caesar.[1] As he was passing a tiny barbarian village in the Alps, one of his companions said, "Is it possible that here too there are rivalries for office, competitions for honours, and jealousies of each other on the part of the leading men?" Caesar replied, "I would rather be first among these people than second among the Romans." This story may be apocryphal; but whether it is or not, it well reflects the spiralling competition which in the end destroyed the rules for the sharing and limitation of power at Rome, and with them the Republic itself. The story of that destruction is familiar, not least from Syme's *The Roman Revolution*. But it also gives us a partial and momentary glimpse of the wider context, made up of a vast range of local communities, within which that competition took place; modern estimates tend to put the population of the early Roman Empire at something like 50 million people.[2]

---

* First published in *Past and Present* 102 (1984): 3–24. This chapter was given as a lecture at the Triennial Meeting of the Hellenic and Roman Societies in 1981. It is printed here essentially in the same form, since for the reasons given in the text the evidence does not in any case allow more than a preliminary exploration of possibilities. I am grateful to Keith Hopkins for comments and suggestions.

1. Plutarch, *Caesar* 11; Plutarch, *Moralia* 206B.

2. R. Syme, *The Roman Revolution* (1939). For population estimates, see, e.g., M. I. Finley, *The Ancient Economy* (1973), 30; K. Hopkins, "Taxes and Trade in the Roman Empire, 200 B.C.–A.D. 400," *JRS* 70 (1980): 117–18.

What consequences did Roman political history have for the populations of the different regions? Suppose, for example, that we ask ourselves not about Caesar and his rivals but about those Alpine villagers. At the time to which the anecdote relates the Alpine passes from Italy into Gaul are reported to have been dangerous and unsecured. Merchants and even Roman armies travelling over them had to pay high tolls to the mountain peoples, and Caesar's efforts to change that had no lasting effect.[3] Yet, by contrast, Vitruvius happens to preserve an instance of how Caesar's operations did serve to integrate one mountain village into a wider economy. One year when he was operating in the foothills of the Alps—probably the eastern Alps, between Aquileia and Virunum—Caesar ordered the local communities to provide supplies. One fortified village (*castellum*) refused and was besieged. Attempts to burn down its wooden towers totally failed, demonstrating the properties of the larchwood of which they were built. In consequence the village earned not only the Latin name "Larignum" but also a trade in larchwood, which by Augustus' time was in use in the towns along the Po and down the coast southwards to Ravenna, Ariminum, Pisaurum, and Fanum.[4]

By contrast, the Salassi of the Val d'Aosta were finally "integrated" by military defeat in 25 B.C.; 8,000 combatants and 36,000 non-combatants were sold as slaves, while a Roman colony was established at Aosta.[5] In this case the intervention of the Roman state was drastic and decisive. Elsewhere it might be more partial, indirect, and indecisive—partial in both senses, for Caesar soon learned in Gaul that the barbarian or semi-barbarian peoples of the west could go in for faction fights just as savage as those at Rome, and he intervened repeatedly in them himself. The same was true in the Alpine area itself. In 49 B.C. Cicero's friend Caelius wearily reported from somewhere in northern Italy that a garrison commander serving in Pompey's forces in the Maritime Alps had been bribed by one faction among the Intimilii to murder a lord leader there named Comitius, who was a former host of Caesar. The people of Intimilium had reacted by taking to arms, and Caelius was obliged to set off with some cohorts through the snow to restore order.[6]

The common characteristic of these cases, all from the Alpine region, is that they show an interaction between the activities of the Roman state in the

3. Caesar, *BG* 1, 10, 4, and 3, 1, 1–2.

4. Vitruvius, 2, 9, 15–16. See J. Sasel, "Castellum Larignum (Vitr. 2, 9, 15)," *Historia* 30 (1981): 254–6, for the suggested identification with *Larix in Itinerarium Antonini*, 276. See now R. Meiggs, *Trees and Timber in the Ancient Mediterranean World* (1982), 248ff.

5. Strabo, *Geography* 4, 6, 7 (205–6); Cassius Dio 53, 25, 2–5; cf. Appian, 3. 17/49–51; *ILS* 6753 (showing that some surviving Salassi were included in the population of the colony).

6. Cicero, *Fam.* 8, 15, 2 (Shackleton Bailey, no. 149).

period of conquests and civil wars, and the political or economic life of local communities. The question posed in this article is: can we gain any serious conception of how and in what ways the apparently earth-shaking events of the period from say 88 to 31 B.C. really affected the social and economic life of ordinary people, grouped in their local communities? The answer, which at any serious level is clearly no, is a reflection of the drastic limitations imposed by the restricted volume, and even more restricted nature, of the evidence surviving from the ancient world. All that is possible is to pick out a number of different dimensions or aspects which are in various ways relevant to trying to understand something about the Mediterranean world in the last half century of the Republic. For instance we may pose the following question: if, as many people assume, we should envisage not a Mediterranean-wide economy, of which inter-regional trade was an essential characteristic, but a network of strictly local economies, how profound an effect could political or military events, or the demands of an ancient state, have had on them? Short-term effects, of course. Even our severely political or military narratives allow us to catch a fleeting glimpse, for instance, of the bakery in Ravenna from which Caesar requisitioned some mules for his journey to the Rubicon in 49 B.C.,[7] or the druggist's shop in Gomphoi in Thessaly, where the leading citizens of the town committed suicide by taking poison as Pompey gave the place over to be ravaged by his troops in 48 B.C.[8]

Sometimes we catch similar glimpses of long-distance trade, such as the export of figs, evidently dried figs, from Caunus in Caria to Italy in the 50s. We know this only because when Crassus was embarking at Brundisium for his Parthian expedition a man was standing in the harbour calling out "Cauneas, Cauneas!"—which to some observers sounded all too like "Cave ne eas" (Beware lest you go).[9] Sometimes we gather even less than that: when Caesar's lieutenant Curio was defeated and killed in the civil war in Africa in 49 B.C. his fleet promptly sailed off, and some of his forces, trying to make their escape, begged to be taken on board the merchant ships which were at anchor in the harbour at Utica. But when the ships came inshore that night, some of the ships' boats were overloaded and sank; and as for the soldiers who did get on board, the majority of those who had any money on them were thrown into the sea by the merchants.[10]

7. Suetonius, *DJ* 31.

8. Appian, *BC* 2, 64/269.

9. Cicero, *Div.* 2, 84; Pliny, *NH* 15, 83. Cicero makes clear that he is talking about figs actually imported from Caunus ("caricas Cauno advectas") and not just a type named after the place. Pliny, *NH* 15, 82, describes various methods of storage.

10. Appian, *BC* 2, 46/187–88.

There the story as we have it stops; it is simply a moment of pathos in Appian's narrative of the civil wars. We hear nothing of the nationality of the merchants, the nature of their cargoes, the size of their ships, or their destination, or destinations. But we do gather something which is quite important. As appears repeatedly in the narratives of this period, the operation of merchant ships between different regions of the Mediterranean is simply presumed as part of the social and economic framework within which military and political conflicts were conducted. Such long-distance trade may have been affected by war and civil war; it certainly did not stop, even in the most immediate areas of conflict. Nor apparently did the day-to-day operations of local inshore fishermen. Or at least, if we want a paradigm of the limited effects of these apparently major conflicts on local economic life, we have it to hand in the splendid anecdote of Sulla and the fishermen of Halae in Greece. When Sulla was in Greece in 84–83, on his way back from Asia to Italy, he went for a cure to Aedepsus in the north of Euboea. When he was walking on the shore there, some fishermen appeared and presented him with a gift of fish. But when he asked where they came from and they replied that they came from Halae, he was furious; for after the victory of Orchomenus in 86 he had ordered the destruction of the towns of Anthedon, Larymna, and Halae. However, on reflection, he forgave them, and the people of Halae, who evidently had abandoned the actual site of the town, gained the courage to return to it.[11] So even where a small town was evacuated or destroyed, the people might continue earning their living almost as if it had not happened.

So should we try the extreme hypothesis that the great conflicts of the six decades down to the battle of Actium in 31 B.C. really made no significant difference at all? That the ordinary world of local communal life, customs, and work just went on unaffected? Again we might use as a paradigm the story which Diodorus tells of his own visit to Egypt in 60 or 59 B.C. about how an Egyptian mob lynched a visiting Roman who had killed a cat.[12]

Egypt was to remain outside direct Roman control until 30 B.C.; and in this case local evidence, in the form of papyri in Greek and Egyptian, might one day make possible a more detailed assessment of whatever changes Roman rule brought about. Here we also have an extra element, the Egyptian monumental and inscriptional evidence—for instance, the remarkable funerary stelae of the high priests of Memphis, which stretch from the third century

11. Plutarch, *Sulla* 26.
12. Diodorus I, 44, I (visit in 180th Olympiad, 60–56 B.C.), and 83, 8–9.

B.C. into the reign of Augustus, and then seem to stop;[13] why, it is not clear. But Egypt is one area where we may one day be able to study change—social, economic, religious—over the period of transition.

Elsewhere we are bound to see things very much from the outside. Gaul, for instance, was another place where there was a sudden and irreversible imposition of Roman rule. But again, have we any idea of what this meant for ordinary social and economic life? We can, of course, turn to classical ethnographic or geographical sources—above all, to the descriptive parts of Caesar's *De bello Gallico* and to Strabo's *Geography*. These are of great interest, for it is quite clear that people in Graeco-Roman society in the first century B.C. were conscious of living surrounded by barbarian peoples with different customs, who were none the less slowly coming under external influences.[14] Well-known passages from Diodorus and Caesar, for instance, illustrate the penetration of Italian trade into Gaul before the conquest.[15] Vitruvius also notes the continued use of wooden or thatched roofs in Spain and Gaul, and of straw and earth ones even at Marseilles.[16] Varro, in his dialogue on agriculture set in Rome, makes one of the speakers report that when he had been in command of an army near the Rhine he had observed an entirely non-Mediterranean type of agriculture: no vines, olives or fruit trees, chalk used as fertilizer, and no salt but a sort of charcoal which was used instead.[17] But even if this is a genuine reminiscence (which is doubtful),[18] it points to a fundamental difficulty. The more specific and concrete, and the more precisely located in space and time a description is, the less it will help us to observe change—or to see whether there were basic changes or not; for that we would need a series of precise reports, descriptions, or documents, which we almost never have. But the more general and systematic such a report is, the less clear it will be whether it is or could have been based on real obser-

13. See D. J. Crawford, J. Quaegebeur, and W. Clarysse, *Studies on Ptolemaic Memphis* (1980).

14. E.g., on the ethnography of the Celts, see J. J. Tierney, "The Celtic Ethnography of Posidonius," *Proc. Roy. Irish Acad.* 60 (1960): 189–275; A. D. Momigliano, *Alien Wisdom: The Limits of Hellenization* (1975), chap. 3; D. Nash, "Reconstructing Poseidonius' Celtic Ethnography: Some Considerations," *Britannia* 7 (1976): 111–26.

15. Diodorus 5, 26, 3 (Italian traders exchanging wine for slaves); Caesar, *BG* 1, 1, 3, and 2, 15, 4 (lesser impact of traders on Belgic north). For the background, see, e.g., G. Clemente, *I Romani nella Gallia meridionale II–I sec. a.C.: politica ed economia nell'età dell' imperialismo* (1974).

16. Vitruvius 2, 1, 4.

17. Varro, *RR* 1, 7, 8.

18. For acute problems over this, see P-W, s.v. "Tremellius" (5).

vation. The geographer Strabo, for instance, repeatedly says that the Gauls have now (under Augustus) given up war and taken to agriculture.[19] That does indeed suggest large changes; but we know both that the Gauls already practised agriculture and that there was a whole series of revolts down to the 20s A.D. So how much is such a generalization worth?

In the case of Gaul, however, we can gain some elements of an answer from archaeology, and especially numismatics. In central Gaul a marked phase of urbanization had been under way since the early first century B.C. The Gallic communities—which Caesar calls *civitates* and which it is misleading to call "tribes"[20]—minted coins in various combinations of gold, silver, and bronze or tin-copper alloy. In the 50s the minting of precious-metal coinage greatly increased, apparently for the payment of troops. Afterwards gold coins ceased, and silver was greatly reduced. Two explanations are offered: firstly, silver, and even more gold, was soaked up by indemnities paid to Rome after the conquest by Caesar in the 50s; secondly, troops were no longer needed, so precious metal coinage was no longer struck to pay them. In the urbanized central areas Celtic bronze coins, in small denominations, continued to be minted, implying that they were in daily use. But specifically Roman coins are hardly found in the central part of Gaul until the middle of the first century A.D. Where they were in use was in the north-east, where the legions were stationed.[21]

Here at least we have significant evidence, which has however to be interpreted in the light of large-scale hypotheses both about the nature of Roman rule, and the structure of the local communities. We can also see Gallic soldiers, mainly cavalry, serving all over the Mediterranean in the period of the civil wars, in a variety of Roman forces, with Juba I in Africa and notably with Cleopatra; these last were transferred by Octavian to King Herod of Judaea in 30 B.C., and a Gallic unit was still in his service when he died in 4 B.C.[22] Again we cannot tell what effects, if any, this service abroad had on

19. Strabo, 4, 1, 2 (178); 1, 5 (180); 1, 11–14 (185–89); 3, 5 (194); 4, 2 (195–96).

20. So J. Harmand, "La Gaule indépendante et la conquête," in C. Nicolet, ed., *Rome et la conquête du monde méditerranéen* II (1977–78), 706.

21. D. Nash, "Plus ça change . . .: Currency in Central Gaul from Julius Caesar to Nero," in R. A. G. Carson and C. M. Kraay, eds., *Scripta Nummaria Romana: Essays Presented to Humphrey Sutherland* (1978), 12–31. For the background, see D. Nash, *Settlement and Coinage in Central Gaul, c. 200–50 B.C.*, 2 vols. (*BAR* Supp. ser. 39, 1978).

22. E.g., Suetonius, *DJ* 24 (V Alauda); Caesar, *BC* 1, 39, 2; 1, 51, 1; 3, 4, 4; 3, 22–3; [Caesar], *B. Alex.* 17, 3; [Caesar], *B. Afr.* 6, 3; 19, 3–4; 20; Appian, *BC* 2, 70/91, and 4, 88/373. For Juba I's 2,000 Spanish and Gallic cavalry, see Caesar, *BC* 2, 40, 1. For Octavian's transfer of 400

Gallic society; but we do know that even before Caesar, Aquitanians had served in Spain with the dissident Roman governor Sertorius in the 70s B.C., that they had returned home and were available to lead their fellow country-men in resistance to Caesar's forces in 56.[23] We have clear evidence also of Caesar's interventions in Gallic political life, and his grants of citizenship and other favours to leading Gallic aristocrats, like the two Allobrogan brothers to whom he had given large sums of money and stretches of captured land at home, and had appointed to local offices — and who then deserted to Pompey before the battle of Pharsalus.[24] Other families showed a better sense of sur-vival, and the C. Iulius Rufus who dedicated the Roman arch at Saintes in A.D. 19 was the grandson of a man whom Caesar had made a Roman citi-zen.[25] But it still remains completely uncertain what degree of continuity or change in property relations or social structure characterized Gaul after the conquest, even at the level of the richer members of the major *civitates*.[26]

But even if we could reach some secure generalizations about the upper classes of Gaul, we would have to remember two things. The first is the vast differences of habits and culture between social classes even within the already conquered areas. Varro for instance claims to have observed in bar-barian Illyricum (roughly Yugoslavia) how a peasant woman would step aside from work, give birth to a child, and continue with her toil.[27] But a few decades earlier Poseidonius had reported being told of just the same thing among workers hired for digging on an estate in Liguria belonging to a friend of his from Massilia.[28]

These workers in Liguria, whose customs seemed totally foreign or bar-barian to their own employer, were at least within a wage-earning economy, receiving a daily wage in cash just like those in many of the New Testament parables; and they were thus linked quite closely to the trans-Mediterranean

---

Gauls to Herod in 30 B.C., see Josephus, *BJ* 1, 20, 3 (397), and Josephus, *AJ* 15, 7, 3 (217). For Herod's funeral, see Josephus, *BJ* 2, 33, 9 (672), and Josephus, *AJ* 17, 8, 3 (198).

23. Caesar, *BJ* 3, 23, 5–6.

24. Caesar, *BJ* 3, 59–61, and 79.

25. *CIL* XIII, 1063; cf. *I. L. de Gaule*, no. 148.

26. For contrast, see J. F. Drinkwater, "The Rise and Fall of the Gallic Iulii: Aspects of the Development of the Aristocracy of the Three Gauls under the Early Empire," *Latomus* 37 (1978): 817–50; E. M. Wightman, "Peasants and Potentates: An Investigation of Social Structure and Land Tenure in Roman Gaul," *AJAH* 3 (1978): 97–128.

27. Varro, *RR* 2, 10, 9.

28. Strabo, 3, 4, 7 (155). See *Poseidonius* I: *The Fragments*, ed. L. Edelstein and I. G. Kidd (1972), T.23 and F.269.

world of the landowning classes of the Greek cities. The man who paid their wages could be a friend of Poseidonius, the great philosopher from Apamea in Syria, who taught in Rhodes and visited Rome. In that they were unlike the peoples in north-west Spain whom Strabo describes, living on goat meat, acorns, and butter made out of olive oil; Strabo, speaking of these peoples, also gives us one of the earliest descriptions of couvade, noting that in this region, when a child was born, the father retired to bed and was looked after by the wife.[29] But to come back to the main point, the second thing we have to remember is that it was not only these mountain peoples in the distant interior of Spain who remained unsubjugated until Augustus' reign. Our convenient maps of the Roman provinces in this period are a polite fiction, for in hilly areas much closer to the coast of the Mediterranean itself there remained free peoples. Even if we ignore those areas like Illyricum where there was an unconquered hinterland,[30] there was still brigandage in Corsica and Sicily in Strabo's time, while Diodorus twice asserts that the peoples of central Sardinia had never been conquered by either Carthage or Rome.[31] That recalls Cicero's famous campaign of 51 B.C., as the Roman governor of Cilicia (southern Turkey), first against the fortified villages of the Amanus, which were captured and burnt, and then against the "free Cilicians" (Eleutherocilices) of Pindenissum "who had never yielded obedience even to the kings"—the Seleucid kings, that is. Those captured at Pindenissum were put on sale, and Cicero reported to Atticus that 120,000 sesterces had been realized from the sale so far.[32]

Much modern discussion of the supposed social and economic effects of Roman conquest is dominated by the presupposition of the mass transfer of slaves to Italy. But populations captured in war were sold on the spot, or at least in the same region (like the Salassi, mentioned earlier, who were sold at Eporedia in northern Italy). Some will simply have been ransomed, others sold locally, like the Jews who had been captured by Cassius and were currently in slavery in Tyre, Sidon, Antioch, and Aradus, and whose release Antonius ordered in 42 B.C. Whatever major social effects the wars of this period had, it was not by the direct transfer of whole populations before

29. Strabo, 3, 3, 7 (155); 4, 17 (165).

30. For Illyricum, see Appian, *Ill.* 12; and note [Caesar], *B. Alex.* 48, 1–3 (Gabinius attacking *castella*, and driven back to Salona): Cicero, *Fam.* 5, 10a–b (Shackleton Bailey, nos. 256, 258) (Vatinius trying to gain a triumph against the Dalmatians).

31. See Strabo, *Geography* 5, 2, 7 (224) (Corsica); 6, 2, 6 (273) (Sicily); Diodorus, 4, 30, 4–6, and 5, 15, 3–5 (Sardinia).

32. Cicero, *Fam.* 2, 10, 3 (Shackleton Bailey, no. 86), and 15, 4, 9–10 (no. 110); Cicero, *Att.*, 5, 20, 3–5 (no. 113).

sale.[33] Those slaves who reached Italy—as, of course, large numbers did—did so via the medium of the slave trade; for instance, we meet one Publicius on his way through Etruria in 83, bringing slaves for sale from Gaul to Rome.[34] Whatever the overall economic character of the slave trade—and obviously it involved a net import of slaves into Italy—it was certainly not a simple one of the extraction of value by Rome. For the immediate profits from the sale of captives into slavery were normally made by Roman generals and soldiers wherever they were on campaign; only some of the value thus realized will have reached Rome or Italy. Other profits will have been made by the middlemen who traded in slaves. If these slaves eventually found their way to Italy it will have been by purchase, involving an outflow of cash.

However, even if we see the existence of pockets of unintegrated, or unsubjugated, peoples within the supposedly provincial areas as an indication of the limits of the Roman state's real functions, their villages *might* at any time be captured and burnt, and their populations sold into slavery. To return to the Alpine region once again, we find Decimus Brutus, as proconsul of Cisalpine Gaul (northern Italy) in 43 B.C., writing casually to Cicero, "I have advanced against the Inalpini with my army, not so much seeking the title of Imperator as wishing to satisfy the soldiers. . . . I have captured many fortified villages and devastated many."[35]

These small-scale internal conquests, like the major external ones of Lucullus, Pompey, and Caesar, were thus one means by which the state, as embodied in an ambitious proconsul, might drastically intervene in a local society and economy, with either temporary or permanent effects. As is obvious, the pace of these interventions accelerated enormously in the course of the first century B.C. At the beginning of the century, indeed, we could well follow Strabo's view that the main economic and social effect of Roman predominance, at least in the eastern Mediterranean, was negative—namely, the weakness of the major Hellenistic powers and the failure to replace them with anything else; piracy and the slave trade thus raged unchecked until substantially ended by Pompey's massive operations in 67 B.C.[36] In the early first century B.C., after all, Rome directly ruled (i.e., raised taxes from) no more than Italy itself, with Sicily, Sardinia, and Corsica; part of Spain and the route to it through southern Gaul; a small island of territory in North

---

33. Josephus, *AJ*, 14, 304–23. See H. Volkmann, *Die Massenversklavungen der Einwohner eroberter Städte in der hellenistisch-römischer Zeit* (1961), 105–10.

34. Cicero, *Quinct.* 24.

35. Cicero, *Fam.* 11, 4 (Shackleton Bailey, no. 342).

36. Strabo, 14, 5, 2 (688–89).

Africa; and, in the east, Macedonia, Greece, and the province of "Asia" (the western coast of Turkey and its hinterland). When Ptolemy Apion left the kingdom of Cyrene (eastern Libya) to Rome in 96, no action was taken. What this meant for the character of life in Cyrenaica is now vividly illustrated by a decree from Berenice (Benghazi).[37] It honours a public-spirited citizen named Apollodorus: "Firstly, immediately after the death of the king, when Berenice was vigorously besieged by the wrongdoers [probably, political dissidents], as a result of the prevailing absence of magistrates in office he was called upon to command the young men [the town's military force], and, enduring every danger, restored conditions to a state of complete peace." Subsequently the city, which was walled, endured two successive raids by pirate fleets, and Apollodorus performed further services, as he seems to have done later also in the period of the imposition of effective Roman control in the 60s.

It is important to remember that the idea that the freedom of the Greek city-state had disappeared at the moment of Alexander's conquest is a fantasy. The Greek cities, like the Gallic, Punic, and Iberian *civitates* of the West, were political and military communities which had no option but to make political and diplomatic choices, could and did withstand sieges, and were expected to send military and naval contingents to assist their allies, including Rome. We can see this clearly in two of the earlier documents from the great new dossier of inscriptions from Aphrodisias in Caria (south-west Turkey). One document honours a citizen of Aphrodisias, named Artemidorus, who was chosen to lead the force of citizens, *paroikoi* (non-citizen inhabitants) and slaves which the city sent to aid the Roman general Quintus Oppius when he was besieged by King Mithridates of Pontus in Laodicea in 88 B.C.; a further one is a letter of Oppius written later from the island of Cos, acknowledging the city's services and promising to do whatever he can in its interests.[38] The cities of Asia, the Aegean, and Greece were faced with a choice, between Mithridates and Rome, in which considerations of self-interest, internal political factors, Mithridates' propaganda as to the relief of debts and the freeing of slaves, and hatred of Roman exploitation, official and unofficial, all played a part.[39] So, on the one hand, we have to see the world in terms

37. J. M. Reynolds, "A Civic Decree from Benghazi," *The Society for Libyan Studies: Fifth Annual Report* (1973–4), 19–24; re-edited by J. M. Reynolds in J. A. Lloyd, ed., *Excavations at Sidi Khrebish, Berenice-Benghazi, Libya Antiqua,* Supp. 6 (1982), 234, no. 3.

38. J. M. Reynolds, *Aphrodisias and Rome* (1982), docs. 2, 3.

39. For the details, which cannot be discussed here, see T. Reinach, *Mithridates Eupator, König von Pontos* (Leipzig, 1895); D. Magie, *Roman Rule in Asia Minor* (1950), chap. 9. For

of the choices made by these local communities; on the other, we have to remember that Rome was not the only imperialist power, and that Roman control was fluctuating and incomplete throughout most of the century.

For a brief moment in 87–86 B.C., indeed, at the height of Mithridates' westward expansion, Rome controlled nothing east of the Adriatic except parts of Greece and Macedonia. To understand the impact of states on the Mediterranean economy in this period we do therefore have to take into account the fact that more than one state was involved. Mithridates was, of course, by far the greatest challenge—Cicero may not have been wholly misleading when he said in 66 B.C. that with the threat of another invasion of the province of "Asia" grazing had been abandoned, the fields had remained unsown, and the volume of shipping had declined, and that credit had collapsed in Rome during the invasions of 88 B.C.[40]

The communities of the Mediterranean, especially the cities of the Greek East, had diplomatic relations with a variety of kings as well as with Rome. Aphrodisias, for instance, maintained contacts with Nicomedes of Bithynia,[41] as Athens did with Ariobarzanes of Cappadocia, who rebuilt the Odeum,[42] or Rhodes with Hiempsal of Numidia.[43] In the north, Bosporus in the Crimea had looked to Mithridates in his early years for protection against the Scythians;[44] and a famous inscription from Dionysopolis on the west coast of the Black Sea shows how one of its citizens, named Akornion, went on an embassy to Burebista, "the first and greatest of the kings in Thrace" (i.e., the king of the Dacians, who were based in present-day Rumania) and secured his friendship for the city. When the king took him as a confidant and sent him as an ambassador to Pompey, encamped at Heraclea Lyncestis in northern Greece in 49–48 B.C., Akornion took the opportunity to secure the interests not only of the king but also of his own city.[45] They were not to know that Pompey would soon be murdered on the sands of Egypt.

Or, again, there was the empire briefly created by King Tigranes of Armenia in Cilicia, Syria, and Phoenicia, in probably 83–69 B.C.; the expansion

---

Athens, note also E. Badian, "Rome, Athens and Mithridates," *AJAH* 1 (1976): 105–28; C. Habicht, "Zur Geschichte Athens in der Zeit Mithridates VI," *Chiron* 6 (1976): 127–42.

40. Cicero, *Leg.Man.* 14–15, and 19.

41. Reynolds (n. 38), doc. 4, a letter of (probably) Nicomedes IV of Bithynia to the city.

42. Vitruvius 5, 9, 1; *OGIS* 354.

43. V. N. Kontorini, "Le roi Hiempsal II de Numidie et Rhodes," *AC* 44 (1975): 89–99.

44. See Z. W. Rubinsohn, "Saumakos: Ancient History, Modern Politics," *Historia* 39 (1980): 50–70.

45. *Syll.*[3] 762; *IGBulg.* 13.

of Pharnaces' kingdom in Asia Minor from his territory on the coast of the
Black Sea in 48–47 B.C.; or the Parthian invasion of Syria and Asia Minor in
40 B.C. The city of Mylasa in Caria resisted this invasion and found its people
slaughtered or enslaved, its city burnt along with its temples, lands ravaged
and farmsteads burnt down.[46] A year or two after the war the city of Aphrodisias was seeking the restoration of slaves who had fled the city at that time,
as well as free men against whom information had been laid and who were
due for punishment. Nor could anyone have told how long-lasting might be
the effects of the restoration by Antonius in the 30s B.C. of much of the empire which the Ptolemies had ruled from Alexandria in the third century—
Phoenicia, Coele Syria, Cilicia, Cyprus, part of Crete, Cyrene.[47]

This brief selection of the possible political alternatives which faced Mediterranean communities may serve to emphasise three points; firstly, that they
were very likely to face violent domination and exaction of tribute from
some direction, and often from more than one in successive periods; secondly, that freedom itself, if gained—or if it arrived as the result of a power-
vacuum—might be expensive and dangerous; and, thirdly, that exploitation
and exaction by Rome, however gigantic its scale (which nobody will deny),
was not necessarily a worse situation from the point of view of an individual
community. Distance might lend a degree of enchantment, and it is clearly
attested that the people of Caunus in Caria, when put under the jurisdiction
of Rhodes by Sulla, perhaps in 81 B.C., sent an embassy to the Senate to argue
that they should pay taxation to Rome instead. Even clearer is the case of
the Greek cities in the area around Judaea, for which the coming of Roman
rule in the 60s B.C. meant liberation and restoration after their oppression
by the Hasmonean kingdom.[48] Or, at the other end of the Mediterranean,
there is the case of Zama, whose people refused entry to their king Juba I
on his retreat from the defeat at Thapsus in 46 B.C.; they were rewarded by
Caesar, but were ordered to go on paying to Rome the tributes and indirect
taxes which they had paid to the king, and became part of the province of
Africa.[49] They at least seem to have been no worse off. The people of the
small town of Parada in Africa, however, made exactly the same deduction
from the news of Caesar's victory, with fatal results: Scipio's cavalry, in flight

46. Strabo, *Geography* 14, 2, 24 (60); R. K. Sherk, *Roman Documents from the Greek East*
(1969), no. 59.

47. For the controversial and obscure details of Antonius' "donations," see E. Schürer,
The History of the Jewish People, ed. G. Vermes and F. Millar, I (1973), 288 n. 5.

48. For Caunus, see Cicero, *QF* 1, 1, 33; Strabo, *Geography* 14, 2, 3 (652); for Judaea,
Schürer (n. 47) 240.

49. [Caesar], *B. Afr.* 91–92 and 97.

from Thapsus to Utica, took the town by force, made a bonfire in the forum and burnt the inhabitants on it alive.[50]

That may lead us to a fourth basic point about the nature and scale of Rome's impact on the Mediterranean world in this period. It is an essential feature of the late Republic, beginning with Sulla's notorious exactions in Asia in 85 B.C., that the individual communities were faced with competing demands for services or military support, with the ultimate threat of annihilation and physical destruction, not only as between Rome and rival powers, great or small, but between rival elements of the Roman state itself. It was precisely by being divided against itself, in Asia and Greece in the 80s, in Spain in the 70s, and almost everywhere in the 40s and 30s, that the Roman state made its most exorbitant demands on the mosaic of local economies off which it lived. In the nature of the case these demands were often contradictory. In 46 B.C., for instance, the people of Sulci in Sardinia, no doubt having no choice, produced supplies for a fleet under Nasidius, an opponent of Caesar; later Caesar sailed in, fined them a large sum as a punishment, raised their tribute in kind from one-tenth to one-eighth of their produce, and confiscated the property of some of their citizens.[51] What all this meant in both political and economic terms for the communities of the Mediterranean does indeed come before us most clearly of all in Caesar's *Civil War*, and the unjustly neglected works of the Caesarian corpus, which carry the story of the civil war down to 45 B.C.; indeed these Caesarian works are the best introduction which we have to the Mediterranean world as it was in the 40s. More particularly, it is these works which show the clearest consciousness both of the dependence of the rival Roman armies on the political allegiances of the provincial communities, and of their absolute dependence—like all other armies, of course—on the economies of the areas in which they were operating. Let me take what seems to me a model example of the contradictory demands made by the conflicting elements of the Roman state on a regional economy: we find in the *African War* that in 46 B.C. Caesar could not find enough wheat in Africa because, so it was said, in the previous year all the ploughmen had been conscripted as soldiers by the Pompeians and no harvest had been produced; such corn as there was in Africa was stored in well-guarded cities, and so there was nothing for it but to rely on imported wheat—if only the trading ships (*naves onerariae*) could find the right place and make a safe landing.[52]

50. *B. Afr.* 87, 2.
51. *B. Afr.* 98, 2.
52. *B. Afr.* 20–21.

So, on the one hand, Caesar's account indicates a considerable short-term effect of civil war on a local agricultural economy. On the other it takes us to a quite different theme, the question of long-distance trade by sea, which turns up everywhere in our narrative sources as an assumed part of the background against which the conflicts of the Roman revolution take place. Pompey, for instance, fled from Pharsalus in 48 B.C. and boarded a trading ship sailing from Thessaly along the coast to Amphipolis, from where he crossed to Mytilene;[53] Herod the Great, fleeing from the Parthians in 40 B.C., reached Alexandria and took a trading vessel round the coast to Pamphylia and then Rhodes, from where he went on to Brundisium.[54] In 43 B.C. Lentulus reported (privately to Cicero and publicly to the magistrates, Senate, and people of Rome) that Dolabella had rounded up 100 merchant ships on the coast of Lycia (southern Turkey), none of less than 2,000 amphorae (or some 52 tons) burthen, and would use them to take his army to Syria.[55] I need not continue with examples, since no accumulation of examples will give us any idea of the scale of seaborne trade or (still less) of its importance within the total economy. What is clear is simply that its presence could be assumed everywhere; in what way the operations of the state affected its direction or content remains very obscure. No doubt we should assume that the steady flow of tribute corn, carried to Rome from Sicily, Sardinia, and Africa in private merchant vessels,[56] substantially affected the overall pattern of trade; to put it at its simplest, the ships bringing wheat to Rome must presumably have carried something in the opposite direction. But no one commented on these developments at the time. It is only later sources which provide some generalizations about trade in this period: Pliny the Elder, talking about the increasing import of Greek wines to Rome in the first century, implies that the volume of the trade could have been substantial; for instance, he records that Hortensius in 50 B.C. left over 10,000 jars of Chian wine in his will.[57] Pliny also seems to imply that it was in the 50s that Italian olive oil was first exported to the provinces; by his own time, the later first century A.D., the olive was cultivated well into the interior of Gaul and Spain.[58] All that contemporary sources can provide is illustrative examples of the movement of luxury

53. Plutarch, *Pomp.* 73–74; compare Cato taking a trading vessel from Thessaly to Aenus in 67 B.C.: Plutarch, *Cat. Min.* 11.

54. Josephus, *AJ* 14, 14, 2–3 (375–78).

55. Cicero, *Fam.* 12, 14, 1, and 15, 2 (Shackleton Bailey, nos. 405–6).

56. See G. E. Rickman, *The Corn Supply of Ancient Rome* (1980).

57. Pliny, *NH* 14, 95–98.

58. Pliny, *NH* 10, 1–3.

goods, wines, and slaves, whose direction was—or so it seems—quite un-affected by questions of political control or contemporary military or naval operations. In the 50s ships sailing from the kingdom of Egypt to Puteoli in Italy might carry papyrus, linen, and glass. In Verres' time as governor of Sicily, 73–71 B.C., ships both from "Asia," which was a province, and from Syria, Tyre, and Egypt, which were not within the provincial area, came into Sicily, bringing Tyrian purple, pearls, Greek wines, and slaves from Asia.[59] Verres himself, according to Cicero, was able to acquire and send home goods worth 1,200,000 sesterces. Cicero's list gives some hint of the varied forms of product which might embody sufficient value to be worth transporting by sea: gold, silver, ivory, purple cloths, cloth from Malta, a large quantity of coverings, tableware from Delos, Corinthian vases, corn, and 400 ampho-rae of honey.[60] This last is of some interest, for it suggests that any product which could be satisfactorily stored could enter long-distance trade by sea, however modest the original units of production may have been. The ships coming from the East will also have arrived, in 73–71 B.C., at what must have been the height of the operations of the pirates—which, therefore, while they must have hindered trade, clearly did not stop it altogether. By con-trast, states seem rarely if ever in this period to have intervened deliberately in trade except by way of requisitioning; the one explicitly mentioned ex-ception is Pompey's attempt in 65–64 B.C. to prevent ships sailing from the Mediterranean to Mithridates' only remaining possession, the Crimea—his objective was to achieve by famine what he had not finally achieved by war.[61]

In other words, so far as we know, the Roman state did not systematically intervene in seaborne trade; the significance of the effects of its activities on the structure or direction of trade remains quite uncertain. Moreover, as Michael Crawford has argued, it seems that Romans or Italians did not try to increase the profits of empire by exporting their own products to their subjects; the Italian exports which can be traced archaeologically—pottery (as always)—went predominantly to places where Roman soldiers were sta-tioned or Italian traders settled (such as Delos).[62] However, if that is so, then the extensive colonization which is one of the most distinctive activities of

---

59. Cicero, *Rab. Post.* 40; Cicero, *Verr. II* 5, 145–6.

60. *Verr. II* 2, 176, 183, 185.

61. Plutarch, *Pomp.* 39.

62. M. H. Crawford, in A. Giardina and A. Schiavone, eds., *Società romana e produzione schiavistica*, 3 vols. (1981), III, 271–83; cf. A. Tchernia, "Italian Wine in Gaul at the End of the Republic," in P. Garnsey, K. Hopkins and C. R. Whittaker, *Trade in the Ancient Economy* (London, 1983), 87–104.

the Roman state in the Caesarian and Augustan period should have had some marginal effect on long-distance trade.

The idea that the empire was expanded in the interests of trade—that is, for securing profitable markets for exports—is surely wholly anachronistic. Cicero does however firmly assert in his speech *For the Manilian Law*, delivered in 66 B.C., something which is related, but fundamentally different: that Rome had often gone to war to protect its own traders or shipowners overseas.[63] At the level of conscious expression it is only in the imperial period that we find (say) Pliny the Elder pointing to the relevance of the universal domination of Rome to the availability of all the different varieties of plants or the expansion of trade: "Who would not admit that, now that intercommunication has been established throughout the world, life has been advanced by the interchange of commodities and by partnership in the blessings of peace, and that even things that had previously lain concealed have all now been established in general use?"[64] But for the period concerned all that is clear is that inter-regional shipping was an accepted part of the social and economic scene. Its importance in the total economy may have been small. But we cannot know how its volume or its direction altered in the period.

In any case the general direct rule of the whole of the Mediterranean area and southern Europe which prompted Pliny's complacent observations was nowhere near being attained even by the end of the period of the civil wars. At the moment of the victory of Actium in 31 B.C., which secured a period of unchallenged rule for Augustus, lasting until his death in A.D. 14, the Alps and Illyricum were still unsubdued military areas, Thrace (roughly Bulgaria and European Turkey) was a client kingdom, and most of Asia Minor (present-day Turkey) was divided between the client kingdoms of Galatia, Cappadocia, and Pontus. Judaea had reverted from being a provincial area to being a client kingdom under Herod the Great, while Mauretania was to become a kingdom again in 25 B.C. under the rule of Juba II. Our overall conception of the effects of state activity on Mediterranean society in this period thus has to allow for the fact that Roman rule was both incomplete and, at certain periods, liable to contract.

However, if we look at the broad lines of the Roman state's impact on social and economic life in the late Republic, a number of very general points can be established. Firstly, even in the established Empire of the second century A.D. Roman provincial government never succeeded in extracting taxa-

63. Cicero, *Leg. Man.*, 5 and 11.
64. Pliny, *NH* 14, 2 (Loeb trans.); cf. 37, 3.

tion or services from all the areas nominally within its borders. Some seventy years after the Pontus region in northern Turkey had become a province, the historian Arrian, as governor, reported to Hadrian in the 130s that the immediate neighbours of the coastal city of Trapezus were a people called the Sanni, very warlike, very hostile to Trapezus, living in fortified positions, practising brigandage, and indifferent to the payment of the tribute (paid in beeswax according to Pliny) which they in principle owed to Rome.[65] We would do well to see all ancient kingdoms and empires as no more than changing patchworks of control.

Secondly, in certain respects it has to be conceded that the distinction between directly ruled areas (i.e., provinces) and ones which were outside the area of Roman domination hardly mattered. One of the prime characteristics of the Roman civil wars from the 70s to Actium was the way in which the competing parties demanded naval and military forces not only from provinces but from all the areas within the Roman sphere of influence. Again, some examples will suffice. From within a province, Cicero reports that Fonteius, as a proconsul of Gaul in 74–72, "ordered the provision of large forces of cavalry for the wars which the Roman people was then conducting throughout the world, large sums of money for their pay, and a very large quantity of corn for the Spanish war" (against Sertorius).[66] From outside the provincial area Lucullus was collecting ships from Cyprus, Phoenicia, Rhodes, and Pamphylia in 85 B.C.;[67] 300 cavalry from the kingdom of Noricum arrived in Italy to help Caesar in 49 B.C., while in the next year cavalry from King Cotys of Thrace fought on the Pompeian side in Thessaly; and from Alexandria in 48/7 B.C. Caesar called, among other forces, for cavalry from Malchus of Nabataea (Arabia).[68] There is no need to recall the various royal forces which took part in the civil war in Africa in the 40s or to give lists of the ethnic units which served at Pharsalus in 48 B.C.,[69] at Philippi in 42, and at Actium in 31. Brutus' and Cassius' forces at Philippi, for instance, included both Celts from the west and Galatians from Galatia in Asia Minor, Celtic-speaking people who had settled there in the third century B.C.[70] In the case of fleets, it is well known that Rome continued to rely on the system of requiring maritime cities to provide small naval contingents, and main-

65. Pliny, *NH*, 21, 72; Arrian, *Periplus*, 11.
66. Cicero, *Font.* 13.
67. Plutarch, *Luc.* 56.
68. Caesar, *BC*, 1, 18, 5, and 3, 36, 4; [Caesar], *B. Alex.*, 1, 1.
69. Appian, *BC* 2, 70–71.
70. Appian, *BC* 4, 88/373.

tained no "Roman" fleet of its own; one remark of Cicero's seems to imply that the cost might be taken out of the cash revenues due to Rome.[71]

The civil wars thus involved the calling out of local forces, often it is true not very large, and their despatch all over the Mediterranean; we see a nice reflection of this in the inscription from Cyzicus (north-west Turkey) in which someone records his dream about the capture and enslavement of a friend of his who had sailed off in a city trireme to fight alongside Caesar in North Africa in 46 B.C.[72] It is not difficult to envisage the local, short-term effects of the requisitioning of forces, men and supplies. We can note the 30,000 Galatians requisitioned to carry corn for Lucullus' campaigns in Asia Minor in 73 B.C.,[73] or read Plutarch's vivid description of the requisitions in Greece before the battle of Actium in 31 B.C.: Antonius' trierarchs pressed into service passing travellers, mule drivers, people working on the harvest, and young men of military age; the cities were stripped of their money, slaves, and beasts for transport, and Plutarch's great-grandfather used to recall how the whole population at Anticyra was impressed to carry sacks of corn down to the sea. But when news came of Antonius' defeat, his officials and soldiers immediately fled and the people shared out the grain.[74] Thus the short-term local effects of Roman exactions could be felt both inside and outside the provincial area, and may often have been overcome without great difficulty. Whether the scale of the requisitioning of troops and fleets and their movement around the Mediterranean was sufficient to have any profound long-term effects is not clear. As always, we are hopelessly handi-capped by not knowing how to conceive of the economy as a whole, or about the scale of the normal movement of men, goods, and money within it.

The mention of money leads to the third general point. So far the theme of Roman taxation, extortion, and extra exactions in money has deliberately been left aside. If we now turn to this, there are a number of considerations which indicate that their effects on the total economy of the region may have been more variable and more ambivalent than is often presumed. Firstly, as was emphasised earlier, the mere fact that local communities paid taxes in cash or kind represents nothing new and distinctive in itself, except in Gaul. Secondly, many of the most extreme and notorious instances are themselves reflections of the particular civil war situation—that is, the maximizing of the rapid extraction of value by one arm of the Roman state in order to gain

---

71. Cicero, *Verr. II* 1, 89.
72. *Syll.*³ 763.
73. Plutarch, *Luc.* 14.
74. Plutarch, *Ant.*, 62 and 68.

resources to fight against another: for instance, Sulla's impositions in Asia in 85 B.C.,[75] Scipio's in Syria and Asia in 48 B.C., self-righteously described by Caesar,[76] and Caesar's own in Syria in 47 B.C.[77]

These cases will represent the rapid accumulation of value mainly in order to pay troops in the field; the ultimate overall effects will then have depended on where the troops went and what happened to them (civilians are not necessarily without resources as against passing soldiers, and we should not forget the Caesarian soldiers being thrown overboard in the harbour at Utica in 49 B.C.). Some exactions took the form of seizing static wealth in the shape of temple treasures or of precious metal ornaments; it was then turned into coin, and used to pay troops.[78] The effect will thus have been to some degree inflationary. The most obvious and well-known example is the process by which, after Cleopatra despoiled the temples of Egypt of accumulated treasures, Octavian captured them in 30 B.C. (without even the odium of impiety), carried out extensive further exactions in Alexandria, and brought the proceeds to Rome in 29 B.C.; there, presumably now in the form of coin, they caused a rise in prices and a fall in interest rates.[79]

That is only one of several well-known instances where vast accumulations of value in the form of precious metal were physically transported to Rome; we have only to think of the triumph of Pompey in 61 B.C.,[80] or the 600 million sesterces "from booty" (*ex manubiis*) displayed in Caesar's triumph in 46 B.C.[81] Yet that sum itself represents only about twice the level of the largest individual fortunes recorded from Rome. Moreover, we may still ask what sort, or scale, of loss to the economies of the various conquered regions was represented by the removal of the type of spoils in precious metal or other valuables which it was physically possible to bring to Rome. That must remain an open question.

75. Plutarch, *Sull.* 25; Appian, *Mith.* 62–63.

76. Caesar, *De bello civili*, 3, 31–32.

77. Dio, *Roman History*, 43, 49, 1–2.

78. For removal of wealth from temples, see, e.g., Diodorus, 38/9, 7; Plutarch, *Sull.*, 12 and 19; Pausanias 9, 7, 6 (Sulla in Greece); Josephus, *AJ* 14, 7, 1 (105–9) (Crassus from the temple in Jerusalem); Dio 42, 49, 1–2, and 43, 39, 4–5 (Caesar in Spain in 49 and 47). For the conversion of precious-metal ornaments into coin, see, e.g., Appian, *BC* 4, 64/273–75 (Tarsos, 43 B.C.), and 5, 6/26 (the cities of Asia, referring back to Brutus' and Cassius' exactions before Philippi). For comparative cases, see F. Millar, *The Emperor in the Roman World* (1977), 151.

79. Dio 51, 17, 6–8, and 21, 5.

80. Pliny, *NH* 37, 12–18; Plutarch, *Pomp.* 45; Appian, *Mith.* 116.

81. Velleius 2, 56, 2; cf. Appian, *BC* 2, 102.

It is certain that, in principle at least, the sums annually collected in cash in the provinces as taxation were also supposed to be sent physically to Rome.[82] But at the same time substantial sums were sent out from Rome, being issued to quaestors or proconsuls for expenditure in the provinces: for instance the 12 million sesterces given to Verres for purchases of corn in Sicily;[83] or, better, the pattern revealed earlier by Verres' conveniently brief accounts as quaestor in 84 B.C.: "received 2,235,417 sesterces; given out for *stipendium* [pay], corn, the legates, the proquaestor, the praetorian cohort, 1,635,417 sesterces; deposited at Ariminum 600,000 sesterces."[84] In this case some two-thirds of the total sum was spent locally and the rest deposited locally, its subsequent fate being unknown; the same procedure could have taken place in a province — note the 18 million sesterces granted to Piso as proconsul of Macedonia in 57 B.C.[85] — and could therefore have involved the redistribution of at least some of Rome's tax revenue in a different part of the Mediterranean. We see a neat example of such a redistribution, for instance, in Asinius Pollio's report to Cicero of an event in Spain in 43 B.C.: "Balbus the quaestor, having accumulated a large sum of money, and a large quantity of gold, and having gathered in more money from public exactions, and without even giving the pay to the soldiers, has set off from Gades and crossed to the kingdom of Bogud in Morocco."[86]

We cannot compile anything like a balance sheet of Roman public finance in the late Republic.[87] But even the most sceptical would have to agree that there was a very large net inflow of spoils, tribute cash, and corn into Italy, and primarily to Rome. But Roman soldiers, who were paid in coin, were nearly all stationed in the provinces, and corn was also bought in some provinces by the state.[88] Vast amounts of moveable wealth were also displaced from one region to another by the efforts of the Roman state, and above all when its energies were maximized by its being divided against itself. It is also clear that the volume of Roman minting at successive periods corresponded

82. See, e.g., Velleius 2, 62, 3: "the moneys . . . which were being transported to Rome by the quaestors"; Cicero, *Fam.* 12, 14–15 (Shackleton Bailey, nos. 405–6); Nicolaus of Damascus, in *FGrH* no. 90, frag. 130, XVIII/55.

83. Cicero, *Verr. II* 3, 163.

84. *Verr. II* 1, 36.

85. Cicero, *Pis.*, 86.

86. Cicero, *Fam.* 10, 32 (Shackleton Bailey, no. 415).

87. For serious attempts to do so, see esp. Tenney Frank, *Economic Survey of Ancient Rome* I (1933), 322–47; M. H. Crawford, *Roman Republican Coinage* (1974), 694–707.

88. For the outflow of expenditure from Rome, see M. H. Crawford, "Rome and the Greek World: Economic Relationships," *Econ. Hist. Rev.*, 2nd ser., 30 (1977): 42–52.

above all to the scale of military effort.[89] Large sums may however have been raised in a province and spent there without ever being transferred physically to Rome. In other cases state funds or the spoils of conquest may perhaps have moved directly from one province to another, whether officially or unofficially. Our picture of the profits of conquest and their use perhaps does not yet take enough account of Suetonius' description of Caesar's financial and diplomatic dealings while he was engaged on the conquest of Gaul: "He was no less energetic in gaining the attachment of kings and provinces throughout the world, offering some of them thousands of captives as a gift, offering others, without the authority of Senate or People, the dispatch of auxiliary forces where and when they wished, and adorning the prominent cities of Italy, Gaul, and Spain, as well as Greece and Asia, with splendid public works."[90]

In other words, if we could analyse the overall economic effects of the convulsive activities of late republican Rome, we would find highly complex patterns, only one of which would be the steady movement of coins, corn, slaves, and valuables to Rome and Italy. But we cannot analyse it anyway, and probably never will be able to; the best attempt to do so, for one large region, namely the Greek-speaking eastern Mediterranean, remains the last part of Michael Rostovtzeff's *Social and Economic History of the Hellenistic World*. Rostovtzeff's methods and historical views, and the connection between them and his unparalleled capacity for assembling information, have never yet received the critical study they deserve. But it would not be inappropriate to compare his two great social and economic histories, of the Roman Empire (1926) and of the Hellenistic world (1941), with Braudel's *The Mediterranean and the Mediterranean World in the Age of Philip II*, which has been the subject of so much discussion.[91] Any critical appraisal of Rostovtzeff, moreover, would be highly unjust if it did not accept that we

89. Crawford (n. 87), 640–707; cf. H. Mattingley, "Coinage and the Roman State," *NC* 17 (1977): 199–215; Hopkins (n. 2), 106ff.

90. Suetonius, *Div.Iul.* 28.

91. F. Braudel, *The Mediterranean and the Mediterranean World in the Age of Philip II*, trans. S. Reynolds, 2 vols. (1972–73); M. Rostovtzeff, *The Social and Economic History of the Roman Empire* (1926); M. Rostovtzeff, *The Social and Economic History of the Hellenistic World*, 3 vols. (1941). I know of no major retrospective analysis of Rostovtzeff's two great works. For a sympathetic and perceptive sketch, see A. D. Momigliano, "M. I. Rostovtzeff," in his *Studies in Historiography* (1966), 91–104. On Braudel, apart from the well-known essay by J. H. Hexter, "Fernand Braudel and the Monde Braudellien," in his *On Historians* (1979), 61–145, see now S. Kinser, "Annaliste Paradigm? The Geohistorical Structuralism of Fernand Braudel," *Amer. Hist. Rev.* 86 (1981): 63–105.

have failed to go beyond him. The greater analytical sophistication which has since been achieved, or at least claimed, has not been matched by a comparable capacity to confront social and economic models with the empirical data which might serve to test them.

There are, however, at least some areas where progress could be made. We could look further at the archaeology of public buildings, as for instance the late John Ward Perkins did a few years ago, showing that Roman-style public buildings cannot be traced archaeologically in the western provinces until the time of Augustus.[92] But of course the archaeological evidence never tells the whole story—we know for instance that in fact there was a basilica at Corduba by the middle of the first century B.C., for Cassius Longinus was giving justice there in the winter of 48/7.[93] Alternatively we could study the movements of amphorae and other pottery products around the Mediterranean.[94] We could concentrate on those areas, like the Greek cities of Asia Minor, or Egypt, where there are real concentrations of local documents. But above all we might hope for general studies of the actual production, distribution, and use of all types of coinage—Celtic, Spanish, North African, and Greek, as well as Roman—over the whole area; in other words, we might see how far the coins would yield a monetary, as opposed to a numismatic, history.[95] Such a history would still have to recall the primitive and laborious means by which metal could be mined, minted, and moved around, and could not ignore Cicero's assumption that sums paid to Sicilian cities for corn will have been brought to them on the backs of mules.[96]

But, finally, if serious analyses of the social and economic context of the Roman revolution are not yet available, we can at least see the nature and the limits of the effects of these great changes in the lives of a few individuals.

92. J. B. Ward Perkins, "From Republic to Empire: Reflections on the Early Provincial Architecture of the Roman West," *JRS* 60 (1970): 1–19.

93. [Caesar], *B. Alex.* 52, 2.

94. Note, for instance, D. Manacorda, "The Ager Cosanus and the Production of the Amphorae of Sestius: New Evidence and a Reassessment," *JRS* 68 (1978): 122–31; and see also A. Giardina and A. Schiavone, eds., *Società romana e produzione schiavistica*, II (1981), and the survey article by J. Paterson, " 'Salvation from the Sea': Amphorae and Trade in the Roman West," *JRS* 72 (1982): 146–57.

95. For example, Nash, "Plus ça change" (n. 21); Nash, *Settlement and Coinage in Central Gaul* (n. 21); M. H. Crawford, "The Financial Organisation of Republican Spain," *NC* 9 (1969): 79–93; R. C. Knapp, "The Date and Purpose of the Iberian Denarii," *NC* 18 (1977): 1–19; cf. A. Giovannini, *Rome et la circulation monétaire en Grèce an IIe siècle avant Jésus-Christ* (1978).

96. Cicero, *Verr. II* 3, 183.

I conclude with one such individual, Philotas of Amphissa, who is known to us from the pages of Plutarch's *Life of Antonius*. He was born in Amphissa, near Delphi, in about the mid-50s B.C., and will have been a child and then adolescent at the time of the great civil war battles of Pharsalus and Philippi, in 48 and 42. By the mid-30s his education at home was complete, and he set off to Alexandria, still the capital of the Ptolemaic kingdom, to pursue the study of medicine. There he got to know a cook at the court of Antonius and Cleopatra, and saw one day in the kitchen eight wild boars roasting, at different stages of readiness; their highnesses were unpunctual, it was explained, but still liked their wild boar done to a turn. Later Philotas was doctor to Antonius' son by Fulvia, and afterwards returned home to Greece, to pursue his profession and tell endless stories to Plutarch's grandfather.[97]

Philotas' life thus touched briefly on the major events of the period, but was not fundamentally affected by them. His career was a symptom of the fact that the entire communal and cultural basis of the life of the Greek cities survived, damaged and depressed but intact, through the period of the civil wars; they were thus able to adjust with ease to the new and immediately evident fact of monarchy after the battle of Actium in 31 B.C. A recently published inscription from Ephesus, for instance, records a man who, within not more than a year or two of Octavian's being voted the name "Augustus" in 27 B.C., had "supervised the setting up of 'the Augustus' [that is, a statue of him] and the dedication of the sanctuary."[98] But the conscious, political adjustment to changed circumstances is a different story, some of which can indeed be told.[99] For the real social and economic history of the world in which the Roman revolution took place, however, I wish that I could see how to do better than the friend of Plutarch's grandfather, with his endless recital of anecdotes. To do better, however, we would need a model, or models. But what models are available to help us understand the history of a region made up of innumerable communities at very different stages of development, within which longer-term changes were overshadowed for contemporaries, as they are for us, by the demands of competing states and factions and the needs and effects of war?

---

97. Plutarch, *Ant.* 28. I owe to Dr. W. E. H. Cockle a number of items of evidence indicating that wild boar were known in Egypt and were hunted there: e.g., Theophrastus, *Hist. pl.* 4, 12, 4; *P.Ryl.* II, no. 238 (A.D. 262).

98. *SEG* XXVI 1243.

99. For this, cf. F. Millar, "State and Subject: The Impact of Monarchy," in F. Millar and E. Segal, eds., *Caesar Augustus: Seven Aspects* (1984) (chapter 12 in this volume).

PART III

The Augustan Revolution

CHAPTER TEN

Triumvirate and Principate*

Introduction

More than thirty years after its publication *The Roman Revolution* still stands unrivalled, not as the "definitive" account of the emergence of a monarch from the ruins of the Republic but as something far more than that, the demonstration of a new method in the presentation of historical change. The aspect of this method which has found most imitation is, of course, prosopography; and it is indeed essential to it. But far more important is the use made of contemporary literature to mirror events, and to analyse and define the concepts and the terms in which the events were seen by those who lived through them.

It is the common characteristic, perhaps even the definition, of great works of history that they invite imitation and offer a challenge, not just to apply their methods and standards to other areas, but to pursue their own conclusions further. The present chapter is gratefully offered as an attempt to portray with a different emphasis some aspects of the establishment of Octavian as a monarch, first by demonstrating the extent to which the institutions

* First published in *JRS* 63 (1973): 50–67. An earlier version of this chapter was given at a research seminar in Berkeley in the autumn of 1968, and part of a more recent version at the Scuola Normale Superiore at Pisa in January 1973. It is offered here first and foremost as a tribute to Sir Ronald Syme; secondly as an attempt to make some preliminary remarks about the unpublished Triumviral documents from the excavations by Professor Kenan Erim at Aphrodisias, which Miss J. M. Reynolds has very kindly allowed me to use; and thirdly as the last of a series of preliminary studies towards a book to be called *The Emperor in the Roman World*. I am most grateful for critical comment (and general disagreement) to Professors E. Badian and G. W. Bowersock in Harvard and A. D. Momigliano and E. Gabba in Pisa, and to Miss Reynolds for generous advice and assistance. [The note has been left as it stood in 1973. *The Emperor in the Roman World* was published in 1977, and J. M. Reynolds, *Aphrodisias and Rome* was published in 1982.]

of the *res publica* remained active in the Triumviral period, and secondly by redefining the change which culminated in 27 B.C., precisely by asking again in what terms it and the "new order" (*novus status*) which emerged from it were seen by contemporaries.

Monarchy is an infinitely complex phenomenon, in each case unique to the particular society from which it springs. The complexity is only increased when it emerges from a centuries-old aristocratic republic whose web of customs, rights, and traditions is dignified by moderns with the title of a constitution; and further when it immediately involves the direct relationship of the monarch to a vast range of regions and communities of varying cultures and political characters. This is the essential new factor, foreshadowed by Pompey during his command in the East, and briefly in Rome by Caesar as dictator. Moreover it allows us to simplify, and to focus a large part of the discussion on a single criterion of monarchy, the issuing by the monarch of pronouncements which are themselves treated by his subjects as effective legal acts. It is all-important to stress the difference between these and pronouncements which either complete some collective legal process, or merely promise that such a process will take place. Among such effective pronouncements the personal judicial verdicts of the monarch have a particular significance. Considerations such as these will be vital in determining the relevance of the Triumviral period to the emergence of monarchy, and the nature of the change completed in 27 B.C.

The Triumvirate and the *Res Publica*

Nobody, then or since, could dispute that the Triumviral period was profoundly marked by violence, illegality, and the arbitrary exercise of power. This view was openly expressed at the time by the jurist Cascellius, who refused to give a legal formula in respect of properties granted by the Triumvirs, "considering all of their grants outside the realm of law."[1] Even Octavian himself admitted this, abolishing (whatever that may mean) all that had been done unlawfully and unjustly up to his sixth consulate in 28 B.C.[2] None the less, if we rely too uncritically on the famous, but also typically emotive, rhetorical, and imprecise, phrase of Tacitus which introduces his reference to this "abolition"—"and then continuous discord for twenty years, no custom, no law" (*exim continua per viginti annos discordia, non mos, non ius*)[3]—we shall miss important features of the Triumviral situation.

1. Val. Max. 6, 2, 12.
2. Dio 53, 2, 5; cf. Tac., *Ann.* 3, 28, 3.
3. Tac., *Ann.* 3, 28, 1.

It is necessary to emphasise first how little can be confidently deduced from the brief accounts we have of the establishment of the Triumvirate, which in this respect resemble the accounts of the "settlement" of 27.[4] Moreover the evidence we have relates partly to the pact of Bononia and partly to the Lex Titia itself. In spite of a very useful discussion,[5] it is necessary to review the main points here.

For the actual powers of the Triumvirs, none of our earliest sources—Livy as represented in the *Epitome*, Augustus himself in the *Res Gestae*, and Velleius Paterculus—gives any help.[6] Nor does the opening narrative section of Suetonius' *Divus Augustus* (12–13) or his later references (27, 96), or the descriptions of the pact and the proscriptions in Plutarch's *Cicero* (46) and *Antonius* (19–20), or in Florus (2, 15). So it is important to emphasise that the narrative sources on which we depend for our conception of the formation of the Triumvirate and the powers of its members are essentially Appian and Dio. From Appian (*BC* 4, 2/4–7, on the pact of Bononia) we learn that their power was to be equal to that of the consuls and to last for five years. They were "to appoint" the city magistrates at once for each of the next five years. They were to divide the governorships of provinces and "have" the different regions separately. Nothing is said about how the government of the provinces would actually work, except (in 3/9) that Lepidus was to be consul for the following year, to remain in Rome and to govern Spain through others. When Appian (in 4, 7/27) comes to describe the passing of the tribunician Lex Titia itself he repeats only the detail that their power was to be consular and for five years.

Dio, describing Bononia (46, 55, 3–4), mentions the five-year term, the right to give offices (*archai*) and honours (*timai*), and the division of the provinces; he does, however, add some sort of definition of their powers—"they should manage all public business, whether or not they made any communication about it to the people and the Senate." He adds, still describing Bononia, that they agreed on executions of their enemies (46, 56, 1). When mentioning their subsequent actions in Rome he makes only a passing allusion to the Lex Titia—"the measures which they had dictated and forced through assumed the name of law" (47, 2, 2). It is thus evident that our major sources for these events are not only remote from them in time but lacking in clarity. Only the *Epitome* of Livy tells us formally that the Lex Titia gave a legal basis

4. For the direct evidence on the provincial aspects of the settlement of 27, see *JRS* 56 (1966): 156–57 (chapter 11 in this volume).

5. V. Fadinger, *Die Begründung des Prinzipats: quellenkritische und staatsrechtliche Untersuchungen zu Cassius Dio und der Parallelüberlieferung* (Diss. Munich, 1969), esp. 31–83.

6. See Livy, *Epit.* 120; *Res Gestae* 1, 7; Vell. Pat. 2, 69.

to the proscriptions; only Aulus Gellius (14, 7, 5) records that the Triumvirs had "the right to convene the senate"; and only the *Fasti Colotiani*[7] give us the terminal date of the five-year period of the Triumvirate—"[M. A]emilius, *M. Antonius* [erased], Imp. Caesar, triumvirs for the ordering of the *res publica*, from the fifth day before the Kalends of December to the day before the sixth Kalends of January following." These *Fasti*, which the erased name of Antonius show to have been inscribed before September 30 B.C., thus make clear that the Triumvirate was due to expire on December 31, 38 B.C.

What remains quite obscure is what effects the appointment of triumvirs for the ordering of the *res publica*—*triumviri rei publicae constituendae*—was expected to have on the assemblies, the Senate, and the annual magistracies. Least obscurity attaches to the question of elections and of appointments to provincial commands, which are explicitly stated to have been within the powers of the Triumvirs. But was *every* annual magistracy in the period filled by Triumviral appointment? And, if so, did this mean that the centuriate and the tribal assemblies actually ceased to meet for electoral purposes until 27 B.C.? Or might they have met to elect formally lists of candidates put forward by the Triumvirs? A number of important articles on the elections under Augustus ignore the problems of the Triumviral period.[8] Only the valuable study of R. Frei-Stolba traces the fortunes of the elections from the Republic through the Caesarian and Triumviral periods, to the Empire.[9] There is of course abundant evidence to show arbitrary use of the power of appointment by the Triumvirs, including gross affronts to Republican custom in certain years. At the end of 43 they appointed two suffect consuls, one of them a praetor in office, who was replaced by one of the aediles; and five days before the end of the year they sent the praetors off to provinces, and appointed replacements.[10] In 42 Dio speaks of them as appointing the city magistrates for several years in advance.[11] In 40 suffect consuls and praetors were again appointed right at the end of the year, and an aedile to replace one who died on the last day of December.[12] In 39 the Triumvirs are recorded as

7. A. Degrassi, *Inscriptiones Italiae* XIII, 1: *Fasti Consulares* (1947), 273–74.

8. A. H. M. Jones, "The Elections under Augustus," *JRS* 45 (1955): 9 = *Studies in Roman Government and Law* (1960), 27; P. A. Brunt, "The Lex Valeria Cornelia," *JRS* 51 (1961): 71; B. M. Levick, "Imperial Control of the Elections under the Early Principate," *Historia* 16 (1967): 207.

9. R. Frei-Stolba, *Untersuchungen zu den Wahlen in der römischen Kaiserzeit* (1967). On the period from 42 to 28 B.C., see pp. 80–86.

10. Dio 47, 15, 2–3.

11. Dio 47, 19, 4.

12. Dio 48, 32, 1 and 3.

making appointments to magistracies several years ahead and to the consulate for eight years, subsequently making additions and subtractions to the list. Dio carefully emphasises that it was at this point that the arbitrary appointment of suffect consuls became regular, and underlines the continuity with established imperial practice.[13] Similarly, when agreement was temporarily reached with Sextus Pompeius in the same year, its terms included praetorships, tribunates, and priesthoods for his followers, and a consulate and the position of *haruspex* (diviner) for himself (he was deposed from both in 37).[14] The following year saw the culmination of the period of disturbance of the republican magistracies.[15] Sixty-seven praetors were appointed in the course of the year, and a boy was made quaestor.[16] Under the next year Dio notes continual multiplication of office-holders, and gives the reason, namely that the offices were valued not for themselves but as the necessary preliminary to provincial commands.[17]

In the following years such irregularities were greatly reduced,[18] though suffect consulates continued (Octavian abandoning his consulate in 33 on the first day).[19] The suffect consulate in 30, for which, as Plutarch says, Octavian "chose" Cicero's son as his colleague,[20] ended the systematic use of suffect consulates for several decades. The abandonment of this practice was surely intended as a sign of approaching normality.

The extensive powers of appointment exercised by the Triumvirs naturally led to the distribution of appointments as favours, and to requests for them from interested parties. So Plutarch mentions that Octavia after her rejection by Antonius continued to assist men sent by him "in quest of office or on other business" to obtain their requests from Octavian (*Ant.* 54); while Aelian has the incident of a runaway slave who was given the praetorship by Antonius, and was recognized by his former master while "he was sitting on tribunal and dispensing justice in the Roman Forum."[21] If we can trust

---

13. Dio 48, 35, 1–3. Under 31 B.C. Dio duly notes that the arrangement of eight years before had been that Octavian and Antonius should be consuls, 50,10, 1.

14. Dio 48, 36, 4; 54, 6.

15. I am indebted to Professor Badian for emphasising to me the importance of indicating the extent to which Triumviral irregularities increased or decreased in the course of time.

16. Dio 48, 43, 2.

17. Dio 48, 53, 1–3.

18. One may note a couple of suffect praetors in 33, Dio 49, 43, 7.

19. Appian, *Illyrica* 28/80; Dio 49, 43, 6.

20. Plut., *Cic.* 49.

21. Aelian, *Apospasmata* 66. Cf. *Dig.* 1, 14, 3.

a curious anecdote in Dio,[22] the right of patronage was extended even beyond the Triumvirs; for he records that Statilius Taurus was rewarded by the people for completing his theatre in 30 B.C. and celebrating the event with a gladiatorial show, by being granted the right to select one of the praetors each year.

None the less, there remain a few indications that the ritual of the elections continued, and even that some places were filled by election. Dio mentions that there were no aediles in 36 B.C. for lack of candidates.[23] In the proscriptions, according to Appian, one praetor was killed holding an assembly in the Forum, and another fled while canvassing the voters for the quaestorship for his son. In this case the son revealed his father's hiding place, and was rewarded by the Triumvirs with both his father's property and an aedileship.[24] The first part of the latter story is confirmed by Valerius Maximus.[25] Similarly, according to Plutarch (*Cic.* 49), it was when Antonius was conducting an assembly in December 43 that Cicero's head and hands were brought to him. One story in Appian (*BC* 4, 41/173) records that the people elected a man as aedile in this period.

But although appointment by patronage was clearly normal, the theory that the republican magistrates, once in office, should exercise their traditional functions persisted throughout the period. When the soldiers imposed an agreement on Octavian and L. Antonius at Teanum in 41 B.C., one of its conditions was that the consuls should exercise their traditional powers (*ta patria*) without hindrance from the Triumvirs.[26] Similarly, when Octavian's fortunes turned in 36, "he allowed the annual magistrates to administer a great part of the *res publica* in the traditional ways." [27] While these references clearly indicate that full normality was not actually achieved, it is none the less important to stress the extent to which the traditional duties of the magistrates in fact continued. Sacrifices were carried out,[28] games and festivals conducted,[29] and public buildings constructed and dedicated.[30] As is

22. Dio 51, 23, 1.

23. Dio 49, 16, 2.

24. *BC* 4, 17–18/68–70.

25. Val. Max. 9, 11, 6.

26. Appian, *BC* 5, 20/79.

27. Appian, *BC* 5, 132/548.

28. Dio 51, 21, 1–2 (Valerius Potitus, suffect consul of 29).

29. Dio 48, 32, 4; Vell. Pat. 2, 79, 6, M. Titius "giving games in the theatre of Pompey," presumably as suffect consul in 31; Dio 48, 20, 2, Agrippa as praetor in 40 giving the *ludi Apollinares*.

30. Dio 49, 42, 2, Aemilius Lepidus Paullus, suffect consul of 34, dedicating the Basilica Aemilia; 49, 45, 1–5, Agrippa's building programme as aedile in 33.

clear from an anecdote in Appian (*BC* 4, 41/173) and Dio (48, 53, 4), office in Rome continued to demand substantial expenditure. Both the continuation of routine business and its subjection to violent interference are illustrated by Suetonius' story (*Div. Aug.* 27) of a praetor dragged from his tribunal by Octavian's soldiers.

Much more important, however, are the indications that substantial matters were still put through by the consuls. Twice under the year 42, Appian represents Antonius as getting the consul Munatius Plancus to have a safe-conduct voted for someone.[31] Ten years later, as is notorious, the consuls Sosius and Domitius Ahenobarbus resolutely opposed Octavian, and refused his demands for publication of Antonius' Donations of Alexandria;[32] Sosius would have taken direct action against Octavian but for the veto of the tribune Nonius Balbus.[33] Two years after that, it was Cicero's son who, as suffect consul of 30, read the news of the death of Antonius to the people.[34] At about this time, after the conspiracy of the younger Lepidus, a puzzling passage of Appian (*BC* 4, 50/218–19) shows a consul on his tribunal and with his lictors accepting a "pledge" (*vadimonium*) from Lepidus' mother for her appearance before Octavian.

More important than these scattered examples of consular or magisterial action is the evidence of votes by the Senate, or by the Senate and people. First, a number of laws, or popular votes. From 42 we have the Lex Munatia Aemilia enabling the Triumvirs to make grants of citizenship (see no. 5 in the next section), the law for the deification of Julius Caesar, "whom the Senate and the Roman People assigned a place among the Gods" (*ILS* 72, Aesernia);[35] and perhaps a Lex Rufrena.[36] From 40 (?) we have the important tribunician law, the Lex Falcidia.[37] From the mid 30s onwards various honours were voted to Octavian, some abortively;[38] but more significant is the fact that Antonius continued to wish to have his eastern dispositions ratified in Rome (Dio 49, 41, 4). Whether the renewal of the Triumvirate in 37 was ratified, even retrospectively, remains in doubt. In *BC* 5, 93/398, Appian says that they renewed it "no longer asking for the assent of the people" but in

31. Appian, *BC* 4, 37/158; 45/193.

32. Dio 49, 41, 4.

33. Dio 50, 2, 3.

34. Appian, *BC* 4, 51/221.

35. See also Dio 47, 18–19, and Triumviral Documents, no. 6.

36. *ILS* 73 "To the deified Julius by order of the Roman people. It was ordered in the Lex Rufrena"; cf. *ILS* 73a. See *Diz. Epig.*, s.v. "lex," 730–1; Degrassi, *ILLRP* I², 409.

37. Dio 48, 33, 5 etc. *Diz. Epig.*, s.v. "lex" 731–2. See Broughton, *MRR* II, 372.

38. Appian, *BC* 5, 131/543; Dio 49, 15, 5–6; 51, 19–20.

Illyrica 28/80 that the people ratified it. However, in 30 B.C. the Senate and People certainly passed a Lex Saenia allowing Octavian to create patricians,[39] and voted the privilege to Statilius Taurus mentioned above.

The Senate acting without the people in substantive matters appears even more frequently. In 41, according to Florus (2, 16) the senators declared L. Antonius a public enemy. In 40 they condemned Salvidienus Rufus to death, voted the "care" (*cura*) of the city to the Triumvirs,[40] and ratified the grant of the kingdom of Judaea to Herod.[41] In 39 they ratified all the official acts of the Triumvirs down to that time.[42] More traditional functions continued as well; in 37, on the advice of the *pontifices*, the Senate ordered the removal of the bones of a man whom the populace had honoured with burial on the Campus Martius.[43]

Then, ignoring various votes in favour of Octavian,[44] we may note that the Senate declared Antonius a public enemy, presumably in 30 — and that one senator voted against.[45] It was apparently subsequently to this that they voted to take down the image of Antonius and cancel the honours voted to him (Plut., *Cic.* 49); and in 29 to close the gates of the temple of Janus (*RG* 13; Dio 51, 20, 4).

Nobody would argue that the formal exercise of their traditional functions by the Senate and People demonstrates the continuance of the free play of politics. But the evidence does seem to indicate that the institutions of the *res publica* themselves persisted through the Triumviral period. Moreover the Triumvirs not only, as we shall see (texts to nn. 103–4), made repeated promises to restore effective power to the republican institutions, but showed considerable concern to have their actions formally approved and ratified by the traditional organs of the state. This intermingling of the exercise of individual power and of the role and influence of the republican institutions comes out very clearly in the now extensive dossier of Triumviral documents.

---

39. *RG* 8; Tac., *Ann.* 11, 25, cf. Dio 52, 42, 5. For other possible laws of this period, see G. Rotondi, *Leges publicae populi Romani* (1912), 435–41.

40. Dio 48, 33, 2–3.

41. Josephus, *Ant.* 14, 14, 4–5 (384–89). For the date and circumstances, see now E. Schürer, *The History of the Jewish People in the Age of Jesus Christ*, ed. G. Vermes and F. Millar, I (1973), 281.

42. Dio 48, 34, 1.

43. Dio 48, 53, 5–6.

44. E.g., Appian, *BC* 5, 130/538, 541; Dio 49, 43, 6; 45, 1; Appian, *Illyrica* 28/83.

45. Appian, *BC* 4, 45/193.

Triumviral Documents

The documents containing official decisions from the Triumviral period come entirely from the Greek East. In this context it will be sufficient to note their essential contents and their relevance to the way in which decisions were made. To illustrate a certain progression of form and attitude they will be given in chronological order.

1. Letter of Antonius to Hyrcanus and the *ethnos* of the Jewish people, 42/1 B.C. Jos., *Ant.* 14, 12, 3 (306–13).
2. Letter of Antonius to Tyre, 42/1 B.C. Jos., *Ant.* 14, 12, 4 (314–18).
3. Letter of Antonius to Tyre enclosing his edict (διάταγμα). 42/1 B.C. Jos., *Ant.* 14, 12, 5 (319–22).

Josephus notes that similar letters were sent to Sidon, Antioch, and Arados (14, 12, 6 [323]), but does not quote them. The letters which he does quote were evoked by an embassy to Antonius at Ephesus some time after Philippi, which brought a gold crown and asked for the freeing of Jewish prisoners taken in the period of Cassius' domination, and the restoration of lost territories. Antonius accepted these claims at once. In his letter to Hyrcanus he refers to a previous embassy to himself in Rome, discourses extravagantly on Philippi, and orders the release of the captives, the maintenance of grants previously granted by himself and Dolabella (proconsul of Syria in 43 B.C.), and the restoration of lands taken by the Tyrians. Writing to Tyre he emphasises that his opponents at Philippi had not been appointed to their provinces by the Senate, orders restoration, and offers them the opportunity of presenting their case before him when he reaches their vicinity. In the second letter he orders the inscription in a prominent place of a general edict referring to the illegal seizure of Syria by Cassius and the losses suffered by the Jews. Here he uses his full titulature, "Marcus Antonius, *imperator*, one of three men in charge of the *res publica* said." It is to be noted that the issue is brought forward, as so often, by an embassy from an interested party, that the decisions on it are taken directly and individually by the Triumvir concerned, but that some reference is made to the legality of his position.

4. Letter of Antonius to the provincial council (*koinon*) of Asia on the rights of the world-wide association of victorious athletes in sacred games who had won crowns. (?) 41 B.C. *SB* 4224; R. K. Sherk, *Roman Documents from the Greek East* (1969), no. 57.

Antonius refers to two embassies, a previous one when M. Antonius Artemidorus, "my friend and trainer," and the eponymous priest of the association, Charopinus of Ephesus, had approached him in Ephesus and requested the maintenance of its privileges; and a second by Artemidorus asking permission to have the privileges inscribed on a bronze tablet. This letter, preserved on papyrus, is addressed to the provincial council presumably for information and as further protection for the rights of the association. The preexisting role and importance of the provincial council is now clear from a document from Aphrodisias showing that earlier in the century it had sent an embassy to Rome to protest against the excesses of the publicans.[46]

5. A grant (*decretum*?) of citizenship by Octavian (or the Triumvirs?) to Seleucus of Rhosus, (?) 41 B.C. *IGLS* III, no. 718, ii; Sherk, *Roman Documents*, no. 58, ii.

The document is much mutilated, and there is ample room for doubt about both its correct designation and its date. What is significant in this context is that it refers (l. 10) to a Lex Munatia Aemilia, evidently passed by the consuls of 42 B.C., Munatius Plancus and Aemilius Lepidus, in accordance with which the grant is made. There is no indication of date, but it is probably early, as the donor appears as "Caesar Imperator"—Καῖσαρ αὐτοκράτωρ. "Imperator" does not yet appear as a *praenomen*, which it came to do from 38, or possibly 40, B.C.[47] On the other hand, the verb given in line 11 is in the plural, "gave," which has suggested to some that an original which referred to a grant by two or three of the Triumvirs has been tampered with before being inscribed several years later. The aftermath of Philippi remains a reasonable, but not in the least a certain, context for the original grant. More important for our purposes is its justification in terms of a law, its formal and detailed character, and its references (ll. 68–71) to the rights of embassy to the Senate, and to Roman magistrates and promagistrates, and to fines payable to the Roman people.

6. (?) Greek translation of a law establishing ceremonies in honour of the deified Julius Caesar? 41 B.C.? *Forschungen in Ephesos* IV, 3 (1951), 280, no. 24; see now M. Crawford, ed., *Roman Statutes* I–II (1996), no. 35.

The first words (*thelete, keleuete*) translate "velitis, iubeatis" ("May you wish and command") the terminology of a law,[48] and the expression "the deified

46. First published by K. Erim, *PBSR* 37 (1969): 92–95; see T. Drew-Bear, *ZPE* 8 (1971): 285–88, and for a full discussion his "Deux décrets hellénistiques d'Asie Mineure," *BCH* 46 (1972): 435, on pp. 443–71; now, J. M. Reynolds, *Aphrodisias and Rome* (1982), no. 5.

47. See R. Syme, "Imperator Caesar, a Study in Nomenclature," *Historia* 7 (1958): 172 = *Roman Papers* I (1979), 361; R. Combès, *Imperator* (1966), 132–35.

48. Mommsen, *Staatsrecht* III, 312, n. 2. S. Weinstock, *Divus Julius* (1972), 402, suggests, surely wrongly, that this is a letter from the Senate.

Julius" is likely not to have been used until after the vote of divine honours in 42 B.C. (Dio 48, 18–19). Whether the reference to Marcus Antonius relates in any way to his presence in Ephesus in 41 B.C.[49] must remain a matter of speculation.

7. A decree of the senate in response to an embassy, probably from Panamara, Caria. 39 B.C. Sherk, *Roman Documents*, no. 27.

The document is formally dated to August in the consulship of L. Marcius Censorinus and Gaius Calvisius. All that emerges is that a large Greek embassy, probably, but not necessarily, from Panamara itself, made some request which Censorinus put to the Senate, and which was evidently received favourably.

8. Part of a decree of the Senate relating to Plarasa-Aphrodisias, 39 B.C. J. M. Reynolds, *Aphrodisias and Rome* (1982), no. 8 (henceforward *Aphrodisias*).

The decree is dated to the consulship of 39, L. Marcius Censorinus and Gaius Calvisius, and it confirms grants of rights and privileges, including freedom and immunity, to the city, and to the sanctuary (*temenos*) of Aphrodite there, made by Divus Julius, Octavian, and Antonius. Among the provisions are some for the reception of future embassies from the city coming before the Senate. Compare no. 12.

9. Edict of the Triumvirs. 39 B.C.? or soon after. *Aphrodisias*, no. 7.

The document contains the last part (about thirty letters) of each of twelve lines of an edict by two of the Triumvirs. There is no formal indication of date, but the succeeding lines contain references to a war and its effects, which is likely to be the Parthian invasion of 39 B.C., although it may refer also to oppression by Brutus and Cassius.

10. Letter of Octavian to Ephesus, promoted by an embassy from Plarasa-Aphrodisias, 38 B.C.? *Aphrodisias*, no. 12.

Octavian appears with the *praenomen* "Imperator," which suggests a year not earlier than 38, or possibly 40, B.C., and his letter is concerned with restoration after the war of Labienus, which suggests not later than 38. The sufferings of Plarasa-Aphrodisias were detailed to Octavian, he says, by an ambassador, Solon, son of Demetrius, the same man who appears in no. 12. The most striking feature of the letter is that Octavian writes that he has given *entolai*

49. Weinstock (n. 48).

to his colleague Antonius to repair the damage; but this may translate *mandata*, in the sense of a commission, and hence be less dramatic than it at first appears. The letter comes to Ephesus because it has been reported to Octavian that a gold statue of Eros dedicated by Divus Julius, having been looted from Aphrodisias, has been dedicated to Artemis of Ephesus. They are firmly warned to restore it. There is no reference to the institutions of the *res publica*.

11. Letter of Octavian to Stephanus concerning Aphrodisias (and letter of Stephanus to Aphrodisias). 38 B.C.? *Aphrodisias*, nos. 10 and 11.

Octavian instructs someone called Stephanus to protect Plarasa-Aphrodisias, whose interests he has at heart above all other cities in Asia, in the absence of Antonius (this will hardly help to date the letter, for Antonius was only rarely in the province of Asia). The first line adds to the evidence on an interesting figure discussed in some typically illuminating pages by L. Robert,[50] and proves conclusively his view that Zoilus belongs in this period and not in the second century A.D. The documents are notable for Octavian's attachment to Aphrodisias, and the cult of Venus-Aphrodite, which he had inherited from Julius Caesar; he writes that he has "taken" for himself this one city from all Asia. The date will again be about 38 B.C., for Stephanus in his letter refers to the handing-over of free men and slaves and also a gold crown after the war of Labienus.

12. Letter of Octavian to Aphrodisias. 39–34 (39/8?) B.C. Sherk, *Roman Documents*, no. 28A; *Aphrodisias*, no. 6.

This letter to Aphrodisias from a Triumvir whose name is missing was earlier supposed, as in Sherk, *Roman Documents*, to be from Antonius, solely because Asia formed part of "his" territory. But its contents, and the comparison with no. 13, ought to have made it clear that it was from Octavian, even before the discovery of the Aphrodisias dossier. Octavian, as it certainly is, writes in response to a request brought by their ambassador, Solon, son of Demetrius (the same man as in no. 10), for copies of the documents granting them privileges (ll. 22–31). The careful distinction between the different forms of Roman official acts, *decretum* (?), *senatus consultum*, *iusiurandum*, and *lex*, and the reference to the public archives (in the *aerarium*),[51] emphasises again the extent to which the Triumvirs, at least formally, operated within the framework

---

50. L. Robert, "Inscriptions d'Aphrodisias," *Ant. Class.* 35 (1966): 401–32.

51. See *JRS* 54 (1964): 34–35 (= chapter 2 in *Rome, the Greek World, and the East*, vol. 2); cf. M. W. Frederiksen, "The Republican Municipal Laws: Errors and Drafts," *JRS* 55 (1965): 183, on pp. 184–87.

of the *res publica*. The possible limits of the date are indicated by Octavian's titulature as it survives: "consul designate for the second and third time," so between 39 and 34 B.C. If this were the same journey on the part of Demetrius as that which produced no. 10, the document would date to the first year or so of the period.

13. Letter of Octavian to Rhosus, Syria. 36–34 B.C. *IGLS* III, no. 718; Sherk, *Roman Documents*, no. 58, i.

This is a covering letter ordering the filing in the public archives of Rhosus of no. 5 (nos. 16 and 17, which are inscribed on the same stone, were written later than this). Octavian surprisingly omits the title *triumvir rei publicae constituendae*, but is Imperator IV (from 36 B.C.) and consul designate for the second and third time, so 39–34 B.C. The date is therefore 36–34 B.C. He writes "What is written below has been excerpted from a pillar on the Capitol at Rome, and [I ask that it should be] filed in your public records." Copies are also to be sent for registration to Tarsus, Antioch, and Seleucia. The letter is evidence that Octavian's relations with cities in the Greek East were not confined to the special case of Aphrodisias; and, along with nos. 5–7, that Greek cities other than Aphrodisias continued to be in active contact with the institutions of the *res publica* in Rome.

14. Edict of Octavian on the privileges of veterans. 38–33 B.C.?, *BGU* II, no. 628; *CIL* XVI, p. 145. no. 10; Riccobono, *FIRA*² I, no. 56; Cavenaille, *Corpus Papyrorum Latinarum*, no. 103; S. Daris, *Documenti per la storia dell'esercito romano in Egitto* (1964), no. 100.

The edict is quoted in a Latin papyrus of the first century A.D., itself evidently part of a report of legal proceedings. It begins "Imp. Caesar [d]ivi filius trium[v]ir rei publicae consultor(?)" — or "consul ter" (= consul for the third time) or "consul iter." (= consul for the second time) or "constit(uendae) iter(um)" (= to reorganize for the second time) — "said," which seems to suggest a date between 38 and 33. The extremely legalistic terms of the document are noticeable, including for instance a provision for veterans to be enrolled in a certain tribe for the census and for voting purposes.

It will be convenient to complete the dossier with three "post-Triumviral" documents. It is to be emphasised that in all three the titulature of Octavian mentions no public office other than the consulate.

15. Letter of Octavian to Mylasa, Caria, in response to an embassy. 31 B.C. (or 32?). Sherk, *Roman Documents*, no. 60.

Octavian writes to Mylasa as "appointed as consul for the third time." The titulature is puzzling, and the presence of the particle "and" after the word consul perhaps suggests that something has been omitted—he was Imperator V before Actium and VI after it. The expression *may* mean, as it is normally taken, that he was simply consul for the third time, that is, in 31. But might it not be a document of late 32, when (perhaps) his only official position was that of consul designate for the third time? The letter refers to two successive embassies which the Mylasans had sent to report their sufferings and losses in the war. On either of these datings this must refer to the preliminaries of the war of Actium.[52]

16. Letter of Octavian to Rhosus, in response to an embassy. 31 B.C.
    IGLS III, no. 718; Sherk, *Roman Documents*, no. 58, iii.

Octavian writes as Imperator VI (after Actium), consul for the third time (31 B.C.) and "designated (consul) for the fourth time" (for 30), so in the last four months of 31. He mentions that the embassy from Rhosus met him in Ephesus and offered a crown and various honours (Dio indeed refers to his brief visit to Asia before his return to Italy in the middle of the winter of 31/0).[53] He undertakes to do the people of Rhosus further services when he comes to Syria, through which he did subsequently pass in 30 B.C.; and he testifies most emphatically to the constant intercessions which Seleucus, who was one of the ambassadors, had made on behalf of his city.

17. Letter of Octavian to Rhosus, recommending Seleucus. 30 B.C.
    IGLS III, no. 718; Sherk, *Roman Documents*, no. 58, iv.

Octavian writes as consul for the fourth time, but is apparently not yet designated as consul for 29. He refers again to the services of Seleucus as naval commander, and to his immunity, Roman citizenship, and other privileges. He continues in a very significant manner: "I recommend this man to you. For such men render one's benevolence more ready towards their native cities as well. On the assumption therefore that I will gladly do for you whatever is possible for the sake of Seleucus, have confidence, and send to me on whatever matter you wish." Octavian writes as a monarch. If in 30 B.C. he

52. For comparative evidence, see Magie, *Roman Rule in Asia Minor* (1950), 439–40 and notes. If, however, the titulature has been seriously abbreviated, it remains possible that Octavian wrote as consul designate for the second and third time, i.e., in 39–34, and that these embassies too referred to the war of Labienus.
    53. Dio 51, 4, 1–3.

expected or intended any future diminution of his effective power to confer benefits, there is no sign of it here. On the contrary he confidently expects, and even invites, petitions for benefits, which will be addressed to himself personally. It is here, rather than in the documents of the Triumvirate proper, with their recurrent formalism and repeated references to the institutions of the *res publica*, that a pattern appears in which decisions will be made by the untrammelled will and judgement of an individual.

It is striking how exactly these two letters match the assumptions of Virgil in the *Georgics*, which, according to the *Vita* by Donatus (27/91–95), were read to Augustus at Atella in 29: ". . . while great Caesar thunders to the deep-flowing Euphrates and, as victor in war, gives out rights, among the willing peoples and prepares for himself the road to Olympus" (4, 560–62).

Triumviral Functions and the Emergence of Personal Jurisdiction

As we have seen, the only attested formal definition of the Triumvirs' power in relation to the Republican magistrates is that it was to be consular. What the powers of a Triumvir were in Rome therefore remains unclear; and the obscurity is increased by the fact, which Dio carefully notes, that the successive divisions of territory between them never included Rome and Italy. For, as he says with the rather undervalued acerbity with which he records the emergence of monarchy, they were supposed to be striving not to gain Italy but on its behalf.[54] One respect in which they were clearly distinguishable from the consuls while in Italy did emerge in 41 B.C.: the Triumvirs had a praetorian cohort, but the consuls did not.[55] The rest of the apparatus of Triumviral office seems, however, to have been very similar to that of the consuls. An anecdote in Appian shows them seated on the tribunal in the Forum (*BC* 4, 37/157). As we have seen, they were granted the right to convene the Senate; when in 32 B.C. Octavian summoned the Senate and sat on the consuls' bench (Dio 50, 2, 5), and later continued to summon and address it when the consuls had fled (50, 3, 2), it is to be presumed that he was exercising a triumviral right, whether formally lapsed or not. Like other magistrates, they could also issue pronouncements as edicts, of which we have seen some examples among the documents listed above. Such was presumably the

---

54. Dio 48, 2, 1.

55. Appian, *BC* 5, 21/82. Cf. Seneca, *Ep.* 114, 6, the seal being obtained from Maecenas "when he performed the tasks of the absent Caesar." For further evidence, see M. Durry, *Les cohortes prétoriennes* (1938), 76–77; A. Passerini, *Le coorti pretorie* (1939), 30–33.

proclamation quoted by Appian, in which the Triumvirs announced the proscriptions: as given, it begins with the conventional terminology of an edict:
"they say."[56]

However, it was an inevitable product of the situation that embassies, petitioners, and perhaps ordinary litigants should address themselves directly to
the Triumvirs, or to one or two of them, and thereby tend to isolate them
from the environment of Republican institutions, and to create a monarchical situation in which decisions were made by individual pronouncement.
We have already seen a number of instances of embassies to one or other of
them, and the literary sources offer more.[57] Individual petitioners took the
same course. Perhaps the best illustration of the working of government in
the period is provided by the so-called *Laudatio Turiae*.[58] The husband of the
unnamed matron records that he was restored from exile "by the favour and
judgement of the absent Caesar Augustus" ("beneficio et i[ud]icio apsentis
Caesaris Augusti") (the document was inscribed after 27 B.C.), but that in his
absence actual permission for his return had to be sought from Lepidus—
"when seeking my restitution, you petitioned the then present colleague,
Lepidus, and lay on the ground at his feet." In the face of abuse and physical
assault the matron (apparently) managed to quote Octavian's edict of restitution. Similarly, another priceless and undervalued contemporary source,
Cornelius Nepos, in the *Life of Atticus*, records that Atticus' daughter was married to Agrippa, with Antonius acting as mediator "although he might have
increased his possessions through his influence, so far was he [Atticus] from
a lust for money that he only used that influence in begging for the removal
of his friends' dangers or inconveniences" (12, 2). Against this background
there is surely no difficulty in accepting that Virgil in the *First Eclogue* (42–5)
is referring to a successful petition to Octavian:

> Here, Meliboeus, I am that youth for whom our altars smoke twice six
> days and years. Here he was the first to give my plea an answer ("hic
> mihi responsum primus dedit ille petenti"): "Feed, swains, your oxen
> as of old; rear your bulls."

56. Appian, *BC* 4, 8–11/34–44. It is not clear what was the form of the pronouncement
quoted in 4, 38/159, by which Messala was removed from the list of the proscribed. But the
term "edict of proscription," applying to an individual, is attested in Seneca, *De clementia* 1,
9, 5.

57. Plut., *Ant.* 24; Jos., *Ant.* 14, 12, 2 (301); Appian, *BC* 4, 47/201; 5, 52/216.

58. *CIL* VI, 1527 = *ILS* 8393: M. Durry, *Eloge funèbre d'une matrone romaine (éloge dite de
Turia)* (1950), II, lines 21–28.

A major public episode was the petition of the married women (*matronae*) to the Triumvirs over an imposition of a tax, recorded by Valerius Maximus (8, 3, 3) and Appian (*BC* 4, 32–4/136–46): since none of the men would offer their advocacy, Hortensia, the daughter of Hortensius, "pleaded the women's cause before the Triumvirs firmly and successfully: imitating her father's eloquence, she obtained the remission of the greater part of the money demanded from them." According to Appian the scene took place before the tribunal of the Triumvirs in the Forum, and they first had the women driven off by their lictors, and then announced a reduction in the tax on the next day.

It is not an accident that the episode concerns the demand for a benefaction which is granted by the simple pronouncement of the Triumvirs, or that in describing the petition Valerius Maximus resorts to the typical vocabulary of the law court. For precisely one of the characteristics of monarchy is the blurring of the distinction between the issuing of decisions and giving of legal judgements by the holder, or holders, of power. As Mommsen notes,[59] Quintilian alludes to this development in just this period in discussing the occasions and functions of "pleas for mercy" (*deprecationes*) — "Pleas for mercy, which are not in any sense a method of actual defence, can rarely be used, and only before judges who are not limited to some precise form of verdict. Even those speeches delivered before Gaius Caesar and the Triumvirs on behalf of members of the opposite party, although they do employ such pleas for mercy, also make use of the ordinary methods of defence." He continues directly to the situation of speaking before the *princeps* — "But if when pleading before the *princeps* or any other person who has power either to acquit or condemn, it is incumbent on us to urge. . . ."[60]

Summary, semi-judicial procedures for disposing of enemies taken in the field are amply attested for the Triumviral period,[61] right down to Octavian's hearings in 31 and 30.[62] These are of course a crucially important instance of the arbitrary exercise of power in this period. But in the long term, for the fundamental transformation of the Roman state, the development of a routine personal jurisdiction by the holder of individual power is of much greater importance. The complexities of this development, which can be

59. *Strafrecht*, 144, n. 5.

60. Quintilian, *Inst. Orat.* 5, 13, 5–6 (Loeb trans.).

61. The evidence is collected and discussed only, so far as I know, by H. Volkmann, *Zur Rechtsprechung im Principat des Augustus*[2] (1969), 11–50.

62. Val. Max. 1, 7, 7; Plut., *Ant* 72; Dio 51, 2, 4–6; 51, 16, 1.

roughly described as the introduction into the city of Rome of the system
of "investigation" (*cognitio*)[63] by a republican provincial governor, cannot be
discussed here. But it must be emphasised that we have excellent evidence,
which seems to be neglected both in books on Julius Caesar[64]and in those on
the legal procedure of the late Republic,[65] that Caesar as dictator exercised a
routine personal jurisdiction in Rome — "he administered justice most con-
scientiously and most severely," as Suetonius records (*Div. Jul.* 43). The generalization is confirmed by two anecdotes. Valerius Maximus (6, 2 11) tells a
story of Galba, "who dared to accost the deified Caesar in this manner when
the latter, his victories accomplished, was dispensing justice in the forum."
From the same period, after Munda, Seneca (*De benef.* 5, 24) records an incident when a veteran of Caesar's army was engaged in a case before him which
concerned nothing more than a dispute between himself and his neighbour.
It is clear that the fact that the man was a veteran was *not* the reason why the
case came to Caesar. For it is only in the middle of the proceedings that he
succeeds in establishing his identity as such, and hence his claim to a benefaction. Caesar is described as "angry because diverted in the middle of the
investigation by this old story." So the procedure was that of *cognitio*, and the
point at issue an entirely insignificant matter. (Whether it was a civil or a
criminal case is not entirely clear.)

Whether it results from the limited nature of our sources or not, it is a
fact which has not yet received its due emphasis that there is very little evidence for a routine personal jurisdiction by the Triumvirs in minor, non-
political matters, and none at all for its exercise in Rome. The evidence of
Triumviral jurisdiction other than over Roman political enemies in fact all
relates to Antonius. Plutarch's *Life* records "that in his judicial decisions he
was reasonable" (23), and that he often gave judgement "seated on a tribunal" to tetrarchs and kings (58). An example, illustrating the confusion

63. Not "cognitio extra ordinem," an expression which, as indicated in *JRS* 58 (1968):
222, is a grammatical monstrosity, since "extra ordinem" (out of order) is an adverbial
phrase, which can qualify various verbs including "cognoscere" (to investigate), but is not
found as an adjectival phrase. The modern use of the pseudo-concept "cognitio extra ordinem," even in the titles of books — some are listed in M. Kaser, *Das römische Zivilprozessrecht*
(1966), 339 — is a classic instance of the process of nominalization brilliantly discussed by
D. Daube, *Roman Law: Linguistic, Social and Philosophical Aspects* (1969), chap. 1.

64. No trace of the question in the excellent work of M. Gelzer, *Caesar: Politician and
Statesman* (1968).

65. Even A. H. J. Greenidge, *The Legal Procedure of Cicero's Time* (1901), contains no discussion of the jurisdiction of Caesar as dictator.

between judgement and political decision, will be the accusations against Hyrcanus and Herod[66] which preceded the steps which produced documents 1–3. We have two specific instances of cases before Antonius: Lachares, the father of Eurycles, was beheaded by him for robbery (Plut., *Ant.* 67); and Boethus of Tarsos was accused before him of peculation, but evidently acquitted (Strabo 674). That jurisdiction was part of his normal routine seems clear from Appian's description (*BC* V, 76/324) of his emergence from his Athenian holiday over the winter of 39/8 B.C.: standards, guards, and officers were seen at his door, embassies were received, and cases decided.

As regards Octavian, by contrast, who was of course based in Rome, we have no concrete instances of routine jurisdiction, and no general referencee to the issue until we reach the notoriously puzzling reference in Dio (51, 19, 6–7) to a vote in 30 B.C. which allowed him, among other things: "to administer justice on appeal." It is not necessary to discuss the peculiarities of this report, or whether the right was actually accepted by Octavian at this time, and, if so, how it relates to the later exercise of jurisdiction by the *Princeps*. It is important to stress instead what has sometimes been denied[67] — that a routine jurisdiction was subsequently exercised by Augustus himself, not just in the provinces,[68] or on appeal,[69] but in Rome and Italy and as the court of first instance, and in both civil and criminal cases.[70] The routine nature of the work is clear from Suetonius: "he himself gave jurisdiction assiduously and on occasion into the night, and if he were physically too weak would do so with his litter placed on the tribunal, or even lying down at home" (33); "of his country retreats he particularly frequented Tibur, where he very often gave jurisdiction, even in the porticoes of the temple of Hercules" (72).

In this important respect therefore the Triumvirate, so far as our evidence goes, may perhaps mark if anything a slight step back in the development of a monarchic institution which was already known before, in the dictatorship of Caesar, and which was to come into full effect in the principate of Augustus.

66. Jos., *Ant.* 14, 12, 2 (302–3).

67. E.g., by J. Bleicken, *Senatsgericht und Kaisergericht* (1962), 72–73.

68. One may list by way of illustration Livy, *Epit.* 134 (I presume that "he held assizes in Narbo" must refer to Augustus' jurisdiction in 27); Seneca, *Controv.* 10 *praef.* 14; from "senatorial" provinces, Jos., *BJ* 1, 26,4 (531); Suet., *Div. Aug.* 93.

69. Suet., *Div. Aug.* 33.

70. Criminal: Val. Max. 9, 15, 2; Ovid. *Tristia* 2, 127ff.; Dio 54, 15, 4; 55, 7, 2; 56, 23, 2–3; 24. 7; Seneca, *QN* 1, 16, 1; Suet., *Div. Aug.* 24; 33; 45, 1; *Dig.* 48, 24, 1; Strabo 670. Civil: Val. Max. 7, 7, 3 and 4; 9, 15, *ext.* 1; Suet., *Div. Aug.* 97; *Dig.* 8, 3, 35.

The "Restoration of the Republic"

Nothing said thus far is claimed to prove that the period of the Triumvirate was not one where violence and illegality played a crucial role. But the discussion will, it may be hoped, have emphasised that the Triumvirate was an institution which was created by a form of law, and which was superimposed on, but did not replace, the institutions of the *res publica*. In consequence, it exhibited many of the ambiguities in the exercise of authority, and many of the compromises between individual power and traditional institutions which characterise the Principate itself. Moreover, the existence of suspicions and rivalries between the Triumvirs caused them, in the search for political support, to pay repeated lip service to the Senate and the Roman people. Not only did the *res publica* survive, if much weakened, but the "Augustan" revival might be considered to have begun in the later thirties, with the building programme of Agrippa as aedile in 33; and its characteristic archaism is already visible in the use of the Fetial rite to declare war in 32.[71] When Atticus died on the last day of March 32 B.C., and was buried "escorted by all men of substance and by very large crowds of the common people,"[72] the outward appearance of Roman life must have been much as it had always been. It is against this background that we can come back to the two central questions. What really changed in the development from Triumvirate to Principate? And, more important even than the facts of constitutional change, what did men think and say had happened, and how did they characterise the "new order" in which they lived?

As is notorious, our evidence does not serve to resolve unambiguously the question of when the Triumviral powers came to an end, either in strict theory or in practice.[73] All that we can say for certain is that from 31 onwards, indeed until his assumption of the tribunician power in 23, the only actual office or power which the titulature of Octavian/Augustus reveals is that of consul. In this formal and outward aspect the only change in 27 was the appearance of the cognomen "Augustus."

There were of course more substantial changes, but their character and significance still require re-examination against the Triumviral background. In 28 Dio records that Octavian shared the *fasces* with Agrippa and his colleague

---

71. Dio 50, 4, 5.

72. Nepos, *Atticus* 22, 3–4 (N. Horsfall's trans.).

73. For discussions, see Fadinger (n. 5), chap. 2; K. E. Petzold, "Die Bedeutung des Jahres 32 für die Entstehung des Principats," *Historia* 18 (1969): 334; E. Gabba, "La data finale del secondo Triumvirato," *RFIC* 98 (1970): 3.

in the consulate,[74] a gesture evidently intended as a symbol of normality, but one whose significance we cannot interpret for lack of evidence from the preceding period. In the same year, as we have noted (see text to n. 2), he abolished the illegal acts of the Triumvirate and, at the end of it, took the customary oath of a consul leaving office.[75] Tacitus indeed appears to couple with this abolition, and to place in this year, the substantial steps which created the Principate—"Finally Caesar Augustus, when consul for the sixth time, secure in his power, abolished what he had decreed as triumvir and gave us the laws by which we enjoy peace and the rule of a Princeps."[76] As so often with Tacitus, we cannot discern precisely to what he is referring. Augustus himself (*RG* 34) speaks of his sixth and seventh consulates. Dio, however, clearly relates the essential change to the "settlement" of 27.

Of the changes which now took place, those affecting the government of the provinces at least are reasonably clear.[77] The Triumvirs had been empowered to appoint all provincial governors, and we have adequate evidence of their doing so,[78] and of Octavian continuing to do likewise between Actium and 27.[79] But it should be noted that the republican title proconsul (*pro consule*) had not been abandoned,[80] though *legatus pro praetore* (legate with praetorian rank), first attested in the seventies B.C.,[81] is found also, though in Sicily under Sextus Pompeius.[82] More significantly, these proconsuls, although they were the appointees of, and in some sense subordinate to, the Triumvirs, continued to celebrate triumphs[83] (a fact which surprised Dio).[84] In 29 B.C., however, Octavian shared the triumph of Gaius Carrinas (Dio 51, 21, 6), and denied the deposition of the *spolia opima* (spoils removed from an

74. Dio 53 1, 1.

75. Dio 53 1, 1.

76. *Tac., Ann.* 3, 28.

77. Cf. *JRS* 56 (1966), 156–57 (= chapter 11 in this volume).

78. E.g., Appian 5, 129/537; 132/549; Dio 48, 22, 1.

79. E.g., Appian, *BC* 4, 38/161; Dio 51, 23, 2 (cf. Dio 51, 17, 1, Cornelius Gallus left in charge of Egypt).

80. E.g., Degrassi, *ILLRP*[2] I, 433; cf. Broughton, *MRR* II, 369, n. 1; and my n. 83. Documentary evidence for the titles borne by governors is however extremely sparse throughout the Triumviral period.

81. *ILS* 37 = Degrassi, *ILLRP*[2] I, 372.

82. Degrassi, *ILLRP*[2] I, 426.

83. The evidence on triumphs between 43 and 28 B.C. is admirably collected by A. Degrassi, *Fasti Consulares et Triumphales, Inscriptiones Italiae* XIII, 1 (1947), 567–70.

84. Dio 48, 42, 4.

enemy general by the Roman commander who had personally killed him in battle) to Licinius Crassus (Dio 51, 24, 4; cf. Livy 4, 20, 5–7). From 27 B.C. some provincial governors continued to have the title proconsul, and appointment by lot was now restored in their case.[85] But the governors of most of the major military provinces lost this title in favour of *legatus*, and continued to be appointed by Augustus; how soon the full title, "legatus Augusti pro praetore" (a legate of Augustus with praetorian rank), came into regular use is curiously difficult to determine;[86] but "leg. Augusti" appears on coins of P. Carisius in Lusitania in the mid 20s B.C.,[87] and "leg. imp. Caesaris Aug." (*ILS* 929) is used of Articuleius Regulus, governor there in the period A.D. 2–14. The change was thus far from being unambiguously a step in the direction of republicanism; our evidence provides only a single uncertain instance from the Republic of a legate using his commander's name in his title.[88] Moreover, while proconsuls continued for a few years, down to 19 B.C., to celebrate triumphs, no legate appointed by Augustus ever did, or could.

The notion that these two methods of appointment and two forms of titulature reflected a fundamental division of political and administrative responsibility between Princeps and Senate is an illusion.[89] Nor can we tell what formal description was applied to Augustus' position in relation to the imperial provinces. It may be that he was formally proconsul of these provinces while concurrently holding the consulship (Pompey had already been proconsul of Spain—Caes. *BG* 6, 1, 2—when elected consul in 52 while continuing his command; cf. Vell. Pat. 2, 48, 1); but no document gives Augustus or any other emperor the *title* of proconsul until the reign of Trajan.[90] It may be, alternatively, that some formula employing the term "proconsular *imperium*" (*imperium proconsulare*), or a similar expression, was devised; but for

85. Dio 53, 11, 2.

86. I owe this essential point to Professor Badian. The documentary evidence is still very poor for this period. In Hispania Citerior, however, it is clear that "legatus pro praetore" was normal—see G. Alföldy, *Fasti Hispanienses* (1969): 3–13—though Paullus Fabius Maximus, *c.* 3/2 B.C., uses "legat. Caesaris" (p. 9). "[Legatus pro] pr. Augusti Caesaris in [Illyrico]" is used of M. Vinicius, there 10/9 or some years later; see A. Dobo, *Die Verwaltung der römischen Provinz Pannonien* (1968), 16–18. Milestones from Galatia of 6 B.C. have "Commodus Aquila, his *legatus propraetore* being in charge" (*curante Com. Aquila leg. suo pro pr.*); see R. K. Sherk, *The Legates of Galatia* (1951), 24.

87. Alföldy (n. 86), 131.

88. See J. M. Reynolds, "Cyrenaica, Pompey and Cn. Cornelius Lentulus Marcellinus," *JRS* 52 (1962): 99–100, no.7 = *ILLRP*² I, 1234.

89. See Millar (n. 77).

90. Mommsen (n. 48), 2, 778.

that we have no evidence at this stage. It remains entirely open to suggest that the provincial aspects of the settlement of 27 amount, on Augustus' side, simply and solely to the right to appoint legates as governors of most of the major military provinces.

As regards the city magistracies, our evidence tends to suggest that the *form* of republican elections had continued through the Triumviral period (see text to nn. 23–39). If that is correct, and it is not certain, then when Dio asserts (53, 21, 6–7) that electoral assemblies began to meet again from 27 onwards, we may take this as a reference to the recommencement of genuine competition for election, which is clearly attested for the Augustan period; the competition was limited in practice, but not formally, by imperial recommendation (*commendatio*).[91] (Nonetheless, our sources do in certain instances speak of Augustus "offering" or "giving" the consulate to a man.[92]) As regards the holders of the city magistracies, no change was made in their powers in 27, for no formal change had been made in the Triumviral period.

Thus the changes which culminated in 27 were of a fairly limited kind, and not all of them clearly tended towards a revived Republic. But that brings us to our central question: now that we have seen the extent to which the institutions of the *res publica* survived through the Triumviral period, what evidence have we to justify the normal view that 27 saw either a real or a proclaimed "Restoration of the Republic"?[93]

The question involves acute problems as to what terms are used in our sources to describe the change of 27 or the state of affairs resulting from it, and what these terms meant at different periods. When if ever, for instance, was *res publica* used to mean "the Republic" in our sense? It surely has something like that meaning in one passage of Tacitus, referring to the year A.D. 14: "how many were left who had seen the Republic with their own eyes?"[94] But did it have the same meaning in the 20s B.C.? Already in 29 B.C. the Senate and People of Rome had made a dedication to Octavian "the *res publica* having been preserved" (*re publica conservata*).[95] More important perhaps is a passage from the third book of Livy, written precisely in the two years after

91. See works cited in n. 8.

92. Tac., *Ann.* 2, 43 (Calpurnius Piso); 3, 75 (Ateius Capito); Seneca, *De Clementia*, 1, 9, 12 (L. Cinna); *Dig.* 1, 2, 2, 47 (Antistius Labeo).

93. The following argument returns, in greatly expanded form, to some points briefly made in *CR*, n.s., 18 (1968): 265–66.

94. Tacitus, *Ann.* 1, 3, 7.

95. *CIL* VI, 873; *ILS* 81.

27 B.C.[96] Here Livy describes the Senate's reaction to a determined and patriotic speech by L. Quinctius Cincinnatus, consul in 460 B.C.: "the uplifted senators believed that the *res publica* had been restored."[97] "Res publica" here means "the state" or "the condition of public affairs," and certainly cannot mean anything like "the Republic."

This passage also serves to emphasize that, even if it were the case that contemporary sources consistently used "res publica restituta" of the change completed in 27, this is not likely to have meant that "the Republic was restored." In fact it is remarkable, firstly, how little reflection the event has in contemporary literature—nothing in Virgil, Horace or Propertius echoes it—and, secondly, how varied are the expressions used in those literary and documentary sources which do refer to it. The expression "res publica restituta" is used almost certainly in the *Laudatio Turiae* (text to n. 58), ii, 25, "the world having been pacified, [and] the *res publica* restored"; and *possibly* in *the Fasti Praenestini* for January 12:[98]

> [The Senate decreed] that an oak crown should be fixed above the door to Caesar Augustus' house [because he restored the *res publica*] to the Roman people.

It must be emphasised that these two cases are the *only* ones in which the expression is used, or may be used. In Ovid, *Fasti*, under 13 January, a quite different formulation appears (1, 589–90): "all the provinces have been restored to our people, and your grandfather was called by the name Augustus." Alternatively, coins of 28/7 B.C. have "vindicator of the liberty of the Roman people" (*Libertatis p.R. vindex*).[99] What might be taken as a reference to the restoration of political liberty is in fact more precisely a reference to the end of the civil war; the reverse of the coins has "peace" (*pax*), and the *Fasti* note on August 1 "since on this day Imperator Caesar son of the deified Julius delivered the *res publica* from terrible danger."[100]

Our most general statement comes from the loyalist Velleius; in describing the general settlement of affairs after the end of the civil wars he echoes in part the words of Cicero addressing Julius Caesar in *Pro Marcello* 23: "It is for you alone [to do], Gaius Caesar, . . . the courts must be re-established,

96. R. M. Ogilvie, *A Commentary on Livy Books 1–5* (1965), 2.

97. Livy 3, 20, 1.

98. *CIL* I² p. 231; Degrassi, *Ins. It.* XIII, 2 (1963), 112–13.

99. *R.I.C.* I, Augustus no. 10; C. H. V. Sutherland, *Coinage in Roman Imperial Policy, 31 B.C.–A.D. 68* (1951), 31; C. H. V. Sutherland, N. Olcay, and K. E. Merrington, *The Cistophori of Augustus* (1970), 89–90.

100. A. Degrassi, *Inscriptiones Italiae* XIII, 2 (1963), 191 (*Fasti Amiternini*); cf. pp. 31, 135.

credit must be called back, licentiousness must be curbed, population growth must be encouraged; all that has become disintegrated and dissipated must be bound by severe laws." Velleius' version is more detailed and ornate: "The civil wars were ended after twenty years, foreign wars suppressed, peace restored, the frenzy of arms everywhere lulled to rest; validity was restored to the laws, authority to the courts, and dignity to the Senate; the power of the magistrates was reduced to its former limits, with the sole exception that two were added to the eight existing praetors. The old traditional form (*forma*) of the *res publica* was restored."[101] We could reasonably paraphrase this passage as "Augustus restored the *res publica*," but not as "Augustus restored the Republic." The reference to the raising of the number of praetors from eight to ten shows how precise and restricted is the meaning of "the form of the *res publica*" in this context.

Our most valuable source for these events would have been Livy. But while his preface refers to the closing of the gates of Janus in 29 (1, 19, 3), it happens not to refer to the political settlement which followed. However, insofar as we may judge by the *Epitome* 134, when he came to the settlement he described it in neutral terms: "Gaius Caesar, when everything had been put in order, and all the provinces brought within a definite framework, also received the *cognomen* Augustus." It is unnecessary and pointless to go on to list the references in later authors to the settlement of affairs at this time, for our concern is essentially with how it was described and thought of by contemporaries. But we may note the two well-known passages in which Tacitus characterises the development of Octavian from triumvir to princeps:

Ann. 1, 2: After he laid down the name of triumvir, he conducted himself as consul, and as content with (having) the tribunician power with which to protect the plebs.

Ann. 3, 28: Finally Caesar Augustus, when consul for the sixth time (A.D. 28), secure in his power, abolished what he had decreed as triumvir and gave us the laws by which we enjoy peace and the rule of a *Princeps*.

In both of these passages Tacitus alludes to, rather than describes, features of Augustus' position in the 20s B.C. Neither reflects any knowledge of a claim that the Republic had been restored. In fact the only statement in our sources which can be interpreted as making a claim of that sort comes from Augustus himself in *Res Gestae* 34. However well known, his words still need reconsideration:

101. Velleius 2, 89, 3–4.

In my sixth (28) and seventh (27) consulships, after I had extinguished the flames of the civil wars, and had gained control of all things by universal consent, I transferred the *res publica* from my own power [*potestas*] to the discretion [*arbitrium*] of the Senate and the Roman people. For this worthy act of mine I was named Augustus. . . . After this time I stood above everyone else by virtue of my *auctoritas*, but I did not have any more power than the other colleagues serving in office with me.

Augustus' words are carefully chosen: except for the consulates of 27–23, 5, and 2 B.C. he never held any republican magistracy after 27 January. What he says can only be absolved of actual falsehood by being understood to mean, in the strictest sense, that as consul he had no powers greater than those of his successive colleagues. But at all times he held other powers which they did not, in the initial period specifically the right to appoint legates to govern his provinces (see text to nn. 86–88); and after 23 B.C. his occasional consulates were essentially irrelevant to his position.

So we have to be cautious in considering the words he uses to describe the events of 28 and 27. He conspicuously fails to claim any constitutional basis for his power up to that point. But what he does claim is that he transferred the *res publica* to the *arbitrium* of the Senate and the Roman people. We cannot, in interpreting this, disregard the view of our only narrative source for these events, Cassius Dio, who considered that the offer of resignation of his powers made by Octavian in January 27 B.C. was a charade which was deliberately intended to, and immediately did, result in a formal continuation of his control of the state.[102] The word "discretion" (*arbitrium*), again, can refer to a historical fact if it alludes to Octavian's offer and the subsequent vote of Senate and People in January 27 B.C.; but if it carries an implication of a continued political freedom lasting beyond that point, that is another matter.

To Dio, of course, there never was any such event as the restoration of the Republic; for he, like Appian (*Hist.*, *praef.* 14/60), regarded Actium as the moment when monarchy returned to the Roman world.[103] It should, however, be noted that he, Appian, and Suetonius all refer to proposals or promises, made at various times by Octavian and Antonius, which would have amounted to "restoring the Republic." The form of words used is almost always that of *giving back* power:

102. Dio 53, 2, 6–12, 3.
103. Dio 51, 1, 1–2.

36 B.C. Appian, *BC* 5, 132/548: "Caesar . . . said that he would give back the whole *res publica*, if Antonius came back from Parthia."

34 B.C. Dio 49, 41, 6: "Now while Antonius was engaged as described, he had the effrontery to write to the Senate that he wished to give up his office and put the whole administration of the state into the hands of this body and of the people."

32 B.C. Dio 50, 7, 1: "Antonius . . . promised that that within two months after his victory he would relinquish his office and restore to the Senate and people all its authority."

30 B.C. Suetonius, *Div. Aug.* 28: "Twice Augustus thought of giving back the *res publica*: immediately after the fall of Antonius, when he remembered that Antonius had often accused him of being the one obstacle to such a change; and again when he could not shake off an exhausting illness. He then actually summoned the magistrates and the Senate to his house and gave them a financial account of the state of the empire."

29 B.C. Dio 52, 1, 1: "After this they [the Romans] reverted to what was, strictly speaking, a monarchy, although Caesar planned to lay down his arms and to entrust the management of the state to the Senate and to the people."

The last passage serves only as an introduction to the debate of Agrippa and Maecenas, and need not be taken as evidence of an intention by Octavian specifically in 29 to restore power to Senate and People. It should be noted that the earlier passages all refer to unfulfilled public promises from the Triumviral period, and that of Suetonius to an unfulfilled private intention. Suetonius gives no hint of an awareness that it had ever been claimed that the event in question had actually occurred.

However, since men writing in the established Empire could hardly have doubted that they were living under a monarchy, it might reasonably be objected that this has coloured their view of the crucial transitional period. So we may come finally to the essential question—how did the matter seem to contemporaries? First we may note the remarkable frankness with which Cornelius Nepos, writing some time after the death of Atticus at the end of March 32, and apparently after the death of Antonius, characterises the ambitions of the two Triumvirs—"when each of them desired to be the first man [*princeps*] not only in Rome but also in the entire world."[104] This passage was probably written before January 27. But the preface of Vitruvius'

104. Nepos, *Atticus* 20, 5.

De architectura is another matter, for it seems certain that it was written after January 27, and not later than 23 B.C.[105] The tone of his address to Augustus in his preface is therefore of primary importance for assessing the conceptions which obtained in Rome in the 20s:

> When your divine mind and power, Imperator Caesar, put the whole world under its command, your citizens gloried in your triumph and victory: for all their enemies were crushed by your invincible courage and all mankind obeyed your bidding. The Roman people and Senate, liberated from fear, has been guided by your bountiful thoughts and counsels. . . . When I observed that you cared not only about the common life of all men and the constitution of the state, but also about the provision of suitable public buildings. . . . Since, however, it was the heavenly counsel to commit him [Julius Caesar] to the regions of immortality and transfer imperial control to your power.

The passage contains no precise allusions to the current constitutional position. But its unabashed acceptance of the personal dominance of Augustus is unmistakable. Moreover, and this is the essential point, its obsequious flatteries could certainly be disregarded and considered as of no historical significance *if* they had been written under any conditions *except* those supposed by modern scholars, namely a recently proclaimed "restoration of the Republic." Had such a thing been proclaimed, Vitruvius' words would have been grossly undiplomatic—and would not have been written.

The same considerations apply, with rather less force, to a number of passages in Horace and Ovid. None is very precise or significant in itself, and most are less close in time to 27 B.C. than the preface of Vitruvius, but all are incompatible with the hypothesis that Augustus had proclaimed a restoration of the Republic:

Horace, *Odes* I, 12, 49–52: "O father and guardian of the human race, thou son of Saturn, to thee by fate has been entrusted the charge of mighty Caesar; mayst thou be lord of all, with Caesar next in power . . ." and later (58) "second to thee alone shall he with justice rule the broad earth."

105. Vitr. 5, 1, 7, referring to an "temple of Augustus" (*aedes Augusti*) at Fanum, ought to be conclusive, but it has sometimes been suggested on general historical grounds that the expression is impossible in Italy at this date. But other indications show that the work was complete by 23 or 22 B.C.: Schanz-Hosius, *Gesch d. röm. Lit.*[4] II (1935), 387–88; cf. A. Boethius, "Vitruvius and the Roman Architecture of His Age," *ΔΡΑΓΜΑ M.P. Nilsson dedicatum* (1939), 114.

Horace, *Odes* 3, 14, 14–16: "Neither civil strife nor death by violence will I fear, while Caesar holds the earth."

Horace, *Odes* 4, 5, 1–2: "Sprung from the blessed gods, best guardian of the race of Romulus, too long already art thou absent"; cf. 4, 15, 17: "while Caesar guards the state."

Ovid, *Fasti* 1, 531–32: "In the line of Augustus the guardianship of the fatherland shall abide: it is decreed that his house shall hold the reins of Empire."

Ovid, *Fasti* 2, 138–42: "All that exists beneath the canopy of Jove is Caesar's own. . . . Thine was a rule of force: under Caesar it is the laws that reign. Thou didst the name of master bear: he bears the name of *princeps*."

Ovid, *Tristia* 4, 4, 13–16: "Even the father of his country [*pater patriae*]— and what can be more like the behaviour of a fellow citizen?—submits to frequent mention in my verse, nor can he prevent it, for Caesar is the *res publica*, and of the common good I too have a share."

Nothing much needs be claimed for these well-known passages, except that they reveal a perfectly open recognition of the control of the Roman state by one man. With the exception of one of the passages of Ovid (*Fasti* 2, 138–42), none betrays the slightest anxiety to cloak this domination in constitutional forms. Even more emphatic is Horace in *Epistulae* 2, 1, 1–4:

> While you sustain so many and so heavy tasks alone, protect the life of Italy with arms, and adorn it with good customs, reform it by laws, I would be committing a sin against the public interest if by a prolonged discourse I were to interrupt your urgent concerns, Caesar.

Augustus himself objected to being acclaimed publicly as "master" (*dominus*),[106] refused the dictatorship in 22 B.C.,[107] and at the end of his life claimed, somewhat disingenuously as we have seen, to have excelled others only in authority (*auctoritas*). But he too had no hesitation in recognising the facts of his position. In a letter to his grandson Gaius he wrote, "But I pray to the Gods that whatever time is left to me I may pass with you safe and well, with the *res publica* in a flourishing condition, while you are playing the men and preparing to succeed to my position [*statio mea*]."[108] "Res publica" here means just what it does in a letter of Ateius Capito, who died in A.D. 22, referring to the love of liberty which possessed his great rival Antistius Labeo.

106. Suet., *Div. Aug.* 53.

107. *RG* 5; Vell. Pat. 2, 89; Suet., *Div. Aug.* 52; Dio 54, 1, 3–4.

108. Aulus Gellius, *NA* 15, 7, 3 = E. Malcovati, *Imperatoris Caesaris Augusti Operum Fragmenta*[5] (1969), *Ep.* XXII (Loeb trans.).

"But an excessive and mad love of liberty possessed the man, to such a degree that, although, the deified Augustus was then *princeps* and in control of the *res publica* [*rem publicam obtinebat*], he looked upon nothing as lawful, and accepted nothing, unless he had found it ordered and sanctioned by the old Roman law."[109]

Labeo thus saw the principate of Augustus in a light not entirely different from that in which Cascellius had seen the Triumvirate. Moreover, even the complaisant Capito regarded the principate as a state of affairs in which Augustus was "in control of the *res publica*." That the *res publica* had been duly "restored"—*restituta*—by Augustus he would surely have agreed; but he clearly did not suppose that it had ever been given back—*reddita*.

The regimes of Julius Caesar, of the Triumvirs, and of Augustus all had to adjust themselves in differing ways to the *res publica* of Rome and its institutions, whose tenacity in survival was to be one of the most remarkable features of imperial history. The temporary nature of the Triumvirate, its very lack of definition, and the competition for political support between its three, and then two, holders, caused it to be, if anything, more dependent on the Republican institutions than were the regimes of Caesar and of Augustus which preceded and followed it. The victory of Actium, the death of Antonius, and the stabilization of affairs in Rome all marked steps towards, not away from, the establishment of a monarchy; and no good evidence suggests that anybody at the time claimed, or supposed, otherwise.

---

109. Aulus Gellius, *NA* 13, 12, 1–2 (based on Loeb trans.).

CHAPTER ELEVEN

The Emperor, the Senate, and the Provinces*

Our sources for the constitutional settlement and division of the provinces in 27 B.C., and the modification of the settlement in 23 B.C., are notoriously brief and inadequate. Neither Augustus in the *Res Gestae* nor Velleius Paterculus mentions the provincial aspects of either settlement. The earliest source is Strabo (840): "he [Caesar] divided the whole of the empire into two parts, and assigned one portion to himself and the other to the Roman people [military provinces for himself, peaceful ones for the people] . . . and he divided each of the two portions into several provinces, of which some are called 'provinces of Caesar' and the others 'provinces of the people.' And to the 'provinces of Caesar' Caesar sends legates and procurators, dividing the territories in different ways . . . whereas to the 'provinces of the people' the people send praetors or proconsuls [list of public provinces]. . . . But the rest of the provinces are held by Caesar; and to some of these he sends as curators men of consular rank, and to others men of the praetorian rank, and to others men of equestrian rank" (Loeb. trans.). Then there is Suetonius (*Div. Aug.* 47): "The stronger provinces, which could neither easily nor safely be governed by annual magistrates, he took to himself; the others he assigned to proconsular governors selected by lot." Finally there is the account in Cassius Dio (53, 12, 2–3): "while he accepted all the care and the oversight of the public business, on the ground that it required some attention on his part, yet he declared he would not personally govern all the provinces, and that in the case of such provinces as he should, he would not do so indefinitely; and he did in fact, restore[1] to the Senate the weaker provinces, on the ground

* First published in *JRS* 56 (1966): 156–66. An earlier version of this chapter was given to the Open Meeting of the Society for the Promotion of Roman Studies on 6 March 1965.

1. Reimar, followed hesitantly by Boissevain, supplied "to the Senate" ($\tau\hat{\eta}$ $\beta o\upsilon\lambda\hat{\eta}$) at this point, from the texts of Xiphilinus and Zonaras. I am not convinced that this is justi-

that they were peaceful and free from war, while the more powerful . . . he retained, his professed motive in this was that the Senate might fearlessly enjoy the finest portion of the empire."

These are the only accounts of the division of the provinces in 27. For the settlement of 23 our evidence is even poorer, a single sentence in Cassius Dio (53, 32, 5): "They also permitted him to hold once for all the office of proconsul, so that he had neither to lay it down upon entering the *pomerium* [the sacred boundary of the city of Rome] nor to have it renewed again, and they gave him in the subject territory authority superior to that of the governor in each instance."

The paucity of the sources—combined with the fact that they are mainly in Greek—has led to insoluble problems about how Augustus' position was described at the time, or (alternatively) what the nature of his *imperium* vis-à-vis the provinces was. None the less, there is a fair consensus of opinion about the division of the provinces itself, and the nature of the administrative pattern which it produced. This can be summarized as follows: Augustus undertook the administration of a large province, comprising Spain, Gaul, and Syria, for a period of ten years, possibly with proconsular authority. He governed these provinces through legates appointed by, and responsible to, himself. The other provinces were governed by promagistrates responsible to the Senate. Down to 23 Augustus was also consul. In 23, while retaining his province, he abandoned the consulate and accepted "greater *imperium*," which gave him superior authority to promagistrates and enabled him to intervene outside his province when necessary. In normal circumstances, however, control of the provinces was divided between the Emperor and the Senate.[2]

This chapter is not concerned with the formal aspects of the settlements and the division of the provinces (except to note that the word province in the singular is not used by any ancient authority to refer to the imperial provinces as a whole).[3] Its purpose is to examine the standard view of the practical division between the two types of province, and its implications. The

---

fiable. See "'Senatorial' Provinces: An Institutionalised Ghost," *Ancient World* 20 (1989): 1 (chapter 13 in this volume).

2. For this summary I have relied mainly on H. H. Scullard, *From the Gracchi to Nero*[2] (1963), 217–22, which I have used as being an accurate, clear, and succinct account of the accepted view.

3. *A fortiori*, therefore, it is unsound to construe Augustus as the proconsul of a province in respect of which he got recurrent grants of public funds from the Senate; so A. H. M. Jones, *JRS* 40 (1950): 24 = *Studies in Roman Government and Law* (1960), 104.

standard view implies that there were in principle two administrative hierarchies, two separate ladders of responsibility. Legates are seen as something
less than full governors of their provinces, as essentially agents of the Emperor. Proconsuls are held to be, normally, independent of the Emperor but
"responsible" to the Senate. It is implied that the Emperor normally confined
himself to making regulations for the imperial provinces, and the Senate for
the public provinces. Only in exceptional circumstances would an Emperor
intervene in a public province.

In examining the validity of this view we cannot, it is clear, expect much
enlightenment from the three passages in ancient authors which describe
the division of the provinces in 27. All report the official explanation of the
division, the retention of potentially dangerous provinces by the Emperor;
Strabo (and, less clearly, Suetonius) makes the principal distinction that of
the type of governor sent; Dio alone says that the Emperor was to "rule"
(*archein*) his provinces. Strabo and Suetonius say nothing further about the
administrative consequences of the division. Dio does give more detail, in
the extensive general analysis of the imperial regime which he attaches to his
account of the settlement of 27.[4] To take the question any further, we must
do likewise, and examine the evidence available on the differences between
the two types of province and the relation to them of the Emperor and the
Senate.

Proconsuls and *Legati Augusti pro Praetore*

The two types of governor were appointed in quite different ways, and certain formal distinctions were maintained between them. Proconsuls were
assigned to provinces by lot.[5] They assumed their official dress (*insignia*) on
leaving the *pomerium* and retained them until their return, and could perform non-contentious judicial acts on the way to and from their provinces.[6]
They did not wear military dress or a sword, had the number of lictors corresponding to their rank as ex-praetor or ex-consul, and governed for one
year only.[7]

Legati Augusti pro praetore (legates of Augustus with praetorian rank) were
appointed by the Emperor and served until replaced; they assumed their

4. See F. Millar, *A Study of Cassius Dio* (1964), 94–95.

5. In exceptional circumstances, which are not in question here, they might be specially
appointed by the Emperor or the Senate, or prolonged for more than one year.

6. Pliny, *Epp.* 7, 16; *Dig.* 1, 16, 2.

7. Dio 53, 13, 2–4.

official dress only on entering their province, wore military uniform and a sword, and, irrespective of whether they were ex-praetors or ex-consuls, were assigned five lictors.[8]

These formal distinctions apart, it appears that a legate (*legatus Augusti pro praetore*) exercised a full *imperium*[9] within his province no less than did a proconsul; "to him had been entrusted the rods [*fasces*], symbols of magistracy, the praetorian jurisdiction, and the legions," as Domitius Celer observed in relation to Cn. Piso, legate of Syria.[10] Ulpian laid down that any *praeses* (governor) had "in [his] province . . . authority greater than everyone else after the emperor."[11] But were there differences in the contacts of legates and proconsuls with the Emperor?

Mandata from the Emperor

Domitius Celer, in his remarks about Piso, continued: "if an act of hostility occurs in the province, who is more entitled to oppose it with arms than he who has the authority of a legate and received personal *mandata* [codes of instructions]?" Thus legates received *mandata* from the Emperor, as did the prefect of Egypt,[12] the *Idios Logos* (the official in charge of the private account in Egypt) as we know from the preamble of the *Gnomon* (a handbook) and procurators in public[13] and imperial provinces. The earliest detailed evidence we have for the content of imperial *mandata* is given by the Greek inscription from Hama in Syria with an extract from the *mandata* of Domitian to the procurator of Syria.[14] The extract concerns the use of *diplomata* (certificates entitling the bearer to transport services), and the exaction of services by soldiers on the march. The first detailed evidence for *mandata* to senatorial legates comes from Pliny's correspondence with Trajan. The *mandata* Pliny received for his governorship of Bithynia included provisions for the disposition of soldiers, procedures in recruiting, the granting of pardon

8. Dio 53, 13, 6–8.

9. Mommsen, *Staatsrecht* II³, 244: "The governors of the imperial provinces are also holders of an independent higher *imperium*."

10. Tac., *Ann.* 2, 77, 1.

11. *Dig.* 1, 16, 8; 18, 4 (Ulpian, *Lib.* 39 *ad edictum*).

12. Philo, *In Flaccum* 74, "by the *mandata* [sent] to Magius Maximus." Cf. *Dig.* 1, 17, 1, "and this is stated in his *instructions*."

13. Tac., *Ann.* 4, 15, 3, "but if he had usurped the governor's authority and used military force, in that matter his [Tiberius'] *mandata* had been flouted."

14. *IGLS* V, 1998. For the view that the procurator concerned is the procurator of Syria, see *JRS* 53 (1963): 199.

to exiles, and the making of gifts out of city funds.[15] One provision at least of the *mandata*, that forbidding the formation of associations (*hetairiae*), was incorporated in the edict issued by Pliny on his arrival in the province.[16]

A century later than Pliny's governorship of Bithynia, both Cassius Dio and the lawyers clearly attest that imperial *mandata* were issued to all types of provincial official, procurators, legates, and proconsuls.[17] The extension of *mandata* to proconsuls seems in fact to have begun much earlier, for Antoninus Pius, when proconsul of Asia in 135/6, issued an edict based on *mandata*, which must presumably have been those of the Emperor.[18] If these were indeed the *mandata* of Hadrian, one might wonder whether it was not in the *mandata* that Hadrian made the first explicit affirmation of the legal privileges of *decuriones* (city councillors)[19]—or indeed whether the *mandata* in which Trajan released soldiers from the normal rules governing the validity of wills[20] were not also addressed to all provincial governors. [It has since been shown by G. P. Burton, *ZPE* 21 (1976): 63, that the issuing of *mandata* to proconsuls in fact took place from the beginning.]

Correspondence between Legates and the Emperor

There is ample evidence of legates writing letters to the Emperor and receiving letters from him. It is only necessary to quote a few instances by way of example. Augustus relieved a consular legate of his post on grounds of illiteracy when he saw that he had written "ixi" instead of "ipsi";[21] Philo details the correspondence between Petronius, legate of Syria, and Gaius over the placing of the statue of Gaius in the Temple.[22] Similarly we have Marsus, legate of Syria, writing to Claudius about Agrippa I's rebuilding of the walls of Jerusalem,[23] or legates of Gallic provinces writing to Augustus and

15. Pliny, *Epp.* 10, 22, 30, 56, 110–11. See L. Vidman, *Étude sur la correspondance de Pline le Jeune avec Trajan* (1960), 45–46, and A. N. Sherwin-White, *JRS* 52 (1962): 120–21.

16. Pliny, *Epp.* 10, 96, 7.

17. Dio 53, 15, 4; *Dig.* 1, 16, 6, 3; 47, 11, 6 *pr.*; 48, 3, 10; 48, 19, 27, 1–2.

18. *Dig.* 48, 3, 6, 1, "There is indeed extant a chapter of the *mandata* which the deified Pius issued under his edict when he was governor of the province of Asia."

19. *Dig.* 48, 19, 15, "The deified Hadrian forbade the capital punishment of any who were classed as decurions . . . and indeed it is very fully provided in the *mandata* that they are to be punished with the penalty of the Lex Cornelia."

20. Dig. 39, 1, 1 *pr.*

21. Suet., *Div. Aug.* 88.

22. Philo, *Legatio* 207, 248, 254–61, 333–34.

23. Jos., *Ant. Jud.* 19, 326–27.

Nerva.[24] Equestrian officials also might write to the Emperor, as did Classi-
cianus from Britain,[25] or Gavius Bassus, the prefect of the Pontic shore (*praefectus orae Ponticae*), from Bithynia.[26] Two points should be noted about this
correspondence between the Emperor and imperial officials. Firstly, it seems
very rarely to have been initiated by the Emperor; Trajan never communicated with Pliny in Bithynia except in response to letters from him. In
some cases where the actual correspondence with the legate or procurator
was begun by the Emperor, this was stimulated by a communication from
some other source in the province. Tiberius wrote to Pilate when the Jews
had written to him about the shields brought into Jerusalem;[27] Gaius' first
letter to Petronius about the statue was provoked by a letter from Herennius
Capito, the procurator of Jamnia, about the "desecration" of an altar to him
placed in the synagogue there by the Greeks.[28] But even a prolonged dispute
in an imperial province might never be referred to the Emperor. The dispute between the collectors of the tolls (*portoria*) and the city of Histria in
Moesia over the boundaries of the city territory, which produced documents
dating from 47 to the 60s which are collected in the *Horothesia* inscription
of Laberius Maximus of A.D. 100,[29] never reached any Emperor. Secondly,
almost our entire evidence for the correspondence between the Emperor and
officials in imperial provinces comes from literary sources. A single inscription of the first century refers to the establishment of a boundary at Sagalassos in Galatia by the legate and procurator on the basis of a letter from Nero.[30]
The earliest example of the text of an imperial letter to a provincial legate
inscribed by a city does not come until 201, the letter of Severus and Cara-
calla to Ovinius Tertullus, legate of Moesia Inferior, about the immunity of
Tyra.[31] This feature of the evidence is not accidental; it relates directly to the
fundamental distinction of type between imperial and public provinces.

24. Pliny, *NH* 9, 9; Philostratus, *VS* I, 19.

25. Tac., *Ann.* 14, 38, 4–5.

26. Pliny, *Epp.* 10, 22.

27. Philo, *Legatio* 303–5.

28. Philo, *Legatio* 200–207.

29. Abbott and Johnson, no. 68. The dates given here come from D. M. Pippidi, "Das
Stadtgebiet von Histria in römischer Zeit auf Grund der *OPOΘΕΣΙΑ* des Laberius Maximus *(SEG* I, 329)," *Dacia* 2 (1958): 227 = *Epigraphische Beiträge zur Geschichte Histrias in hellenistischer und römischer Zeit* (1962), 133. The full version of both texts of the inscription is
published for the first time by J. H. Oliver, "Texts A and B of the Horothesia Dossier at
Istros," *GRBS* 6 (1965): 143.

30. New text in *Anatolian Studies* 9 (1959): 84–85 = *SEG* XIX, 765.

31. Abbott and Johnson, no. 130 = *FIRA*² I, 86.

Prisoners Sent from Imperial Provinces

Imperial legates on occasion sent prisoners to the Emperor to be judged.[32] The earliest clear instance is that in 4 B.C. when Quinctilius Varus, as legate of Syria, sent the ringleaders of the Jewish rising after the death of Herod to stand trial before Augustus.[33] In 37 Vitellius, legate of Syria, sent Pilate to Rome when accused by the Samaritans.[34] About 52 Ummidius Quadratus, legate of Syria, sent Cumanus the procurator of Judaea, Celer a tribune, and a number of leading Jews and Samaritans to be tried by Claudius.[35] Similarly, Julius Civilis had been sent from Gaul for trial before Nero, presumably in 67 or 68, and was freed by Galba.[36] At about the same time Vespasian advised Agrippa II to send his general (*strategos*), Philippus, to be tried by Nero, on the accusation of the Tyrians,[37] and intended to send Josephus when he fell captive at Jotapata in 67.[38] One of Domitian's last acts was to condemn a *haruspex* (diviner) who had been sent from Germany by the legate, accused of predicting his death.[39]

It is thus clear that it was common for legates to pass on to the Emperor cases involving subversion or danger to the Emperor's person.

The Senate and Proconsuls

What evidence is there for either *mandata* of the Senate to proconsuls or specific communications from the Senate to individual proconsuls while in their provinces? The answer is simple—none.

The Senate and the Public Provinces

If we have no evidence of the Senate instructing or communicating with the proconsuls themselves, do we have evidence of it "administering" the public

32. I ignore here the question of prisoners who had appealed. Compare the discussion in *JRS* 66 (1966): 167ff. by P. D. A. Garnsey.

33. Jos., *Bell. Jud.* 2, 77–78; *Ant. Jud.* 17, 297.

34. Jos., *Ant. Jud.* 18, 88–89.

35. Jos., *Bell. Jud.* 2, 243–46; *Ant. Jud.* 20, 131–36. *Pace* E. M. Smallwood, "Some Comments on Tacitus, *Annals* 12, 54," *Latomus* 18 (1959): 560, I believe that Tacitus' account of these events is just wrong, and cannot be combined with the narrative in Josephus.

36. Tac., *Hist.* 4, 13.

37. Jos., *Vita* 407–9.

38. Jos., *Bell. Jud.* 3, 398.

39. Suet., *Dom.* 16; Dio 67, 16, 2. Compare the precisely similar case of a seer sent from Egypt in 41, Dio 49, 29, 4.

provinces as such? The question needs an answer, for in the orthodox view their control of these provinces was one of the prime functions of the Senate under the Principate.[40] There is in fact one single item of evidence which shows a decree of the Senate (*senatus consultum*) which applied to all proconsular provinces and to these alone. When Pliny in Bithynia was asked to take cases "concerning acknowledgement of children and granting of free-born rights to former slaves," he looked up (*respexi ad*) the relevant decree of the Senate, but found that it covered only provinces governed by proconsuls. It may be noted that it was only from the specific wording, *not* from the very fact that it was a decree of the Senate, that Pliny realized that it applied only to these provinces. Trajan asked him to send on the decree of the Senate, and nothing more is heard of the matter.[41]

This one item of evidence apart, we have a statement of a general principle made by Nero at the beginning of his reign: "Let the Senate retain its old functions! Let Italy and the public provinces take their stand before the tribunals of the consuls, and let the consuls grant them access to the Fathers [i.e., the Senate]: for the armies entrusted to his charge he would himself be responsible."[42] That the Senate did hear embassies from public provinces needs no proof—for instance, that from Baetica in A.D. 25 which asked permission for a temple to Tiberius and Livia.[43] We also have documentary evidence of decree of the Senate passed in response to the requests of communities or individuals within senatorial provinces. For instance there is the decree of the Senate of 112–17 allowing the request of Pergamon for a second series of quinquennial iselastic games in honour of Trajan and Zeus Philios. But this is a mixed case, for the inscription also contains an extract from the *mandata* of Trajan specifying the conditions, and referring to the decree of the Senate, and also a fragmentary letter of Trajan to Pergamon, probably in response to an embassy.[44] There is also the decree of the Senate of 138 permitting the establishment of a fair or market on the Saltus Beguensis in Africa, and that from the reign of Pius allowing Cyzicus in Asia to have a corps of young men (*neoi*).[45]

40. See, e.g., O'Brien Moore, "Senatus," P-W, Supp. VI, 793–95.

41. Pliny, *Epp.* 10, 72–73.

42. Tac., *Ann.* 13, 4, 3.

43. Tac., *Ann.* 4, 37, I.

44. *CIL* III, 7086 = *IGR* IV, 336 = Abbott and Johnson, no. 73. The fragmentary earlier part of the inscription *may* (as supposed in *IGR*) contain a letter of the proconsul enclosing the *mandata* and the decrees of the Senate.

45. *FIRA*² I, 47, 48.

The Senate and the Imperial Provinces

We have thus one piece of evidence showing a decree of the Senate for pub-lic provinces only, and a fair amount showing the Senate dealing with indi-vidual public provinces or with communities within them. Were the Senate's activities confined to such provinces? So far as the specifically law-making functions of the Senate go, the answer is clearly no. There is no suggestion in the sources (apart from the one letter of Pliny) that modifications in pri-vate or public law made by the Senate were valid in only half the Empire. If proof is needed, it is explicitly stated that the *Senatus Consultum Apronia-num*, passed in the reign of Hadrian, allowed legacies to "all communities which are under the rule of the Roman people."[46] Similarly, the preamble of the *Gnomon* of the *Idios Logos* states that its provisions are those laid down by Augustus, with modifications by later Emperors, by the Senate, by prefects, or by the *Idios Logos* himself.[47] Other documents from Egypt show requests for the appointment of a guardian "in accordance with the Lex Iulia et Titia and a decree of the Senate" (*datio tutoris* "e lege Iulia et Titia et ex s.c.").[48]

The text of the *Senatus Consultum Calvisianum* of 4 B.C., establishing a new procedure for cases of extortion (*repetundae*) against provincial governors, comes from a public province, Cyrene, but is prefaced by an imperial edict and clearly refers to all provinces.[49] In A.D. 17 the Senate, voting Germanicus his eastern command, gave him "a greater *imperium*, in all regions he might visit, than those of the governors holding office there by the lot or by im-perial appointment."[50] In 62 the Senate resolved, on the motion of Nero, that it should be forbidden to propose in provincial councils to send embas-sies to the Senate in praise of either proconsuls or imperial legates.[51] Finally, there is the decree of the Senate about reducing the expenses on gladiatorial games (*senatus consultum de sumptibus ludorum gladiatorum minuendis*) of 177–80. The two texts we have of it both come from places in public provinces, Sardis in Asia and Italica in Baetica. But the regulations reducing the price

46. *Dig.* 36, 1, 27; Ulp., *Reg.* 24, 28.

47. See S. Riccobono, *Il Gnomon dell' Idios Logos* (1951), esp. pp. 86–87, also R. Tauben-schlag, *The Law of Greco-Roman Egypt in the Light of the Papyri*[2] (1955), 32.

48. Cavenaille, *Corp. Pap. Lat.* 200, 202, 203 (restored), 205 (restored).

49. *SEG* IX, 8; Ehrenberg and Jones, no. 311. Cf. F. de Visscher, *Les édits d'Auguste décou-verts à Cyrène* (1940), 137–38. I do not share the view of P. A. Brunt, "Charges of Provincial Maladministration under the Early Principate," *Historia* 10 (1961): 189, that this procedure soon lapsed.

50. Tac., *Ann.* 2, 43, 2. Cf. 3, 12, 1.

51. Tac., *Ann.* 15, 22, 1–2.

of gladiators for games given by local officials are explicitly to be applied in both types of province—"let those most honorable men, who are proconsuls . . . and those who govern provinces without being appointed by the lot, be aware."[52] Moreover, there are specific references to games given by priests (*sacerdotes*) in the imperial provinces of the Tres Galliae.

It may be noted also that we do find the Senate dealing with individual places in the imperial provinces. In A.D. 25 it was, it seems, the Senate which heard rival delegations from Lacedaimon and Messenia, although Achaea was then under an imperial legate.[53] Dio records that through Saoterus, the favourite of Commodus, Nicomedia obtained from the Senate permission for a festival and a temple of Commodus;[54] Bithynia had been an imperial province since about 165.[55]

The Emperor and the Imperial Provinces

It is not worth asking whether the Emperor *confined* his activities to the imperial provinces, since no one could suggest that he did. But did he on occasion issue edicts or other regulations for the imperial provinces alone? There is one single item of evidence: in 26 B.C. Augustus excluded Cornelius Gallus, before his condemnation and suicide, from the imperial provinces.[56]

The Emperor and the Provinces in General

We have a number of instances of general edicts or pronouncements by Emperors affecting all the provinces alike. The earliest of these, I would tentatively suggest, is that in the notoriously puzzling Augustan inscription from Cyme in Asia.[57] I would take it that the first, Greek, document is a general pronouncement by Augustus and Agrippa in 27 B.C., ordering the restitution of public and sacred properties in all the provinces. On this view *hekastes eparchias* in line 4 does in fact mean "of every province";[58] and the text in

52. *ILS* 5163 = *FIRA*² I, no. 49; J. H. Oliver and R. E. A. Palmer, "Minutes of an Act of the Roman Senate," *Hesperia* 24 (1955): 320.

53. Tac., *Ann.* 4, 43, 1–6.

54. Dio 72, 12, 2. See F. Grosso, *La lotta politica al tempo di Commodo* (1964), 552.

55. See D. Magie, *Roman Rule in Asia Minor* (1950), chap. 28, n. 7.

56. Suet., *Div. Aug.* 66; Dio 53, 23, 6.

57. *SEG* XVIII, 555; XX, 15, where the bibliography is given.

58. I cannot follow the view of J. H. Oliver, "The Main Problem of the Augustus Inscription from Cyme," *GRBS* 4 (1963): 115, modified in "Augustan, Flavian and Hadrianic

lines 8–9 means "whoever is governor of the (relevant) province," and is a way of referring, without a list of different titles, to the various types of provincial governor. The Greek document is followed by a letter, given in Latin and Greek, from [.] Vinicius, proconsul of Asia, to the city of Cyme. I accept the view of the original editor, H. W. Pleket, that this is L. Vinicius, suffect consul in 33 and thus proconsul probably in 27–26.[59] He takes action on the information of one Apollonides L(ucii) f(ilius) No[raceus] that the "shrine of Liber Pater" has been "possessed" by a private person, "even though the club members wished to restore the cult to the god by order of Augustus Caesar" (ll. 4–5); he also writes that the temple is to be inscribed "Imp(erator) Caesar, son of the deified Iulius, Augustus restored it" (ll. 8–9). Thus, whatever the exact formal status of the pronouncement by Augustus and Agrippa (and it does not fit precisely into any known category), it was regarded in the province as an order of Augustus.[60]

Then we have the edict, dating to 12 B.C.,[61] by which Augustus protected the traditional right of the Jews to send money to Jerusalem. It was issued, it should be noted, at the instance of embassies from the Jews of two public provinces, Asia and Cyrene. The text of the edict, preserved by Josephus,[62] mentions that it is to be inscribed at a place appointed by the provincial council of Asia.[63] A few years later Iullus Antonius, proconsul of Asia, wrote a letter, also reproduced by Josephus,[64] to Ephesus, saying that the Jews had quoted to him the permission granted them by Augustus and Agrippa to observe their ancestral customs, and instructing the Ephesians to behave accordingly. In the same context Josephus gives a letter of Caesar to Norbanus Flaccus, proconsul of Asia, instructing him to let the Jews send money to

---

Praefecti Iure Dicundo in Asia and Greece," *AJPh* 84 (1963): 162, that this refers to a "prefecture" of a *Praefectus iure dicundo* (prefect with civil jurisdiction) in a Greek city.

59. H. W. Pleket, *The Greek Inscriptions in the "Rijksmuseum van Oudheden" at Leyden* (1958), no. 57; see pp. 61–62 and cf. R. Syme, *JRS* 45 (1955): 159.

60. I cannot follow the views of K. M. T. Atkinson, " 'Restitutio in integrum' and 'iussum Augusti Caesaris' in an Inscription at Leyden," *RIDA* 7 (1960): 227, that the pronouncement of Augustus and Agrippa expresses a decree of the Senate, that the second document dates to after 23 B.C., or that "iussum" (order) is not a reference to the first document. Furthermore, as will be shown below, imperial action in Asia was not unusual even between 27 and 23 B.C.

61. For the date, see G. W. Bowersock, "C. Marcius Censorinus, Legatus Caesaris," *HSCPh* 68 (1964): 207.

62. Jos., *Ant. Jud.* 16, 160–65; 162–65 = Ehrenberg and Jones, no. 314.

63. See J. Deininger, *Die Provinziallandtage der römischen Kaiserzeit* (1965), 37, n. 1.

64. Jos., *Ant. Jud.* 16, 172–73 = Ehrenberg and Jones, no. 313.

Jerusalem,[65] and also Norbanus' letter to Sardis, referring to Caesar's *mandata*—"Caesar has written to me, ordering."[66] Philo quotes Norbanus' letter
to Ephesus on the same point—"I therefore write to you to let you know
that this is what he orders to be done."[67] Norbanus might have been the consul of 38 B.C. or of 24 B.C.; the former could have been proconsul in the 20s
or even, most improbably, the 30s.[68] But the man concerned is most likely
the younger Norbanus, who could have been proconsul soon after 12 B.C.[69]

Philo also records that after the death of Sejanus Tiberius wrote to all those
appointed as governors everywhere to reassure the Jews about their rights.[70]
Claudius in 41 also promulgated a general edict confirming the privileges
of the Jews throughout the Empire which he ordered to be inscribed in the
civitates, *coloniae*, and *municipia* in Italy and outside. The edict was promulgated by Claudius, according to Josephus' text, at the request of Agrippa I
and Herod of Chalcis.[71]

Also from Claudius' reign we have the edict about the exaction of transport services (*vehiculatio*), attested on an inscription from Tegea.[72] It explicitly
refers to both Italy and all the provinces, and dates to 49 or 50, after Achaea
had been restored to proconsular rule. In 58 Nero issued an edict about abuses
by tax-collectors—"The Emperor . . . issued an edict that . . . the praetor
at Rome, the propraetors or proconsuls in the provinces, were to waive the
usual order of trial in favour of actions against tax collectors."[73] Vespasian
issued one general edict to all communities that embassies should not number more than three men,[74] and another in 74, on the privileges of doctors
and teachers. This is attested by an inscription from Pergamon in Asia, and is
followed on the same stone by a rescript of Domitian on the same subject.[75]
Domitian issued an edict, evidently of general application, on the immu-

65. Jos., *Ant. Jud.* 16, 166.

66. Jos., *Ant. Jud.* 16, 171.

67. Philo, *Legatio* 315.

68. See D. Magie, *Roman Rule in Asia Minor* (1950), 1580; R. Syme, *The Roman Revolution*
(1939), 303; *JRS* 45 (1955): 159.

69. See E. M. Smallwood, *Philonis Alexandrini Legatio ad Gaium* (1961), 310.

70. Philo, *Legatio* 161.

71. Jos., *Ant. Jud.* 19, 286–91 = Charlesworth, *Documents*, no. 15.

72. *ILS* 214 = Charlesworth, *Documents*, no. 11.

73. Tac., *Ann.* 13, 51.

74. *Dig.* L, 7, 5, 6, "An edict of the deified Vespasian, directed to all cities, ordained that
no more than three be sent on an embassy."

75. *FIRA*² I, 73, 77.

nity of veterans from tolls,[76] and also his famous edict on the uprooting of vines in the provinces. This certainly applied in proconsular Asia, for it was this province which sent an embassy to protest, headed by the great sophist Scopelianus, whose speech so moved the Emperor that he not only revoked the edict but laid penalties on those who failed to plant vines.[77] Finally one might mention Nerva's edict, attested by Pliny, which confirmed all benefactions granted by previous emperors; it applied in all provinces including Bithynia.[78]

The Emperor and Individual Public Provinces or Communities within Them

Pliny in Bithynia found that a modification of the provincial Lex Pompeia had been made by an edict of Augustus (though the edict may have been general).[79] He also sent to Trajan the petition of Nicaea asking for confirmation of the right of claiming possession of the property (*vindicatio bonorum*) of citizens who died intestate, which had been granted (*concessa*) by Augustus; it is probable that the original concession had also been petitioned for by the city.[80] Pliny also mentions an alleged edict of Augustus to Andania in Achaea (though the reading of the name is not certain) on the subject of foundlings (*threptoi*).[81] Similarly, in his letter to the Saborenses in Baetica, Vespasian confirmed the "the right to levy taxes which you claim to have received from the deified Augustus,"[82] while Claudius, writing to the city of Thasos, said "I preserve for you, in accordance with the decisions of the deified Augustus, all the privileges as (were received) from him."[83] (Thasos was then in the province of Macedonia.) Then an inscription on a statue basis from Ephesus reads (the text is repeated in Greek), "By the benefaction of the deified Caesar Augustus, from the income of sacred lands which he donated

76. *FIRA²* I, 76.

77. Suet., *Dom.* 7; Philostratus, *VS* I, 21.

78. Pliny, *Epp.* 10, 58.

79. Pliny, *Epp.* 10, 79–80. The evidence collected by J. Morris, *Listy Filologické* 87 (1964): 317, suggests that the minimum age for magistracies may generally have been lowered to twenty-five by Augustus.

80. Pliny, *Epp.* 10, 83–84.

81. Pliny, *Epp.* 10, 65, 3.

82. *ILS* 6092 = Abbott and Johnson, no. 61 = *FIRA²* I, 74.

83. C. Dunant and J. Pouilloux, *Recherches sur l'histoire et les cultes de Thasos* (1957), 66, no. 179, ll. 7–8.

to Diana, the road was paved when Sex. Appuleius was proconsul"; if the inscription is contemporary with the paving of the road, then Sex. Appuleius
must be the consul of A.D. 14 and proconsul some time under Tiberius.[84]

The edicts of Augustus from Cyrene[85] constitute the standard example of
imperial "intervention" in a public province. The first edict, however, issued
in 7–6 B.C. on the appointment of jurors, was provoked by complaints from
delegations sent by the cities (l. 8). Augustus then gives preliminary *mandata*
until the Senate has conferred on the matter *or* he himself has found a better
solution (ll. 12–13). He in fact lays down the procedure to be followed by
the proconsuls—lines 13–14: "it seems to me that those who are in charge of
the province of Crete and Cyrene will act well and properly if they put forward . . ." We do not know whether he also wrote directly to the proconsul,
or in what terms. The second edict arose, firstly, from the fact that P. Sextius Scaeva, probably but not certainly the proconsul,[86] had sent three men
in chains to Augustus, as having something to reveal on a matter affecting
public safety; and, secondly, from the fact that one of the three had been accused, by a delegation from Cyrene, of removing statues inscribed with the
name of Augustus. Augustus decreed that the man should not leave Rome
until he had investigated the matter. In the third and fourth edicts there is
no indication of how the matter came before Augustus.

Subsequently, there are only rare cases of imperial measures for specific
public provinces, or places within them, in the form of edicts. There is, however, the edict of Paullus Fabius Persicus, proconsul of Asia under Claudius,[87]
which begins with a reference to an edict (*epikrima*) of Claudius, beneficial
not only to the city of Ephesus but to the whole province, which was to
be inscribed on a column in Ephesus. The proconsul announces, after a reference to his own beneficial principles of government, that he will act in
accordance with the model provided by the Emperor, who has all mankind
under his care (II, 1–17). Later he makes brief references to the restoration
of revenues to the temple of Artemis at Ephesus by Augustus (IV, 5–6), and
to a constitution (*diataxis*; *constitutio* in the Latin text) of Vedius Pollio confirmed by Augustus (VI, 10–11; cf. VII, 3–4, VIII, 4).[88] Towards the end of

84. *Jahreshefte Öst. Arch. Inst.* 45 (1960; pub. 1963): Beiblatt, 42.

85. References in n. 49.

86. De Visscher (n. 49), 78, assumes that he was proconsul; P. Romanelli, *La Cirenaica
romana* (1943), 83, leaves the question open.

87. F. K. Dörner, *Der Erlass des Statthalters von Asia Paullus Fabius Persicus* (1935), Greek
text on pp. 37–40. See Magie (n. 68), 545–46.

88. K. M. T. Atkinson, "The 'Constitutio' of Vedius Pollio at Ephesus and Its Analogies,"
RIDA 9 (1962): 261, makes a strong case for the view that "constitutio" means "endowment"

the inscription (VIII, 11–12) he refers to the recognition by Augustus of the privileges (*philanthropa*) of the hymnodes (hymn singers) who performed at the provincial sanctuary at Pergamon.[89]

Finally, one may mention the edict by which in 66–67 Nero summoned the inhabitants of Achaea to the Isthmus to hear his speech granting them freedom.[90] The comparative rarity of imperial edicts affecting specific provinces or places is, however, easily explained. The Emperors normally communicated with cities or provinces by letter, such letters almost never being written except in response to an initiative from below, normally in the form of an embassy from the community. Some of these were in origin formal or diplomatic, like the embassy from Ilium consoling Tiberius on the death of Drusus which Suetonius reveals.[91] Even these were actually heard by the Emperor; Tiberius felt that the Ilian embassy was somewhat belated and replied sarcastically by consoling them on the death of their fellow citizen, Hector. The ambassadors sent by the city of Sardis in 5 B.C. to congratulate Augustus and Gaius Caesar on the latter's assumption of the *toga pura* were instructed also to speak to Augustus about matters of interest to Sardis and the province of Asia.[92]

If we take the Augustan period alone, we find a long series of embassies to Augustus from public provinces, which begins before, and continues unaffected after, the division of the provinces in 27 B.C. In 31 B.C. Octavian wrote in reply to an embassy from Mylasa in Caria.[93] In 29 the ship on which Strabo was crossing the Aegean took on board a fisherman from Gyarus, who was going to request Octavian, then at Corinth, for a remission of tribute.[94] In 26 B.C. Augustus wrote to Chios a letter, which is referred to in a letter to the city from the proconsul of Asia thirty or more years later, in which he confirmed the freedom of the city.[95] In 26 or 25 B.C. the city of Tralles was struck by an earthquake and sent an embassy, including the poet Chaeremon (whose verses on the journey are quoted by Agathias), all the way to Tar-

---

rather than something like "legal enactment," and therefore for abandoning the view that he necessarily held some official position in the province. But even if this is correct I cannot follow her interpretation of the purpose and functioning of the endowment. I am very grateful to Dr. R. P. Duncan-Jones for discussing this with me.

89. See Magie (n. 68), 448 and n. 58.

90. *Syll.*³ 824 = Abbott and Johnson, no. 56 = Charlesworth, *Documents*, Nero no. 2.

91. Suet., *Tib.* 52.

92. *Sardis*, VII, 1, 8, 1. Cf. Deininger (n. 63), 56.

93. *Syll.*³ 768 = Abbott and Johnson, no. 30.

94. Strabo 485.

95. *Syll.*³ 785 = Abbott and Johnson, no. 40 = Ehrenberg and Jones, no. 317.

raconensis to implore Augustus for aid, which he granted.[96] About 25 B.C.,
when the Senate made a treaty with Mytilene, an embassy, including the
poet Crinagoras, may perhaps also have gone to Spain to Augustus.[97] Then in
12 B.C., or just before, came the embassies from the Jews of Asia and Cyrene,
mentioned earlier (text to n. 62), and perhaps in the same year came an embassy from Eresos on Lesbos, possibly to offer consolation on the death of
Agrippa;[98] and in 7–6 B.C. the embassies from Cyrene (text to n. 86). In 6 B.C.
two ambassadors came from the free city of Cnidus to accuse a man (already
deceased) and his wife of the murder of another citizen of the place. Augustus says in his letter to the city that he ordered his "friend" Asinius Gallus (the
proconsul of Asia) to make an investigation and then heard the case himself.[99]
In 5 B.C. there was an embassy from Sardis (text to n. 92). At unknown dates
in the reign embassies came from Athens to secure funds for the completion of the Agora of Caesar and Augustus,[100] from Tegea,[101] and (at some date
between 27 and 11 B.C.) from Mytilene to both Augustus and the Senate.[102]

   In the same reign the imperial provinces produce evidence of embassies
to the Emperor only from Judaea—separately from the Jews and the Greek
cities[103]—after the death of Herod in 4 B.C., from Alexandria in A.D. 13,[104] and
from Tarraco.[105] A compilation of the evidence for embassies in later reigns
would show a similar disparity, though not so marked.[106]

   96. Agathias 2, 17; Euseb; *Chron.* 2, 140–41 Schoene; Strabo 579. Cf. G. W. Bowersock, *Augustus and the Greek World* (1965), 87 and 157.

   97. *IGR* IV, 33 = Ehrenberg and Jones, no. 307. See C. A. Cichorius, *Rom und Mytilene* (1888), 55; Bowersock (n. 96), 36. The notion of an embassy to Spain depends on the view that the phrase "in Tarraco, Iberia" in *IGR* IV, 38, l. 8, refers to such an occasion. But cf. IV, 39, l. 13 where Tarraco is mentioned in a quite different context.

   98. *IGR* IV, 7.

   99. *Syll.*³ 780 = Abbott and Johnson, no. 36 (there is no reference to appeal in the case, as stated there) = Ehrenberg and Jones, no. 312. R. K. Sherk, "C. Asinius Gallus and His Governorship of Asia," *GRBS* 7 (1966): 57, argues (not quite convincingly) that Gallus was at the time merely "a friend of the *princeps*" (*amicus principis*) in Rome, and not proconsul until the following year.

   100. *IG*² II–III, 3175. See Bowersock (n. 96), 96.

   101. *IG* V, 2, 25.

   102. *IGR* IV, 39.

   103. The Jewish people, Jos., *Bell. Jud.* 2, 80; *Ant. Jud.* 17, 300; the Greek cities, Nic. Dam., *FGrH* 90, F 136 (9).

   104. *P.Oxy.* 2435 verso.

   105. Quint., *Inst.* 6, 3, 77.

   106. I rely here on a preliminary collection of the evidence, which could not be pub-

The Emperor and Proconsuls

It has already been noted above (text to nn. 17–19) that Emperors did in fact issue *mandata* to proconsuls as well as to legates. Moreover, some occasions have been mentioned on which an Emperor gave direct *mandata* to proconsuls, Augustus to Norbanus Flaccus and Asinius Gallus, Tiberius to all governors. The Cyrene Edicts I and IV laid down a procedure for the proconsuls, but may not have involved direct *mandata* to them. A further possible case is reported by Tacitus, who says that "some people" recorded that the soldiers who killed Julia in A.D. 14 had been sent not from Rome but by L. Asprenas, the proconsul of Africa, "at Tiberius' initiative."[107] The very fragmentary letter of Claudius to Delphi in 52, which mentions the proconsul Junius Gallio, might indicate consultation of Claudius by him, *mandata* to him, or neither.[108]

The evidence is fuller for the Flavian period. The letter of Titus to Munigua in Baetica, resulting from an appeal by the *municipium* against the judgement of a former proconsul, mentions that he has sent *mandata* to the proconsul—"since I wrote to Gallicanus the proconsul, my friend."[109] Pliny in his correspondence with Trajan mentions letters of Domitian to Lappius Maximus, evidently proconsul of Bithynia, to Avidius Nigrinus and Armenius Brocchus proconsuls (probably of Achaea), and to Minicius Rufus, and of Nerva to Tullius Iustus, both probably proconsuls of Bithynia.[110] Similarly we have on an inscription from Delphi references both by Domitian himself, writing to the Delphians, and by the proconsul, to a letter of his giving *mandata* to the proconsuls; in referring to these the proconsul uses expressions like "by order" and "as the emperor has ordered."[111] Also from Delphi we have a letter of Trajan in which he seems to refer to *mandata* he has given both to the proconsul and to the procurator of Achaea.[112]

From the reign of Hadrian we have the earliest certain evidence of proconsuls writing to consult the Emperor, and receiving answers from him. The *Digest* mentions rescripts of Hadrian to proconsuls of Macedonia,[113] Bae-

---

lished in its present incomplete state. See now *The Emperor in the Roman World*² (1992), chap. 7.

107. Tac., *Ann.* 1, 53, 9.

108. *Syll.*³ 801D.

109. M. Nesselhauf, *Madrider Mitteilungen* 1 (1960): 148; *AE* 1962, 288.

110. Pliny, *Epp.* 10, 58, 65, 72.

111. *Syll.*³ 821 = McCrum and Woodhead, *Select Documents*, no. 463.

112. E. Bourguet, *De rebus Delphicis* (1905), 70.

113. *Dig.* 22, 5, 3, 3.

tica,[114] Crete, and Achaea.[115] Inscriptions record a rescript of Hadrian to the proconsul of Achaia or Macedonia,[116] and a letter from Avidius Quietus, proconsul of Asia, written to Hadrian in 125–126 about a land dispute at Aezani, with the Emperor's reply.[117] Justin and Eusebius quote a letter written in the early 120s to the proconsul of Asia, Minicius Fundanus, in reply to a letter from his predecessor, Silvanus Granianus, about the judicial procedure with regard to Christians.[118]

The evidence available clearly shows a tendency for imperial letters to proconsuls to become more frequent, followed in Hadrian's reign by the beginning of consultation of the Emperor by them. It thus seems proper to conclude that in this respect there was a certain difference between legates and proconsuls, which finally disappeared in the first half of the second century.

Prisoners Sent for Trial by Proconsuls

If P. Sextius Scaeva was, as is probable, proconsul of Cyrene in 7–6 B.C. (text to n. 86), that is the earliest example of a proconsul sending prisoners for trial before the Emperor (the category of prisoners from public provinces accused in the first instance before the Emperor is not considered here). Then, in 65, Tacitus mentions Claudius Demianus "who because of his crimes was imprisoned by Vetus the proconsul of Asia and subsequently released by Nero";[119] and in about 73 the proconsul of Cyrene sent a Jewish rebel, Jonathan, to Vespasian, who condemned him to be burnt to death.[120] The category of prisoners sent by proconsuls is thus less numerous and less clear in its nature than that of men sent by legates, but such a category did exist.

Conclusions

When the evidence is assembled, the notion of two separate administrative hierarchies, whose lines of demarcation were crossed only by the Em-

114. *Dig.* 48, 8, 4, 1–2 = *Coll.* 1, 11, 1 (quoting full text of consultation and reply).

115. *Dig.* 48, 16, 14; 1, 16, 10.

116. *ILS* 5974[a].

117. *OGIS* 502 = *IGR* IV, 571 = Abbott and Johnson, no. 82.

118. Eusebius, *HE* 4, 8, 6; 9, 1–3; Justin, *Apol.* I, 68–69. See W. H. C. Frend, *Martyrdom and Persecution in the Early Church* (1965), 223–25.

119. Tac., *Ann.* 16, 10, 2. There is no reason to think, as presumed by A. N. Sherwin-White, *Roman Society and Roman Law in the New Testament* (1963), 60, that the man had appealed.

120. Jos., *Vita* 424–25; cf. *BJ* 7, 441–50.

peror in occasional "interventions," becomes entirely untenable. The Emperor did not govern the Imperial provinces either as a whole or individually "through" his legates; like proconsuls, the legates governed their provinces themselves. In no sense whatsoever did the Senate "control" the senatorial provinces, and the proconsuls were not "responsible to" it. Both the Emperor and the Senate, predominantly of course the former, made regulations (sometimes jointly) affecting all the provinces. The Emperor could deal directly with provinces of both types or with communities within them. The Senate is not attested as dealing with any imperial province as a whole, but is found dealing with individual places in these provinces. The sole concrete distinctions are in the direct relations between the Emperor and legates and proconsuls. The Emperor, invariably it seems when stimulated by some other source of information, pressure, or complaint from within the province, might initiate correspondence with either type of governor. But legates are attested initiating such correspondence quite commonly in the first century—to make reports or ask advice—while proconsuls began to do so under Hadrian.

The practical consequences of the division of the provinces were thus two, the different methods of appointment and length of tenure of the two types of governor, and the extent and nature of the communications between them and the Emperor—and of these the second disappeared after a century and a half. There was not even a constitutional principle by which the Senate kept to "its" half of the Empire. Tiberius, endeavouring to observe the strictest propriety, rebuked his legates for not sending reports of their achievements to the Senate,[121] and chose to consult the Senate on taxation, the recruitment and discharge of soldiers, the disposition of the legions, and the prolongation of commands.[122] Then we have Tacitus' account of what happened when delegations from the Greek cities of Asia and Cyprus arrived in A.D. 22 to make their claims for rights of asylum for their temples: "[Tiberius] vouchsafed to the Senate a shadow of the past by submitting the claims of the provinces to the discussion of its members."[123] The implication that the delegations had originally come to Tiberius seems to be confirmed by an inscription from Didyma, which was one of the temples involved, honouring a man who had gone as ambassador to the Emperor about the right of asylum.[124] Or one can compare the case mentioned by Suetonius, when some ambassadors from Africa came to the consuls to complain that they

121. Suet., *Tib.* 32.
122. Suet., *Tib.* 30; Dio 57, 7.
123. Tac., *Ann.* 3, 60, 1.
124. *Ins. Didyma* 107.

were being delayed by Tiberius, to whom they had been sent.[125] A similar intermingling of responsibilities is illustrated by Tacitus under 23: "Meanwhile Tiberius . . . was dealing with . . . petitions from the provinces. On his proposal, senatorial decrees were passed to relieve the towns of Cibyra in Asia and Aegium in Achaia, both damaged by earthquake, by remitting their tribute for three years";[126] Asia was, of course, a public, Achaea then an imperial, province. Communities in senatorial (and to a lesser extent in imperial) provinces sent embassies at will to either the Senate or the Emperor. Thus a man from Cos in the Julio-Claudian period is honoured on an inscription for having often been on embassies for his city, at his own expense, to the Emperors, the Senate, and the proconsuls of Asia,[127] while another man from there had often been ambassador just to the Emperors.[128] Then, for instance, under Trajan we find the Bithynians first accusing Q. Varenus before the Senate, and then sending ambassadors with a decree of the provincial council to the Emperor stating that they were dropping the case: one of the ambassadors appeared also before the Senate—"explained their reasons for dropping the prosecution and asked that no decision should be taken before the Emperor held an inquiry." Trajan undertook to enquire into the intentions of the province.[129]

The weakness of the accepted interpretation of the division of the provinces is not merely that it envisages a division of responsibility and authority which simply did not exist. It is rather that it and its implications depend on a number of assumptions about Roman "administration" (a term which itself tends to mislead) which are themselves invalid. If we look at the actual evidence for how the Empire worked, what we see is not an arrangement of compartments, of administrative hierarchies, but an array of institutions, communities, and persons, the relations between which depended on political and diplomatic choices which could be made by any of the parties. What passes for "administration" was in fact largely either jurisdiction and the settlement of disputes, or diplomacy. Moreover, the centralization of *power* in the hands of an individual did not mean the centralization of initiative. On the contrary, the imperial power was largely static or inert, and its activity stimulated by pressures and initiatives from below. What initiatives were taken depended on the standing of individuals and communities, and their

125. Suet., *Tib.* 31.

126. Tac., *Ann.* 4, 13, 1.

127. A. Maiuri, *Nuova Silloge epigrafica di Rodi e Cos* (1925), no. 462.

128. W. R. Paton and E. L. Hicks, *The Inscriptions of Cos* (1891), no. 94.

129. Pliny, *Epp.* 5, 20; 6, 5; 7, 6; 10.

relations with Rome and the Court. It is thus not an accident that so much of the evidence in this chapter concerns the province of Asia, for it was precisely those established, civilized provinces—Asia, Africa, Baetica—which were given over to proconsular rule, whose inhabitants were in a position to make direct approaches to the Emperor. As Dio of Prusa said, addressing his fellow citizens, "If you had not listened, and the proconsuls had paid no attention either, it would not have been difficult for me to write to the Emperor."[130] Thus by a paradox which was the direct result of the nature of the division of the provinces, if the Emperor found himself dealing directly with the affairs of an individual, a community, or a province, these were more likely than not to be from the "public" half of the Empire.

The moral is simple. The Republic, it may be, can be seen from Rome outwards. To take this standpoint for the Empire is to lose contact with reality. Not only the pattern of the literary evidence, or the existence of an immense mass of local documents, but the very nature of the Empire itself, means that it can only be understood by starting from the provinces and looking inward.

130. *Or.* 45, 8.

CHAPTER TWELVE

State and Subject:
The Impact of Monarchy*

In 26 or 25 B.C., as a new Greek inscription records, a citizen of Ephesus was responsible for "the setting up of the *Sebastos* and the dedication of the sanctuary."[1] The reference appears quite casually in a list of holders of priesthoods; but the very casualness of the allusion has a lot to tell us about how people in a Greek city saw the world in the 20s B.C. *Sebastos* was of course to be the established Greek equivalent for *Augustus* and was to reappear on thousands of inscriptions throughout the imperial period. But when this statue was erected it was only one or two years since the name Augustus, never before used for a personal name, had been thought up in Rome, and solemnly voted by Senate and People in 27; voted, that is, as the new additional name of the thirty-five-year-old victor of the civil wars, "Imperator Caesar divi filius," whom we call Octavian. The victory itself, the battle of Actium in which the forces of Antonius and Cleopatra had fled, was only five or six years in the past. Antonius himself had been in Ephesus in the winter of 42/1 B.C. and again in 33/2; and on one of these occasions one of the other six men named in the list of priests had acted as ambassador to him.[2] Then, immediately after the battle, Octavian also had arrived in Ephesus. Chance has preserved the letter which he then had occasion to write to the almost totally insignificant city of Rhosos on the coast of Syria. His words reflect a

---

* First published in F. Millar and E. Segal, eds., *Caesar Augustus: Seven Aspects* (1984), 37–60. I am very grateful to Michael Crawford and Simon Price for corrections and comments.

1. *SEG* XXVI, 1243; *AE* 1975, 799; now *I.K.Eph.* III, 902.

2. *I.K.Eph.* III, 902, ll. 8–10: "Perikles son of Herakleis, by birth Charopinos," certainly to be identified with the Charopinos of Ephesus of R. K. Sherk, *Roman Documents from the Greek East* (1969), no. 57.

relationship which must have been formed at the same moment with scores, perhaps hundreds, of other Greek cities:

> The ambassadors sent by you . . . having come to me at Ephesus, addressed me on the matters on which they had instructions. On receiving them I found them to be patriotic and good men, and accepted the honours and the gold crown. When I come to those parts I will do my best to be of service to you and to preserve the privileges of the city.[3]

Ephesus had thus been for a moment the political focus of the Graeco-Roman world, and no one there could have been unaware that power had just changed hands. But the vote taken in Rome in 27 B.C. was also known in Ephesus, and *Augustus/Sebastos* was already so common a term that "the *Sebastos*" could mean a statue—already ordered, made, and ceremonially installed. Associated with that was a sanctuary (*temenos*); new elements have entered the communal activity, the religious life, and the visible topography of the city.

By implication what I have been saying is that one way to try to approach that crucial turning point which is the reign of Augustus is to look at how the world was represented, or mirrored, in hundreds of communities round the Mediterranean; for there really was a revolution, above all a revolution of consciousness, but it was not only a Roman one. Of course, if we do look, we can only see what there is to be seen. From cities in the Greek world, in North Africa, Italy, or southern Gaul there are written documents, architectural remains, statues, coins. Elsewhere there may be literally nothing, or at best a tale of conquest, seen from the outside.

So all we can do is to examine the inherent logic when Augustus is represented, in word or symbol.[4] Sometimes there is aid from unexpected quarters, for instance a red cow named Thayris. This hitherto unknown constituent of the early Roman Empire stepped into the light of history in the pages of the *Journal of Egyptian Archaeology* of 1982; a papyrus published there records that she was leased out in 26 B.C. by the slave of a Roman citizen resident in Egypt. We know the date because it was "the fifth year of the dominion [*kratesis*] of Caesar, son of a god."[5] Forty years later those citizens

3. *IGLS* III, 718: Sherk (n. 2), no. 58, doc. iii.

4. I am much indebted throughout to the methodology of S. R. F. Price, "Between Man and God: Sacrifice in the Roman Imperial Cult," *JRS* 70 (1980): 28, and to his *Rituals and Power: The Roman Imperial Cult in Asia Minor* (1984).

5. See J. R. Rea, "Lease of a Red Cow Named Thayris," *JEA* 68 (1982): 277.

of Rome who took a stroll round Augustus' Mausoleum would be able to read in the *Res Gestae* (27) that he had added Egypt to the *imperium* of the Roman people. There is a certain contradiction here, and one which neither can be nor should be resolved. But the words in which two people in Egypt dated the purchase of a cow constitute a fact in themselves. So do the words which the lamplighters of Oxyrhynchus had used in taking an oath four years earlier, in 30/29 B.C. This document is particularly important, for it takes us to a level of society which our evidence elsewhere systematically fails to reach; two at least of the four lamplighters, three with Egyptian names and one with a Graeco-Egyptian one, were illiterate. They swore to supply oil for the temple lamps for the current first year of Caesar "in accordance with what was supplied up to the 22nd year which was also the 7th" (*P.Oxy.* 1453). Life and its obligations went on; but one monarch, Cleopatra, had given place to another, called Caesar.

It is easy to object that, however the world was construed in Egypt, the only major Hellenistic monarchy to pass directly into the "dominion" of a single Roman ruler, this is not how things will have seemed in Rome. This view has some truth; but only some. Cornelius Nepos, concluding his biography of Atticus, recorded Atticus' awareness that Octavian and Antonius each desired to be *princeps*, "not just of the city of Rome but of the whole world" (*Att.* 20, 5). This dispassionate neutrality, clearly shared by Nepos himself, was to be perfectly matched in the attitudes shown by one of the common people of Rome when Octavian returned in 29 B.C., two years after Actium. As Octavian approached Rome, among the crowd which came out to meet him there appeared a man with a crow, which duly called out "Ave Caesar Victor Imperator" (Hail Caesar, victorious Imperator). Suitably impressed, Octavian bought the dutiful bird (*officiosa avis*) for 20,000 sesterces. It was then that the man's partner reported the existence of a second crow, which when produced emitted the words "Ave victor imperator Antoni" (Hail Antonius, victorious Imperator) (Macrobius, *Sat.* 2, 4, 29). The story has a lot to tell us. First, the established ritual of greeting important persons could be easily applied to the new situation. Secondly, the single victor who was due to appear could be expected to distribute largesse when honour required it; the sum which the man's partner failed to share is described as a *liberalitas*.

But there is also a much more important message to be gained from this anecdote. What the man exhibits is loyalist *behaviour*, of a sort which he believes to be both appropriate in a public context and advantageous to himself. But in his case, and perhaps in his case alone, we know that he did not feel loyalty, that he was indeed quite indifferent. It is important therefore to stress that in looking at rituals, cults, public expressions of gratitude, the erection of statues, and all those other visible forms of symbolism, we should not ask what people really felt, because we do not know (and in almost all cases cannot in principle know). Some two centuries after Augustus' death, Tertullian was to point out to the pagan world that all their loyalist rituals showed precisely nothing about their real feelings; if (he imagines) their hearts were covered with some transparent material, you would be able to look in and, just as they were acclaiming one emperor, you would see the image already formed there of his rival and successor distributing largesse (*Apol.* 35, 7). There is not, and cannot be, any such privileged view into the hearts of Augustus' subjects. We cannot know either that they felt, or for that matter that they did not feel, the reverence, loyalty, and gratitude which they so lavishly expressed. But we can study the logic of their public actions, and of their words, artefacts, and buildings.

Or, to be more precise, we can study the logic of these things provided both that the communities concerned did once speak, act, or create artefacts and that these, or some reflections of them, have survived. Equally, if we try to look at the actions of Augustus or the Senate in order to see how these actions were represented by their subjects, we can only do so, once again, by courtesy of those whose perceptions have left some trace. The conception we gain is thus bound to be partial. But I would insist that in speaking of perceptions or representations we are talking about an essential aspect of what the Roman Empire "was." Firstly, the emergence of a single ruler from within the Roman republican system had created a constitutional situation which seems to us inherently ambiguous. The symbols and words used in the provinces to represent the new situation thus acquire a particular importance. Secondly, it was because they were internally self-governing political communities that the provincial cities could and did respond to changes of power at the centre. They were both free, and yet also obliged, to choose the correct symbols and responses, precisely because they were typically neither garrisoned by Roman troops nor supervised by any Roman official who was permanently present among them. The civil wars had indeed meant for many places within the Empire, at least at certain moments, that Roman forces and officials might be present as an active, violent, and oppressive force. Whether or not their brutalities and exactions had any serious economic effects, which is not easy to say,[6] the ending of all that after Actium and the conquest of Egypt was a moment which did not pass without notice. Plutarch's great-

6. See F. Millar, "The Mediterranean and the Roman Revolution: Politics, War and the Economy," *Past and Present* 102 (1984): 3 (chapter 9 in this volume).

grandfather, for instance, used to recount how the citizens of Chaeronea had been forced into service to carry down to the sea sacks of grain for the forces of Antonius at Actium. Lashed by the whip, they had already carried one consignment when news came of Octavian's victory. Antonius' agents and soldiers promptly fled, and the citizens shared out the grain (*Ant.* 68). If we want to try to imagine what the blessings of the Augustan peace really amounted to, we could always start by remembering these resilient Greeks digesting the supplies which had come their way.

Within a very few years at the most, there were no Roman legions at all in what became in 27 the province of Achaea, that is, most of present day Greece; and the same was true of many other areas. The single governor of each province, with his staff, might appear from time to time to give justice, but only in the main centres; smaller places therefore would never actually see him at all. Being a subject community of the Roman Empire therefore consisted, firstly, in a symbolic, or diplomatic, adhesion and, secondly, in the obligation to pay tribute. But here too the direct weight of Roman agents was no longer felt in the same way as it had been previously. For the contractors (*publicani*) who had collected the tribute up to the late Republic now disappear, at least from most areas, leaving the communities (as it seems) to pay it themselves.[7] Thus we can actually see the Roman Empire changing shape before the eyes of its subjects if we simply take the example of complaints about taxation. Some time in the late Republic, as a relatively new inscription shows, the cities of Asia, leagued together in their *koinon* (provincial council), made such a complaint; its subject was oppression by the tax collectors who were active in the province, and the step taken was to send an embassy to speak before the Senate in Rome.[8] In 29 B.C., however, two years after Actium, the whole pattern had changed. When the people of the small Aegean island of Gyaros decided to ask for a reduction of their minute annual tribute, they sent an ambassador to make a petition before Octavian, then at Corinth on his way to Rome. The sum concerned was 150 drachmas, or 600 sesterces, a mere fraction of the amount which Octavian was soon to give for a talkative crow (Strabo, *Geog.* 485).

---

7. See E. Badian, *Publicans and Sinners* (1972); for the problems about the ending of the *publicani* system for direct taxation, see P. A. Brunt in A. H. M. Jones, *The Roman Economy* (1974), 180–81. But cf. Cl. Nicolet, "Augustus, Government, and the Propertied Classes," in F. Millar and E. Segal, eds., *Caesar Augustus: Seven Aspects* (1984), 101–3.

8. The inscription from Aphrodisias originally published by K. T. Erim, *PBSR* 37 (1969): 92, has been re-edited by T. Drew-Bear, *BCH* 96 (1972): 443, and J. Reynolds, *Aphrodisias and Rome* (1982), doc. 5.

The islanders' perception of where power now lay must be regarded as having been significant in itself, even if it had been wrong; even if, that is, Octavian will have told them to make their appeal to the Senate. But I rather doubt whether he did. For while we do not know what happened to the fisherman from Gyaros, we do know exactly what Octavian or Augustus wrote, probably some time between 31 and 20 B.C., to the much larger Aegean island of Samos. We know it because they requested him to grant them freedom, including freedom from tribute, and he refused, and in doing so made an unfavourable comparison to Aphrodisias in Caria. The city of Samos, we can safely assume, did not inscribe this reply. But the city of Aphrodisias did. It is therefore worth noting the exact words of this reply, first published in 1982:[9]

> You yourselves can see that I have given the privilege of freedom to no people except the Aphrodisians, who took my side in the war and were captured by storm because of their devotion to us. For it is not right to give the favour of the greatest privilege to all at random and without cause. I am well disposed to you and should like to do a favour to my wife who is active on your behalf, but not to the point of breaking my custom. For I am not concerned for the money which you pay towards the tribute, but I am not willing to give the most highly prized privileges to anyone without good cause.

If freedom had been granted to Samos, we cannot prove that the constitutional machinery of a vote by the Senate would not have been used; indeed it had been used in precisely the grant to Aphrodisias, in 39 B.C., which Octavian/Augustus refers to as if it had emanated solely from his own will.[10] None the less, the implication and logic of the reply is unmistakably that the effective decision belongs to the speaker and has been determined by considerations which are entirely personal to himself. The reference to Livia is also highly important, as we will see. What is significant for the moment

9. Reynolds (n. 8). doc. 13. Miss Reynolds is inclined to date the reply earlier, because of the reference to the war, which she argues to have been that of Labienus. But while, for the reasons she gives, the presence of the name "Augustus" is not significant for dating, the reference to Aphrodisias having taken "my side" (*ta ema phronesas*) seems to me to reflect the situation after Actium. Compare the cases of Sparta and Mantinea, which also took Octavian's side; see G. Bowersock, "Augustus and the East: The Problem of Succession," in Millar and Segal (n. 7), 169. The date must in any case be before Samos successfully gained freedom in 20/19 (Dio 5, 9, 7).

10. Reynolds (n. 8), doc. 8.

is the clear expression of the unqualified right and determination of the
speaker to decide a matter which affected the revenues due to be paid to the
Roman state; and the effort to explain the principles upon which his decision
is based.

I should like to dwell on this point for a moment. In the event, so I believe, the reign of Augustus turned out to have inaugurated almost three
centuries of relatively passive and inert government, in which the central
power pursued few policies and was largely content to respond to pressures
and demands from below.[11] In this, the revolution of consciousness to which
I have referred played a crucial part; that is the consciousness that there was
an individual ruler, whose name and image appeared everywhere (or everywhere that words were written or images made) and to whom appeal could
be made. The step taken by the fisherman of Gyaros embodies exactly that
perception. But in the reign of Augustus there is also something else, which
to me recalls not the relative torpor of the intervening centuries, but the
moralizing and reforming zeal of the tetrarchic period, of Diocletian and
Constantine. From the emphasis on victory, to the use of members of an extended imperial family in military and governmental roles in different parts
of the empire, the obsession with large-scale building projects, the reform
of the basis of taxation, or the level of moralizing self-justification addressed
to the people, a whole series of features unites the two periods. Another feature, which looks forward to the restless journeyings of the tetrarchic courts,
is the active movement round the empire which distinguishes the first part
of Augustus' reign; of the eighteen years after Actium he was in Rome for
about seven.[12]

On one of these journeys, in Gaul in 27 B.C., Augustus took a census of
the people. Our total evidence on this event, the Epitome of Livy (134) and
Dio (53, 23, 5) hardly says more than that; nor does either source make clear
that no *provincial* census, numbering persons and recording property, had ever
been taken before. It is of course only the author of Luke's Gospel who actually states both that there was a universal census and that it was promoted by
an edict from Augustus: "It happened in those days that an edict went out
from Caesar Augustus that all the inhabited world should be censused. This
was the first which took place, while Quirinius was governor of Syria" (2:1).
As Professor Brunt has reminded us, we should not deduce from the scat-

11. See F. Millar, *The Emperor in the Roman World (31 BC–AD 337)* (1977).

12. Return to Rome, 29 B.C.; Gaul and Spain, 27–24 B.C.; in the Greek East, 22–19 B.C.;
in Gaul, 16–13 B.C.

tered and defective nature of our evidence that Luke was simply wrong.[13] At the most he has compressed into a single moment a process spread over many years in different places. As it happened, a census was going on in Syria anyway, under Quirinius, when in A.D. 6 the rule of Herod's son Archelaus was ended, the province of Judaea came into existence, a census was imposed, tribute was demanded, and resistance flared up, never finally to die away until it led to the great revolt and the destruction of the Temple in A.D. 70.[14] Luke's allusion reflects the reverberations of that first census. So, of course, did the questions about tribute which were put to Jesus in Jerusalem. "The coin of the census," "of whom is this image and the inscription?" "give to Caesar the things which are Caesar's"—the language used perfectly reflects a perceived association between census, tribute, coinage, and emperor.[15] In principle, if indeed people in Judaea did believe that they were paying their tribute "to Caesar," it is quite certain they were wrong. Even Egypt, as Augustus claimed, was added "to the *imperium* of the Roman people."[16] But this mistake, like various others which we shall look at, is illuminating just because it is a mistake. Whether tribute did indeed have to be paid in what Matthew calls "the coin of the census," and which all three Gospels identify as a *denarius*—that is, specifically in Roman coins—we, as it happens, do not know. But the image and inscription had been there for all to see since before Actium.

We accept too easily, without surprise, almost without notice, the change which had come about within a very few years in the coinage of the Mediterranean world. Let me just recall the facts in outline. Up to 44 B.C., thirteen years before Actium, there is no certain case of a living Roman being portrayed on a Roman coin. The precedent was set by Julius Caesar in 44, followed by Octavian, Antonius, and Lepidus, in the Triumviral period. But all this time there were other coin issues which did not portray any living

13. See P. A. Brunt, "The Revenues of Rome," *JRS* 71 (1981): 161, on pp. 163–64. Note also T. D. Barnes, *The New Empire of Diocletian and Constantine* (1982), 226–27.

14. See E. Schürer, *History of the Jewish People*, ed. G. Vermes and F. Millar, I (1973), 381–82; 399–427. For the continuity of the resistance movement, M. Stern "Sicarii and Zealots," *World History of the Jewish People*, VIII (1977), 263. Census in Syria: *ILS* 2683.

15. Mark 12:13–17; Math. 22:17–22; Luke 20:21–6. For the significance to the population of the representation of the emperor (as opposed to that of any short-term information—or propaganda—content of coin types), see M. H. Crawford, "Roman Imperial Coin Types and the Formation of Public Opinion," in C. N. L. Brooke, I. Stewart, J. G. Pollard, and T. R. Volk, *Studies in Numismatic Method Presented to Philip Grierson* (1983), 47.

16. *RG* 27; cf. *CIL* VI 702: "Aegypto in potestamem populi Romani redacta" (from the base of the obelisk used for Augustus' sundial, see text to n. 53); cf. Vell. Pat. 2, 39, 2.

person.[17] Then from 31 B.C. onwards almost every single issue of official Roman coinage, in gold, silver, and bronze, portrays Octavian—Augustus.[18] The story of the non-Roman coinage of the Empire is if anything more dramatic.[19] Before 31 B.C. there may have been a few contemporary portrayals of Pompey and Caesar on city coinages; there were a few of Marcus Antonius, and perhaps one of Octavian. But between 31 B.C. and A.D. 14 portrayals of Augustus are known from 189 different places. Though some cities (such as Tyre, a free city) continued to mint without the head of Augustus, and other places produced some coins with and some without his portrait, we should not minimize the colossal change which had come over the symbolic character of the coinage, both Roman and non-Roman. The term "propaganda," often used of coin types and legends, seems to me unhelpful; we know neither who decided these matters nor what reactions they evoked. What we have is once again a set of visible and uncontrovertible examples of how people construed the world in which they lived; or, to put it another way, of the symbols which they thought it appropriate to display publicly. In this light it is therefore of some importance that both Roman and civic coinages of Augustus' reign may also portray other members of his family, Livia, Agrippa Postumus, Gaius and Lucius, and Tiberius.[20] Gaius and Lucius, together or separately, appear on the coins of more than thirty cities.[21]

That fact has its own importance, since, as we will see, it is clearly reinforced by other evidence. For the moment it is enough to say that if provincials on the streets of Jerusalem, or anywhere else in the Empire, imagined their payment of tribute as "giving to Caesar that which was Caesar's," it was a forgivable mistake, and a highly significant one. In fact even the tribute of the imperial provinces did not actually belong to Caesar, whatever some confusing modern theories may have claimed. But with that we have to turn to the division of the provinces in 27 B.C. Here too we will come round in the end to a significant mistake or misconstruction, this time embodied in a major contemporary document. We will also, looking at the new structure

17. See M. H. Crawford, *Roman Republican Coinage* (1974), 734–35; for the gold statue portraying Flamininus, not a *Roman* issue, see p. 544.

18. For the most complete account, see C. H. V. Sutherland and C. M. Kraay, *Catalogue of Coins of the Roman Empire in the Ashmolean Museum* I: *Augustus (c.* 31 B.C.–A.D. 14) (1975).

19. For a very useful survey of the civic coin portraits of Augustus, see S. Walker and A. Burnett, *Augustus: Handlist of the Exhibition and Supplementary Studies, British Museum, Occasional Papers* 16 (1981), 23–24.

20. See, e.g., C. H. V. Sutherland, *Coinage in Roman Imperial Policy, 32 BC–AD 68* (1951), chap. 4, for the representation of different members of Augustus' family on Roman coinage.

21. Walker and Burnett (n. 19), 57–58.

created in 27, see more examples of positive, reforming government from the centre, by Augustus; I think, or at least I hope, that I have not been the only person not to see the accumulated weight of this evidence, some of it quite new.

In January 27 B.C., three and a half years after his victory, Octavian appeared before the Senate and formally offered to lay down his powers. What exactly those powers had been, either as triumvir down to the end of 33 B.C. or in the intervening period, it is perhaps better not to enquire, since the question presents insoluble problems.[22] But his only formal office was that of consul, as it had been since 31, and would remain until 23. The response of the Senate, followed by the People of Rome, was to vote him the new, unheard-of name "Augustus" and various other honours, and to establish a new arrangement for the appointment of provincial governors. If we look at all of this from the angle of the provinces, the new name was very soon current, at least in the major centres. As for the new form of government, we have only one detailed contemporary picture of it, in the last paragraph of Strabo's *Geography* (840): "For when his native country entrusted to him the care of the government, and he was established for life as master of war and peace, he divided the entire territory [of the Empire] into two and allotted one to himself and one to the people." To anyone accustomed to the intricacies of that familiar topic "the Augustan constitution," these words will seem wrong, either a blatant over-simplification or, if taken literally—that is, as referring to the actual words of a constitutional enactment—just false. But, once again, we do have to remember that Strabo was a member of a prominent family in Pontos whose contacts with the leading Romans went back to the time of Lucullus; and that he himself had been in Rome and in the twenties had sailed up the Nile in the entourage of the then prefect of Egypt, Aelius Gallus.[23] If this was how he saw the change in 27 B.C., that is a historical fact in itself; if his words are misleading, they constitute, again, a significant error. Note also that to Strabo the division was not between Augustus and the *Senate*, but between Augustus and the people. The content of the division was that the people "sent" governors of consular or praetorian rank to its provinces, while Augustus sent both governors of consular or praetorian rank (i.e., senators) and also ones of equestrian rank to his provinces. The division, therefore, in Strabo's eyes consisted in the method of appointment of provincial governors. He could not have failed to know,

22. For the author's views, which remain controversial, see F. Millar, "Triumvirate and Principate," *JRS* 63 (1973): 50 (chapter 10 in this volume).

23. On Strabo, see G. W. Bowersock, *Augustus and the Greek World* (1965), 127–29.

but does not make it clear, that senatorial governors in the people's provinces bore the republican title of "proconsul," while those appointed by the emperor bore a title which explicitly referred to their dependence on him, namely *legatus*, or deputy. He could not have failed to know, for the obvious reason that these titles appeared everywhere on public inscriptions. He might perhaps not have known, what Cassius Dio was later to explain so clearly (53, 13–14), that, while the legates were appointed by Augustus and served until he chose to replace them, the proconsuls were chosen by the ancient system of the lot and served for a year only. In their case therefore the right to submit their name to the lot was one which came to them automatically five years after holding the elected office of praetor or consul. The government of these provinces *was* thus conferred by the vote of the people, even if indirectly, and imperial patronage played no part. But legates were appointed by imperial patronage, and their public title proclaimed this fact.

Whereas under the Triumvirate, or so it seems, all governors had been appointees, now a man could once again become proconsul of the great and rich province of Africa or Asia, while owing nothing to anyone's patronage. Was this however always clearly perceptible to the class of educated Greeks who, like Strabo, accepted the fact of Roman dominance and ran their own cities within its framework? It does not seem so. One of the most famous of Augustan documents is the great dossier which records how in 9 B.C. the cities of Asia celebrated the new era by agreeing to start all their separate annual calendars from Augustus' birthday, 23 September.[24] The proposal, indeed instruction, for this had actually come from the proconsul of Asia himself, Paullus Fabius Maximus, the descendant of a prominent republican family.[25] In response to his sycophantic epistle the *koinon* (provincial council) of Asia duly passed a decree making the new arrangements; in it it alluded to their proconsul in the following terms: "the proconsular benefactor of the province, sent by his [Augustus'] right hand and judgement."

So here is another significant mistake; even this distinction, between appointees and non-appointees, could vanish from the perspective of the leading citizens of a rich and civilized province. However, I have so far expressed myself as if this division in the method of appointment of governors, together with the new name "Augustus," were all that there was, from a provincial point of view, to the settlement of 27 B.C. That is indeed exactly what I think; the idea that there were ever two separate spheres of authority or ad-

24. The fullest discussion of the various texts is U. Laffi, "Le iscrizioni relativi all' introduzione nel 9 a. C. del nuovo calendario della provincia d'Asia," *Stud. Class. e Or.* 16 (1967): 5.

25. *PIR*² F 47; see R. Syme, *History in Ovid* (1978), chap. 8.

ministrative activity, that of the emperor and that of the Senate, in relation to the provinces is just a modern fiction.[26] Indeed it is even more of a fiction than I once thought. For I did for a time suppose that while the emperor from the beginning gave a set of instructions (*mandata*) to the legates whom he sent out, he did not do so for proconsuls until about the end of the first century A.D. They therefore, on this view, preserved a certain functional independence.[27] But Dio states quite clearly that Augustus began to issue instructions to proconsuls, as well as to his own appointees, already in 27 B.C. (53, 15, 4). Recent evidence strongly suggests that Dio was right. A recently re-edited letter of Domitius Corbulo, as proconsul of Asia under Claudius (*AF* 1974, 629), refers to the *entolai*, "instructions," which must surely be those of the Emperor; and that is confirmation enough.[28] Beyond that, two other new items of evidence, of the greatest importance, illustrate the way in which codes of instruction from Augustus, issued to provincial governors or officials, filtered down to affect the lives of communities and individuals in the provinces.

The first is the bilingual edict of Sextus Sotidius Strabo Libuscidianus, issued when he was legate of Galatia early in Tiberius' reign.[29] It is indeed clear that he had been appointed as legate by Augustus, and had continued in office after the Emperor's death and deification in A.D. 14. The subject matter of the edict is the local application, to the city of Sagalassus and its surrounding region, of an immensely complex set of rules relating to the right of official travellers to requisition transport at fixed prices, and to demand free accommodation up to specific limits. The governor's dependence on the rules drawn up by the Emperor is heavily stressed in his opening paragraph:

> It is the most unjust thing of all for me to tighten up by my own edict that which the Augusti, one the greatest of gods [Augustus], the other the greatest of emperors [Tiberius], have taken the utmost care to prevent, namely that no one should make use of carts without payment. However, since the indiscipline of certain people requires an immediate punishment, I have set up in the individual towns and villages a

26. See F. Millar, "The Emperor, the Senate and the Provinces," *JRS* 56 (1966): 156 (chapter 11 in this volume); see also W. K. Lacey, "Octavian in the Senate, January 27 BC," *JRS* 64 (1974): 176.

27. Millar (n. 26), 157–58; (n. 11), 314–17.

28. G. P. Burton, "The Issuing of Mandata to Proconsuls and a New Inscription from Cos," *ZPE* 21 (1976): 63.

29. Published by S. Mitchell, "Requisitioned Transport in the Roman Empire: A New Inscription from Pisidia," *JRS* 66 (1976): 106; *AE* 1976, 653; *SEG* XXVI, 1392.

register of those services which I judge ought to be provided, with the intention of having it observed, or, if it shall be neglected, of enforcing it not only with my own power but with the majesty of the best of princes [in Greek the "Saviour *Sebastos*," namely Augustus] from whom I received instructions [*entolai/mandata*] concerning these matters.

Behind the confused and self-deprecating language it is evident that a positive code of rules had been drawn up by Augustus, had been embodied in the *mandata* which the legate had originally received, and had been confirmed by Tiberius. There is every reason to suppose that similar instructions were issued by Augustus to governors of all types.

Another code of instructions issued by Augustus was the *Gnomon*, or handbook, for the Roman official in Egypt who was in charge of the *Idios Logos*, the "private account," which absorbed vacant or confiscated properties. We know it best from a selection of its most commonly applied clauses, found on a papyrus of the mid-second century. The preamble of this text runs: "A summary of the *gnomon* which the deified Augustus delivered to the administration of the *Idios Logos* and of the additions made from time to time by emperors or Senate or the prefects or *Idioi Logoi* of the time." The code imposed very detailed regulations concerning personal status, the rights of the Emperor to vacant property, and the confiscation of property after condemnation. If this text seems far away from Augustus himself, we come a great deal closer (once again) with a newly published papyrus which contains extracts from the code, and was written before the middle of the first century A.D. (*P.Oxy.* 3014).[30]

If we think of status, and the rules relating to it, we must inevitably think of the citizenship. By what seems to be a paradox, but is in fact typical of the imperial system, imperial patronage was precisely the instrument which opened the Roman citizenship to the provinces. In that sense the citizenship provides a perfect example of that ambivalent relationship analysed by Andrew Wallace-Hadrill, in which statuses and ranks in the republican system themselves provided the content of patronage by the emperor.[31]

As regards Augustus and the citizenship there are three points to make. Firstly, the disposal of the citizenship by Caesar and Augustus served to distribute around the provinces individuals with the Roman *nomen* Julius, living symbols of the unseen emperor's influence. Secondly, it was Augustus, in the third of his edicts inscribed in the market-place of Cyrene, who laid down the all-important principle that gaining Roman citizenship would not

30. S. Riccobono, *Il Gnomon dell'Idios Logos* (1950); see Millar (n. 11), 159.
31. A. Wallace-Hadrill, "Civilis Princeps: Between Citizen and King," *JRS* 72 (1982): 32.

of itself affect a man's obligations to his home community; it was precisely this principle which was to determine the political and social structure of the Empire for the next two centuries.[32] Thirdly, there is yet another relatively new document, the bronze tablet from Banasa in Morocco. For this reveals that Augustus, with what we can begin to see as an obsession with documentation (compare Suet. *Aug.* 101), had started an archive (*commentarius*) which was to record the names and details of every single person granted the Roman citizenship by himself and (as it turned out) subsequent emperors, at least up to Marcus Aurelius.[33]

The citizenship could thus be exported to the provinces, and the details recorded. But so too could existing citizens. We perhaps do not emphasize sufficiently that the age of Caesar, the Triumvirs, and Augustus is not merely the first but the only period in Roman history which saw the state engaged in active and large-scale settlement of citizens outside Italy. The scale and the geographical range of the establishment of veteran colonies makes this one of the important direct effects ever achieved by government in the ancient world; as Augustus claims in the *Res Gestae*, 120,000 men were already in the colonies by 29 B.C., and the colonies themselves were by the end to be found in Africa, Sicily, Macedonia, Spain, Achaea, Asia, Syria, Gallia Narbonensis, Pisidia, and Italy itself (*RG* 15; 28). Once again, these complex human movements and rearrangements did not just happen. They were subject to direct supervision by Augustus himself. Our evidence that detailed plans, and records of grants of land (significantly called the *liber beneficiorum*, book of grants), remained in the imperial archives "subscribed by the hand of the founder" must relate in the first instance to Augustus himself. Edicts of Augustus attempted to regulate the consequences of the immense disturbances to property and legal rights which were inevitably caused: "There are also certain edicts of Augustus, by which he indicated that wherever he had taken lands from the territories of other cities and assigned them to the veterans (i.e., of a particular colony), nothing else pertained to the jurisdiction of that colony except what had been given and assigned to the veterans." All this information comes from that invaluable, but obscure and complex source, the writings of the Roman land measurers.[34] Each individual colony

32. See F. Millar, "Empire and City, Augustus to Julian: Obligations, Excuses and Status," *JRS* 73 (1983): 76 (= chapter 16 in *Rome, the Greek World, and the East*, vol. 2).

33. First published by W. Seston and M. Euzennat, "Un dossier de la chancellerie romaine: la *Tabula Banasitana*, étude de diplomatique," *CRAI* (1971): 468; see, e.g., A. N. Sherwin-White, *JRS* 63 (1973): 86; *AE* 1971, 534.

34. *Corpus Agrimensorum Romanorum* I, ed. Thulin, 165–66 and 82–83; Millar (n. 11), 263–64.

might also get letters of instruction; giving judgement over disputed land in
A.D. 82, Domitian was to recall: "The letter of the deified Augustus, a most
diligent *princeps* and most indulgent towards his *quartani* [the veterans of the
fourth legion settled at Firmum], in which he advised them to make a record
of, and sell, all their unassigned plots." "I do not doubt," Domitian concludes,
"that they obeyed such salubrious advice."[35]

In Italy, so Suetonius records (*Aug.* 46), the twenty-eight colonies, once
founded, used to be visited by Augustus, who would equip them with buildings and public revenues. Elsewhere the imperial will could still be felt at a
distance. Another relatively new document, from the colony of Alexandria
Troas, refers to "the works carried out in the colony by the order of Augustus," as well as to the levy conducted by him and Tiberius in Rome, and to
military decorations granted by Germanicus (*AE* 1973, 501). We should not
treat as banal the fact that a Latin inscription from the north-west corner of
Turkey should recall specific actions on the part of three different members
of the imperial house.

Even outside the colonies we come across many traces of both individual
decisions and general rules issued by Augustus and affecting the cities of the
Empire: in the western Mediterranean, for instance, various benefits granted
to the obscure community of the Vanacini in Corsica, or revenues (*vectigalia*)
to the equally obscure Saborenses in Spain.[36] The apparent source of authority for general rules had changed also. I say apparent authority, because
we can rarely be quite certain whether or not some constitutional processes
did not precede, or perhaps follow, pronouncements by Augustus. For an
example of that problem we may look again at the famous document from
Kyme in Asia, first published in 1958.[37] What I think is certain about this
much-debated text is as follows. Firstly, Augustus and Agrippa, as consuls in
27 B.C., issued some form of general pronouncement ordering the restitution
of sacred or public properties which were illegally in private possession. Secondly, a man from Kyme approached the proconsul of Asia and demonstrated
that a shrine in Kyme was illegally in private possession. Thirdly, the proconsul wrote to the magistrates of Kyme to say that the shrine was to be restored
in accordance with the order (*iussum*) of Augustus, and was to have an inscription saying "Imperator Caesar Divi filius Augustus has restored [it]." The

35. *CIL* IX, 5420; *FIRA*² I, no. 5.

36. *FIRA*² I, 72; 74.

37. *SEG* XVIII, 555; Sherk (n. 2), no. 61; *I. K. Kyme* no. 17 (with restorations which
seem to me ill advised). See most recently N. Charbonnel, "À propos de l'inscription de
Kymé et des pouvoirs d'Auguste dans les provinces au lendemain du règlement de 27 av.
n.è.," *RIDA* 26 (1979): 177.

document has a much wider significance than the tedious debates about it have allowed. Firstly, if it really does reflect a general pronouncement concerned with sacred and public property in all provinces, then it seems to be the earliest attested case of such an intervention in the history of Roman rule outside Italy. Secondly, if (as many have argued) a decree of the Senate (*senatus consultum*) or some other collective constitutional act preceded and authorized the pronouncement by Augustus and Agrippa, then it has vanished, even from the perspective of the proconsul himself. What is more, Agrippa, who really did have some role, has also vanished. The more constitutionalist one's assumptions about the original process, the more striking is the concentration by the proconsul on the figure of Augustus: "Imperator Caesar Divi filius Augustus has restored it."

The inscription is also an example of how an imperial ruling could have its effect not by direct enforcement but by being known and being used by an interested party. Both the man in the street and the proconsul act on assumptions which reflect a new map of the world. Above and behind the governor is the unseen figure of the emperor, whose word, if known, can be used to enforce local effects.

How, or if, the emperor's word would become known to his subjects is a monstrous problem, still too little discussed. One way, of course, in those areas where at least some were literate, was the public inscription. But it was not the Roman state or its agents which normally created these, but any city which felt moved to do so. This is the case even with the most general, the most reformist, and the most clearly propagandist pronouncement of Augustus which we have, namely the last of the five edicts inscribed in Greek in the market-place of Cyrene. The procedure involved, namely the passing of a decree of the Senate under Augustus' influence, aptly reflects the uneasy collaboration of Emperor and Senate; the aim, to establish a simpler process for gaining restitution of money improperly acquired by governors, is typical of Augustus' reforming and moralizing spirit. The tone of paternalistic propaganda addressed to the people might belong to Diocletian. The preamble runs:[38]

> Imperator Caesar Augustus, Pontifex Maximus, holding the tribunician power for the 19th time, says:
>   The decree of the Senate passed . . . with myself being present and being named jointly as author, being relevant to the security of the allies of the Roman people, I have decided, so that it may be known to all of whom we have the care, to send to the provinces and to sub-

38. *SEG* IX, 8, v; Sherk (n. 2), no. 31.

join it to my own edict, from which it will be clear to all who dwell in
the provinces how much concern is exercised by myself and the Senate
that none of those subject to us should endure any improper injury or
exaction.

This is in fact the earliest known Roman pronouncement which explicitly
addresses itself to the attention of all the inhabitants of the empire. Though
the body of the document is a decree of the Senate, it is Augustus' name and
titles which occupy the first two lines, and Augustus' words which make up
the first paragraph. Those who could read would read them first. Those who
could not, could have seen a statue of the emperor; the second edict records
that the removal of such a statue, along with others, from public places had
already been the subject of accusations within the city (*SEG* IX, 8, ii).

With that we come back to our starting point, the symbolic presence of
the emperor, in word and physical representation, in the provincial community; or rather in those Greek or Latin cities where the "epigraphic habit," as
Ramsey MacMullen has called it,[39] was entrenched, and where statues were
made. That should bring us in its turn to the imperial cult, or to the confusing nexus of different acts and ceremonials which go under that heading.
But the evidence is too complex, and anyway may well evoke "tedium and
distaste." Let me therefore make a few brief points.

Firstly, the notion that the cults directed to emperors evolved from those
for Hellenistic kings is hardly even a half-truth. There is nothing anywhere
to suggest that the *scale* of cult acts for Hellenistic kings had ever approached
that which immediately appeared for Augustus. Few cults of deceased Hellenistic kings still lingered on, and only a modest range of evidence attests
cults or games or shrines for even the major Roman figures of the late Republic. The sudden outburst of the celebration of Octavian/Augustus was a new
phenomenon.[40] Nicolaus' remarks on the temples and sacrifices for Augustus
by cities and provinces (*FGrH* 90 F 125) are all the more important because
written in the 20s B.C. It was new first in its wide diffusion at the city level
and above all in the creation, from 30/29 B.C. onwards, of provincial cults,
with common temples of Roma and Augustus, common annual games associated with them, and annual high priesthoods. Everyone knows that these
arrangements were formally permitted to the provinces of Asia and Bithynia
by Octavian in 30/29 B.C. (Dio 51, 20, 6–9). What deserves equal emphasis is
the fact that he subsequently took a detailed interest in the practical arrange-

39. R. MacMullen, "The Epigraphic Habit in the Roman Empire," *AJPh* 103 (1982): 233.
40. See esp. K. Tuchelt, *Frühe Denkmäler Roms in Kleinasien* I: *Roma und Promagistrate*
(1979), and Price (n. 4, 1984).

ments. For instance, in the early days of the provincial cult in Asia a choir assembled to sing hymns to the emperor; I am not sure whether I wish that a text of such a hymn had survived. At any rate Augustus subsequently laid down arrangements for the expenses of the choir to be shared by the cities of the province.[41] In Syria there is nothing to suggest that a provincial league already existed, as it had in Asia, or that there were any surviving cults of the Seleucids. Indeed, until a few years ago there was no evidence even of the existence of a provincial cult in Syria under Augustus. But now we know there was, and that the first high priest was a man personally honoured by the emperor. This is how the man, Dexandros, appears in an inscription from Apamea in honour of his great-grandson: listing distinguished ancestors, the inscription continues "And above all Dexandros, the first man to have been priest of the province, his great-grandfather [who] by the decree of the deified Augustus, because of his friendship and loyalty to the Roman people, was inscribed as a friend and ally on bronze tablets on the Capitol."[42] The inscription shows the honours given to a local notable associated with the cult of the emperor; and it is also another example of the use by Augustus of the apparatus of the Roman *res publica*.

The provincial cult was not, even in Asia, a natural development from a long tradition, but an organized novelty, soon exported, as we now know, to Syria, and also, as has always been known, to Gaul. At the level of the city also, the dossier of 9 B.C. from Asia can simply assume that there will be Kaisareia at least in the assize-centres, and "Caesarean" games apparently everywhere; city cults of Augustus are in fact attested in thirty-four places in Asia, a figure never again approached in the case of any later emperor.[43] Once again the reign of Augustus can be seen not only as a beginning, but as a phase in itself. Equally distinctive is the scatter of cults for other members of the imperial family, matching their appearance on both Roman and civic coins (see text to nn. 20–21). For example, an inscription published in 1962 revealed a priest of Augustus, Gaius, and Agrippa on Samos,[44] and one of 1972 a priest of Agrippa Postumus and Hermes at Iasos in Caria (*AE* 1974, 628).

But we do not need these passing allusions to perceive the importance of the imperial family in the new political system. We can go back to the

41. F. K. Dörner, *Der Erlass des Statthalters von Asia Paullus Fabius Persicus* (1935), col. viii, lines 11–19; *I. K. Ephesos* Ia, nos. 17–19; 18d, lines 11–19.

42. J. P. Rey-Coquais, "Inscriptions grecques d'Apamée," *Ann. Arch. Arab. Syr.* 23 (1973): 39, no. 2; *AE* 1976, 678; see *BE* 1976, 718.

43. Price (n. 4, 1984), chap. 3.

44. P. Herrmann, "Die Inschriften römischer Zeit aus dem Heraion von Samos," *Ath. Mitt.* 75 (1960, app. 1962): 68 no. 1, part B.

long-known oath of Gangra in Paphlagonia, the same oath which was being sworn in the country districts at the *Sebastea* and at Neapolis in the *Sebasteon*, at the altar of the *Sebastos*. The opening words were "I swear by Zeus, Ge, Helios, all the gods and goddesses and the Sebastos himself to be loyal to Caesar Sebastos *and his children and his descendants.*"[45] Perhaps these are after all just ignorant Greeks from the interior of Asia Minor, accustomed to royal dynasties. So let us take the inhabitants of the Roman colony of Narbo in Provence—by now called in full Colonia Iulia Paterna Narbo Martia—and the exact words of the oath (*votum*) which they took in A.D. 11: "That it should be good, fortunate, and auspicious for Imperator Caesar divi filius Augustus, Pater Patriae, Pontifex Maximus, holding the tribunician power for the 34th time, *and his wife and children and his family* and the Senate and People of Rome and the *coloni* and *incolae* of the Colony." Even on an altar to the *numen* (spirit) of Augustus, erected in recognition of his settlement of divisions in the town, they did not have to select just these elements, in that order.[46]

If we turn to yet another relatively new document, we can see that the emphasis on the imperial family could seem appropriate, not just to provincial communities but to a senatorial official fulfilling a public role in his province. Thus the town of Messene passed a decree to honour the *quaestor pro praetore* of Achaea, Publius Cornelius Scipio, who "being filled with unexcelled good will to Augustus *and all his house*" had conducted the Kaisareia in lavish style and, learning the news of Gaius Caesar's campaigns in the East, had carried out a public sacrifice for his safety (*SEG* XXIII, 206 = *AE* 1967, 458). When Gaius died, what significance was to be attached to the event? We can judge best from the second of the two famous inscriptions from Pisa, or rather the "Colonia Obsequens Iulia Pisana," a place already equipped with an Augusteum and a Flamen Augustalis (a temple and priest of Augustus):[47]

> When the news was brought that Gaius Caesar, the son of Augustus, Pater Patriae [father of his country], Pontifex Maximus, guardian of the Roman Empire, and governor [*praeses*] of the whole world, grandson of the deified . . . had by a cruel fate been seized from the Roman people, when already designated as a most just *princeps* and closest to the qualities of his father, and the only protector of our colony.

45. *IGR* III, 137; *OGIS* 532; *ILS* 8781; cf. P. Herrmann, *Der römische Kaisereid* (1968), esp. 96–97.

46. *ILS* 112. See P. Kreissel, "Entstehung und Bedeutung der Augustalität. Zur Inschrift der *ara Narbonensis* (*CIL* XII, 4333)," *Chiron* 10 (1980): 291.

47. *ILS* 140. See, e.g., A. R. Marotta d'Agata, *Decreta Pisana* (*CIL* XI, 1420–21) (1980).

We ought to recall, listening to these words, that those who composed them came from precisely that Italian middle class which Jones once supposed to have been the group most attached to the republican constitution.[48]

New documents allow us to hear more and more of the words which people felt to be publicly appropriate under Augustus, or which he uttered to them. We should not brush these words aside as insincere (which we cannot know and, in any case, is irrelevant) or as misapprehensions of some privileged reality which is knowable in some other way. For these public expressions *are* a significant part of what we can know of the reality of the Roman Empire for those who lived in it. Instead we should be impressed by the suddenness and extent of the creation of a symbolic relationship between the new source of power and the provincial communities. It is possible to see entire town centres, say at Athens, or at Lepcis Magna,[49] which were transformed under Augustus by the erection of buildings related to the emperor and his household.

I have concentrated on provincial towns, and the rituals, images, and words in which they represented the imperial power; on the role of senatorial governors in reinforcing that same message; and on the relatively active role of Augustus himself in addressing his words to the people. But in fact there was nowhere where the impact of monarchy was more emphatic than in Rome itself. There is no need for a catalogue of buildings. Let us take one of our best examples of the continued functioning of *res publica*, namely the law passed in 9 B.C. to define offences against the acqueducts: "The Consul, T. Quinctius Crispinus, duly put the question to the people and the people duly passed a vote in the Forum, before the Rostra of the temple of the deified Julius on the thirtieth day of June. The Sergian tribe was to vote first."[50]

The consul spoke from the new Rostra, decorated with the spoils of Actium, and placed in front of the temple of Julius Caesar; completed in 29 B.C., the temple occupied a central point in the old Forum, blocking off the Regia from the large open space including the Comitium. The temple therefore rose behind the consul as he had the law read out; if the doors were open, the crowd would have been able to see the statue of the deified Caesar within. To the right, some at least of the crowd could see the new arch of Augustus

48. A. H. M. Jones, "The *Imperium* of Augustus," *JRS* 41 (1951): 112 = *Studies in Roman Government and Law* (1960), 1.

49. See T. L. Shear, "Athens: From City-State to Provincial Town," *Hesperia* 50 (1981): 356; E. Smadja, "L'inscription du culte impériale dans la cité: l'exemple de Lepcis Magna au début de l'Empire," *Dial. d'hist. anc.* 4 (1978): 171.

50. Frontinus, *De aquae ductu* 2, 129 (Loeb trans.).

dedicated in 19 B.C. If they looked further round to the right they could see
the Basilica Iulia, begun by Caesar and completed by Augustus. Directly behind them stood the old Rostra, shifted to a new position by Julius Caesar.
Those at the back, if a large enough crowd had come, could see on their left
the new Senate house, the Curia Iulia, begun by Caesar and finally dedicated
by Octavian in 29 B.C., which was attached to the outside of one of the porticoes of the vast new Forum Iulium.[51] From further over to their left they
might have been aware of work going on to complete the Forum of Augustus with the temple of Mars Ultor; as yet, however, they had been spared
its programmatic re-reading of Roman history in terms of legendary ancestors and kings, together with historical *summi viri* (foremost men), that is to
say, those *duces* (generals) whose individual achievements had brought the
imperium of the Roman people from insignificance to greatness.[52]

If they were still unclear as to what symbolic message was being delivered, they could always have taken a walk to the north end of the Campus
Martius, past the Saepta and Pantheon built by Agrippa, past the Ara Pacis,
dedicated in January of that very year (9 B.C.); and parallel with it—probably
dedicated at the same time—the monstrous sundial marked out by Augustus over some 150 metres of the Campus, its shadow provided by an obelisk
brought from Heliopolis, which stood, with its base, some 30 metres high.[53]
They could then have contemplated the hideous mass of Augustus' Mausoleum;[54] at some 88 metres across the base, it was the largest Roman tomb so
far known, begun perhaps in the late 30s or at the latest in 28 B.C., that is,
just before the chance was solemnly offered for Senate and People to exercise their discretion (*arbitrium*). By 9 B.C. the Mausoleum already contained
the remains of two members of the imperial family, Marcellus and Agrippa,
and would very soon receive those of Drusus. A quarter of a century later,
once Augustus' ashes had also been placed there, the passer-by was to have
the chance to read his *Res Gestae*, inscribed on bronze tablets attached to pil-

51. See P. Zanker, *Forum Romanum: die Neugestaltung durch Augustus* (1972).

52. See P. Zanker, *Forum Augustum: das Bildprogramm* (1968); Degrassi, *Ins. It.* XIII. 3:
Elogia (1937). See S. R. Tufi, "Frammenti delle statue dei summi viri nel Foro di Augusto,"
Dial. di Arch. 3 (1981): 69. For the *duces*, Suet. *Aug.* 31.

53. See E. Buchner, *Die Sonnenuhr des Augustus* (1982).

54. For the Mausoleum, see, e.g., R. A. Cordingley and I. A. Richmond, "The Mauso-
leum of Augustus," *PBSR* 10 (1927): 23; K. Kraft, "Der Sinn des Mausoleums des Augustus,"
Historia 16 (1967): 189 = *Gesammelte Aufsätze zur antiken Geschichte und Militärgeschichte* (1973),
29 (for the view that building began in the late 30s and was complete by 28 B.C.); J.-C.
Richard, " 'Mausoleum': d'Halicarnasse à Rome, puis à Alexandrie," *Latomus* 29 (1970): 370.
See J. M. C. Toynbee, *Death and Burial in the Roman World* (1971), 144–45.

lars standing in front of it. Unlike modern scholars, this passer-by could also, from time to time, lift up his eyes from the text and observe, at a height of some 40 metres above where he was standing, the bronze image of Caesar Augustus which rose over the tomb. Returning to the text, he was probably not clever enough to read it as a republican document.

CHAPTER THIRTEEN

"Senatorial" Provinces:
An Institutionalized Ghost[*]

In Memoriam Ronald Syme

As the fiftieth anniversary of the publication of *The Roman Revolution* approaches, a renewed interest has been felt in the very profound "revolution" referred to, which with extraordinary speed transformed the exercise of power, the functions of the organs of the *res publica* (all of which, in some sense at least, survived), the nature and accessibility of the Roman citizenship, and the perception on the part of the peoples of the Empire as to what was the nature of the political system within which they lived. The vivid, but nonetheless ambivalent, reflection of the new order in what we label "Augustan" literature also remains a fruitful, if treacherous, field of study. But the most important new light on this great transformation has certainly come from the demonstration of the wholly new "language" of Roman art and architecture provided by the major book of Paul Zanker, *Augustus und die Macht der Bilder* (1987), the Jerome Lectures of 1983–84, translated as *The Power of Images in the Age of Augustus* (1988). We can safely say that Augustan Rome will never look the same again.

In the face of this other Roman "revolution," it may seem perverse to go back to one of those dry and tedious questions of constitutional terminology which are calculated to recall all too clearly the sterile debates on the niceties of "the Augustan constitution," which used to be so common in learned journals. Nonetheless, I hope that it can be proved that the exercise is illuminating. For it shows, firstly, how modern scholars have imposed on the ancient evidence an item of terminology, "the senatorial provinces" ("die senatorischen Provinzen") for which the ancient sources themselves offer not the slightest justification. Secondly, we may recall that it has long since been demonstrated that the supposed division into "Imperial" and "Senatorial"

[*] First published in *Ancient World* 20 (1989): 93–97.

provinces corresponds to no division of administrative practice or of political responsibility, but simply reflects the method and conditions of appointment and the length of tenure of *legati Augusti pro praetore* (legates of Augustus with praetorian rank) on the one hand and of proconsuls on the other.[1] That issue does not, I think, need to be rehearsed again, and will be not re-argued here. But it is highly significant that nonetheless the term "senatorial provinces" has remained in use as a common description of those provinces which from 27 B.C. onwards reverted to being governed by proconsuls selected by lot and serving normally for only one year.[2] For the unreflecting imposition of this term not only flies in the face of the ancient evidence but expresses a lingering presumption—of a very profound kind—about the Roman revolution itself. That is to say, that the political and constitutional system as against which, or from within the framework of which, a monarch emerged was one in which the sovereign element had been the Roman Senate. Therefore, in so far as the "settlements" of 27 B.C. and after, which gave constitutional expression to Augustus' monarchic position, were compromises, they were compromises between the Senate and the Emperor. Consequently, as then hardly needs to be argued, the division of the provinces carried out in 27 January must have been a division between Emperor and Senate.

But it was not. The sovereign body in the Roman *res publica*, to which the *imperium* and the provinces belonged, was not the Senate but the Roman people. As our only contemporary source makes quite explicit, it was the people to whom Augustus gave back certain provinces in 27 B.C. as part of the termination of the Triumviral system. And those provinces were henceforward to be known as *publicae provinciae* (public provinces), or even more explicitly as *provinciae populi Romani* (the provinces of the Roman people).

Before the evidence is set out in more detail, it may be relevant to recall some features of the public vocabulary, or public ideology, of the early Principate already discussed in relation to the Tabula Siarensis and Tabula Hebana of A.D. 19, two major inscriptions, which together present a single text of almost limitless importance.[3] Firstly, the whole Empire, and not merely the

1. F. Millar, "The Emperor, the Senate and the Provinces," *JRS* 56 (1966): 156 (chapter 11 in this volume), with revisions in *The Emperor in the Roman World* (1977), 313ff., and in "State and Subject: The Impact of Monarchy," in F. Millar and E. Segal, eds., *Caesar Augustus: Seven Aspects* (1984) 37, esp. 45ff. (chapter 12 in this volume).

2. See, for instance, the generally excellent commentary on Suetonius, *Divus Augustus* by J. M. Carter (1982), 163ff. (on chap. 47, 1).

3. F. Millar, "Imperial Ideology in the Tabula Siarensis," in J. González, ed., *Estudios sobre la Tabula Siarensis, Anejos de Archivo Español de Arqueología* 9 (1988): 11 (chapter 15 in this volume), with some further points in "Government and Diplomacy in the Roman Empire

public provinces, belonged in principle to the Roman people, and it was to its *imperium* or *potestas* that the Emperor or members of his family were seen as making newly acquired areas subject: "I added Egypt to the *imperium* of the Roman people" (*RG* 27, 1); "Egypt having become subject to the power of the Roman people" (*Aegypto in potestatem populi Romani redacta*, *ILS* 91); "Tiberius Caesar . . . made Cappadocia tributary to the Roman people" (Vell. Pat. 2, 39, 3). Both areas were to be governed not even by senators but by *Equites* appointed by the Emperor. In the same way Gaius Caesar was conceived of after his death as having been conducting a campaign "beyond the furthest territories of the Roman people" (*ILS* 140, ll. 10–11).

Furthermore, one of the important revelations of the Tabula Siarensis is that in A.D. 19 an army commanded by a legate of Augustus in one of the provinces of Caesar was also conceived of as an army of the Roman people. For the text refers back to the disaster under Quinctilius Varus in A.D. 9, and to Germanicus' supposed revenge for that defeat, in just these terms (Fr. I, ll. 14–15): "the military standards having been retrieved and the treacherous defeat of the Roman people avenged" (*receptisque signis militaribus et vindicata frau[dulenta clade] exercitus p(opuli) R(omani)*). There was therefore a clear, wider sense in which the formal sovereignty in the whole Roman empire lay not yet with the Emperor himself but with the Roman people.

It is with these considerations in mind that we ought to look again at the evidence we have for the nature of the division of the provinces in 27 B.C. and for subsequent transferrals of provinces from one system to the other. Our earliest and most explicit description, and the only one provided by a contemporary, is that given by Strabo in the concluding chapter of his *Geography*. His conception of the nature of the division is quite unambiguous: "he [Augustus] divided the entire territory [of the empire] in two, and assigned one half to himself, and the other to the people" (*Geog.* 840). He continues by explaining that the more peaceful provinces were assigned to the people (*toi demoi*, again); the two halves of the Empire were subdivided into separate provinces, "of which some are called [provinces] of Caesar and others [provinces] of the people." The rest of what Strabo says concerns the method of appointment to the two types of province, and there is no allusion to the Senate. The Emperor appoints the governors of his provinces, while it is the people which sends (*pempei*) praetors or consuls to its part. Strictly speak-

during the First Three Centuries," *Int. Hist. Rev.* 10 (1988): 345, 348. The Tabula Siarensis is reprinted, but without division into lines, as *AE* 1984, 508. Note also the very helpful translation of the combined text in R. K. Sherk, *The Roman Empire: Augustus to Hadrian* (1985), no. 36. See now M. Crawford, ed., *Roman Statutes* I (1996), no. 37/8.

ing, he ought to have spoken of ex-praetors and ex-consuls, and he makes no reference to the use of the lot. But he is correct in that the praetorship or consulship, gained by popular election, was a necessary and sufficient condition—bar only the use of the lot—for being the proconsul of a public province (*demosia eparchia* in Strabo).

There is no further description of this division in our sources (none is supplied by Velleius) until we come to Suetonius' *Life of Augustus*, where a reference to the lot duly appears: "the others he [Augustus] assigned to proconsuls selected by lot" (*ceteras [provincias] proconsulibus sortito permisit, Div. Aug.* 47). Again the emphasis is on the method of appointment, and there is no reference to the Senate as a body. Where such a reference does appear, though only in a tangential way, is in Cassius Dio's account of the same arrangement: here it is said that Augustus "gave back" (*apedoke*) the more peaceful provinces, without it being said to whom.[4] Dio adds the comment that he did so notionally so that the Senate (*gerousia* here) might have the untroubled benefit of the fairest part of the empire (53, 12, 2–3). He then lists those provinces which were to be those of the people and Senate (12, 4). This is, of course, an allusion to the Senate; but such an allusion, as part of a phrase equivalent to *Senatus Populusque Romanus* (*SPQR*), has a sense quite different from one which would imply an administrative or constitutional competence of the Senate per se. If that needed a demonstration, it is provided a few lines later (12, 7), when Dio says that Augustus subsequently gave back Cyprus and Narbonensis to the people (*demos*, cf. 54, 4, 1). The same combined term, as used in Dio's Greek, also reappears a couple of chapters later (14, 5), when he speaks of the quaestors appointed by lot and the (occasional) legates sent to the provinces called "those of the People and Senate." The implications of this phrase are thus quite clear: the provinces concerned were those where the system long established in the Roman *res publica* prevailed, whereby appointment to specific provinces was made by lot.

Only at one moment in his detailed description of the provincial system does Dio speak as if the provinces governed by proconsuls of consular or praetorian rank were in some way the collective concern of the Senate as such. Here (53, 14, 1–2) he is contrasting the fact that emperors sometimes appointed to "their" provinces governors who were still in their year of office as praetor or consul. By contrast Augustus assigned to the Senate for its part, and to ex-consuls, the provinces of Africa and Asia, and the remaining ones to ex-praetors, but with the strict rule that allocation by lot should not take

4. As was noted in *JRS* 56 (1966): 156, the words τῇ βουλῇ appear in the versions of Xiphilinus and Zonaras at this point, but not in the transmitted text of Dio.

place until five years had elapsed after the relevant magistracy in the city. Whatever Dio means to imply here about the role of the Senate as a whole, the context of the reference is clearly to the process of appointment of proconsuls, and not to any wider administrative function.

In his books on the Augustan period Dio is otherwise quite consistent in speaking of the non-imperial provinces as being "of the people."[5] Only once later does he (or rather, strictly speaking, Xiphilinus) use a different terminology: when C. Iulius Severus was sent as legate to the previously public province of Pontus and Bithynia in circa 134, Lycia-Pamphylia "was given to the Senate and the lot" (69, 14, 4).

Of course, it cannot be claimed that there is complete consistency and lack of ambiguity in the language which our narrative sources use; for if that were so, the confusion which this chapter attempts to clear up would never have arisen. So, for instance, when Suetonius wants to say that Claudius returned Achaea and Macedonia to rule by proconsuls, he does so in language which fits the traditional presuppositions very well: "He gave back to the Senate the provinces of Achaea and Macedonia, which Tiberius had taken to himself" (*Div. Claud.* 25, 3). Dio, however, interprets this same transfer (on my hypothesis correctly) as meaning that he restored these governorships to the system of appointment by lot (60, 24, 1).

But in spite of these ambiguities, the fact remains that no text known to me speaks of the proconsular provinces as being "senatorial," or as being the provinces "of the Senate." More important, however, is the fact that a perfectly clear alternative designation for them, with wholly different connotations, is perfectly well attested. To Tacitus these provinces were *publicae provinciae* (public provinces, *Ann.* 13, 4, 3). More specifically still, to Gaius, writing in the middle of the second century, the provinces were still divided into provinces of the Roman people and provinces of Caesar (*provinciae populi Romani* and *provinciae Caesaris*). This division was relevant first of all to the vehicles for the dissemination of Roman law, and the specification of those office-holders who possessed the right of issuing edicts (*ius edicendi*): "the same is true of the edicts of the curule aediles, whose jurisdiction in the provinces of the Roman people is held by the quaestors; for quaestors are not sent at all into the provinces of Caesar" (*Inst.* 1, 1, 6). It is true that with Gaius, as with all other jurists, we have to remind ourselves that what we are reading is not the expression of a perfectly codified entity called "Roman

5. Dio 53, 15, 3: "those which are his, and those which are the people's"; 55, 28, 2: "In the provinces of the people"; 54, 7, 5: "although also these provinces (*ethne*) belong to the people."

Law," but a work of scholarly interpretation which allowed a lot of room for personal theorizing, sometimes of an antiquarian character, and for ex post facto excogitation of general principles designed to explain existing, or indeed no longer existing, practices. Hence Gaius, alone of all the jurists known to us, goes on to develop a quite eccentric theory about the ownership of provincial land, based on the division of the provinces into two types. We can, he says, cause a place (*locus*) to become sacred (*religiosus*) by interring a corpse there, but not, however, if the area concerned is provincial: "But some people claim that on provincial ground a place cannot become sacred [i.e. in this way] since the full ownership [*dominium*] of such land belongs to the Roman people or to Caesar; we, on the other hand, can only acquire possession or usufruct there" (2, 6–7). He does indeed seem to mean that on this theory full ownership (*dominium*) depended on whether the province concerned was Caesar's or the people's. For a little later he produces another distinction which is unique to himself: "To this category belong provincial lands, of which some are called *stipendiaria* and others *tributaria*. *Stipendiaria* are those located in these provinces which belong to the Roman people; *tributaria* are those located in those provinces which are believed to belong to Caesar" (2, 21).

It is not necessary here to discuss whether there could be any justification for Gaius' distinction between *praedia stipendiaria* and *praedia tributaria*, or to dwell on the expressions found quite frequently in the writings of the classical jurists, which reflect their perception of Roman law as being based still on the sovereignty of the Roman people.[6] Enough has been said to demonstrate the fragility of any supposed textual justification for the expression "senatorial province," a term which retains an established place even in the standard modern work on the Senate of the imperial period.[7] The fact that this pseudo-technical expression conveys presuppositions about administrative practice which our evidence does not support is reason enough for suggesting that we should cease to use it. But there are far more significant reasons than that. For if we were instead to speak, as our sources do, of the public provinces or the provinces of the Roman people, we would thereby remind ourselves that the inherited framework to which Augustus adjusted him-

6. See, for instance, Gaius, *Inst.* 1, 53: "It is not allowed either to Roman citizens or to others who are under the *imperium* of the Roman people . . ."; 4, 28: "the public revenues of the Roman people"; *Dig.* 43, 8, 3 (Celsus): "The shores over which the Roman people has *imperium* I consider to belong to the Roman people"; 49, 15, 24 (Ulpian): "Enemies are those on whom the Roman people has publicly declared war, or who have themselves [declared war] on the Roman people."

7. R. J. A. Talbert, *The Senate of Imperial Rome* (1984), 392–407.

self with such skill consisted not just of the Senate but of the *res publica* as a whole or, in political terms, the *Senatus Populusque Romanus*. After all, that is precisely what, in his posthumously published *Res Gestae*, Augustus tells us himself: "I transferred the *res publica* from my own power [*potestas*] to the discretion [*arbitrium*] of the senate and the Roman people" (*RG* 34). Too little attention is paid to the subtle choice of terminology deployed here. For the exercise of what is here described, looking back over more than four decades, as *arbitrium* by the Senate and People, had consisted in an apparently free vote to entrust certain major provinces, for a period of ten years, to the newly named Augustus.[8] A choice, an act of *arbitrium*, had, formally speaking, been made. Hence the precise, and extremely revealing, terms in which Ovid was to celebrate this moment in the *Fasti*, notionally addressing Germanicus: "all the provinces [*omnis provincia*] have been restored to our people, and your grandfather was called by the name Augustus" (1, 589–90). *Omnis provincia* here does not mean "die gesamte Staatsgewalt" (so Bomer *ad loc.*); it means what it says. Moreover, whatever the *Fasti Praenestini* for this day, 13 January, said, it certainly alluded to an act of redistribution by Augustus to the Roman people.

Indeed, even the provinces of Caesar remained, on a wider definition, subject in principle to the *imperium* of the Roman people. This constitutional conception too is firmly embedded in the *Res Gestae*, for example, 26.1: "I extended the territories of all the provinces of the Roman people." Nonetheless, the distinction between *provinces* whose governors were *legati Augusti pro praetore* nominated by the Emperor and those governed by proconsuls accompanied by quaestors, both appointed by lot on the traditional system, was a real one, and justified the custom of calling the first group "the provinces of Caesar" and the second "the public provinces," or "the provinces of the Roman people." We should now abandon the wholly illegitimate expression "senatorial provinces," and adopt one or other of these two expressions: but preferably, following both Strabo and Gaius, *provinciae populi Romnani*. The use of this expression would further serve to remind us that, fifty years later, the last word on the Roman revolution has yet to be said.

8. For the most careful modern treatment of these procedures, see W. K. Lacey, "Octavian in the Senate, January 27 B.C.," *JRS* 64 (1974): 176, suggesting convincingly that the key element was a senatorial debate and vote *de provinciis consularibus* ("concerning the proconsular provinces"). Whether the people also voted on this specific point is unclear, but they certainly did on the honours granted in mid-January to Octavian/Augustus; Dio 53, 12, 1; *RG* 34, 1, and Lacey, "Octavian in the Senate," 181.

CHAPTER FOURTEEN

Ovid and the Domus Augusta:
Rome Seen from Tomoi*

From Triumviral to Augustan Literature

The greatest works of what we normally call "Augustan" literature were produced by writers who came to maturity in the Triumviral period, and were
already established as major authors before January 27 B.C., when "Imperator
Caesar Divi filius," whom we like to call "Octavianus," gained the unprecedented cognomen "Augustus." By that moment the *Eclogues* and *Georgics* of
Virgil were already written, as were the *Epodes* and *Satires* of Horace and
book I of the *Elegies* of Propertius. Livy had composed his sombre preface,
and probably the whole first pentad, in the later Triumviral period, around
the time of Actium or soon after.[1]

We might thus wish to see these writers not as "Augustan" but as "Triumviral," along (for instance) with Sallust, and the much underestimated
Cornelius Nepos (whose *Life* of Atticus is the most illuminating prose work
for the 40s and 30s),[2] not to speak of Vitruvius, whose *De Architectura* does
not address the dedicatee as "Augustus." Several of the key monuments of
"Augustan" Rome were equally dedicated before the name "Augustus" was

* First published in *JRS* 83 (1993): 1–17. This chapter represents a version of my Presidential Lecture to the Roman Society, given on January 7, 1992. I am very grateful to the
Editor, Andrew Wallace-Hadrill, and the Editorial Committee for valuable and salutary
criticisms, and to the Editor for providing his own translations of the Latin. But for the
author's obstinacy, the criticisms offered would have served to reduce the defects of the
paper somewhat further.

1. Livy 4, 17–20, see Ogilvie to the passage, and see esp. R. Syme, "Livy and Augustus,"
HSCPh 64 (1954): 27 = *Roman Papers* I (1979), 440, and T. J. Luce, "The Dating of Livy's
First Decade," *TAPhA* 96 (1965): 209.

2. See F. Millar, "Cornelius Nepos, 'Atticus' and the Roman Revolution," *Greece and Rome*
35 (1988): 40 (chapter 7 in this volume), and now esp. N. Horsfall, *Cornelius Nepos: A Selection,
including the Lives of Cato and Atticus* (1989).

acquired: the Mausoleum on the Campus Martius, the temple of Apollo Pala-tinus, and the Curia Julia.[3] Equally, the impulse to repair the ancient temple of Iuppiter Feretrius on the Capitol had come from Atticus, who had died in 32 B.C.[4]

But if we decided to identify this crucial and creative period in the his-tory of Roman culture as "Triumviral,"[5] which writers can we designate as truly and unambiguously "Augustan"? The great "Augustans" Virgil, Horace, Propertius, and Livy[6] emerge as Triumviral, and in their later works could be thought of as "post-Triumviral." If anyone is to qualify as Augustan through and through, it is Ovid, born in 43, whose writing starts in the 20s and extends into the early years of Tiberius. He is "Augustan" not merely in a chronological sense, but in a far more profound one, of the expression in some (not all) of his works of an overt literary commitment to the new regime (of true *personal* commitment we can never know, and should not at-tempt to speak). The poetry of exile, this chapter suggests, expresses not the voice of the subversive dissident, but that of the outraged loyalist whom the regime has rejected and was never to accept back.

The earlier *Heroides* and the first version of the *Amores* apart, Ovid's major surviving works belong, in the form in which we have them, to the very mysterious and rather neglected last two decades of Augustus' life: the *Ars Amatoria*, the *Fasti*, the *Metamorphoses*, the *Tristia*, and *Epistulae ex Ponto* 1–3, with *Epistulae* 4 stretching from a year before Augustus' death to two years after it. All of them manifest an intense concern to incorporate appropri-ate reflections of the major monuments and successes of the regime, in a laborious and explicit way which had not been characteristic of the poets of half a generation earlier. As Jasper Griffin has brilliantly demonstrated, these writers found ways of honouring the new regime, while delicately distanc-ing themselves from it.[7] By contrast, Ovid's works have to negotiate the in-superable task of incorporating appropriate allusions to Augustus, while also giving due recognition to his associates and successors, potential or actual.

These considerations might allow us, as a way of relocating Ovid, and

3. For this phase, see P. Zanker, *Augustus und die Macht der Bilder* (1987), chaps. 2–3.

4. Millar (no. 2), 40 and 51.

5. For the suggestion that the period from 43 to 28 B.C. might be so termed, see R. Syme, *History in Ovid* (1978), 169.

6. For difficulties in seeing Livy as "Augustan," see T. J. Luce, "Livy, Augustus and the Forum Augustum," in K. A. Raaflaub and M. Toher, eds., *Between Republic and Empire: In-terpretations of Augustus and His Principate* (1990), 123.

7. J. Griffin, "Augustus and the Poets: 'Caesar qui cogere posset,'" in F. Millar and E. Segal, eds., *Caesar Augustus: Seven Aspects* (1984), 189.

thus re-evaluating how we should read him, not only to separate him from the earlier, less than truly "Augustan" writers, but to re-attach him to others, whose adult lives or whose works also bridge the divide between Augustus' regime and what one might think of as the "post-Augustan" phase of Tiberius' reign, that is, the years dominated by Livia, up to her death in A.D. 29. This period of approximately three decades, from the dedication of the temple of Mars Ultor in 2 B.C. to the death of Livia, and the disgrace of the widow and children of Germanicus, is marked by the most emphatic public assertions of "Augustan" values and historical claims, along with their proclamation as lessons for future generations, and simultaneously by systematic uncertainty and unease about the role of other members of the imperial house—and (given the deaths of many of them) by the repeated necessity to reflect on what might have been. The combination of triumphalism and anxiety is perfectly caught by Velleius Paterculus, coming towards the end of the *History* which he dedicated to M. Vinicius, *consul ordinarius* of A.D. 30; for he emphasises the unhappy coincidence, in 2 B.C., of the dedication of the temple of Mars Ultor with the disgrace of the elder Julia:[8]

> At in urbe eo ipso anno, quo magnificentissimis gladiatorii muneris naumachiaeque spectaculis Divus Augustus, abhinc annos triginta, se et Gallo Caninio consulibus, dedicato Martis templo animos oculosque populi Romani repleverat, foeda dicta memoriaque horrenda in ipsius domo tempestas erupit.

> But in the City, in the year, thirty years ago, in which Divus Augustus, in his own and Gallus Caninius' consulship, marked by the most magnificent shows of gladiatorial games and a sea battle the dedication of the temple of Mars, and sated the minds and eyes of the Roman people, a storm, foul to speak of and horrible to recall, broke out under his own roof.

Velleius Paterculus himself offers the most illuminating comparison to Ovid, and one of the chief purposes of this chapter will be precisely to suggest the significance of this thirty-year period as embracing them both. In Latin epigraphy likewise, this "late-Augustan" and "post-Augustan" period might also be seen as representing a distinct phase, marked by the production of long and complex inscribed texts, which can be seen not merely as counterpoints to the literature of the period, but as a sub-branch of literature in themselves. They too exhibit that same curious mélange of triumphalism, anxiety,

---

8. Velleius 2, 100, 2. For his repeated allusions to the consulate of M. Vinicius, see *PIR*[1] 5, 445.

and unfulfilled hopes. The reign of Augustus itself, of course, is reflected in an explosion of epigraphic commemoration, as Géza Alföldy has recently demonstrated.[9]

This particular phase would thus begin with the dedication in 2 B.C. of the temple of Mars Ultor, along with the surrounding Forum Augustum, adorned with statues of the generals (*duces*) who had made the Roman people great from small beginnings. The surviving inscribed *elogia* ("eulogies") which accompanied the statues simply do not match what Livy had already written about the achievements of these same *duces*, a point which underlines how far Livy was from offering the canonical "Augustan" text. For Suetonius records that Augustus informed the people in an edict how they were to read these statues and their inscriptions: they were to serve as a model, by which appropriate conduct should be demanded of himself while he lived, and of the *principes* of succeeding ages.[10]

The formation of an ideology of the proper role of *principes* is reflected in other inscriptions of the following years. First there is the Greek inscription from Messene giving an exaggerated view of Gaius' achievements in the East ("learning that Gaius Caesar, the son of Augustus, was fighting the barbarians for the safety of all mankind").[11] Then come the two long inscriptions from Pisa expressing the mourning of the colony for Lucius (A.D. 2) and Gaius (A.D. 4).[12] The sense of a future which was not now to come about is particularly clear in the latter case: *crudelibus fatis ereptum populo Romano, iam designatu[m i]ustissumum ac simillimum parentis sui virtutibus principem* (by the cruel fates snatched from the Roman people, already designated, as the most just, and most similar to his parent's virtues, *princeps*). We know, of course, of one aspect of the elaborate forms of commemoration devised in Rome itself for Gaius and Lucius, namely the addition to the centuriate assembly of ten new centuries named after them; the measure was embodied in the Lex Valeria Cornelia passed by the ordinary consuls of A.D. 5, L. Valerius Messalla Volesus and Cn. Cornelius Cinna Magnus. It is no more than an accident that we have no text of this law itself and can perceive it only through the Tabula Hebana of Tiberius' reign.[13]

That sense of a future which could not now come about is of course felt

---

9. G. Alföldy, "Augustus und die Inschriften: Tradition und Innovation. Die Geburt der imperialen Epigraphik," *Gymnasium* 98 (1991): 289.

10. Suetonius, *Div. Aug.* 31, 5; see Luce (n. 6).

11. *AE* 1967, no. 458; *SEG* XXIII, no. 206; see esp. J. E. G. Zetzel, "New Light on Gaius Caesar's Eastern Campaign," *GRBS* 11 (1970): 259.

12. *ILS* 139–40; A. R. Marotta d'Agata, *Decreta Pisana* (*CIL* XI, 1420–21) (1980).

13. See, still, P. A. Brunt, "The Lex Valeria Cornelia," *JRS* 51 (1961): 71.

also in the most famous inscribed document of the period, the *Res Gestae* of Augustus (chap. 14): "filios meos, quos iuve[nes m]ihi eripuit fortuna" (my sons, whom fortune snatched from me in their youth). But the two texts share more than that, for the *Res Gestae* itself is simultaneously both "Augustan" and "Tiberian." As a *text*, it is a composition of the Emperor's last years, culminating in the award of the designation "Pater Patriae" (father of his country) in 2 B.C. and completed in A.D. 13 (chap. 35).[14] But as an *inscription* it is Tiberian, put up after Augustus' death (we do not know exactly when), at the entrance to the Mausoleum, and then copied—again we do not know exactly when—in provincial towns. All the copies which we happen to have come from Asia Minor. It remains uncertain whether local copying was specifically enjoined, as we now know was the case for the text of the measures passed in Rome to commemorate Germanicus. But those latter measures, revealed by the Tabula Siarensis, also show that it was not an idle guess on the part of Zvi Yavetz to suggest that a text of this period celebrating the virtues and achievements of a deceased member of the imperial household might have been specifically designed for the edification of the "youth" (*iuventus*) of the next and future generations. For Tiberius formally stated to the Senate in December A.D. 19 that his testimony (*testimonium*) to Germanicus' services would be "utile iuventuti liberorum posterorumque nostrorum" (useful for the youth of our children and descendants).[15] But the combined text of the Tabula Siarensis and the longer-known Tabula Hebana, conveniently overlapping to produce 176 lines of official Tiberian prose, is also simultaneously "Augustan" and "Tiberian." For, as mentioned earlier, it rehearses the legislation put through in A.D. 5 by the two ordinary consuls, adding ten new centuries to the centuriate assembly, and uses that as the model for the addition of five further centuries in memory of Germanicus. If a law had been required for that previous enactment, so it would be for these measures. So the Tabula Siarensis records that the Senate advised the incoming consuls of A.D. 20 to have its votes incorporated as soon as possible in a law passed by the people: "Utique M. Messalla, M. Aurelius Cotta Maximus, cos. designati, cum magistratum inissent, primo quoque tempore cum per auspicia liceret, sine binum trinumve nundinum prodictione, legem ad populum de honoribus Germanici Caesaris ferendam curent" (and that M. Messalla and M. Aurelius Cotta Maximus, consuls designate, when they enter their magis-

14. See now E. S. Ramage, *The Nature and Purpose of Augustus' Res Gestae* (1987).

15. *AE* 1984, no. 508, fr. B, col. 2, l. 17, of the combined text in M. Crawford (ed.), *Roman Statutes* I (1991), no. 37/8. See Z. Yavetz, "The *Res Gestae* and Augustus' Public Image," in Millar and Segal (n. 7), 1. Note the excellent English translation of the whole text provided by R. K. Sherk, *The Roman Empire* (1988), no. 36.

tracy, at the first moment permitted by the auspices, without a declaration of notice of a double or triple nine-day period, should see to the taking to the people of a law about the honours of Germanicus Caesar).[16] The full name of the first of the consuls was "M. Valerius Messalla Messallinus," and of his colleague, "M. Aurelius Cotta Maximus Messallinus"; they were respectively (as it seems) the grandson and the son (by a different wife) of M. Messalla Corvinus, the consul of 31 B.C. All three names bring us close to the life and works of Ovid. One of the consuls of A.D. 5 had been another Messalla, apparently not related.[17] The public adulation and exaltation of the imperial house was in no small measure the work of long-established republican families — as well as of their associates, like Ovidius Naso.

The Tabula Siarensis also takes us back to the public celebration of Augustus, and almost certainly to the year after his death. For it records that the arch ("ianus") which was to be erected in the Circus Flaminius was to go on the spot where statues had already been dedicated to Divus Augustus and the Domus Augusta by Gaius Norbanus Flaccus. The occasion is very likely to have been Flaccus' consulate as *ordinarius* in A.D. 15. If so, the combination of attention to the recently deified Augustus and to the wider imperial house finds a close reflection both in Ovid's poetry and in another key inscription of the same period.[18]

The dossier of major inscriptions of this very distinctive period is now augmented by the extremely important text, also from Baetica, recording the proceedings of the Senate after the suicide of Cn. Calpurnius Piso in A.D. 20.[19] But that remarkable reflection of the same combination of adulatory triumphalism on the one hand and of fear, uncertainty, and (now) unfulfillable hopes on the other is also matched in two other literary works of the period, which need to be mentioned briefly before we turn to the later works of Ovid.

The first is the *Facta et Dicta Memorabilia* (Memorable deeds and sayings) of Valerius Maximus, a work which is only now beginning to be accorded the prominence which it deserves.[20] For it is a perfect reflection, composed under

16. *Roman Statutes*, no. 37/8, fr. B, col. 2, ll. 27–30.

17. For these genealogical connections, by their nature beyond the ability of the present writer to grasp in detail, see R. Syme, *The Augustan Aristocracy* (1986), chaps. 15–17 and tables 9–10.

18. *AE* 1984, no. 508, fr. I. For this connection see already F. Millar, "Imperial Ideology in the Tabula Siarensis," in J. González and J. Arce, eds., *Estudios Sobre La Tabula Siarensis* (1988), 11 (chapter 15 in this volume).

19. W. Eck, A. Caballos, and P. Fernandes, *Das Senatusconsultum de Cn. Pisone Patre* (1996).

20. See Y. Maslakov, "Valerius Maximus and Roman Historiography: A Study of the

Tiberius, of the moralising deployment of *exempla* from the Roman past in Augustan historiography. The opening address to Tiberius sets the tone:

> Te igitur huic coepto, penes quem hominum deorumque consensus maris ac terrae regimen esse voluit, certissima salus patriae, Caesar, invoco, cuius caelesti providentia virtutes, de quibus dicturus sum, foventur, vitia severissime vindicantur.

> You therefore do I invoke in this undertaking, Caesar, in whose power the common will of gods and mankind wished the government of sea and earth to be, by whose celestial providence the virtues, of which I am about to speak, are fostered, and vices are most severely punished.

But here too, as is well known, a powerful note of anxiety and of danger narrowly averted, makes itself felt. For in 9, 11, *ext.* 4, Valerius launches into an invective against someone who had conspired against the current emperor.

> Tu videlicet efferatae barbariae immanitate truculentior habenas Romani imperii, quas princeps parensque noster salutari dextera continet, capere potuisti? . . . sed vigilarunt oculi deorum . . . et in primis auctor ac tutela nostrae incolumitatis ne excellentissima merita sua totius orbis ruina conlaberentur divino consilio providit.

> Could you indeed, a being more savage than the monstrosity of wild barbarity, have taken over the reins of the Roman empire, which our princeps and parent holds in his salutary right hand? But the eyes of the gods were vigilant . . . and above all the author and guardian of our security took provision by his divine counsel to prevent his most excellent services from collapsing in the ruin of the whole globe.

Generally taken to refer to Sejanus, and hence to date the work after A.D. 31, this invective may well, as Jane Bellemore has suggested, refer to the conspiracy of Libo Drusus in A.D. 16.[21] If so, then the whole text may date to the earlier years of Tiberius; we might therefore all the more easily see it too as a work which was, both in inspiration and in actual date, "post-Augustan." Precisely because it is *intended* to represent conventional wisdom, its importance for the ideology of the period can hardly be exaggerated.

One limiting factor in any attempt to locate the *Dicta et Facta* within the

exempla Tradition," *ANRW* 2.32.1 (1984), 437, and now esp. W. Martin Bloomer, *Valerius Maximus and the Rhetoric of the New Nobility* (1992).

21. J. Bellemore, "When Did Valerius Maximus Write the *Facta et Dicta Memorabilia*?," *Antichthon* 23 (1989): 67.

formulation of early imperial ideology is the fact that its author hardly reveals anything of himself, whether as regards geographical origin, social standing, or life-history. Precisely the opposite is true of the writer who, in part for that very reason, offers by far the most revealing comparison to Ovid (and indeed to Valerius Maximus), namely Velleius Paterculus. His work, dedicated as we saw to the consul of A.D. 30, M. Vinicius, also gains its importance precisely from its deliberate conventionality, from its attempt both to retell the main events of Roman history and to give due emphasis to its salient features.

But in this case there is an extra dimension, in that he gives sufficient prominence to his ancestors and his own career, to reveal himself as the perfect example of what Syme saw as a fundamental feature of "the Roman revolution": the long-delayed absorption of Rome by "the whole of Italy" (*tota Italia*), or in other terms, the large-scale entry of "the local nobility" (*domi nobiles*) of Italy into the equestrian order and the Senate itself.[22] Velleius ought to have been the hero, or anti-hero, of *The Roman Revolution*, as the local dignitary who entered the Senate in the last part of Augustus' reign, after equestrian military service; and then, in writing his *History*, did his best to direct adulation appropriately to both successive emperors, sometimes with unintentionally comic effects.[23] Looking in another direction, we could see Velleius as the successful counterpart to Ovid, his older contemporary — that is, as the Italian local dignitary who followed the career which Ovid rejected, reached the Senate, wrote what at the relevant moment (just before the fall of Sejanus) seemed to be required by the regime, and left descendants who rose to the consulship. To suggest the significance of the family and the man, only the barest details need be given here.[24]

A remote ancestor on the maternal side had been Decius Magius, a pro-Roman Capuan who played a part in the Second Punic War; by the early first century B.C. the family was settled in Aeclanum, and Velleius' great-great-great(?) grandfather, Minatius Magius, fought on the Roman side in the Social War; his two sons became praetors in Rome; a later member of the family, a contemporary of Velleius, will be the Marcus Magius Maximus from Aeclanum who was praefectus Aegypti in the period A.D. 11–14. On the

---

22. See G. V. Sumner, "The Truth about Velleius Paterculus: Prolegomena," *HSCPh* 74 1970): 252; A. J. Woodman, *Velleius Paterculus: The Caesarian and Augustan Narrative (2.41–93)* (1983), and *The Tiberian Narrative (2.94–131)* (1977).

23. Contrast the much-quoted passage on the "restoration" of the *res publica* by Augustus (2, 89) with that on the same achievement on the part of Tiberius (2, 126).

24. S. Demougin, *Prosopographie des chevaliers romains julio-claudiens* (1992), no. 88 (the father); no. 108 (Velleius himself).

paternal side, the grandfather, Gaius Velleius, was a *praefectus fabrum* (prefect of engineers) and juror (*iudex*) in the late Republic; of his sons, one was a senator (and an assistant prosecutor in the prosecution of Cassius), while Velleius' father remained an equestrian, and was *praefectus equitum*, apparently in Germania. If we follow the recent discussion by Ségolène Demougin, the father will have been born in the 50s B.C.; hence it makes sense that Velleius himself began his military career as a military tribune under P. Vinicius and L. Silius in Thrace and Macedonia about 2 B.C. (he may thus have been some fifteen years younger than Ovid). Then, after further service, still as military tribune, with Gaius Caesar in the East, he served as *praefectus equitum* with Tiberius in Germany. In A.D. 7 he entered the Senate as quaestor, evidently at a later age than the norm of twenty-five. In A.D. 14, as his own testimony shows, he was, along with his brother, Magius Celer Velleianus, the emperor's candidate (*candidatus Caesaris*) for the praetorship of A.D. 15, "commended" both by Augustus before his death and then by Tiberius (2, 124, 3–4). Just before this (124, 2), Velleius had recorded the long reluctance of Tiberius to take up the position of emperor: "solique huic contigit paene diutius recusare principatum, quam ut occuparent eum, alii armis pugnaverant" (to him alone it befell to refuse the principate almost longer than others have fought with arms to seize it). There is thus no earlier witness to this reluctance—except Ovid.

Velleius' ancestry and career would of themselves give him a significant place in Roman history, even if he had not gone on to write his patriotic and value-laden account of it. Its structure and emphases would deserve much fuller analysis, especially if taken seriously as the perfect expression of "post-Augustan" ideology. But in this context it will be enough to stress the paucity of the account of Gaius and Lucius, compared with the importance given to the return and adoption of Tiberius (2, 102–4); the low profile of Germanicus, and the unmistakable, if muted, unfavourable comparison between him and Drusus, the son of Tiberius (2, 125, 4); the elaborate justification of the prominent role of Sejanus, in spite of his relatively modest origins and equestrian rank (2, 127–28); and the rhetorical evocation of the pain caused to Tiberius by Agrippina, the widow of Germanicus, and her son Nero (2, 130): "Quam diu abstruso, quod miserrimum est, pectus eius flagravit incendio, quod ex nuru, quod ex nepote dolere, indignari, erubescere coactus est!" (How long did his heart burn with an inflammation, more wretched for being concealed, because of the grief, the indignation, and the shame he was forced to suffer through his daughter-in-law and his grandson!). In keeping with the tone of combined triumphalism and anxiety which marks the literature of this period, the work ends with a prayer to Iuppiter Capitolinus, Mars Gradivus, and Vesta to preserve Tiberius as long as possible—and then

grant him capable successors: "destinate successores quam serissimos, sed eos
quorum cervices tam fortiter sustinendo terrarum orbis imperio sufficiant,
quam huius suffecisse sensimus, consiliaque omnium civium aut pia [fovete
aut impia opprimite?]" (mark out successors as far as possible in the future,
but ones whose shoulders are broad enough to bear the government of the
world as bravely as we have seen his do, and whatever the plans of all citizens,
if pious [promote them, if impious suppress them?]).

Ovid in Rome

There were of course at least three profound differences between Velleius and
another local dignitary of the Augustan period, Ovidius Naso from Sulmo.
Firstly, Ovid though he began a career as a senator, did not pursue it; secondly, his very prominent position in Rome ended suddenly in disgrace and
exile, from which (so far as we know) he was never to be recalled; and, thirdly,
he was a writer of genius, capable of the highest achievements in a succession
of different poetic genres.

But the undeniable fact of his literary genius, combined with his eventual
fall and exile, should not tempt us to see him as always having been, in social
and political terms, at some distance from the regime, as having preserved
a real spiritual and artistic independence, or as having been in some sense a
rebel whose non-compliance was ultimately punished. This chapter suggests
that the truth is otherwise: that Ovid should be clearly contrasted with the
great "post-Triumviral" writers of the earlier part of Augustus' reign; and that
he belongs not with them but, in social origin, in attachment to a strongly
loyalist senatorial family, and in the overt "Augustanism," found in some of
his later works, with the "post-Augustan" Velleius. Far from being expressions of spiritual resistance, the poems of exile should be read as the protests
of a rejected loyalist, whose rightful place, in Rome and in relation with leading senatorial families, has wrongly been denied him. The poetry both of
the decade before his exile in A.D. 8, and of the decade after it, incorporates
"Augustan" features, in a way in which the works of the "post-Triumviral"
writers do not.

This is, of course, no place to rehearse all that is known of Ovid's origins,
career, and earlier works.[25] But it is important to stress how prominent an
example he is of the local dignitary who might have ascended to the heart of
the senatorial order in Rome. As we all know, an inscription of the Augustan

25. Only the key references will be given. The evidence has often been collected, most
recently in *PIR*² o 180.

period reveals that the first ever Roman senator to come from the territory of the Paeligni was Q. Varius Geminus from Superaequum Paelignorum:[26] "is primus omnium Paelign(orum) senator factus est et eos honores gessit" (he was the first of the Paeligni to become senator and held these offices). The earliest of the offices listed in his career (*cursus*) will have been the presenatorial post in the vigintivirate, *decemvir stlitibus iudicandis* (one of a board of ten men for judging law-suits), and he went on to be praetor, and a praetorian legate and proconsul. That no earlier Paelignian had risen so far lends much greater significance to the fact that Ovid (and his brother) might have done so. Like Velleius, Ovid lays repeated emphasis on his place of origin (*patria*), Sulmo, and on the (equestrian) rank which he inherited (e.g., *Tr.* 4, 10, 3–8), though in fact no *Roman* rank can have gone back more than two generations (at the most) of the family; for Sulmo, as Ovid himself recalls, had been non-Roman and on the allied side in the Social War (*Amores* 3, 15, 5–10). In the 20s B.C., Ovid was in Rome and, like his brother, assumed the wide stripe on the toga (*latus clavus*), a sign that he was intending to enter the Senate. It seems to have been after his brother had died in 24 B.C. that Ovid held the post of *tresvir* (one of the "three men" in charge either of capital cases, *capitales*, or of the mint, *monetales*) in the vigintivirate (the board of twenty), and was preparing for a senatorial career—only then to reject it in favour of poetry (*Tr.* 4, 10, 27–40).

The conclusion is inescapable that Ovid belonged to one of the most prominent families of the whole Paelignian region. That he rejected a senatorial career was a personal choice; he remained a member of the equestrian order, later regretfully recalling from Tomoi how he had ridden in the annual parade (*transvectio*) on July 15 (*Tr.* 2, 89–90): "at, memini, vitamque meam moresque probabas / illo, quem dederas, praetereuntis equo" (But, I recall, you used to approve my life and morals, when I rode past on the horse you had granted me).

He also enjoyed the personal friendship and encouragement of one of the most prominent of all Augustan senators, M. Valerius Messalla Corvinus, who had shared the consulship with Imperator Caesar Divi filius in the year of Actium. True social equality there surely was not; but at the same time we should avoid at all costs importing into our conceptions of how Latin literature was written the wholly irrelevant categories of "patronus" and "cliens." [27]

26. *ILS* 932.

27. There is no room here to argue this proposition. I will merely state baldly that (for instance) it wholly vitiates the otherwise interesting paper by G. Williams, "Did Maecenas 'Fall from Favour'? Augustan Literary Patronage," in Raaflaub and Toher (n. 6), 258.

As countless examples show, comfortably-off persons of equestrian origin, whether from Rome itself, like Atticus, or from a *municipium*, like Cicero, belonged, in social, economic, and cultural terms, to the same broad band of educated landowners as did senators, even those who were *nobiles*. In the crucial year 2 B.C., which it is suggested should be seen as beginning the "late-Augustan" phase of Latin literature, it was Messalla Corvinus who proposed in the Senate that Augustus should receive the appellation "Pater Patriae."[28] But it is Augustus himself who records that it was not only the Senate and the Roman people who awarded this honour, but also the equestian order, acting as a corporate body (*RG* 35). If this piece of loyalism involved some form of vote or resolution, it is the only such act attested on the part of the order, and must thus have been of great significance. In the *Fasti* Ovid does not fail to note this also, carefully using the first-person plural to signal his own participation (*Fasti* 2, 127–28): "Sancte pater patriae, tibi plebs, tibi curia nomen / hoc dedit, dedimus nos tibi nomen, eques" (Reverend father of the fatherland, the plebs, the senate and we, the equites, gave you this name)—and goes on to a laborious comparison of Augustus first to Iuppiter and then to Romulus, in which the latter clearly comes off worse (129–144).

These same years witnessed the emergence of Ovid as a poet in whose works emphatic, unambiguous, and highly developed expressions of loyalty to the regime would play (at least) a very marked part. It would be absurd to claim that other currents, or ambivalences of attitude, can nowhere be found in Ovid's poetry of this period; critical ingenuity can in any case discover these in any text. What is claimed as significant here is simply that Ovid's writing of this period is marked by deliberate, highly developed, and overt expressions of loyalism. For instance, in the revision of the *Ars Amatoria*, which seems to belong in 1 B.C.,[29] Ovid inserted, as Glen Bowersock has shown, a reference to the sea battle of "Athenians and Persians," which Augustus put on in 2 B.C. in the newly created *naumachia* (an artificial lake for giving waterborne displays); and he went on to expound its connection with Gaius' mission to the East to confront the Parthians (*AA* 1, 171ff.).[30] Ovid does not forget (202–3) to bring in both Mars and the prospective deification of Augustus: "Marsque pater Caesarque pater, date numen eunti: / nam deus e vobis alter est, alter eris" (Father Mars and Father Caesar, send him off with

---

28. Suetonius, *Div. Aug.* 58.

29. For the dates (as in all that follows), Syme (n. 5), 19–20.

30. G. Bowersock, "Augustus and the East: The Problem of the Succession," in Millar and Segal (n. 7), 169.

your blessing: for of the two of you, one is a god, and one will be). This long passage gains all the more significance from being so evidently a deliberate insertion in the new edition.

The newly dedicated temple of Mars Ultor and the surrounding Forum Augustum were, of course, to receive their fullest literary exposition in the *Fasti* (5, 550–78), of which six books were completed before Ovid's exile, to be partially revised during it. Little more need be said of this work here, except to note Syme's dating of the first version to A.D. 1–4;[31] for its status as the most systematic attempt at writing poetry which was not only "Augustan," but which placed the new regime laboriously in the framework of inherited cults and of newly revived antiquarian learning, needs no emphasis. To say this is not to deny that no tensions or ambivalences in the treatment of Augustus and his regime are present in the text.[32] It is to assert that in its overall, overt programme and structure it represents a new phase in "Augustan" literature. If we are to understand the revolution of consciousness brought about by the emergence of a monarch from within the traditional *res publica*, it is here, and not with the great writers of a generation, or half-generation, earlier, that we should begin.

As an "Augustan" work, the *Fasti* involved both the evocation of an inherited (or reinvented) set of rituals, and a due emphasis on novelty, that is, the role of Augustus, of the members of his household, and of his actual *domus* (in the literal sense of a "house") on the Palatine (e.g., 4, 943–54). But, while never achieving the intended twelve books (*Tr.* 2, 549–50), the work was none the less revised in exile, then acquiring (among other things) a dedication to Germanicus. Like other works of the period, it thus finishes up by exhibiting a systematic uncertainty as to what, or who, the proper focus of loyalty should be. That object was in any case a moving target, repeatedly transformed by death, and by reversals of fortune among members of the *domus Augusta* (in the sense of "household"). Some aspects of the *Fasti* as we have it will even reflect revisions made after Augustus' own death.[33]

If the *Fasti* sets out systematically to place Augustus within the frame-

31. Syme (n. 5), 21–22.

32. See, e.g., A. Wallace-Hadrill, "Time for Augustus: Ovid, Augustus and the *Fasti*," in M. Whitby, P. Hardie, and M. Whitby, eds., *Homo Victor: Classical Essays for John Bramble* (1987), 221; the essays collected in *Arethusa* 25.1 (1992), *Reconsidering Ovid's Fasti*; and D. C. Feeney, "*Si licet et fas est*: Ovid's *Fasti* and the Problem of Free Speech under the Principate," in A. Powell, ed., *Roman Poetry and Propaganda in the Age of Augustus* (1992), 1.

33. So, e.g., G. Williams, *Change and Decline: Roman Literature in the Early Empire* (1978), 54–55 — though I cannot see why the main passage quoted, *Fasti* 4, 19–62, must have been written after A.D. 14. *Fasti* 1, 531–36, is a much clearer case (see text to n. 47).

work of inherited tradition, the same is also true of Ovid's greatest work, the *Metamorphoses*. Looking back in *Tristia* 2 on his poetic achievement before his exile, Ovid, if anything, rather understated just how profoundly shaped by Augustan loyalism this work had been (555–62):

> Dictaque sunt nobis, quamvis manus ultima coeptis
> defuit, in facies corpora versa novas.
> atque utinam revoces animum paulisper ab ira,
> et vacuo iubeas hinc tibi pauca legi,
> pauca, quibus prima surgens ab origine mundi
> in tua deduxi tempora, Caesar, opus:
> aspicies, quantum dederis mihi pectoris ipse,
> quoque favore animi teque tuosque canam.

We sang too, though the final touch was missing from the undertaking, / of bodies transformed into new appearances. / If only you put your anger briefly from your mind, / and in an idle moment have a few lines from this work read to you: / a few, in which starting from the first origin of the world / I spun out a work down to your time, Caesar. / Then you will see how much heart you put into me, / and with what wholehearted support I sing of you and yours.

As Denis Feeney has recently shown, it is not merely that Ovid's brilliant retelling of myths of transformation does in fact culminate in the deification of Julius Caesar and the prospective deification of Augustus. It is that the entire work is framed by the very recent Roman institution of the legal transformation of humans into deities.[34] Thus book 1 introduces the extremely bold reversal of representing Iuppiter as summoning all the gods to conclave in a context which is explicitly compared to the Palatine (1, 170–6): "hic locus est, quem si verbis audacia detur, / haud timeam magni dixisse Palatia caeli" (this is the place which, if my words be allowed some boldness, I should not fear to call the Palatine of the great heaven). Soon after comes a crucial reference to the murder of Caesar, and the continuing *pietas* (piety) shown to Augustus by his people, as by the other gods to Iuppiter (199–205). But even that hardly prepares the reader for the culmination in books 13–15, in which Aeneas is to play the central role, with diversionary sub-plots, before the emphasis shifts to Romulus, and then Numa (with further sub-plots); then to the importation of the cult of Aesculapius—and finally, by

---

34. See D. C. Feeney, *The Gods in Epic: Poets and Critics of the Classical Tradition* (1991), chap. 5.

another daring conceit, to the deification of Caesar. Caesar, unlike Aesculapius, was a native of Rome; but, more than that, it was not so much his own deeds which had won him divinity, but his progeny (*progenies*) (15, 745–51): "neque enim de Caesaris actis / ullum maius opus, quam quod pater exstitit huius" (nor is there among Caesar's acts any greater achievement than that he proved father of this man). The claim that what had been involved was natural, biological succession is now re-emphasised again. Were any of Caesar's triumphs greater than that of having fathered so great a man: "quam tantum genuisse virum"? (752–58). Not only the Triumvirs, but the Roman people, who passed the law of 42 B.C., and with them the natural father of Augustus, have all vanished, to leave Augustus both as the real son of Caesar, and the sole author of his divine status. The passage moves to the most vivid of all literary evocations of Caesar's murder, and then turns, in a prophecy uttered by Juppiter, to Augustus. But the prophecy also looks forward to the prospective accession of Tiberius, and finally focuses on to Divus Iulius and his temple (15, 832–42):

> Pace data terris animum ad civilia vertet
> iura suum legesque feret iustissimus auctor
> exemploque suo mores reget inque futuri
> temporis aetatem venturorumque nepotum
> prospiciens prolem sancta de coniuge natam
> ferre simul nomenque suum curasque iubebit,
> nec nisi cum senior Pylios aequaverit annos,
> aetherias sedes cognataque sidera tanget.
> hanc animam interea caeso de corpore raptam
> fac iubar, ut semper Capitolia nostra forumque
> divus ab excelso prospectet Iulius aede.

Peace once brought to the earth, he will turn his mind / to civil justice, and, most just of law-makers, will carry laws, / and by his own example will control morals; and looking ahead to future / ages and coming generations / will order offspring born of a saintly wife / to bear both his name and his cares; / nor, till in old age he has matched the years of Nestor, / will he touch the etheral seat and the stars that share his blood. / Meantime, make this soul snatched from the murdered body / into a star, so that for ever our Capitol and forum / Divus Iulius may look forth from his lofty temple.

If, as has been claimed, Julius Caesar had indeed not been given a very prominent place in earlier Augustan literature, that is not so in Ovid. Equally, in-

attention to his memory cannot have reflected popular perceptions. For since
29 B.C. the new temple of Divus Iulius had occupied one pole of the central axis of the Forum.[35] But Ovid's exploitation of the symbolic landscape
of Rome is not yet complete. In his final prayer he evokes, as he does in the
Fasti (4, 949–54), the cohabitation of Vesta, Apollo, and Augustus himself on
the Palatine, linking the three in a single complex line of great conceptual
boldness—"et cum Caesarea tu, Phoebe domestice, Vesta" (and you, domestic Phoebus, together with Caesarian Vesta, 865)—and looks forward once
again to the prospective deification of Augustus (861–70).

In the last part of the *Metamorphoses* the delicacy, restraint, and indirect-
ness which Virgil had deployed in linking the Julian house to the legendary
origins of Rome has vanished, to be replaced, as in the *Fasti*, by an overt
loyalism, as well as by a creative use of the now "Julian" topography of the
centre of Rome. What remained for the poems of exile was an intensifica-
tion of these elements, a repeated evocation of changes of power, both those
which might happen and those which already had; and something new, in
the *Epistulae ex Ponto* at least: a representation of the relationship of Augustus, and then of Tiberius, to the successive holders of the consulate, to the
Senate, and to the Roman people.

Ovid in Tomoi

As to how Ovid came to be exiled, this chapter has no suggestion to offer to
add to the scores already canvassed. It is important instead to stress his high
social position, as an equestrian who might have chosen a senatorial career,
and who had personal connections to the family of Messalla Corvinus. Messalla had died in A.D. 8, and Ovid had written the eulogy (*elogium*) delivered
at his funeral (*Ex P.* 1, 7, 29), just as he had composed the wedding hymn (*epi-
thalamium*) for the marriage of Fabius Maximus, consul of 11 B.C. (1, 2, 133).
The notions of "patronus" and "cliens" give a quite distorted impression of
such relationships, and of the social standing of a local dignitary and Roman
equestrian like Ovidius Naso. Such a person, whether he wrote poetry or
not, was a member of the political class, a man (necessarily) of independent
wealth, and of high, but not the highest, rank.

It will have been of real practical importance that Ovid, though ordered
to live in Tomoi, had been, as he explicitly says, merely exiled (*relegatus*), and
had not been subject to condemnation. Whatever stage the developing rules

---

35. See P. White, "Julius Caesar in Augustan Rome," *Phoenix* 42 (1988): 334.

about the confiscation of the property of the condemned had reached by A.D. 8, Ovid will have kept his property and income.[36]

Beyond that, as to the real circumstances which attended him in exile, and the real extent of actual communications between him and Rome, we have no "evidence" external to the *Tristia* and *Epistulae ex Ponto* themselves. What we have instead is the poetic evocation of a personal disaster, and equally a series of poetic evocations of appeals made to persons in Rome in the hope of getting his exile ended—along with representations of public events, of public ceremonials, of the assumption of office by consuls, and of personal relationships at the centre of power, in Rome itself. A real "history" of relations and communications between Ovid and persons in Rome cannot be written. We may suppose, for instance, that the poems of the years A.D. 8 to 16 were indeed actually carried to Rome, though by whom we do not know; and were read there, though again we do not know by whom. But all that the poems present, as regards such communications is, for instance, an *anticipatory* portrayal of the journey of his "book" (*liber*) to Rome and its reception there (*Tr.* 1, 1); or a poem written in the person of the book itself as it records its (prospective) tour of the Forum, the Palatine, and the nearest part of the Campus Martius (*Tr.* 3, 1). We cannot even be sure that poems which represent themselves as directed to well-placed intermediaries to intercede with the ultimate holder of power were in reality delivered to those persons.

At the same time, the poems are, without qualification, evidence for the transmission of news from Rome to the outer fringes of the Empire. Ovid may mislead his readers into forgetting that Tomoi, far from being "Getic," was a long-established Greek city, which will have had much the same diplomatic relations to governors and emperors as any other; and equally his continued personal contacts with Roman society, presumably transmitted by letters carried by messengers, may have kept him more precisely up-to-date than might have been expected of someone living on the shore of the Black Sea. In that sense he provides simultaneously both an "insider's" and a provincial "outsider's" view, or representation, of the march of events in Rome. But information about those events does reach him: about triumphs, about who will hold the consulship, about the death and deification of Augustus. In some ways his poetic recreations of these distant events, happening in an urban context which is intensely familiar, are actually more important for the historian than mere eyewitness accounts. For, firstly, they are the work of an extremely well placed loyalist (or author of loyalist expressions), whose

36. *Tr.* 2, 131–37; 4, 9, 12; 5, 2, 56–58; 2, 21.

writing from after his exile shows profound continuities, in general and in detail, with that from the years before it. And, secondly, by being compelled to re-imagine what was occurring in Rome he confers on it a generic significance which a mere report might lack.

The poems "addressed" to named persons are very important for historians, not because they actually "are" petitions for intercession (we do not know whether they were or not), but because they are remarkably vivid representations of the central role which the arrival of monarchic power had conferred on petitioning; and because, more precisely, they are testimony to the already established significance of what Richard Saller has called "brokerage": the custom of directing appeals and requests to well-placed intermediaries, who—it was to be hoped—would intercede with the real holders of power.[37] Precisely because of the importance of brokerage in their structure, the poems in *Ex Ponto* in particular go beyond the representation of the imperial house and the structure of power within it, to speak of leading senators and their imagined relationship to the regime. Ovid's evidence is thus of immense complexity and significance, all the more important for reflecting a period at the end of Augustus' reign and the beginning of Tiberius' which is relatively little known.

As is obvious, the representation of public scenes and political relations in Rome is only one aspect of the poetry of exile;[38] and even as regards this aspect I pick out here merely a few examples of three overlapping themes: emperor and public in Rome, consuls and the emperor, and the changing structure of the imperial house.

Emperor and Roman People

I begin with an event which never occurred, the triumph over Germany which Ovid was expecting in A.D. 10.[39] As indicated earlier, events and interconnections which had literally to be imagined, and presented in poetic form, could be thought of as even more significant than those, described at second hand on the basis of actual reports, which had in reality already occurred, like the triumph of A.D. 12 to which we come next.

Writing the poem in question (*Tr.* IV, 2), Ovid explicitly represents him-

---

37. R. Saller, "Promotion and Patronage in Equestrian Careers," *JRS* 70 (1980): 44, and *Personal Patronage in the Early Empire* (1982).

38. For the fullest recent discussion see H. B. Evans, *Publica Carmina: Ovid's Books from Exile* (1983).

39. Syme (n. 5), 38–39.

self, the exiled outcast, as speculating about whether a victory had already been achieved, or perhaps even a triumph already held; but though Tiberius and Germanicus did campaign in Germany in A.D. 10 and 11, and imperial salutations were gained for Augustus and Tiberius, no great victory was achieved, and no triumph was held. Ovid could still imagine what it would be like, or would have been, to be there (1–26):

> Iam fera Caesaribus Germania, totus ut orbis,
> victa potest flexo succubuisse genu.
> altaque velentur fortasse Palatia sertis,
> turaque in igne sonent inficiantque diem,
> candidaque adducta collum percussa securi
> victima purpureo sanguine pulset humum,
> donaque amicorum templis promissa deorum
> reddere victores Caesar uterque parent.
> et qui Caesareo iuvenes sub nomine crescunt,
> perpetuo terras ut domus illa regat,
> cumque bonis nuribus pro sospite Livia nato
> munera det meritis, saepe datura, deis,
> et pariter matres et quae sine crimine castos
> perpetua servant virginitate focos;
> plebs pia cumque pia laetetur plebe senatus,
> parvaque cuius eram pars ego nuper eques:
> nos procul expulsos communia gaudia fallunt,
> famaque tam longe non nisi parva venit.
> ergo omnis populus poterit spectare triumphos,
> cumque ducum titulis oppida capta leget.
> vinclaque captiva reges cervice gerentes
> ante coronatos ire videbit equos.
> et cernet vultus aliis pro tempore versos,
> terribiles aliis inmemoresque sui.
> quorum pars causas et res et nomina quaeret,
> pars referet, quamvis noverit illa parum.

(1) Already before the Caesars wild Germany, like the whole world, / may have fallen in defeat on bended knee. / Maybe the high Palatine is veiled in garlands, / and incense crackles in the fire and dyes the day, / and the white victim smitten in the neck by the lifted axe / throbs purple blood to the ground, / and the gifts they had promised to the temples of the friendly gods / the victors, each a Caesar, may be making ready to present; / together with the young men who

grow under the name of Caesar, / to ensure the household rules the earth for ever. /

(2) Livia too with her good daughters in-law may be making for her son's safety / the offerings she will always make to the well-deserving gods; / likewise the matrons and the chaste ones / who preserve the sacred hearths with their perpetual virginity, / and the loyal plebs, and with the loyal plebs the Senate / and the knights of whom I was once a small part. / This common joy passes me by in distant isolation, / and none but slight news penetrates so far. / So then all the people will have managed to watch the triumphs, / and will read on placards the names of leaders and cities captured. /

(3) They will see kings with chains about their captive necks / walking before the garlanded horses. / Here they will see the expressions fittingly downcast. / There fearsome scowls of men beside themselves. / One viewer will ask for names and stories and explanations; / the next will give them, little though they know.

Ovid, who could not be there, devotes much of the poem, in the lines which follow (27–46), to an imagined interpretation of the scene given by one spectator to another; the technique is strikingly similar to Polybius' use of spectators' reactions as a way of giving meaning to the events in his *History*.[40] One figure which needed to be identified will have been a representation of the conquered Germania (43–44): "crinibus en etiam fertur Germania passis, / et ducis invicti sub pede maesta sedet" (Look—even Germany is borne along with her hair flying wild, / and sits sadly at the foot of the invincible leader). This evocation will naturally recall the images of conquered nations, above all Britannia herself, from the Sebasteion of Aphrodisias.[41]

If the crowd could not identify the symbolic figures carried in the procession, it was possible (as equally, in permanent form, at Aphrodisias) to read the names, and pass on the information to others. At the end of the poem (67–74) Ovid returns to the theme of his own absence from among the spectators; but earlier, in the passage quoted, he has also recalled once again his proper, if now lost, place as a member of a privileged order, one of the groups whose rejoicing gives meaning to the event (15–16).

In the context of a triumph, however, it must be striking that the only member of the imperial house who is actually named in this passage is Livia

---

40. J. Davidson, "The Gaze in Polybius," *JRS* 81 (1991): 38–39.

41. R. R. R. Smith, "The Imperial Reliefs from the Sebasteion at Aphrodisias," *JRS* 77 (1987): 88; "*Simulacra Gentium*: The *Ethne* from the Sebasteion at Aphrodisias," *JRS* 78 (1988): 50.

(11–14), identified as offering sacrifices, along with her unnamed daughters-in-law (Agrippina and Livilla), for the safety of her equally unnamed son (Tiberius); with equal emphasis, she is associated with mothers and the Vestal Virgins.[42] The imperial family is seen expressly as a collectivity, and as located within traditional Roman society.

The prospect of change and a shift of power in the Augustan house is already implicit, even explicit. Augustus and Tiberius appear only as "Caesar uterque" (both emperors), and far more emphasis is laid, in remarkably un-ambiguous language, on the prospective rule of the next generation, Germanicus and Drusus (9–10). In noting Ovid's bold use of the verb *regere* (to rule as king), we should also recall that, like the entire scene (which never occurred), *domus illa* (that household) was a construct, made up, in default of other unfulfilled possibilities, by reluctant adoptions.

The other triumph which Ovid was to evoke was at least a real one, that celebrated by Tiberius over Illyricum, on October 23, A.D. 12.[43] In the first of two poems on this triumph (*Ex P.* 2, 1), he provides another evocation of the spectators watching the procession (21–48), and a prediction of a future triumph by Germanicus (49–63). But the following poem (2, 2) is the more concrete and, in various ways, the more significant. Firstly, it is addressed to M. Valerius Messalla Messallinus, consul of 3 B.C., and the elder son of Messalla Corvinus, with an allusion to his brother, M. Valerius Cotta Maximus. Like many poems in *Ex Ponto* it has the form of a request for intercession, or "brokerage," which is to be based on close connection of the prospective intercessor with the emperor, and is to deploy the eloquence inherited from his famous father (41–52):

> verbaque nostra favens Romana ad numina perfer,
> non tibi Tarpeio culta Tonante minus,
> mandatique mei legatus suscipe causam:
> nulla meo quamvis nomine causa bona est.
> iam prope depositus, certe iam frigidus aeger,
> servatus per te, si modo servor, ero.
> nunc tua pro lassis nitatur gratia rebus,
> principis aeterni quam tibi praestat amor.
> nunc tibi et eloquii nitor ille domesticus adsit,

42. See N. Purcell, "Livia and the Womanhood of Rome," *PCPhS* 212 (1986): 78.

43. The date is given by *AE* 1922, no. 96 (from Praeneste, Degrassi, *Ins. It.* 13.2, p. 135, a fragment of the *Fasti Praenestini*): "Ti. Caesar curru triumphavit ex Ilurico" (Ti[berius] Caesar, riding in a chariot, triumphed over Illyricum [on the same day of the year as the second battle of Philippi]; see Syme (n. 3), 40–41.

> quo poteras trepidis utilis esse reis.
> vivit enim in vobis facundi lingua parentis,
> et res heredem repperit illa suum.

As a favour take my words to the Roman powers / whom you worship no less than the Thundered on the Tarpeian rock, / and as my emissary take up my brief, / even though no plea in my name is good. / All but abandoned, ailing and chill indeed, / if I am saved, it will be by you. / Now may my flagging fortunes rely on the influence you enjoy, / thanks to the love for you of the eternal prince. / Now summon up your family's brilliant eloquence, / which has made you useful to trembling defendants. / For in you lives on your father's gift of speech, / and has found in you a true heir.

The triumph itself is then suggested as an appropriate moment for the presentation of a request and once again stress is laid on the collective role of the imperial house (67–74):

> tempus adest aptum precibus. valet ille videtque
> quas fecit vires, Roma, valere tuas.
> incolumis coniunx sua pulvinaria servat:
> promovet Ausonium filius imperium;
> praeterit ipse suos animo Germanicus annos;
> nec vigor est Drusi nobilitate minor.
> adde nurum neptemque pias natosque nepotum
> ceteraque Augustae membra valere domus.

The time is right for prayers. He is flourishing, and sees / that your strength, Rome, that he built up himself, is flourishing too. / A wife in good health guards his couch; / his son pushes forward the western front. / Germanicus is older than his years in spirit; / the vigour of Drusus matches his nobility. / Add a pious daughter-in-law and granddaughter, and grandsons with sons, / and that all the members of the Augustan house are in good health.

Again Livia comes first, though here unnamed, followed by Tiberius, also unnamed; then Germanicus and Drusus, followed by Livilla and Agrippina (unnamed), and the "sons of his grandsons." That is the sons of Germanicus—Nero, Drusus, and the just-born Gaius; and (perhaps) the infant son of Drusus, who was to die in A.D. 15.[44]

Tiberius, the actual *triumphator*, continues to play a strikingly anonymous

44. Dio 57, 14, 6.

role, alluded to only in the "triumphant foot of Caesar" (*Caesareum . . . pedem*) of line 78. More prominence is given to the two sons of Messalla themselves, evidently taking part in the triumph, and to the traditional setting in the Forum—the temple of Castor and Pollux (to whom the two brothers are compared), and (as before) the temple of Divus Iulius (81–84):

> quem pia vobiscum proles comitavit euntem,
> digna parente suo nominibusque datis,
> fratribus adsimiles, quos proxima templa tenentis
> divus ab excelsa Iulius aede videt.

With him ride you and your pious progeny, / worthy of their father and the names they bear, / like the twin brothers who occupy the temple / next to the lofty one from which Divus Julius looks on.

The "triumph" poems are another reminder of the fact, only partially modified by the arrival of monarchy, that Rome was a traditional public stage on which the actors (now including the female members of the imperial house) played out their roles in public, in the open air, before an audience made up of the Roman people. Within that same context the holders of the traditional magistracies also played their roles; in the new context of monarchy, they could be assumed on the one hand to be in a position to influence the ruler, but they were known on the other to be subject to his patronage. The interplay of public ceremonial and private influence was well known to Ovid, who (once again) can evoke it in advance, without waiting for mere reports.

Consuls and the Emperor

So, if we turn to the second of the three themes picked out from the exile poetry, the occupation of the consulate, we find Ovid in A.D. 13 looking forward to the consulate as *ordinarius* which Sextus Pompeius is to hold throughout A.D. 14 (*Ex P.* 4, 4, 23–42). He imagines the crowd on January 1 filling Pompeius' house to bursting; the procession to the Capitol and the sacrifice of oxen; the entry to the Senate house and the customary speech by the new consul; and then the return to his house, accompanied through the streets by the whole Senate. Here too, the public framework is profoundly traditional, and much of what is imagined could have taken place centuries before. But one element may be new. Was it already acknowledged, in formal public ceremonial, that the consulate was a gift from the emperor? What is certain is that the anticipated speech in the Senate by the new consul was to include expressions of thanks both to the gods and to the emperor (39): "*egeris et* meritas superis cum Caesare grates" (you will have offered due thanks to the gods along with Caesar). Were the thanks which he would give going to be offered for the peaceful and victorious state of the empire? Or, as later consuls would do, specifically to the emperor for the gift of the consulship itself?

In this poem that is left unspecified. But no such doubt remains when Ovid turns, in perhaps the latest poem in the collection, to imagine in advance (once again) the suffect consulship of C. Pomponius Graecinus, which would begin in July A.D. 16, and would last to the end of the year; and then the coming consulate as *ordinarius* of his brother, C. Pomponius Flaccus, due to start on January 1, A.D. 17. Ovid must be writing towards the middle of A.D. 16 (*Ex P.* 4, 9). Once again, addressing Graecinus, Ovid imagines the public ceremonials and sacrifices of the first day, adding only (18) the role that he himself, as an equestrian (*eques*), would play there if he could: "consulis ante pedes ire iuberer eques" (I would be ordered to go as a knight before the feet of the consul). But in this case he also goes on to imagine the daily public functions of the consul, in the Forum or the Senate, or sacrificing on the Capitol—and perhaps then there might be a place for a prayer on behalf of Ovid (41–52):

> mente tamen, quae sola loco non exulat, usus
> praetextam fasces aspiciamque tuos.
> haec modo te populo reddentem iura videbit,
> et se decretis finget adesse tuis;
> nunc longi reditus hastae supponere lustri
> credet, et exacta cuncta locare fide:
> nunc facere in medio facundum verba senatu.
> publica quaerentem quid petat utilitas;
> nunc pro Caesaribus superis decernere grates,
> albave opimorum colla ferire boam.
> atque utinam, cum iam fueris potiora precatus,
> ut mihi placetur principis ira roges!

In my mind, which alone is not in exile, / I shall see your robes and fasces. / It will see you one moment giving justice to the people, / and imagine itself to witness your decrees. / Next it will believe you to be putting to auction the revenues of a long cycle, / and to be contracting out everything with impeccable honesty; / next to be delivering an eloquent address in the Senate / enquiring what the public interest requires; / next to be decreeing thanks to the gods for the Caesars, / and to be smiting the white necks of choice oxen. / If only, when you have prayed for higher things, / you would ask for emperor's anger against me to abate!

But it is towards the middle of this poem that Ovid offers his most striking contribution to our conception of how the consulate was now understood, in using the utmost ingenuity to express the idea that its dignity was even increased by its being in the gift of another. As to the latter point, there here is no ambiguity at all. Ovid is referring to both of the two consulships to be held by the brothers (65–70):

> qui quamquam est ingens, et nullum Martia summo
> altius imperium consule Roma videt,
> multiplicat tamen hunc gravitas auctoris honorem,
> et maiestatem res data dantis habet.
> iudiciis igitur liceat Flaccoque tibique
> talibus Augusti tempus in omne frui.

Mighty though he is, and though Mar's Rome / sees no power higher than the supreme consul's, / yet the gravity of its author multiplies this honour, / and the gift shares the majesty of its giver. / Both Flaccus and yourself may now enjoy the benefit / of Augustus' judgement for all time.

The language is unambiguous: the Emperor is the author (*auctor*) of the honour, and the consulship itself a gift (*res data*) which partakes of the majesty (*maiestas*) of the giver.

Metamorphoses in the Imperial Houshold

But "Augustus," whose favourable judgements both brothers will, it is hoped, continue to enjoy, is not of course Augustus, now dead, but Tiberius. Tiberius may perhaps have claimed that he would reserve this cognomen only for writing to kings;[45] but if so, Ovid, like everyone else in the Empire, did not believe it. It was not however that detailed news did not reach him in Tomoi. In the sixth winter of his exile (A.D. 14/15) he was able to claim that he had written a poem in the Getic language (*Getico sermone*) on the deification of Augustus and the delayed accession of Tiberius. The poem which embodies this claim (*Ex P.* 4, 13), reflecting the reports of the events of summer A.D. 14 which had reached Tomoi by the following winter, is thus by far the most

45. Suetonius, *Tib.* 26, 2.

immediate testimony to the confused and hesitant process by which Tiberius took up the "reins of empire"—those same "reins" which Valerius Maximus, perhaps writing not long after, recorded as having nearly been seized from Tiberius by a conspirator.[46] Ovid writes as follows (25–33):

> nam patris Augusti docui mortale fuisse
> corpus, in aetherias numen abisse domos:
> esse parem virtute patri, qui frena rogatus
> saepe recusati ceperit imperii:
> esse pudicarum te Vestam, Livia, matrum,
> ambiguum nato dignior anne viro:
> esse duos iuvenes, firma adiumenta parentis,
> qui dederint animi pignora certa sui.

For I taught how, though father Augustus had been mortal / in body, his spirit had departed for the heavenly abodes; / that one matched his father in virtue, who, offered the reins / of empire, took them after frequent refusal; / that you, Livia, were the Vesta of chaste matrons, / whether worthier of son or husband none can tell; / that there were two young men, firm props for their parent, / who had given sure guarantees of their spirit.

The language which Ovid uses is, not surprisingly, very close to that of a revised passage which appears in book 1 of the *Fasti*, again as part of a prophecy of the rule of the Augusti, put in the mouth of Carmentis (529–36):[47]

> tempus erit, cum vos orbemque tuebitur idem,
> et fient ipso sacra colente deo,
> et penes Augustos patriae tutela manebit:
> hanc fas imperii frena tenere domum.
> inde nepos natusque dei, licet ipse recuset,
> pondera caelesti mente paterna feret;
> utque ego perpetuis dim sacrabor in aris,
> sic Augusta novum Iulia numen erit.

Time will be, when the same one will protect you and the globe, / and sacrifice will be offered by the god himself, / the guardianship of the land will remain with the Augusti: / it is the god's will for this house to hold the reins of empire. / Hence the grandson of a god and son of a god, though he may himself refuse, / will carry his

46. Text to n. 21.
47. Cf. n. 33 and related discussion in text.

father's burden with celestial mind; / and just as I shall one day be
sanctified with perpetual altars, / so shall Iulia Augusta become a
new deity.

Here too the reins of empire (*imperii frena*) make their appearance; and, here
too, a real prominence is give to Livia, appearing in the *Fasti* with her new
name "Augusta," while in *Ex Ponto* she is again associated with Vesta and the
mothers. Once again, in both passages, stress is laid on the (artificial) continuity of the imperial house. Here too, Ovid's perceptions were specifically
prompted from Rome, and from the inmost circles of the "Augustan aristocracy." Norbanus Flaccus' public dedication in the Circus Flaminius of statues
of Divus Augustus and the Domus Augusta (see text to n. 18) was matched
by the fact that Cotta Messallinus, before Augustus' death, had sent Ovid a
set of silver statuettes of Augustus, Tiberius, and Livia, intended—or certainly deployed by Ovid—as objects of worship (*Ex P.* 2, 8, 1–10). But now,
in the same poem addressed to Pomponius Graecinus about his consulate,
Ovid proclaims that in the shrine of Caesar (*sacrum Caesaris*) in his house not
only Livia and Tiberius but Germanicus and Drusus have their place, all duly
receiving his daily worship (4, 9, 105–12):

> nec pietas ignota mea est: videt hospita terra
> in nostra sacrum Caesaris esse domo.
> stant pariter natusque pius coniunxque sacerdos,
> numina iam facto non leviora deo.
> neu desit pars ulla domus, stat uterque nepotum,
> hic aviae lateri proximus, ille patris.
> his ego do totiens cum ture precantia verba,
> Eoo quotiens surgit ab orbe dies.

Nor is my piety unknown: the land that shelters me sees / that in my
home there is a shrine of Caesar. / By him stand pious son and
priestess wife, / no slighter powers now he has become a god. / No
part of the house is missing, each of the grandsons stands there, / one
by his grandmother's side, the other by his father. / To them time and
again I offer incense and words of prayer, / as often as the day rises
from the east.

Rome Seen from Tomoi: The Insider's View from Outside

Ovid's exile, however unfortunate for him, offers still unexploited resources
for us. For, on the one hand, he was the close associate of prominent sena-

torial families which not only made their peace with the new regime, but played a central part in constructing an adulatory ideology for it. Secondly, while he did indeed step aside from the senatorial career which his younger contemporary, Velleius Paterculus, followed, he remained high up in Roman society. What is more, the poetry of his last ten years in Rome might be seen as the most "Augustan" of all, as the only large body of verse to devote itself overtly to the celebration of the new regime. But it is precisely, I wish to suggest, this previous role as an indefatigable and poetically resourceful loyalist which provides the background against which we should read the "late-Augustan," or "post-Augustan," poetry of Ovid's exile. For circumstances forced him to devote his extraordinary talents to a construction or representation of Rome, its public life, the role of the leading senators, and the place within it of the imperial family, which is all the more important for being both well informed and yet almost wholly "imagined." There is, of course, far more to this evocation than the isolated examples put forward here.

Ovid, writing from Tomoi, was thus simultaneously the rejected loyalist "insider" and the provincial "outsider," catching the distant echoes of political change. He makes himself, of course, rather more distant, in a true sense, than he really was. For although Tomoi was indeed a frontier city, outside which the territory of barbarian peoples began, it was itself a Greek city like any other,[48] a fact which achieves only a brief reflection in the poetry which he wrote there (*Ex P.* 4, 14, 47–48).

Seen in a different light, therefore, as the witness writing from "outside," Ovid reflects the close attention to the changing shape of the imperial house, and the anxieties as to how to react after the death of Augustus, which might be felt in any Greek city. How those distant realities were construed and expressed must itself be fundamental to the nature of the immediately "post-Augustan" Empire as understood by us. The most vivid parallel to the exiled Ovid's insistent loyalism is the rather neglected oath of loyalty from Palaipaphos in Cyprus.[49] The inhabitants of this small Greek city also had to do what they could in A.D. 14. They did not need to feel so marginal to the Empire as the people of Tomoi, and were not exposed to the bitter cold of the Black Sea coast, or the raids of barbarians; and what is more, they could (and did) claim

48. See esp. D. M. Pippidi, "Tomis, cité géto-grecque à l'époque d'Ovide?," *Athenaeum* (1968): 250 = *Parerga: écrits de Philologie, d'epigraphie et d'histoire ancienne* (1984), 189. For the inscriptions, see *Inscriptiones Scythiae Minoris Graecae et Latinae* II: *Tomis et territorium* (1987).

49. T. B. Mitford, "A Cypriot Oath of Allegiance to Tiberius," *JRS* 50 (1960): 75; *SEG* XVIII, no. 578; *AE* 1962, no. 248. See P. Herrmann, *Der römische Kaisereid* (1968), esp. 102–3.

a special link to "the descendant of Aphrodite, Sebastos Theos Kaisar" (the Deified Caesar Augustus). None the less, it is worth recalling that they were in fact situated some one-and-a-half times as far from Rome, as the crow flies, as Tomoi, and were faced with the same need to construe an unprecedented situation. What is more, they too had heard that there was some hesitation in the new emperor's acceptance of the imperial nomenclature, and duly left in the inscribed text of their oath of loyalty two gaps into which they might later insert the word "Autokrator"—if the new emperor later turned out to have taken the *praenomen* "Imperator" after all. But, more important, they laid a heavy emphasis on the (fictional) continuity of the imperial house: some honours (it is not clear which) would be voted "along with the other gods, to Roma, to Tiberius Caesar, son of Augustus, Augustus, and to the sons of his blood, and none other of all." The ideological force of the new monarchy was indeed remarkable: poetry and prose, inscriptions in both Greek and Latin, coins both Roman and non-Roman, and images both Roman and provincial, had all come to express an elaborate series of constructions of an imperial "family" which was itself a succession of constructions.

CHAPTER FIFTEEN

Imperial Ideology
in the Tabula Siarensis[*]

The importance of the Tabula Siarensis is first of all, quite simply, that it presents an extensive new text in Latin from the early Empire. Moreover, as a text, it can be considered as a single document along with that contained in the Tabula Hebana, and the three smaller fragments from Rome.[1] For, as was evident from the outset, the last nine lines of the Tabula Siarensis contain the beginnings of the first six lines of the Tabula Hebana. We thus have at our disposal a single, but not continuous, text of some 160 lines; it therefore represents one of the most substantial pieces of Latin prose from the early imperial period to be preserved in documentary form.

I emphasise the use of the word "text." The creation of a text is one thing, which in this case is a function of the central organs of the Roman *res publica*. The creation of the *inscription* is a separate question, which involves a range of different issues: these include the despatch of the text to a particular locality, or the spontaneous acquisition of it by the community concerned; the nature of the political community which gave instructions for the inscribing of the bronze tablets; the motivation for this action and (where possible) the nature of the urban setting in which the tablets were to be displayed; the availability of persons technically qualified to carry out the work of incising the text on bronze; and the wider questions of literacy, and the public, or social, function of extensive texts displayed in Latin in a provincial context.

I emphasise the distinction between text and inscription in order to make clear that what I propose to discuss is the text; and by text I mean the com-

---

* First published in J. González and J. Arce, eds., *Estudios sobre la Tabula Siarensis* (Madrid, 1988), 11–19. I am grateful for comments and improvements to the members of the symposium, and especially to Prof. J. S. Richardson.

1. *CIL* VI, 31199; now in M. Crawford, ed., *Roman Statutes* I (1996), no. 37/8.

350

bined text made available by the two tablets, from Heba and Siarum, together, along with the fragments from Rome. In novelty and significance this
text far outweighs, for instance, that of the new decree of the senate of the
same year, A.D. 19, from Larinum,[2] or even the extensive bilingual edict of a
governor on *vehiculatio* (the exaction of transport services), issued probably a
couple of years earlier, and inscribed in Pisidia.[3] In scale the new combined
text can be compared with the 280 or so lines of the *Res Gestae* itself. There
are several points of contact between the two, to which I will return. For
the moment let me simply emphasise again, in the case of the *Res Gestae*, the
distinction between text and inscription. As a text, the *Res Gestae* is in every
sense an Augustan composition, written by Augustus himself, perhaps in a
first draft soon after 2 B.C., and in its final form in the last year of his life. But
as an *inscription* it too is early Tiberian, set up outside the Mausoleum, and
then copied for re-inscription in a number of provincial centres. Whether
this copying and re-inscription were spontaneous or followed instructions
from the Senate for the distribution of the text is precisely a question raised
by analogy by the new text from Siarum.

What I wish to say therefore concerns not Baetica, where the inscription
was created, but the nature of the Roman *res publica* as it was in the early Empire, and specifically in the early years of Tiberius. By nature I mean in the
first instance its explicit nature, or the conception of the state as expressed
publicly by those who played a role in it. In this respect the new text presents
a view of the emperor, the imperial family, of Rome—its institutions and its
urban monuments—which can both be compared and contrasted with that
provided by another set of texts from the same years, the *Tristia* and *Epistulae ex Ponto* of Ovid.[4] Here too, but of course in a very different way, the
structure of public and political life at Rome is mirrored in a provincial environment.

Let me just illustrate one aspect of this parallel between the *tabula* and
Ovid, two sources which speak to us from opposite ends of the Empire: that
is the emphasis on the *domus Augusta* (the Imperial family). The text of the
decree of the Senate passed in December A.D. 19 records that statues of Divus
Augustus and the Domus Augusta had already been dedicated by Gaius Norbanus Flaccus in the Circus Flaminius; as Professor González suggests, the

2. *AE* 1978, 145; see B. Levick, "The Senatus Consultum from Larinum," *JRS* 73
(1983): 97.

3. S. Mitchell, "Requisitioned Transport in the Roman Empire: A New Inscription from
Pisidia," *JRS* 66 (1976): 106; *AE* 1976, 653; *SEG* XXVI, 1392.

4. For the historical and chronological framework, R. Syme, *History in Ovid* (1978).

year must be that of Flaccus' consulship, in A.D. 15 along with Drusus Caesar. In the same year Ovid addressed *Ex Ponto* 4, 9, to Pomponius Graecinus, consul designate for A.D. 16: in it he records that his house in Tomoi displayed his *pietas*, for it contained a shrine with images of the newly deified Augustus, as well as of Tiberius, Livia, Germanicus, and Drusus—lest any member of the family be lacking (4, 9, 105–10).

More generally, the new text serves to emphasise a number of important features of the structure of the early imperial state. The first and most important of these is the continuing significance of the passage of legislation by the people. I believe indeed that our entire conception of Roman political history has been distorted by an excessive emphasis on the importance of the Senate, as opposed to the Roman people. I have argued this for the second century,[5] and hope to do so elsewhere as regards the last years of the Republic; in the latter case in particular it was successive laws passed by the people which were the main agent of change, and represented the crucial steps which brought about the domination of Caesar and hence the foundation of the empire.

As regards the early Empire itself, Professor P. A. Brunt has recently emphasised the importance of the role of the Senate, and the fact that our sources will often attribute to an emperor measures which had in fact to be put into effect through a vote of the Senate.[6] This is indeed true and important; but the same considerations apply also to the votes of the people, whether in the centuriate assembly or the tribal assembly of the thirty-five tribes. The new text affords a precise example. Tacitus, *Annals* 2, 83, recording in summary form some of the honours voted in memory of Germanicus at the end of A.D. 19, does not explicitly say by whom these honours were voted. But, given his general dependence on the *Acta Senatus* (the proceedings of the Senate),[7] it would always have been natural to suppose that he was implicitly referring to a vote of the Senate. What we would *not* have presumed is that this vote was to be followed, early in A.D. 20, by a law put to the people by the incoming consuls (fr. b, 2, ll. 27–30): "And that M. Messala, M. Aurelius Cotta Maximus, the consuls designate, when they entered office—on the first occasion as far as the auspicies allow—without giving notice of two or three *nundinae* [three eight-day periods], should see that a law [*lex*] on the hon-

5. "The Political Character of the Classical Roman Republic, 200–151 BC." *JRS* 74 (1984): 1 (chapter 4 in this volume); "Politics, Persuasion and the People before the Social War (150–90 BC)," *JRS* 76 (1986): 1 (chapter 5 in this volume).

6. P. A. Brunt, "The Role of the Senate in the Augustan Régime," *CQ* 34 (1984): 423.

7. See R. Syme, "Tacitus: Some Sources of His Information," *JRS* 72 (1982): 68.

ours for Germanicus Caesar be presented to the people." As J. S. Richardson points out to me, this part of the new text can also be seen from the opposite perspective. That is to say, it shows that, even as regards the most formal aspects of procedure, the Senate can now act as if the consent of the people could be assumed in advance. As the passage which precedes these lines also shows, the measures also included provisions for honours to be offered by or in the name of the urban plebs, including statues of Germanicus "with an inscription of the Roman plebs" (*Tab. Siar.* fr. b, 2, ll. 7–10). None the less, it remains significant that these provisions were still, in however cursory a fashion, to be embodied by the consuls in a law and put before the people.

What the people subsequently voted had a dual character, in this respect presumably mirroring the Lex Valeria Cornelia of A.D. 5: that is to say the people both voted honours for the deceased and instituted a novel element in the constitution, the new centuries composed of senators and *equites*, which would henceforth form a part of the centuriate assembly as an electoral assembly. We know from Cassius Dio (37, 28, 1–3; 58, 20, 3–4) that the centuriate assembly continued to meet on the Campus Martius at least until his own time, the early third century. There is no reason to suppose that the new centuries did not continue to form a part of what Pliny the Younger was to call the *sanctissimum carmen* (the most sacred ritual) of the assembly (*Pan.* 92, 3). As I indicated earlier, what is at issue here is the formal structure of the *res publica* and the relations of its component parts, not the question of the real location of political power. As the evidence of Ovid itself shows, as early as the end of Augustus' reign and the beginning of that of Tiberius, it was openly acknowledged that the consulate at least was in fact in the gift of the emperor. In the same poem which was mentioned earlier, addressed to Pomponius Graecinus, consul designate for A.D. 16, and concerning the prospective consulate of his brother, Pomponius Flaccus, in A.D. 17, Ovid says: "Grand as the consul is — and Rome, the city of Mars, sees no *imperium* higher than that of the supreme consul — none the less the dignity [*gravitas*] of the author [*auctor*] increases the honour, and that which is given partakes of the majesty of the giver" (*Ep. ex Ponto* 4, 9, 65–67). Few texts more perfectly express the delicate ambiguity of the early imperial state.

The formal structure of the centuriate assembly, which was to continue to meet on the Campus Martius to elect consuls and praetors for at least two centuries more, was one component of the law (*rogatio*) to be put forward in January A.D. 20. The other was the range of honours and forms of commemoration for the deceased Germanicus. Those clauses which survive in the last part of the Tabula Hebana include, firstly, permanent provisions for changes in the annual rituals of the city, such as the putting out of the curule chairs of

Germanicus Caesar in the theatres during the *ludi Augustales* (ll. 51–52); when the temple of Divus Augustus was finished, these chairs would be kept there, and in the mean time in that of Mars Ultor. The provisions also include specific arrangements (ll. 54–55) for the day (i.e., the expected day in A.D. 20) when the bones, or rather the ashes, of Germanicus would be interred in the *tumulus*; that done, the *magistri* of the *sodales Augustales* were subsequently to make offerings (*inferiae*) there on the anniversary of his death each year. The building described as *tumulus* is of course what we call the Mausoleum of Augustus. The references to *inferiae* offered to the shade (*manes*) of Germanicus (as to those of Gaius and Lucius) which appear in the fragmentary opening lines of fragment b, column 2 of the Tabula Siarensis are to mark this same anniversary; it follows that the Mausoleum will thus have been described, in the missing lines, simply as *tumulus*, and not as *tumulus Germanici Caesaris*.

The use of a law, in A.D. 19 as in A.D. 5, and almost certainly in A.D. 23 for Drusus, to validate honours for deceased members of the imperial house, of course mirrors the similar use of laws to grant powers and honours to them during their lives. It is not necessary to multiply examples of this: the *Res Gestae* itself records the laws by which Augustus received the tribunician power for life in 23 B.C. (10, 1), or by which the consulship in advance was decreed for Gaius and Lucius (14, 1). Other evidence shows, for instance, that it was by a law that Tiberius had received a general *imperium* in the provinces in A.D. 13.[8]

On such occasions, as with posthumous honours, even when a law was in fact passed by the people, this fact may not always be specifically recorded by our narrative source. No law is mentioned, for instance, when Tacitus briefly alludes to Tiberius' request, evidently addressed to the Senate, for proconsular *imperium* for Germanicus in A.D. 14 (*Ann.* 1, 14). But the precedents, that is to say, that of the previous year and that of the *imperium* voted for Agrippa (*P.Col.inv.*, no. 4701 = *P.Köln* 249), show that it is almost certain that such a law was in fact subsequently passed. Moreover, since we now know from the Tabula Siarensis that Tacitus ignored the passing of such a law early in A.D. 20, we can be reasonably certain that he did so also in relation to the posthumous honours of Drusus, the son of Tiberius, in A.D. 23 (*Ann.* 4, 9). As Oliver and Palmer suggested,[9] it is the honours which were then voted to Drusus which appear in the Tabula Ilicitana; the Tabula Siarensis now strongly suggests that this fragmentary text also is that of a law.

8. Velleius 2, 121, 1; Suetonius, *Tib.* 21.

9. J. H. Oliver and R. E. A. Palmer, "The Text of the Tabula Hebana," *AJPh* 75 (1954): 225, on pp. 248–49.

Tacitus is thus guilty of some distortion in his account of events in Rome, in focusing so exclusively on the Senate, and on scenes and votes in the Senate. So are we, and in some respects more so. Tacitus at least was quite clear that provinces governed by proconsuls appointed by lot were called "public provinces" (*publicae provinciae*) (*Ann.* 13, 4). We frequently call them "senatorial" provinces. But the only contemporary description of the division of the provinces as it was under Augustus, that of Strabo in the *Geography* (840), states unambiguously that the division, which in any case related only to the method of appointment, was between the Emperor and the *demos*, that is the Roman people.[10]

The new text also happens to illustrate perfectly the fact that the distinction between the two types of province was not an administrative one. The Senate, to be followed by the people, determines the emplacement of monuments in the imperial province of Syria and on the Rhine, both of which were areas to which the emperor sent legates (*legati*) selected by himself (*Tab. Sia.* fr. a, 1, ll. 23–37; *CIL* VI, 31199a = *Roman Statutes*, no. 37/8, Rome fr. a). The arrangements for the distribution of the text to provincial colonies and for its posting-up by provincial governors (*Tab. Sia.* fr. b, 2, ll. 24–27) also make no distinction between the two types of province.

The empire as a whole in any case remained, in the official language of the time, the attribute of the Roman people, in which formal sovereignty still resided. Augustus himself in the *Res Gestae* makes this clear: "I extended the territories of all the provinces of the Roman people" (26, 1); "I added Egypt to the *imperium* of the Roman people" (27.1): "The peoples of Pannonia, who have never seen armies of the Roman people before my principate [*ante me principem*], having been defeated [subdued] by my son Tiberius Nero, I brought under the *imperium* of the Roman people" (30, 1). Sometimes the expression of sovereignty is indeed blurred; that is to say, the emperor may appear in this text, the *Res Gestae*, not merely as an agent of the sovereign Roman people but as a second sovereign: "*my* army compelled the Dacian peoples to submit to the *imperium* of the Roman people" (30, 2); or "The peoples of Germany through their envoys sought my friendship and that of the Roman people" (26.4). None the less, the essential military role which is stressed in the *Res Gestae* is that of the *imperator* who achieves his conquests *for* the Roman people, whose *imperium* is thus increased: "Egypt having become subject to the power of the Roman people," as Augustus expressed it on the bases of two obelisks which he installed in Rome (*ILS* 91). Velleius Paterculus, writing a few years after the composition of the text which the Tabula

10. F. Millar, "The Emperor, the Senate and the Provinces," *JRS* 66 (1966): 156 (chapter 11 in this volume).

Siarensis reveals, faithfully concurs. His list of provinces added to the Empire ends with Cappadocia: "Tiberius Caesar . . . made Cappadocia tributary to the Roman people" (2, 39, 3).

The greatness and imperial domination of the Roman people was of course central to Augustan ideology. But so too was the conception that this greatness had been brought about by the agency of a long line of famous *duces* (generals), stretching back to the Foundation. Exactly this was the lesson which Augustus explicitly stated that he wanted to be drawn from the statues of the *summi viri* (the foremost men), each with its brief inscribed record of achievements, which he placed in the Forum Augustum surrounding his new temple of Mars Ultor. These statues enshrined the memory of the *duces*: "who transformed the empire of the Roman people from the smallest into the greatest" (qui imperium p[opuli] R[omani] ex minimo maximum reddidissent). But their purpose was not to be merely commemorative, for Augustus stated in a edict that he had designed all this in order that their example might lead to the demand by the citizens for the observance of the same standard both by himself and by the *principes* of subsequent ages (Suetonius, *Div. Aug.* 31).

This interrelated set of concepts is perfectly reflected also in the Tabula Siarensis. The arch to be placed in the Circus Flaminius was to be adorned with *signa* (statues) of the *devictae gentes*, that is, those conquered by Germanicus. On the front the arch was to bear an inscription recording that it had been dedicated to the memory of Germanicus Caesar by the Senate and the Roman people, because he had conquered the Germans in war and driven them out of Gaul; he had recovered the military standards and had avenged the treacherous slaughter of an "army of the Roman people"; when Gaul had been restored to order he had been sent to the East as proconsul. This title, found also in *CIL* VI, 31199a = *Roman Statutes*, no. 37/8, Rome fr. a, remains puzzling. But its use in this context confirms the correctness of the use of *anthupatos* (proconsul) in the edict issued by Germanicus in Alexandria (*Sel. Pap.* 2, no. 211). He had then regulated the provinces and kingdoms, following the *mandata* (instructions) of Tiberius Caesar Augustus, until "he finally met his death for the *res publica*" (fr. a, 1, l. 18: *ob rem p[ublicam] mortem obisset*). The heroic role is that of the individual, Germanicus; but the army had been that of the Roman people and the cause which he had been serving is that of the *res publica*.

This theme was taken up when the ashes of Germanicus reached Rome and were placed in the *tumulus Augusti* (as Tacitus calls it). Tiberius informed the people that in the past many illustrious Romans had died for the *res publica* (*ob rem publicam obisse*); moreover a decent restraint in mourning was appro-

priate to an *imperator populus*. But the people none the less compared the more
extravagant and open mourning for Germanicus' father Drusus in 9 B.C.: on
that occasion the body had been surrounded by the portraits (*imagines*) of the
Claudii and the Iulii, there had been public lamentation in the Forum, and
a funeral oration from the Rostra. Where, the people asked in A.D. 20, were
the ancient customs, the effigy laid on the pyre, the songs (*carmina*) and eulogies (*laudationes*) designed to preserve the memory of his valour (*ad memoriam
virtutis*) (Tacitus, *Ann.* 3, 4–6)?

As the popular reactions reported by Tacitus implied, the Roman funeral
was designed both to recall the past and provide exhortation for the future.
If the interment ceremonies for Germanicus were indeed, as Tacitus implies,
regarded as not meeting the expected standards for public commemoration, even Tacitus admits that the funeral procession of Tiberius' son Drusus,
three years later, was of exceptional splendour; it was marked by portraits
of Aeneas, the originator (*origo*) of the Iulia Gens; of all the Alban kings; of
Romulus, the founder of the city; and of the Sabine aristocracy (*nobilitas*),
Attus Clausus and the later Claudii (*Ann.* 4, 9). This list comes very close to
that of the foremost men whose statues adorned the two apses of the Forum
Augustum. The ideology of the Augustan regime still dominated the public image of the next reign, and formed the standard by which it would be
judged.

Indeed, it was precisely the comparison between the elder Drusus' funeral
in 9 B.C. and that of Germanicus which, as Tacitus implies, so struck the
people of Rome in A.D. 20. But, as the Tabula Siarensis now shows, Tacitus' report of official reactions on the news of Germanicus' death, before the ashes
arrived, is very abbreviated and incomplete. It is not only, as we saw, that he
omits altogether the law passed by the consuls early in 20. Even his brief account of the honours for the deceased (*Ann.* 2, 83) hardly does justice to the
complexity of what the Senate voted in December of A.D. 19. The measures
which were then taken included, for instance, the laying down of a detailed
sculptural programme for the new arch which was to be erected in the Circus
Flaminius (*Tab. Siar.* fr. a, 1, ll. 9–21). These lines represent the only documentary account which we have, which records the decision-making process
by which the ideological and propaganda function of an arch in Rome was
consciously determined. Apart from the statues representing the defeated
peoples (*devictae gentes*) and the commemorative inscription, already mentioned, the arch was to be surmounted by a statue of Germanicus in a triumphal chariot (*currus triumphalis*), and on either side of him there were to
be statues of his father Drusus, his mother Antonia, probably his wife Agrippina, his sister Livia, his brother Claudius (here called Tiberius Germanicus),

and his male and female children. The programme is notable for the prominence which it gives to the female members of the family, a feature which
deserves further consideration elsewhere. The prominence here given to the
Claudii Nerones makes a striking contrast with the fate which befell most
of those mentioned within the next two decades. Even by the time Velleius
Paterculus was completing his *History* in A.D. 30, and piously adverting to the
pain caused to Tiberius by Agrippina and her eldest son (2, 130, 4), this arch
in the Circus Flaminius must have been somewhat embarrassing. It would
also be interesting to know in what way the unwarlike Claudius was represented on this triumphal arch. No one could have expected that a quarter of
a century later it would be he who would have a number of *devictae gentes*
in the new province of Britain to his credit, and would be celebrating a triumph of unparalleled splendour: or that far away in Aphrodisias in Caria they
would feel moved to create the first ever symbolic representation of Britannia, in the form of a bas-relief of her being conquered and subjected by the
victorious Claudius in person.[11]

   All this is of course extremely significant for the public ideology of Tiberius' reign. But it all represents, none the less, words and honours directed
towards the imperial house, by the Senate and People. What then of words
actually issued by members of the imperial family? Tacitus, as we saw, complained that when the ashes of Germanicus arrived, there was a conspicuous
lack of the songs (*carmina*) and eulogies (*laudationes*) designed to preserve the
memory of his valour (*Ann.* 3, 5). But in fact, as the new text reveals, such
laudationes had taken place, but earlier, in December A.D. 19, and within the
walls of the Senate. Drusus Caesar, the son of Tiberius, delivered one oration, and it was agreed that "the text of it, which he had read in the next
meeting of the Senate" (*libellus, quem in proxumo senatu recitasset*) should be
inscribed on bronze and put up in public. Before that, on December 16, the
date of the earlier of two decrees of the Senate passed this month in relation
to Germanicus, Tiberius himself had also delivered a *laudatio*: this too was to
be inscribed and put up in public. The reasons for doing so are explained in
detail: "because [the text] contained not only a *laudatio* but an account of his
whole life [*vitae totius ordinem*] and a true record of his *virtus*"; moreover "he
himself [Tiberius] had testified in the same text [*libellus*] that he would not
wish to conceal his desire [that this should be done], and judged that it was
useful to the young of the next generation and those of our posterity [*utile
iuventuti liberorum posterorumque nostrorum*] (*Tab. Siar.* fr. b, 2, ll. 11–19).

   11. K. Erim, "A New Relief showing Claudius and Britannia from Aphrodisias," *Britannia*
13 (1982): 277. See R. R. R. Smith in *JRS* 77 (1987): 88.

Here again we have a direct expression, reflecting the words of Tiberius himself, of the explicit continuation of Augustan ideology: the achievements of Germanicus, like those of the *summi viri* commemorated in the Forum Augustum, were to serve as a model for posterity. But there may also be a more specific connection; if this is so, we have a case where the new text casts light back on the propaganda, or rather retrospective propaganda, of Augustus himself.

What readership had Augustus had in mind in composing his *Res Gestae*? Was not this text also, set up outside his Mausoleum, intented to offer a model of conduct for future generations? Looking at this question a few years ago in his chapter in the volume *Caesar Augustus*,[12] Zvi Yavetz considered various possibilities, and then suggested that it was really directed to the *iuventus* of Rome and Italy. Like Syme in the *Roman Revolution*, he was of course thinking of the pre-war dictatorships, of Hitler and the *Hitlerjugend*. Various reviewers of the book found difficulty in accepting this suggestion;[13] indeed it could at that moment have been no more than a suggestion, even a jeu d'espirit, with no concrete basis in evidence. But fortune sometimes favours those who have the courage to speculate, and who do so with a feeling for the nature of a society in the past. The Tabula Siarensis had already been discovered when Yavetz spoke at the colloquium to honour the eightieth birthday of Sir Ronald Syme in 1983; the book of essays on Caesar Augustus and the text of the Tabula were published almost simultaneously in 1984.[14] The Tabula thus provides precisely the explicit confirmation which had previously been lacking: it proves that it was possible, within the political culture of the early imperial state, to express the idea that a record of individual achievement might indeed be conceived of as a model offered to the *iuventus* of the next and succeeding generations. Not the least of the many benefits of this extraordinary text, for which we owe a debt of gratitude to Julián González, is that it makes us look again at the reign of Augustus.

12. Z. Yavetz, "The Res Gestae and Augustus' Public Image," in F. Millar and E. Segal, eds., *Caesar Augustus: Seven Aspects* (1984), 1, on pp. 14–20.

13. E.g., T. P. Wiseman, *TLS*, August 24, 1984, 950; J. J. Paterson, *G&R* 32 (1985): 92–93; A. Wallace-Hadrill, *JRS* 75 (1985): 248–49.

14. J. González and F. Fernández, "Tabula Siarensis," *Iura* 32 (1981, app. 1984): 1; J. González, "Tabula Siarensis Fortunales Siarenses et Municipia Civium Romanorum," *ZPE* 55 (1984): 55. Cf. also J. Arce, "*Tabula Siarensis*; primeros comentarios (I)," *Arch. esp. de arqu.* 57 (1984): 149; J. González, "Addenda et corrigenda," *ZPE* 60 (1985): 146. See now *AE* 1984, 508.

CHAPTER SIXTEEN

The Roman City-State
under the Emperors, 29 B.C.–A.D. 69 *

This chapter must begin with a confession. I have always felt unsure as to
how we should approach the central narrative of events in Rome in the first
century and a half of imperial rule. Whose history should we be attempting
to write? That of the successive emperors? Of the Senate in its new situation? Of the population of Rome? Of the wider body of Roman citizens?
Or of all the peoples whom Rome ruled or had contact with? In particular,
I find Tacitus' *Annales* profoundly unsatisfying. For a start, we must ask why
he made the deliberate choice to call the work *Annales*, as he does: "But let
no one compare our *Annales* with the writing of those who recounted the
ancient deeds of the Roman people."[1] We will come back to this comparison
later, for the frame of reference which is implied is fundamental to the historical writing of the early Empire. But it was also a deliberate choice, as is
implied by the title *Annales*, to structure the work by years, and to introduce
at the beginning of each year the names of the annual pair of *consules ordinarii*
(by whom the year was dated). As regards the history of what we call the
Republic, there had been a good reason for this: for it was the two consuls,

---

* First published in F. Muecke, ed., *Sidere mens eadem mutato: The Todd Memorial Lectures,
1976–1997*, Prudentia Supp. (1998), 113–34. I am very grateful to the University of Sydney
for the honour of being invited to give this paper as the Todd Memorial Lecture, delivered
on 17 November 1997, and to Princeton University, where it was given as the Magie Lecture on 24 March 1998. It represents the text of the lecture as given, with the addition of a
few footnotes containing essential references. There is a mass of further evidence, old and
new, relating to the *res publica* of the first century A.D., and I hope to return to the topic in
more detail elsewhere.

1. *Ann.* 4, 32, 1: "sed nemo annales nostros cum scriptura eorum contenderit, qui veteres
populi Romani res composuere."

360

during their year of office, who commanded the two main Roman armies; in other words it was they who expanded, or failed to expand, the *imperium* of the Roman people. But in spite of this, even in the Republic itself, the idea of writing "annalistic," year-by-year history could seem inadequate, mere chronicling without proper analysis of intentions and reasons. Precisely this view had been expressed by Sempronius Asellio in the preface to the *res gestae* which he wrote in the second half of the second century B.C. But we can encounter his words now only because they were quoted by Aulus Gellius, writing in the middle of the second century A.D.[2]—and thus only a few decades after Tacitus had finished his *Annales*. In short, a highly educated senatorial orator, like Tacitus, writing in the earlier second century, must have known that it might seem oddly old-fashioned to write "annalistic" history.

So, to call the work *Annales* was a deliberate choice, and a very paradoxical one. For the consuls of the imperial period did not lead armies, but held office in Rome, and usually not even for the whole year. One thing they did do was to preside in the Senate. As to what else they did, the evidence now available shows, for instance, that they gave jurisdiction and dealt with contracts for public revenues and expenditures. But if they were ever, like Domitius Corbulo or Iulius Agricola, to get the chance to command armies, it was after their consulship, sometimes long after, and only when appointed by an emperor. Their campaigns when in their provinces could extend over several years.

So choosing to write *Annales* was a controversial decision for a senator of the early second century, and one which, as Tacitus himself found, caused various difficulties: in some years, as he complains, nothing much happened in Rome;[3] in other periods campaigns on the frontiers did not really make sense if divided up year-by-year.[4] These are some of the reasons why I have always found it hard to discern what the purpose and subject of Tacitus' *Annales* really is. But one aspect of how the work is constructed is clear, and has become incomparably clearer as a result of dramatic recent discoveries of new evidence. That is that, to a quite extraordinary extent, the narra-

2. Aulus Gellius, *Noct. Att.* 5, 18.

3. See, e.g., *Ann.* 13, 31, 1: "In the year in which Nero was consul for the second and L. Piso for the first time few things worth recording occurred, unless it pleases one to fill volumes with the praise of the foundations and beams of the huge amphitheatre which Caesar constructed on the Campus Martius; for it has been judged fitting the *dignitas* of the Roman people that illustrious deeds should be assigned to *Annales*, whereas the aforementioned events to the daily journal of the city."

4. See, e.g., *Ann.* 14, 29, 1.

tive of events in Rome which Tacitus presents is built up from a chain of scenes in the Senate. This was argued in a splendid article by the late Sir Ronald Syme, published when its author was a mere 79.[5] It is clear throughout the *Annales* how Tacitus has followed in detail the sequence of exchanges and speeches in the Senate; what is more, as has long been known, he has edited and re-written the original speeches for insertion in his own narrative. I hardly need to refer to the two classic cases where we have both at least some of the original text and also its representation, or re-presentation, by Tacitus: I mean, of course, Claudius' speech about the right of prominent Roman citizens from Gaul to seek senatorial rank, of which we have the original text on the famous inscription from Lyons;[6] and the debate on the conferment of honours on Pallas, from which Pliny the Younger quotes verbatim.[7] In the former case, both the text of Claudius' actual speech and Tacitus' version of it represent something very characteristic both of the ideology of first-century Rome and of our means of access to it. That is, the use of the republican past, its history, its institutions, and its values, as a frame of reference for debates about the present. When we encounter these debates as represented by Tacitus, of course, we are ourselves engaging in a sort of multi-level dialogue: there is our engagement with Tacitus' text; his engagement with the oratory of the emperor and the Senate in the Julio-Claudian period; and their engagement with the institutions and values of the Republic as they understood them. I will mention only two further examples: the speech by Cremutius Cordus in *Annales* 4 on the tradition of free speech in Roman historiography;[8] and the debates in *Annales* 3 on the rules relating to the Flamen Dialis.[9]

The Senate is therefore the main stage on which the action recorded in the *Annales* of Tacitus takes place, and the question which Tacitus poses is above all the following. How did the senators conduct themselves in the shadow of autocracy? Some responded to the new political structure by adulation, or by self-interested accusations directed against other senators; but others did so by self-conscious adherence to traditional standards, or by an unyielding attachment to liberty (*libertas*), meaning both dignity of conduct and free-

5. R. Syme, "Tacitus: Some Sources of His Information," *JRS* 72 (1982): 68 = *Roman Papers* IV (1988), 199.

6. The Tabula Lugdunensis, *ILS*, 212; *Ann.* 11, 23–25. See esp. M. T. Griffin, "The Lyons Tablet and Tacitean Hindsight," *CQ* 32 (1982): 404.

7. Pliny, *Epp.* 7, 29 and 8, 6 (verbatim quotations found in paras. 6–7 and 13); *Ann.* 12, 53.

8. *Ann.* 4, 34.

9. *Ann.* 3, 58–59; 71.

dom of speech. The best analysis of this theme is still, in my view, Chaim Wirszubski's book *Libertas*, published in 1950.[10]

As we will see later, recent evidence gives us very clear and specific reasons for thinking that Tacitus' concentration on the Senate is excessive. For we can now see, much more clearly than before, how the Senate was only one element in a much wider context, even if we think only of Rome and its inhabitants. Firstly, there are the very complex institutions of the *res publica* itself, or what I have called in the title "the Roman City-State." It is a strange paradox, but I think a real one, that as a result of both new and not-so-new discoveries, we now know more about the working of the *res publica* under the emperors than we do for the Republic proper.

Then, because Roman public life really was public and took place almost entirely in the open air, we have to think of the topography of the city of Rome itself and, above all, of its public buildings and public spaces, of the functions performed by them, and of the meanings and associations attached to them. Some of these buildings and designated spaces were centuries old, like the Circus Maximus, the temple of Iuppiter on the Capitol, or the Campus Martius, in its role as a meeting place for the assembly, or of course the Forum Romanum itself. But the huge building programmes which had been undertaken from the late Republic onwards, from wholly new building to restructuring or renovation, had transformed the centre of the city, and with that the very contexts in which the business and communal life of the *res publica* was conducted. We have only to think of the theatres of Pompey and Marcellus, the temple of Divus Iulius in the Forum Romanum, the Forum of Caesar with the temple of Venus Genetrix, or the Forum of Augustus with the temple of Mars Ultor.

The monumental centre of Rome does, of course, play a significant part in Tacitus' narratives, for instance in the *Historiae*, in his powerful accounts of the last hours of both Galba and Vitellius, or of the burning of the Capitol in December 69, and its subsequent restoration.[11] But we also find the major buildings of Rome forming the subject of debates and exchanges in the Senate, as represented in Tacitus' narrative, for instance under A.D. 22, when Lepidus asked permission to restore at his own expense what Tacitus calls "the Basilica Pauli, Aemilia monumenta." The reference is to the massive basilica on the north side of the Forum Romanum which is normally known as the "Basilica Aemilia." What it should properly be called is the subject of

10. Ch. Wirszubski, *Libertas as a Political Idea at Rome during the Late Republic and Early Principate* (1950).

11. *Hist.* 1, 39–42 (Galba); 3, 67–68; 84–86 (Vitellius); 3, 70–72; 4, 53 (Capitol).

heated debate among moderns, not worth entering into now.[12] As Tacitus says, Lepidus was setting out deliberately to live up to the tradition of his family's munificence; by contrast, since there was no member of the family to do it, it was Tiberius who promised to restore the theatre of Pompey. He took the occasion, when speaking in the Senate, to praise the services and vigilance of Sejanus, and the Senate duly voted that a statue of Sejanus should be set up in the theatre.[13]

That vote reflected another new feature of senatorial business, and one which had only entered the standard repertoire of senatorial debates in the very late Republic, and then the Caesarian and Triumviral period. This was the emphasis on formal, public marks of honour, usually in both visual and written form (for we can be quite certain that the base for Sejanus' statue will have borne an inscription in his honour). The elaboration of visible forms of honour for emperors themselves, and their families, hardly needs emphasis here. Equally, the forms of self-representation—or of representation by others—which were now open to senators were the subject of a brilliant chapter by Werner Eck published in 1984.[14] But what needs stressing is the self-conscious awareness in early imperial culture of the potential ideological significance of forms of publicly inscribed writing. *Annales* 3 offers a perfect example. When Tiberius wrote to the Senate to ask for a vote of the tribunician power for Drusus, adulatory votes of statues, altars, temples, and arches were merely a routine response. But one senator went further and proposed that monuments should from now on bear the names not of the consuls but of the holders of the tribunician power; and another went too far, in suggesting that the texts of the decree of the Senate passed that day should be put up in golden letters in the Curia.[15] We shall see that a self-conscious attention to memorialisation in the form of carefully displayed public writing was not in itself an aberration but was precisely an innovation which was entirely characteristic of the imperial age.[16] So too was the placing of hon-

12. See E. M. Steinby, "Il lato orientale del Foro Romano," *Arctos* 21 (1987): 139; E. Carnabucci, *L'angolo sud-orientale del Foro Romano nel manoscritto inedito di Giacomo Boni* (1991); T. P. Wiseman, "Rome and the Resplendent Aemilii," in H. D. Jocelyn, ed., *Tria Lustra* (1993): 181; *LTUR* I (1993), s.vv. "Basilica Aemilia"; "Basilica Fulvia."

13. *Ann.* 3, 72.

14. W. Eck, "Senatorial Self-Representation: Developments in the Augustan Period," in F. Millar and E. Segal, eds., *Caesar Augustus: Seven Aspects* (1984), 129 = W. Eck, *Tra epigrafia, prosopografia e archeologia* (1996), 271.

15. *Ann.* 3, 57.

16. See esp. G. Alföldy, "Augustus und die Inschriften: Tradition und Innovation. Die

orific statues. Thus under A.D. 23 a brief sentence in the Annales records that the Senate voted that Lucilius Longus should receive a *censorium funus* (public funeral appropriate to a censor) and a statue in the Forum of Augustus, both at public expense.[17] That was one sign of the re-shaping of the topography of public space in the centre of Rome. We see this much more clearly, however, at the death of L. Volusius Saturninus in 56. Tacitus, in recording this, notes only the good reputation which Volusius had preserved through his ninety-three years. But the damaged inscription recording his posthumous honours, found at the family villa at Lucus Feroniae, reveals a whole new, or almost new, topography of public honour.[18] The Senate had voted a public funeral, with the provision that *vadimonia* (pledges to appear in court) for that day should be postponed; then there were to be three triumphal statues, a bronze one in the Forum of Augustus, and two marble ones in the "new" temple of Divus Augustus; also three "consular" statues, one in the temple of Divus Iulius, one in the Palatium, and a third in the forecourt (*area*) of (the temple of) Apollo, within view from the Curia (meaning where the Senate now often met, at the temple of Apollo on the Palatine); next, there was to be a statue of him in augural dress at the Regia; then a mounted statue near the Rostra; and finally one of him seated on his official seat, to be placed in the Portico of the Lentuli, beside the theatre of Pompey.

Almost all the architectural features mentioned had come into existence in the previous hundred years. Nor is it the case that, as we might expect, these new monumental elements were just that, with no significance for the operations of society or government. The opposite is shown by unexpected evidence, namely the wax tablets from Murecine recording business affairs at Puteoli in the middle of the first century A.D. Now properly edited by G. Camodeca, these documents record a whole series of *vadimonia* given by parties to legal proceedings who are due to go to Rome to appear before the praetor.[19] As usual, old and new elements combine. Another text which Camodeca has re-edited in the same volume shows that the urban praetor would still put up his edict in the old Forum, "under the Porticus Iulia, in

---

Geburt der imperialen Epigraphik," *Gymnasium* 98 (1991): 289, and *Studi sull'epigrafia augustea e tiberiana di Roma* (1992).

17. *Ann.* 4, 15, 1–3.

18. *Ann.* 13, 30, 4. For the inscription, see esp. W. Eck, "Die Familie der Volusii Saturnini in neuen Inschriften aus Lucus Feroniae," *Hermes* 100 (1972): 461, and S. Panciera in M. T. Boatwright et al., *I Volusii Saturnini: una famiglia romana della prima età imperiale* (1982), 83–84.

19. G. Camodeca, *L'archivo puteolano dei Sulpicii* I (1992).

front of his tribunal."[20] But all of the actual *vadimonia* are for appearances at different sections of the Forum of Augustus, each identified by its most prominent monumental element: "at Rome in the Forum Augustum before the triumphal statue of Cn. Sentius Saturninus, at the fifth hour;" "in front of the altar of Mars Ultor;" "before the statue of Gracchus at the column nearest to the steps;" "before the statue of Diana Lucifera, at column X." Here we go beyond the monuments themselves, to catch a glimpse of the open-air functioning of the administration of justice as it affected the man in the street, and indeed (potentially) in the streets of all the small towns of Italy. The public space in question was a new one, opened only a few decades earlier, and the different parts of it were distinguished by the honorific statues which stood there.

This routine jurisdiction by annual office-holders, which was essential to the working of society, only surfaces occasionally in literary sources, and usually when an emperor is in some way involved. Thus, early in his reign, so Tacitus says, Tiberius would take his seat on the praetor's tribunal, but at the far end of it, so as not to displace the magistrate from his curule seat; as a result, the verdicts issued gave less weight to influence and the pleas of the powerful.[21] But emperors too followed the model of the roles fulfilled by the annual republican magistrates and made a point of taking their seats in public to give jurisdiction. While he was giving justice in the Forum in 51 Claudius was assailed by a crowd complaining of the price of corn, and only just escaped via the nearest door to the Palatine.[22] This was of course the old Forum, the Forum Romanum. But he might do the same in the new Forum Augustum. Suetonius tells the splendid anecdote of how, when Claudius was giving justice there, he was powerfully attracted by the smell of a banquet which was being set out for the college of priests called the Salii in the nearby temple of Mars (Ultor); so he quitted the tribunal, mounted to the temple, and reclined along with the priests for the meal.[23]

The custom of the Salii dining together was presumably ancient — but we have to be careful, for another feature of the history of the Roman *res publica* is that a very large proportion of what we are told of its early history and institutions in fact comes from sources written under the emperors (think of the *Fasti* of Ovid for a start). I cannot pursue this topic here, nor go into the complex and varied forms in which civil and criminal jurisdiction actu-

20. Ibid., 49.
21. *Ann.* 1, 75, 1; see Suetonius, *Tib.* 33.
22. *Ann.* 12, 43, 2; Suetonius, *Div. Claud.* 18.
23. Suetonius, *Div. Claud.* 33.

ally operated in Rome in the early Empire. It is in fact only now, with the publication of the tablets from Puteoli, and also from reading the Flavian municipal law, of which a large new section was published in 1986, that we can begin to see what we call "Roman law" actually functioning in the classical period itself. It is of some significance that the Flavian municipal law, known from inscribed bronze tablets of Domitian's reign, found in Spain, repeatedly refers back to the procedures for jurisdiction in Rome.[24]

I must leave that topic, not least because I am still too confused myself as to how the various elements of jurisdiction in Rome in the first century really functioned. But in thinking of the routine of jurisdiction we are extending our attention to the citizens of the res publica: "citizens" in one sense means the population of the city itself; in another, it includes all the adult males in Italy; and, in another, not only them but all those outside Italy who enjoyed the Roman citizenship. Citizens from the provinces were still relatively few. But there were now Roman colonies in the provinces, and one of the really important revelations provided by new documents comes from the Tabula Siarensis, a bronze tablet from Baetica recording the public commemoration of Germanicus after his death in 19. For in this document the Senate advises the consuls to put up a text of its decree, and instructs the ambassadors of the *municipia* (cities with Roman-style constitutions) and colonies to copy it and to send it "to the *municipia* and colonies of Italy, and to those colonies which are situated in the provinces."[25] Italy was now in some respects something like a nation-state, with citizen off-shoots in the provinces. In other respects, what still mattered most, and what in a real sense constituted the active citizenry of the *res publica*, was the population of Rome. All Roman citizens, wherever they lived, belonged in principle to one or other of the ancient thirty-five tribes. But inscriptions put up in Rome in honour of Germanicus and Drusus in A.D. 23 could represent the source of these honours as being "the urban plebs of the 35 tribes," as if the two categories were essentially identical.[26] Tacitus himself was of course to begin his *Annales* with the words "Urbem Romam," and there was a real sense in which the essential subject of Roman history could still be seen as the city, its institutions, and its people: in short, as the history of a strange and anomalous sort of city-state, which on the one hand had extended its citizenship to all of Italy and beyond,

24. J. González, "The Lex Irnitana: A New Copy of the Flavian Municipal Law," *JRS* 76 (1986): 147. The three main texts are printed separately in J. González, *Bronces jurídicos romanos de Andalucia* (1990): 51–52 (Irnitana); 101–2 (Salpensana); 111–12 (Malacitana).

25. For the Tabula Siarensis, see nn. 41–42. The section quoted is fr. (b), col. II, ll. 23–24.

26. *ILS*, 168 (Drusus); 176 (Germanicus). See esp. C. Nicolet, "Plèbe et tribus: les statues de Lucius Antonius et le testament d'Auguste," *MEFR*(A) 97 (1985): 799.

and on the other ruled a great empire. But the most marked anomaly was of course that this city-state was now itself ruled by an emperor, and all of its complex institutions were transformed by that fact. But yet it is absolutely clear from contemporary documents, including the Tabula Siarensis, that in formal terms the Roman Empire was still seen "as the *imperium* of the Roman people."[27] Augustus himself embodied this conception in his *Res Gestae*: "I added Egypt to the *imperium* of the Roman people."[28] It is also the case, as we shall see soon, that new evidence brings out, in a way which had not been clear before, to what extent popular participation—and popular voting— was still essential to the way that the *res publica* worked. To call it a "city-state" is certainly to beg many questions. But it does serve to do two things: to direct attention to public institutions other than the Senate itself; and to stress the power and importance of popular reactions to events in Rome. The "history" of Rome in the Empire, as under the Republic, is, or should be, the history of a whole community.

This element, the population of the city of Rome, is of course vividly present from time to time in Tacitus' narrative. In one particular respect, however, both in Tacitus' narrative and in other accounts, there is a new feature which was missing from the Republic: the presence of soldiers stationed in the city, and with that is the capacity of the state to control or repress popular reactions by force. The role of military forces in Rome is heavily marked in the first few pages of the *Annales*: for instance, the watchword given to the praetorian cohorts, a guard stationed at the Palatine, soldiers escorting Tiberius to the Forum and the Curia. Then, after an edict from Tiberius warning the people not to demand that Augustus, like Divus Iulius, should be cremated in the Forum rather than the Campus Martius, came the day of Augustus' funeral itself, with soldiers acting, as Tacitus says, like a garrison. After the long years of the first reign, Tacitus alleges, some people commented that military protection was hardly needed to ensure that his funeral would be peaceful.[29]

None the less, as the narrative progresses, Tacitus comes to a number of different occasions where crowd reactions, even violent ones, are significant. Even here, however, he is selective. If I may digress for a moment, it is odd how little use we make, in analysing the Julio-Claudian period, of a vast range of evidence in the *Naturalis Historia* of Pliny the Elder, who was born

---

27. F. Millar, "Imperial Ideology in the *Tabula Siarensis*," in J. González, ed., *Estudios sobre la Tabula Siarensis* (1988), 11.

28. *RG* 27.

29. *Ann.* I, 7–8.

in the 20s, and finished his work in the 70s, long before Tacitus. Out of a vast store of material I pick out a couple of stories, both from around the time of Pliny's birth. First, there is the anecdote of the raven which was hatched on the roof of the temple of Castor and Pollux on the Forum, and which then attached itself to a cobbler's shop in the vicinity, and which learned to talk; each morning it would fly down to the Rostra and salute by name Tiberius, Germanicus, and Drusus, and then the Roman people on its way past. When it was killed, as a result of a dispute between its owner and a neighbour, its killer was driven out, and the bird's funeral was celebrated by a vast crowd, with two Ethiopians carrying the coffin, and a trumpeter going in front. The body was burned on a pyre on the Via Appia.[30] Then, from a few years later, A.D. 28, comes the story of the loyal dog which belonged to a man who was executed because he was a friend of Nero, the son of Germanicus. The dog followed his master to the prison (*carcer*) and still persisted when he was cast down the Gemonian Steps; finally, when the body was thrown into the Tiber, the dog swam after it, "while a crowd poured out to witness the *fides* [loyalty] of the animal."[31] These stories give a much deeper impression of popular feeling, and of popular attachment to members of the imperial family, than anything in Tacitus. So they serve to prepare us for Tacitus' report from A.D. 29 of how, when a letter from Tiberius attacking Agrippina the elder and her son Nero was read in the Senate, a crowd carrying images of these two surrounded the Senate, praising the emperor, and shouting that the letter was a forgery, and that the attack on the house of Germanicus was being made without his knowledge.[32] The crowd reappears, as a passive witness or an active participant, at quite a number of points in Tacitus' narrative. In 62, for instance, popular protests seemed momentarily to have prevented Nero's divorce of Octavia and his marriage to Poppaea. The people rejoiced, went up to the Capitol and offered worship to the gods. They threw down images of Poppaea, bore statuettes of Octavia on their shoulders, decked them with flowers, and placed them in the temple. Crowds had even filled the Palatium, when units of soldiers were sent out to disperse them, and Poppaea was restored to her position.[33]

But of all the scenes in which Tacitus reflects the force of popular feeling, the most powerful is the account of the news of the death of Germanicus in Syria in A.D. 19, the subsequent arrival of his ashes, brought by his widow

30. Pliny, *NH* 10, 60/121–22.
31. Pliny, *NH* 8, 68/145.
32. *Ann.* 5, 3–4.
33. *Ann.* 14, 60, 6–61, 2.

Agrippina, and in the next year the trial of Cn. Piso on a charge of treasonable actions against him, culminating in his murder. For anyone who was in
Britain in the first week of September 1997, it is absolutely impossible now to
read this narrative without thinking of the death of Diana, Princess of Wales,
of the enormous popular reaction, of the way in which everything closed
on the day of the funeral, of the *laudatio funebris* (funeral oration) which, for
good or ill, was heard by more people than any other in the history of the
world, of the tens of millions of flowers which were laid not just at the royal
palaces but at sites all over the country, and of the several million people who
lined the route on the day of the funeral. There was also a darker note, the
widespread suspicion that at the very centre grief was not felt with the same
intensity as it was on the streets.[34]

So it is, with of course even darker overtones, in the pages of Tacitus in
book 2 of the *Annales*. News comes that Germanicus is ill, and rumours circulate of foul play: for he, like his father Drusus, had been put out of the
way because they had thought of restoring equality and liberty to the *populus
Romanus*. "This popular talk was so inflamed by the actual news of his death,
that before the edict of the magistrates, before the decree of the Senate, by
the spontaneous adoption of a *iustitium* [a cessation of all public business],
the forums were deserted, and houses closed."[35]

Then Tacitus comes in a single paragraph (2, 83) to the posthumous honours for Germanicus which were now thought up and *decreti*—the word implies that they were voted specifically by the Senate. We will come back to
this passage, for it is here, in the light of the Tabula Siarensis, that the limitations of Tacitus' account begin to show up. He then goes on, in book 3, to
describe the events of the following year, when huge crowds of mourners
awaited Agrippina at Brundisium when she arrived with Germanicus' ashes,
and filled every town along the route, weeping and offering sacrifices. Germanicus' adoptive brother Drusus and his real one, the future emperor Claudius, along with Germanicus' children, met the cortege at Tarracina. The
two consuls of A.D. 20, and "a large part of the people [of Rome]" also came
out along the road. Tiberius and Livia did not, and nor did Germanicus'
mother Antonia, for reasons which Tacitus could not discover. Then came
the funeral:[36]

34. For the comparison, see the illuminating remarks by Jasper Griffin and Miriam Griffin, "Show Us you Care, Ma'am," *New York Review of Books*, 9 October 1997, 29, and in
Omnibus 35 (January 1998): 1.

35. *Ann.* 2, 82, 1–4.

36. *Ann.* 3, 1–4. The passage quoted is chap. 4.

The streets of the city were crammed, torches blazing across the Campus Martius. There were the soldiers in arms, the magistrates without their insignia, the people arranged by tribes—they shouted that the *res publica* had fallen, that there was no hope left, so vigorously and openly that you would think they had forgotten their rulers. Nothing, however, pained Tiberius more than the feelings of the people inflamed in support of Agrippina. They called her the glory of the *patria*, the sole descendant of Augustus, the only representative of ancient values. Turning to the heavens and the gods, they prayed that her children would be safe, and survive their enemies.

Perhaps I can leave this all too loaded narrative there, except just to note Tacitus' account of popular comparisons of the funeral of Germanicus with the much more elaborate and traditional one which had been accorded to his father Drusus—and to mention the excellent book by Harriet Flower, published in 1996, on ancestor masks and their role in Roman society.[37] Tacitus' account concludes with Tiberius' edict urging the people to restrain their grief, as not being in accordance with Roman tradition, and to resume normal life.[38]

Later, Tacitus comes to Piso's leisurely return to Rome, and his trial in the Senate, on a charge of the murder of Germanicus, and of a whole series of treasonable acts, committed while Germanicus was on a special mission to settle affairs in the Eastern provinces, and Piso was the regular governor (*legatus*) of Syria.[39] Here too, a popular reaction is recorded during the proceedings. A crowd surrounded the Curia, and shouted that they would not keep their hands off Piso if the Senate did not condemn him. In a typical use of symbolism, they took statues of Piso to the Gemonian Steps and would have smashed them but for the intervention of the emperor.[40]

Before the trial reached a conclusion, Piso committed suicide. Tacitus' narrative then devotes several paragraphs to subsequent senatorial debates, directed to dissociating his widow, Plancina, and his two sons from their father's alleged crimes, and to preserving their status.[41]

These two separate stages in the events which took place in Rome in the aftermath of the death of Germanicus are the two moments which are now illuminated, in a quite remarkable way, by new documents. The two stages

37. *Ann.* 3, 5; H. Flower, *Ancestor Masks and Aristocratic Power in Roman Culture* (1996).
38. *Ann.* 3, 6.
39. *Ann.* 3, 9–18.
40. *Ann.* 3, 14, 5–6.
41. *Ann.* 3, 16–18.

are, firstly, the votes of the Senate in December A.D. 19, following on the arrival of the definitive news of his death; and, secondly, the debates in the Senate which took place after Piso's suicide, and a year later, in December A.D. 20.

It would take volumes to explore the significance of the two texts concerned for both the institutions and the ruling ideology of the early Principate. In a quite real sense our study of the period has to begin all over again, and what is said here touches only on a few salient points, which do however really tell us something new about what "the Roman city-state under the emperors" was. For the documents not only fill in a mass of detail about the working of the *res publica*—the communal institutions of Rome—under Tiberius, and the way in which these were being affected by the existence of an emperor. They also show that Tacitus' picture of events simply leaves out the constitutional role which was still exercised by the Roman people. We like to think of Britain as a democracy, and beyond doubt it was popular feeling which dictated the form and the extent of public mourning in Britain in September 1997. But there was no place, before death or after, for actual voting by the people.

Rome on the other hand was, as it may seem, an autocracy, tempered to some extent by republican traditions and values as maintained by the Senate. But in Rome, as we now know, both the position which Germanicus occupied at the time of his death and the honours for his memory which were decided on posthumously were the subject of *leges* (laws) put to the people and voted on by them.

The first of the two documents, that of December A.D. 19, is a single incomplete text, which is preserved, apart from a few fragments, in two quite separate inscriptions, discovered in different countries several decades apart. The last sixty-two lines of the text are found on the bronze tablet known as the Tabula Hebana, found in Tuscany, and published in 1947. The bulk of the earlier part comes from the Tabula Siarensis, namely fragments of a bronze tablet found in Andalucia, the Roman province of Baetica, and first published as a coherent text in 1984. An overlap of a few lines makes it certain that the two main *inscriptions* contain large parts of what was originally a single *text*. It was this which, as we saw earlier, was issued from Rome to the cities of Italy and the *coloniae* of the provinces. It was also to be put up "in as prominent place as possible" by the provincial governors.[42]

It is rather remarkable that it was a whole twelve years after the publica-

42. Fr. (b), col. II, ll. 26–27, trans. Crawford.

tion of the first full text of the Tabula Siarensis[43] before anyone published a combined text of both the two main inscriptions and the fragments. This is now available, along with an English translation, in the major work edited by Michael Crawford, *Roman Statutes*.[44] But there has still been no full study of the combined text of some 150 lines. Along with the composite decree of the Senate embodying the various votes of the Senate after Piso's death, to which we will come in a moment, it represents by far the best evidence which we have for the public ideology, the rhetoric, and the evolving institutions of the early Empire.

Only a few features of the text can be underlined here: the self-conscious emphasis on the propagation of the approved public ideology through the putting-up of written texts, in Rome, Italy, and the provinces; the new political and ceremonial topography of Rome, with the "tumulus," which we call the Mausoleum, the temple of Apollo on the Palatine, where the Senate now regularly met, the temple of Mars Ultor, and the as yet unbuilt temple of Divus Augustus; the new elements of the religious calendar, with the Ludi Augustales, instituted in A.D. 14; the new role of the *equites* belonging to the *decuriae* (panels) of jurymen, who now had a place in the constitutional order, voting in the centuriate assembly in new centuries along with the senators. I will not dwell on the details concerning voting. It is enough to mention that the Tabula Hebana confirms what we knew anyway from Pliny the Younger and Cassius Dio, that meetings of the assemblies for voting in elections continued through the Julio-Claudian period, and indeed long after it.[45] When Tacitus wrote baldly that in A.D. 14 "the elections were then for the first time transferred to the *patres* [the Senate],"[46] he was referring to the practice of arranging a single list of names to go before the people. But the vital *principle* remained in force, that public office could only be conferred by a popular vote.

43. J. González, "Tabula Siarensis, Fortunales Siarensis et Municipia Civium Romanorum," *ZPE* 55 (1984): 55; *AE* 1984, no. 508; González (n. 24), no. 11.

44. M. H. Crawford, ed., *Roman Statutes* I–II (1996), nos. 37–38 (vol. I, pp. 507–43).

45. Pliny, *Pan.* 63, 2: "The Roman people saw you [Trajan] in that ancient seat of its power; you endured that long ritual of the assembly" (Vidit te populus Romanus in illa vetere potestatis suae sede; perpessus es longum illud carmen comitiorum); 92, 3: "we were proclaimed [consuls] by your voice so that for our public honours the same person [yourself] came forward as our sponsor in the Senate house and our returning officer in the Campus" (tua voce renuntiati sumus, ut idem honoribus nostris suffragator in curia, in campo declarator existeres). Cassius Dio 37, 28, 3; 53, 20, 4.

46. *Ann.* 1, 15, 1.

The Tabula Hebana had already revealed, half a century ago now, that the new voting arrangements set up in A.D. 19 to commemorate Germanicus had been modelled on those instituted in A.D. 5 to commemorate Gaius and Lucius. The formal procedure then had been a law, a lex, which had been put to the people by the consuls of that year: "in conformity with the law which Lucius Valerius Messalla Volesus [and] Gnaeus Cornelius Cinna Magnus carried."[47] Thus in A.D. 5 a change in the constitution had required the passing of a law by the people meeting in their assembly. So it would again in A.D. 19/20, after Germanicus' death. But you would not know this from Tacitus' narrative. If we go back to the relevant chapter (2, 83), we find that he gives a quite detailed summary of many of the steps which we can now see as attested in a contemporary document. But two vital aspects are missing: firstly, there is no reference in Tacitus to the new voting arrangements; and, secondly, all the honours are represented as being voted (*decreti*) by the Senate. But this picture is incomplete. One of the most striking features of the Tabula Siarensis is that it shows that in December 19 the Senate formally advised the incoming consuls of A.D. 20 to incorporate all the steps taken in a law which should be put without delay to the people:[48]

> That M. Messalla and M. Aurelius Cotta Maximus, the consuls designate, when they had entered office — on the first occasion as far as the auspices allow — without giving notice of two or three *nundinae* [three eight-day periods], should see that a statute on the honours for Germanicus Caesar be presented to the people.

No such law appears in Tacitus' account of the year 20; for him the decisions of the Senate were enough.

Exactly the same point is brought out by the inscribed record which contains a consolidated, or composite, version of the various votes of the Senate passed a year later, in December A.D. 20, and after the suicide of Piso. This text, much better preserved, and in a number of different copies, has been the subject of an exemplary edition, with German translation and historical commentary, by Werner Eck, Antonio Caballos, and Fernando Fernández.[49]

47. E.g., Tabula Hebana, ll. 10–11: "by the law which L. Valerius Messala Volesus and Cn. Cornelius Cinna Magnus carried."

48. Tabula Siarensis, fr. (b), col. II, ll. 27–9, trans. Crawford.

49. W. Eck, A. Caballos, and F. Fernández, *Das senatus consultum de Cn. Pisone patre*, *Vestigia* 48 (1996). Note also the parallel Spanish edition, A. Caballos, W. Eck, and F. Fernández, *El "senado consulto" de Cne. Pisone padre* (1996). See now also the extended discussion, with an English translation of the text, by M. Griffin, "The Senate's Story," *JRS* 87 (1997): 249.

Here too there are endless revelations concerning (for instance) the sycophantic public rhetoric of the period, the topography of Rome, the early
history of the *fiscus* (the emperor's treasury), the conduct of funerals and the
role of *imagines* (portraits), the importance attached to inscriptions, the administration of justice, and the role of the praetors who then managed the
Aerarium, the public treasury in Rome. But I will leave all that aside, to focus
on another aspect in which Tacitus' narrative is revealed to be incomplete. In
his account of the year 17, Tacitus had recorded that by the *decretum* (decree)
of the Senate Germanicus had been entrusted with the provinces "which are
divided by the sea" (that is, the eastern provinces), and also had been granted
an *imperium* superior to that of the governor in any area which he visited.[50]
But, as the new text now shows (ll. 29–30), that was not the whole story.
The initiative for the appointment of Germanicus to his eastern mission had
indeed come from Emperor and Senate: Germanicus "had been sent by our
princeps on the *auctoritas* of this *ordo* [the Senate] to put in order the condition of transmarine affairs." Piso ought therefore to have seen himself, in his
role as legate of Syria, as being a helper (*adiutor*) of Germanicus. But instead
he had neglected not only the *maiestas* of the Domus Augusta but also the *ius
publicum*, the public law. For he had been subordinated to Germanicus in his
role and status as proconsul, and not just as any proconsul, but as one invested
with special powers by a law:[51]

> To that proconsul, concerning whom a law [*lex*] had been put to the
> people to the effect that, to whatsoever province he came, he should
> possess a superior imperium to him who governed that province *pro
> consule*, given that in all matters a greater *imperium* should attach to
> Tiberius Caesar Augustus than to Germanicus Caesar.

This last provision beautifully confirms the reality of the tensions which
marked the imperial house in the 20s of the first century. Other aspects of
the law are puzzling—why did it refer only to governors *pro consule*, and how
did it apply to someone like Piso, who was not a proconsul but a *legatus*? But

50. *Ann.* 2, 43, 2: "tunc decreto patrum permissae Germanico provinciae quae mari divi-
duntur, maiusque imperium, quoque adisset, quam iis qui sorte aut missu principis ob-
tinerent."

51. *Senatus consultum*, ll. 32–35: "neclecta | maiestate domus Aug(ustae), neclecto etiam
iure publico, quod adlect(us) pro co(n)s(ule) et ei pro co(n)s(ule), de quo | lex ad populum
lata esset, ut in quamcumq(ue) provinciam venisset, maius ei imperium | quam ei, qui eam
provinciam proco(n)s(ule) optineret, esset, dum in omni re maius imperi|um Ti. Caesari
Aug(usto) quam Germanico Caesari esset."

these are minor points compared to the essential. Both of the two new texts reveal as never before that there was still a *res publica*, in which, in a certain formal sense, the sovereign was the Roman people. One could describe the Roman system of the first century as an autocracy, as an empire, as a constitutional monarchy, as a nation-state, as a city-state, as a *res publica*, even as a sort of democracy, in which constitutional power could only be conferred by the votes of the people. Few political systems have been quite so complex a mixture of old and new, autocratic and popular, monarchic and communal. I am not arguing that within the Roman system of the first century A.D. the people still had any real power to choose—and, in any case, when Germanicus' son Gaius was murdered in A.D. 41, the people were to show unambiguously that they wanted an emperor.[52] But I am arguing that, in a formal sense, legislation, constitutional change and the occupation of office all still required validation by a vote of the people. I am also arguing that Tacitus' concentration on the effective votes in the Senate does tend to obscure this aspect of what the Roman *res publica* now was. Reading Tacitus is still essential. But we can now go beyond, or behind, his narrative to encounter new Latin texts which we can call "documents," but which are also powerful evocations of contemporary oratory. Far from being objective reports, they are literary constructions in themselves, and no less so for being inscribed on bronze tablets. It is these remarkable, and in many ways profoundly repellent, texts expressing the official version of the relationship between the *res publica* and the imperial house, which should now provide our starting point in studying the Roman city-state under the emperors.

52. This emerges beyond question from the important narrative account of the murder of Gaius and the steps which led to the accession of Claudius given by Josephus, *Ant. Jud.* 19, 1, 1–4, 6 (1–273). See esp. the discussion, translation, and commentary by T. P. Wiseman, *Death of an Emperor*, Exeter Studies in History 30 (1991).

Index

This index, compiled by the editors, is meant to give clues and keys to the string of thoughts and ideas developed over the years in Fergus Millar's articles on the study of ancient history, the Roman Republic, and the Augustan Principate: names, institutions, events, and dates are all subservient to this principle.

Actium, battle of: as turning point, 10, 295, 299–300

Acts of the Christian Martyrs, 35–36

Administration, Roman: false assumptions about, 290–91

Alexander (the Great), 10, 28–30

Ancient world. *See* Graeco-Roman civilization

Anthropology and Roman history, 19

Antiquarianism in Rome and its political significance, 183–84, 192–94, 199, 326–27; and Valerius Maximus, 326–27; and Ovid's *Fasti*, 333

Asoka (emperor in India and Afghanistan) and his edicts, 30, 45, 48

Atticus (110/9–32 B.C.), 183–99. *See* Political neutrality and quietism

Augustan ideology: resembles ideology of Tetrarchic monarchy, 298, 307; moralizing tone of, 324–25, 356, 359; recreated and made more significant in poetic forms, 337–49 passim. *See also* Ovid; Public space in Rome

Augustinus (St. Augustine), 32–33

Auxiliary forces (*auxilia*), 212–13

Cambridge Ancient History IX^2: *The Last Age of the Roman Republic, 146–43 B.C.* (1994): conceptual and historiographical problems, 200–205, 214. *See also* Method of inquiry

Careers, official: senatorial and equestrian, 74–79; absence of specialisation and fixed rules of promotion for, 77–79. *See also* Euergetism; Imperial letters; Prosopography

Census: in Italy, 211; associated with the emperor, 298–99

Centuriate assembly (*comitia centuriata*), 89; transformation of, 93–94, 110

Christianity and Graeco-Roman culture, 28–29, 32–33, 35–37

Cicero's writings: reactions to a political system, not descriptive of it, 148, 155. *See also* Method of inquiry

Citizenship, Roman, 15, 20–21, 56–59, 213, 250, 367; imperial grants of, 304–5; without derogation to local citizenship, 305. *See also* Italy: Roman citizenship; Sovereignty of the Roman people

Civil Wars. *See* Roman Revolution; Political neutrality and quietism

Classics: definition of, 26; and extending literary "canon," 33–37

Comitium. *See* Sovereignty of the Roman people: physical manifestation of

Concilium plebis (plebeian assembly), 94–95

Contio (public speech, public meeting). *See* Oratory, public

Curia: relatively slight evidence for early history of, 103–4

Deification of emperors: prefiguration and culmination of, in Ovid's *Metamorphoses*, 334–36

Democracy in Rome, 131–32, 138–42, 150, 158, 164–65; absence of representative principle in, 138, 177; existence of debate in public meetings (*contiones*) in, 181–82. *See also* Sovereignty of the Roman people

Devolution of state functions: by patronage under the Republic, 187–88

Digest, 33

Double negative: principle of, in evaluating evidence, 48, 50–51, 73

Egypt: and papyri, 28, 40

Electoral competition and canvassing, 111, 113, 124–32 passim, 165–66, 178; and bribery (*ambitus*) and public expenditure, 127–28, 174; our ignorance of technicalities of voting in, 128–31; role of advocacy in, 129–30; and elections vs. appointment by lot, 131–32. *See also* Gladiatorial shows offered to the people; Office and office-holders; Sovereignty of the Roman people

Embassies: to Senate, 114–15, 278; to Triumvirs, 249–51; to emperor from public provinces, 285–87, 289–90

Epigraphy. *See* Inscriptions

Equestrian class: and *dignitas*, 185, 186; and republican antecedents of imperial "civil service" posts, 187–88; absence of social barrier between, and senators, 190–91; chose not to enter Senate, 191

Euergetism, 67, 75. *See also* Careers, official

Exempla: use of, in Augustan Rome. *See* Antiquarianism in Rome and its political significance

Factions (*factiones*) in Roman politics: as misleading term, 134, 148

Fasti (lists): of consuls (*consulares*) and of generals who won triumph in Rome (*triumphales*), 14–15, 72, 194

Forum: functions performed in, 90–91, 97, 99, 101–3, 208–9; monumentalization of, 101–4, 144–45; as public stage, 117, 125, 141–42, 143–45, 171; imperial monopolization of, 194, 311–12

Gelzer: *Die römische Nobilität* (1912). *See* "Patrician-plebeian governing class" (*nobilitas*); Patronage and clientage in Rome

Genealogical interest in Rome: as symptom of transition to monarchy, 192–95. *See* Republicanism under the emperors

Gens, Roman: not proven to be a significant element in society, 126

Gladiatorial shows offered to the people, 97, 108, 125

Graeco-Roman civilization, 25–37; nearness of, to modern, 1–5; languages of, 4–5, 11, 28–37; physical and literary remains of, 4–7; historical approaches to, 7, 12–18; money and coins of, 7–9, 21, 220; military aspect of, 9–11; beginning of, 26–27; end of, 33; Jewish and Christian texts' place in, 34–36. *See also* Inscriptions

Greek City: inscriptions about, 63–70, 72

Greek language: dominance of, in East, 31; in Roman inscriptions, 71–2. *See also* Asoka; Christianity and Graeco-Roman culture; Inscriptions; Koine; Septuagint

History and historiography. *See* Method of inquiry

Impact of Roman rule: and direction of trade and valuables, 228–36; limited, 231, 296; not felt only where direct rule existed, 231–32

Imperial cult: as organized novelty on a scale previously unknown, 308–9; and emphasis on imperial family, 310–11. *See also* Deification of emperors

Imperial epigraphy, 323–26, 348–49; elaborate public display as memoralisation in both visual and written forms of, 355–57, 364–65, 373–76; expressing the official version of events, 374–76

Imperialism, Roman: determined by the political system, 109–10; from the point of view of the people, 166–69

Imperial letters, 75–76; of appointment (*codicilli*), 75–76; as source of imperial history, 76; as almost always written in response to initiative from below, 285

Imperial provinces: tribute from, did not belong to emperor, 299, 300. See also *Legati Augusti pro praetore*; Provinces; Public provinces

Inscriptions, 14, 21–22, 36, 39–81 passim; as distinctive feature of Graeco-Roman civilization, 39, 80–81, 308; *corpora* and collections of, 40–43, 70, 72, 73; geopgraphical extension, 42–43; as literary texts, 52–61, 350–59; honorific, 67, 72, 74–75, 79. *See also* Prosopography; Careers, official

—Latin, 70–81, 350–51; limitations and partiality of, 41, 61–63, 76; Semitic, 42–43; multilingualism of, ill served

in collections, 43–51; linguistic aspect of, 46; and republican laws, 155–56; vs. the "text" of the "inscription," 350–51. *See also* Double negative; Greek City; Imperial epigraphy; Imperial letters

Italian confederation: as misnomer, 119. *See also* Italy

Italy: republican history of, 10, 20–21; languages, 47–51; Greek influence in, 48–50; and inscriptions, 72; Rome and the Italian communities, 119–20; Roman citizenship, 158–61, 209–12; absence of, in *Cambridge Ancient History* IX², 210–12; lack of distinction between, and provinces, 212–13

Josephus, 29, 34
Judaea and Judaism, 28–29, 34; languages of, 42

Koine (common Greek language of post-Alexander period), 47

Latin, language, literature and culture of, 25–27, 30–37, 47, 49–50, 71; in West, 72–73; Latin Bible, 35
Legati Augusti pro praetore (governors in imperial provinces), 262; formally distinguished from proconsuls, 273–74, 289; exercised, like proconsuls, full *imperium* in provinces, 274, 289; initiate correspondence with emperors, 275–76, 286; appointed by imperial patronage, 302
Legislation. *See* Sovereignty of the Roman people
Livia Augusta. *See* Monarchical forms of government, emergence of—imperial household

Magistrates. *See* Office-holders
Mandata: issued by emperors to both *legati*

Augusti pro praetore and proconsuls, 274–75, 287, 303

Mediterranean. *See* Roman revolution: Mediterranean context of

Method of inquiry, 106–8, 111–12, 132, 137–38, 143–44, 147–48, 164–66, 167–68; concerning last century of Roman Republic 200–214; and Mediterranean in Roman Revolution, 217–37; model(s) required for interpretation of anecdotes, 237; and Empire, 290–91; and impact of monarchy, 295; and problems of annalistic history, 360–61; and history of Rome as history of a community, 368

Mob. *See* Violence in later Roman Republic

Monarchical forms of government, emergence of
—blending between making decisions and pronouncing legal judgements, 257
—dating documents by imperial era, 293–94, 302
—development of routine personal jurisdiction, 257–59
—division of responsibilty with Senate, an illusion, 262, 271–91 passim, 302–3
—imperial household (Domus Augusta), 340–43, 345–47, 351–52, 357–58; prominence of female members in, 323, 342, 347, 358. *See also* Imperial cult: emphasis on imperial family; Ovid
—imperial portraits on coinage, 299–300
—intercessions with the ruler, 189, 254, 256–57; intercessions with the ruler through well-placed individuals ("brokerage"), 338, 341
—occasional appointment of consuls by Augustus, 263
—petitions to emperor, 255, 296–97
—planned colonies of Roman citizens in Empire, 305–6. *See also* Citizenship, Roman

—praetorian cohorts, 255
—reflected in Augustan sources, 267–69. *See also* Ovid
—symbolic presence of emperor in Empire, 292–94, 308–11; in Rome, 311–13, 314, 336
—taxation and tribute associated with emperor, 299

Monarchy, Roman, 242, 270, 290–91; centralization of power does not mean centralization of initiative in, 290–91; and passive and inert government, 290–91, 298; emerged within republican system 295, 314; republican institutions and magistracies provide the content of imperial patronage in, 304, 343–45; anxiety about succession in, 323–26, 333, 345–49; formally *res publica* or city state, 360–76 passim. *See also* Deification of emperors; Imperial cult

Municipal laws (so-called): in Italy, 71; in Spain, 73

Near East, 11, 28–30
Nomenclature, 47–48

Office and office-holders, 118, 122–24, 144; competence and sphere of activity of, 113–14; as accountable to the people, 116–18, 122, 140–41, 153–54; and descent, wealth, and social fluidity, 126–27; public munificence of, correctly interpreted, 174–77; and favour conferred by the people, 178. *See also* Electoral competition and canvassing; Senate: recruitment of

Onomastics. *See* Nomenclature

Oratory, public, 143, 146, 171, 178, 180–82, 203

Ovid (Augustan poet *par excellence*), 321–23, 330, 348–49; as distinct from great post-Triumviral writers, 321–23, 330; belongs with post-Augustan Velleius Paterculus, 328–30; as "rejected loyalist," 330–49 passim; declines senatorial career, 331, 336. *See also* Augustan ideology; Deification of emperors

Palestine. *See* Judaea and Judaism

Papyri, 36–37, 40. *See also* Egypt; Near East

"Patrician-plebeian governing class" (*nobilitas*): shortcomings of concept of, 91–93, 104–6, 111, 126–27, 191–92. *See also* Patronage and clientage in Rome

Patricians, 88–89, 96, 104

Patronage and clientage in Rome: as modern construct, 92, 111, 124–25, 131, 137–38, 145–46, 149; as irrelevant for history of Latin literature, 331–32, 336; and imperial patronge, 343. *See also* Devolution of state functions; Monarchical forms of government, emergence of—intercessions with the ruler

Petitions and petitioning. *See* Monarchical forms of government, emergence of

Political neutrality and quietism: as new civil ideology: 186–90, 197–99, 294–95

Politics, Roman: and individualistic character of the politician, 143–44, 148–52; as not without ideological content, 148–50

Polybius' interpretation of the Roman Republic, xiii–xv, 111–12, 132, 141–42, 150

Private duty (*officium*) replacing public duty. *See* Political neutrality and quietism

Proconsuls (governors of public provinces), 273–74, 317–18; receive *mandata* from emperors, 275, 287, 303; correspond with emperors, 287–88; chosen by lot, 302; overshadowed by emperor, 306–7. See also *Legati Augusti pro praetore*; Provinces; Public provinces

Prosopography, imperial and republican, 12–16, 76–77; and criticism of abuse, 77–79, 96–97, 105, 107, 134

Provinces, division of, in 27 B.C.: ancient sources concerning, 271–72, 273, 300–303; and modifications in 23 B.C., 272; and standard view of implications of modifications, 272–73; had only formal and practical consequences (no division in responsibility), 273–74, 289, 301–2, 315, 355; untenability of standard view of, 273–91 passim, 302–3; wrongly interpreted as compromise with Senate rather than with people, 315. *See also* Administration, Roman; *Legati Augusti pro praetore*; *mandata*; Proconsuls; Public provinces

Public expenditure in republican Rome. *See* Electoral competition and canvassing; Office and office-holders; Self-representation of individuals in public

Public provinces: routinely subjected to regulations made by emperors, 280–86, 288–90; misnamed "senatorial," 301, 314–20 passim. *See also* Embassies; Proconsuls; Provinces; Senate, imperial

Public space in Rome: monumentalised, transformed, and monopolized by emperors, 311–13, 314, 336, 363–64. *See also* Forum

Republicanism under emperors: crystallized, 194–95; and immortalized in stone in Augustus' Forum, 195–96, 199; immortalized in restoration of temples, 196–97; used as framework to debate the present, 362. *See also* Sovereignty of the Roman people: recognised and emphasised under the monarchy

"Restoration of the Republic": did not take place in 27 B.C., 260–70; not attested or implied in contemporary sources,

264–65, 267–69; not attested or implied in later sources, 265, 266; not claimed in 27 B.C., 270. See also *Legati Augusti pro praetore*; Provinces

Roman history: myth and reality in, 85–90; Mid-Republican (390–218 B.C.), 85–108 passim; of Classical Republic (200–151 B.C.), 109–42 passim, 168; from 150 to 90 B.C., 143–61 passim; of late Republic (70–50 B.C.), 162–82 passim; of late second century B.C. to 70 B.C., 168–70. See also *Cambridge Ancient History* IX²; Method of inquiry

Roman people. *See* Sovereignty of the Roman people

Roman Revolution, 150; Mediterranean context of, 215–37; misinterpreted due to emphasis on Senate, 352. *See also* Syme, Ronald

Roman rule. *See* Impact of Roman rule

Rostovtzeff: *Histories*, 16, 61, 202, 235–36

Rostra. *See* Sovereignty of the Roman people: physical manifestation of

Self-representation of individuals in public, 87, 97, 106, 108, 151, 175–77

Senate, imperial: activities of, not confined to the public provinces, 277–80, 288–90; ceremonial character of decisions of, 350–59 passim, 364; as stage of Tacitus' Annals, 361–63. *See also* Proconsuls; Provinces; Public provinces

Senate, republican: misnamed "aristocracy" or "oligarchy," 87, 92, 95–96, 141, 164, 191; recruitment of, 104,133; role of in foreign affairs, 114; as exercising governmental functions, but not a government, 114–15, 132–36, 148, 150, 163–64; topics for future research on, 205–8; not sovereign element in Roman state, 315. *See also* Factions in Roman politics; "Patrician-plebeian governing class";

Patronage and clientage in Rome; Senate, imperial

Septuagint (Greek version of Bible), 29, 34

Shapor I (A.D. 241–72) and his *Res Gestae*, 45–46

Social War of 90–87 B.C.: as turning point, 10, 160–61, 169, 177, 209–12

Sovereignty of the Roman people, 95, 98–108 passim, 111–42 passim; 143–61 passim, 162–82 passim; physical manifestation of, 90–91, 101–4, 106–8, 140; in the popular courts, 112, 117–18, 136–37; in declaring war and making treaties, 115, 136; in colonization, 120–21; in bestowing and withholding citizenship, 122, 151–52; over public funds and property, 154, 167; denied by modern scholars, 164; over resources of Empire, 169–77; recognised and emphasised under the monarchy, and attested in imperial documents, 315–20 passim, 352–56, 368, 373–76; in Roman law as seen by jurists, 319; over both public and imperial provinces 320. *See also* Democracy in Rome; Electoral competition and canvassing

Subscriptio (informal type of imperial reply to petitions), 76. *See also* Monarchical forms of government, emergence of — petitions to emperor

Syme, Ronald, 12–13, 15–16; *The Roman Revolution*, 241–42, 314

Tacitus: as frequently imprecise, 242, 261, 354, 355, 357; and deliberate choice of *Annals* as title, 360–62; concentrates excessively on Senate, 363, 376; occasional appearance of the populace in, 368–71; leaves out constitutional role of the people, 372–76

Tribal assembly (*comitia tributa*), 89, 94

Tribes (*tribus*), 92–94, 110

Tribunes: as champions of plebs, 96–98, 102, 169–70. *See also* Sovereignty of the Roman people

Triumvirs and the Triumvirate: obscurities left by ancient accounts of "constitutional powers" of, 243–45, 255; exercise of patronage and favouritism under, 245–46; and persistence of republican institutions and forms, 246–48, 255–56; deference of, to republican forms attested in the documents, 249–53; contrasted with monarchical forms of government, 253–60

Violence in later Roman republic: as expression of popular or crowd politics, 179

Xanthos: trilingual inscription from, 44–46